University of Chicago
Readings in Western Civilization

9
Twentieth-
Century Europe

Edited by John W. Boyer and Jan Goldstein

John W. Boyer and Julius Kirshner, General Editors

Readings in Western Civilization

℧ Vere dignum

University of Chicago Readings in Western Civilization
John W. Boyer and Julius Kirshner, General Editors

1. **The Greek Polis**
   Edited by Arthur W. H. Adkins and Peter White

2. **Rome: Late Republic and Principate**
   Edited by Walter Emil Kaegi, Jr., and Peter White

3. **The Church in the Roman Empire**
   Edited by Karl F. Morrison

4. **Medieval Europe**
   Edited by Julius Kirshner and Karl F. Morrison

5. **The Renaissance**
   Edited by Eric Cochrane and Julius Kirshner

6. **Early Modern Europe: Crisis of Authority**
   Edited by Eric Cochrane, Charles M. Gray, and Mark A. Kishlansky

7. **The Old Regime and the French Revolution**
   Edited by Keith Michael Baker

8. **Nineteenth-Century Europe: Liberalism and Its Critics**
   Edited by Jan Goldstein and John W. Boyer

9. **Twentieth-Century Europe**
   Edited by John W. Boyer and Jan Goldstein

University of Chicago
Readings in Western Civilization

John W. Boyer and Julius Kirshner, General Editors

9 Twentieth-Century Europe

**Edited by John W. Boyer
and Jan Goldstein**

The University of Chicago Press

Chicago and London

Eric Cochrane, 1928–1985

ἀθάνατος μνήμη
Immortal memory

John Boyer is professor of history at the University of
Chicago, and an editor of the *Journal of Modern History.*

Jan Goldstein is associate professor of history at the
University of Chicago.

The University of Chicago Press, Chicago 60637
The University of Chicago Press, Ltd., London
© 1987 by The University of Chicago
All rights reserved. Published 1987
Printed in the United States of America
96 95 94 93 92 91 90 89 88 87   5 4 3 2 1

Library of Congress Cataloging-in-Publication Data
Main entry under title:

University of Chicago readings in Western civilization.

  Includes bibliographies and indexes.
  Contents: 1. The Greek polis / edited by Arthur W.H.
Adkins and Peter White — 2. Rome: late republic and
principate / edited by Walter Emil Kaegi, Jr., and
Peter White —   — 9. Twentieth-century Europe /
edited by John W. Boyer and Jan Goldstein.
  1. Civilization, Occidental—History—Sources.
2. Europe—Civilization—Sources.   I. Boyer, John W.
II. Kirshner, Julius.   III. Readings in Western
civilization.
CB245.U64   1986   909'.09821   85-16328
ISBN 0-226-06934-6 (v. 1)
ISBN 0-226-06935-4 (pbk. : v. 1)

ISBN 0-226-06953-2 (v. 9)
ISBN 0-226-06954-0 (pbk. : v. 9)

Contents

Series Editors' Foreword

This series is the result of almost four decades of teaching the History of Western Civilization course at the College of the University of Chicago. The course was founded in its present form in the late 1940s by a group of young historians at Chicago, including William H. McNeill, Christian Mackauer, and Sylvia Thrupp, and has been sustained during the past twenty-five years by the distinguished teaching of Eric Cochrane, Hanna H. Gray, Charles M. Gray, and Karl J. Weintraub. In the beginning it served as a counterpoint to the antihistorical and positivistic thrust of the general education curriculum in the social sciences in the Hutchins College. Western Civilization has since been incorporated as a year-long course into different parts of the College program, from the first to the last year. It now forms part of the general intercivilizational requirement for sophomores and juniors. It is still taught, as it has been almost constantly since its inception, in discussion groups ranging from twenty to thirty students.

Although both the readings and the instructors of the course have changed over the years, its purpose has remained the same. It seeks not to provide students with morsels of Western culture, nor to nourish their moral and aesthetic sensitivities, and much less to attract recruits for the history profession. Its purpose instead is to raise a whole set of complex conceptual questions regarding the nature of time and change and the intended and unintended consequences of human action and consciousness. Students in this course learn to analyze past events and ideas by rigorously examining a variety of texts. This is in contrast to parallel courses in the social sciences, which teach students to deploy synchronic and quantitative techniques in analyzing society, usually without reference to historical context or process.

Ours is a history course that aims not at imparting relevant facts or exotic ideas but at providing students with the critical tools by which to analyze texts produced in the distant or near past. It also serves a related purpose: to familiarize students with major epochs of that Western historical tradition to which most of them, albeit at times unknowingly, are heirs. The major curricular vehicle of the course is the *Readings in Western Civilization*, a nine-volume series of primary sources in translation, beginning with Periclean Athens and concluding with Europe in the twentieth century. The series is not meant to be a comprehensive survey of Western history. Rather, in each volume, we provide a large number of documents on specific themes in the belief that depth, not breadth, is the surest antidote to superficiality. The very extensiveness of the documentation in each volume allows for a variety of approaches to the same theme. At the same time the concentrated focus of individual volumes makes it possible for them to serve as source readings in more advanced and specialized courses.

Many people contributed to the publication of these volumes. The enthusiastic collaboration and labors of the members of the Western Civilization staff made it possible for these *Readings* to be published. We thank Barbara Boyer for providing superb editorial direction to the project and Mary Van Steenbergh for her dedication in creating beautifully text-edited manuscripts. Steven Wheatley's advice in procuring funding for this project was invaluable. Members of the University of Chicago Press have given their unstinting support and guidance. We also appreciate the confidence and support accorded by Donald N. Levine, the Dean of the College at the University of Chicago. Above all, we are deeply grateful for the extraordinary dedication, energy, and erudition which our late colleague and former chairperson of the course, Eric Cochrane, contributed to the *Readings in Western Civilization*.

We are grateful to the National Endowment for the Humanities for providing generous funding for the preparation and publication of the volumes.

John Boyer and Julius Kirshner

General Introduction

The history of Europe in the twentieth century is one of distressing events, uneasy interludes, and terrible destruction, but at the same time of proud and valiant attempts to defend and eventually to restore humane order to European civilization. It is also *our* century, and as it is the most recent of times, comprehending its meaning is a difficult, perhaps impossible, and certainly controversial task. In this volume we have concentrated mainly on developments in politics and culture, although the documents we have chosen cannot help but reveal something of the social and economic problems that weighed so heavily on the minds of contemporaries. Adhering to the pattern of this series as a whole, we have made no attempt to cover all the important subjects that fall under the heading indicated by our title. We have instead been guided by the principle that well-chosen and suggestive texts can serve to illuminate larger themes and issues and that they are especially effective at the introductory level.

This volume is organized chronologically around four key periods of a century twice punctuated by world war: pre-1914, 1914–1919, the interwar years, and post-1945. While *Twentieth-Century Europe* can stand alone, we have designed it with the final two sections of *Nineteenth-Century Europe* in mind, namely, what historians have come to call the "German problem" in modern history, and the emergence of mass political movements on the right and left directed against the liberal center. More generally, volume 9 continues the theme, begun in volume 8, of the shifting fortunes of the liberal state, which is traced here from its nadir in the 1930s to its reconstitution after 1945. In this sense the two volumes do constitute an intellectual unity and can be used together with profit.

The first section of this book explores a range of popular mentalities on the eve of the Great War, all of which reflected intense dissatisfaction with the middle-class liberal values dominant at the time. Heard here are the voices of aesthetic modernism (the *Futurist Manifestos*), of generational consciousness and rebellion among the young (Massis and de Tarde,

The Young People of Today), and of modern feminism (Mabel Atkinson's *The Economic Foundations of the Women's Movement*). These documents highlight movements which not only emerged with special force in the early twentieth century, but which have since become decisive features of the cultural map of the whole century. The last two documents in this section illustrate the diametric opposites of revanchist nationalism and socialist internationalism before 1914. General Friedrich von Bernhardi's *Germany and the Next War* and the transcript of the final meeting of the executive of the Second Socialist International offer a dramatic contrast between those who wanted to destroy the nineteenth-century world through military force in the name of a fantasied past, and those who wanted to defend it through reasoned deliberation in the name of a progressive future.

Topic 2, on the war itself, opens with two documents indicating the fate of European Socialism during the war: the statement on war credits presented by the German Social Democrats in the Reichstag on 4 August 1914, after Germany had declared war on France, and Rudolf Hilferding's critique of right-wing collaboration within the Social Democratic party, which also presents Hilferding's famous concept of "organized capital- ism." Selections from the work of Walther Rathenau and Marshal Henri Pétain suggest the profound transformational effect of the war on society and economy and the growing role of the state bureaucracy, and espe- cially its military component, in civil society—trends which proved irre- versible and made the war a watershed in the history of the Western state. A poignant exchange between Alfred Zimmern and Edward Grigg, both members of the Round Table movement, introduces the problem of the multiplicity of "wars" which actually constituted the Great War, as seen by optimists at home and those in the trenches. Representing the most articulate group of British neo-imperialists in the twentieth century, these documents also signal implicitly the crisis which England and its demo- cratic empire would endure as a result of the war. The section concludes with three contemporary analyses of the catastrophe by Sigmund Freud, Max Weber, and John Maynard Keynes.

We have chosen to give special emphasis to the interwar years, a pe- riod of political and economic chaos and cultural upheaval which D. C. Watt has recently characterized as constituting a "European civil war." [1] Our consideration of the 1920s and 1930s, topic 3, is divided into four large subtopics. The first concerns the emergence of two categorically radical alternatives to the nineteenth-century liberal state, Central Euro-

---

1. Donald C. Watt, "The European Civil War," in Wolfgang J. Mommsen and Lothar Ket- tenacker, eds., *The Fascist Challenge and the Policy of Appeasement* (London, 1983).

pean fascism and Soviet totalitarianism. Texts by Hitler, Mussolini, and Stalin address the motives, means, and consequences of mass terroristic politics, and may be used to consider the similarities, as well as the differences, among forms of dictatorship in the twentieth century. The embattlement of the democracies in the overlapping realms of domestic and international affairs is explored in the next subtopic by means of three illustrative cases: Léon Blum's speech at Tours in 1920 pledging "to guard the old house" of French democratic socialism against the claims of Soviet communism; Gustav Stresemann's commentaries on the treaties of Locarno, which for an all-too-short period in the later 1920s seemed to guarantee peace in Europe by reintegrating a now democratic Germany into the collective polity of the European Great Powers; and Neville Chamberlain's and Winston Churchill's speeches in the House of Commons during the Munich Crisis in October 1938, the one for, the other against, appeasing the dictators.

A brilliant intellectual and artistic creativity accompanied, and seems to have been spurred on by, the dark intensity of the historical situation of the interwar years. Hence we have devoted the remaining parts of topic 3 to the contributions of intellectuals and artists. Texts by Julien Benda, Antonio Gramsci, Simone Weil, and Arthur Koestler provide a series of contrasting reflections on the role of the intellectual in general and especially in critical and trying times. The depictions of the intellectual contained here range from the voice of disinterested rationality; to the shaper of the new revolutionary and, eventually, hegemonic culture; to the individual whose awareness entails personal accountability for the sufferings of the lowest; to the idealist who tends not to recognize his own fallibility.

The exploration of cultural ferment in the 1920s and 1930s is continued in selections from four prominent artistic innovators and cultural critics, all of whom tie their aesthetic values to the political circumstances of the day. André Breton discusses surrealism's critique of the bourgeois outlook and the movement's affinity with communism; Walter Gropius articulates the essential principles of an architectural modernism which he regarded as fundamentally democratic in nature; Virginia Woolf ponders the perennial scarcity of women writers and, in the process, connects fascism with a particular view of gender; and Walter Benjamin traces the changing technology of art and describes how its modern technology has been differently incorporated into the politics of fascism and of communism.

Finally, topic 3 presents a pair of documents written by participants in the final stage of the Viennese Renaissance of the early twentieth century. They illuminate the fate of nineteenth-century liberal and socialist ideals in the 1930s. The empirical study, conducted by Paul Lazarsfeld, Marie

Jahoda, and Hans Zeisel, of the small rural town of Marienthal during the Depression is profoundly indebted to the tradition of Austro-Marxism. Friedrich von Hayek's *The Road to Serfdom* (although written in England) is similarly beholden to the heritage of Austrian liberalism. Both—an ethical socialism and an ethical individualism—not only offer analyses of the anarchy of the 1930s, but also represent values influential in the reconstruction of the public order in the 1950s. Both texts are also the work of European scholars who later had prominent careers in the United States (as did several other authors in this volume), suggesting the significance of the intellectual migration of the 1930s in bringing yet another wave of talented Europeans who enriched the New World.

Topic 4 begins with a consideration of society at "point zero," a phrase referring to the moral and physical deterioration of Europe during the war and given concrete meaning by Bruno Bettelheim's deposition in 1945 before the United States government investigators on the brutal regimen of the Nazi concentration camps. Continuing in the same vein, Jean-Paul Sartre's *Existentialism Is a Humanism* explicates the philosophy that was to prove most compelling in the postwar era—a philosophy which posits a world stripped bare of all comforting illusions and makes it the ground from which any authentic human action must begin.

Topic 4 then surveys courageous (and successful) attempts by moderate socialist and moderate conservative politicians to reestablish institutions *and* values of social justice and liberal order in Europe and to create an economic union of states which would prevent a reversion to the bitter nationalism of the 1930s. Following a speech by Sir William Beveridge which conveys the significance and moral purpose of his plan for social insurance, a plan which inspired much of the work of the postwar Labour government in Great Britain, we offer two sets of related texts. First, we explore the evolution of the "German problem" in Western Europe after 1945 with texts which discuss the return of economic prosperity and political democracy to postwar Germany. Ludwig Erhard's account of the Social Market economy presents the economic philosophy of the Christian Democratic Union, the major conservative party of postwar Western Germany and the heir not only of the German Center Party, but, in some respects, of German Liberalism as well. This is followed by the German Social Democrats' *Bad Godesberg Program* (1959), an announcement by the leading Socialist party of nineteenth-century Europe of its conversion from a class-based advocate of revolutionary transformation to a sponsor of pluralistic social reform, willing to accept, if uneasily, the basic assumptions of modern capitalism. We then offer texts from the work of Jean Monnet and Charles de Gaulle, representing Monnet's labor of love on behalf of the European Economic Community and de Gaulle's vision of the role of the French political nation in postwar Europe. Are the two visions—a Europe beyond nations and a Europe of proud, free nations—compatible? This has been and will remain a serious question facing Europeans in the coming century.

A coda—with texts by Hannah Arendt, Michel Foucault, and Raymond Williams—reflects back on the first sixty years of the twentieth century, and, in a larger sense, speculates on the nature and fate of Western civilization. For Arendt the "dark times" of modern history can be understood by means of concepts found in ancient Greek philosophy, Arendt's testimony to the enduring wisdom and strength of the Western intellectual tradition. For Foucault the modes of power developed in the West include not only those in the political sphere which produce overt subjection, but those in the sphere of knowledge, which constitute our very subjectivity: in this view the Western intellectual tradition lays traps of its own, which vastly complicate the problem of human emancipation. For Williams, finally, the "long revolution" of the nineteenth and twentieth centuries involves a process of sustained democratization which should not rest with the self-satisfactions of material prosperity, consumer capitalism, and political consensus.

While our volume concludes with Europe in the 1960s and early 1970s, by implication these texts move Europe forward into the last quarter of our century by indicating a dilemma Europeans now face. Does the achievement of social liberal consensus, economic integration, and a balance of military terror in (and among) most European states mean the end of "progress" as the nineteenth century understood it? Has Condorcet's Tenth Stage been concluded? Or have the last forty years of modern history merely served to "close" one epoch of impressive material reconstruction, so that a new epoch of creative innovation may be born?

1
Mentalities on the Eve of the Great War

1. The Futurist Manifestos

The Futurist movement was founded in 1909–10 by a group of young Italian artists and writers who sought to break decisively with contemporary artistic canons and with the civilization of liberal, bourgeois values of post-Risorgimento Italy and to launch a new avant-garde of dynamic and violent art. Led by the Milanese poet and editor F. T. Marinetti (the author of the original manifesto, which appeared in the Paris newspaper *Le Figaro* in February 1909), the group included painters like Carlo Carrà, Umberto Boccioni, Luigi Russolo, Gino Severini, and Giacomo Balla as well as musicians and photographers like Francesco Balilla Pratella and Anton Giulio Bragaglia. By 1914 the canon of Futurist manifestos included statements on music, photography, and architecture, in addition to those on poetry, painting, and sculpture.

Pontus Hulten has suggested that Marinetti's ideas derived from a combination of social Darwinism and evolutionism, with a dose of technologism thrown in: "Marinetti called Futurism an 'aesthetic of violence and blood.' His cult of strength was related to his faith in evolution and optimism. He derived his ideas from Social Darwinism and from evolutionism in the natural sciences of the nineteenth century, but gave them an extreme interpretration, not realizing until it was too late the dangers of dehumanization, of *fisicofollia,* and of replacing human values with the concept of energy. . . . War was to be the remedy and the agent for great changes. Even if much of Marinetti's worship of violence was there for its shock effect . . . the events of the Thirties and Forties tragically illustrated what he had written." [1]

In aesthetic form and in cultural purpose Futurism has often been considered an offshoot of cubism, although the Futurist painters strove vig-

1. Pontus Hulten, "Futurist Prophecies," in *Futurismo e Futurismi* (Milan, 1986), p. 19.

orously to preserve their own collective and individual independence. The Futurist movement must be seen, however, as part of larger trends in modernist aesthetics and generationalist rebellion in the first decade of the twentieth century. As Joshua Taylor has noted of their influence, "the Futurist principle of 'dynamism' as an expressive means, the painters' emphasis on process rather than on things (for which they cited the teachings of Henri Bergson as authority), and their emphasis upon the intuition and its power to synthesize the manifold experiences of sense and memory in a coherent 'simultaneity,' had profound effects on other movements: the Constructivists and their various branches, the English Vorticists, and subsequently on Dada and Surrealism." [2]

The Futurists ardently supported the entry of Italy into the First World War, yet the war crushed the opportunity for anarchic creativity which the group had enjoyed between 1909 and 1914. Some of the leading members were victims of the fighting; others like Marinetti tried unsuccessfully to revive the tradition after 1918. Marinetti did succeed, however, in offering his personal prestige to Mussolini's *Fasci di Combattimento* in 1919, leading to the putative, if uneasy, connection between fascism and Futurism often noted in the 1920s.

Foundation and Declaration of Futurism

We had been up all night, my friends and I, under the oriental lamps with their pierced copper domes starred like our souls—for from them too burst the trapped lightning of an electric heart. We had tramped out at length on the luxurious carpets from the East our inherited sloth, disputing up to the farthest boundaries of logic and blackening much paper with frenzied writing.

An immense pride swelled our chests because we felt ourselves alone at that hour, alert and upright like magnificent beacons and advance guard posts confronting the army of enemy stars staring down from their heavenly encampments. Alone with the stokers tending the infernal fires of great ships; alone with the black phantoms that poke into the red hot bellies of locomotives launched at mad speed; alone with the drunks reeling with their uncertain flapping of wings around the city walls.

Suddenly we started at the formidable sound of the enormous double-

2. Joshua C. Taylor, "Introduction: The Futurists," *History of Western Civilization. Topic X: Problems of the Twentieth Century* (Chicago, 1964), p. 106.

From Marinetti's *Futurist Manifesto,* translated from the Italian for an earlier edition of this volume.

decked trams that jolted past, magnificent in multi-colored lights like villages at holiday time that the flooded Po has suddenly rocked and wrenched from their foundations to carry over the cascades and through the whirlpools of a flood, down to the sea.

Then the silence deepened. But while we were listening to the interminable mumbled praying of the old canal and the creaking bones of the moribund palaces on their mossy, dank foundations, we suddenly heard automobiles roaring voraciously beneath our windows.

"Let's go!" I said, "Let's go, friends! Let's get out. Mythology and the Mystic Ideal are finally overcome. We are about to witness the birth of the centaur and soon we shall see the first angels fly! . . . The doors of life must be shaken to test the hinges and bolts! . . . Let's take off! Behold the very first dawn on earth! There is nothing to equal the splendor of the sun's rose-colored sword as for the first time it slashes through our millennial darkness! . . ."

We went up to the three snorting beasts to pat lovingly their torrid breasts. I stretched out on my machine like a corpse on a bier; but I revived at once under the steering wheel, a guillotine blade that menaced my stomach.

The furious sweep of madness took us out of ourselves and hurled us through streets as rough and deep as stream beds. Here and there a sick lamp in a window taught us to mistrust the fallacious mathematics of our wasted eyes.

I cried, "The scent! The scent is enough for the beasts! . . ."

And like young lions we pursued Death with its black pelt spotted with pale crosses, streaking across the violet sky so alive and vibrant.

Yet we had no ideal lover reaching her sublime face to the clouds, nor a cruel queen to whom to offer our bodies, twisted in the forms of Byzantine rings! Nothing to die for except the desire to free ourselves at last from our too exigent courage!

And we sped on, squashing the watchdogs on their doorsteps who curled up under our scorching tires like starched collars under a flatiron. Death, domesticated, overtook me at every turn to graciously offer me a paw, and from time to time it would stretch out on the ground with the sound of grinding teeth to make soft caressing eyes at me from every puddle.

"Let's break away from wisdom as from a horrible husk and throw ourselves like pride-spiced fruit into the immense distorted mouth of the wind! Let's give ourselves up to the unknown, not out of desperation but to plumb the deep pits of the absurd!"

I had hardly spoken these words when suddenly I spun my car around with a drunken lurch like a dog trying to bite his tail, and there all at once coming towards me were two cyclists, wavering in front of me like two equally persuasive but nevertheless contradictory arguments. Their stupid dilemma was blocking my way. . . . What a nuisance! Ouch! . . . I stopped short and to my disgust was hurled, wheels in the air, into a ditch. . . .

Oh! maternal ditch, filled almost to the top with muddy water! Fair factory drainage ditch! I avidly savored your nourishing muck, remembering the holy black breast of my Sudanese nurse. . . . When I got out from under the up-turned car—torn, filthy, and stinking—I felt the red-hot iron of joy pass over my heart!

A crowd of fishermen armed with their poles, and some gouty naturalists were already crowding around the wonder. With patient and meticulous care they rigged up a tall derrick and enormous iron grapnels to fish out my automobile like a great beached shark. The machine emerged slowly, shedding at the bottom like scales its heavy framework of good sense and its soft upholstery of comfort.

They thought it was dead, my fine shark, but the stroke of my hand was enough to restore it to life, and there it was living again, speeding along once more on its powerful fins.

So, with face smeared in good waste from the factories—a plaster of metal slag, useless sweat, and celestial soot—bruised, arms bandaged, but undaunted, we declare our primary intentions to all *living* men of the earth:

Initial Manifesto of Futurism (20 February 1909)

1. We shall sing the love of danger, the habit of energy and boldness.
2. The essential elements of our poetry shall be courage, daring and rebellion.
3. Literature has hitherto glorified thoughtful immobility, ecstasy and sleep; we shall extol aggressive movement, feverish insomnia, the double quick step, the somersault, the box on the ear, the fisticuff.
4. We declare that the world's splendour has been enriched by a new beauty; the beauty of speed. A racing motor-car, its frame adorned with great pipes, like snakes with explosive breath . . . a roaring motor-car, which looks as though running on shrapnel, is more beautiful than the *Victory of Samothrace*.
5. We shall sing of the man at the steering wheel, whose ideal stem transfixes the Earth, rushing over the circuit of her orbit.

From Joshua C. Taylor, *Futurism* (New York: Museum of Modern Art, 1961), pp. 124–27.

6. The poet must give himself with frenzy, with splendour and with lavishness, in order to increase the enthusiastic fervour of the primordial elements.

7. There is no more beauty except in strife. No masterpiece without aggressiveness. Poetry must be a violent onslaught upon the unknown forces, to command them to bow before man.

8. We stand upon the extreme promontory of the centuries! . . . Why should we look behind us, when we have to break in the mysterious portals of the Impossible? Time and Space died yesterday. Already we live in the absolute, since we have already created speed, eternal and ever-present.

9. We wish to glorify War—the only health giver of the world—militarism, patriotism, the destructive arm of the Anarchist, the beautiful Ideas that kill, the contempt for woman.

10. We wish to destroy the museums, the libraries, to fight against moralism, feminism and all opportunistic and utilitarian meannesses.

11. We shall sing of the great crowds in the excitement of labour, pleasure and rebellion; of the multi-coloured and polyphonic surf of revolutions in modern capital cities; of the nocturnal vibration of arsenals and workshops beneath their violent electric moons; of the greedy stations swallowing smoking snakes; of factories suspended from the clouds by their strings of smoke; of bridges leaping like gymnasts over the diabolical cutlery of sunbathed rivers; of adventurous liners scenting the horizon; of broadchested locomotives prancing on the rails, like huge steel horses bridled with long tubes; and of the gliding flight of aeroplanes, the sound of whose screw is like the flapping of flags and the applause of an enthusiastic crowd.

It is in Italy that we launch this manifesto of violence, destructive and incendiary, by which we this day found *Futurism,* because we would deliver Italy from its canker of professors, archaeologists, cicerones and antiquaries.

Italy has been too long the great market of the secondhand dealers. We would free her from the numberless museums which cover her with as many cemeteries.

Museums, cemeteries! . . . Truly identical with their sinister jostling of bodies that know one another not. Public dormitories where one sleeps for ever side by side with detested or unknown beings. Mutual ferocity of painters and sculptors slaying one another with blows of lines and colour in a single museum.

Let one pay a visit there each year as one visits one's dead once a year . . . That we can allow! . . . Deposit flowers even once a year at the feet of the *Gioconda,* if you will! . . . But to walk daily in the museums with our sorrows, our fragile courage and our anxiety, that is inadmissible! . . . Would you, then, poison yourselves? Do you want to decay?

What can one find in an old picture unless it be the painful contortions of the artist striving to break the bars that stand in the way of his desire to express completely his dream?

To admire an old picture is to pour our sensitiveness into a funeral urn, instead of casting it forward in violent gushes of creation and action. Would you, then, waste the best of your strength by a useless administration of the past, from which you can but emerge exhausted, reduced, downtrodden?

In truth, the daily haunting of museums, of libraries and of academies (those cemeteries of wasted efforts, those calvaries of crucified dreams, those ledgers of broken attempts!) is to artists what the protracted tutelage of parents is to intelligent youths, intoxicated with their talent and their ambitious determination.

For men on their death-bed, for invalids, and for prisoners, very well! The admirable past may be balsam to their wounds, since the future is closed to them . . . But we will have none of it, we, the young, the strong, and the living *Futurists!*

Come, then, the good incendiaries, with their charred fingers! . . . Here they come! Here they come! . . . Set fire to the shelves of the libraries! Deviate the course of canals to flood the cellars of the museums! Oh! may the glorious canvases drift helplessly! Seize pickaxes and hammers! Sap the foundations of the venerable cities!

The oldest amongst us are thirty; we have, therefore, ten years at least to accomplish our task. When we are forty, let others, younger and more valiant, throw us into the basket like useless manuscripts! . . . They will come against us from afar, from everywhere, bounding upon the lightsome measure of their first poems, scratching the air with their hooked fingers, and scenting at the academy doors the pleasant odour of our rotting minds, marked out already for the catacombs of the libraries.

But we shall not be there. They will find us at length, one winter's night, right out in the country, beneath a dreary shed, the monotonous rain-drops strumming on the roof, cowering by our trepidating aeroplanes, warming our hands at the miserable fire which our books of today will make, blazing gaily beneath the dazzling flight of their images.

They will surge around us, breathless with anxiety and disappointment, and all, exasperated by our dauntless courage, will throw themselves upon us to slay us, with all the more hatred because their hearts will be filled with love and admiration for us. And Injustice, strong and healthy, will burst forth radiantly in their eyes. For art can be nought but violence, cruelty and injustice.

The oldest amongst us are thirty, and yet we have already squandered treasures, treasures of strength, of love, of courage, of rugged determination, hastily, in a frenzy, without counting, with all our might, breathlessly.

Look at us! We are not breathless . . . Our heart does not feel the slightest weariness! For it is fed with fire, hatred and speed! . . . That surprises you? It is because you do not remember even having lived! We stand upon the summit of the world and once more we cast our challenge to the stars!

Your objections? Enough! Enough! I know them! It is agreed! We know well what our fine and false intelligence tells us. We are, it says, only the summary and the extension of our ancestors. Perhaps! Very well! . . . What matter? . . . But we do not wish to hear! Beware of repeating those infamous words! Better lift your head!

We stand upon the summit of the world and once more we cast our challenge to the stars!

F. T. Marinetti
Editor of *Poesia*

Futurist Painting: Technical Manifesto (11 April 1910)

On the 8th of March, 1910, in the limelight of the Chiarella Theatre of Turin, we launched our first Manifesto to a public of three thousand people—artists, men of letters, students and others; it was a violent and cynical cry which displayed our sense of rebellion, our deep-rooted disgust, our haughty contempt for vulgarity, for academic and pedantic mediocrity, for the fanatical worship of all that is old and worm-eaten.

We bound ourselves there and then to the movement of Futurist Poetry which was initiated a year earlier by F. T. Marinetti in the columns of the *Figaro*.

The battle of Turin has remained legendary. We exchanged almost as many knocks as we did ideas, in order to protect from certain death the genius of Italian Art.

And now during a temporary pause in this formidable struggle we come out of the crowd in order to expound with technical precision our programme for the renovation of painting, of which our Futurist Salon at Milan was a dazzling manifestation.

Our growing need of truth is no longer satisfied with Form and Colour as they have been understood hitherto.

The gesture which we would reproduce on canvas shall no longer be a fixed *moment* in universal dynamism. It shall simply be the dynamic sensation itself [made eternal].

Indeed, all things move, all things run, all things are rapidly changing.

A profile is never motionless before our eyes, but it constantly appears and disappears. On account of the persistency of an image upon the retina, moving objects constantly multiply themselves; their form changes like rapid vibrations, in their mad career. Thus a running horse has not four legs, but twenty, and their movements are triangular.

All is conventional in art. Nothing is absolute in painting. What was truth for the painters of yesterday is but a falsehood today. We declare, for instance, that a portrait [to be a work of art] must not be like the sitter and that the painter carries in himself the landscapes which he would fix upon his canvas.

To paint a human figure you must not paint it; you must render the whole of its surrounding atmosphere.

Space no longer exists: The street pavement, soaked by rain beneath the glare of electric lamps, becomes immensely deep and gapes to the very centre of the earth. Thousands of miles divide us from the sun; yet the house in front of us fits into the solar disk.

Who can still believe in the opacity of bodies, since our sharpened and multiplied sensitiveness has already penetrated the obscure manifestations of the medium? Why should we forget in our creations the doubled power of our sight, capable of giving results analogous to those of the X rays?

It will be sufficient to cite a few examples, chosen amongst thousands, to prove the truth of our arguments.

The sixteen people around you in a rolling motor-bus are in turn and at the same time one, ten, four, three; they are motionless and they change places; they come and go, bound into the street, are suddenly swallowed up by the sunshine, then come back and sit before you, like persistent symbols of universal vibration.

How often have we not seen upon the cheek of the person with whom we were talking the horse which passes at the end of the street.

Our bodies penetrate the sofas upon which we sit, and the sofas penetrate our bodies. The motor-bus rushes into the houses which it passes, and in their turn the houses throw themselves upon the motor-bus and are blended with it.

The construction of pictures has hitherto been foolishly traditional. Painters have shown us the objects and the people placed before us. We shall henceforward put the spectator in the centre of the picture.

As in every realm of the human mind, clear-sighted individual research has swept away the unchanging obscurities of dogma, so must the vivifying current of science soon deliver painting from academic tradition.

We would at any price re-enter into life. Victorious science has nowadays disowned its past in order the better to serve the material needs of our time; we would that art, disowning its past, were able to serve at last the intellectual needs which are within us.

Our renovated consciousness does not permit us to look upon man as the centre of universal life. The suffering of a man is of the same interest to us as the suffering of an electric lamp, which, with spasmodic starts, shrieks out the most heartrending expressions of colour. The harmony of the lines and folds of modern dress works upon our sensitiveness with the same emotional and symbolical power as did the nude upon the sensitiveness of the old masters.

In order to conceive and understand the novel beauties of a futurist picture, the soul must be purified [become again pure]; the eye must be freed from its veil of atavism and culture, so that it may at last look upon Nature and not upon the museum as the one and only standard.

As soon as ever this result has been obtained, it will be readily admitted that brown tints have never coursed beneath our skin; it will be discovered that yellow shines forth in our flesh, that red blazes, and that green, blue and violet dance upon it with untold charms, voluptuous and caressing.

How is it possible still to see the human face pink, now that our life, redoubled by noctambulism, has multiplied our perceptions as colourists? The human face is yellow, red, green, blue, violet. The pallor of a woman gazing in a jeweller's window is more intensely iridescent than the prismatic fires of the jewels that fascinate her like a lark.

The time has passed for our sensations in painting to be whispered. We wish them in future to sing and re-echo upon our canvases in deafening and triumphant flourishes.

Your eyes, accustomed to semi-darkness, will soon open to more radiant visions of light. The shadows which we shall paint shall be more luminous than the high-lights of our predecessors, and our pictures, next to those of the museums, will shine like blinding daylight compared with deepest night.

We conclude that painting cannot exist today without Divisionism. This is no process that can be learned and applied at will. Divisionism, for the modern painter, must be an INNATE COMPLEMENTARINESS which we declare to be essential and necessary.

Our art will probably be accused of tormented and decadent cerebralism. But we shall merely answer that we are, on the contrary, the primitives of a new sensitiveness, multiplied hundredfold, and that our art is intoxicated with spontaneity and power.

WE DECLARE:

1. THAT ALL FORMS OF IMITATION MUST BE DESPISED, ALL FORMS OF ORIGINALITY GLORIFIED.

2. THAT IT IS ESSENTIAL TO REBEL AGAINST THE TYRANNY OF THE TERMS "HARMONY" AND "GOOD TASTE" AS BEING TOO ELASTIC EXPRESSIONS, BY THE HELP OF WHICH IT IS EASY TO DEMOLISH THE WORKS OF REMBRANDT, OF GOYA AND OF RODIN.

3. THAT THE ART CRITICS ARE USELESS OR HARMFUL.

4. THAT ALL SUBJECTS PREVIOUSLY USED MUST BE SWEPT ASIDE IN ORDER TO EXPRESS OUR WHIRLING LIFE OF STEEL, OF PRIDE, OF FEVER AND OF SPEED.

5. THAT THE NAME OF "MADMAN" WITH WHICH IT IS ATTEMPTED TO GAG ALL INNOVATORS SHOULD BE LOOKED UPON AS A TITLE OF HONOUR.

6. THAT INNATE COMPLEMENTARINESS IS AN ABSOLUTE NECESSITY IN PAINTING, JUST AS FREE METRE IN POETRY OR POLYPHONY IN MUSIC.

7. THAT UNIVERSAL DYNAMISM MUST BE RENDERED IN PAINTING AS A DYNAMIC SENSATION.

8. THAT IN THE MANNER OF RENDERING NATURE THE FIRST ESSENTIAL IS IN SINCERITY AND PURITY.

9. THAT MOVEMENT AND LIGHT DESTROY THE MATERIALITY OF BODIES.

WE FIGHT:

1. AGAINST THE BITUMINOUS TINTS BY WHICH IT IS ATTEMPTED TO OBTAIN THE PATINA OF TIME UPON MODERN PICTURES.

2. AGAINST THE SUPERFICIAL AND ELEMENTARY ARCHAISM FOUNDED UPON FLAT TINTS, AND WHICH, BY IMITATING THE LINEAR TECHNIQUE OF THE EGYPTIANS, REDUCES PAINTING TO A POWERLESS SYNTHESIS, BOTH CHILDISH AND GROTESQUE.

3. AGAINST THE FALSE CLAIMS TO BELONG TO THE FUTURE PUT FORWARD BY THE SECESSIONISTS AND THE INDEPENDENTS, WHO HAVE INSTALLED NEW ACADEMIES NO LESS TRITE AND ATTACHED TO ROUTINE THAN THE PRECEDING ONES.

4. AGAINST THE NUDE IN PAINTING, AS NAUSEOUS AND AS TEDIOUS AS ADULTERY IN LITERATURE.

We wish to explain this last point. Nothing is *immoral* in our eyes; it is the monotony of the nude against which we fight. We are told that the subject is nothing and that everything lies in the manner of treating it. That is agreed; we, too, admit that. But this truism, unimpeachable and absolute fifty years ago, is no longer so today with regard to the nude, since artists obsessed with the desire to expose the bodies of their mistresses have transformed the Salons into arrays of unwholesome flesh!

We demand, for ten years, the total suppression of the nude in painting.

> Umberto Boccioni, *painter* (Milan)
> Carlo D. Carrà, *painter* (Milan)
> Luigi Russolo, *painter* (Milan)
> Giacomo Balla, *painter* (Rome)
> Gino Severini, *painter* (Paris)

2. Henri Massis and Alfred de Tarde,
The Young People of Today

Les Jeunes Gens d'aujourd'hui—literally the "young people of today" but
in fact intended to refer only to the young men—is one of the most famous "opinion polls" in history. Undertaken by two young intellectuals,
Henri Massis and Alfred de Tarde, who wrote under the pseudonym
"Agathon" (Socrates' disciple), it purported to be an objective survey of
Parisian students between the ages of eighteen and twenty-five at a variety
of elite educational institutions: the *lycées,* the Ecole Normale Supérieure,
and the university faculties. But the authors, and Massis in particular,
were far from neutral researchers and sought rather to find in the students
they interviewed corroboration of their own views. The survey, which
was first published in a Paris newspaper in 1912 and appeared in book
form a year later, attracted a great deal of attention. Its main themes
were even incorporated into two novels of the day, the last installment of
Romain Rolland's *Jean-Christophe* (1912) and Roger Martin du Gard's
Jean Barois (1913).

Massis and de Tarde's fundamental finding was a variant on the great
nineteenth-century theme of father-son conflict: they stressed again and
again the stark contrast between the generation born around 1890 and its
predecessor. The paternal generation had been steeped in the values of
the Enlightenment: rationalism, faith in science, distrust of religion, hatred of war. The new generation scorned these values as tepid, even lifeless. The selections from *The Young People of Today* reprinted below
describe and analyze the values of their elders and those that they embraced instead.

While "generation" was hardly a new word, sustained talk about generations and the consciousness of being the member of a generation began in Europe only in the decade or so before the First World War. *The
Young Men of Today* was one of the salient examples and main popularizers of this mode of thinking, which included the use of "generation"
both as an analytic tool and as a polemical device.

Introduction

"There is something new about the young"—such is the unanimous perception. The courageous attitude of the young people who are coming of

From Agathon (pseud. for Henri Massis and Alfred de Tarde), *Les Jeunes Gens d'aujourd'hui,* 4th ed. (Paris: Plon, 1913), pp. i–iv, 1–9, 11–12, 16–20, 22–36, 65–68,
70–79, 94–100, 111–12, 116–19. Translated for this volume by Kent Wright.

age today has impressed all of their elders. Parents experience an unsettling surprise, for every being aspires above all to produce its own likeness. But their teachers rejoice in them, for in them they see an auspicious impulse of the race.

Is it possible, however, to speak of a "new generation"? A generation presupposes a community of traits, an interconnection, a secret agreement, an ensemble "in which each person is moved by a common effort." Is it true that young people are united by common tendencies, by an ideal different from that of their predecessors, that a single internal impulse, if not a single doctrine, fashions their souls, that a single hope uplifts them? And if it is true, to what extent is it true? That is the object of our investigation. We have undertaken it with a burning curiosity, too burning not to require of us complete honesty and candor, and we have completed it in a mood of joy and confidence.

But first, what do we mean by "youth"? We have focused our research on young men between the ages of eighteen and twenty-five years. It is after graduating from the *lycée,* during one's years in the *grandes écoles,*[1] before submitting to the demands of a career, that one's moral character is formed and the intellectual directions to which one will remain faithful all one's life are chosen. Among these young men, those who are approaching their twentieth year seemed to us genuinely to represent an original type. Thus we wish to sketch a portrait of the generation born around 1890.

Is this to say that everyone with that approximate birthdate displays distinctive traits? We could hardly make such a claim. We are concerned here only with cultivated young men, those whose true thoughts we were in a position to learn and whose confidences we could receive. To be frank, this is a study of elite youth. Perhaps a broader investigation, extended to all young Frenchmen, those of the workshops, the poorer neighborhoods, the fields, as well as those coming out of institutions of higher learning, would have yielded different results. But, in fact, the numerical majority has only a secondary importance, even a misleading one, for once a doctrine has won over the crowd, it has begun to die in the eyes of the philosopher; its present triumph insures that it will not dominate the future. And it is the future which interests us here. Its secret should not be sought among the

1. The *grandes écoles* are a number of separate, state-run educational institutions in Paris for professional training in specialized subjects. Admission is by rigorous competitive examination. Since the nineteenth century, these schools, entered after graduation from the *lycée,* have been regarded as among the most elite in the French system, presumably turning out the best minds in France and assuring their graduates of an eminently respectable and often brilliant career. The schools include the Ecole Normale Supérieure, for the training of *lycée* professors and renowned for the quality of its instruction in philosophy; the Ecole Polytechnique, for engineering; and the Ecole Nationale d'Administration, for the training of high-level civil servants.—ED.

multitude, but in the innovating elite, the leaven of the unformed masses. It is the beliefs of intellectuals which, many years afterward, orient public consciousness, and through it, politics, morality, and the arts. That is why we thought it appropriate to examine those among the young who will probably govern the destinies of the nation in politics, the army, literature, industry, and administration. Make no mistake about it, we did not attempt to draw a portrait of the average young man of 1912, but rather to sketch the features of the best young men and to describe the *new type of intellectual elite*.

Finally, a word on the form of our investigation. You will not find here a series of responses to a questionnaire prepared in advance and distributed haphazardly among relatives and friends. Nothing is more futile than such a series of opinions, which are not so much contradictory as incoherent, in which each respondent tries to outshine his neighbor. We have frequented the society of and have questioned a large number of young men in the schools, Faculties, *lycées,* chosen among the most representative of their group. We have verified their assertions by the observations of their teachers. Lastly, we have read the pages in which certain of them have expressed themselves.[2]

Chapter 1

The Taste for Action

Eckermann records this remark of Goethe: "In all epochs of regression and dissolution, minds are preoccupied with themselves, while in epochs of progress they are oriented towards the external world." And the Master of Weimar thus condemned his own century: "Our time is one of regression, it is personal." A vigorous thought, but one that needs to be clarified. Goethe did not intend to proscribe the inner life merely for the sake of activity. He wanted to distinguish those pessimistic periods, in which the vital forces impede and dissipate themselves, from those of optimism and vitality, in which some great external object binds these forces together and concentrates them. That is the point which concerns us here.

---

2. In the present publication we have made use of the investigations parallel to our own in the *Revue des Français,* the *Revue hebdomadaire,* the *Temps,* and the *Gaulois.* The study from the *Temps,* directed by Emile Henriot, has recently appeared as a book entitled *What Young People Dream of.* It can be usefully consulted, above all with regard to the new literary doctrines.

Finally, in order to verify our conclusions further, we sent our essay to twenty young men, spokesmen of literary or political groups, asking if their sentiments coincided with our own, and to what extent. The results of this test of our investigation can be found in the appendix. The confirmation that we received proves the general truth of our description. [Massis and de Tarde's note.]

The Pessimism of the Elders

Pessimism was the distinguishing mark of the generation that came of age around 1885. We possess a unique testimony to this, a kind of moral inventory drawn up by one of the most perceptive minds of this time: the *Essais de psychologie contemporaine* of Paul Bourget.

Convinced that "the state of mind peculiar to one generation is contained in embryo in the theories and dreams of the preceding generation," Bourget surveyed the works of the masters who had guided the youth of that time and concluded with resignation: "It seems to me that all these works are pervaded by the same unhappy influence, which, to express it in a single word, is profoundly and unceasingly pessimistic." Whether one speaks of [Baudelaire's] *Les Fleurs du Mal,* [Flaubert's] *Madame Bovary,* . . . or [Huysman's] *A Rebours,* there exists, in these diverse writings, the same feeling of discouragement, "a deadly fatigue of living, a dejected perception of the vanity of all effort."

In each soul there resounded the hopeless avowal that Taine, at the age of twenty, confided to Prévost-Paradol: "This systematic discouragement which has overcome me with respect to thought, has done so as well with respect to love. I do not hope. No thoughtful man can hope." The dilettantism of a Renan, or a Goncourt, was merely a powerlessness to make choices or to love, and it ended in a kind of desolate negation. In Flaubert, Tolstoy, Turgenev, and Loti, the magic spell of far-away or lost civilizations disordered sensibilities that were no longer guided by any tradition. The analytical spirit of a Stendhal, an Amiel, a Dumas, doomed the heart to aridity, and the extreme aristocratism of Renan in his *Dialogues* was not alone in concealing an arrogant despair.

One must reread these *Essais:* they are even richer in meaning, if we use them not only to satisfy our curiosity about the past, but also to serve in the examination of our present sensibility. For the sick people to whom this book was addressed have been succeeded by healthy men, who will find in its pages everything to which they are most opposed. If reading it annoys them, it may also throw some light on their own situation. . . .

A Sacrificed Generation

It was a transitional sacrificed generation. Coming after that of the Second Empire, which was full of materialistic pride and scientific credo, and which was vanquished in 1870, it truly bore the entire weight of the defeat. It was forced to make the overwhelming effort of revising its deepest beliefs. It experienced the worst grief, humiliation, and doubt. At least, its self-effacement prepared and made possible the present generation, which did not have to triumph over so many obstacles in order to reestablish life vigorously on new certitudes.

The most terrible wounds of the defeat were felt, not immediately, but many years after the war. In the wake of such a catastrophe there is first a brief explosion of vitality; the tasks of material recovery keep everyone busy. It does not appear as if intellectuals recognized, at the outset, the humiliation of the nation, or that they doubted themselves; or that artists made any effort to disavow their former sources of inspiration. The *Soirées de Medan* prolonged the naturalist aesthetic; the Parnasse of 1876 resumed that of 1860. The war itself became the object of commentary in the manner of Flaubert or the Goncourt brothers. It was only later, around 1880, that what one might call the *ideology of defeat* began to be expressed. It then seemed "that the defeat had not been merely an episode, but that it continued, that we would be defeated anew every day, indefinitely, until the moment that we had restored the French patrimony in its integrity."

This profound disheartenment was translated into an incensed idealism, which exalted pure intellect at the expense of strength. Illusory revenge, the revenge of wounded pride! A real impotence consoles itself with the dream of an ideal power. The fettered will forges for itself an imaginary liberty within a spiritual world. If strength was victorious—so goes the argument—that was only because strength is evil, because the world is hostile to the spirit. Let us therefore take refuge in a lofty indifference, which at least safeguards the rights of this vainglorious and sovereign intellect.

It would be cruel not to admit that there was something heroic in this attitude. In many circles it preserved an ideal of high culture that, while useless, was not without grandeur. But the very excess of this intellectual absolutism cut them off from life, from all human emotion. The sole reality which did not disillusion them was one they thought they found in themselves: they made a system out of egoism. "Since it is necessary to live," wrote Alfred Vallette in the first issue of the *Mercure de France* (1892), "we will oppose to desolate and universal negation this resolute affirmation: ME." Did a coherent inner world result from this doctrine? Quite the contrary, it only brought them back to the void from which it claimed to deliver them.

The Conflict between Thought and Action

The problem which obsessed this entire generation was the supposed *antinomy of thought and action*. Our predecessors believed themselves to be the victims of what Bourget called "the poison of analysis." A phantom problem which depleted their best forces. All their activity was consumed in a search for a reason, almost an excuse to act. As an adolescent, Taine was already distressed by this conflict, which paralyzed his existence. "Reason counsels me to remain immobile," he wrote to his friend Prévost-

Paradol, "and nature orders me to act." This hopeless contradiction haunted him to the end. . . .

Now this formidable problem, which confounded an entire generation, has been resolved by the youth of today. Or to put it better, the problem has resolved itself, and disappeared. The famous contradiction, through which their elders secretly savored the pathos of their lives, seems to them to be a pure intellectual mirage. It no longer confines them to a pleasurable inertia; indeed, they all but resent it as a lie.

For isn't the antinomy of thought and action a problem only for beings of a spent and anemic sensibility, in whom no vital instinct gives rise to vigorous affirmation? A thoughtful nature, truly rich in life and love, breaks the circle, withdraws from the eternal oscillation, and strives towards a belief, a synthesis, a dogmatism that is the precursor of action. . . .

Strange detour of pride! [The previous generation] took their incapacity for living to the point of congratulating themselves for it. They sincerely considered it to be the logical extension and end result of many centuries of thought. They declared that they were "sick of civilization." But this was surely an abuse of words. For is not a civilization an integrated system of ideas and sentiments, a harmonious ensemble of beliefs, that is, by definition, a barrier against doubt and despair, a reason for acting, a kind of "predestination"?

To find an excuse for the defeat of their deepest energies, they gladly turned to the then-famous thesis of the decadence of the Latin races. They proclaimed that the most idealistic and refined peoples are for that very reason condemned to die, and that the highest cultivation of the mind is only the brilliant sign of its agony. They believed in deadly hosts, the decrepitude of races, in the irresistible waning of life in those mysterious, amorphous, and inconsistent organisms. They prostrated themselves before those so-called historical laws which are unceasingly belied by history, and thus rightly mocked the newcomers, freed from the obsession of time-honored atavisms!

All these traits—pessimism, intellectual pride, scorn for the active life, the acceptance of an impending and irreparable fall—were united in *dilettantism,* "the very intelligent and at the same time very sensuous disposition of mind, which inclines us towards various forms of life in turn, and persuades us to sample all of these forms, without fully giving ourselves over to any." *Dilettantism* means the dispersal of being, by which the bundle of our energies is unbound; it is the inability to choose, or, to put it better, it is the lack of love. Because he samples everything, while devoting himself to nothing, the dilettante naturally considers himself to be superior to the believer. Renan gave expression to this self-satisfaction in a famous passage from *Saint Paul:* "We should like to imagine a skeptical Paul, shipwrecked, alone, abandoned and betrayed by his people, who had arrived at the disillusionment of old age. It would please us to see the scales fall from his eyes a second time, and our sweet unbelief would have its revenge if the most dogmatic of men had died sorrowful and disheartened, but let us say tranquilly, on some seashore or road in Spain, saying to himself: *Ergo erravi.*" The accent of this passage was able secretly to move our fathers, but it is unbearable to the young people of today. The sweet unbelief that seeks revenge on faith because it believes itself to be superior, this smiling apotheosis of doubt, appeared to them as a limitation of their being; not a limitation of the intellect, but one of the heart and of the will. . . .

The Optimism of the New Generation

How energetically are the young people of today raising themselves up on the morose foundation of the previous generation!

We are struck first by their confidence in themselves. They have banished doubt. The spirit which guides them is one of affirmation and creativity. For them this spirit is like a clean bill of health for the soul, like a positive current which travels to the mind from their whole being. It is not enough to say that these young men are optimists, for optimism is merely a doctrine: here, it is a matter of an originality of temperament, which reveals itself as a state of plenitude and vitality.

We have seen in their predecessors the fashionable concern to be duped by nothing. They, on the contrary, are the dupes of joyous life, if being "duped" is indeed the correct expression for conforming to life's demands in order to get the most out of it. "He who believes is worth more, counts for more, than he who doubts. If he is mistaken—too bad, it's a waste of energy, but at least it is energy." They accept the minimum amount of illusion that underlies all activity.

Their sensibility is realistic: it submits itself to fact of its own accord. Of course the resigned fatalism of the intellectuals of 1890 also appeared as a submission to fact; but in reality it was merely the pouting of disenchanted idealists. They *surrendered,* the new generation *accepts.* To surrender is to flee from responsibility; to accept is to embrace wholly. To surrender is to close in upon oneself; to accept is to bring will and energy to completion. From the start our young people have a very clear grasp of the possible and the practical. Besides, the perception of freedom, which a Bergson restored to them, intensifies their lust for life. Constraint only spurs them on. The words of Vauvenargues seem to sum up their experience: "The world is what it must be for an active being: *full of obstacles.*" . . .

In a word, what characterizes their attitude is the *taste for action.* . . . Consciously or instinctually, [the new generation] is anti-intellectual; it does not approach life as an intellectual debate, that is, as a debate in

which only rational considerations are at stake. . . . Doubtless it is necessary to see in this, besides certain mental habits which arise from the growing practice of sports, the influence of American philosophy (James, Whit-
man). [The new generation] endorses the words of Emerson: "Life is not a
dialectic . . . It is neither intellectual nor critical, but vigorous." . . . Are
these young people less intelligent [than their predecessors]? No, but less
in love with intellect. The only speculation worthy of interest in their view
is the one which asks "What is there to do?" and "How should it be
done?" . . .

Chapter 2

Patriotic Faith

The sentiment which underlies all these youthful attitudes, which unanimously accords with the deepest tendencies in their thought, is that of patriotic faith. That they are possessed of this sentiment is unequivocal and
undeniable. Optimism, that state of mind which defines the attitude of
these young people, manifests itself from the outset in the confidence
which they place in the future of France: there they find their first motive
for acting, the one which determines and directs all their activity.

The young men of today have read the word of their destiny in this
French soul, which dictates to them a clear and imperious duty. There
seems to be nothing unnatural or out of the ordinary in this, and yet some
sort of shame or modesty prevents us from declaring it. The novelty of such
an attitude appears remarkable only by contrast. Our elders, left uncertain
and destitute by the war, searched in vain for the words which would restore to them the divine virtue of joy in effort and hope in struggle. This
anxious, and soon guilty, quest led them down the most dangerous paths.
Let us pause and go back a few years, in order to retrace their steps.

An Eclipse of Patriotism around 1890

Here are the documents. We are not reprinting the words of our predecessors for the cruel pleasure of condemning them; we are not assuming the
role of accusers. We know quite well that there was something of the cun-
ning revenge of a humiliated patriotism at the root of the humanitarian
internationalism that the "intellectuals" of 1890 proudly professed. But
there is one point we want to make palpable: the misunderstanding between
those arriving on the scene and those who preceded them.

Thus let us open the *Mercure de France,* where the young elite of
twenty years ago expressed themselves. In one of the first issues (1891) we
are struck by the provocative title of an article: "The Patriotic Plaything."
The author [Rémy de Gourmont] who later became the guiding spirit of the

review, was then unknown: "Personally," he writes, "in exchange for those God-forsaken lands"—he was speaking of Alsace and Lorraine—"I would give neither the pinky of my right hand, which I use to balance my hand when I write, nor that of my left hand, which I use to flick the ashes from my cigarette. . . . It seems to me that it has gone on long enough, the joke about these two little enslaved sisters, dressed in mourning and kneeling at the foot of a border marker, crying like little heifers instead of going out to milk their cows. . . ." Still further: "Perhaps the day will come when they will find us at the border; we will go without enthusiasm; it will be our turn to kill each other, and we will do so with a true displeasure: 'To die for the fatherland'—but we are singing other ballads, we are cultivating a different kind of poetry. If it is necessary to sum it up in a phrase, so be it. *We are not patriots.*"

Let us not yield to the indignation which these pages arouse in us. Who does not sense the disconsolate bitterness of this confession, which is intended to be so pugnacious? One must have violently despaired of one's country, one must have been sorely wounded by actual events, to have resorted to the arrogant consolation of sovereign egoism. This willful callousness is really the avowal of a still open wound! In the end, it is still idealism, but of the most deceptive sort. . . .

More fervent than these aesthetes, students turned this humanitarianism into a doctrine of action. Their master was Tolstoy, with his dreams of fraternal love and peace between men. This was the heroic period, if one can put it that way, of antimilitarism in the universities.

We possess a remarkable testimony to this: we refer to the study that one of the most sincere "intellectuals" of the Sorbonne, Frédéric Rauh, conducted with his students at the Ecole Normale, in order to find out if "patriotism is a reasonable sentiment and if it can withstand the scrutiny of factual examination." Ah, what a fine massacre! All the grounds on which the patriotic sentiment is justified are treated in turn as "high-sounding generalities," "superstitions," "literary and artistic doctrines." Nothing escapes the pitiless "scientific method," as if patriotism, which plumbs the depths of belief and feeling, could ever be its object. "Patriots do not count," says Rauh, "they are pure sentimentalists." What's more: "Nationalists do not share my convictions. Their doctrine is in contradiction with the opinions I hold. I see no need to hide internationalism in France under a bushel-basket."

In short, this socialistic professor's study attempted to show that "conscience can sacrifice the nation to an idea": at the very least, it endeavored to put "the fatherland at the service of internationalism." . . .

Such is the astonishing word-play taught at the Sorbonne scarcely ten years ago. They supported the nation on condition that it served the humanitarian ideal, and, finally, they sacrificed it to that end! Such phrases can be taken as excellent touchstones. And from the start, the pacifist sophistries of these intellectuals seemed impious or puerile to all the young people we examined and to whom we proposed them as a test. "No one would any longer dare to write them," said Monsieur de Mun when reprinting them, "or even to think them." Read at a meeting of *lycée* students, these ideas "brought forth, particularly on the faces of the young, an expression of profound amazement." It is thus a fact that the new generation does not put the ideal ahead of the nation, but instead *fuses* the two into a single faith.

The Reawakening of the National Instinct

In fact, we no longer find students who profess antipatriotism in the Faculties or the *grandes écoles*. At the Polytechnique, at the Normale, where only yesterday the antimilitarists and the disciples of Jaurès were so plentiful, even at the Sorbonne, which boasted of so many cosmopolitan elements, the humanitarian doctrines are no longer making new converts. At the Law Faculty, at the School of Political Sciences, national sentiment is lively, indeed almost impassioned. There the words "Alsace-Lorraine" inspire long ovations, and professors refer to German methods[3] with caution, for fear of murmurs and hisses. This is horseplay, no doubt, but it indicates that the new generation does not accept the notion of the superiority of German science, the conviction in which their teachers were formed. . . .

This magnificent renaissance of the virtues of the race has only become clearer since 1905, the "arrival of the new generation." "At that time," Monsieur Désiré Ferry, president of the Republican Union of Students in Paris, tells us, "a shudder was felt throughout France. Youthful energies drew themselves up: at eighteen years of age, we were little Frenchmen, filled with haughty pride, determined no longer to endure a humiliation." A dawn, an expanding dawn rose over the darkness of that autumn of 1905, when our young people understood that the German threat was present.[4] . . .

The patriotism of French youth was thus deepened and fortified. Last

3. The reference is to the scientific methods for the study of the humanistic disciplines—e.g., the use of philology for the criticism of textual sources—pioneered by German scholars during the nineteenth century. These had recently been adopted at the Sorbonne, in part out of the conviction that the Germans had become intellectually superior to the French and that the latter needed to catch up.—Ed.

4. In 1905 the German Kaiser, while on a Mediterranean trip, had debarked in Tangier and expressed principled opposition to the French policy which placed Morocco in a French sphere of influence. The episode initiated the so-called First Moroccan Crisis, one of a series of European diplomatic crises in the decade before the outbreak of World War I.—Ed.

summer young men fearlessly envisaged war: throughout the entire country, they communicated their confidence.

"Let it be known," says Monsieur Tourolle, president of the General Association of Students, "let it be known that the entire youth of France has arisen to a man, to respond to the German insult." And when they spoke of the Franco-German Treaty, the fifteen hundred students of Paris, without political distinction, all agreed to protest the surrender of the Congo to Germany: "We are not in agreement," they declared, "with those who diminish the empire or the prestige of the nation! Let the generation of those who govern take the sole responsibility!" . . .

Heroism and War

Consider something even more significant. Students of advanced rhetoric in Paris, that is, the most cultivated elite among young people, declare that they find in warfare an aesthetic ideal of energy and strength. They believe that "France needs heroism in order to live." "Such is the faith," comments Monsieur Tourolle, "which consumes modern youth."

How many times in the last two years have we heard this repeated: "Better war than this eternal waiting!" There is no bitterness in this avowal, but rather a secret hope. . . .

War! The word has taken on a sudden glamour. It is a youthful word, wholly new, adorned with that seduction which the eternal bellicose instinct has revived in the hearts of men. These young men impute to it all the beauty with which they are in love and of which they have been deprived by ordinary life. Above all, war, in their eyes, is the occasion for the most noble of human virtues, those which they exalt above all others: energy, mastery, and sacrifice for a cause which transcends ourselves. With William James, they believe that life "would become odious if it offered neither risks nor rewards for the courageous man."

A professor of philosophy at the Lycée Henri IV confided to us: "I once spoke about war to my pupils. I explained to them that there were unjust wars, undertaken out of anger, and that it was necessary to justify the bellicose sentiment. Well, the class obviously did not follow me; they rejected that distinction."

Read this passage from a letter written to us by a young student of rhetoric, Alsatian in origin. "The existence that we lead does not satisfy us completely because, even if we possess all the elements of a good life, we cannot organize them in a practical, immediate deed that would take us, body and soul, and hurl us outside of ourselves. One event only will permit that deed—war; and hence we desire it. It is in the life of the camps, it is around the fire that we will experience the supreme expansion of those French powers that are within us. Our intellect will no longer be troubled in the face of the unknowable, since it will be able to concentrate itself entirely on a present duty from which uncertainty and hesitation are excluded."

Above all, perhaps, how can one ignore the success that accounts of our colonialists have had among the young intellectuals under consideration here? The expeditions of Moll, Lenfant, and Baratier arouse their enthusiasm; they search in their own unperilous existences for a moral equivalent to these bold destinies; they attempt to transpose this intrepid valor into their inner lives.

Some go further: their studies completed, they satisfy their taste for action in colonial adventures. It is not enough for them to learn history: they are making it. A young student from the Normale, Monsieur Klipfell, who received his teaching degree in literature in July of 1912, requested to be assigned to active service in Morocco, as a member of the Expeditionary Corps. We can cite many a similar example. One thinks of Jacques Violet, a twenty-year-old officer, who died so gloriously at Ksar-Teuchan, in Adrar: he was killed at the head of his men, at the moment of victory, in a grove of palm trees; among his belongings, they found a pair of white gloves and a copy of *Servitude and Military Grandeur;* it was thus that he went into combat.

Need we recall the adventures of the colonial military artillery lieutenant Ernest Psichari, the grandson of Renan, who abandoned his studies at the Sorbonne, along with the thesis he had begun on the bankruptcy of idealism, in order to lead a French operation in the African bush. "Africa," he wrote, "is one of the last places where our finest sentiments can still be affirmed, where the last robust consciences have hope of finding an outlet for their activity." He adds: "From extreme barbarism we passed into a condition of extreme civilization. . . . But who knows whether, by one of the reversals common in human history, we will not return to the point from which we began? The moment will come when benevolence ceases to be fruitful and becomes enfeebling and cowardly."

For such young men, fired by patriotic faith and the cult of military virtues, only the occasion for heroism is lacking.

The Influence of Sport and Travel

Moreover, everything has reinforced this audacious ideal and encouraged this resurrection among the new generation. In the popular imagination, the exploits of our aviators are the symbols of the courage and the unceasing vitality of our race, and they nourish patriotic sentiment. It is worth pointing out that a few years ago aviation promoted the humanitarian dream; it was interpreted as bearing the promise of an imminent elimination of boundaries between countries. Yet today it heightens awareness of those boundaries, and the airplane, in the eyes of the populace, is first and foremost an engine of war.

Sports, too, have exercised an influence on the patriotic optimism of young people that can hardly be neglected. The moral benefit of sport, by which I mean team sports such as soccer, which is so popular in the *lycées,* lies in the fact that it develops a spirit of solidarity, the experience of a common action to which each individual will must agree to sacrifice itself. On the other hand, sports promote the military virtues of endurance and cool self-possession, and sustain the young in a bellicose atmosphere.

Finally, the practice of travel, far from weakening the idea of fatherland, transforms it and gives it shape. Those who travel feel most keenly the opposition between foreigners and themselves. They become aware of their differences: "Each time that I find myself abroad," a young student of literature told us, "I experience within myself the truth and strength of patriotic feelings." . . .

Chapter 4

A Catholic Renaissance

It is evident that the cult of character and personality and a taste for moral discipline are among the deepest tendencies of the new generation. This temperament, which predisposes one to prefer human qualities, the realities of feeling and action, to abstract ideas and systems, leads these young men even further, bringing them back to the most profound source of action, the religious life.

Let us clear up one possible source of confusion at once. It is not a matter here of a vague religiosity, without foundation or framework, like that fashionable among the writers of 1890, a sort of delicate and mystical idealism for the use of unbelievers. It is the traditional and straightforward form of Catholicism that is endorsed by the religious sensibility of the new generation.

The religious aspirations of the young intellectual elite, the subjects of our inquiry, have nothing in common with that Tolstoyan and anarchical form of piety [of the 1880s and 1890s]. . . . That cloudy mysticism quickly degenerated into humanitarianism; its devotees dreamt of fraternity, of universal solidarity, of the union of all churches. . . . That vague and anarchical sensibility, that cult of gentle sweetness and suffering, that enfeebled piety, has no hold on the youth of today. Their religious sentiment needs a clear and definite casing into which its living abundance can be inserted; it seeks out discipline in order to insure its liberty; it accepts the traditional positions because they seem to offer "a marvelous framework of amplitude, breadth, and flexibility for receiving and organizing the discoveries of the present." . . .

Intellectual Youth and Catholicism

Consider an important fact, one whose significance can hardly be exaggerated. At the same time that anticlericalism is progressing among the people, and even winning adherents from the bourgeois classes, who are more and more indifferent to their traditions, the cultivated elite is spontaneously disavowing it; and the young intellectuals who seemed in the thrall of anticlerical doctrines twenty years ago, today find themselves drawn ever closer to Catholicism.

Let us recall those pages of confession from *The Disciple,* in which Robert Greslou analyzes the causes which lead to a loss of faith: "I knew that the young teachers who came to us from Paris, with the prestige of having gone to the Ecole Normale, were all skeptics and atheists." Now, at that same Ecole Normale, there are at the moment some forty students, which is to say almost one-third of the total, who are practicing Catholics. We do not mean Catholics by upbringing, but Catholics by conviction and way of life, faithful to the prescriptions of the church, who for the most part belong to Confraternity of St. Vincent de Paul in their parish. If it is noted that eight or ten years ago one could not find three or four practicing Catholics at the Ecole Normale, this progress can hardly be attributed to a random effect in the recruitment of students. Another significant fact, which we will take up shortly: in this group, contrary to what one might think, there are slightly more students of science than students of literature. . . .

Moreover, we almost always encounter converts among the young believers. As one of them remarks: "They did not seek for long. One or two years at the most, and here they are, in faithful submission to the Church." The point is that they no longer take pleasure in a prolonged "crisis of the soul." As soon as the problem of life is posed to them, they identify it with the problem of religion; for, among all the conceptions bequeathed to them by their elders, they search in vain for "an object noble and strong enough to earn their devotion." These young realists need "the stability, the profundity, the inexhaustible richness of religion." To them Catholicism appears less as a speculative philosophical system than as a rule, a doctrine of moral and social action. . . .

The Decline of Positivism

In order to understand the original meaning of this Catholic renaissance, we would have to return to its earliest beginnings; but this would, at the same time, require us to sketch the philosophic developments of the last twenty years. Such a project deserves an entire volume: here we can do no more than provide a very brief summary.

A superficial observer, seeing the documents gathered in the course of our investigation, would no doubt exclaim: "In an epoch of unbelief, in which criticism is sovereign, how is a reawakening of faith possible? Isn't the present-day world devoid of mystery, to use the phrase of Berthelot? How many times have we heard that science was going to replace dogma?"

The whole generation whose teachers were Renan and Taine began by being unconsciously imbued with a belief in the absolute truth of our positive knowledge and, in turn, the supreme value of science, which it made the objects of an enthusiastic and passionate cult. And many a young man, twenty years ago, would have joined in the declaration of Renan: "I would bet my life a hundred times over, and my eternal salvation as well, on the scientific truth of the rationalist thesis!" They expected that science, conceived as the sole mistress of truth, would in the future fulfill all the needs of man, that it would entirely replace the archaic spiritual disciplines. In a splendid fervor, they condemned all true philosophy, all metaphysics, as a sort of vague daydream about incorporeal objects, imperceptible to our senses; religion, finally, seemed to be "overturned in every respect by the rational and irrefutable system of modern science." In these methods they sought a rule of conduct, of morality, of sociology, and even of politics.

But after proudly claiming to have uncovered the principles of life itself by means of the intellect, this generation was rudely restored to humility. The great issue for them was the passage from the absolute to the relative. "This deified science was crushed by the weight of its own triumph," and its inability to go beyond the *order of relations,* its utter powerlessness to explain the origin, the ends, and the foundation of things had finally to be admitted. Beyond it lay the unknowable, before which the human mind could only come to a halt, hopelessly. Thus science led only to nothingness. When reading contemporary philosophers, the *Disciple* of Bourget acknowledged with a dark melancholy: "I perceived the universe as it is, pouring forth, without beginning or end, the inexhaustible flow of phenomena."

The human spirit cannot abide in relativity, and relativism had to engender, in this entire generation, a profound moral distress, a brooding pessimism, a lack of confidence in our destiny, which in effect condemned it to impotence. Thought turned against itself; its poverty was born of its limitless ambition; and, for having believed too exclusively in the strength of analysis and logic, it was "forced at the end of its efforts to admit defeat in face of the only questions which no man is permitted to ignore."

The generation which immediately followed, whose anxieties were expressed, it seems, by Maurice Barrès, understood, in a moving fashion, "the difficulty of doing without an absolute morality"; at the very least, this generation expressed a deep repugnance for the materialism and the destructive dialectic of its elders. Barrès became their mentor, for having shown them that an act of faith was necessary for the higher operations of the spirit. "Roemerspacher," he says in his *Déracinés,* "affirms the true, the beautiful, the good, as elements which are necessary to him and towards which both the curiosity of his mind and the outpouring of his heart aspire. All that this soul of good will needs is for someone to propose to it an acceptable religious formula." Maurice Barrès attempted to do so, with his cult of traditional heroes, and his religion of the soil and the dead. His work was highly educational and salutary in that it restored a sense of veneration; but it still bore the mark of "a generation established upon relativity": it could not fully satisfy the new generation, which no more had to overcome moral dilettantism than it had to reclaim the illusory prestige of scientific idolatry. This was a necessary stage, a consolation that had a certain efficacy, but some of the young people had already discovered its insufficiency.

Thus it was that a profound ideological movement placed all problems and, at the same time, our concepts of knowledge and of life in a new light.

While the systems which preceded it were positivist and intellectualist, the new philosophy began with a subtle and forceful critique of the nature of scientific truths and of the value of the intellect as the faculty of knowing.

According to Bergson, the proper domain of the intellect and its creation—science—is not the living, but the material and inorganic world. "The world of life and of the soul does not depend, in what is essential to it, on scientific knowledge, but on a special knowledge, which is properly philosophic or metaphysical"—that is, *intuition*. Bergson thus affirms the priority over reflective activity of a more obscure and richer activity, which consists in the faculty of seizing life directly, of sympathizing with it. With this clear demarcation between two orders of knowledge, we are able to "open knowledge to all the riches of reality, and at the same time, reintegrate the sense of mystery, with its thrill of higher, disquieting concerns."

Now this distinction between science and deep or intuitive knowledge, the one limited to making contact with things, the other attempting to comprehend them, is extremely important. The domain of science is thus no longer that of the true, but rather that of the useful: its role is to assist in our transformation of the material world, to help us satisfy our practical needs; and in this domain—but in this domain only—it can attain the absolute. Beyond this, it remains radically, profoundly powerless to solve the problem of human life.

For philosophers such as Boutroux, Henri Poincaré, Le Roy, Blondel, science is thus something infinitely less real than philosophy. It is a kind of arbitrary symbolism, internally consistent and integrated in its ongoing development, to be sure, but which does not have to trouble itself with explaining the basis of things. It has only to establish a system of coherent relations, an intelligible discourse, in view of certain practical ends. Scientific law is presented as a convenient translation of the external world; it is no longer a decree, which, in divesting man of his liberty, claims to determine his conduct. Thus delivered from the servitude of determinism, souls find themselves face-to-face with life, ready to govern themselves according to their own powers.

Modern religious apologetics receive a new impulse from this philosophy. For the apologists of twenty years ago, the central point was to reconcile faith and reason. Convinced of the universality of evolutionary explanation, they attempted a Darwinian interpretation of the Holy Scriptures. Positivism itself was used by someone like Brunetière to return *to the road of belief.* All their effort went into finding an agreement between religious dogma and a science that was henceforth to be regarded as infallible.

Such a reconciliation now appears meaningless both to the new apologists and to these young men whom the Catholic faith has rallied: they think that the development of religion and of science takes place on two separate and independent planes. And for the most part they declare themselves to be less worried about exegesis than about the true foundation of the religious life: deep personal experience. A young physician wrote the following to us: "This experience is always persuasive when it is wholehearted. And once we have found that experience, the rest of our life, though upset and confused when we began, is reorganized little by little in accordance with a new and obviously true perspective. It is from the vantage point of life, from the human point of view, that we approach the religious problem." . . .

Chapter 5

The Critique of Political Values

The point on which [the new generation of intellectuals] all concur is the critique of political values. The present parliamentary regime is in disfavor. A large number of young people heed those who repeat passionately: "Government by parties is only the reign of accident and incoherence; it impedes any uniform plan of national development; it degrades individual morality by destroying all responsibility." The argumentative vigor of the attacks of the neo-monarchists of the Action Française has given a kind of revolutionary novelty to doctrines which, twenty years ago, would have been judged those of a backward party, intellectually bankrupt and irreparably in decline. At the other end of the political spectrum, a doctrine equally conducive to order, speaking in the name of the proletariat, has taken up a similarly bitter campaign against democracy; the young find something healthy and forceful in the syndicalism of Georges Sorel.

Now it would be childish to deny that the republican idea is experiencing a crisis in the consciences of many young men. . . . In the heated polemics which the bicentennial of the birth of Jean-Jacques Rousseau provoked last June, Rousseau the artist and writer receded to the background, while Rousseau the political figure became the object of violent attacks. Some students from a right bank *lycée* addressed a letter to Maurice Barrès, in which they declared that they "repudiate, with the great majority of Frenchmen, the philosophy of the citizen of Geneva." No less telling is the investigation made at the time by an important journal into young people's attitude towards Rousseau. They condemned him as a sentimental anarchist, as the metaphysician of the rights of man.

If the adversaries of the government have won over so many ardent hearts, it is only because events have, for many years now, readily confirmed their theses. One must bear in mind that the whole development of today's youth has been dominated by the cruel experience of the humiliation France suffered at the hands of a foreign power; it will then be explicable that the young have listened with fervor to those doctrinaires who regarded the nation as the highest reality, and who conceived of, discussed "and expected to resolve all remaining questions in terms of the national interest." Public perils have determined their political attitude. Civil strife and ideological struggles have sapped the energy of the government, which found itself surprised by the threat from abroad. The landing of Kaiser Wilhelm at Tangier is an event of central importance in the history of our values. This wound to national pride, deep and hidden, set working in our blood a secret ferment whose effects suddenly burst forth at the time of the incident at Agadir. The transformation was so complete that it astonished our leaders, who had had no intimation of it. . . .

Conclusion

The elegant, skeptical philosopher of yesteryear smiles and says to us, "Your investigation is curious, but it doesn't unsettle me. It even strengthens me in my conclusions. For any observer with a grain of historical sense could have predicted the movement you describe. After a period of pessimism, nervous exhaustion, and humanitarian daydreams, the inevitable rhythm of the generations called to life this healthy and confident generation, so eager for reality and so full of a mad, patriotic optimism. Don't you know that young people almost always violently oppose the attitudes of their elders? Hence I can't get too alarmed about a younger generation governed so passionately by an ideal contrary to my own, and I can be assured of the return, some ten or fifteen years from now, of the forces that are today so manifestly in decline."

We can't deny the value of this mode of reasoning. It would be foolhardy to dispute that a secret force of contradiction is at the origin of great currents of thought and sentiment. Writing about our investigation in *L'Humanité*,[5] Marcel Sembat quoted this line from Taine and took comfort in it: "Great public propensities are always transitory. Because they are great, they are gratified; and because they are gratified, they expire." But it must be recognized that we are not now in the presence of a mere intellectual fashion. The taste for action, for the practical life and for moral and religious discipline is something very different from a snobbish attitude. The principle of change is very much deeper: it is in the inmost being, in the will. . . .

Ah! doubtless some moralist will say, I see subtleties in this which worry me; this younger generation is not at all as unselfish as you seemed at first to say. My God! there is no virtue that, depending upon the temperament of the possessor, cannot degenerate into a defect. The love of sport can lead to the cult of brutal valor, to the wrongful disdain for the scruples and weaknesses of the heart. The concern for practical necessities can similarly conduce to a repudiation of that certain elegance of style dear to our race, and some people are already lamenting the decline of the inquiring and refined mind nicely shaded with irony. Finally, a too exclusive preoccupation with one's career can entail a deplorable hurry for success.

Perhaps the young people of tomorrow will hear only too well the wish that Barrès puts in the mouth of Philippe in *Les Amitiés françaises:* "Be active and a little harsh. May you not have too much heart!" Barrès was calling not for less feeling, but for less nervous disorder, less distraught lyricism, less of those passionate transports which are, besides, so well-suited to an arid soul. He wanted steady, well-regulated feeling armed against the enticements of desire and growing strong through its contact with real order. Only, inured against the onslaughts of a soft and effeminate sentimentality, such a generation would probably be less full of pity than its predecessor.

On the other hand, it declares itself gifted for the greatest and most rugged task, that of organizing things. It organizes the individual life in accordance with a moral discipline while waiting to organize the country in accordance with a political discipline. In all matters, it is characteristic of its spirit to make order and hierarchy, just as its predecessor made disorder and chaos. Its intellect has the appetite for classification and the taste for the enduring. That is why we cannot listen to those fretful people who, already predicting the excesses of this realistic tendency, fear the future triumph of a bourgeois spirit, intolerant and caring nothing for culture. Yes, perhaps some day it will be necessary to rediscover the benefits of intellec-

5. The newspaper of the French Socialist Party.

tualism. But while waiting, one consideration will dictate the conclusion that we draw—one only, but one strong enough to counterbalance the useless hand-wringing of the malcontents.

What in our eyes surpasses everything else today is the idea of the national recovery. Our attentive readers will have recognized its invisible presence in each line of this book. This idea must prevail over that deep and painful feeling associated with a humiliated and weakened fatherland whose vital forces are threatened. All around, we sense this self-affirmation, this "renaissance of French pride. . . ."

And since nothing can be more useful for the renewal of the fatherland than a generation that is athletic, realistic, unideological, virtuous, and fit for economic struggles, since nothing can better insure the revitalization and the health of the race, we must credit the hopes of this generation, the so mysterious intimation it possesses of its boldness and of its future triumph. We must be in communion with it with respect to the faith that animates it, a faith that is all French and French above all.

3. Mabel Atkinson, *The Economic Foundations of the Women's Movement*

Mabel Atkinson (1876–1958) was a member of the Fabian Society and a leading proponent of the Fabian Women's Group which was founded in 1908. By profession a journalist and a lecturer in economics at Armstrong College, Newcastle-upon-Tyne, Atkinson was a founder of the Fabian Society's Summer School, the voluntary residential session devoted to the study of social science and politics. In Margaret Cole's words, Atkinson was "something of a stormy element in Edwardian Fabianism, a very truculent member of the Fabian Women's Group and a supporter of the Fabian Reform Committee."[1] Atkinson was also a vigorous supporter of the women's suffrage movement, serving as the Group's liaison with several women's suffrage groups and leading her colleagues in refusing to pay taxes on the grounds of "no taxation without representation." She continued to participate in Fabian politics until after the First World War, when she left Britain for South Africa.

Until the founding of the Women's Group, the Fabian Society's record on feminist issues was uninspired and occasionally benighted. Even Beatrice Webb was on record against women's suffrage, a position she later regretted having taken. In 1907 a group of feminist Fabians, led by Maud Pember Reeves, forced the revision of the Fabian Society's program so

1. Margaret Cole, *The Story of Fabian Socialism* (London, 1961), p. 349.

that it now included a demand for "the establishment of equal citizenship for men and women," and in early 1908 they formally constituted the Women's Group. In addition to participating in feminist demonstrations and, as a result of subsequent political protests, seeing many of its members arrested or harassed, the Group also organized lectures and conferences on issues of concern to women and sponsored a series of investigative publications on the professional and social status of women in Great Britain.

Atkinson's *The Economic Foundations of the Women's Movement* was originally delivered as a lecture before the full Fabian Society in early 1914. Her text, part of which is reprinted below, is an example of the Group's efforts to combine science and social protest toward the betterment of women's social as well as political rights.

The Spiritual Aspect of the Women's Movement

Purely economic causes are never sufficient to account entirely for any great revolt of the human spirit. Behind every revolution there lies a spiritual striving, a grasping after an ideal felt rather than seen. Most emphatically is it true that there is a social impulse independent of economic conditions, which has over and over again asserted itself in the demand for the emancipation of women. All the greatest seers and prophets have insisted on the equal value of men and women, and on the right of women to control their own lives. Four centuries before Christ, Plato claimed that in the life of the State women, as well as men, should take their place; and in all the records of Christ's conversations, which the Gospels have handed down to us, there is not one hint that he advocated that subordination of women on which his disciples later on insisted. In Rome also, at the Renaissance, and at the time of the French Revolution, powerful voices were raised in denunciation of the subjection of women.

These demands were, however, only sporadic. At most they affected a small class. It was not until the nineteenth century that the demand of women for political, economic, and educational freedom was heard among any considerable mass of the people. This extension of the demand for emancipation was due to economic changes, to those alterations in human control over environment which are associated with the substitution of mechanical power for human energy in the making of commodities, and with

From *The Economic Foundations of the Women's Movement*, by M. A., Fabian Tract No. 175, Fabian Women's Group Series, No. 4 (London: The Fabian Society, 1914), pp. 2–3, 5–11, 13–24. Reprinted by permission of the publisher. Footnotes deleted.

the development of powerful and smoothly working machines in place of human hands and simple tools.

The Effect of the Industrial Revolution

Probably when Hargreaves invented his spinning jenny, and when Arkwright established his first cotton mill, in which the power of water took the place of the easily wearied arms of humanity, they had no conception of the fact that they were preparing the way for the greatest revolution in human society which has ever taken place since man learnt the use of fire. Yet nothing less was the truth, for then first men learnt how to utilize for their service the energies of the universe without previously absorbing them into their own bodies or into the bodies of domesticated animals in the form of food. Before the end of the eighteenth century man did indeed use water power on a small scale for grinding corn, and the capricious force of the wind for the same end and for propelling sailing vessels. But the energies of steam and electricity and petrol were lying dormant or running to waste all around him, while he sweated at the forge or the loom, and was hauled slowly over badly made roads by the straining sinews of horses. Now throughout human society inanimate forces are at work, harnessed at last successfully to the service of man, shaping iron and steel plates, setting to work looms and printing presses, propelling enormous trains of waggons, urging leviathan ships across the ocean.

Before this mighty revolution, whatever alterations man wanted made in his world must be made through his own physical exertions; now he sets to work the energies of his environment to remould that environment according to his needs. From himself there is demanded merely the brain work of planning and directing and the nervous strain of tendence on the marvellous machines. It is true that in our badly arranged social system (all of whose concepts of property, contract, wages, and labor are still adjusted to the pre-machine era) the increased control over nature has brought but little advantage to the mass of the workers. But the full effects of the substitution of inanimate for human energy have not yet been seen, and will ultimately work themselves out into conditions of life vastly different from those which we know at present.

Women before the Industrial Revolution

Of all the changes introduced by the industrial revolution there is none greater than the alteration brought about in the position of women. Many people believe that it was only in the nineteenth century that women began, on a large scale, to work for their living. There could be no greater mistake. All the evidence goes to show that before the eighteenth century women, with few exceptions, worked as hard and as long as men did. In the sixteenth century women not only helped their husbands in farm work, but they toiled at spinning and carding of flax and wool as a by-industry of their own. Few nineteenth century women could work harder than the wife of a sixteenth century husbandman. . . .

The Family as the Economic Unit;
Marriage an Industrial Partnership

. . . [B]efore the industrial revolution women took a full share in industrial work. The basis of their work, however, was quite different from what it is today. Speaking generally, before the industrial revolution the economic unit was the family, and not the individual. So much was this the case, that in the censuses of 1811, 1821, and 1831 it was assumed that all the members of the family would practise the same occupation. Much of the work done by women in the family was of a domestic nature for the immediate service of their husbands and children, and not for profit. In technical language it was the production of use values, and not of exchange values. . . .

But it would be a mistake to assume that women never worked for profit. . . . It is common to find a woman carrying on the farm or shop of her husband after his death, and the farmer's wife, who has been already described, was her husband's working partner in his business enterprise as well as his housekeeper and servant. In fact, before the nineteenth century marriage was an industrial partnership as well as a relation of affection. The women worked, and worked hard, contributing much to the wealth of England, which was sold in her markets. This situation must have served to modify considerably the harshness of the common law, which decreed the husband's entire control of his wife's property. . . .

The Alteration of the Economic Basis of the Family

. . . Now what was the effect of the industrial revolution on the position of women in relation to these economic activities of the family? Briefly, the answer is that the introduction of machinery, by taking work out of the home and establishing the factory, the railway, and the mine as the organs of industry, broke up the family as an economic unit and diminished the amount of production for use carried on within the home. Brewing, baking, butter-making, spinning, weaving, even—to a large extent—the making of clothes, have ceased to be activities of the family; and increasingly housewives are finding that it is cheaper and more convenient to hand over jam making, laundry work, even window cleaning and floor polishing, to agencies that exist independently of the home. This is an inevitable development. Modern machinery and the use of artificial sources of power immensely cheapen production, but they can only be used by organizations bigger than the family group. So that the economic basis of the family has altered more within the last hundred years than in the whole course of Christian civilization preceding that time. . . .

The Changed Position of Women

But different classes of women were affected very differently. Among the wealthier people attempts were made to preserve the subordination of women to the family unit, although the economic justification for that dependence had ceased. Among the poor the necessity for the women's contribution to the family income was so strong that they were drafted into the new forms of industrial life without any consideration of their powers or capacities. To put it shortly, parasitism became the fate of the middle class women, ruthless exploitation that of the working class women. The latter were absorbed in large numbers by the new factories, as were also the children, who equally had worked as parts of the family unit; and the first stage of machine production saw the women and children workers cruelly and shamelessly sacrificed to the demands of profit.

The Exploitation of the Working Women

There is no need to repeat this oft told story, but it may be pointed out that the previous close relation of the women and children to the family unit had rendered them incapable of asserting themselves against the powers of capital and competition. And the low wages which they received made them dangerous rivals of the men and no longer co-operators with them. No one during the first agitation for the Factory Acts seems to have realized that the general labor of women and children pulled down the wages of men. The conditions became so bad that dead in the face of a public opinion more strongly individualistic than has ever been the case either before or since, the State was forced to constitute itself the established guardian of the women and children, and to bring into existence all the machinery of the Factory Acts, by which, first in the textile industries and in mining, later on in all branches of machine production, and still later in practically the whole field of industry, an attempt was made to preserve women and children from the degradation and suffering due to over long hours and work in unsanitary conditions. The problem is, of course, not yet fully solved. In the industrial world the cheap labor of women is continually threatening new industries. Since these women believe themselves inferior

to men, and since most of them expect to marry early and regard their occupation only as a makeshift, they are naturally willing to work more
cheaply than men, and so constitute a perpetual menace to the masculine
standard of life, while they themselves are subjected to conditions unfit for
human beings. It cannot be wondered at that under these circumstances
many social reformers regard the work of women outside the home as an
evil development. For women in the industrial world are frequently forced
to be blacklegs. Moreover, the conditions of modern large scale industry
are determined not by the needs of the human beings who work in it, but by
the demands of the machinery, and are therefore often unsuitable for
women (equally so, in all probability, for men). In the early days of the
movement for State regulation of industry, that innovation on the doctrine
of *laissez faire* which then prevailed was justified on the ground that
women were not free agents. Men, it was asserted, could and should stand
out for themselves against the power of their employers. The State ought
never to interfere in the wages contracts formed by its citizens among
themselves, but women and children were not citizens. They were weak,
ignorant, easily exploited. Further, they represented in a special way the
human capital of the nation. The men might be used from generation to
generation and the life of the race would still continue, but a nation which
lived upon the labor of its women and children was doomed to degeneration.

The Parasitism of the Middle Class Women

In this view there is, of course, a truth which must never be forgotten. But
it ignores another part of the problem, that which confronted the other
class of women. The middle class women had so awful and so bitter an
experience that for a time they were quite unable to appreciate the need of
State protection for women. The result for them of the introduction of machinery was altogether opposite to the effect produced upon the industrial
women. As the economic functions of the family diminished, the daughters
of lawyers, doctors, wealthy shopkeepers, and manufacturers did not work
out new forms of activity for themselves. It would have been against the
dignity of their fathers and brothers to permit them to do so. Moreover, it
would have diminished their chances of marriage, and would have involved
a breach with the people who were nearest and dearest to them. They remained within the family group, occupied in the insignificant domestic duties that still remained and in the futilities of an extraordinarily conventional social intercourse. Dusting, arranging the flowers, and paying calls
were the important duties of their existence. The married middle class
woman had indeed, as wife and mother, a definite place and important re-

sponsibility, though the decay of household activities and the growing habit of living in suburbs, quite apart from the man's business, lessened at every point her contact with the social world and cut even her off more than had ever been the case previously from intercourse with the spheres of industry and commerce. But the unmarried woman, forbidden during her years of greatest vitality and strongest desire for new scenes and fresh interest to find any channels for her energies, save those of "helping mamma" and "visiting the poor," suffered intensely from the inactive parasitism forced upon her. Exploitation brings great suffering; but suffering as acute, though more obscure, is experienced by those whose growing powers and growing need for human contacts are dammed within them by an incomprehensible social fiat, resting really on conditions that had passed away a generation earlier. The only escape from this enforced inactivity and dependence was through marriage. The middle class woman, in fact, was regarded solely from the standpoint of sex. There was no way by which she might satisfy her natural wish to use the welling energies within her other than by becoming the mistress of a household. Naturally, therefore, she often regarded "to be settled" as an end to be aimed at, quite apart from the personality of the man who offered to make her his wife. And the irony of the situation was that to the finer spirits who refused to acquiesce in this degradation of love to the economic plane, there was no other alternative than an existence which became "that useless, blank, pale, slow-trailing thing" of which one of Charlotte Brontë's heroines so bitterly complains.

The Surplus of Women

As the nineteenth century wore on other tendencies came into play which further increased the hardships of middle class women. The presence of a surplus of women in the middle classes made itself more and more apparent. Probably the cause of this is the emigration of young men, rendered necessary by our enormous colonial development; but it may be that some other and more subtle cause is at work. Exact statistics are difficult to give, as our statistics are not based on class distinctions. But certain conclusions can be drawn, as Miss Clara Collet first pointed out, from the distribution of unmarried males and females over certain ages in different boroughs of London, which to some extent are peopled by different classes of the community. The following table shows how striking the difference is, and how the surplus of females tends to accumulate in the better off districts. Some have urged that these surplus females are really domestic servants. But the number of female unmarried domestic servants over thirty-five is comparatively small.

Number of unmarried males and females between the ages of
thirty-five and fifty-five in three wealthy and three poor London
boroughs, as given in the Census of 1911.

	Males	Females
Hampstead	1,559	4,655
Kensington	2,785	11,395
Chelsea	1,414	3,688
Woolwich	1,861	1,526
Shoreditch	1,689	1,004
Bethnal Green	1,635	1,320

Putting the same facts in another way, for every 100 unmarried men
between thirty-five and fifty-five there are in Hampstead 291 unmarried
women of the same ages, in Kensington 409, and in Chelsea 260; while in
Woolwich to every 100 unmarried men of these ages there are 81 unmarried women, in Shoreditch only 59, and in Bethnal Green 81.

We can cite also an article by Miss Hutchins in the *Englishwoman*,
June, 1913, in the course of which she says: "Another means of comparing
the prospects of marriage in different social strata is by comparing the proportion of single women in the age group 25–45 in rich and poor districts
respectively. In making this comparison we must allow for the numbers of
domestic servants, who of course very considerably augment the proportion of single women in the wealthy residential districts. The following
table shows that, even if we subtract all the domestic indoor servants from
the single women in the age group (which is over-generous, as a small but
unknown proportion of them are certainly married or widowed), the single
women in Hampstead, Kensington and Paddington are a considerably
higher proportion than in Stepney, Shoreditch and Poplar. These districts
have been 'selected' only in the sense that they were the first that occurred
to the writer as affording a marked contrast of wealth and poverty."

Number and proportion of single women and domestic indoor
servants in every 100 women aged 25–45 in certain
London boroughs. (Census of 1911.)

	Number	Per cent. of Women aged 25–45	Difference of percentage
HAMPSTEAD			
Single Women	11,483	57.3	
Domestic Servants	6,534	32.6	24.7
KENSINGTON			
Single Women	21,967	56	
Domestic Servants	13,431	34.2	21.8

	PADDINGTON		
Single Women	13,711	46.6	
Domestic Servants	6,473	22.1	24.5
	POPLAR		
Single Women	4,406	19.5	
Domestic Servants	506	2.2	17.3
	SHOREDITCH		
Single Women	2,923	18.1	
Domestic Servants	340	2.2	15.9
	STEPNEY		
Single Women	7,158	18.4	
Domestic Servants	1,207	3.4	15

This table also brings out the extraordinary difference between the proportions of women of the most marriageable period of life married in rich and in poor districts. The same fact is illustrated by the following table, comparing the number of married, single and widowed women among the population living "on private means" and among the general population. The comparison is suggested by Miss Hutchins, but the table used by her in the *Englishwoman* cannot be reproduced here as the new Census does not give the information in the same way.

Number and percentage of single, married and widowed women
over 20 years of age in the population living on private means
and in the general population in England. (Census of 1911.)

	Living on Private Means		General Population	
	Number	Percentage	Number	Percentage
Unmarried	136,705	46.5	3,448,442	30.2
Married	23,724	8.1	6,610,173	57.9
Widowed	133,698	45.4	1,364,715	11.9
Total	294,127	100	11,423,330	100

No doubt the figures in this table are distorted by the number of widows who owe their private means to their widowhood, but even allowing for this it is remarkable to discover that the percentage of married women in the general population is so much greater than in the population living on private means.

But statistical evidence is really not necessary. All hostesses and organizers of middle class social functions know well that one of the constant difficulties with which they have to contend is the over supply of women.

The Salaried Middle Class

Another new element in the position of the middle class woman arises from the fact that her men relations tend to become salaried officials in place of independent merchants and employers. This means not only that the women can no longer take part in the economic activities of their men relations, but that, in the event of the death of the latter, their position is far more precarious. A business or a shop goes on even after the death of a husband or father who established or inherited it, but when a salaried official dies his family are altogether deprived of the support which he afforded them.

Can He Afford to Get Married?

And again, if a wife is no longer of any direct economic value, if, on the contrary, she is an expense, then men, in many cases probably with reluctance, must defer marriage until they can afford that luxury. To a middle class man before the industrial revolution, as indeed to the men of the working class at present, marriage was not a thing "to be afforded." A wife was a partner, bringing to the relation of wedlock economically, as well as in other and more emotional ways, as much value as she received. But the middle class bachelor contemplating marriage today realizes that he must be prepared to double, or more than double, his expenditure, while his wife adds nothing to the income. Therefore he defers marriage, finding often an outlet to his emotions in other directions (it would be interesting to endeavor to trace the relation between prostitution and the use of machinery), and the girl who should be his mate withers unwanted in the "upholstered cage" of her parents' home. Therefore in the nineteenth century the middle class woman had fewer chances of marriage, was less needed in the family life if unmarried, and was liable to find herself when that family life came to an end through the death of a father or brother stranded resourceless on the world.

The Tragedy of the Surplus Women

It is heartrending to think of the hidden tragedies which these sociological changes brought in their train, the mute sufferings of the women, who, unmated and workless, felt themselves of no value or importance to the world around them. What wonder that in the end a revolt came, and women insisted that in the great world of human activities outside the family they, too, must have place and power. . . .

The First Feminist Movement

The first feminist movement emerged into the open at the time of the Reform Bill of 1867. If its origin is grasped, its peculiar characteristics will be easily understood. It was on the whole a demand of elderly unmarried women for the right to freer activities, as the alternative to an impracticable ideal of marriage and motherhood for every woman. Therefore it is not astonishing that these early feminists tended on the whole to ignore differences of sex, since those differences had been made the pretext for condemning them to a condition of parasitism, against which a healthy human being was bound to revolt. It was natural enough that these pioneers of the women's movement should insist upon their likeness to men, should demand the right to the same education as men received and the entrance to the same professions as men followed. In their revolt against the degradations which sex parasitism had brought in its train, it was not unnatural that in their dress and bearing they should neglect the grace and charm which a normal man will always desire in women. It was not unnatural either, when they found a section of the public advocating in industry special protection of women by law, that they should regard this as another form of the masculine exclusiveness from which they themselves suffered, so that to them the right of a woman to be a doctor and the right of a woman to work underground in a mine should present themselves as similar demands. Being but middle class women, influenced by the progressive ideals of their class, they were mostly Liberals, and to their special dread of the exclusion of women from human activities, other than those conditioned by sex, was added the strong individualism of the Liberalism of the period. Therefore they naturally set themselves in opposition to the demand for factory legislation, and there arose in consequence misunderstandings between two sections of reformers, the echoes of which have persisted to our own time.

Its Attitude towards Marriage

The attitude towards marriage of these early feminists has also been much misunderstood. There were, no doubt, a certain number among them who were indifferent or opposed to marriage; but most of them found themselves driven into hostility to normal family relations, mainly because these were used as an argument to convince them that the alterations in the position of women which they desired were impossible. When a woman, struggling for education and the right to work for herself, was met by the objection: "If you learn Greek or if you become a doctor no one will marry you," is it astonishing that she answered, "I don't care if no one does"? Moreover, as has been already said, the pioneers came mostly from the class of "superfluous women." They knew well that marriage was far from being the certainty or the likelihood which their opponents always assumed it to be. The alternative for them was not work *or* marriage, but work and money of their own *or* a spinstered existence in their fathers' houses. Therefore, naturally most of them put out of their minds, with what bitterness few people have realized, the possibility of marriage and motherhood, and turned instead to develop their own intellectual and spiritual forces, devoting themselves to public work and to the struggle for that independent living which is so sweet to the woman who has revolted against parasitism.

Economic Independence

Few men understand what importance the modern middle class woman attaches to her economic independence. To men the right to earn a livelihood does not present itself as a hardly won and cherished privilege, but as a tiresome necessity. They may have earned an income with difficulty, but, at least, when they earned it it was theirs to spend as they would. But many women, even wealthy women, dressed in gorgeous raiment, with servants and horses and carriages at their command, never know what it is to be able to spend a guinea on the gratification simply of their own tastes. The money that they receive comes from father or husband, and must be spent as father or husband approve. Workers in the feminist movement are perfectly familiar with the well-dressed and prosperous-looking woman who declares, "Yes, I quite agree with you. I have often thought these things myself, and I wish I could help, but my husband does not approve of Women's Suffrage, and I have no money except what I get from him." The life of the professional woman is often toilsome and often lonely, but the power of self-direction and self-activity which economic independence brings with it counts for much, and few women who have realized what sex-parasitism means, and have succeeded in emerging from it will ever willingly return to it.

The Two Sections of the Women's Movement

So, at the present time there are two main sections in the modern women's movement—the movement of the middle class women who are revolting against their exclusion from human activity and insisting, firstly, on their right to education, which is now practically conceded on all sides; secondly, on their right to earn a livelihood for themselves, which is rapidly being won; and, thirdly, on their right to share in the control of Government, the point round which the fight is now most fiercely raging. These women are primarily rebelling against the sex-exclusiveness of men, and regard independence and the right to work as the most valuable privilege to be striven for.

On the other hand, there are the women of the working classes, who have been faced with a totally different problem, and who naturally react in a different way. Parasitism has never been forced on them. Even when the working class woman does not earn her own living in the world of industry—though practically all the unmarried girls of the working classes do so—her activities at home are so unending, and she subconsciously feels so important and so valuable, that she has never conceived of herself as useless and shut out from human interests, as was the parasitic middle class woman. What the woman of the proletariat feels as her grievance is that her work is too long and too monotonous, the burden laid upon her too heavy. Moreover, in her case that burden is due to the power of capitalistic exploitation resulting from the injustice of our social system. It is not due, or not, at least, to any considerable extent, to the fact that the men of her class shut her out from gainful occupations. Therefore, among the working women there is less sex consciousness. Evolving social enthusiasm tends to run rather into the channel of the labor revolt in general than into a specific revolution against the conditions alleged to be due to sex differences. The working woman feels her solidarity with the men of her class rather than their antagonism to her. The reforms that she demands are not independence and the right to work, but rather protection against the unending burden of toil which has been laid upon her. A speaker at a working women's congress said once, "It is not work we want, but more love, more leisure to enjoy life, and more beauty." These facts explain the relative lukewarmness of working class women in the distinctively feminist movement, and one of the possible dangers of the future is that the working class women in their right and natural desire to be protected against that exploitation which the first development of machinery brought with it, should allow themselves to drift without observing it into the parasitism which was the lot of middle class women. If the exclusion of married women from all paid work were carried out; if the unmarried women were at the same time prevented from following all those occupations which reactionary male hygienists choose, without adequate investigation, to assume to be bad for women; if at the same time the growth of the public supply of schools and other agencies for the care of children were to go on and the number of children in each family were to continue to diminish; if the home, by reason of the development of machinery and large scale production, were to lose all those remaining economic activities which are carried on within it, then working women might come to live through the same experience as the middle class women have already known.

Sex-consciousness among Working Women

But changes are proceeding in this situation. The consciousness of their rights and wrongs as a sex is arising among the working class women. They are beginning to see the possibility that even in the fight against capitalist exploitation, on which the men of their class are now entering, their specific interests may be overlooked. The shocking disregard of the needs of women by the Insurance Act has given them a clear proof of this. The great calamity against which the working class woman needs insurance is the death of her husband and bread winner; yet it is commonly stated that in the bargain with the big insurance societies the Government simply threw overboard the plans for a form of insurance which would make more secure the position of widows and orphans. Again, the home-staying working class woman finds that the Government cares little for her health, and makes practically no provision for her care should she fall ill, save in the one case of maternity benefit, and that, by curious irony, was originally to be paid to the husband and not to herself, save where the woman was herself a wage earner. Moreover, the development of social legislation is throwing heavier burdens on the working woman, and is yet making scant provision for her special needs. There are clubs, lectures, holidays provided for men, for boys, for young girls; but for the married working woman how little is done? A few schools for mothers, still mainly supported by private charity, in the poorest districts is about the sum total; yet all the while it is she who bears the burden of the insurance paid by her husband, for it comes in nine cases out of ten out of her housekeeping money. It is she who has to send the children to school clean and tidy and has to keep the great appetites of growing boys satisfied; it is she who is regarded as responsible for buying inflammable flannelette, for not providing fireguards or separate cradles for the babies, and whatever else a Government of men may choose to impose on her. So that there is appearing also among the working women an understanding of the fact that their interests are not altogether safe in the hands of men, though the working class women will never probably arrive at the intense consciousness of sex antagonism which characterizes some sections of the middle class feminists, and is due to men's callous disregard of their claims as human beings.

Changed Views among the Middle Class Women

At the same time among the middle class women, too, the situation is altering. Many of them are realizing that to earn their own living is not always the joy it had appeared at first, for the living may be so meagre as to provide, at the cost of perpetual toil, only the merest food and shelter. Although the number of girls among the middle classes who are working for their living is steadily increasing, every now and then one comes across a young woman who finds the rigor of her work and the fierce competition too much for her, and hastens back gladly to the parasitic shelter of her relatives' roof. The lower sections of professional women, in short, are coming to understand the possibilities of exploitation, and are dimly beginning to feel rather than to comprehend the fact that work may be so monotonous and so ill-paid that even their human qualities, and much more their feminine attractiveness, will be beaten out of them in the process of earning their living.

And among the whole community the growth of collectivist feeling is bringing us to realize that State regulation of the conditions of labor is a necessity, and therefore we seldom find now among the feminists that embittered opposition to factory legislation which caused so many difficulties in the seventies and eighties. It is realized on all hands that the position of women in industry is not an exceptional one; that men, too, need protection against over-long hours of work, low wages, and insanitary conditions; and that, therefore, women are not accepting an inferior position in demanding the intervention of the State to secure for them suitable conditions of work.

They Want Both Work and Marriage

An even more momentous change is occurring in the attitude towards marriage. The first generation of feminists did not so much oppose marriage as ignore it; but there is now coming into existence a second generation of advanced women, few at present, but destined to increase. Most of them know nothing at first hand of the old struggles. They have gone to high schools and colleges, and education has come to them as naturally as to their brothers. Many under the care of feminist relatives have been carefully trained to win the economic independence for which their mothers and aunts agonized in vain. And now these younger women find themselves face to face with a new set of problems. The fierceness and bitterness of the old struggles caused the first set of feminists to put the question of marriage and the supposed special disabilities of their sex altogether on one side. Today many of these elder women, looking at their young relatives in receipt of independent incomes, doing work that is of real value to the world, and enjoying in such matters as foreign travel, theatre and concert going, and the cultivation of friendships a degree of freedom which they had longed for as unattainable, wonder what difficulties the young women of today can possibly have to contend with. But there are fundamental human instincts which can be disregarded only for a time. The problem of the modern professional woman is that she is forced to reconcile two needs of her nature which the present constitution of society makes irreconcilable. She wants work, she wants the control of her own financial position, she wants education and the right to take part in the human activities of the State, but at the same time she is no longer willing to be shut out from marriage and motherhood. And the present organization of society means that for most women the two are alternatives. In almost all occupations the public acknowledgement of marriage means for a woman dismissal from her post and diminished economic resources. This is the case in practically all the Government posts: women civil servants, including even factory inspectors and school inspectors, are compelled to resign on marriage. Even the women school medical officers of the L.C.C. are now forced to sign a contract stating that they will retire on marriage, and although the same rule is not so strict in private business, there, too, it is rare for married women to be employed. Most women, that is to say, can only continue to preserve that economic independence, so keenly appreciated and won by such fierce struggles, on condition of compulsory celibacy and, what to many women is far worse, compulsory childlessness. Against this state of things a revolt is beginning which so far is barely articulate, but which is bound to make itself heard in public before long. What women who have fully thought out the position want, is not this forced alternative between activity in the human world and control of their own economic position on the one hand and marriage and children on the other, *but both*. The normal woman, like the normal man, desires a mate and a child, but she does not therefore desire nothing else. Least of all does she desire to sink back into a state of economic dependence and sex parasitism. Women do not want either love *or* work, but both; and the full meaning of the feminist movement will not develop until this demand becomes conscious and articulate among the rank and file of the movement.

Can Child-bearing Women Earn Their Living?

Now there can be no denying the fact that this demand will raise many difficulties. Some writers, chief of whom is that extraordinarily suggestive and interesting American, Charlotte Perkins Gilman, assume that with improved conditions of household management and the development of large scale housekeeping and publicly managed crèches and nursery schools it will be possible even for childbearing women to continue to earn their own living in such a way that they will be able not only to keep themselves during this period, but to contribute their share towards the bringing up of children, and this without any injury to the children. To the writer this seems a very optimistic attitude. It may, perhaps, be practicable for a few exceptional women, who possess sufficient ability to earn large incomes and have sufficient energy to endure, without breaking down, the twofold strain of working for a living and bringing children into the world. But it is obvious that for the vast majority of women regular work on exactly the same terms as those which men now submit to in office or factory is most undesirable for women during at least six months of the pre-natal and post-natal life of each child. If the child is to be nursed by its mother, as it should be, probably in most cases an even longer period of rest should be taken. The common sense of mankind knows well that just as increasing civilization leads to an increasing protection of children, so, too, it should mean more care for young mothers. During the child-bearing years the welfare of the child should have the precedence over all other considerations. But this does not mean that the woman need be incapacitated for earning her own living during her whole married life. It is not marriage that prevents a woman from working. On the contrary, the married woman who is leading a normal and healthy life is likely to do better work and be a more satisfactory person than the spinster. The real hindrance is not marriage, but motherhood. Most people assume that the two are identical; but should absorption in maternal duties extend over the whole of married life? The days have gone past (one hopes never to return) when the married woman had a child every one or two years during the whole of the fertile period of life. The modern family, it seems probable, will not consist in the future of more than three or four children, and even if one made the assumption that the woman should devote herself entirely to the care of the children until the youngest reached school age, there would still remain many years of her life during which she would be strong and fit for work. Indeed, one of the most pathetic sights of today is the middle aged woman whose children have ceased to afford her complete occupation. They are absorbed in school life and in the training for their future occupations. The husband, too, gives up his time to his work and his sport, and the woman of forty or fifty, still at the height of her maturity, stronger perhaps, and certainly wiser, than she was in her youth, is left stranded by the current of life, with no interests outside her family; whilst by the family the necessary task of being "company to mother" is resented and evaded. How much happier would such women be if, when their children no longer needed all their time, they could return to activities outside the household; and how much richer would humanity be if it could avail itself of the services of such women. A type might come into existence, of which only one or two instances have yet appeared, of mature women who, as girls, had worked for themselves and known what human life, as opposed to sex life, meant; who then had lived through the normal feminine experiences of being sought in marriage, loved, and made mothers of children; and who, ripened and enriched by these experiences, returned in middle age to the activities of the world, knowing—because they have lived through—both sides of life. How enormously valuable such women would be in education and in the medical profession, where, indeed, even now a few of them may be found.

The Problem of the Future

So, then, the problem before the future is to secure for women freedom and independence, the right to control their own destinies, and yet to make it possible for the same women to be wives and mothers. The solution of this problem will not be easy. It cannot be attained through the methods advocated by either of the schools of thought that now hold the field; neither by the feminists of the more old fashioned sort, on the one hand, who simply demand for women the same rights as men possess, ignoring all the inevitable differences of sex; nor, on the other hand, by those who believe that sex is the only characteristic of women that matters, and disregard in her the human nature that she shares with man. Neither independence alone nor protection alone will meet the case. . . .

The Endowment of Motherhood

. . . No act of citizenship is more fundamental than the act of bringing into the world and protecting in his helpless infancy a new citizen, and therefore the most reasonable solution of the problem, though it may not be applicable in every case, is that women during the period when these activities must absorb their whole energies should be supported by a State endowment, but that this State endowment should not continue longer than the time during which they are so absorbed, and that at the end of that time they should be free to return to their former vocations.

Such a system would at one blow solve innumerable difficulties. If childbearing is protected by the State, it would not be unreasonable for the State to impose on the women who are possible mothers certain restrictions with regard to the activities which they may follow. Moreover, if the husband is no longer solely responsible for the support of his wife and her children, marriage will become easier among precisely those classes where we desire to encourage it. At the same time, if the dependence of women on marriage disappeared, and with it the inevitable accompanying subordination of their own wishes to their husbands' marital demands, we should establish the most reasonable check on the increase of the population, namely, the woman's natural dislike to excessive and unwished-for childbearing. That decline of the birth rate among the classes with the highest standard of comfort which exists at present would be checked by the greater facilities for marriage, yet, on the other hand, there would be no danger of the too large families which are due to the dependence of women, and which give rise to over population. At present the distribution of children presents the same inequality as the distribution of wealth; some people have far too many at the same time that others have too few. Another problem which would in time disappear is the inequality of the wages of men and women. The great argument which now weighs with the popular mind in favor of this inequality is the alleged fact that most men have dependants, while most women have not. Unfortunately, this is by no means always true; and, moreover, this theory overlooks the fact that in a certain number of instances, at all events, women compete with men, and therefore if a lower level of payment is established for women, they will drive the men out altogether, as they have done in typewriting, and are in process of doing in elementary school teaching. What we want to work towards is a system whereby all adult human beings not incapacitated by some specific cause shall work for their living and be paid for it, no distinction of sex being made where similar work is done by men and women. Then the young, the aged, and those adults who for some special reason are unable to earn their living, should be supported by the State from the surplus funds available when rent and interest have been absorbed by the community; a system of which we have already made a beginning in old age pensions on the one hand, and maintenance scholarships on the other. And among the most honored and respected of all those endowed by the State should be the women who are rendering to it the greatest possible service, that, namely, of ushering into the world its future citizens. But their reward for this service should only cover the time when their maternal duties prevent them from taking any part in industry.

This is coming to be realized more and more clearly as the ultimate ideal of the feminist movement, and what we have to do at present is, while not straining our adhesion to it unduly in the face of the conflicts of the present situation, to attempt no changes in the law which will make our ultimate attainment of it impossible; so that we should watch very carefully any development which may result in intensifying the dependence of women outside the childbearing years. It cannot be denied that the demands of some eugenists who are unable to believe that the necessary protection for motherhood can be given save through absolute dependence on a husband may make in this direction, and the increasing tendency of local authorities and government departments and of some philanthropic employers to exclude women from employment simply because they are legally married is equally a danger.

Socialism and Feminism

It will be seen that these changes in the status of women cannot come about in our present individualistic society. In the first place, under the existing state of competition in business a woman who drops out for the childbearing period can hardly expect to be reinstated, and the world will probably honestly have to face the fact that certain readjustments, not otherwise desirable, must be made in order that the mother may not be penalized in her later economic life by reason of her motherhood. Even among elementary school teachers today a married teacher who frequently demands leave of absence because of her approaching confinement finds herself at a serious disadvantage. The absence and subsequent return of the married women to their work will no doubt be inconvenient, but the inconvenience must be faced, and the women as far as possible be placed at no disadvantage, if we are to put a stop to our present practice of the deliberate sterilization of the ablest and most independent women.

Such a system could be deliberately and consciously introduced into the public services; it could be imposed on private enterprise by factory legislation, though with much greater difficulty. But it is the development of Socialism, and that alone, which can make it possible throughout the whole fabric of society for the normal woman to attain her twin demands, independent work and motherhood. It is only Socialism which can make the endowment of the women during the maternal years a possibility, that endowment being one of the first charges on the surplus value or economic rent which the State will absorb; and until the State has made itself master of the land and the capital of this country, it will not have an income big enough to enable it to provide adequate endowments for the childbearing women. Therefore it becomes clear that the only path to the ultimate and most deep lying ends of the feminist movement is through Socialism, and every wise feminist will find herself more and more compelled to adopt the principles of Socialism. But the wise Socialists must also be feminists. The public spirit of willingness to serve the community which will be necessary if the Socialist principles are to work must be inculcated into children from their earliest days. Can they be so inculcated by women who know nothing of the activities of the world beyond the four walls of their homes? Women, too, must be citizens and fully conscious of the privileges and duties of their citizenship if Socialism is to be attained. Not least among the duties of that citizenship should be what Plato long ago demanded of his women guardians:—that they should bear children for the service of the State.

4. Friedrich von Bernhardi, *Germany and the Next War*

Friedrich von Bernhardi (1849–1930) was the son of the noted military writer of the Bismarckian period, Theodor von Bernhardi. Entering the Prussian army in 1870, he was stationed with a regiment of hussars and took part in the Franco-Prussian war as a young lieutenant. From 1873 to 1877 Bernhardi was assigned to the famous War Academy, the institution which trained General Staff Officers. In 1898 Bernhardi was appointed chief of the military history section of the German General Staff and promoted to the rank of general in 1901. He retired from active service in 1909. In 1912 Bernhardi published *Deutschland und der nächste Krieg,* an unusually provocative commentary on Germany's position in Europe and on the possibility, indeed the inevitability, of a coming European war. Although some later German historians have dismissed Bernhardi's views as eccentric and as having little or no relationship with German war plans or strategic thinking, the German revisionist historian Fritz Fischer saw Bernhardi's visions as summarizing "the intentions of official Germany with great precision." [1] In either case, Bernhardi's book enjoyed an enormous popular success with the German reading public, running through five editions in a single year. As Wolfgang Mommsen has noted, "the response to this book was extraordinary and its effect was multiplied by reviews of the book in numerous right-wing newspapers," even though the book was censored by both the Social Democratic and Liberal press and in spite of the German Foreign Office's efforts to counteract its sensationalism. [2] Translated into English, it became, after August 1914, along with Treitschke's books and essays, a favorite source for Allied propagandists attempting to illuminate the true nature of "German militarism" in the First World War.

Introduction

The value of war for the political and moral development of mankind has been criticized by large sections of the modern civilized world in a way

1. Fritz Fischer, *Germany's Aims in the First World War* (New York, 1967), p. 34.

2. Wolfgang J. Mommsen, "The Topos of Inevitable War in Germany in the Decade before 1914," in Volker R. Berghahn and Martin Kitchen, eds., *Germany in the Age of Total War* (Totowa, N.J., 1981), p. 32.

From Friedrich von Bernhardi, *Germany and the Next War,* translated by Allen H. Powles (New York: Longmans, Green, and Co., 1914), pp. 9–14, 76, 102–14.

which threatens to weaken the defensive powers of States by undermining the warlike spirit of the people. Such ideas are widely disseminated in Germany, and whole strata of our nation seem to have lost that ideal enthusiasm which constituted the greatness of its history. With the increase of wealth they live for the moment, they are incapable of sacrificing the enjoyment of the hour to the service of great conceptions, and close their eyes complacently to the duties of our future and to the pressing problems of international life which await a solution at the present time.

We have been capable of soaring upwards. Mighty deeds raised Germany from political disruption and feebleness to the forefront of European nations. But we do not seem willing to take up this inheritance, and to advance along the path of development in politics and culture. We tremble at our own greatness, and shirk the sacrifices it demands from us. Yet we do not wish to renounce the claim which we derive from our glorious past. How rightly Fichte once judged his countrymen when he said the German can never wish for a thing by itself; he must always wish for its contrary also.

The Germans were formerly the best fighting men and the most warlike nation of Europe. For a long time they have proved themselves to be the ruling people of the Continent by the power of their arms and the loftiness of their ideas. Germans have bled and conquered on countless battlefields in every part of the world, and in late years have shown that the heroism of their ancestors still lives in the descendants. In striking contrast to this military aptitude they have today become a peace-loving—an almost "too" peace-loving—nation. A rude shock is needed to awaken their warlike instincts, and compel them to show their military strength.

This strongly-marked love of peace is due to various causes.

It springs first from the good-natured character of the German people, which finds intense satisfaction in doctrinaire disputations and partisanship, but dislikes pushing things to an extreme. It is connected with another characteristic of the German nature. Our aim is to be just, and we strangely imagine that all other nations with whom we exchange relations share this aim. We are always ready to consider the peaceful assurances of foreign diplomacy and of the foreign Press to be no less genuine and true than our own ideas of peace, and we obstinately resist the view that the political world is only ruled by interests and never from ideal aims of philanthropy. "Justice," Goethe says aptly, "is a quality and a phantom of the Germans." We are always inclined to assume that disputes between States can find a peaceful solution on the basis of justice without clearly realizing what *international* justice is.

An additional cause of the love of peace, besides those which are rooted in the very soul of the German people, is the wish not to be disturbed in commercial life.

The Germans are born business men, more than any others in the world. Even before the beginning of the Thirty Years' War, Germany was perhaps the greatest trading Power in the world, and in the last forty years Germany's trade has made marvellous progress under the renewed expansion of her political power. Notwithstanding our small stretch of coast-line, we have created in a few years the second largest merchant fleet in the world, and our young industries challenge competition with all the great industrial States of the earth. German trading-houses are established all over the world; German merchants traverse every quarter of the globe; a part, indeed, of English wholesale trade is in the hands of Germans, who are, of course, mostly lost to their own country. Under these conditions our national wealth has increased with rapid strides.

Our trade and our industries—owners no less than employés—do not want this development to be interrupted. They believe that peace is the essential condition of commerce. They assume that free competition will be conceded to us, and do not reflect that our victorious wars have never disturbed our business life, and that the political power regained by war rendered possible the vast progress of our trade and commerce.

Universal military service, too, contributes to the love of peace, for war in these days does not merely affect, as formerly, definite limited circles, but the whole nation suffers alike. All families and all classes have to pay the same toll of human lives. Finally comes the effect of that universal conception of peace so characteristic of the times—the idea that war in itself is a sign of barbarism unworthy of an aspiring people, and that the finest blossoms of culture can only unfold in peace.

Under the many-sided influence of such views and aspirations, we seem entirely to have forgotten the teaching which once the old German Empire received with "astonishment and indignation" from Frederick the Great, that "the rights of States can only be asserted by the living power"; that what was won in war can only be kept by war; and that we Germans, cramped as we are by political and geographical conditions, require the greatest efforts to hold and to increase what we have won. We regard our warlike preparations as an almost insupportable burden, which it is the special duty of the German Reichstag to lighten so far as possible. We seem to have forgotten that the conscious increase of our armament is not an inevitable evil, but the most necessary precondition of our national health, and the only guarantee of our international prestige. We are accustomed to regard war as a curse, and refuse to recognize it as the greatest factor in the furtherance of culture and power.

Besides this clamorous need of peace, and in spite of its continued justification, other movements, wishes, and efforts, inarticulate and often unconscious, live in the depths of the soul of the German people. The agelong dream of the German nation was realized in the political union of the greater part of the German races and in the founding of the German Empire. Since then there lives in the hearts of all (I would not exclude even the supporters of the anti-national party) a proud consciousness of strength, of regained national unity, and of increased political power. This consciousness is supported by the fixed determination never to abandon these acquisitions. The conviction is universal that every attack upon these conquests will rouse the whole nation with enthusiastic unanimity to arms. We all wish, indeed, to be able to maintain our present position in the world without a conflict, and we live in the belief that the power of our State will steadily increase without our needing to fight for it. We do not at the bottom of our hearts shrink from such a conflict, but we look towards it with a certain calm confidence, and are inwardly resolved never to let ourselves be degraded to an inferior position without striking a blow. Every appeal to force finds a loud response in the hearts of all. Not merely in the North, where a proud, efficient, hard-working race with glorious traditions has grown up under the laurel-crowned banner of Prussia, does this feeling thrive as an unconscious basis of all thought, sentiment, and volition, in the depth of the soul; but in the South also, which has suffered for centuries under the curse of petty nationalities, the haughty pride and ambition of the German stock live in the heart of the people. Here and there, maybe, such emotions slumber in the shade of a jealous particularism, overgrown by the richer and more luxuriant forms of social intercourse; but still they are animated by latent energy; here, too, the germs of mighty national consciousness await their awakening.

Thus the political power of our nation, while fully alive below the surface, is fettered externally by this love of peace. It fritters itself away in fruitless bickerings and doctrinaire disputes. We no longer have a clearly-defined political and national aim, which grips the imagination, moves the heart of the people, and forces them to unity of action. Such a goal existed, until our wars of unification, in the yearnings for German unity, for the fulfilment of the Barbarossa legend. A great danger to the healthy, continuous growth of our people seems to me to lie in the lack of it, and the more our political position in the world is threatened by external complications, the greater is this danger.

Extreme tension exists between the Great Powers, notwithstanding all peaceful prospects for the moment, and it is hardly to be assumed that their aspirations, which conflict at so many points and are so often pressed forward with brutal energy, will always find a pacific settlement.

In this struggle of the most powerful nations, which employ peaceful methods at first until the differences between them grow irreconcilable, our German nation is beset on all sides. This is primarily a result of our geographical position in the midst of hostile rivals, but also because we have forced ourselves, though the last-comers, the virtual upstarts, between the States which have earlier gained their place, and now claim our share in the dominion of this world, after we have for centuries been paramount only in the realm of intellect. We have thus injured a thousand interests and roused bitter hostilities. It must be reserved for a subsequent section to explain the political situation thus affected, but one point can be mentioned without further consideration: if a violent solution of existing difficulties is adopted, if the political crisis develops into military action, the Germans would have a dangerous situation in the midst of all the forces brought into play against them. On the other hand, the issue of this struggle will be decisive of Germany's whole future as State and nation. We have the most to win or lose by such a struggle. We shall be beset by the greatest perils, and we can only emerge victoriously from this struggle against a world of hostile elements, and successfully carry through a Seven Years' War for our position as a World Power, if we gain a start on our probable enemy as *soldiers;* if the army which will fight our battles is supported by all the material and spiritual forces of the nation; if the resolve to conquer lives not only in our troops, but in the entire united people which sends these troops to fight for all their dearest possessions.

These were the considerations which induced me to regard war from the standpoint of civilization, and to study its relation to the great tasks of the present and the future which Providence has set before the German people as the greatest civilized people known to history.

From this standpoint I must first of all examine the aspirations for peace, which seem to dominate our age and threaten to poison the soul of the German people, according to their true moral significance. I must try to prove that war is not merely a necessary element in the life of nations, but an indispensable factor of culture, in which a true civilized nation finds the highest expression of strength and vitality. I must endeavour to develop from the history of the German past in its connection with the conditions of the present those aspects of the question which may guide us into the unknown land of the future. The historical past cannot be killed; it exists and works according to inward laws, while the present, too, imposes its own drastic obligations. No one need passively submit to the pressure of circumstances; even States stand, like the Hercules of legend, at the parting of the ways. They can choose the road to progress or to decadence. "A favoured position in the world will only become effective in the life of nations by the conscious human endeavour to use it." It seemed to me, therefore, to be necessary and profitable, at this parting of the ways of our development where we now stand, to throw what light I may on the different paths which are open to our people. A nation must fully realize the probable consequences of its action; then only can it take deliberately the great decisions for its future development, and, looking forward to its destiny with clear gaze, be prepared for any sacrifices which the present or future may demand. . . .

Germany's Historical Mission

. . . Duties of the greatest importance for the whole advance of human civilization have thus been transmitted to the German nation, as heir of a great and glorious past. It is faced with problems of no less significance in the sphere of its international relations. These problems are of special importance, since they affect most deeply the intellectual development, and on their solution depends the position of Germany in the world.

The German Empire has suffered great losses of territory in the storms and struggles of the past. The Germany of today, considered geographically, is a mutilated torso of the old dominions of the Emperors; it comprises only a fraction of the German peoples. A large number of German fellow-countrymen have been incorporated into other States, or live in political independence, like the Dutch, who have developed into a separate nationality, but in language and national customs cannot deny their German ancestry. Germany has been robbed of her natural boundaries; even the source and mouth of the most characteristically German stream, the much lauded German Rhine, lie outside the German territory. On the eastern frontier, too, where the strength of the modern German Empire grew up in centuries of war against the Slavs, the possessions of Germany are menaced. The Slavonic waves are ever dashing more furiously against the coast of that Germanism, which seems to have lost its old victorious strength.

Signs of political weakness are visible here, while for centuries the overflow of the strength of the German nation has poured into foreign countries, and been lost to our fatherland and to our nationality; it is absorbed by foreign nations and steeped with foreign sentiments. Even today the German Empire possesses no colonial territories where its increasing population may find remunerative work and a German way of living.

This is obviously not a condition which can satisfy a powerful nation, or corresponds to the greatness of the German nation and its intellectual importance. . . .

World Power or Downfall

. . . If we look at these conditions as a whole, it appears that on the continent of Europe the power of the Central European Triple Alliance and that of the States united against it by alliance and agreement balance each other, provided that Italy belongs to the league. If we take into calculation the imponderabilia, whose weight can only be guessed at, the scale is inclined slightly in favour of the Triple Alliance. On the other hand, England indisputably rules the sea. In consequence of her crushing naval superiority when allied with France, and of the geographical conditions, she may cause the greatest damage to Germany by cutting off her maritime trade. There is also a not inconsiderable army available for a continental war. When all considerations are taken into account, our opponents have a political superiority not to be underestimated. If France succeeds in strengthening her army by large colonial levies and a strong English landing-force, this superiority would be asserted on land also. If Italy really withdraws from the Triple Alliance, very distinctly superior forces will be united against Germany and Austria.

Under these conditions the position of Germany is extraordinarily difficult. We not only require for the full material development of our nation, on a scale corresponding to its intellectual importance, an extended political basis, but, as explained in the previous chapter, we are compelled to obtain space for our increasing population and markets for our growing industries. But at every step which we take in this direction England will resolutely oppose us. English policy may not yet have made the definite decision to attack us; but it doubtless wishes by all and every means, even the most extreme, to hinder every further expansion of German international influence and of German maritime power. The recognized political aims of England and the attitude of the English Government leave no doubt on this point. But if we were involved in a struggle with England, we can be quite sure that France would not neglect the opportunity of attacking our flank. Italy, with her extensive coast-line, even if still a member of the Triple Alliance, will have to devote large forces to the defence of the coast to keep off the attacks of the Anglo-French Mediterranean Fleet, and would thus be only able to employ weaker forces against France. Austria would be paralyzed by Russia; against the latter we should have to leave forces in the East. We should thus have to fight out the struggle against France and England practically alone with a part of our army, perhaps with some support from Italy. It is in this double menace by sea and on the mainland of Europe that the grave danger to our political position lies, since all freedom of action is taken from us and all expansion barred.

Since the struggle is, as appears on a thorough investigation of the international question, necessary and inevitable, we must fight it out, cost what it may. Indeed, we are carrying it on at the present moment, though not with drawn swords, and only by peaceful means so far. On the one hand it is being waged by the competition in trade, industries and warlike preparations; on the other hand, by diplomatic methods with which the rival States are fighting each other in every region where their interests clash.

With these methods it has been possible to maintain peace hitherto, but not without considerable loss of power and prestige. This apparently peaceful state of things must not deceive us; we are facing a hidden, but none the less formidable, crisis—perhaps the most momentous crisis in the history of the German nation.

We have fought in the last great wars for our national union and our position among the Powers of *Europe;* we now must decide whether we wish to develop into and maintain a *World Empire,* and procure for German spirit and German ideas that fit recognition which has been hitherto withheld from them.

Have we the energy to aspire to that great goal? Are we prepared to make the sacrifices which such an effort will doubtless cost us? or are we willing to recoil before the hostile forces, and sink step by step lower in our economic, political, and national importance? That is what is involved in our decision.

"To be, or not to be," is the question which is put to us today, disguised, indeed, by the apparent equilibrium of the opposing interests and forces, by the deceitful shifts of diplomacy, and the official peace-aspirations of all the States; but by the logic of history inexorably demanding an answer, if we look with clear gaze beyond the narrow horizon of the day and the mere surface of things into the region of realities.

There is no standing still in the world's history. All is growth and development. It is obviously impossible to keep things in the *status quo,* as diplomacy has so often attempted. No true statesman will ever seriously count on such a possibility; he will only make the outward and temporary maintenance of existing conditions a duty when he wishes to gain time and deceive an opponent, or when he cannot see what is the trend of events. He will use such diplomatic means only as inferior tools; in reality he will only reckon with actual forces and with the powers of a continuous development.

We must make it quite clear to ourselves that there can be no standing still, no being satisfied for us, but only progress or retrogression, and that it is tantamount to retrogression when we are contented with our present place among the nations of Europe, while all our rivals are straining with desperate energy, even at the cost of our rights, to extend their power. The process of our decay would set in gradually and advance slowly so long as the struggle against us was waged with peaceful weapons; the living generation would, perhaps, be able to continue to exist in peace and comfort. But should a war be forced upon us by stronger enemies under conditions unfavourable to us, then, if our arms met with disaster, our political downfall would not be delayed, and we should rapidly sink down. The future of German nationality would be sacrificed, an independent German civilization would not long exist, and the blessings for which German blood has flowed in streams—spiritual and moral liberty, and the profound and lofty aspirations of German thought—would for long ages be lost to mankind.

If, as is right, we do not wish to assume the responsibility for such a catastrophe, we must have the courage to strive with every means to attain that increase of power which we are entitled to claim, even at the risk of a war with numerically superior foes.

Under present conditions it is out of the question to attempt this by acquiring territory in Europe. The region in the East, where German colonists once settled, is lost to us, and could only be recovered from Russia by a long and victorious war, and would then be a perpetual incitement to renewed wars. So, again, the reannexation of the former South Prussia, which was united to Prussia on the second partition of Poland, would be a serious undertaking, on account of the Polish population.

Under these circumstances we must clearly try to strengthen our political power in other ways.

In the first place, our political position would be considerably consolidated if we could finally get rid of the standing danger that France will attack us on a favourable occasion, so soon as we find ourselves involved in complications elsewhere. In one way or another *we must square our account with France* if we wish for a free hand in our international policy. This is the first and foremost condition of a sound German policy, and since the hostility of France once for all cannot be removed by peaceful overtures, the matter must be settled by force of arms. France must be so completely crushed that she can never again come across our path.

Further, we must contrive every means of strengthening the political power of our allies. We have already followed such a policy in the case of Austria when we declared our readiness to protect, if necessary with armed intervention, the final annexation of Bosnia and Herzegovina by our ally on the Danube. Our policy towards Italy must follow the same lines, especially if in any Franco-German war an opportunity should be presented of doing her a really valuable service. It is equally good policy in every way to support Turkey, whose importance for Germany and the Triple Alliance has already been discussed.

Our political duties, therefore, are complicated, and during the Turco-Italian War all that we can do at first is to use our influence as mediators, and to prevent a transference of hostilities to the Balkan Peninsula. It cannot be decided at this moment whether further intervention will be necessary. Finally, as regards our own position in Europe, we can only effect an extension of our own political influence, in my opinion, by awakening in our weaker neighbours, through the integrity and firmness of our policy, the conviction that their independence and their interests are bound up with Germany, and are best secured under the protection of the German arms. This conviction might eventually lead to an enlargement of the Triple Alliance into a Central European Federation. Our military strength in Central Europe would by this means be considerably increased, and the extraordinarily unfavourable geographical configuration of our dominions would be essentially improved in case of war. Such a federation would be the expression of a natural community of interests, which is founded on the geographical and natural conditions, and would insure the durability of the political community based on it.

We must employ other means also for the widening of our colonial territory, so that it may be able to receive the overflow of our population. Very recent events have shown that, under certain circumstances, it is possible to obtain districts in Equatorial Africa by pacific negotiations. A financial or political crash in Portugal might give us the opportunity to take possession of a portion of the Portuguese colonies. We may assume that some understanding exists between England and Germany which contemplates a division of the Portuguese colonial possessions, but has never become *publici juris*. It cannot, indeed, be certain that England, if the contingency arrives, would be prepared honestly to carry out such a treaty, if it actually exists. She might find ways and means to invalidate it. It has even been often said, although disputed in other quarters, that Great Britain, after coming to an agreement with Germany about the partition of the Portuguese colonies, had, by a special convention, guaranteed Portugal the possession of *all* her colonies.

Other possible schemes may be imagined, by which some extension of our African territory would be possible. These need not be discussed here more particularly. If necessary, they must be obtained as the result of a successful European war. In all these possible acquisitions of territory the point must be strictly borne in mind that we require countries which are climatically suited to German settlers. Now, there are even in Central Africa large regions which are adapted to the settlement of German farmers and stock-breeders, and part of our overflow population might be diverted to those parts. But, generally speaking, we can only obtain in tropical colonies markets for our industrial products and wide stretches of cultivated ground for the growth of the raw materials which our industries require. This represents in itself a considerable advantage, but does not release us from the obligation to acquire land for actual colonization.

A part of our surplus population, indeed—so far as present conditions point—will always be driven to seek a livelihood outside the borders of the German Empire. Measures must be taken to the extent at least of providing that the German element is not split up in the world, but remains united in compact blocks, and thus forms, even in foreign countries, political centres of gravity in our favour, markets for our exports, and centres for the diffusion of German culture.

An intensive colonial policy is for us especially an absolute necessity. It has often been asserted that a "policy of the open door" can replace the want of colonies of our own, and must constitute our programme for the future, just because we do not possess sufficient colonies. This notion is only justified in a certain sense. In the first place, such a policy does not offer the possibility of finding homes for the overflow population in a territory of our own; next, it does not guarantee the certainty of an open and unrestricted trade competition. It secures to all trading nations equal tariffs, but this does not imply by any means competition under equal conditions. On the contrary, the political power which is exercised in such a country is the determining factor in the economic relations. The principle of the open door prevails everywhere—in Egypt, Manchuria, in the Congo State, in Morocco—and everywhere the politically dominant Power controls the commerce: in Manchuria Japan, in Egypt England, in the Congo State Belgium, and in Morocco France. The reason is plain. All State concessions fall naturally to that State which is practically dominant; its products are bought by all the consumers who are any way dependent on the power of the State, quite apart from the fact that by reduced tariffs and similar advantages for the favoured wares the concession of the open door can be evaded in various ways. A "policy of the open door" must at best be regarded as a makeshift, and as a complement of a vigorous colonial policy. The essential point is for a country to have colonies of its own and a predominant political influence in the spheres where its markets lie. Our German world policy must be guided by these considerations.

The execution of such political schemes would certainly clash with many old-fashioned notions and vested rights of the traditional European policy. In the first place, the principle of the balance of power in Europe, which has, since the Congress of Vienna, led an almost sacrosanct but entirely unjustifiable existence, must be entirely disregarded.

The idea of a balance of power was gradually developed from the feeling that States do not exist to thwart each other, but to work together for the advancement of culture. Christianity, which leads man beyond the limits of the State to a world citizenship of the noblest kind, and lays the foundation of all international law, has exercised a wide influence in this respect. Practical interests, too, have strengthened the theory of balance of power. When it was understood that the State was a power, and that, by its nature, it must strive to extend that power, a certain guarantee of peace was supposed to exist in the balance of forces. The conviction was thus gradually established that every State had a close community of interests with the other States, with which it entered into political and economic relations, and was bound to establish some sort of understanding with them. Thus the idea grew up in Europe of a State-system, which was formed after the fall of Napoleon by the five Great Powers—England, France, Russia, Austria, and Prussia, which latter had gained a place in the first rank by force of arms; in 1866 Italy joined it as the sixth Great Power.

"Such a system cannot be supported with an approximate equilibrium among the nations." "All theory must rest on the basis of practice, and a real equilibrium—i.e., an actual equality of power—is postulated."[3] This condition does not exist between the European nations. England by herself rules the sea, and the 65,000,000 of Germans cannot allow themselves to sink to the same level of power as the 40,000,000 of French. An attempt has been made to produce a real equilibrium by special alliances. One result only has been obtained—the hindrance of the free development of the nations in general, and of Germany in particular. This is an unsound condition. A European balance of power can no longer be termed a condition which corresponds to the existing state of things; it can only have the disastrous consequences of rendering the forces of the continental European States mutually ineffective, and of thus favouring the plans of the political powers which stand outside that charmed circle. It has always been England's policy to stir up enmity between the respective continental States, and to keep them at approximately the same standard of power, in order herself undisturbed to conquer at once the sovereignty of the seas and the sovereignty of the world.

We must put aside all such notions of equilibrium. In its present distorted form it is opposed to our weightiest interests. The idea of a State system which has common interests in civilization must not, of course, be abandoned; but it must be expanded on a new and more just basis. It is now not a question of a European State system, but of one embracing all the States in the world, in which the equilibrium is established on real factors of power. We must endeavour to obtain in this system our merited position at the head of a federation of Central European States, and thus reduce the imaginary European equilibrium, in one way or the other, to its true value, and correspondingly to increase our own power.

A further question, suggested by the present political position, is whether all the political treaties which were concluded at the beginning of the last century under quite other conditions—in fact, under a different conception of what constitutes a State—can, or ought to be, permanently observed. When Belgium was proclaimed neutral, no one contemplated that she would lay claim to a large and valuable region of Africa. It may well be asked whether the acquisition of such territory is not *ipso facto* a breach of neutrality, for a State from which—theoretically at least—all danger of war has been removed, has no right to enter into political competition with the other States. This argument is the more justifiable because it may safely be assumed that, in event of a war of Germany against France and England, the two last-mentioned States would try to unite their forces in Belgium. Lastly, the neutrality of the Congo State must be termed more

3. Treitschke.

than problematic, since Belgium claims the right to cede or sell it to a non-neutral country. The conception of permanent neutrality is entirely contrary to the essential nature of the State, which can only attain its highest moral aims in competition with other States. Its complete development presupposes such competition.

Again, the principle that no State can ever interfere in the internal affairs of another State is repugnant to the highest rights of the State. This principle is, of course, very variously interpreted, and powerful States have never refrained from a high-handed interference in the internal affairs of smaller ones. We daily witness instances of such conduct. Indeed, England quite lately attempted to interfere in the private affairs of Germany, not formally or by diplomatic methods, but none the less in point of fact, on the subject of our naval preparations. It is, however, accepted as a principle of international intercourse that between the States of one and the same political system a strict non-interference in home affairs should be observed. The unqualified recognition of this principle and its application to political intercourse under all conditions involves serious difficulties. It is the doctrine of the Liberals, which was first preached in France in 1830, and of which the English Ministry of Lord Palmerston availed themselves for their own purposes. Equally false is the doctrine of unrestricted intervention, as promulgated by the States of the Holy Alliance at Troppau in 1820. No fixed principles for international politics can be laid down.

After all, the relation of States to each other is that of individuals; and as the individual can decline the interference of others in his affairs, so, naturally, the same right belongs to the State. Above the individual, however, stands the authority of the State, which regulates the relations of the citizens to each other. But no one stands above the State; it is sovereign, and must itself decide whether the internal conditions or measures of another State menace its own existence or interests. In no case, therefore, may a sovereign State renounce the right of interfering in the affairs of other States, should circumstances demand. Cases may occur at any time, when the party disputes or the preparations of the neighbouring country become a threat to the existence of a State. "It can only be asserted that every State acts at its own risk when it interferes in the internal affairs of another State, and that experience shows how very dangerous such an interference may become." On the other hand, it must be remembered that the dangers which may arise from non-intervention are occasionally still graver, and that the whole discussion turns, not on an international right, but simply and solely on power and expediency.

I have gone closely into these questions of international policy because, under conditions which are not remote, they may greatly influence the realization of our necessary political aspirations, and may give rise to hostile complications. Then it becomes essential that we do not allow ourselves to be cramped in our freedom of action by considerations, devoid of any inherent political necessity, which only depend on political expediency, and are not binding on us. We must remain conscious in all such eventualities that we cannot, under any circumstances, avoid fighting for our position in the world, and that the all-important point is, not to postpone that war as long as possible, but to bring it on under the most favourable conditions possible. "No man," so wrote Frederick the Great to Pitt on July 3, 1761, "if he has a grain of sense, will leave his enemies leisure to make all preparations in order to destroy him; he will rather take advantage of his start to put himself in a favourable position."

If we wish to act in this spirit of prompt and effective policy which guided the great heroes of our past, we must learn to concentrate our forces, and not to dissipate them in centrifugal efforts.

The political and national development of the German people has always, so far back as German history extends, been hampered and hindered by the hereditary defects of its character—that is, by the particularism of the individual races and States, the theoretic dogmatism of the parties, the incapacity to sacrifice personal interests for great national objects from want of patriotism and of political common sense, often, also, by the pettiness of the prevailing ideas. Even today it is painful to see how the forces of the German nation, which are so restricted and confined in their activities abroad, are wasted in fruitless quarrels among themselves.

Our primary and most obvious moral and political duty is to overcome these hereditary failings, and to lay a secure foundation for a healthy, consistent development of our power.

It must not be denied that the variety of forms of intellectual and social life arising from the like variety of the German nationality and political system offers valuable advantages. It presents countless centres for the advancement of science, art, technical skill, and a high spiritual and material way of life in a steadily increasing development. But we must resist the converse of these conditions, the transference of this richness in variety and contrasts into the domain of politics.

Above all must we endeavour to confirm and consolidate the institutions which are calculated to counteract and concentrate the centrifugal forces of the German nation—the common system of defence of our country by land and sea, in which all party feeling is merged, and a strong national empire.

No people is so little qualified as the German to direct its own destinies, whether in a parliamentarian or republican constitution; to no people is the customary liberal pattern so inappropriate as to us. A glance at the Reichstag will show how completely this conviction, which is forced on us by a study of German history, holds good today.

The German people has always been incapable of great acts for the common interest except under the irresistible pressure of external conditions, as in the rising of 1813, or under the leadership of powerful personalities, who knew how to arouse the enthusiasm of the masses, to stir the German spirit to its depths, to vivify the idea of nationality, and force conflicting aspirations into concentration and union.

We must therefore take care that such men are assured the possibility of acting with a confident and free hand in order to accomplish great ends through and for our people.

Within these limits, it is in harmony with the national German character to allow personality to have a free course for the fullest development of all individual forces and capacities, of all spiritual, scientific, and artistic aims. "Every extension of the activities of the State is beneficial and wise, if it arouses, promotes, and purifies the independence of free and reasoning men; it is evil when it kills and stunts the independence of free men."[4] This independence of the individual, within the limits marked out by the interests of the State, forms the necessary complement of the wide expansion of the central power, and assures an ample scope to a liberal development of all our social conditions.

We must rouse in our people the unanimous wish for power in this sense, together with the determination to sacrifice on the altar of patriotism, not only life and property, but also private views and preferences in the interests of the common welfare. Then alone shall we discharge our great duties of the future, grow into a World Power, and stamp a great part of humanity with the impress of the German spirit. If, on the contrary, we persist in that dissipation of energy which now marks our political life, there is imminent fear that in the great contest of the nations, which we must inevitably face, we shall be dishonourably beaten; that days of disaster await us in the future, and that once again, as in the days of our former degradation, the poet's lament will be heard:

> O Germany, thy oaks still stand,
> But thou art fallen, glorious land!
> Körner

5. Stenographic Protocol of the Last Meeting of the International Socialist Bureau of the Second International

On 29 July 1914 the executive Bureau of the Socialist International convened in Brussels in an emergency session to discuss the threat of war in

---

4. Treitschke, *Politik,* i., & 2.

Europe and possible responses which European socialist parties might make. The meeting came in the wake of the Austrian declaration of war against Serbia on 28 July; its conclusion on 30 July occurred on the day of the Czar's order for a general mobilization of Russian military forces which helped to trigger the fateful chain of events resulting in the Great War.

The Second International was both a political institution and a moral ideal, a federation of nationally autonomous parties and an international association with an agenda of implicitly European-wide concerns. Founded in 1889 in Paris, on the centennial of the French Revolution, the International brought together the leaders of all the major and many of the minor socialist parties of Europe for consultations and congresses. Not all of the member parties were strictly "Marxist," but the leading role played by the German and Austrian Social Democrats lent to the International a broad (and equivocally conservative) Marxist aura.

One of the avowed goals of the International was to fight against militarism and war as a vehicle for aggrandizement in European international affairs. Discussion of possible actions against war constituted an important part of the debates of the congresses held in Stuttgart in 1907, in Copenhagen in 1910, and in Basel in 1912. Yet the valence of nationalism and the successful (if "negative") integration of the socialist parties into their respective civic cultures proved overpowering in 1914. The debates of the final meeting of the Bureau manifested the tension between internationalist ideals of pacifism and the stark realities of fear of organizational survival.

Particularly candid were the remarks of the great leader of the Austrian Social Democrats, Victor Adler, who acknowledged the severe limitations facing his multiethnic party during the crisis. Adler had devoted his life to creating a modern socialist party in the Hapsburg Empire, a party which faced at first hand the kind of nationalistic tensions which were spared most of Adler's colleagues, except perhaps in their theorizing. Ironically, the original source of the war crisis—the assassination of Archduke Franz Ferdinand at Sarajevo on 28 June 1914 by young Bosnian terrorists, themselves products of generationalist nationalism in the Balkans—led to the destruction both of the Hapsburg state and of the party which, beyond all ideological consistency, had tried to defend that state's multinational integrity.

Since it was impossible in late July 1914 to proceed with the congress of the International scheduled for Vienna, a plan was developed in Brussels to summon an emergency congress in Paris. This too became a victim of the rush toward war in early August, to which most European Socialists actively or passively acceded.

Because of the critical international situation and the threat of war between Serbia and Austria the members of the International Socialist Bureau were summoned on 26 July by telegram to a session of the Bureau held on 29 and 30 July 1914 in the Maison du Peuple at Brussels.

Wednesday morning, 29 July

Chairman: Comrade Emile Vandervelde.
Members of the Executive Committee present:

Great Britain	James Keir Hardie, Bruce Glasier, Dan Irving
Germany	Hugo Haase, Karl Kautsky
Austria	Dr. Victor Adler, Dr. Friedrich Adler
Bohemia	Edmond Burian, Anton Nemec
France	Jean Jaurès, Edouard Vaillant, Jules Guesde, Marcel Sembat, Jean Longuet
Italy	Angelica Balabanoff, Morgari
Spain	Fabra-Ribas, Corralès
Russia	Ilya Rubanovich, Pavel Axelrod
Latvia	P. Winter, Otto Braun
Poland	Rosa Luxemburg, Walecki
Denmark	Stauning
Holland	Troelstra
Belgium	Emile Vandervelde, Edouard Anseele, Louis Bertrand, Camille Huysmans
Switzerland	Karl Moor, Robert Grimm

Comrade Henri de Man acted as interpreter.

The first item to be discussed was whether the press should be allowed to be present.

Vaillant: At the last session of the Bureau the press was not admitted. Only members of the Bureau were allowed to be present. The same procedure might be adopted on this occasion.

Vandervelde agreed. It could be dangerous to admit the press. A communiqué could be issued. *(Adopted)* . . .

Vandervelde proposed that the representatives of the countries involved in the conflict should report on the situation.

Guesde: Let the delegates of the national sections present be given the floor.

Jaurès: Let us proceed in the order of events. Let us first hear Austria,

From Georges Haupt, *Socialism and the Great War: The Collapse of the Second International,* translated by M. Jackson (Oxford: Oxford University Press, 1972), pp. 250–65. Reprinted by permission of Oxford University Press. Footnotes deleted.

Bohemia and Serbia, then Russia, France, Germany, and so on. *(Adopted)*

Victor Adler: I shall not tell you the things that you all know. But let me say that Austria's provocative note came as much of a surprise to us as to everyone else. We were of course forewarned by the various diplomatic moves. But we did not expect war. Although Serbia has accepted the principal points of the Austrian ultimatum, a few points excepted, war is with us.

The party is defenceless. To say anything else would mean deceiving the Bureau. One must not be misled by the news. We now see the result of years of class agitation and demagogy. Demonstrations in support of the war are taking place in the streets. There will be a new situation in our country which is full of national problems and contrasts. What this new situation will be nobody knows. The south Slav question, Serb agitation in Bosnia, all this has naturally had a detrimental effect on Serbia. With us hostility towards Serbia is almost natural. I personally do not believe that there will be a general war. In Austria people want to finish Serbia. Let us look at the situation as it affects the party. We cannot ward off the threat. Demonstrations have become impossible. One risks one's life in the process and must expect to be imprisoned. That we may have been through before. But our whole organization and our press are at risk. We run the danger of destroying thirty years' work without any political result. Is it not dangerous to encourage Serbia inside our own country? Are we not taking on a great responsibility by wanting to make the Serbs believe that Austria is threatened by revolution? We must protect the proletariat against such an infection. We must protect our institutions. Ideas of striking, etc., are mere fantasies. The matter is very serious and our only hope is that we alone will be the victims, that the war will not spread. Even if it remains localized the party is in a very sad position. Our enemies will be fortified and encouraged by their successes. We have had the pleasure of being allowed to organize the international congress in our country. We made careful preparations for it. The Austrian proletariat without distinction of nationality has looked forward impatiently to this congress. It is sad but there is nothing to be done about it. We hope that the Bureau believes us when we say that we could not have acted differently. We want to save the party. What the Bureau can do and we together with it is to condemn the guilty and to attempt to localize the conflict.

Our industry is likely to be militarized; every refusal to work will be dealt with under martial law.

In spite of everything we hope that the great war will be avoided. To believe this may mean believing in a miracle but we hope nevertheless.

Haase: I want to make a very important announcement. People ask what the proletariat is doing at this critical moment. If the bourgeois press is to be believed the proletariat remains chauvinistic. But the following telegram which I have just received from Berlin clearly proves the contrary.

Haase then read the text of a telegram signed by Braun saying that in Berlin on the previous day thousands of workers had demonstrated against the war and for peace at twenty-seven crowded meetings and in the streets.

Nemec described the situation in Bohemia where there had been pro-war demonstrations by the bourgeoisie. The bourgeoisie regarded the war as the result of the policy of recent years. But one must not forget that the steps which the Austrian Government had taken against Serbia had made the situation more critical still. In his view the Serb socialists were in favour of union with Austria. The bourgeoisie regarded war as a means of reducing the influence of social democracy. Together with the German socialists of Austria his comrades had considered the possibility of a general strike. Both parties had come to the same conclusion; their organizations were at stake.

Victor Adler hoped that the Bureau would not make any fatal decisions although the Bureau's decision would tip the scales. The Austrian party would see what measure of responsibility it could shoulder.

Jaurès wanted information about prospects in Bosnia-Herzegovina and among the Croats. What did the Hungarians expect from the war?

Victor Adler: The Croats are Catholic. The Serbs are Orthodox. The Croats are very loyal to the dynasty. The Serb element does not predominate in Bosnia. There are Croats and Mohammedans. It was the Croats who organized a pogrom against the Catholic clergy. As regards Hungary the Magyars are against the Slavs, particularly against the Rumanians.

Who governs Austria at present? The Emperor is like a prisoner. Policy is made by Berchtold and Tisza. In Hungary the situation is very confused. It is certain that part of the working class has been carried away by militant ideas. From the point of view of Austria's interest one must also bear in mind Serbia's demands concerning Bosnia.

Haase: It was difficult for us to leave our respective countries at this moment. We must return immediately and therefore, if possible, conclude the session this evening.

Vandervelde: We are counting on several of you for the meeting this evening. Your absence would cause great disappointment.

Keir Hardie: Why finish today? It would be a mistake to conclude this session in too much of a hurry.

Vaillant: How can we stop now? Come what may we must not go our various ways until we have finished, this afternoon or tomorrow morning.

Huysmans: Vaillant thinks that we shall achieve nothing today. That means that we must meet again tomorrow morning.

Rosa Luxemburg: We must act quickly and with determination. Let us issue no manifesto but decide on the congress. Let us then try to finish today.

Haase thought that a manifesto was required. If it was necessary for them to stay they would stay. Diplomats always acted quickly. Let them do the same.

Nemec: Adler maintains that the Serb element does not predominate in Bosnia. The opposite is true. The majority in Bosnia consists of Serbs. We in Prague are not afraid of the struggle, we are only afraid of the destruction of our party.

Wednesday afternoon, 29 July

The meeting opened at 3.15 p.m.

Haase: I propose that the International shall assemble for the congress at Paris not later than the end of next week. It is for the International to prove that it is alive. This congress must make an impression on the workers of all countries, on the political situation in all countries. We must prove that the International is not a negligible quantity. Let us use what influence we have. If at Paris Russians, Austrians, Frenchmen, Germans, Italians, and so on jointly raise their voice in protest we can have the satisfaction of having done our duty. We do not know whether we shall be successful but we must do our duty.

Vaillant: This congress will not be an extraordinary congress but an ordinary congress. The French will be very happy to act as your hosts. You can start today taking the necessary steps to open on Sunday week at Paris the congress that should have taken place at Vienna.

Irving regretted both proposals. It was understandable that the congress should be transferred to another place. But the British were unhappy about the change of date. The number of delegates would be very different from that expected in Vienna.

Huysmans: Let us be precise. We shall organize this congress on the lines of the one at Basle. We cannot make France bear the entire costs of the congress. Let us delete alcoholism, unemployment, and the increase in the cost of living from the agenda and retain only imperialism and immediate political issues, such as the deportation of our South African comrades. We must accept the proposed date. Some of the Africans are already in Europe. It is possible to wire to America. The duration of the congress will be limited and there will be no commissions.

Vandervelde: Let us take the points one by one. First the place, then the date, then the costs and finally the organizational details. First the place: does anybody propose any city other than Paris?

Keir Hardie: Paris was not proposed. London would also be suitable.

(Paris was agreed upon)

Angelica Balabanoff: Vaillant says that the congress will not be an extraordinary one. But if we meet now it will be an extraordinary congress.

Can the Bureau not take an immediate decision? In my opinion it would be better to postpone the congress and not to meet. We must not turn the congress into nothing but a demonstration. We must decide on action.

Jaurès: The International Socialist Bureau will agree upon the form of the anti-war demonstration and the sovereign congress will take the final decision. It will adopt whatever agenda and resolution it wants to adopt. The decisions of the congress cannot be made conditional on the present session. We need the congress. Its deliberations and its resolutions will give the proletariat confidence. The cancellation of the congress would be a big disappointment to the proletariat. To hold it at Vienna has become impossible; but that is not enough reason to cancel it. We must convene the congress as soon as possible at Paris. If it could be done tomorrow then we should do it tomorrow. The congress can open on Sunday 9 August with a big demonstration. A vast mass of people will be present. Thereby we shall all have contributed to the work for peace.

Bruce Glasier: The British reject the proposal to change the date of the congress. They would have no objection if it was possible to prevent the war by any form of direct action. But the socialists in the countries concerned are impotent. We all esteem our Austrian comrades but we think that they should have said: let us sacrifice our property to do our duty. As regards the congress we think that it will be attended by only a few delegates. No trade union delegates will be able to come.

Haase asked the British to bear in mind that extraordinary circumstances demand extraordinary measures. It had been impossible to foresee the congress. It was equally difficult for all to attend. If Germany and France were embroiled in a conflict the congress could not take place. Therefore it was very difficult to arrange things. When Jaurès spoke of the sovereignty of the congress, of hearing all views, there was agreement that it was the duty of the International Socialist Bureau to take measures that would prove the usefulness of the congress. They must be united at the congress. Therefore they must avoid all disputed questions, for example that of the general strike in the case of war and similar issues. Let the International Socialist Bureau act accordingly.

Victor Adler: Haase's proposal offers a solution. The congress must meet as soon as possible. There have been doubts about the location. We could have chosen a city in Switzerland but big demonstrations would have been impossible there. If even so the congress should happen too late it will not be because of us. I am in favour of Haase's date. To reply to Bruce Glasier: I do not know how I could have reported differently. It is my responsibility to report without worrying about what people think. Let our English colleagues believe us when we say that our position is very difficult, much more difficult than theirs and they see difficulties even in sending delegates two weeks earlier to a congress. It is not a question of property; it is a question of our arms which we do not want to lay down before we have taken action on behalf of the International. I did not think that at a moment such as this it was necessary to sing our own praises. But if that is what is wanted from us I apologize for not having done so and ask you to despise us no longer.

Irving: If we have spoken of difficulties they concern not only Britain but also the other nations.

Keir Hardie: If the only argument in favour of advancing the date of the congress is to hold an anti-war demonstration I cannot support the proposal. This is not a sufficient reason. We must keep the agenda. The items on it are of lasting interest whereas the war may pass. Keeping the agenda means not changing the date of the congress. Let us first discuss the agenda. The discussion will show whether or not to keep to the old date.

Vandervelde: Let us take a vote because a discussion will take too long. If it would take the powers as long to organize the war as it takes us to organize the war on war we could sleep in peace.

I therefore put to the vote: 9 August or the original date.

(9 August is adopted with the British and the Italians voting against.)

Agenda

Troelstra: This congress cannot be considered as extraordinary. We cannot turn it into a second Basle Congress. This would suggest that the Basle Congress had had no result. Consequently it would be a contradiction not to discuss the other points. If we debate imperialism we must also debate the general strike, the behaviour of the bourgeoisie in times of peace, and so on. Let us move the congress but let us not alter the agenda.

Vaillant: We have changed the place and date of the congress. Let us keep the agenda. If that means that the congress is not an extraordinary congress it will nevertheless be one because of the circumstances. This we must take into consideration. What worries the international proletariat most at present is the threat of war. How can the war be avoided, limited, or prevented? Therefore we must place the question of war at the top of the agenda. How can we discuss the question of the rising cost of living if there is a famine as a result of the war? How can we discuss imperialism if war is there? Let us therefore put at the top, above imperialism, the steps to be taken against the war and let us keep the original agenda. Thereby we shall satisfy the proletariat and the public and do our duty.

Vandervelde: The question of the war certainly overshadows everything. If the threat is removed we shall have our congress.

Rosa Luxemburg considered that the procedure adopted at Paris should be the same as at Basle. The question of the war overshadowed everything and therefore they must above all focus on that point. The other items would suffer as a result. They would be dealt with quickly and without the necessary interest.

Rubanovich: Today we must take steps against the war which we shall not prevent once it is there. In this respect we have never entered into an obligation *vis-à-vis* the proletariat. We must hold the congress. That is certain. We are conscious of the seriousness of the moment and agree with Troelstra's proposal to adhere to the agenda for which we have prepared ourselves. But in view of the situation let us begin with the question of imperialism and the steps to oppose the war.

Sembat agreed with Vandervelde that it was possible to combine the proposals of Vaillant and Troelstra. If necesssary the other items could be deleted from the agenda of the congress. If not, the congress would be a conference and an anti-war demonstration.

Keir Hardie proposed that imperialism and the war on war should not be dealt with under the same agenda item. It was necessary to distinguish and to discuss two very different problems: the present situation and imperialism—the future.

Kautsky did not think that in ten days there would be universal peace. In those circumstances it would be impossible for his delegation to travel to Paris to discuss questions which could be discussed later. At present they could not stay long abroad. Therefore there should be no discussion of the possibility of future wars. He thought that future wars would be prevented if the present war was averted.

Jaurès: The situation is critical. The French accept both suggestions. At the beginning they thought that the agenda should be adhered to. The Germans propose that nothing but the war should be discussed. Perhaps the best solution is the one suggested by Vandervelde. Another difficult question is how there can be any discussion at Paris. If I have understood Adler correctly questions on which there is no agreement should be avoided. Our comrades, like Haase, know that one can say what items should be put on the agenda but not what will be said. The French have received clear instructions. They must speak. To discuss problems on which there is no agreement is a matter of tact. It is impossible to avoid the question of the general strike. This always happened, even at Basle. Nevertheless agreement was reached. Let the discussions in the commissions be related to the work of plenaries. Let us prove that we have enough tact to know how to organize.

Sembat proposed to close the discussion on that item.

Haase proposed to put everything on the Paris agenda but to add as a first item: the war and the proletariat. The first item would thus have a bearing on the present situation. The congress had the right to change the agenda if it thought that this was desirable.

Keir Hardie: The present situation and the future must be dealt with separately. There will be a misunderstanding.

(Haase's proposal was adopted) . . .

The meeting examined the political situation created by recent events; it listened to and discussed reports by the delegates from the countries where war rages or threatens to rage. It decided unanimously not to postpone the congress scheduled for 23 August at Vienna but on the contrary to advance its date; at the suggestion of the German delegates, enthusiastically supported by the French delegates, it was decided that the congress shall meet on 9 August at Paris, that the agenda shall not be changed and that the first item shall be: "The war and the proletariat."

Vandervelde read out a telegram from the Paris *Temps,* indicating that the situation had become more critical.

Axelrod considered it unnecessary to discuss Russia's position *vis-à-vis* Austria or the possibility of a clash. The main task was to find out whether Russian social democracy was capable of anti-war action. For about ten years Russia had been in a state of revolution and he did not think that it was necessary to wait much longer for the second act of the affair. In his opinion the masses would again rise to oppose the war. What was the party's position now? A few days ago they had had strikes of a revolutionary character. On the one hand the party was weakened. The organization had suffered big losses because of the present strike. But the prestige of the socialist idea had risen enormously. They could say with certainty that revolution would break out if there was a war.

He read out the following statement by the Russian socialists:

> The attempts that are made outside Russia, namely in Austria, to create the impression that in case of war between Russia and Austria there would be a pro-Austrian revolt in Russian Poland, are completely misleading.
>
> About Galicia we know nothing. But all our information, particularly that provided by our comrades from Russian Poland, is unanimous: any popular movement that emerges in Russian Poland as the result of a war will form part of the Russian empire's revolutionary movement whose aim is autonomy for Russian Poland and a democratic Russia.

Rubanovich: The Russian situation is different from that in Austria. We are a secret and unorganized party. Our preoccupations therefore differ. Tsarism is isolated in Europe and seeks diversions. What is its aim? The mobilization shows that its designs are bellicose. A comedy has been enacted in Russia which we shall one day reveal with the help of the bourgeoisie. We cannot enter into formal commitments. The Russian proletariat is more revolutionary than the party. There is no doubt that if there is a war the situation will become more revolutionary still. And then, if necessary, the party will have recourse to highly effective means.

Haase: We know the Austrians well enough to understand their attitude. We know their tactics. They have seen the situation from uncomfortably close quarters. Their attitude of passivity and resignation is wrong, firstly because this passivity renders no service to social democracy and secondly because it does nothing to solve the present crisis. If they oppose the war now they will have public opinion on their side after the war. The population will realize that social democracy did not lose its head at the critical moment. I cannot believe that the proletariat's demonstrations strengthen the government's militant attitude. If anything they will, in my opinion, weaken it. I appreciate that great difficulties are involved, but those are my impressions. I hope that the decisions taken at this session and those that will be taken at Paris will not cause further difficulties for the Austrians.

As for Germany the government says that it was not consulted. That may be so. But we knew two weeks before the publication of the Austrian note to Serbia that Austria would in the end present Serbia with an ultimatum. We can be blamed for not having spoken out then. We did not do so because we could not believe that it would happen. The German Government closed its eyes so as to have a free hand when the conflict came. The *Temps* telegram suggests that Germany influenced Austria. We know that Germany wants peace but if Russia intervenes Germany must also intervene. The story about the conversation which I am alleged to have had with the Chancellor is a pure fabrication. The Government has made no attempt to influence the social democrats who were notified by a representative of the Government. Everything that might lead to war is being avoided. Nor have we stopped our activities. Our demonstrations have even benefited by being treated neutrally. Our rallies were tolerated. The most militant element is the liberal bourgeoisie which is anti-Serb and on the side of Austria. But the ruling class and the great industrialists are opposed to the war. The press of the military party declares that Germany has no interest whatsoever in war. But if Russia attacks Germany will intervene. There is no doubt about that. The social democrats are exploiting the present situation. We shall not cease our activities. We shall demonstrate more and make our protests even more anti-militaristic.

Keir Hardie proposed that there should be a meeting the following day. *(Adopted)*

Jaurès wanted to examine the question of what pressure could be exerted.

France was unanimous in condemning Austria's action and the hypocritical pretexts used by Austria to reject Serbia's reply which was anyway too accommodating. Austria wanted war and wanted to destroy the small nation. That fact had created universal indignation. The Catholic militarists who, as Catholics, had considerable sympathy for Austria expressed their disapproval. As regards Germany there was not one Frenchman in a hundred thousand who would admit that Germany had not been kept informed. Germany might not have been handed the text of the note but there was no doubt that it was determined to take Austria's side on the occasion of the first incident. Two days before the transmission of the note a German journalist attached to the German embassy in Paris had said: "I am leaving because there will be a big to-do over the Austro-Serb incident." The view therefore was that Germany knew everything. They therefore knew what the Triple Entente's powers of resistance were. "If we give way Germany's prestige will have been enhanced without war." That was how people argued in Germany. Had the governments reached such a nadir of weakness that they failed to see the danger? They were all agreed. The greatest conceivable misfortune awaited them.

The French Government wanted peace. It would support Britain in its attempts to mediate. It had exerted pressure on Russia so as to avoid a worsening of the situation. All that they could do now was to look out for new and unfavourable influences. Their theme should be: they were not committed to any action nor bound by any treaty. He rejoiced to hear about their German comrades' peace demonstrations and thanked them sincerely for their efforts. In France it was thought that Germany would attack France even if the French did not follow Russia. As far as they were concerned that attitude implied no *arrière-pensée* of war. They wished to prove that to their comrades and asked them to believe the French. If they succeeded in solving their terrible predicament they could be satisfied.

Morgari described the situation in Italy which proved that Italy had not remained loyal to the Triple Entente. The national antipathies were sufficiently well known. It was impossible to predict the attitude of the Italian proletariat to the general strike, etc. Italy understood the difficulties of the Austrians. But it was not those difficulties that counted. The Italian socialists had experience of that during the Tripoli war. They had been insulted and slandered. But after the war their prestige had increased.

The meeting rose at 20.30 hours.

Thursday morning, 30 July

Bruce Glasier regretted the absence of Keir Hardie who together with the other British comrades had been very disappointed by yesterday's debate.

Too much preference had been given to the French and the Germans and not enough attention had been paid to the British. The capitalist world regarded Britain as a power but the International Socialist Bureau did not. People in Britain at present were not seriously concerned with the consequences of the Austro-Serbian war. It was true that they felt the economic repercussions of the Balkan war but they did not think that they would be affected by the present war. The British wanted peace. The whole of the Cabinet wanted peace. So did the working class. Militarism and war had been attacked at every trade union congress. Even if part of the population was swept off its feet the trade union and socialist movement would continue to fight that trend.

Vandervelde: The British comrades are wrong in thinking that no attention has been paid to them. There is a misunderstanding here. Whereas in Britain the speaker who stands up has the floor, here it is the chairman who calls upon the speaker who is first on his list. Furthermore it was agreed that delegates should be allowed to speak in order of the importance of their country in the present conflict.

Vandervelde read out the following resolution proposed by Haase:

At its meeting of 29 July, the International Socialist Bureau heard
delegates from all the nations threatened by the world war describe
the political situation in their respective countries. It unanimously
calls upon the proletarians of all the countries concerned not only
to continue but to intensify their demonstrations against war and for
peace. The German and French proletarians will make every effort, as
they have done in the past, to make their governments exert pressure
on their allies, Austria and Russia, so that these two countries cease
to threaten world peace.

The congress convened at Paris will be a powerful expression of
this pacifist determination of the world proletariat.

. . .

(The final text of the resolution was adopted unanimously)
It read:

At its meeting of 29 July, the International Socialist Bureau heard the
delegates from all the nations threatened by the world war describe
the political situation in their respective countries. It unanimously
calls upon the proletarians of all countries concerned not merely to
continue but to intensify their demonstrations against war and for peace
and for a settlement of the Austro-Serb conflict by arbitration.

The German and French proletariats are invited to put more pressure than ever on their governments to ensure that Germany exerts a
moderating influence on Austria and that France persuades Russia not
to intervene in the conflict. The proletarians of Great Britain and Italy
for their part will support these efforts with all their energy.

The congress urgently convened at Paris shall give powerful expression to this pacifist determination of the world proletariat.

. . .

Rosa Luxemburg proposed the following resolution which was adopted unanimously:

The International Socialist Bureau warmly welcomes the revolutionary attitude of the Russian proletariat upon whom it calls to persevere in its heroic anti-Tsarist efforts which provide the most effective guarantee against the threat of a world war.

Vandervelde closed the session and convened the International for the Sunday after the next at Paris.

2
European Society during the War

6. Hugo Haase, Speech in the Reichstag on War Credits

The outbreak of the First World War ended an epoch of extraordinary
material progress and relative political peace in European civilization,
and ushered in forty years of unparalleled economic instability and political violence from which European society, much chastened and, in international terms at least, far less hegemonic, only now (in the 1980s) seems
to be fully recovered. The question of the responsibility for the war constituted a major point of polemical and eventually historiographical debate from 1914 until well into the 1960s. From the first outpouring of
self-justificatory "white" or "blue" or "red" books by the belligerent
Powers, through the massive documents projects of the interwar period
and the controversial and often poisoned debate about "war guilt" of the
1920s and 1930s, and finally in various streams of post-1945 revisionism
(most notably, perhaps, that engendered by Fritz Fischer with his *Griff
nach der Weltmacht* [1961]), the debate about the "causes" of the war has
inevitably been caught up in and defined by the larger issues of its horrific moral consequences and its monumentally destructive outcome. The
history of the First World War, like that of the French Revolution, has
thus come to be read both "forward" and "backward," as an exercise in
the historical analysis of an ongoing series of discrete events, policies,
and structural processes, and yet as a lucrative opportunity for retrospective ethical judgments and moral appraisals of the self and the other
in European history.

That Germany's peculiar pattern of national development since the
1850s and its conduct of international relations since the 1890s, its militaristic blustering and provocative economic expansion, its entrapment in
and sponsorship of an unstable alliance system, its dependence on and yet
genteel bullying of its increasingly desperate Austro-Hungarian partner,

all became primary occasions for the war is doubted today by no serious historian. Nor can the programs of annexationist "war aims," as they were conceived between 1914 and 1917 by the German government, by private ideological interest groups in German society, and especially by the German High Command, be wholly divorced from the political culture of late Imperial politics on the eve of the war. But the origins of the First World War are far more complex than any unilinear or mono-national theory of innocence or guilt can possibly explain. Perversely, even the European socialist parties must bear their share of "guilt," if not in "starting" the war, then in allowing it to begin. The early component of that which, today in the 1980s, may be most satisfying about the civic structure of the various West European polities—their successful cooptation and integration of the European working classes into their value systems—may be seen as a "cause" of 1914 as well as a consequence of 1945.

Among the immediate challenges of the war crisis was, therefore, the conundrum which it presented to socialist parties throughout Europe, parties who had committed themselves before 1914 to formal programs of democratic internationalism, while they drew nourishment from their own integration—positive or negative—into nineteenth-century bourgeois civic cultures defined by national boundaries and infused with national values. The dilemma of the German Social Democratic party in August 1914 was perhaps the most poignant, although by no means singular. When the failure of diplomatic efforts to maintain the peace was finally apparent, the leadership of the Social Democratic party met to discuss its official reaction to the Imperial German government's war policy. By an overwhelming majority (78 vs. 14), the party's parliamentary delegation voted on 3 August to support the government's request for war credits, rather than to resort to passive opposition against the war.

Hugo Haase, who along with Friedrich Ebert was cochairman of the Social Democratic party, was one of the small minority who opposed this decision (as his trenchant comments during the debate of the International, in document 5 above, anticipated). Haase was born in East Prussia in 1863, the son of a middle-class Jewish family. A trial lawyer and intellectual who made his reputation by defending socialists persecuted for political reasons, Haase did not hold, as did the more conservative Ebert, a functionary position in the party bureaucracy in Berlin. Ideologically on the party's left-center, Haase resisted the tide of civic patriotism which overwhelmed many of his colleagues in August 1914, but he nevertheless bowed to party discipline. On the insistence of his colleagues Haase agreed to present to the special session of the Reichstag called for 4 August a statement which summarized the majority's reasons for voting war credits, even though he personally disagreed with its arguments. The final version of this statement, printed below, was drafted by a special party commission, consisting of Eduard David, Karl Kautsky, Ludwig Frank, Otto Wels, and Gustav Hoch, of whom the right-wing David appears to have played an especially prominent role.[1]

Carl Schorske has noted that the decision of the German Social Democrats to approve war credits on 4 August 1914 "was taken in an atmosphere somewhat reminiscent of that of another August 4—that of 1789, when the nobility of France, seized by a paroxysm of fear, voted away its privileges and, in effect, publicly renounced its own principles of social organization. As in 1789 the hard facts of political life—above all the threat of force against the nobility—operated to strengthen the left wing of the second estate, so in 1914 the cold facts favored the right wing of the German Social Democratic Party."[2]

Hugo Haase's disenchantment with the war grew precipitously over the next three years, however, and at Gotha in April 1917 he led other left-wing, antiwar deputies in establishing the Independent Social Democrat Party (USPD). During the Revolutionary autumn and winter of 1918–19, Haase played a critical role in curbing violence, while trying, albeit unsuccessfully, to force the majority Socialists led by Ebert to remain loyal to their own revolutionary ideals. In October 1919 Haase was shot by a mentally deranged worker, a victim of what was soon to become a pattern of violence which undercut political stability in the Weimar Republic.

Gentlemen, upon the instruction of my parliamentary club, I would like to make the following declaration. We stand before a fateful hour. The consequences of the imperialistic politics which brought on an era of competitive armaments and the intensification of the conflicts among the nations, have swept over Europe like a tidal wave. The responsibility for this situation rests upon the advocates of this politics. (Very true! [by the Social Democrats]) We reject any complicity in it. (Bravo! [by the Social Democrats]) Social Democracy has fought this fateful development with all its

1. Compare *Das Kriegstagebuch des Reichstagsabgeordneten Eduard David 1914 bis 1918*, ed. Susanne Miller (Düsseldorf, 1966), pp. 6–10; and Philipp Scheidemann, *Memoiren eines Sozialdemokraten* (2 vols.; Dresden, 1928), 1: 254.

2. Carl E. Schorske, *German Social Democracy 1905–1917: The Development of the Great Schism* (Cambridge, Mass., 1955), pp. 290–91.

From *Verhandlungen des Reichstags. XIII. Legislaturperiode. II. Session,* vol. 306 (Berlin, 1916), pp. 8–9. Translated for this volume by John W. Boyer.

powers, and up to the final moment it has worked to maintain the peace, by huge demonstrations in all countries (spirited bravo by the Social Democrats), especially in ardent agreement with our French brothers. (More lively applause by the Social Democrats) Its efforts have been in vain.

We now confront the cold, hard reality of war. We are threatened by the terrors of enemy invasion. We have today not to decide for or against war, but rather to deal with the question of the means requisite for the defense of our country. (Spirited agreement from the bourgeois parties) We now have to think of the millions of our fellow citizens who, without any fault of their own, have been dragged into this fate. (Very true! [by the Social Democrats]) They will be the most severely affected by the devastations of the war. (Quite right! [by the Social Democrats]) Our passionate wishes go with our brothers, without respect to party, who have been called to the colors. (Lively bravo and handclapping from all sides) We also remember the mothers who must give up their sons, and the women and the children who are deprived of their bread-winners and who, in addition to the fear for their loved ones which they must endure, are threatened by the terrors of hunger. These people will soon be joined by tens of thousands of wounded and maimed soldiers. (Very true!) To support all these people, to ease their lot, to alleviate this immeasurable misery, this we think is our compelling obligation. (Spirited agreement by the Social Democrats)

For our people and for its future in freedom much, if not everything, is at stake in the event of a victory by Russian despotism, a despotism which is defiled with the blood of the best of its own people. (Spirited shouts: Very true! [by the Social Democrats]) It is necessary to avert this danger and to guarantee the culture and independence of our own country. (Bravo!) Under these circumstances, we are carrying out what we have always emphasized—in the hour of danger we will not leave our own fatherland in the lurch. (Spirited bravo) In this we feel we are in agreement with the International, which has always recognized the right of each people to national independence and self-defense (Quite correct! [by the Social Democrats]), just as we condemn with it every war of conquest. (Very good! [by the Social Democrats])

We demand that as soon as the goal of security is achieved and our adversaries are disposed toward peace, the war be ended by a peace settlement which will make friendship possible with the nations who are our neighbors. (Bravo! [by the Social Democrats]) We demand this not only in the interest of international solidarity, which we have always championed, but also in the interest of the German people. (Very good! [by the Social Democrats]) We hope that the cruel school of the sufferings of war will awake in new millions a loathing of war and win them over to the ideals of socialism and international peace. (Spirited bravo by the Social Demo-

crats) Led by these principles, we will vote for the war credits which have
been demanded. (Lively applause by the Social Democrats)

7. Rudolf Hilferding, *A Co-Partnership of Classes?*

Rudolf Hilferding (1877–1941) was one of the most prominent Social
Democratic theorists of the early twentieth century. The son of a Jewish
insurance employee who had come to Vienna from Austrian Poland, Hilferding studied medicine at the University of Vienna. As a student he
joined a circle of socialist students who soon became the core of the
second generation of intellectual leaders within modern Austrian Social
Democracy, usually referred to as the Austro-Marxists (Otto Bauer, Max
Adler, Karl Renner). Like many of his generation, moreover, Hilferding
also moved easily between the fraternal worlds of Austrian and German
socialism. In 1904 Hilferding published his first work, *Böhm-Bawerks
Marx-Kritik,* an analysis of the critique of Marx's thought which the Austrian liberal economist Eugen von Böhm-Bawerk had published in 1896.
In 1906 Hilferding taught economics at the Socialist party school in
Berlin and soon thereafter became an editor at *Vorwärts,* the major Socialist daily in Berlin. In 1910 Hilferding published *Das Finanzkapital,*
a classic analysis of the evolution of finance capitalism, a form of centralized capitalism which, given the regulation and planning accompanying the emergence of cartels, monopolies, and interlocking control networks of banks and big industry, might prepare the way for socialism.

In August 1914 Hilferding, like his friend Hugo Haase, opposed the
decision of the German Social Democrats to vote for war credits. He
criticized the hegemony of more conservative views within the party
leadership in his forceful essay "A Co-Partnership of Classes?" published
in October 1915 in the Austrian Socialist journal *Der Kampf.* A translation of this essay is presented below. In addition to its trenchant critique
of what Hilferding felt to be accommodation to power politics and the
state, this article contains Hilferding's first mention of "organized capitalism." By this concept Hilferding referred to a structural process by
which the modern bureaucratic state and modern finance capitalism
would pursue, at times in a collaborative framework, defensive, monopolistic strategies for regulation, planning, and social stabilization, and
thereby make industrial capitalism more stable as well as more rational.
At the same time, since this strategy made the line between politics and
economy more fluid, "organized capitalism" also opened up long-term
possibilities for the Social Democrats to achieve socioeconomic transformation by political-legal means. According to Charles Maier, Hilferding

thought that eventually "a workers' majority might simply collectivize the networks that the economy and state had already generated without violence and upheaval."[1] Yet earlier in his career Hilferding expressed radical ambivalence about collaboration with bourgeois nationalist elites which would strengthen the new, managerial war state.

Beginning in early 1916 Hilferding worked as an Austrian military doctor in a field hospital on the Italian front. At the end of the war, however, he returned to Berlin, where he joined the secessionist Independent Social Democratic party (USPD). Hilferding refused to follow many of his USPD colleagues into the German Communist party, however, choosing instead to reenter the Social Democratic party. From 1924 to 1933 Hilferding was a member of the Reichstag and the editor of the Socialist monthly *Die Gesellschaft.* In August 1923 he was appointed Reich Finance Minister in the cabinet led by Gustav Stresemann (see below, document 19). He also served in the same capacity in the cabinet of Hermann Müller in 1928–29, the last republican government of the Weimar Republic. Following Hitler's accession to power, Hilferding fled to Denmark and then Switzerland and eventually in 1938 to France. After the Nazi invasion of France, Hilferding was handed over by the Pétain government to the SS in February 1941. He died in Paris while in the custody of the Gestapo.

If someone should still be of the opinion that the war has pulled the rug out from under the old antagonisms between opportunism and radicalism within the labor movement, the actual facts should long ago have taught him otherwise. In reality the situation is exactly the reverse. Just before the outbreak of the war it could still appear as if the unambiguous nature of social and political development would increasingly blunt these antagonisms, antagonisms which were always active, even if under changing forms, in the labor movement of all nations. The war has changed this situation completely. Certainly not in terms of a permanent easing of social conflicts within existing society—the postwar period will soon destroy such illusions—but rather, in that the war has helped the ideology of opportunism to an unsuspected victory, so that today the labor movement is everywhere under the dictatorship of the right wing within the Socialist party. And it is only natural that this favorable opportunity will be ex-

1. Charles S. Maier, "The State and Economic Organization in the Twentieth Century," in *Experiencing the Twentieth Century,* ed. Nobutoshi Hagihara, Akira Iriye, Georges Nivat, and Philip Windsor (Tokyo, 1985), p. 107.

From Rudolf Hilferding, "Arbeitsgemeinschaft der Klassen?" *Der Kampf* 8 (1915), pp. 321–29. Translated for this volume by John W. Boyer.

ploited by those politicians who even before the war were striving to change the direction of party tactics and who advocated a form of politics which in its ultimate consequences would have to lead to the transformation of a fundamentally revolutionary movement (the goal of which was the complete reorganization of society) into a reformist movement, whose task would be to accommodate the labor movement to capitalist society, fundamentally to recognize the existing powers, especially the contemporary state power—in short, to integrate even the working class within the existing social and state order. Whoever denies this conflict and pretends that these politics during the war were only a passing episode, again to become outmoded, so that nothing stands in the way of a return to older tactics, deceives himself or desires to deceive others about the magnitude and significance of this conflict. For the stance taken toward the war constitutes, because it does after all involve a decision of world-historical importance and impact, nothing less than the touchstone for reckoning the spiritual strength of Social Democratic convictions in the face of the ruling ideology, and the measure of the intellectual independence of the working class, which forms the precondition for its political and social emancipation. The victory of the ideology of opportunism is, therefore, a danger for the future of the labor movement, because certain tendencies of the development of capitalism are supported with its help, which stand in the way of the realization of socialism.

1

The course of social development has in all essential aspects taken place according to those forms already anticipated by the prophetic vision of genius expressed in the *Communist Manifesto,* the necessity of which was then demonstrated in *Capital.* But the social-psychological effect of this development on the behavior of the working class could not be discerned with the same acuteness, precisely because such behavior is the subjective reflection of objective tendencies and thus not easily understood. Marx saw above all (and, in his own time, could hardly have seen otherwise) the revolutionary tendencies of capitalism. What he underestimated (and what we followers for so long after him still underestimate) were the possibilities of accommodation within capitalist society, which were brought about precisely through the struggle of the working class, the Social Democratic and trade union movement. The spiritual, moral, and material improvement which the labor movement has brought to the oppressed class, which was vegetating in deepest misery, and the elevation of the worker from the status of a "talking tool" to that of a human being have at the same time made capitalism more tolerable for the working class. In fact these only made capitalism capable of survival. This improvement has strengthened the working class physically and spiritually; has made it more capable of struggle and more self-confident than any oppressed class ever was, but at the same time it has moderated any immediate revolutionary impulse, resulting from the complete intolerability of an existence unworthy of a human being. Out of the capitalism of infanticide and starvation, the labor movement, through unceasing political and union struggles, has fashioned a capitalism which has become incapable of realizing its worst tendencies towards pauperization. It has thus protected capitalism from a revolution by desperate (but also inferior and uncultivated) masses. To express it paradoxically: the counterrevolutionary effects of the labor movement have weakened the revolutionary tendencies of capitalism.

The most recent phase of the development of mature capitalism has generated additional tendencies toward self-preservation on its own. The rapid development of world capitalism since the middle of the nineties of the last century has shortened the periods of depression and has moderated chronic unemployment. Since this time the most developed capitalist countries— Germany and the United States—have no longer known an industrial reserve army in the conventional sense; both constantly require the importation of foreign laborers for agriculture and industry, who then bear the primary brunt of crises. Finance capital—the domination of a monopolistically organized industry by a small number of large banks—has the tendency to moderate the anarchy of production and contains the nucleus for a transformation of the anarchic-capitalistic economic order into an organized-capitalistic economic order. The enormous strengthening of state power, which finance capitalism and its politics have engendered, works in the same direction. Instead of a socialist victory, a society seems possible which possesses an organized economy, to be sure, but one organized in an authoritarian rather than a democratic manner. On top of it would stand the combined forces of capitalistic monopolies and the state. Beneath it the laboring masses would be hierarchically arranged to serve as civil servants in the process of production. In place of the overcoming of capitalist society by socialism would come a society of organized capitalism, a society better suited to the immediate material needs of the masses than was previously the case.

The events of the war, if one disregards for a moment the democratic-proletarian countereffect, can only strengthen these tendencies. What has been called War Socialism—and in reality this is only a monstrous strengthening which capitalism gains by the power attendant upon its organization—works in this direction. Moreover, the executive authority of the state which likewise has enormously increased its power and above all its self-confidence through the war will encourage these tendencies, if only for financial reasons (state monopolies!).

And we are now seeing an ideology arise within the leadership of the working class which must also encourage such a development. Some people are now preaching to the working class that there exists a commonality of their interests with those of the ruling classes, and especially with those of the state itself. The conception of the opposition between imperialistic power politics and a democratic transformation of the totality of domestic and foreign politics is receding—above all under the overwhelming impression of the enormous strength of state power—behind the hope for the satisfaction of the immediate material interests by social reformist measures. In other words: the struggle for democracy recedes, and its success appears, like that of socialism itself, no longer to be an immediate, practical goal of proletarian politics. And this is happening at a time when the fundamental significance of democracy in the face of the prevailing form of power politics emerges more unmistakably than ever before, not only as a condition of peace between nations, but also for the preservation and reconstruction of the International. The question of democracy becomes all the more burning, since upon its solution also depends that of the other issue, namely, whether the future belongs to organized state capitalism or to democratic socialism. Democracy is being put aside and social policy emphasized, because one expects that this satisfaction of the material interests of proletarian daily life will encounter minimal resistance, since in principle it changes nothing in the structure of present-day society and in the power relationships of the classes. And there can be no doubt that this strategy of resignation or of a falsely understood harmony of interests also finds its support within the German working class.

But if this is how things now stand, then to confront this strategy is the most urgent task which we have to undertake within the party. And the working class is done an ill-service by those who wish to hinder and to restrict the settlement of this conflict—the most serious and historically the most important one which has occurred within the labor movement since its inception—or by those who want to poison the discussion from the outset through irrelevant insinuations about motives, and do not even shrink from the methods of the *Reichsverband*.

To be sure it would be un-Marxian, if one imagined that only by theoretical arguments or by an appeal to democratic convictions one could bring about a decision. We know how bourgeois democracy and liberalism in Germany were ruined after the satisfaction of the material needs of the bourgeoisie. If we cherish the hope that we shall succeed in protecting proletarian democracy from a similar fate, this hope is based not on the superiority of our arguments, not on the passion of our conviction of the necessity of democracy (which today glows more fervently than ever within us). Rather, it derives from the insight that as an immediate effect of the war, tendencies will arise again (which we are not at the moment in a position to set forth), which will convince the working class that the principled politics and tactics, which we represent, alone correspond to its true and enduring interests.

No matter what the more or less consistent advocates of social opportunism would like to imagine, and completely apart from what they are consciously aware of, if socialist opportunism represents all those efforts aimed at conserving capitalism, all that is directed toward the accommodation of the working class to capitalism and the accommodation of capitalism to the immediate, elementary, and material interests of the workers, then we Marxists must once again take on the role which Marx posed for us in the *Communist Manifesto:* to represent that which is of enduring import despite the momentary interests of the proletariat; and to comprise the driving element of the labor movement. And we do not doubt that the masses will finally decide in our favor and thus in favor of democratic socialism. This is because we represent nothing other than—and it would be hypocritical not to state the source of our pride and defiance even after the most daunting of experiences—the theoretical consciousness of their true interests, and the recognition of the historical necessity and world-historical mission of the working class.

2

The magnitude of the antinomy between the opportunistic and the principled approach to the coming tasks, and to the spirit of proletarian politics in general, comes quite clearly to mind when we examine the peculiar literary phenomenon of ten professors and ten Social Democrats writing about "The Working Class in the New Germany." [2] This publication is a kind of literary harbinger of the future cooperation of the classes. The editors, Dr. Friedrich Thimme, Director of the Library of the Prussian House of Lords, and Comrade Karl Legien, Chairman of the General Commission of the German Unions, argue in their introduction:

> Again and again the wish has been expressed recently that the unity and the concord of all the German people—which has revealed itself so magnificently during the world tempest—should be salvaged from the misery of war for the coming peace. But the doubt has also made itself heard as to whether such a lasting unity of our nation is at all possible, considering the manifold social and economic antagonisms, the differences among the classes and the parties, and above all the

2. Friedrich Thimme and Karl Legien, eds., *Die Arbeiterschaft im neuen Deutschland* (Leipzig, 1915).—ED.

deep cleavage that exists between the bourgeois classes and Social Democracy. About hope and doubt, in the final analysis, only the future will be able to decide. But nothing can be more important than to make up one's mind today about the possibility and the conditions of a spiritual co-partnership between the intellectual worlds of the bourgeoisie and the Socialists. The present publication owes its genesis to this perception.

To be sure, the collaborators knew nothing about one another:

> It is self-evident that the individual contributors, who had altogether no knowledge of the essays of the others, are only responsible for their own articles; also, both editors cannot and will not take responsibility for all that has been said on the one side or the other. So far as opinions and views in the articles are concerned, the editors have given the authors a completely free hand and have only stressed that polemics against other parties or individual persons be avoided as much as possible.

Now certainly no one will want to take this disavowal of responsibility in a completely literal fashion. When men whose names are of repute in the labor movement support a literary undertaking through their collaboration and thereby surely work for its diffusion, then they simply do bear responsibility for the entire project; it may be ascribed to their own imprudence if they have not previously ascertained on behalf of what cause they have given their support. But this responsibility is really easy to bear, for the editors are quite satisfied by the outcome. On the whole, say Dr. Thimme and Comrade Legien in the foreword, "it turns out—no one will be able to avoid the impression—that the cooperative effort between the bourgeois and socialist writers which was attempted here for the first time on such a broad scale produced, notwithstanding all the natural diversity of views, such a measure of mutual understanding that the hopes for a joint, successful collaboration in and on the new Germany can only be invigorated anew."

Let us therefore also try to arrive at such an understanding. As is well known, the Germans made their bourgeois revolution not, as the English and French did, in real life, but in philosophy. It is therefore consistent with our entire past history if socialist reformism does not send ministers into the government at this point, as in France and England, but, in the beginning at least, produces a book together with some professors. That the persons in question are professors, and not bourgeois politicians, obviously lessens the value of the co-partnership. For one really should suppose that professors ought to realize their accomplishments in their specific areas of scholarship while our comrades ought to do so in the realm of politics. The co-partnership would appear more understandable to us if it were bourgeois politicians, rather than bourgeois scholars, who had marked out the area of common effort. One would rather know the how and where of collaboration, if, instead of these professors, Messrs. Heydebrand, Zedlitz, Spahn, and Bassermann had shown us what unites them with Social Democracy.[3] For whatever the views of scholars in the area of politics may be, they are in any case disadvantaged by being of little importance in the harsh world of political facts. For that reason they certainly have the advantage of a standpoint rather more exalted than that of ordinary politicians. "One certainly knows," Börne once remarked, "how heavenly it is for all the German savants to be placed at such a lofty standpoint, for up there in the clouds, there are no police." And even if the malicious explanation given by Börne certainly no longer holds true—the police having long since raised themselves to the sublime vantage point of the professors and thus having become omnipresent—a cooperative venture which found only the approval of the professors would still remain wholly in the clouds, unless the professors at the same time represented a truly concrete politics, precisely in regard to the main point. So far as this is concerned, they are certainly the spokesmen of bourgeois politics, and hence the publication deserves political notice.

3

Now what is this essential point, what is it that runs as the common element through all the contributions of the bourgeois savants? What fills them with that feeling of good fortune, about which the historian at the University of Berlin, Professor Meinecke, speaks so enthusiastically? It is the belief that, as Professor Oncken puts it, Social Democracy will never again be able to shed the realization that the power of the German workers is tied to the power of the German state.[4] According to Oncken, just now in Germany it is in a linkage of the historical authoritarian powers of the state with the tendencies and needs of the broad masses that "all progress of the classes is comprehended, and the further realization of this problem is a

3. Ernst Bassermann (1854–1917), lawyer and chairman of the German National Liberal party from 1905 until his death; Peter Spahn (1846–1925), jurist and chairman of the Reichstag delegation of the Catholic Center party from 1912 until 1917; Oktavio von Zedlitz (1840–1919), Prussian Free Conservative party leader from 1907 until 1918; Ernst von Heydebrand (1851–1924), landowner and leader of the Conservative party in Prussia from 1906 until 1918.—ED.

4. Friedrich Meinecke (1862–1954), German historian, was professor of history at the University of Berlin, and editor of *Historische Zeitschrift*. Hermann Oncken (1860–1945), a German historian, was professor of history at the University of Heidelberg and, in 1905–6, visiting professor at the University of Chicago.—ED.

matter which will also be a concern of the future. The idea of the state at that point will also overcome the anti-statist manner of thinking and the international orientation of pure Marxism within Social Democracy."

What this means one can best appreciate from the comments of the professor of public law in Berlin, Anschütz, who takes the most concrete position about these political problems.[5]

In capitalist society the state is above all an organization for domination at home, and an organization of power abroad. It is the ideal of democratic socialism to transform the state into the self-administration of a classless society which consciously regulates production in the interests of and according to the needs of all of its members. The abolition of class conflict also eliminates tension among the states, which arises from the conflict of capitalist interests, and thus also makes the organization of power superfluous. The war has presented to the peoples of the world this opposition between the prevailing form of power politics, from which the war arose directly, and the politics of democracy as the true political problem.

And now let us look at what position the professors take on this problem. Right at the beginning of his essay on "Thoughts about Future State Reforms" Professor Anschütz writes:

Whoever reflects today on the future responsibilities of our domestic politics, on the guiding principles and goals of state reform in Germany, must begin by frankly acknowledging the most supreme of all state necessities: the resources of power needed by our fatherland to maintain its independence and strength, its prestige and significance in the world. In this we want to be united, now in midst of the war, just as we always want to remain united after the war. We do not want any "new orientation" on this point, but rather a simple holding fast to the grand, fundamental idea: the fatherland over everything else, to the fatherland all power and resources necessary to preserve it, to enhance it. Whoever is incapable of offering this avowal, to them we cannot concede the right to discuss with us anything further, for one can only confer about the extension and improvement of a house with someone who wants to allow that house to stand, not with someone who wants to demolish it, to destroy it.

Let us say this with all possible decisiveness and determination: our concern for the strongest of all state powers, for the armed forces, for the army and the fleet must and will in the future stand more than ever at the centerpoint of our domestic state program. We should not shrink from the catchword that now makes itself felt in the conscious-

---

5. Gerhard Anschütz (1867–1948), German jurist and professor of law at the universities of Tübingen, Berlin, and Heidelberg. Anschütz was later noted for his commentary on the Weimar constitution, which went through fourteen editions up to 1933.—ED.

ness of everyone who thinks these thoughts. Let us acknowledge openly and freely the *militarism* which is mortally hated, slandered, and defamed by our enemies and—let us not deceive ourselves—also by the greatest part of the still-neutral world. Militarism belongs to the formative factors of our political system; for us it is a necessity of life in every sense. We must hold firmly to it! For the word "militarism," which in the wider world is widely propagated about us as a term of abuse and loathing (and not least by those who are more militaristic than we are or who would at least like to be), should be for us a badge of honor! . . .

We must remain militarily strong on land and sea and become still stronger, stronger than any other nation of equal size . . . In the future the military power of our people will, in all probability, be more intensely exerted than before the war, it will have to be exerted to the point of exploiting totally the available military energies and abilities of the people. That means above all the complete, total realization of the principle of universal compulsory military service, which up to now, all excuses to the contrary, has to a significant extent only existed on paper. . . . The strengthening of the army will have to be matched by similar measures for our naval forces. We cannot stick with the present naval law; the experiences of the war demand a new naval program. . . .

This enthusiastic acknowledgment of prevailing power politics, this unconditional affirmation of the imperialistic focus of the power of the state is for Anschütz, as it is for the other professors, the obvious precondition of all other reform activity. It is characteristic that Herr Anschütz would already like to outlaw all those who are not willing to accept this assumption—which up to now has not been the assumption of the Social Democrats—as new *Reichsfeinde* [enemies of the realm], who would have no say in the reconstruction of the social order. It is characteristic of Anschütz that he is the stout ideologist of the practice already commencing of confirming in office those Social Democrats who are well behaved as jurymen, city aldermen, reserve officers, and even as university instructors, while throwing the wicked Social Democrats in jail.

For the time being we satisfy ourselves, however, with the observation that the co-partnership inaugurated here has been conceived by one side to mean that nothing essential should be changed in the basic foundations of the ruling form of politics; and we now want to see what else is being contemplated in terms of reform. Herr Anschütz outlines a complete program for the state, which is intended to repress political particularism, especially that in Prussia, and strengthen the idea of the Empire. The program looks like this:

The Imperial administration must become the only, the exclusive Imperial government—an Imperial government culminating in the Emperor, managed by his ministers, the Imperial Chancellor and the State Secretaries (whose responsibility toward the Reichstag should be more sharply emphasized and, by appropriate arrangements, be expanded), upon which devolve the sovereign powers now exercised by the Bundesrat. The Bundesrat will go from being an executive to being a parliamentary factor; it will become an influential Upper House, standing next to the Reichstag, which at the same time will discharge the functions of a state council. Through this the Emperor will for the first time truly become that which he now falls somewhat short of being: the monarchic head of the Empire, of all the German people. This enhancement of empire is surely in accordance with the intentions of the overwhelming majority of the people—quite certainly if one, as just demanded, brings the principles of constitutionalism strongly to bear in the ministerial organization of the Imperial government and in its relationship to parliament. . . . A German Empire, as genuinely monarchical as it is sincerely constitutional, that is the goal of the future. It was the dream of our fathers, of those who first paved the way in the years 1848 and 1849 for German unity and freedom, it was the plan of the Frankfurt National Assembly: the Empire placed on a democratic basis and with democratic institutions.

To achieve this goal a reform of the Prussian electoral franchise is also necessary. The ideal would be the expansion of the Reichstag franchise over Prussia. If this cannot be achieved all at once, so says Professor Anschütz, one may have to be satisfied with partial reforms. The first and most minimal reform would be the introduction of direct, secret elections. Then might come "a franchise of plural or multiple votes (which would, however, not be constructed merely as a privilege for the propertied), or if worst comes to worst, another, more democratic demarcation between the classes of voters, the latter being retained as such." A preponderance of Social Democracy need not be feared. For "is perchance the will of the House of Deputies the law in Prussia, and not, on the contrary, only just that which also finds the agreement of the House of Lords and the state government?" And in fact, even if the plan of another professor to appoint workers to the Upper Houses [of the various German legislatures] is implemented, these chambers would surely remain protected from all too great a Social Democratic influence.

The enhancement of the Empire, the conversion of the single chamber system into a dual system in the Empire, a plural franchise in Prussia—it is all there. Sober progress can begin, the dreams of 1848 will come true, as promised again and again, in the not-too-distant future, and simultaneously the basis will be secured for the co-partnership of classes. My darling, what more could you want?

But even for this "more" provision is made. Among the collaborating professors are a number of those Socialists of the Chair, who even before the war already championed social reforms. They rightly see in the experiences of the war new evidence of the usefulness of social reform precisely for the purposes of state power. They advocate, therefore, in their essays the continuation and expansion of social reform, in the course of which one could, to be sure, wish that much had been more sharply defined. In particular, the demand for a law limiting the hours of the working day is missing. They expect that the behavior of the Social Democrats, and especially the unions, will eliminate the resistance of the state authorities to a program of social politics and to the freedom of action of the labor associations. Some of them go still a step further and see in the tendencies toward state capitalism a welcome compromise between individualist-bourgeois and socialist-proletarian principles. They look forward with confidence to the positive cooperation of the working class in all these economic spheres of activity and demand for that reason equality of rights for the workers in politics and administration. Jaffé even sees in this exclusively economic direction of activity of the working class an impulse which will divert it from the alleged overestimation of political activity.[6] This conception appears very characteristic to us because it demonstrates how much questions of political principle, the resolution of which for us is the most important point, count for these bourgeois authors as if they have already been actually decided by the victory of the power of the state as it has manifested itself during the war.

Basically it is the old doctrine of the Social Monarchy of the Hohenzollerns, which we encounter here in a somewhat more impersonal form, stripped of the polemical profile against Social Democracy, from which one no longer anticipates the rejection of this point of view. After a recognition of the existing institutions of the state, the "co-partnership in the new Germany" will be inaugurated between the workers and the professors in the area of social reform. And certainly one will gladly greet this intercession by the professors for equality of political rights and for social reforms, even if one may surely not assess their influence on the leading capitalist classes and their political representatives too highly.

6. Edgar Jaffé (1866–1921), German economist. A student of Gustav Schmoller and Adolf Wagner, Jaffé was coeditor with Max Weber and Werner Sombart of the *Archiv für Sozialwissenschaft und Sozialpolitik*. In November 1918 Jaffé was appointed minister of finance in the revolutionary government of Kurt Eisner in Bavaria.—ED.

4

Now what about the advocacy of the Social Democratic world view in this book, for which ten contributors were appointed, after all? It is embarrassing to discuss this matter. Ten socialists and not one word about socialism, ten democrats and not one word about democracy! Or, rather, the word may well have been used occasionally, but of its spirit there is no trace. Not that our spokesmen perchance said something against our program or the views of our party. The demands which we have to make on the social policy programs of the state or on the municipalities are discussed in detail and with the usual expertise, while political equality in the Empire and the state is treated as something whose rightness and necessity is obvious. In addition, the feat which Social Democracy has accomplished for wartime strategy is described in detail and with satisfaction. So writes Comrade Noske:[7]

> German Social Democracy not only accommodated itself to harsh necessity. The allegation which has been made—that the Social Democrats, in order to save their political associations and their newspapers (which are worth millions and which employ thousands of white-collar workers) and in order to protect their union organizations from being disadvantaged, made with silent reluctance the best of a bad situation when they voted for war credits—is totally false. On the contrary, the party avoided, on the basis of its most honest convictions, any injury to German interests and, with total surrender of energy, property, and blood, whenever possible tried to protect the people and the fatherland from harm.

And further:

> On the basis of firm conviction, the great majority of Social Democratic newspapers made it their business to emphasize decisively the justice of the struggle conducted by Germany, as one forced upon our people. More than a million copies of these Social Democratic papers reach the nation every day. Many thousands of copies reach the trenches and the battlefront. The Social Democratic press enjoys a particularly great trust on the part of its readers. Most of our newspapers have made it their business to fortify confidence in the cause of our fatherland; to awaken understanding for the inescapable economic damages which are consequences of the war; to allay the resentment which each day arises anew over the inflation in prices; and to maintain the highest level of self-sacrifice on the part of our warriors. Even when it opposed

7. Gustav Noske (1868–1946), German Social Democratic politician and a leading figure of the party's right wing during World War I. Noske was active in repressing the Spartacist revolt in January 1919 and served as minister of defense in the first Weimar Cabinet.—Ed.

blunders in the judgment of foreign countries or when it demanded
(or, as the case may be, opposed) domestic political measures, the
Social Democratic press proved itself a judicious sponsor of the cause
of Germany.

And about the behavior of the unions Noske writes:

> The German unions have manifested a very special measure of devo-
> tion to the fatherland as well as the most sympathetic behavior toward
> the great distress of the entire nation by putting aside the wishes and
> demands of their members. As organizations devoted to economic
> struggle, they have become large and strong by overcoming the most
> tremendous obstacles which the industrialists, the governments, and
> the administrative authorities piled up against them. Their best rule of
> battle has always been to exploit every propitious opportunity which
> presented itself in order to achieve an advantage. But under the chang-
> ing conditions during the war the unions have maintained the *Burg-
> frieden* in an extremely strict fashion. In view of the distress of the
> fatherland, the organized workers have renounced their struggle to
> gain advantages by exploiting their indispensability—a thing they
> were in a most promising position to do. And the workers' organiza-
> tions did substantially more for the fatherland. They used their great
> resources for the purpose of counteracting seething discontent, since
> they helped their destitute members through difficult times of unem-
> ployment by providing relief benefits which were usually far beyond
> the limits established in their regulations. The numerous wage struggles
> in England during the war show that a different pattern of behavior
> would have been possible.

Similar comments can be found in most of the other Social Democratic
contributions.

The most comprehensive endorsement of the co-partnership of classes
is, no doubt, expressed in the remarks of Winnig, when he writes:[8]

> The mass of the people knows and feels that the fate of the nation and
> its organized expression—the state—is also their fate. They no longer
> marvel at the state as a primordial power hovering above the water, but
> rather recognize its dependence upon the freely working forces of the
> people as a whole; and they strive and struggle to breath more and
> more of their own nature into the state. They feel themselves to have
> a share in economic, political, and cultural terms in this community,
> as expressed in the state, and feel themselves bound to it. Their eco-
> nomic well-being depends on the condition of the national economy,
> which needs freedom of movement in order to develop. Only then can

---

8. August Winnig (1878–1956), German Social Democratic union leader. Winnig was a
member of the right-wing faction of the party during the war.—ED.

their union organizations favorably influence wage and working conditions—when trade and commerce prosper. It is in this way that the mass of the working class is interested in the fate of the national economy and through this in the political importance of the state community. It therefore feels itself united solidly with the totality of the people in defending against the dangers which threaten this community from abroad.

Here some very dubious concessions are assuredly being made to the doctrine of the harmony of the classes, which defined the behavior of old English trade unionism. Winnig is only being consistent with such ideas when he views the International not as the necessary precondition for and the means of making possible proletarian class politics in each individual state, but rather as an expedient organization for the improved representation of separate demands (especially social-political demands, whose realization encounters less resistance on an international level than on a state-by-state basis). Such international relationships are then, to be sure, in principle no different from the international organizations of the agrarians or the bi-metallists, which permits easy proof that the international sentiments of the proletariat and the nationalist convictions of the bourgeoisie are not opposed to each other.

However, all this, even if it is far removed from our own view, is not the critical issue for us here. Our question concerns something different. We have seen how at bottom the works of the professors all end with an enthusiastic acknowledgment of the fundamental features of the prevailing form of power politics. And over against this situation it would not be unjustified to expect to hear from the representatives of our world view an equally outspoken confession of faith on behalf of socialism and democracy. But, unfortunately, there is no talk of this kind. As to the great reorganization of the world, to which we think the working class is called, which the World War has set as the immediate task of the working class's politics, nothing is said. Only from the polemic which Professor Meinecke puts forth on behalf of power politics against our "pacifistic" basic demands does one hear about the principles concerning the relationships of nations which are peculiar to socialism. No one says that such comments would have been impossible for our comrades under the spell of the *Burgfrieden*. That is perhaps true for us at this point. If, however, in such a declaration our representatives were not able to speak openly, then they should have remained totally silent. That they *could* have spoken out, however, is demonstrated by the comments of the bourgeois professors, who bluntly approached the fundamental problems without timidity. In truth such a discourse would, of course, have been difficult to reconcile with the purpose of the book. If one wants a co-partnership, then that certainly means renouncing those things which fundamentally separate the classes. And the fundamental issue, that which really separates the classes, is today not social reform and not the confirmation in office of jurors or city aldermen—indeed, it is not even the Prussian franchise reform—but rather one's attitude about the power of the state. The fundamental question is: power politics and imperialism, or democracy and socialism. Since our party comrades have left this question aside, they have abandoned the political field to the bourgeois professors without a struggle, and it is their fault that at the end of the book—the bourgeoisie gets the last word!—Herr Thimme is able to proclaim the future positive political stance of Social Democracy toward the state.

To take up here what has been omitted there, to show what consequences socialism should draw from the great catastrophe, what powerful, universal responsibilities will be placed on democracy, if it is not to relinquish all real effectiveness for a long time to come—all this is unfortunately denied to us at this point. We must content ourselves with warning of the dangers for the party and its character, as we have hitherto known and loved it, which grow out of the political frugality, resignation, and despair about our real responsibility, which is evident to us in the comments of the Social Democratic authors. And with this the significance of the book is exhausted for us. This spiritual co-partnership became possible only because in the area in which the professors actually assumed the point of view of the bourgeois world—the area of power politics—the Social Democrats did not really face up to them. In other areas, like that of social-political reform, the Social Democrats and the professors concur on many of the goals (even if not the motives), but there the professors unfortunately do not represent the leading strata of the bourgeoisie. And so the co-partnership will indeed have to remain "spiritual," because it will never become real. For reality after the war will have less in common with that of the war than the "Realpolitiker" today would like to believe.

Alfred Zimmern and Edward Grigg. Introduction: The Round Table on England in the War

Alfred Zimmern and Edward Grigg were members of the Round Table, a circle of politicians, civil servants, and university scholars from England and the Dominions organized under the sponsorship of Alfred Viscount Milner in 1909–10 to stimulate discussions and influence policy on the future of English imperialism. Based originally on the experiences of Milner's protégés in working for the unification of South Africa, the Round Table attracted a group of bright young Englishmen, most of whom were products of elite colleges at Oxford, intent on charting a comprehensive, federative structure of governance for the Empire. One of their main goals was the drafting of a memorandum outlining their proposition for a new charter of Imperial union, known as "the Egg," whose principal author was to be Lionel Curtis. Philip Kerr (later Lord Lothian) was a prominent member of the circle, many of the members of which emerged from Milner's "Kindergarten," as the stable of talented young men who worked for Milner during his tenure as high commissioner for South Africa between 1897 and 1905 came to be known. The Round Table was one of the most influential and powerful private groups in modern English politics. Lloyd George himself remarked in October 1921 that "it is a very powerful combination—in its way perhaps the most powerful in the country." [1]

Edward Grigg (1879–1955) was born in Madras, India, and trained at New College, Oxford. He served as a journalist for the *Times* and for *Outlook* and eventually as head of the colonial department of the *Times* from 1908 to 1913, during which time he became involved in the Round Table movement. In 1913 he joined Philip Kerr as editor of the *Round Table* magazine, a position he relinquished for service in the British army in France in 1914. In 1920 he succeeded Kerr as private secretary to Lloyd George, after service as military secretary to the Prince of Wales. He was elected to Parliament as a Liberal in 1922, serving until appointed Governor of Kenya in 1925. In 1933 he returned to Parliament as a national conservative, serving until 1945. During the Second World War he worked as joint parliamentary undersecretary in the War Office and as minister resident in the Middle East. He was created Baron Altrincham in 1945.

Alfred Zimmern (1879–1957) joined the Round Table movement slightly later than Grigg. The son of an assimilated German-Jewish merchant from Frankfurt who had emigrated to England after the Revolution of 1848, Zimmern was (like Grigg, Kerr, and Curtis) trained at New College, Oxford, where after graduation he was Fellow and Tutor until 1909. A friend of Graham Wallas, Sidney Webb, and other English social reformers, Zimmern became active in the Workers' Education Association movement in Oxford and London before the war. From 1912 to 1915 he worked as a staff inspector for the Board of Education. His connection to the Round Table was as an advisor on social as well as political policy issues. Upon the outbreak of the war Zimmern wrote patriotic essays for various publications, including Kerr's and Grigg's *Round Table,* but joined the Reconstruction Committee as a temporary official in 1916 and in

1. *Lord Riddell's Intimate Diary of the Peace Conference and After, 1918–1923* (London, 1933), p. 330.

1918 became a member of the Political Intelligence Department of the Foreign Office. In 1919 he became a professor of international relations at Aberystwyth in Wales, and in 1930 he was named Montague Burton Professor of International Relations at Oxford. A liberal internationalist, Zimmern was a strong supporter of the League of Nations. During the 1920s and 1930s he served as director of the School of International Studies in Geneva. Zimmern received a knighthood in 1936.

The two documents below are (1) selections from an essay which Zimmern drafted for the *Round Table* in 1915 on the domestic consequences of the war in England and (2) a private letter of Edward Grigg to Philip Kerr, written from the trenches in France, commenting on Zimmern's assumptions and arguments.

---

8. Alfred Zimmern, *The War and English Life*

Foreign observers, reading the news day by day, must have found it difficult, during the past months, to form any coherent impression of the state of the popular mind in this country. The daily Press gives the foreground; and that foreground presents the confusion and want of harmony inevitable in a free country where men have been accustomed to think and say what they like, and even to say what they like without thinking. But the news that can be summarized and cabled day by day is not English history, or even the raw material of English history. Real history is to be found in the background, in the movement of large impersonal forces and in the influences that affect the life and spirit and temper of the body of the people. An attempt will, therefore, be made in this article to describe some features at least of this background and to deal with various factors which, though unrecorded in the daily Press, are occupying the mind and attention of the great mass of the population. Its object is frankly neither to defend nor to impugn, but rather to hold up a mirror—to give a faithful and sympathetic picture of opinions and developments which have not everywhere been sufficiently understood. It relates mainly to England proper.

1. The Temper of the People

Anyone whose duties or friendships caused him to move about in recent months among various social classes, passing from West-End drawing-rooms to working-class homes, cannot fail to have been struck by what seems at first sight a remarkable fact—the noticeably greater cheerfulness

From *The Round Table* 6 (1915/1916), pp. 56–64, 80–85. Reprinted by permission of the publisher.

among the poor than among the rich. There can be no doubt that just now, on the whole, to put it in military language, the *morale* of the working class is better than that of the well-to-do. Both are equally determined to pursue the war to a successful end, and both are equally ready to make the sacrifices required; but the temper of the working class is distinctly the more buoyant and confident of the two. In the great war a hundred years ago Wordsworth noted the same phenomenon, and gave expression to it in lines which those who know England in all her moods will be glad to recall in the present crisis:

> These times touch monied Worldlings with dismay:
> Even rich men, brave by nature, taint the air
> With words of apprehension and despair:
> While tens of thousands, thinking of the affray,
> Men unto whom sufficient for the day
> And minds not stinted or untilled are given,
> Sound, healthy Children of the God of Heaven,
> Are cheerful as the rising Sun in May.

This contrast is due to a variety of causes. But undoubtedly the most important factor underlying it is simply the old English feeling that if a difficult job has to be done it is best done in good spirits. Despite political labels, the working class is, and is always likely to remain, the most difficult section of the population to move. Workpeople are slow to adjust themselves to a new situation; they have little imagination and little capacity for the rapid assimilation of ideas; they "hold fast to that which is good," to accepted standards of conduct, or wages, or comfort, or opinion; but when they move they move with an irresistible momentum. It took them many months to "realize" the war. While nimbler brains were redrawing the map of Europe, or discussing the possibilities of a reconciliation with a contrite Germany, workpeople were still questioning their consciences as to whether we ought to be at war at all. For, like the Americans, they had been living in a world in which war had no place, a world that was "beyond war," and it cost them a great spiritual effort—great in proportion to the depth and sincerity of their Christian ideals—to realize that the actual world in which the Germans and Magyars compel us to live falls far below the standard of their fixed opinions or the hopes of their dreams. It was not till the sinking of the "Lusitania" that the last doubts as to the cause at stake were dispelled. Since the "Lusitania" it has not been a question of working-class opinion, but of national resolve: not a question of discussing details or calculating chances, either of diplomacy or strategy, but of going cheerfully on through an unknown future till the world is rid of a monstrous evil.

This war has reduced the whole of civilized mankind to the habitual mental condition of the wage earner, who can never be quite certain of his future beyond the end of next week. Well-to-do people find this trying, and are apt to grumble at the prolongation of the strain. Poor people are used to it. In fact, the war has brought an alleviation of their position. In ordinary times the sense of the uncertainty of their situation is not relieved by any feeling of the importance and dignity of their work. Today workmen realize that their occupation has a direct bearing on the national well-being, and thousands of men are conscious for the first time in their lives that labour—their labour—is the foundation of the State. Workpeople, in fact, once they had accepted the fact of war, with all the change in their standards and ideals that it involved, were mentally better prepared to meet it and bear its trials. They know by hard experience that life is a severe and difficult pilgrimage, that trouble is certain by the way, and that every bit of fortune or happiness is something to be thankful for. Not hoping for sensational victories from the first, they have not been disillusioned by their absence. The fact of war itself was their disillusionment.

Kitchener's Army is the outward and visible testimony of this working-class outlook at its best. Its quiet endurance, its obstinate but unassuming determination, its free-spokenness and good fellowship, its unfailing and unforced cheerfulness, rising to boisterous humour when things look blackest, are as essentially English today as when Shakespeare immortalized them in his English plays. "In ancient days," as the King's proclamation reminds us, "the darkest moment has ever produced in men of our race the sternest resolve." "The customs of a free people are part of its liberty," wrote a great French political thinker in a famous chapter on this country, which has shown itself at least twice to be prophetic. Kitchener's Army, the largest voluntary force ever raised in history, is the triumph of the customary English way of doing things. The working classes, from whom the great majority of its men are drawn, are proud of what has been thus characteristically achieved, and hope to achieve more still and in sufficient measure. Whether their hopes will be fulfilled through Lord Derby's scheme for canvassing everyone of military age whose work is not of direct use to the State still remains to be seen.

But there are other reasons besides custom which determine the attitude still held by important sections of workpeople on the question of compulsory service. They are frankly afraid of its reaction upon industrial conditions. The mental furniture of the English workman is often not very considerable; opinions and prejudices he may adopt and again discard, from politicians or from the newspapers, on a variety of topics: but what may be called his "fixtures," the fixed ideas which lie beyond the reach of argument, are few and immovable. One of these is a dislike of the intervention of the military in domestic affairs. In the eyes of Englishmen, as Montesquieu remarked in the chapter already quoted, "military men are regarded as belonging to a profession which may be useful but is often dangerous." The English are an incurably civilian people. Our island position and our traditions have made us so. Military law may be necessary, but we do not regard it as law, as the deep impression made by the death of Miss Cavell has shown. The mere suggestion that the methods of compulsory service might be applied in the workshop as in the Army has reawakened suspicions which were first roused by the use of the military in the English and French railway strikes a few years ago. Compulsory enlistment in order to secure enough men to keep our fighting forces at full strength is an expedient which Labour would be readily open to consider; so many men have already gone that the demand for equality of sacrifice is one which finds an echo in thousands of working-class homes; but military law in the workshop is something which workpeople regard as in quite a different category. Unfortunately, the two are associated, not only in the minds of their proposers, but in the actual facts of the case; and herein lies the real crux of the controversy which has arisen.

The advocates of compulsory service are, many of them, sincere and patriotic men. They are pleading their cause not with any sinister ulterior object, such as the reduction of soldiers' pay, or the creation of a weapon wherewith to break strikes after the war, but with the sole desire of saving the country and winning the war. But their object is frankly not simply to secure more men but to secure men in what they consider a more advantageous and economical way, by arming the Executive with general powers enabling it to call up men according to their status and occupation. Such a programme would automatically and of necessity carry the element of compulsion into the workshop, for it would give the Executive power to render strikes as impossible as they are under a similar system on the Continent. Moreover, serviceable men in exempted occupations would only be exempted so long as they were needed. In other words, it would be the employer, or rather, in actual practice, the foreman, who would stand between them and the Army. Such a situation would put into the hands of private employers a power which they have never claimed, and which public opinion in this country is democratic enough not to allow them to exercise without control. It is because workmen can foresee these results of the introduction of military law, and feel that the advocates of compulsory service (whose motives they undoubtedly misunderstand) do not understand the working-class point of view or sufficiently respect the traditional British sentiment underlying it, that they view their proposals with such grave distrust.

Working people have already had some foretaste of what compulsory enlistment would mean. In the early days of the war, when trade was bad and the Army seemed the only alternative to destitution, employers of labour frequently dismissed men, telling them to join the Army, and in the districts, happily few in number, where the staple industry has suffered through the war, the practice has remained a common one and has not unnaturally provoked considerable resentment and alienation of feeling. Men feel that it is unjust and incompatible with the whole spirit of English life and of the voluntary system. After the first months and even weeks of the war, however, employment improved so rapidly that the position was soon reversed. Men out of work had no difficulty whatever in finding employment, while employers became more and more reluctant to lose workmen, and munition firms had eventually to be prohibited in the Munitions Act from "pilfering" labour from their competitors by the offer of higher wages. Lord Derby's scheme has, however, brought about a change in the attitude of employers, who are now receiving authoritative advice as to the relative importance of their businesses in the national economy. At the same time, voluntary enlistment has become more and more a matter of the deliberate choice of the individual citizen, and its unlooked-for success is likely to leave a permanent mark on English life in a new and deeper sense of the relationship between the State and the individual. Englishmen have always been patriots, but they are only now learning, in the fullest sense, what it means to be citizens.

Another factor which has not tended to allay working-class apprehension is the working of the Munitions Act. As passed, that Act was the result of an agreement arrived at in conference between Mr. Lloyd George and the Trade Union representatives, and it was arranged that Labour should have fair representation both on the Local Committees which were to be responsible for the local organizing work under the Act and on the special tribunals which were to penalize its breaches. In practice the Act has worked out very differently from what was expected either by its author or by the Trade Union leaders. The Local Committees, having finished their preliminary organizing work, have fallen into abeyance, while the Munition Tribunals have suffered in working-class estimation from the fact that the so-called Labour representative is nominated by Whitehall instead of being representative of local labour opinion. Partly as a result of this, and of the comparative ineffectiveness of the Labour representatives in handling the difficult and novel points that have arisen, there has been a good deal of friction which better handling might have avoided. Trouble has arisen especially on the clause forbidding the employment of workmen within six weeks without a certificate from their last employer, which obviously leaves an opening for vexatious treatment. Difficulties such as these were only to be expected and are not incapable of fair adjustment; it

would indeed be deplorable if such precedents for the equal partnership of
Capital and Labour as the Local Committees and the Munition Tribunals
were allowed to pass away without an effort to extend and develop the spirit
which gave rise to them.

These various considerations may serve to explain the course of proceedings at the most authoritative and representative of recent working-
class deliberative gatherings—the Trades Union Congress held at Bristol
in the second week of September. Three resolutions relating to the war
were brought forward and carried with practical unanimity. One supported
the action of the Labour Party in cooperating with the other political parties in the national recruiting campaign. Of the other two one related to the
prosecution of the war and the other to compulsory service; their wording
is so characteristic that it is worth giving in full:

1. "That this Trades Union Congress, whilst expressing its opposition (in accordance with its previously expressed opinions) to all systems of militarism as a danger to human progress, considers the present
action of Great Britain and her Allies as completely justified, and expresses its horror at the atrocities which have been committed by the
German and Austrian military authorities, and the callous, brutal, and
unnecessary sacrifice of the lives of non-combatants, including women
and children, and hereby pledges itself to assist the Government as far
as possible in the successful prosecution of the war."

2. "That we, the delegates to this Congress, representing nearly
three million organized workers, record our hearty appreciation of the
magnificent response made to the call for volunteers to fight against
the tyranny of militarism.

"We emphatically protest against the sinister efforts of a section of
the reactionary Press in formulating newspaper policies for party purposes and attempting to foist upon this country conscription, which
always proves a burden to the workers, and will divide the nation at a
time when absolute unanimity is essential.

"No reliable evidence has been produced to show that the voluntary system of enlistment is not adequate to meet all the Empire's
requirements.

"We believe that all the men necessary can, and will, be obtained
through a voluntary system properly organized, and we heartily support and will give every aid to the Government in their present efforts
to secure the men necessary to prosecute the war to a successful issue."

To the Continental mind, accustomed to regard universal compulsory
service as the only thorough way of organizing national defence, the two
resolutions may not appear to hang together—may even seem incompatible
and illogical. To this the only answer that can be made is that the two expressions of opinion do in fact hang together in the minds of their authors.

But he would have a poor knowledge of the temper of Englishmen—and especially of that Puritan layer in English life from which these resolutions mainly emanate—who could deduce from them any weakening in the national determination to carry the war through to a successful end. Working-class opinion, though neither angry nor bitter, and, in spite of the gutter Press, quite devoid of racial hatred, is more united and determined on the issues of this conflict than over any struggle in English history. . . .

4. The Industrial Outlook

This attempt to review some of the domestic problems preoccupying the minds of the people at the present time would not be complete without a glance ahead; for the question of the future relations of Capital and Labour, under the altered circumstances brought about by the war, is already much in men's minds, and has, in fact, been responsible for some of the most serious difficulties which have arisen.

Every thoughtful working man realizes that great difficulties are looming ahead for the working class after the war. Its growing strength before the war and the strong strategic position it occupied in its earlier stages will be the measure of its economic weakness then. The sudden cessation of war-contracts, which are employing several millions of workers, the demobilization of the Army, the weakening of the financial resources of the Trade Unions by the loss of contributions from members on war service, the presence in the Labour market of thousands of new recruits, difficult to organize, imperfectly trained, yet skilled enough to be available as black-legs, seem likely to create a problem such as the working-class has never—not even after Waterloo—had to deal with before. It is clear that Labour will not be able to face it alone, without an understanding with Capital and active help from the State; just as Capital was not able by itself to face the unprecedented situation created by the demand for munitions. As the three parties were called into partnership by the problems of the war, and Labour forebore to press its full economic advantage by making concessions on the right to strike and on the Trade Union rules, so the partnership must be continued and extended in the effort to set the trade of the country on its feet again after the war. The prosperity of the next fifty years may, and probably will, depend on the rapidity with which our economic system adjusts itself to the new conditions. All three parties have a joint interest in the national task of recuperation, and if it is thwarted or even delayed by mutual suspicion and bickering and by the absence of considered plans, much of the sacrifice of the war will have been in vain.

It is too early to discuss in detail the problems that will arise; but certain main facts are already clear, and can be briefly stated.

Both Capital and Labour have much to learn. They have to adjust their minds to a totally new situation in which past landmarks and shibboleths will avail them little. In some form or other the problems which divided the nation before the war will still await solution. But to go back to pre-war conditions will be impossible. The nation will have lived through a great experience, a few years of crowded life embodying a century of development, which will have left its mark on every field of the national life— spiritual, social, economic and political. All sorts and conditions of people will have met and mingled, and will have learnt to know and respect one another's opinions and prejudices. Feelings of bitterness and suspicion born of isolation and segregation will often have been dissipated, even if only for a time, in the fellowship of common work. Vast new sections of the community—notably women in every class—will have become conscious of powers hitherto untried, and eager for wider fields of activity. Others, formerly classed as unskilled, will have become accustomed to a broader horizon and a higher standard of physical health and will be unwilling to sink back into the ancient groove. Great strides forward will have been made in the organization of production—not only in the munition trades but in the other trades affected by the war. Even agriculture, as a result of high prices and the shortage of labour, will find itself equipped, in part at least, with scientific labour-saving machinery.

These are facts which Labour must boldly face and to which it must wisely adjust its attitude. Labour, like the country as a whole, has everything to gain by improved and more scientific production, if only its temporary injurious reactions can be kept under control. Improvements in production mean, or could mean, fair remuneration to the worker and reasonable hours, and it rests with the working class and its leaders and with public opinion to see to it that they do. Restrictions on production and the policy of ca'canny benefit neither the workman nor the industry nor the State. The best that can be said of them is that they may serve to avert evils (such as the reduction of piece-work rates) which the workers consider to be impending; but there are other and better ways of combating such dangers as this. Labour will never rise to its full stature in the State, it will never achieve an industrial constitution worthy the name of Democracy, till workmen boldly claim the problems of the working conditions and processes of their industry as *their* problems, and treat attempts to meet them, whether by improved production or "scientific management" or whatever may be the particular suggestion, not as something imposed on them from above, but as their own concern, on which they should be consulted as a matter of right and on which they should offer responsible advice, not simply from the point of view of their own personal convenience, but as partners with Capital in the working of the industry and of the community as a whole. It is not enough for Labour to have the power of Veto, as exercised by the Strike. The people of England controlled the Executive by their power to veto supplies generations before they gained the positive rights of democratic self-government. Something more than blank negation is needed from Labour—a real understanding of the problems which each industry has to meet and a readiness to confer with and give considered advice to the industrial executive on matters within their competence. The more Capital and Labour can be brought together, not simply to strike a "collective bargain" over the disposal of the surplus profit, but actually to discuss the problems of the industry or service which is their common concern, the better it will be for Trade Unionism, for British Industry and for the security and prosperity of the State.

The attainment of such a position presupposes the abandonment by Capital of certain patriarchal notions of proprietorship, still cherished in many quarters, and a willingness to meet the representatives of the workers on the common ground of industrial service. It presupposes no less a change of attitude and organization within the ranks of Labour itself. It implies the spread of broader and more democratic forms of organization within the Trade Union world, the elimination of relics of monopoly and privilege and craft-selfishness, the ready association of craft with craft in the pursuance of common ends, an eagerness to welcome new classes of members and to make them free of the fellowship, a readiness to bridge what has been too often in the past the impassable gulf between skilled and unskilled and between men and women, and, above all, a closer attention to the development of the industrial training and education by which alone the dignity and prosperity of the craft or industry can be maintained. In some of these directions progress can already be recorded. The executive of the English railways have at last broken with a bad past by consenting to negotiate directly with the representatives of the National Union of Railwaymen, while the Union, on its side, followed by the Railway Clerks' Association, has opened its doors to women workers, realizing that only by common membership and association can the new recruits be initiated into the spirit of the service.

But if Labour has much to learn, if it is to weather the coming storm, Capital has even more. If the moral for Labour is maximum production, as the only way to make up for the waste of wealth during the war, the moral for Capital is maximum taxation, as the only way of meeting the State's new burden of debt. The war has made Capital scarce, and in the natural course it will make it dear: the rate of interest is already and is likely to remain unusually high. But what Capital demands and, owing to its international character, can succeed in exacting in interest it will have to yield in taxation. The investing public must realize that it cannot in justice be allowed to enjoy to the full the advantages arising out of its economic position, just as Labour did not enjoy to the full the advantage arising out of the scarcity value of its services. The old easy, affluent days have passed away from this country for long years ahead. Long may England still remain, what Mr. Lloyd George once described her, "the best place in the world for a rich man to live in": but wealth will be asked to contribute in unprecedented measure to the service of the State. The gross inequality of the distribution of wealth in this country has long been felt to be a standing evil; but many have acquiesced in it, not simply out of selfish slothfulness but because they distrusted the remedies proposed and the spirit of class-bitterness which often seemed to actuate their promoters. They felt uneasy about "great possessions," which seemed to separate them from the mass of their fellow-countrymen: but they felt still more uneasy over the designs of those who proposed to despoil them. Henceforward, if we are to pay our way as a nation, there must be, what England has not known for a century, a real simplicity of life in all classes, and an approximation, if not of incomes, at least of standards of living. If we are to avoid reverting to a struggle between the classes no less fruitless and even bitterer than before the war, the excesses of both ends of the scale, the luxury at the top and the destitution at the bottom, must be sloughed off by the State. New habits will bring new horizons, as the war has brought to so many already: and England, fortified by a more firmly knit association of all classes of her citizens, may yet lead the way in the solution of the industrial problems with which the civilized world will be everywhere confronted. The "sophisters and the calculators," the subjects of Burke's everlasting derision, may demonstrate by their statistics that England after the war will be an immeasurably poorer community. The duty rests upon Englishmen to show that her very loss of riches has made her richer in the things that count.

9. Edward Grigg, Response to Alfred Zimmern

Copy of a letter from Captain E. W. M. Grigg to Mr. Kerr, 23 December 1915.

It is not you who are disgraceful about letters but me. I have simply been unable to write any since I came back from leave—which, incredible as it seems, is six weeks ago. The reasons are various, but the chief is that I have a great deal of work to do and am always dog-tired in the intervals—

From a letter of Grigg to Philip Kerr, 23 December 1915 (copy), *Robert Brand Papers,* box 3, Bodleian Archives, Bodleian Library, Oxford, pp. 1–7. Reprinted by permission of Mr. John Grigg.

dog-tired in the literal sense, with the proper dog-remedy prompt at hand of curling up and going to sleep. That is, out of the trenches. In the trenches life is, of course, much harder than it was in the summer, and the nights with all their possibilities are prodigiously long—as I am sure you have felt on guard at home. I used to write quite a lot of letters in the trenches, but now—apart from having more to do—there are all sorts of obstacles like mud and cold hands and no light—and these have hitherto quite defeated my efforts to keep letters up. But I am beginning to master the innumerable small troubles which beset one in a slimy dug-out, and I hope I shall do better in future.

The Hun is on the whole where we are, but we have been giving him an awful time—raiding his line at night and bombarding it and his billets by day—and I think he is beginning to meditate retaliation in some form. The Battalion—or at least a small patrol from it—brought back a prisoner from a night-raid not long ago—an untrained Bavarian land sturmer who was unashamedly glad of having finished his bit in the war. My Grenadiers looked vast and furious around him when they brought him to my dug-out door and shewed up suddenly in the little column of light coming out of it. There they told me an artless story of how they had scuppered his comrades (who had attempted to resist) and caught him asleep. A horrid awakening! And then, as they marched him off again, I observed them giving him a cigarette. Really the British soldier is one of the most lovable things in creation. It's against Army orders to give cigarettes to prisoners, but their enemies are no sooner down and out than they must pick them up and comfort them. And I think every incident of that kind does more to teach the Hun what we really are than millions of arguments.

This reminds me of Zim's article. I was much upset to hear that and your article had led Oliver[1] to make a protest, and I hope it has all been cleared up satisfactorily. But I see what upset him—or I think I do—and (to be quite truthful) have some sympathy with it. Zim's article was as good as it could be in one way, i.e., as a sympathetic picture of the higher-minded working-class world—and it was written with all his charm and persuasiveness. But three things seem to me quite out of perspective in it. The first was the comparison on the second page. The real contrast is not between monied worldlings and spiritual paupers—but between human beings (rich or otherwise) who have risked and sacrificed a great deal and

---

1. Kerr's article referred to here was "The Harvest of the War," *Round Table* 6 (1915–16): 1–32. F. S. Oliver (1864–1934) was an English businessman and publicist who wrote an influential popular biography of Alexander Hamilton. He was active in the Round Table movement from its inception. For his criticisms of Kerr and Zimmern, see Oliver to Kerr, 6 December 1915, *Round Table Papers* (Administration 1916), Bodleian Library, MS. Eng. Hist., c. 780.—ED.

human beings (poor or otherwise) who have so far risked and sacrificed very little—indeed are in many ways better off than they were before the war. I am not crabbing Zim's working-man, but really we should all be equally cheerful optimists in his case. Neither do I hold a brief for monied worldlings—but Bob[2] (to take an instance) is presumably by comparison one of that ilk, and I would rather have his kind of pessimism any day than the British working-man's present kind of optimism as a national asset in war. I won't labour the point. One could discuss it over miles of ground. The sum of my criticism is simply that the picture is out of perspective—a wrong rendering of the facts.

My next point is an old one. It is simply that Zim's "working-class" is too much the high-minded and aspiring working-class representation whom he tends to meet. Zim, bless his heart, idealizes everything he comes across. It is a splendid gift, I think it is the right method too, of getting at the changed world we all want to see. But it's a wrong method in what is set forward as a presentation of facts. The facts are otherwise, and his chosen working-men friends do not yet represent more than a fraction of their class.

You and Zim will say—How do I know? My answer is that I have been living in daily intimate association with a varied assortment of human beings from the working-class for the last nine months. They depend on me, and I depend on them. We hold each others' lives in our unworthy hands at all hours of the day and night—especially the night. Most important of all, I read all their letters, however intimate—because I have to—and I can't help having a pretty clear idea of the letters these are answers to.

Now really all the world from which these letters and their writers spring is not in the least the working-class world of Zim's picture. It is much more childish, much less thoughtful, much more primitive. It doesn't look beyond the horizon of the individual and his small human circle, nor can it, for it hasn't the eyes or the understanding. People certainly ought to know that there is such a thing as the labour world Zim writes about. They ought to know, too, that the aspiring element in the labour world is the power in it that will make its history. But they ought not to be invited to suppose that the aspiring element is as yet in any way representative.

Finally—and this criticism is closely mixed up with the last—they ought not to be told that the achievement represented by Kitchener's armies is anything to be very proud of yet. When, oh when, will people begin to realise that armies are not made, mainly by members, but by the spirit in which the members come. Here at least I know what I am talking about.

2. Robert Brand (1878–1963). Educated at New College, Oxford, Brand was a member of Milner's "Kindergarten" in South Africa and a founding member of the Round Table.—Ed.

The passage on p. 59 about the spirit of that new army—"Its quiet endurance, its obstinate but unassuming determination, its free-spokenness and good fellowship, its unfailing and unforced cheerfulness, rising to boisterous humour when things look blackest"—is certainly a brilliant summing up of the sentimental attitude of that army towards itself. It is the view popularised by the daily press. But it isn't true, because at present the greater part of that army loses all those qualities when faced by its real task. We are having fresh units of K's army attached to us for instruction every week. We absorb them into our system, take them into the firing line with us, and endeavour to give them the benefit of our experience—officers to officers, N.C.O.'s to N.C.O.'s, men to men. See the two things side by side, the old and the new, the democratic army and the supposedly Prussianified Brigade, and you will find Zim's catalogue of qualities much better illustrated in the old than in the new. If the new armies really represent the English spirit, God help us. We are lost. *But they don't. We* represent it and we shall get it into them by degrees, when they have forgotten the rot they have written and listened to about themselves.

And now for my last grouse—which applies to your article as well as to Zim's. You and I and Zim have never doubted for a moment that Germany's forces are the forces of darkness, and ours the forces of light. The R.T. cannot say that too often or too well. But I think we are in some danger of confusing the cause with the want of effort behind it, and thereby of misjudging what we are still called upon to do to make our cause prevail. As to the future, your argument and Zim's is sound enough. I agree with it heartily. But it is no use our seeing more clearly into the future of human society, it is no use our having a way to it which others have not, if we do not prove ourselves morally equal to our enlightenment—if you understand what I mean. We are in some danger of being the Rosebery of nations. Taking national effort as a moral asset apart from the merits of the national cause, Germany is still immeasurably our superior. Zim's article is redolent of our weakness. Every one in England—from recruits to Trade Unions, and from Trade Unions to Ministers, has the idea of contrast uppermost in his mind. We can all be patriots at a price—the recruit on a large scale of separation allowance and pay. The Trade Unions on a guarantee of this or that right, the Minister on a careful calculation of the political risks he can take. It is only us out here, the real army, which understands that it is up to the neck; that whether the current seems favourable, and this temperature of the water agreeable, or not, we have to swim our best; in fact, that there is nothing under Heaven which we may not be ordered to do and which we will not then do to our last breath. But what a small part of the nation the real army is, and how far from that spirit is K's army—even the best. The officers attached to me have found they would rather not come round the trenches again, thank you, tonight; they were tired and would go to sleep. They have wondered whether this or that regulation were not too hard on the men, and the men have justified these speculations indicating their opinions by their acts. From top to bottom they fail to understand what kind of enemy they are set against, and what it will take to prove superior to him. And they reflect the nation, they reflect Zim's buoyant working-class in the moral failure that state of mind implies. Judged by effort, Germany is immeasurably our superior, as we are hers, judged by cause. And France is greatly superior to us both, because she shares our cause and has something even finer than German moral.

I have been greatly depressed lately, and mainly by the constant association with the Company from some unit of K's army. We are never by ourselves now, but have to combine the education of the new troops with the task of holding the line. I assure you it doesn't make life easier. Either in billets or in the firing line.

And my depression is not due to their quality as soldiers. That is poor enough, but it can be put gradually right. It is due to their moral quality and attitude of mind—a microcosm of the great human society from which they come and on which we of the R.T. base such great hopes. Add "He that seeks his life shall lose it and he that loses his life shall save it" to the other great text you quoted at the end of your article. It needs more emphasis at present than the other—for which the time is hardly yet (in its political application of course).

I have never doubted—and do not doubt now—that we shall win the war. But I begin to fear for the first time that we shall end it the moral inferiors, not only of our chief ally, but also of our chief enemy, *despite the wrongness of his cause and the rightness of ours.* And what will our cause be worth in our hands if that is our true state.

So, Philip and Zim, please in your next articles don't flatter the English mind too much. It wants hard words more than soft just now.

I hope this rigmarole will convey something of my feelings. They are very strong, but I have no time to make them quite clear.

10. Walther Rathenau, *Germany's Provisions for Raw Materials*

Walther Rathenau (1867–1922) was the son of Emil Rathenau, a German engineer who, by acquiring Edison's patents for the production of electric light bulbs, was able to establish the huge German General Electric Company. Trained in the physical sciences at Berlin, Rathenau's remarkable success as an industrialist and banker launched him into the highest circles of Imperial German society. In addition to his role as a "grand master of capitalism" (Hartmut Pogge von Strandmann) Rathenau also had serious ambitions as a social critic and philosopher, contributing regularly to Maximilian Harden's *Die Zukunft*. Eventually he would publish several major books—*Zur Kritik der Zeit* (1912), *Zur Mechanik des Geistes* (1913), *Die Neue Wirtschaft* (1918), *Von kommenden Dingen* (1917)— articulating his vision of a future where social technocracy, anti-materialist cultural renewal, and corporatist economic planning would guarantee human progress while preserving free enterprise.

Upon the outbreak of the First World War Rathenau served briefly as head of the *Kriegsrohstoffabteilung* (KRA), a special war materials section in the Prussian War Ministry responsible for securing stocks of strategic materials vital for German war production. Although he resigned from this post in 1915, Rathenau had made a fundamental contribution to the German war effort. After Germany's defeat Rathenau became a supporter of the new Republic, serving as Minister for Reconstruction in 1921 and briefly as Foreign Minister in 1922. As an assimilated Jew, Rathenau was a special target for nationalist terrorism. On 24 June 1922 he was assassinated by rightist thugs.

In the following speech given before a political group called the German Society 1914, Rathenau describes the work of the KRA in the early months of the war. This organization presented a hybrid of private planning and state supervision, utilizing a new type of private-public corporation (War Raw Materials Corporation) which had the responsibility of registering, purchasing, and distributing raw materials. In November 1916 control of the KRA was shifted from the War Ministry itself to the new War Office through which the German Supreme Command under Hindenburg and Ludendorff sought to control the German war economy. In the view of its historian, Gerald Feldman, the KRA was "undoubtedly the most successful economic organization created by Germany during the war."[1] In spite of Rathenau's patriotic rhetoric, however, the trend toward state intervention was broadly secular. The decisive role of the Ministry of Munitions in Britain, the program of supply and labor controls in France, the interventions of the War Ministry in Austria—all testify to the growing role of the modern bureaucratic state in the management of wartime economy and society.

---

1. Gerald D. Feldman, *Army, Industry and Labor in Germany, 1914–1918* (Princeton, 1966), p. 51.

Address before the German Society 1914 on 20 December 1915

The object of my paper is to report to you a new departure in our economic warfare which has no precedent in history, which will have a decided influence on the war, and which in all probability is destined to affect future times. In its methods it is closely akin to communism and yet it departs essentially from the prophecies and demands resulting from radical theories. It is not my purpose to give an account of a rigid system based on theories, but I shall relate how this system grew out of our actual life, first taking concrete form in a small group, then affecting ever widening circles, and finally bringing about a complete change in our economic life. Its visible result is a new department attached to the War Ministry which places our whole economic life in the service of the war.

I should not like to limit our report to our actual work, but I wish to make you acquainted with its romantic aspect. Men are working together united only by a common purpose, men enlisted from all parts of the Fatherland, from all professions, working for the welfare of the country, giving freely and without reserve what they possess in experience, energy, and inventive power.

"Organization and administration of raw materials!" Abstract terms, lifeless words, and yet terms of great significance if we fully realize their meaning. If we look around us: our tools and building materials, our clothing, our food, our armaments, our means of transportation, all depend on foreign materials, for the economic life of all nations is closely interrelated. . . .

Even more serious is the problem of armament and defense, above all in a country surrounded and blockaded by the enemy. Daily we hear the food question discussed. And yet our country is able to produce 80 per cent of what is needed. Completely surrounded and cut off, we may be restricted, but we cannot be annihilated. The case is totally different regarding the raw materials needed for warfare: to be cut off from all such sources of supply might spell destruction.

Look at a map of Europe and study the location of the Central Powers; it is as though a demon had drawn the boundaries, for only a very few strategic points need to be taken by our enemy, and the colossal area will be cut off. It is true we have access to three seas, but what are they? They are landlocked inland seas. The Baltic is accessible only through a channel; the

From *Fall of the German Empire 1914–1918*, vol. 2, translated, as an abridged version of the original, by David G. Rempel and Gertrude Rendtorff and edited by Ralph Haswell Lutz (Stanford: Stanford University Press, 1932), pp. 77–91. ©1932 by the Board of Trustees of the Leland Stanford Junior University. Copyright renewed 1960 by Ralph Haswell Lutz. Reprinted by permission of the publishers.

North Sea is blocked by the English Channel, by the Orkney and Shetland Islands; the Mediterranean Sea is blocked both in the east and in the west. And back of these landlocked seas there is in the north but a poor country unable to give us a plentiful supply of materials needed, and in the south beyond the Mediterranean Sea the desert, not crossed by railways or trade routes that might bring us in contact with the great centers of productivity.

When on August 4 of last year England declared war our country became a beleaguered fortress. Cut off by land and cut off by sea it was made wholly self-dependent; we were facing a war the duration, cost, danger, and sacrifices of which no one could foresee.

When three days had passed after England had declared war I could no longer stand the agony. I called on the Chief of the War Department, Colonel Scheuch, and on the evening of the same day I was kindly received by him. I explained to him that I was convinced that the supply of the absolutely needed raw materials on hand could probably last only a limited number of months. Colonel Scheuch shared my opinion that the war would be one of long duration, and so I was forced to ask him, "What has been done and what can be done to avert the danger that Germany will be strangled?"

Very little had been done in the past, but much has been done since the interest of the War Ministry has been aroused. Returning home deeply concerned and worried I found a telegram from von Falkenhayn,[2] then Minister of War, asking me to come to his office the next morning.

This was Sunday, August 9. I expressed my thanks to the Minister, telling him that I was astonished that he, at the time of mobilization, could afford to find leisure to acquaint himself with the thoughts of outsiders. Pointing to his desk he said: "The desk is cleared. The great work has been done, our mobilization has been carried out; not a single claim for exemption from military service has been made and I am free to receive visitors."

Our discussion lasted the greater part of the forenoon, and when it was ended the Minister of War had decided to establish an organization, no matter whether great or small, provided it had authority and was efficient and able to solve the problem which we were facing. In that moment the Prussian Minister of War was bold enough to take upon himself the responsibility for a decision which meant the turning-point in that matter which I am discussing here.

I was about to take leave, but the Minister detained me by making the unexpected demand that I should undertake to organize the work. I was not prepared for this; I asked for time to think the matter over, but my request

2. Erich von Falkenhayn (1861–1922) was Chief of the German General Staff from 1914 to 1916 and from 1913 to early 1915 Prussian minister of war.—ED.

was not granted; I had to consent, and a few days later I found myself installed at the War Ministry.

The *Kriegs-Rohstoff-Abteilung* (War Raw Materials Section) was established by ministerial decree. There were to be two directors: a retired colonel, a man of great experience, representing the War Ministry in matters demanding expert military knowledge; and myself, whose duty it was to create the organization. We were located in four small rooms, working with the assistance of a secretary whose practical experience was of great value.

The first problem was to find men. I approached my friends and induced my colleague of the General Electric Company, Professor Klingenberg, to join us in the capacity of vice-president. I also gained the co-operation of my friend, von Moellendorff,[3] who had been the first to point out in private conversations the sore spot of our economic situation. We were now five, and the work could begin.

The first problem was the question of available supplies. It was necessary to ascertain the period of months for which the country was provided with the indispensable materials. Any further action depended on that. Opinions received from the great industries were quite contradictory.

Having asked the authorities if statistics might be furnished, I was informed that such statistics might be worked out but that it would probably take six months to do so. When I stated that I must have them within a fortnight because the matter was urgent I was assured that that was quite impossible. Yet I had to have them; and I had them within fourteen days.

We were forced to take a daring step, namely, we had to rely on a hypothesis. And this hypothesis proved to be reliable. We started with the assumption that the store of supplies available for the whole country would be approximately equal to the available supply stored by any large group of industries. The War Ministry did business with some 900 or 1,000 concerns. If we found out to what extent these industries were supplied with the various materials needed by them, we might expect to ascertain data for the entire country. Fractions did not matter; what we wanted were round figures. The experiment was successful. After two weeks we saw light; after three weeks we were sure of our facts. Few of the materials needed for the army were available in quantities sufficient for a year (and since that time the yearly demands of the army have substantially increased); in most cases they were considerably less.

At first we were concerned with only a small number of materials. The whole fields of foodstuffs and of liquid fuel were excluded; included was

3. Wichard von Moellendorff (1881–1937) and Georg Klingenberg (1870–1925) were collaborators of Rathenau in the General Electric Company.—ED.

everything called "raw materials." The official definition gave the following interpretation: "Such materials as are needed for the defense of the country and which cannot be produced within the country at all times and in sufficient quantities." At first hardly more than a dozen of such indispensable materials were enumerated; the number, however, increased from week to week and has now passed the hundred mark.

So far we had but little data, but we had a foundation to work on. We had learned to what extent the country was supplied, and by degrees we began to see the problem in its entirety. But we did not yet know how the problem was to be solved.

Four measures appeared feasible and worth trying out for reconstructing our economic policies so as to afford proper protection for the country.

First: Coercive measures had to be adopted regarding the use of all raw materials in the country. No material must be used arbitrarily, or for luxury, or for anything that is not absolutely needed. The needs of the army are of paramount importance and everything must be directed toward that ultimate end. That was our first and most difficult task.

Secondly: [Author's omission].

The third way of solving the problem was through manufacture. Anything indispensable and not procurable must be manufactured within the country. New methods of manufacture had to be invented and developed wherever the old technique was inadequate.

And now the fourth measure: Materials difficult to obtain must be replaced by others more easily procurable. It is not ordained that this or that object must be made of copper or of aluminum; it may be made of some other material. Substitutes must be found. Instead of using the time-honored materials for our household goods, etc., we must use new substances, and articles must be manufactured that do not require so much raw material.

Such were the measures that we seized upon; they were not solutions, yet were possibilities, and they gave us hope.

On the other hand, we faced insurmountable opposition.

Our laws regulating the economic and industrial life in war time had hardly been changed since the time of Frederick the Great. According to the letter of the law we were given about as much leeway as though the law, shorn of its theoretical terms, had said: if a captain of cavalry comes into a village, he may ask the chief magistrate of the place for barley, and if the magistrate should raise difficulties, he, under certain conditions, may take the barley himself. That, in a nutshell, is about all the law that we found.

And there were other difficulties.

To solve the problems confronting us we needed the co-operation of many bureaus and of the several Federal Governments. During the first few days we received very encouraging replies from the three ministries of war outside of Prussia, expressing their willingness to permit Prussia to establish the organization. That meant considerable simplification. But we had to carry on negotiations with many more bureaus, authorities, and officials.

The very fact that the problem was not understood caused many difficulties. Up to the present the German people believe that the supply of raw materials takes care of itself. The food question is being discussed all day long; the question of raw materials is hardly mentioned. Even now it is hard for us to realize what the situation was at the beginning of the war. For the first six months no one had any idea what we were trying to do. The Parliament, meeting in November 1914, considered us to be a kind of commercial agency charged to see that leather and wool became cheaper. That questions were at stake on which war and peace, victory or defeat depended, no one seemed to see and many fail to see today. We suffered under these conditions. In industrial circles our inquiries were sometimes considered to be offensive and unpleasant interference with the industrial situation. We were accused of injuring certain peace industries.

We were forced to advance slowly, step by step. Yet I may say that, after all, all authorities have supported us, that the people have finally come to understand that our organization is able to take up any problem, however difficult it may be, and can find new ways to solve the problems.

But the beginning was difficult. . . .

[Rathenau next discusses the problem of personnel at great length. The work started by five men who had four rooms at their disposal had grown to such dimensions that sixty rooms were used. At the time when the report was given a whole block of buildings on Hedemannstrasse was occupied. The problem of getting hold of the right men and of keeping them, as told by Rathenau, was probably not very different from the situation in Washington in 1917–18. The passage is not without humor. Thus: "Professors would call, telling us that everything was quite wrong and that we must start all over again. Then members of the Parliament would come, suggesting that everything was indeed quite wrong, and that what the professors had told us was also quite wrong, and that we must start all over again. But, except for a terrible amount of writing, no real harm was done."]

We now come to the solution.

The first question was to establish a legal basis. I have already alluded to the defective and incomplete state of our laws. It was necessary to establish and formulate new and fundamental ideas upon which the reorganization of our economic life could rest. The term "sequestration" (*Beschlagnahme*) was given a new interpretation, somewhat arbitrarily, I admit, but supported by certain passages in our martial law. At a later period our interpretation was sanctioned by law.

"Sequestration" does not mean that merchandise or material (*Ware*) is seized by the state but only that it is restricted, i.e., that it no longer can be disposed of by the owner at will but must be reserved for a more important purpose (or, that it must be put at the disposal of a higher authority). The merchandise must be used for war purposes only: it may be sold, manufactured, shipped, transformed; but no matter what is done to it, it always remains subject to the law that it must be used for war purposes only.

At first many people found it difficult to adjust themselves to the new doctrine. We were often told that we had made the great mistake of not confiscating everything. I do not mention this assertion with the idea of contradicting it, for it needs no contradiction. If we had requisitioned the goods of even a single branch of industries, e.g., of the metal industries (that is to say, if we had requisitioned all copper, tin, nickel, aluminum, antimony, wolfram, chrome) we should have become owners of millions of lots of goods and every day innumerable inquiries would have been received demanding to know what was to be done with this or that parcel of goods? Is it to be rolled, drawn, or cast? Who is to get it? There is much demand! On the other hand, all manufacturing would have come practically to a standstill until such a time as all goods could have been reapportioned. And the responsibility of accounting for goods worth many milliards of marks would have rested on us.

The interpretation formulated by us for the term "sequestration" has stood the test and will remain a potent factor in our economic warfare. The new doctrine, however, entailed grave dangers. For when goods are sequestered, peace industries must come to a stop. A manufacturer of metal goods whose store of metals has been sequestered no longer can manufacture peace articles; he must depend on war work. His whole plant and his machinery, his methods, and his products must be readjusted. He has to begin all over again. Our industries underwent a terrible period of trial and hardship, especially those in the field of metallurgy, chemistry, and the textile materials.

In those trying weeks of 1915 when the new order had just gone out, my colleagues of the General Electric Company came to me and said: "Do you know what you have done? Sixty thousand men will be without bread."

But the crisis is past. For two months we gave the industries a certain amount of leeway, though with a heavy heart. Who could tell whether or not the release of a single ton of saltpeter would decide the fate of a battle or of a beleaguered fortress? But somebody had to take the responsibility and we have not shirked doing it.

Within two months German industrial life was readjusted. It was done quietly, without a breakdown, with self-confidence and energy, and with magnificent efficiency. That, gentlemen, speaks highly for the German in-

dustries and must never be forgotten. Not France, nor England, nor the
United States, nor any of our enemies or our quasi-enemies will ever do the
same.

So much regarding sequestration. Its effect was the reorganization of
our industries. And now I approach the second factor.

We were aware that our economic life had to be remade. We knew that
new forms and methods must be found for the distribution of materials.
But how was that to be done?

The army and the navy must retain absolute freedom to do business with
whom they choose. We could not tell them: you will receive orders from us
as to with whom you may deal. On the other hand, the concern receiving
orders from the Government must be furnished the needed material. New
agencies had to be created for gathering, storing, and distributing the material circulating in a new form through the arteries of German commerce.
A new system had to be created, that of the *Kriegswirtschafts-Gesellschaf-
ten* (War Industries Corporations). Today we are as accustomed to them as
if they had been handed down from time immemorial. But at first they appeared so paradoxical that, even in our intimate circle, otherwise so harmonious, there was difference of opinion as to the possibility and practicability of this new organ.

On the one hand, it meant a step in the direction of state socialism. For
commerce was no longer free, but had become restricted.

On the other hand, it meant the attempt to encourage self-administration of our industries. How were such contradictory doctrines to be made
to agree?

With more or less benevolence we have been afterward informed what
course we ought to have taken: we should not have founded companies but
should have added to the existing government apparatus. Today criticism
has become silent. If anyone is still skeptical let him go to the War Metal
Corporation or to the War Chemical Corporation. If he sees the beehive,
thousands of men at work, a constant stream of visitors, if he watches the
amount of correspondence, of shipments, and of payments, he will realize
that this work could not have been done within the framework of government administration; it had to be left to professional experts and to self-
administration.

The system of war corporations is based upon self-administration; yet
that does not signify unrestricted freedom. The war raw materials corporations were established under strict government supervision. The corporations
serve the interests of the public at large; they neither distribute dividends nor
apportion profits; in addition to the usual organs of stock companies, a board
of governors and a supervising committee, they have another independent
organ, a committee of appraisement and distribution, made up of members

selected from various chambers of commerce, or of government officials. This committee serves as intermediary between the stock companies, representing capitalism, and the Government—an economic innovation which may be destined to become generally accepted in future times.

Their duty is to amass raw materials and to direct the flow of supply in such a way that each manufacturing concern is furnished the needed materials in quantities corresponding to the orders it receives from the Government and at prices fixed for such materials.

These corporations were not always kindly received by the industrials.

The metal industries were comparatively friendly. They asked: "A stock company which makes no profits? What is the good of that? So far, we have attended to our business alone and we are quite able to do so in the future." Nevertheless, they acquiesced, partly to do me a personal favor and partly, I presume, because they thought that no harm was done.

It was different with the chemical industries. They are the great captains of industry along the Rhine, proud, charged with great responsibilities, commanders of whole armies of workingmen. One of them, a man of great influence, went about in the Rhenish provinces warning the people against new experiments. But finally a constituent assembly was held in the Hofmannhaus, Berlin. At first everything went smoothly, but toward the end the discussion became heated. When the gentlemen saw that saltpeter would have to be restricted, a scene was enacted which reminded one somewhat of Paris in 1789. Nevertheless the corporation was founded, and today we must express our gratitude to the chemists for their efficient cooperation. This model German industry, which at first found it somewhat difficult to adjust itself to the new order, has, I venture to say, subsequently, by its initiative and inventive genius, by its courage and perseverance, reached the highest place in our economic warfare system.

Almost every week saw new corporations coming into existence. Metal was the first; then jute, wool, worsted, rubber, cotton, leather, hides, flax, linen, and horsehair—partly stock companies, partly holding companies. . . .

We were hard at work. On the one side the mountain of sequestered material grew and continual negotiations with the great industries were necessary. On the other hand, our organization took shape . . . when a new task of greatest importance, yet greatly desired and welcome, had to be met.

Our victorious armies had advanced. Belgium and part of France had been conquered. In Russia the sky had cleared. . . .

A business of enormous proportions was thus added to our department which even then had itself assumed gigantic dimensions. Then we were confronted with a new danger. I must now lay before you our greatest problem, the problem of nitrates; but I shall not give you exact figures.

It is well known that the most important explosives used in warfare are nitrous compounds, that saltpeter is a nitrous compound, and that, consequently, war is, to a certain extent, a problem of nitrates.

At the beginning of the war our supply of nitrates was not unsatisfactory. I shall use fictitious figures selected to indicate proportions. Let us imagine that at the outbreak of the war we had in the country 90 tons of nitrogen, and let us further assume that 50 more tons were expected in Antwerp or Ostend; that would give us a total of 140 tons at our disposal. Supposing that we used 10 tons a month, we should thus have a supply sufficient for 14 months. I repeat that my figures are merely chosen to serve as proportional numbers.

The situation was quite hopeful. September came and the methods of warfare changed. Again and again we checked our figures on the basis of the data furnished by those using saltpeter. We always reached the same conclusion: our calculations are correct.

All of a sudden it dawned upon us: suppose the war at the eastern front assumes the same dimensions as the war in the West? Suppose the war will last longer and will surpass in magnitude anything that we are able to imagine at present? Will, under such conditions, the supply of nitrate suffice? There was no answer.

It was an anxious moment when I laid these considerations before the Minister of War requesting permission to build as many factories as the chemical industries were able to construct.

The Minister of War, von Wandel, always quiet, energetic, and farsighted, authorized me at once to take up negotiations with the chemical industries.

Preliminary work of great importance had been done in the field. His Excellency Fischer and Privy Councillor Haber had studied the problem of producing nitrate on a large scale, and the chemical industries were by no means surprised when they were asked to establish factories.

The construction of a large number of factories was decided upon and the chemists, bold and confident, were willing to undertake actual construction work even before I could give them the contract authorized by the Treasury. Construction was finished before the contract was signed. That was about Christmas [1914]. Nitrates had now become a German product; we no longer needed the world. The most difficult technical danger of the war had been averted.

But while the factories were building the information came from the front: 10 tons no longer suffice, we need 16; 16 tons no longer are enough, we need 21, soon 27, and so on—I shall not give any more figures for fear that my proportional numbers might indicate to what extent the demands had increased. But I may say that the original store had by that time been reduced to insignificant proportions. Had we deferred building until the time when the situation had become critical, a dangerous point would have been reached and that at a time when the offensive in Galicia demanded enormous supplies of ammunition.

Chemical products, especially nitric acid, were and are by far the most important of our products. But a large number of other products were added to our department: factories for refining metals and for used materials were erected; methods for extracting metals from ore were improved; and electrolytic and electrothermic works were established or enlarged, partly by the War Raw Materials Section and partly by the Raw Materials corporations.

In the midst of all these activities we were given another task which, in reality, had no direct bearing on the mobilization of the country, yet which we had to assume, as there was no one else to solve the problem.

I have mentioned before that Parliament, in November, considered us to be an agency charged to lower market prices. To be present at the meeting of the Committee of the Parliament but not to be able to defend one's self was not exactly a pleasure. The gentlemen were justly annoyed because some of the raw materials had become very dear, and, indeed, we thought the same. But they did not know that our foremost care had been to avert depletion before we could consider the question of prices, after all, a matter of secondary importance. Immediate redress was demanded.

In the meantime we had found ways and means and were approaching the solution. We started by fixing maximum prices for metals. That was a difficult undertaking. Not only the more important metals had to be considered but also their alloys, used materials, and half-finished products. After protracted negotiations a table was agreed upon, not entirely liked by industry and commerce, but against which no really serious protest could be raised. This table was adopted by the Federal Council. We then succeeded in fixing maximum prices for a group of goods, an undertaking which experts had thought to be impossible, the group of wools and wool products. . . .

While the fixing of maximum prices was more or less a departure into the field of general economics, we were on our own ground when the question of obtaining and introducing substitutes and surrogates was taken up.

The materials used for the Prussian uniforms had to be changed. Worsted and other goods were added. Rare materials no longer could be used for helmets, buttons, and other accessories. In manufacturing ammunition zinc and steel were employed, replacing rare materials. Metals heretofore not used for such purposes were now introduced for the making of electrical apparatus. Many products thus became cheaper. New and large chemical works were constructed for the manufacture of known or hitherto unknown substitutes. Even the textile industries adopted the system of utilizing used materials. Today there are but few branches of industry using exclusively the same materials as before the war. Many have profited by the reorganization.

I shall now give you a short description of the work of the War Raw Materials Section as it was at the beginning of the year [1915].

A central section was in charge of the general administration and gave directions. It negotiated with the Government, planned all new measures and orders, prepared the reports for the War Minister, conferred with industrial groups, members of the Reichstag, and interested parties, studied economic and juridical questions, employed the personnel, had charge of the archives, edited the quarterly reports, and had general responsibility for the whole organization.

In addition there were the various departments in charge of the various materials, assisted by and co-operating with the several raw-material companies, their subdivisions and branch organizations.

We had departments for metals, chemicals, cotton, wool, jute, rubber, leather, hides, lumber, and organic products. These departments represented the economic part of our organization.

The department of sequestration (*Beschlagnahmestelle*) regulated the flow of the sequestered materials, had charge of the legal side, conferred with the owners, and, with the assistance of supervisors, saw to it that our measures were obeyed. At first it served as our statistical bureau, but this work was later transferred to other departments. The department of sequestration employed a very large staff; their printed matter was daily sent to the General Commandos for distribution throughout the country.

A separate department for shipping, bookkeeping, and auditing was needed. Tens of thousands of freight cars were constantly employed to fill more than two hundred warehouses. These depots had to be equipped and guarded. The materials had to be loaded, shipped, unloaded, controlled, distributed, and accounted for.

A shipping bureau made use of a special trust company (*Treuhandgesellschaft*) to supervise freight rates, and of a clearinghouse, probably the largest in all Germany. It kept track of all shipments; watched them at the large central depots in Haspe, Frankfurt, and Mannheim; and supervised their transshipment, their arrival in the warehouses, and their final distribution to the many factories where the wares were used.

On April 1, 1915, I was able to turn over the Section to the Prussian Ministry of War as a going concern, working smoothly. I was greatly pleased when the majority of my co-workers stayed with the Government. Under the direction of my successor, Major Koeth, the department has grown enormously. Many new organizations have been added and the whole system has been perfected. Judged by its personnel and by the extent of its work, it is, with the exception of the War Ministry and the Ministry of Railways, equal to any governmental department in Prussia. It differs from them all in that it has grown up within eight months. It is served by a staff of more than five hundred officials, the raw-materials companies employing in addition, together with their branch organizations, a staff of several thousands. . . .

The English blockade has failed. More than that, England has suffered. England's greatest worry is, at the present time, her unrestricted free trade. England is able to buy and she does buy, yet she fears every purchase made by her subjects in foreign countries. For every purchase, whether it be tea or saltpeter, endangers her economic balance. Every purchase must be paid for and as full payments cannot be made by wares (many of her industries formerly working for the export trade are now engaged in the manufacture of ammunition), every purchase means that English money flows into foreign countries.

German commerce circulates within the country. This state of our economic life was forced upon us, but we have adjusted ourselves to it. In some respects it has harmed us. But it has also strengthened us in that we now enjoy the whole benefit of the cycle. Our goods are produced within our boundaries and they are consumed within our boundaries. Nothing goes beyond these boundaries unless it be the cannon ball hurled by our artillery. Whatever the state consumes is paid for by the state in cash. The money thus paid is returned to the state in the form of bonds and once more enters into the cycle. The state has become a commercial unit.

Our methods will leave their impress on future times. I do not wish to take up the social question. Nor is it my intention to discuss to what extent our methods may affect the whole field of general economy, or whether they might possibly result in a reform of capitalism. One effect is felt even now: our valuation of political economy has changed—we have developed a new conception of raw materials. Many substitutes will continue to be used; home products will be employed where formerly we depended on imported materials; many foreign products we shall, I trust, no longer need, among them saltpeter; sulphur must no longer be imported. Our economic life will become more independent in a double sense: we shall no longer be obliged to rely on the good will of the vendors nor on that of our creditors whom we must pay and who, under certain conditions, by increasing their tariff rates, might have the power to depress the value of our payments, i.e., the value of our exported goods.

Such considerations will gain in weight and will result in a new economic doctrine, the doctrine of the necessity of protecting our raw materials (*Begriff des Rohstoff-Schutzes*). The more foreign markets will be closed to us by protective tariffs or by chauvinism, the more we must take care of our economic balance. Unnecessary and superfluous purchases made in foreign countries must be paid for by exports, and such enforced exporting may mean a loss to us. Our neighbors are left free to depreciate our finished products by protective tariffs while we must import their raw materials. Thus mercantilism appears in a new form, not aiming to increase our export to ever larger dimensions, but to make export pay. Up to the present time, we were accustomed to what we called "protective tariffs"; we are now evolving a new doctrine, the doctrine of "protection of raw materials." It is a matter of vital concern to the state when saltpeter is imported from Chile while it can be manufactured just as cheaply, or nearly as cheaply, out of German air. The state cannot remain indifferent if a metal is bought and paid for in America when a substitute of equal value can be produced at home.

The protection of raw materials will become a generally accepted doctrine, and Germany's economic life will be benefited by it.

These are considerations affecting future times. Future times will also have to decide upon the fate of that organization which I have described.

The Raw Materials Section will not cease to function in peace time; it will be made the nucleus of an Economic General Staff (*wirtschaftlicher Generalstab*). Names will change. It is possible that the term "Kriegswirtschafts-Abteilung" will be used, for it is that now. We cannot and must not be drawn again into a war without being economically prepared. The years of peace must be employed with utmost energy for this preparation. We must constantly keep informed of our supplies of essentials. Our stores must be equal to our needs. Depots of enormous size must be maintained. That will require considerable statistical and clerical work. Arrangements must be made for the smooth and automatic readjustment of these organizations in war time, whereas in this war coercion had to be employed. A general economic mobilization plan must be worked out.

If we look at our organization in its totality and inquire how Germany could succeed where England faltered and Lloyd George failed, I may offer the following answer:

First of all, we made an early start. As soon as it was approached, the War Ministry boldly decided to identify itself with us and that at a time when other economic questions had not yet been touched. And, in fostering us, the War Ministry has never failed to exert its power and the genius for which it has always been known.

Secondly, our organization has always remained well centralized and unified. It has never been turned over to commissions, committees, or experts. It has never been decentralized by bureaucratic methods. There was a central will endowed with authority. Committees are good when you want advice but not good when you want to create.

The third factor is German idealism. A group of men was found ready to trust a common leader, working without remuneration, without contract, impelled by enthusiasm, offering their strength and their intellect because they knew that their country needed them. Co-operating in the spirit of democratic and friendly companionship, frequently working quite independently, this select group has created a new economic life for Germany. It had the support of our industry, young and elastic, ready to act, equal to the demands of the time, able to perform what had seemed impossible.

The highest and last factor, however, is purely a human trait. For the human soul rises far above mechanical attainments, as it alone has the power to create and to lead onward. I refer to human trust and to human confidence. I have to thank three Prussian Ministers of War for the confidence which they have bestowed upon our men and our work. Such trust is a sign of genius—I might call it ethical genius—and it would be hard to find it in another country. It speaks well for the German and the Prussian system that such human relationship could be given and received in the service of our economic life and in the defense of our country.

11. Henri Philippe Pétain, *A Crisis of Morale in the French Nation at War*

The refusal of French troops to continue combat in the spring of 1917 represented the most dramatic expression of an attitude which was common among all participants in the horrific trench warfare of World War I. The account below was composed by Marshal Henri Philippe Pétain (1856–1951), the French commander credited with quelling the mutinies as well as with leading the earlier successful defense of Verdun. Pétain went on to play a leading role in the final stages of the war as commander in chief of French forces in 1917–18.

In July 1940, Pétain, who had made little effort in the 1930s to disguise his contempt for "politics" and his suspicion of the parliamentary system, gained a less heroic reputation as head of the French government at Vichy which collaborated with Nazi Germany.[1] In 1945 he was convicted of collaboration and sentenced to death, a sentence General de Gaulle commuted to life imprisonment.

In these memoirs Pétain represents the perspective of the officers against whom French soldiers rebelled, rather than that of the mutineers themselves. Nonetheless his narrative can be read as a valid description

1. Richard Griffiths has noted that Pétain was "the father figure for most anti-democratic projects" in the later 1930s in France. Richard Griffiths, *Marshal Pétain* (London, 1970), p. 172.

of the conditions leading to the mutiny and the actions taken by the discontented troops. Pétain's statements on how order was finally restored to
the French army are more subjective, but offer a fascinating portrait of
military attitudes toward the civilian world—the public and private "home
front"—during the Great War.

---

1. The Symptoms
. . .

Exhaustion and Grievances at the Front

The criminal propaganda campaign conceived in the interior spread gradually to the front, where it found well-prepared soil. For the troops, at the
end of two years of a terrible war, were physically and morally in an utterly
exhausted state, and needed little urging, if encouraged, to complain of
hardships which a spirit of discipline had hitherto caused them to bear in
silence. . . .

Irregularity of Leave Foremost among the grievances was *the irregularity
of leave and the inadequacy of leave transport arrangements.* In many
units the rosters were incomplete or wrongly drawn up, and the mistakes
made gave colour to complaints of injustice and unfairness. New intakes
were able to get back to their families before veterans who had been far
longer in the line. Officers were more favourably treated than the men.
From February 1917 on, because of the imminence of the offensive, leave
in the majority of units was cut down and sometimes stopped altogether.
Then, when the attacks ended, it was impossible to re-establish the normal
allocations in the divisions which had been engaged. Thus from the start of
the mutinies the soldiers' mail is full of allusions to what the men considered to be a serious injustice: "I expect to be home before the end of the
month; that is what the revolt has been about . . ." "For several days nerves
in the company had been on edge; there were complaints about the unfair
allocation of leave . . ." "The most serious grievance which brought this
trouble about was the question of leave."

Even the lucky ones who did enjoy a reunion with their families returned with a deplorable impression of the conditions of their journey.
They complained of uncomfortable trains, unprotected from the weather,
always late and held up for hours in stations without shelters. They re-

From Sir Edward Spears, *Two Men Who Saved France: Pétain and De Gaulle,* translated
by Rivers Scott (London: Eyre & Spottiswoode, 1966), pp. 76–84, 86–94, 97, 99–111,
119–20, 122–23; ©1966 by Sir Edward Louis Spears. Reprinted with permission of Stein
and Day Publishers and Methuen London.

ported that there was nothing to prevent men indulging in acts of indiscipline for there were no police to be seen anywhere. The people who had it all their own way were the racketeers, who reigned supreme.

Poor Food, Increasing Drunkenness The soldier on leave, like the soldier at the front, marches on his stomach; and the fighting man, always hungry and always thirsty, and with a purse bulging with cash that he had no choice but to save, was an easy prey for the shoals of sharks who followed him wherever he went. He knew he was being cheated, but complained, and *he held it against the army that his basic rations were so inadequate.* What these rations were lacking in, most of all, was variety. They were often especially deficient in green vegetables. *They were badly prepared,* for the most part by "old sweats," who were chosen as cooks whatever their lack of skill or inclination. In cantonments, the dishes they served to their compulsory customers were invariably unappetising. When it was a question of getting meals up to the trenches, the distances involved and the *inadequacy of the equipment* available meant that when the food arrived it was congealed, dried up, dirty, and often absolutely disgusting.

The divisional co-operative canteens, instituted on 2nd November 1916, were not yet doing much good and could not supplement the inadequate rations. As soon as the men came out of the line and arrived in camp, they made a dive for the local shops with the intention of buying up whatever foodstuffs were offered them at whatever price, content with requiting those who fleeced them with a few oaths and finding in the experience new fuel for their resentments. The fact was, of course, that they had *too much spare cash.* . . . The craftiest dodges were used by the troops to procure alcoholic drinks, then strictly prohibited, the men being encouraged in this by many of the local inhabitants turned wine-merchants for the duration. Men would not hesitate to walk miles, where necessary, for the purpose of filling their water-bottles with *pinard. Drunkenness became general,* with the most deplorable effect on good order and military discipline.

Faulty Organisation of Rest Billets It can be stated that the misuse of the rest periods out of the line was largely due to *the discontent which the men felt at the allocation of these,* to which they felt they had a right, and which in any case they sorely needed. They felt that by misusing the rest periods when they got them they were making up in some way for the delays they had suffered.

It is undeniable that there were many units which, from Verdun and the Somme onwards, had been kept in the front line almost continuously, with no respite in which battle-shattered nerves could be restored. Other units, on the contrary, were kept in the rear for months at a time, too long not to lose their familiarity with danger and too long not to arouse bitter jealousy in the ranks of units less favoured. . . .

Another source of grievance was that the rest-quarters behind the line, usually in villages now three-quarters reduced to rubble, were totally without comfort, while the lack of any permanent staff in these places, and the rapid succession of different units in and out of them, made it impossible for them either to be looked after or kept up, or even for the billets themselves to be fairly allocated. *The best were monopolised by permanent personnel, generally belonging to rear formations.* . . .

Apparent Uselessness of the Sacrifices Undergone The intense suffering the combatant endured and the continuous nature of his ordeal do certainly seem to have been too often overlooked. Ever since the stabilisation of the front the war had become an obscure plodding grind, *with none of the old excitement or idealism left to relieve it.* It may be true that it called for a less violent sort of effort than did the fighting in open country. But against this it demanded inexhaustible patience, maintained under constant fire, amid mounds of rotting corpses, now in a sea of filthy mud, snow and rain, now in a desert of sun-scorched chalk, clay and sand. *This was a war of constant small engagements, of sorties of men against the barbed wire defences of well-entrenched machine-gun emplacements. The successes achieved were temporary and costly,* and the corpses left lying in No Man's Land after each one served to remind the survivors of the futility of their sacrifice. There were more important attacks, made in the hope of achieving "the break-through." But on every occasion, after a few trenches had been overrun, they foundered against carefully prepared second lines of defence, before which it became apparent that their efforts had been in vain and all was to begin again.

With such bitter disappointment as the only result of their sacrifice, *it began to be felt by the fighting troops that the High Command had no understanding of what could be done* and persisted in courses which experience had shown to be hopeless. A breakout into open country and a resumption of the "war of movement" seemed no longer possible. Confidence in a "military victory" was badly shaken. For a short time "economic victory" was canvassed instead, but this in its turn proved a source of disillusionment and no one could see any hope of ending the war.

In spite of the resounding success of our defence of Verdun and our brilliant counter-offensives at Douaumont, Vaux and the Somme, it was bitterly evident to the front-line troops that the basic position of the two sides remained unchanged. At the beginning of the third winter of the war they felt deeply the burden of their fatigue. They were nervous, impatient and restless. They grumbled. They wrote home that they wondered "if the war would ever end"; that "they were fed up"; that "the amount of ground still to be covered was appalling"; that it was not true to claim that we were stronger than the Boche; that they no longer had any idea why they were fighting; and, finally, that it was time those in command of them explained the reasons for such massacres. . . .

Defeatist Attitude and Lack of Initiative on the Part of Certain Officers
Faced with all this, what was the attitude of the officers? A handful responded with courage and energy. The great majority bowed before the storm and awaited events.

Practically all the old peacetime officers, who had won the respect and affection of their men and had proved their worth in the handling of their troops in action, had gone. Their replacements had had to pick up what training they could as they went along. They lacked authority to stand firm when the trouble began and to prevent its spreading by the dignity of their attitude and the force of their example. They had been faced with the same tests and experienced the same hardships as their men. They had the same private worries and were beset by the same doubts.

As for the senior officers and generals, the constant threat of being stellenbosched, inhibited and demoralised them. *Many commanders were no longer prepared to furnish their superiors with candid and full reports either about events in their sectors or the moral or material condition of their units.* To insure themselves against trouble they often descended to suppressing details capable of showing up their units in a bad light, and even to distorting the facts. Some went so far as to carry out a shameless bluff and to exploit the heroism of their men to obtain minor successes out of all proportion to the risks involved.

False Optimism and Rashness in the Direction of the War

Adoption of a Strategy of Boldness and Risk This obsession with rapid results, coupled with disregard of the risks involved, was for some time the characteristic attitude of the French Command. It is here that we approach the most delicate aspect of our study, since it will be largely critical. Yet we feel it essential to speak out unambiguously if the lessons which the crisis of 1917 hold for the future are to be clearly brought out.

It is certainly true that, *at this point of the war, there was no reason to doubt that victory could be achieved so long as we confined ourselves to the possible and the practicable*—two words that were constantly on everybody's lips and should have inspired the country's leaders with a suitable programme. Unfortunately the solution decided upon to resolve the crisis in command in December 1916 and the plan of campaign which our Allies agreed to at our insistence were more than ever the product of hysterically high hopes *and of fantastic strategic over-confidence.*

The offensive fixed for the spring was planned and discussed in the full glare of publicity and presented to all as a campaign of rapid movement and far-distant objectives which was intended to force a decision. This would come, it was claimed, within forty-eight hours: the attackers would be able to sweep without difficulty or impediment through the point of rupture and beyond. . . . Such, however, was not the opinion of those who would have to carry out the plan. The mere conception of such an operation was entirely contrary to the experience acquired in two years of war at the cost of appalling sacrifices.

Weakened Authority of the High Command Graver still, *the planners were in extraordinary and strange contradiction with themselves. Having accepted the principle of a policy and a strategy based on boldness and risk, they did not hesitate to undermine the confidence which was so essential to success.* The War Council held at Compiègne on 6th April, 1917, was a real blunder, and it would have been wiser not to voice the doubts concerning the plan's success which emerged at the Conference. A ban should at least have been imposed on the Press comment, to protect the prestige of those entrusted with the nation's fate. This was not done and *the whole Press of every political shade of opinion reported the doubts that had been raised* and the agonising questions which had been posed.

Relaxation of the Severity of Military Justice It was against this background that *the refusal to face the likelihood of a crisis in morale and to take the preventive measures the Command was clamouring for revealed itself as the official attitude.* And since the campaign for military disobedience was being allowed to develop unchecked, one may fairly ask whether any measures of repression were being taken at all.

On the outbreak of war it had been considered necessary to revise the existing legislation to enable offences against discipline to be energetically and swiftly dealt with. . . .

These provisions, although unquestionably severe, had been regarded by previous responsible governments as both necessary and just. Now they were or were about to be gradually withdrawn, despite the Commander-in-Chief's protests. . . . The desire for the introduction of lenient measures overrode reason. French generosity followed its natural and irresistible bent. The result was that the convictions by Military Courts for offences against military discipline rose from 14,479 in 1915 to 24,953 in 1916, then rocketed the following year, to a new peak figure of 37,842.

The Law of 27th April, 1916, suppressed the special Courts Martial and re-established the admissibility of evidence of extenuating circumstances and the right to give suspended sentences. It further deprived the military courts of their right to try civilians, except for crimes and offences touching on national defence.

A Decree of 8th June, 1916, reintroduced the right of appeal against the death sentence. . . .

2. The Crisis

Towards the end of April 1917, the fortune of war appeared to turn against the Allied armies after having smiled on them for a brief moment. The dazzling hopes of the early spring, which the German withdrawal to the Hindenburg Line, America's entry into the war, and the anticipated impact of the Franco-British offensives had caused the leaders of the Coalition to hold out, were dashed to the ground. *The grand strategic triumph on which so much had been staked turned into a series of dearly-bought minor successes in a prolonged campaign of merciless attrition.* Russia defaulted and her army began to disintegrate. The newspapers reported, often with approval, the early revolutionary measures—the setting up of workers' and soldiers' committees, the abolition of saluting and of military ranks. . . .

**First Incidents between 29th April and 17th May. Reorganisation
of the French High Command. Gravity and Rapid Extension of
the Crisis.**

On 29th April an infantry regiment stationed at Mourmelon was ordered up the line to the sector of the Moronvilliers Heights, where it had carried out attacks on the 17th April and subsequent days and from which it had been withdrawn for a short period of rest only five days before. It was known to the men that they would be employed in a new offensive. They also knew that their division was being sent back into action when other major formations which had also taken part in the attack of 17th April were still resting far from the front. Two or three hundred men, almost all from the battalion chosen to lead the new offensive, failed to appear when their unit was leaving for the front and then announced that they would not march. The unit's officers and NCOs proved incapable of quelling the outbreak, which, however, was put down by the divisional commander within twenty-four hours.

News of this incident soon got round and other mutinous outbreaks followed. On 4th May a number of sudden desertions occurred among members of an infantry regiment in action in the Chemin-des-Dames area. In the quarters of a colonial regiment due to take part in an attack in the same sector *the men noisily refused to fight,* an action clearly provoked by the circulation of leaflets on which were blazoned such inflammatory slogans as "Down with the War!", "Death to the Warmongers!", etc. On 16th and 17th May serious trouble of a similar nature broke out in a battalion of Chasseurs, and in an infantry regiment in a reserve position on the Aisne. These unhappy incidents multiplied to a point where *the safety and cohesion of the whole army were in jeopardy.*

It was precisely on this same date, the 17th, that the French High Command was reorganised. Its first duty was to assess objectively the seriousness of the trouble so as to weigh the gravity of its task. It saw the deadly virus of indiscipline spreading. It received alarming reports from all sides. They poured in—almost uninterruptedly, alas! . . .

29th, 30th and 31st May: The situation deteriorated and indiscipline spread to the majority of the regiments of eight divisions and to a colonial artillery regiment, all of which had been in action in the Chemin-des-Dames sector or were about to be sent back there.

1st, 2nd and 3rd June: *Zenith of the crisis.* In fifteen to twenty units belonging to sixteen divisions, either in action or resting in the same area, men of all arms were involved for three days in the most violent outbreaks of disorder. . . .

Example of a Premeditated and Methodically Planned Mutiny in [the 129th Infantry] Regiment: 28th–30th May

This was an example of a type of mutiny *conceived in cold blood, systematically organised and obstinately conducted* in an infantry regiment which up to that moment had been regarded as quite first class. Planned over a long period, it developed without a hitch, and in an atmosphere of total assurance.

This unit had taken part in May 1916 in the first attempt to recapture Fort Douaumont, where it showed great courage and sustained heavy losses. From June 1916 to February 1917 it was almost continuously in the line in the tough Eparges sector, exposed to constant shelling, surprise attacks and enemy mines. At this point *symptoms of serious physical and moral exhaustion* became noticeable in its ranks—symptoms which affected the junior officers as well, and to which their superiors, up to the regimental and brigade commanders themselves, appeared to pay too little regard, whereas it should have made them doubly watchful and active, doubly willing to show themselves and take personal risks, to give encouragement and set an example. Action had been taken against certain of these officers whose grip on the situation had been notoriously feeble, and in February 1917 the unit was withdrawn for a rest. By the spring, there were grounds for hoping that when it returned to the fighting line it would once more justify its former reputation. But this moment was delayed, since the grand plan for a strategic exploitation of the attack of 16th April failed to materialise, and *the regiment was left in inglorious inactivity near Paris.* There the men, too closely in touch with the rear, were affected by the bad spirit in the interior. . . . And when, on Whit Sunday, the lorries arrived to bring this agreeable and restful existence to an end, and trundle them off to the dreaded destination of Laffaux, the harrowing farewells overcame their sense of duty. It was then that *they began to be influenced by the propaganda directed at them at the departure point, and to believe—what they were always being told—that they would be fools indeed to go and get themselves killed when so many others had apparently refused to march.*

On 28th May, at the end of its journey, the regiment installed itself in three small villages in a sector to the south of Soissons.

After the midday meal, "*la Soupe,*" between 150 and 180 men attended a meeting in one of the hamlets, listened to a number of inflammatory speeches, fell in on the road in marching order, and coolly informed their company officers, when these arrived to disperse them, *that they refused to go up to the line. They had,* they said, *had enough of the war. They wanted a cease-fire immediately* and thought the Deputies had been wrong in December not to negotiate on the German proposals. They claimed that as Russia crumbled, leaving the German war-machine free to re-mass on the French front, the Government were simply pulling the wool over people's eyes, and that in fact everyone knew that the Americans would not be able to come into the war in time to be of any use. The fighting soldiers, they complained, were not getting proper leave; their rations were inadequate, their wives and children were "starving to death." *They were no longer willing to sacrifice their lives when shirkers at home were earning all the money, taking the women around in cars, cornering all the best jobs, and while so many profiteers were waxing rich.*

The mood of these demonstrators was calm and resolute. They were not drunk. They wanted their protest reported to the Government. They still respected their officers and dispersed when these told them to do so.

Misled by the ease with which they appeared to have won this round, the officers, from the divisional commander down to the most junior second lieutenants, spent the night of the 28th/29th advising each other that the best line to adopt *was one of patience and accommodation.* . . .

This made it possible for the demonstrators of the day before to assemble again on the morning of the 29th and form themselves into a column—this time some 400 strong. Most of these had got themselves up to look like *strikers,* and appeared with walking sticks, flowers in their button-holes, and unbuttoned jackets. They marched in turn to the quarters of each of the two other battalions. There they were joined in the course of the morning by several hundred more supporters. By the end of the midday meal there were more than 800 of them, from every unit in the regiment. They answered to a bugle, and in due course moved off to rally support from the regiment next in line. Their discipline was excellent. They had been told by their leaders to do nothing which might provoke violence and to confine themselves to signifying *their fixed and unalterable determination to take no part in any further costly attacks.* They made this point firmly to the Divisional Commander. "You have nothing to fear, we are prepared to man the trenches, we will do our duty and the Boche will not get through. But we will not take part in attacks which result in nothing but useless casualties." . . . About mid-afternoon they reached the quarters of the neighbouring regiment. Here the mutineers were fewer in number but much wilder. They urged them to be calm and to maintain respect for their officers. Then, *led on as usual by some extremely skilful organisers,* who seem from the evidence to have acted like true mob leaders throughout, they decided to continue their impressive march round the other units of the division and then to go on and capture some trains in which to set off for Paris with their own crews in the drivers' cabs. But, if necessary, they were prepared to march on the capital by stages in order to bring their demands before the Chamber of Deputies. Meanwhile they returned to their own cantonments for the night.

At dawn on the 30th, under orders from the High Command, motor convoys arrived at the camps to act as transport for the three battalions. This time all the officers were at their posts, and with tougher instructions. They shouted louder than the agitators and made their men obey them. The mutineers put up some resistance but did board the lorries. On the journey they continued their attempts at incitement, and tried to stir up the troops they met on the way. They made "hands up" and "thumbs down" signs. They whistled. They sang the Internationale. They waved bits of red cloth. They distributed leaflets containing the text of their refusal to fight and encouraged others to follow their example.

On the evening of the 30th and on the following days the regiment was halted in isolation from other units, then moved to the Verdun sector by train. The rebellious spirit persisted, but the demonstrations became less frequent. The High Command split up the battalions, and during the month of June *Courts Martial were held.* A corporal and three privates were sentenced to death for "deserting their post and refusing to obey orders in the presence of the enemy." The regiment itself supplied the firing squads and several detachments for the expiatory ceremony, which took place without incident on 28th June. *On 29th June, the regiment was stripped of its col-*

ours. The battalion to which the leading spirits of the mutiny had belonged was disbanded on 16th July, and the necessary new postings among the officers took place.

That was the end of it. In July the two remaining battalions gave an honourable account of themselves at Verdun. In 1918 the regiment was reconstituted. It was twice mentioned in dispatches, received back its colours, and was decorated with the lanyard of the Croix de Guerre on the very spot where the 1917 mutinies had taken place. . . .

General Character of the Crisis from June to September The mutinies took many forms . . . and reached their peak on 2nd June, when seventeen outbreaks were reported. The situation remained serious up to 10th June, with an average of seven incidents a day. During the rest of the month the daily average was one. In July the total fell to seven incidents altogether, in August to four, and in September to one.

Altogether, *151 incidents were recorded and examined, of which 110 were concerted outbreaks of genuine gravity. . . .*

3. The Remedies

Since it was they who had allowed this evil to well up and reach the proportions of a flood, it was now the responsibility of the civil power to cut it off at its source and to make good the damage which it had caused to the national interest. While still reeling from the shock of their disillusion in the spring of 1917, they appeared determined not to fail in this task, the difficulty as well as the importance of which they fully recognised. Having reorganised the High Command of the armies, they gave it their full confidence. It was for the High Command to take the necessary steps to restore the balance of our fortunes in face of the enemy. It was the responsibility of the Government to supply it with the means it required, and to give it unfailing support; and this it promised to do.

The High Command lost no time in setting to work. It had a clear understanding of the causes of the crisis, and was determined to tackle them one after the other in whatever order circumstances might dictate.

The aims of its immediate measures were as follows:

To reaffirm the authority of military law and to secure the immediate arrest of the principal trouble-makers;

To stiffen the morale of the officers and to lay down a line of conduct which they must follow in order to regain the confidence of their men;

To protect the armies against contamination from the interior;

To draw up a new set of operational directives in conformity with what could actually be achieved.

Then would follow longer-term measures to be applied systematically to cure the disease and prevent its recurrence.

These would be as follows: With regard to the morale of the troops, no pains would be spared in providing for the welfare of the men who were bearing so much, in keeping them contented and raising their spirits by a fair allocation of military honours and leave, by improving the rations, combating drunkenness, and encouraging saving; and also, finally, by the efficient supervision of rest arrangements and rest camps;

In general, the spirit prevailing in the country at large and the lead to be given to the national Press would both continue to be closely studied;

On the tactical level, efficient training would be reintroduced, so that the troops engaged in future operations could look forward to achieving greater successes with fewer losses and would be given fresh confidence that they possessed the means to win.

It may be of interest to take the items of this list in order, and to study how the High Command's measures made themselves felt and the support afforded it by the Government.

Immediate Measures

Re-establishment of the Authority of Military Law and Action Taken against the Guilty In the grave circumstances of the moment, the most urgent necessity was that the activity of the principal trouble-makers should be broken on the spot. *Mutineers, drunk with slogans and alcohol, must be forced back to their obedience, and every means must be used to reduce to impotence the criminals who had exploited the distress of the fighting troops.*

The Commander-in-Chief, from the moment he took up his post, directed all his activities to this end, and, first by word of mouth, in the course of his tours of inspection, and afterwards in his written orders, demanded an attitude of inflexible firmness. . . .

. . . [T]he penalties imposed were severe. *The first to feel their force were the commanders of all units who had shown weakness incompatible with their duty and had failed to react after the first moment of surprise.* Two generals, nine lieutenant-colonels, fourteen battalion commanders and eighteen lieutenants or second lieutenants were deprived of their commands, being either relegated to less important posts, stripped of their temporary ranks, or posted elsewhere.

At the same time, on its own initiative or by goading the Government into action, the High Command worked to *reestablish most of the measures for suppressing indiscipline in the armies which had been gradually whittled away in 1916 and 1917.*

On 1st June, with the Government's authorisation, it ruled that, *wher-*

*ever the gravity of the crime demanded prompt and exemplary punishment,
an accused man should be brought straight before a Court Martial, without the benefit of preliminary proceedings,* and that proof of guilt supplied
by direct examination of the accused should be deemed to be sufficient. In
a capital case, once the sentence had been confirmed, either through the
failure of the accused to lodge an appeal within the limits of the time
allowed by law, or because his appeal had been rejected, it was laid down
that the formation to which the Court Martial was responsible should telegraph to GHQ stating its reasons for demanding immediate execution of
sentence; and that this sentence should be carried out as soon as the Commander-in-Chief had telegraphed giving the agreement of the Head of
State. . . .

On 11th June the Minister of War notified the Commander-in-Chief that
the *military authority would no longer be required to submit the transcript
of a capital trial to the President of the Republic, if the requirements of
discipline and national defence absolutely demanded that a sentence be
carried out without delay* and if the sentence in question was for concerted
or collective crimes, inciting men to go over to the enemy or join in an
armed rebellion, dereliction of duty, usurpation of authority, or, finally, the
commission of any destructive act endangering defence, the supply of provisions, or munitions of war. In any of these cases, *sentence of death
would be carried out as soon as the authorisation of the Commander-in-
Chief had been requested and obtained by telegram.* . . .

The exceptional measures agreed to by the Civil Power for the emergency were only conceded for a short period. *On the 14th July they were
revoked and the milder legislation introduced in 1916 and 1917 was revived.* The emergency measures were, however, in force long enough to
enable the most urgent measures of repression to be taken and to bring the
crisis under control.

Altogether, between May and October, 412 men were condemned to
death by the Courts Martial, 203 of whom were sentenced in June, 386 for
offences against military law or for acts of rebellion and twenty-six for
common law offences. In consequence of the large number of free pardons
and commuted sentences, *only seven men were, in fact, executed immediately, by order of the Commander-in-Chief, and only forty-eight after the
Head of State had confirmed the sentence.* . . .

**Measures to Restore a Proper Spirit among the Officers and Confi-
dence among the Men** To influence the healthy elements in the army and
to restore the lost confidence of the officers, the Commander-in-Chief published a Note on 19th May. This read:

I consider it time to draw the attention of all officers to the importance of maintaining high morale in the commissioned ranks.

Officers who have displayed heroic courage for almost three years hesitate to inform their superior officers of the difficulties they face in carrying out their duties, for fear of being taxed with faint-heartedness.

The result of this timid reluctance to speak out is that senior commanders persist with plans which would unquestionably have been altered or postponed had they been better informed. Often, preparations for an attack have been made in the absence of such necessary information.

It is up to commanding officers to adopt an attitude which will abolish this tendency.

A superior officer, in his relations with his subordinates, must at all times show himself approachable and friendly, willing to help them in finding solutions to the difficulties that hamper their work, ready to pass on any useful information and even to invite it.

In present-day conditions of warfare the murderous fire-power of modern weapons means that nothing can be left to chance. Planning for even the smallest operation must be undertaken in the minutest detail, and demands the co-operation and goodwill of all concerned.

Once, however, the preparations are complete, the decisions made and the orders given, the operation must be carried through with a vigour and determination which holds nothing back.

An attitude of kindliness and goodwill on the part of commanders is in the noblest tradition of the French army and in no way excludes firmness.

It is when such an attitude is lacking in a unit that an unfortunate and blameworthy spirit tends to arise. Men with a chip on their shoulder confide their bitterness to the don't-cares and the incompetents, and a discontented, restless and potentially dangerous mood is gradually built up.

The proper person to receive an officer's confidence is his chief. The chief must justify the confidence reposed in him—a confidence founded on mutual respect and on a common love of country.

I regard it as a matter of first importance that all relationships between officers should be guided by these principles.

At every level, immediate efforts were made to spread these ideas by word of mouth, using the medium of frequent, informal chats, unconstrained by considerations of rank. *The Commander-in-Chief himself took the lead in this, visiting a different unit at the front every day.* After inspecting it, he would gather around him the officers, NCOs, and a number of other ranks, talk to them frankly and as man to man, inviting them to forget about his rank for a few moments and to speak to him openly in their turn. He would give them his views on the general situation, speaking of the *confidence in victory* which their Allies possessed, until his listeners really felt it for themselves, and painting a picture of innumerable American troopships looming up on the horizon and making for the coasts of France. He brought within the compass of each man's understanding the basic aims of his *strategy* and how he intended to change the character of operations in order to make them less costly to our own troops and more deadly to those of the enemy. . . .

Finally, he concluded these talks by giving *tangible tokens of his goodwill to the fighting men.* He distributed the *Croix de Guerre,* the Military Medal and the Cross of the Legion of Honour lavishly to all those he wished to distinguish, calling them out from the ranks and decorating them on the spot without further formalities or citations. He also distributed souvenirs, small gifts of practical value, tobacco, and so forth. Then he would tour the camp, telling the local CO to make this or that improvement. He inspected the kitchens, to make sure that the food was adequate in quality as well as quantity to satisfy the men's needs. He checked the leave rosters. In fact, in every one of these matters, he endeavoured to spur the officers on to greater efficiency while at the same time taking care not to degrade them in the eyes of their men by the way he put his questions or made his comments.

The officers, inspired by this example, acquired a better understanding of the importance of the part assigned to them and recaptured an enthusiasm which many of them had lost. *The officers, at all levels from the generals and the staff down, now looked after the men's needs and took care not to send them into action without insuring that they had adequate support and that when they withdrew from the line to rest camps both their rations and their billets were as good as they could be.* The NCOs, in the fulfilment of their duties, were once more able to look to the officers for the backing which had too often failed them when the discouragement was at its height. Given this sort of support and direction, they recovered *a taste for acting on their own initiative* and tried once more to work with their superiors as useful members of the team. . . .

Protection of the Armies against Contamination from the Interior This restoration of confidence would only bear fruit if means were found to *protect the combatants from the effect of propaganda from the interior.*

As trouble spread from unit to unit, a strict watch was organised on doubtful elements in the army and an attempt made to extend this surveillance to cover the whole country. Telegraphic warnings were issued by GHQ to all formations concerned, naming suspects on whom the Special Service had information and giving details of their positions. The actions, contacts and correspondence of these men were watched with care, in an effort to prevent them from launching or continuing their work of pacifist propaganda and from passing on orders from organisers at home. For without question the danger came chiefly from the rear, and *the Commander-in-Chief considered it essential that the Government should launch an action parallel to his own to extirpate on the home front known centres of infection.* On the 22nd, 25th, 29th and 30th May and on 2nd June he informed the Minister that leaflets protesting against the continuation of the war had been distributed in large quantities to men on leave so that they could be distributed in the trenches and stuck up in stations and billets. Their texts constituted a whole programme of subversion. "Enough have died: Peace . . . Our womenfolk claim peace and their rights . . . etc. . . . etc. . . ." They were printed by the "Unions of Building Workers and Navvies" and distributed by "The Committee for the Defence of the Trade Union Movement" and "The Committee for the Resumption of International Relations," which had its headquarters in Paris, at 33 rue Grange-aux-Belles. The most energetic measures were urgently needed, the Commander-in-Chief declared, "to suppress this intolerable propaganda at its source and the most energetic measures must be taken to this end."

The last of the letters cited above, that of June 2nd, listed *the steps which the Government must take:*

(a) It should control and discipline the home-front organisations whose aim was to stir up disturbances in the army and cause it to revolt and mutiny; expel suspected neutrals; imprison the nationals of enemy powers who were still moving freely about the country; and arrest all agitators and bring them to trial.

(b) Exercise censorship and direction of the Press; forbid it to criticise the High Command, the shortages of equipment, the system of allocating periods of leave and rest; see that more discretion was exercised in reporting the Russian revolution, strikes in France and peace propaganda; and emphasise the great advantage to be expected from the intervention of the United States.

(c) Hasten the review of capital sentences by the Head of State.

(d) The gangs of condemned prisoners, the companies of Bulgarian and native labourers, all of them centres of indiscipline and demoralisation, must be sent to southern Algeria and Tunisia.

Anticipating the Government's decisions, the Commander-in-Chief took it on himself to send a telegram on 27th May putting Paris out of bounds to all men on leave from the African battalions, the Foreign Legion and other special formations too easily led astray and liable by their mere presence to aggravate any unrest either in the city itself or on the trains. As regards other formations, he ordered leave in Paris to be restricted to those who would be staying there in their own homes. He made all necessary provisions so that men without families or unable to reach them who had formerly been put up in the capital itself by various welfare organisations should be offered similar hospitality in the provinces by the same organisations or their equivalents on the spot, by local families, or by farmers prepared to bring home with them comrades in the same walk of life.

At all his interviews with members of the Government, whose measures he considered both too feeble and too slow, the Commander-in-Chief never ceased to call for *speed in closing down dangerous committees and groups of trouble-makers, in particular to prohibit trades union activities by mobilised men, which were illegal, and intolerable from the disciplinary point of view, and for the banning in the interior of all meetings not held for strictly professional purposes.* In his interviews with Ministers he insisted that however repugnant such measures might be to politicians profoundly attached to democratic principles and the defence of freedom, they were none the less essential at this critical hour, when the task was to save democracy itself from enslavement, which would certainly ensue if the weakness of the French nation continued and grew worse! . . .

Return to a Realistic Strategy Finally the Commander-in-Chief considered it most urgent to prescribe the scope of future operations which would follow the disastrously ineffective spring offensives. It was with this objective that he issued his Directive No. 1 of 19th May: "The balance of opposing forces on the northern and north-eastern fronts," he wrote, "means that a break-through followed by strategic exploitation is not at present a practical possibility. For the moment, therefore, we must apply our efforts to wearing down the enemy with the minimum of losses to ourselves." . . .

. . . [T]he aim was to obtain from a flexible strategy results hitherto sought from the tactical engagement of the troops. In modern warfare, even more than in that of the past, *much bloodshed can be avoided where several battles are skilfully and systematically directed in combination rather than where everything is staked on the hazard of one brutal and murderous attempted breakthrough, developed at length and with blind obstinacy at a single point.* With their limited but soundly-based experience in matters of warfare, the soldiers of 1917 understood this very well. They enthusiastically welcomed these operational reforms, and from the moment they felt the first practical effects of Directive No. 1 their morale rose strikingly.

Long-Term Measures

[Pétain describes policies taken to improve the granting of awards and leaves, to improve rations and to reduce drunkenness, as well as to allocate rest periods in a more equitable manner.]

General Supervision of the Country's Morale Despite all these precautions, the armies would still be exposed to contamination from the interior if a strict watch was not continually kept on the rear. . . .

On 23rd June the Commander-in-Chief wrote to the Minister of the Interior to inform him of a serious recurrence of the pamphlet propaganda campaign: "Enough have died: Peace!" . . . "The Russian Revolution and what Socialists should be doing about it" . . . "Spreading the Gospel" . . . "A Call to the People of Paris: Peace without Annexations!" . . . "Down with the War" . . . etc. . . . etc. "The Committee for the Resumption of International Relations and the Committee for the Defence of the Trade Union Movement," the Commander-in-Chief concluded, "seem to me to be playing a particularly harmful role. I call upon you urgently to take the necessary steps to suppress this renewed agitation."

On 9th July he asked the Minister of the Interior and the Minister of War *to see that he was supplied with regular information about subversive activities in the interior, so that he would be able to take steps to prevent them spreading among the troops or at least to counter their effects without delay.* In letters of 12th and 23rd July the two Ministers replied that they agreed to this request in principle.

In practice, the information supplied to the Commander-in-Chief was both spasmodic and incomplete, and he complained about this to the Minister of War on 28th July: "I am thus left in total ignorance of the present direction of the pacifist propaganda campaign and of the demonstrations in support of it. . . . I remain powerless against its machinations. . . . I ask you to put pressure on the Minister of the Interior to have the exchange of information about the pacifist campaign between the Security Department and my Intelligence Branch resumed. . . ." . . .

The clash between the Commander-in-Chief and the Minister of the Interior, which occurred for a short time in the days which followed the disturbances and was concerned with the steps needed to prevent their return, sprang from the difference between the two men's points of view. Both, no doubt, were equally concerned for the safety of the country, but the one had seen the danger at less close range than had the other, had not measured its full importance, and had bowed once more *to the Frenchman's unshakeable habit of putting respect for the liberty of the individual above all else, of wanting to let bygones be bygones and show mercy to those who had failed.* But the hour when such an attitude could be countenanced had not yet struck, and those at the front were determined to oppose it with unremitting persistence and vigour. These things deserve to be said, and to serve as lessons for the future. . . .

Despite his repeated efforts, it was only gradually that the Commander-in-Chief obtained acceptance of his principal demands. He managed to preserve his right to direct weekly access to the Minister of the Interior, but had no success, throughout the whole of the summer, in getting the centres of agitation extirpated root and branch. Thus it was that on 23rd September he was once more addressing the Minister of War on the harm done at the front by the circulation of the "Bonnet Rouge," and the bad effects of this journal on the morale of its regular readers.

Control of the National Press Being powerless to take the firm action he would have liked against these organs of defeatism, *the Commander-in-Chief turned his attention to the national Press,* fortunately the largest and most influential section of newspapers, *and attempted to steer it along the right path.* His aim was to persuade it to ban all pessimistic articles and, while obviously not overdoing it, to act as the mouthpiece of a spirit of healthy optimism.

To this end, "Press missions" were set up in July. Journalists and writers, with officers acting as guides, were taken on visits to units at interesting points of the front. Their articles, which gained in accuracy as a result, were submitted at GHQ to the scrutiny of officers appointed by the Commander-in-Chief and acting on his directions. The "copy" then passed to the Censor's office in Paris, now reorganised on lines acceptable to the Commander-in-Chief and in accordance with his views.

Since the Press did not always take kindly to this guidance and control, the Commander-in-Chief had to return to the subject on many occasions in his letters to the Minister of War. "It is essential," he wrote on 23rd August, "that what the troops read in the newspapers should provide them with grounds for perseverance and enthusiasm and not for scepticism and bitterness. . . . Tactful direction must be applied to the Press to persuade it to be less critical and more factual in its reports, and to remember that the blank spaces resulting from the Censor's excisions only leave the reader free, in a very harmful way, to imagine goodness knows what. . . ." On 20th October he expressed a wish that the newspapers should devote less space to their favourite theme of "our victorious army" and more to articles which placed due emphasis on "the ever increasing weight of our allies' contribution and the certain prospect of a victorious peace which could alone be counted on to bring general prosperity and ensure the recovery of our industry, trade and agriculture." On 30th November he underlined the danger of giving too much publicity to the Courts Martial then in progress, and to events in Russia, which had a demoralising effect.

The Commander-in-Chief continued to send the Government such suggestions right up to the end of the war, in a constant effort to prevent the nerves of the soldiers, now raw with weariness, from being harmfully worked upon. And when publications detrimental to morale slipped through the Censor's net in Paris and percolated through from the interior to the armies, they were seized in accordance with detailed regulations brought to the notice of Army Group commanders in Notes of 7th and 15th October, 1917.

12. Max Weber, *Between Two Laws*

Max Weber (1864–1920) was a man of vast learning whose scholarship was closely coordinated with his deep concern for political and social developments in Germany and the world. Born in Erfurt, he grew up in Berlin where his family moved in 1869. Weber's father rose to prominence in the National Liberal party and the Weber home became an important meeting place for leading figures in German society and politics.

In 1882 Weber entered the University of Heidelberg to study law. He joined a student fraternity and took to dueling and beer drinking with alacrity, but also entered into wide-ranging studies in the fields of economics, history, philosophy, and theology. At this time he also came under the influence of his uncle, Hermann Baumgarten, a professor of history in Strassburg and a Liberal who had endorsed Bismarck in 1866 only to become disillusioned in the 1880s with the consequences of Bismarck's caesaristic rule (Baumgarten was also one of Treitschke's most vigorous domestic critics). Baumgarten's example helped Weber to begin to question the self-satisfied National Liberalism of his father and to assume the stance of an independent critic whose primary concern was the security and power of the German state.

In 1884 Weber enrolled in the University of Berlin, writing a dissertation on the law of medieval trading associations. Having decided on an academic career rather than the practice of law, Weber habilitated in 1891 with a study on Roman agrarian history. He became an associate professor at Berlin in 1893, but was called to a professorship in economics at Freiburg in 1894 (for Weber's inaugural speech, "The National State and Economic Policy," see volume 8 of this series, document 41).

Shortly after Weber assumed a chair at the University of Heidelberg, he endured a protracted period of serious mental problems—insomnia, anxiety, and exhaustion—forcing him to withdraw from teaching. In 1902 he had sufficiently recovered to resume a career as a scholar, although not a teacher. He began to publish important writings on the nature and method of the social sciences and the sociology of religion. By 1913 he had completed most of his masterpiece, a treatise on general sociology published posthumously, *Economy and Society*.

At the outbreak of the war in 1914 Weber was carried away by the general nationalist enthusiasm, but later became a stern critic of German policies, especially the declaration of unrestricted submarine warfare in 1917. Following the end of the war he became a strong supporter of constitutional democracy and attempted to enter politics. He ran for office, without success, but played an important role in drafting the constitution of the Weimar Republic.

The following letter of Max Weber to Gertrud Bäumer was published in the periodical *Die Frau* in February 1916. It was written as an answer to an article by a Swiss pacifist, published earlier in the same magazine. It formed part of a discussion series which had the title "The Laws of the Gospel and the Laws of the Fatherland."

May I contribute to the debate about the meaning of our war by emphasizing one aspect of the problem whose importance, I am certain, you will appreciate: *our responsibility in the face of history.* This may sound melodramatic; the matter itself is plain:

A numerically "greater" nation, a nation organized as a power-state, finds itself, by the very fact of being such a nation, confronted with tasks totally different from those entrusted to nations like the Swiss, the Danes, the Dutch, the Norwegians. This certainly means in no way that a nation which is "little" in regard to numbers and power should be considered less "valuable" or less "important" in the forum of History. Such a nation just has different duties and, therefore, different chances of cultural self-realization. You are familiar with Jacob Burckhardt's assertion of the diabolic character of power which has perplexed so many of his readers. But this characterization of power is quite in tune with those cultural values that are the particular heritage of a nation like the Swiss who cannot shoulder the burdens carried by great military nations (and has no historical obligation to do so). We ourselves cannot be too grateful to destiny that there are Germans who live outside the national power-state. Not plain middleclass virtues alone and genuine democracy (which never has been achieved yet in any great power-state), but other much more intimate and yet eternal values can flourish only on the soil of communities that renounce political

From Max Weber, *Gesammelte Politische Schriften,* 2d edition (Tübingen: J. C. B. Mohr, 1958), pp. 139–42. Translated by C. W. Mackauer.

power. The same is true even of certain artistic values: such a true German as Gottfried Keller never could have found his quite peculiar, unique form in the middle of a war-camp; and a war-camp our state has to be.

On the other hand, no nation, once organized as a great power, can shun its proper tasks. Future generations, our own descendants in particular, will not blame the Danes, the Swiss, the Dutch, the Norwegians if, without a struggle, the rule over the world—and that ultimately means the determination of the character of the civilization of the future—should be divided between the ordinances of Russian officials on the one side and the conventions of Anglo-Saxon "society" on the other—perhaps with some touch of Latin *"raison"* added for good measure. But *we* could be blamed. And justly so. For we are a power-state and we, therefore, in contrast to the "little" nations, can in this contest throw our weight into the scales of history; so we, not they, must in the eyes of history—and that means: of posterity—carry the sacred burden of standing firm against the inundation of the world by these two powers. Should we shirk this duty, then the German Empire would be a costly and vain luxury, harmful to civilization; we never ought to have indulged in it, and we should get rid of it as quickly as possible and should replace it with a political order similar to that of the Swiss: we should dissolve our state into small, politically impotent cantons (perhaps each centered around a princely court to take care of the arts); and we should sit back and wait to see how long our neighbors allow us to enjoy this idyllic cultivation of little-nation values which, in this case, we never should have forsaken. But it would be a grave mistake to believe that a political entity like the German Empire could espouse, through a *voluntary* decision, a pacifist policy of the Swiss brand, i.e., that it could confine itself to blocking, by means of a brave militia, any violation of its frontiers. The Swiss are, at least in principle, not in the way of any other state's urge for expansion, not only because of their lack of power but because of their geographical situation as well—although even they may, if we should be defeated, immediately be exposed to the demands of Italian annexationism. The very existence of a great power, however—and we cannot help being one—is an obstacle in the way of other power-states, especially in the way of the Russian peasant's hunger for more land (which is rooted in his lack of civilization) and of the power interests of the Russian state-church and bureaucracy. I cannot see how these conditions could have been changed. Austria certainly was among all great countries the one most free from any desire for expansion, and *for this very reason*—what is so often overlooked—the most endangered. We had no choice but either to grasp the spokes of the wheel, at the last possible moment before Austria was destroyed, or to look quietly on and have the same wheel crush ourselves a few years later. If it is not possible to turn the Russian urge for expansion into a different direction again, these conditions will remain the same in times to come. That is our destiny, and all pacifist talk will not change it. And it is equally obvious that, even if we wanted, we could not in the past and cannot in the future betray, *without disgrace,* the decision that we once had made—at the time when we created our Empire—nor escape from the duties which we accepted with that decision.

The pacifism of American "ladies" (of both sexes!) is truly the most disgusting "cant" that (in perfectly good faith) was ever pronounced and advocated from the lofty height of a tea table—with the pharisaism of the parasite who pockets his war profits and looks down on the barbarians in the trenches. Even the antimilitaristic "neutrality" of the Swiss and their repudiation of the power-state occasionally contains more than a bit of a truly pharisaical lack of understanding for the tragic dilemma involved in the historical duties of a nation that finds itself in the position of a power-state. Yet, in spite of this, we remain objective enough to see that behind this attitude there lies a sincere conviction which unfortunately, because of our peculiar destiny, we Germans of the Empire cannot accept as our own.

But the Gospel one should leave out of this controversy—or one should fully accept it. If one does this, there can be only Tolstoy's conclusion, no other. Whoever receives a single penny of rent that others have to pay (directly or indirectly), whoever possesses or consumes anything tainted with the sweat of another man's toil—he feeds his life from the spoils derived from that loveless and pitiless economic struggle for existence which in bourgeois language is called a "peaceful effort in the service of civilization." It is just another form of the struggle of man against man in which, year after year, not millions but hundreds of millions are stunted in body and soul, are wiped out, or, at least, are condemned to lead an existence that, alas, is infinitely more deprived of any recognizable "meaning" than the defense of the honor (and that means nothing but the inescapable historical duties) of one's own nation by all—the women as well as the men, for they, too, are "soldiers" if they do their duty. The attitude of the Gospels in this connection is in the decisive points absolutely unambiguous: the Gospels are in opposition not just to war (they do not even especially mention it), but ultimately to all and any laws of the social world in so far as it wants to be a world of secular "civilization," i.e., a world of strictly human beauty, dignity, honor, and greatness. Those who do not draw these consequences—Tolstoy himself has done so only when he was about to die—should know that they are bound to the laws of the secular world which include, for all foreseeable future, the possibility and inevitability of wars for power, and that only within the framework of these laws they can fulfill the "demand of the hour." But this demand has been and is different for the Germans in Germany and for the Germans in Switzerland. This will always be so. For whatever participates in the achievements of the power-state, is entangled in the laws of the "power-pragma" that rules over all political history.

John Stuart Mill, this old sober empiricist, has said that on the basis of experience alone one does not reach the idea of *one* God—it seems to me: least of all a God of charity—but the idea of polytheism. It cannot be denied: whoever lives in the "world" (in the Christian meaning of this term) can derive from his personal experience no other conclusion but that of a struggle among a multiplicity of values, each of which, taken by itself, seems to demand absolute loyalty. Man must choose which one of these gods he wants to serve and has to serve, or, perhaps, at what time he should serve the one and at what time the other. But always he will find himself in conflict with one or several of the gods of this world, and especially far away from the God of Christianity—at least that God who was proclaimed in the Sermon on the Mount.

13. Sigmund Freud, *Thoughts for the Times on War and Death*

Regarded as one of the most powerful influences on twentieth-century Western thought, Sigmund Freud (1856–1939) was born in Moravia (in what is now Czechoslovakia) and lived almost the whole of his life in the city of Vienna, arriving there at the age of three and moving only in 1938, when he sought refuge in London from Nazi persecution. A physician by training, Freud laid the foundations for the new discipline he called psychoanalysis—a discipline which focuses upon the exploration of the unconscious aspects of the mind—during the 1890s. He originally intended psychoanalysis as a mode of cure for the nervous patients, especially hysterics, who seemed to be proliferating at the turn of the century and who had proven resistant to all standard modes of medical treatment. But Freud soon began boldly to enlarge the scope of his creation. *The Interpretation of Dreams* (1900) applied to a manifestation of normal mental functioning—dreams—some of the insights Freud had gained in his work with hysterics, and it thus went a long way towards transforming psychoanalysis from a theory of psychopathology to a theory of general psychology. *Three Essays on the Theory of Sexuality* (1905) presented a psychoanalytic theory of child development, and *Totem and Taboo* (1913) offered a psychoanalytic anthropology, treating the origins of such cultural products as religion and moral injunctions. In the essay reprinted below, written in 1915 and inspired by Freud's own civilian experience of the first year of the Great War, Freud uses psychoanalytical tools to speculate about the basis of civilization itself.

At this date, Freud postulated two human instincts: libido and the ego-preservative instinct. By 1920, in part as a response to the First World War, Freud would revise this scheme, postulating instead the two instincts of libido and aggression. The latter instinct would be given pride of place when Freud returned to the subject of his 1915 essay in the now classic *Civilization and Its Discontents* (1930). Freud's essays on civilization reveal, more clearly than his clinical studies, the tragic nature of his vision—that is, the unending conflict he perceived between the light of science and reason and the darkness lurking within human nature.

---

1. The Disillusionment of the War

In the confusion of wartime in which we are caught up, relying as we must on one-sided information, standing too close to the great changes that have already taken place or are beginning to, and without a glimmering of the future that is being shaped, we ourselves are at a loss as to the significance of the impressions which press in upon us and as to the value of the judge-ments which we form. We cannot but feel that no event has ever destroyed so much that is precious in the common possessions of humanity, confused so many of the clearest intelligences, or so thoroughly debased what is highest. Science herself has lost her passionless impartiality; her deeply embittered servants seek for weapons from her with which to contribute towards the struggle with the enemy. Anthropologists feel driven to declare him inferior and degenerate, psychiatrists issue a diagnosis of his disease of mind or spirit. Probably, however, our sense of these immediate evils is disproportionately strong, and we are not entitled to compare them with the evils of other times which we have not experienced.

The individual who is not himself a combatant—and so a cog in the gigantic machine of war—feels bewildered in his orientation, and inhib-ited in his powers and activities. I believe that he will welcome any indica-tion, however slight, which will make it easier for him to find his bearings within himself at least. I propose to pick out two among the factors which

From Sigmund Freud, "Thoughts for the Times on War and Death," in *The Standard Edi-tion of the Complete Psychological Works of Sigmund Freud,* edited and translated by James Strachey (London: Hogarth, 1951), pp. 275–300. Footnotes deleted. Reprinted by permis-sion of Sigmund Freud Copyrights, the Institute of Psycho-Analysis, and the Hogarth Press. See also *Collected Papers,* vol. 4, authorized translation under the supervision of Joan Riviere (New York: Basic Books, 1959), pp. 288–317.

are responsible for the mental distress felt by non-combatants, against
which it is such a heavy task to struggle, and to treat of them here: the
disillusionment which this war has evoked, and the altered attitude towards
death which this—like every other war—forces upon us.

When I speak of disillusionment, everyone will know at once what I
mean. One need not be a sentimentalist; one may perceive the biological
and psychological necessity for suffering in the economy of human life,
and yet condemn war both in its means and ends and long for the cessation
of all wars. We have told ourselves, no doubt, that wars can never cease so
long as nations live under such widely differing conditions, so long as the
value of individual life is so variously assessed among them, and so long as
the animosities which divide them represent such powerful motive forces
in the mind. We were prepared to find that wars between the primitive and
the civilized peoples, between the races who are divided by the colour of
their skin—wars, even, against and among the nationalities of Europe
whose civilization is little developed or has been lost—would occupy mankind for some time to come. But we permitted ourselves to have other
hopes. We had expected the great world-dominating nations of white race
upon whom the leadership of the human species has fallen, who were
known to have world-wide interests as their concern, to whose creative
powers were due not only our technical advances towards the control of
nature but the artistic and scientific standards of civilization—we had expected these peoples to succeed in discovering another way of settling misunderstandings and conflicts of interest. Within each of these nations high
norms of moral conduct were laid down for the individual, to which his
manner of life was bound to conform if he desired to take part in a civilized
community. These ordinances, often too stringent, demanded a great deal
of him—much self-restraint, much renunciation of instinctual satisfaction.
He was above all forbidden to make use of the immense advantages to be
gained by the practice of lying and deception in the competition with his
fellow-men. The civilized states regarded these moral standards as the
basis of their existence. They took serious steps if anyone ventured to tam-
per with them, and often declared it improper even to subject them to examination by a critical intelligence. It was to be assumed, therefore, that
the state itself would respect them, and would not think of undertaking anything against them which would contradict the basis of its own existence.
Observation showed, to be sure, that embedded in these civilized states
there were remnants of certain other peoples, which were universally unpopular and had therefore been only reluctantly, and even so not fully, admitted to participation in the common work of civilization, for which they
had shown themselves suitable enough. But the great nations themselves, it
might have been supposed, would have acquired so much comprehension

of what they had in common, and so much tolerance for their differences, that "foreigner" and "enemy" could no longer be merged, as they still were in classical antiquity, into a single concept.

Relying on this unity among the civilized peoples, countless men and women have exchanged their native home for a foreign one, and made their existence dependent on the intercommunications between friendly nations. Moreover anyone who was not by stress of circumstance confined to one spot could create for himself out of all the advantages and attractions of these civilized countries a new and wider fatherland, in which he could move about without hindrance or suspicion. In this way he enjoyed the blue sea and the grey; the beauty of snow-covered mountains and of green meadow lands; the magic of northern forests and the splendour of southern vegetation; the mood evoked by landscapes that recall great historical events, and the silence of untouched nature. This new fatherland was a museum for him, too, filled with all the treasures which the artists of civilized humanity had in the successive centuries created and left behind. As he wandered from one gallery to another in this museum, he could recognize with impartial appreciation what varied types of perfection a mixture of blood, the course of history, and the special quality of their mother-earth had produced among his compatriots in this wider sense. Here he would find cool, inflexible energy developed to the highest point; there, the graceful art of beautifying existence; elsewhere, the feeling for orderliness and law, or others among the qualities which have made mankind the lords of the earth.

Nor must we forget that each of these citizens of the civilized world had created for himself a "Parnassus" and a "School of Athens" of his own. From among the great thinkers, writers and artists of all nations he had chosen those to whom he considered he owed the best of what he had been able to achieve in enjoyment and understanding of life, and he had venerated them along with the immortal ancients as well as with the familiar masters of his own tongue. None of these great men had seemed to him foreign because they spoke another language—neither the incomparable explorer of human passions, nor the intoxicated worshipper of beauty, nor the powerful and menacing prophet, nor the subtle satirist; and he never reproached himself on that account for being a renegade towards his own nation and his beloved mother-tongue.

The enjoyment of this common civilization was disturbed from time to time by warning voices, which declared that old traditional differences made wars inevitable, even among the members of a community such as this. We refused to believe it; but if such a war were to happen, how did we picture it? We saw it as an opportunity for demonstrating the progress of comity among men since the era when the Greek Amphictyonic Council proclaimed that no city of the league might be destroyed, nor its olive-groves cut down, nor its water-supply stopped; we pictured it as a chivalrous passage of arms, which would limit itself to establishing the superiority of one side in the struggle, while as far as possible avoiding acute suffering that could contribute nothing to the decision, and granting complete immunity for the wounded who had to withdraw from the contest, as well as for the doctors and nurses who devoted themselves to their recovery. There would, of course, be the utmost consideration for the non-combatant classes of the population—for women who take no part in war-work, and for the children who, when they are grown up, should become on both sides one another's friends and helpers. And again, all the international undertakings and institutions in which the common civilization of peace-time had been embodied would be maintained.

Even a war like this would have produced enough horror and suffering; but it would not have interrupted the development of ethical relations between the collective individuals of mankind—the peoples and states.

Then the war in which we had refused to believe broke out, and it brought—disillusionment. Not only is it more bloody and more destructive than any war of other days, because of the enormously increased perfection of weapons of attack and defence; it is at least as cruel, as embittered, as implacable as any that has preceded it. It disregards all the restrictions known as International Law, which in peace-time the states had bound themselves to observe; it ignores the prerogatives of the wounded and the medical service, the distinction between civil and military sections of the population, the claims of private property. It tramples in blind fury on all that comes in its way, as though there were to be no future and no peace among men after it is over. It cuts all the common bonds between the contending peoples, and threatens to leave a legacy of embitterment that will make any renewal of those bonds impossible for a long time to come.

Moreover, it has brought to light an almost incredible phenomenon: the civilized nations know and understand one another so little that one can turn against the other with hate and loathing. Indeed, one of the great civilized nations is so universally unpopular that the attempt can actually be made to exclude it from the civilized community as "barbaric," although it has long proved its fitness by the magnificent contributions to that community which it has made. We live in hopes that the pages of an impartial history will prove that that nation, in whose language we write and for whose victory our dear ones are fighting, has been precisely the one which has least transgressed the laws of civilization. But at such a time who dares to set himself up as judge in his own cause?

Peoples are more or less represented by the states which they form, and these states by the governments which rule them. The individual citizen can with horror convince himself in this war of what would occasionally cross his mind in peace-time—that the state has forbidden to the individual the practice of wrongdoing, not because it desires to abolish it, but because it desires to monopolize it, like salt and tobacco. A belligerent state permits itself every such misdeed, every such act of violence, as would disgrace the individual. It makes use against the enemy not only of the accepted *ruses de guerre,* but of deliberate lying and deception as well—and to a degree which seems to exceed the usage of former wars. The state exacts the utmost degree of obedience and sacrifice from its citizens, but at the same time it treats them like children by an excess of secrecy and a censorship upon news and expressions of opinion which leaves the spirits of those whose intellects it thus suppresses defenceless against every unfavourable turn of events and every sinister rumour. It absolves itself from the guarantees and treaties by which it was bound to other states, and confesses shamelessly to its own rapacity and lust for power, which the private individual has then to sanction in the name of patriotism.

It should not be objected that the state cannot refrain from wrong-doing, since that would place it at a disadvantage. It is no less disadvantageous, as a general rule, for the individual man to conform to the standards of morality and refrain from brutal and arbitrary conduct; and the state seldom proves able to indemnify him for the sacrifices it exacts. Nor should it be a matter for surprise that this relaxation of all the moral ties between the collective individuals of mankind should have had repercussions on the morality of individuals; for our conscience is not the inflexible judge that ethical teachers declare it, but in its origin is "social anxiety" and nothing else. When the community no longer raises objections, there is an end, too, to the suppression of evil passions, and men perpetrate deeds of cruelty, fraud, treachery and barbarity so incompatible with their level of civilization that one would have thought them impossible.

Well may the citizen of the civilized world of whom I have spoken stand helpless in a world that has grown strange to him—his great fatherland disintegrated, its common estates laid waste, his fellow-citizens divided and debased!

There is something to be said, however, in criticism of his disappointment. Strictly speaking it is not justified, for it consists in the destruction of an illusion. We welcome illusions because they spare us unpleasurable feelings, and enable us to enjoy satisfactions instead. We must not complain, then, if now and again they come into collision with some portion of reality, and are shattered against it.

Two things in this war have aroused our sense of disillusionment: the low morality shown externally by states which in their internal relations pose as the guardians of moral standards, and the brutality shown by individuals whom, as participants in the highest human civilization, one would not have thought capable of such behaviour.

Let us begin with the second point and try to formulate, in a few brief words, the point of view that we wish to criticize. How, in point of fact, do we imagine the process by which an individual rises to a comparatively high plane of morality? The first answer will no doubt simply be that he is virtuous and noble from birth—from the very start. We shall not consider this view any further here. A second answer will suggest that we are concerned with a developmental process, and will probably assume that the development consists in eradicating his evil human tendencies and, under the influence of education and a civilized environment, replacing them by good ones. If so, it is nevertheless surprising that evil should re-emerge with such force in anyone who has been brought up in this way.

But this answer also contains the thesis which we propose to contradict. In reality, there is no such thing as "eradicating" evil. Psychological—or, more strictly speaking, psycho-analytic—investigation shows instead that the deepest essence of human nature consists of instinctual impulses which are of an elementary nature, which are similar in all men and which aim at the satisfaction of certain primal needs. These impulses in themselves are neither good nor bad. We classify them and their expressions in that way, according to their relation to the needs and demands of the human community. It must be granted that all the impulses which society condemns as evil—let us take as representative the selfish and the cruel ones—are of this primitive kind.

These primitive impulses undergo a lengthy process of development before they are allowed to become active in the adult. They are inhibited, directed towards other aims and fields, become commingled, alter their objects, and are to some extent turned back upon their possessor. Reaction-formations against certain instincts take the deceptive form of a change in their content, as though egoism had changed into altruism, or cruelty into pity. These reaction-formations are facilitated by the circumstance that some instinctual impulses make their appearance almost from the first in pairs of opposites—a very remarkable phenomenon, and one strange to the lay public, which is termed "ambivalence of feeling." The most easily observed and comprehensible instance of this is the fact that intense love and intense hatred are so often to be found together in the same person. Psycho-analysis adds that the two opposed feelings not infrequently have the same person for their object.

It is not until all these "instinctual vicissitudes" have been surmounted that what we call a person's character is formed, and this, as we know, can only very inadequately be classified as "good" or "bad." A human being is seldom altogether good or bad; he is usually "good" in one relation and "bad" in another, or "good" in certain external circumstances and in others decidedly "bad." It is interesting to find that the pre-existence of strong "bad" impulses in infancy is often the actual condition for an unmistakable inclination towards "good" in the adult. Those who as children have been the most pronounced egoists may well become the most helpful and self-sacrificing members of the community; most of our sentimentalists, friends of humanity and protectors of animals have been evolved from little sadists and animal-tormentors.

The transformation of "bad" instincts is brought about by two factors working in the same direction, an internal and an external one. The internal factor consists in the influence exercised on the bad (let us say, the egoistic) instincts by erotism—that is, by the human need for love, taken in its widest sense. By the admixture of *erotic* components the egoistic instincts are transformed into *social* ones. We learn to value being loved as an advantage for which we are willing to sacrifice other advantages. The external factor is the force exercised by upbringing, which represents the claims of our cultural environment, and this is continued later by the direct pressure of that environment. Civilization has been attained through the renunciation of instinctual satisfaction, and it demands the same renunciation from each newcomer in turn. Throughout an individual's life there is a constant replacement of external by internal compulsion. The influences of civilization cause an ever-increasing transformation of egoistic trends into altruistic and social ones by an admixture of erotic elements. In the last resort it may be assumed that every internal compulsion which makes itself felt in the development of human beings was originally—that is, in the *history of mankind*—only an external one. Those who are born to-day bring with them as an inherited organization some degree of tendency (disposition) towards the transformation of egoistic into social instincts, and this disposition is easily stimulated into bringing about that result. A further portion of this instinctual transformation has to be accomplished during the life of the individual himself. So the human being is subject not only to the pressure of his immediate cultural environment, but also to the influence of the cultural history of his ancestors.

If we give the name of "susceptibility to culture" to a man's personal capacity for the transformation of the egoistic impulses under the influence of erotism, we may further affirm that this susceptibility is made up of two parts, one innate and the other acquired in the course of life, and that the relation of the two to each other and to that portion of the instinctual life which remains untransformed is a very variable one.

Generally speaking, we are apt to attach too much importance to the innate part, and in addition to this we run the risk of over-estimating the total susceptibility to culture in comparison with the portion of instinctual life which has remained primitive—that is, we are misled into regarding men as "better" than they actually are. For there is yet another element which obscures our judgement and falsifies the issue in a favourable sense.

The instinctual impulses of other people are of course hidden from our observation. We infer them from their actions and behaviour, which we trace back to *motives* arising from their instinctual life. Such an inference is bound to be erroneous in many cases. This or that action which is "good" from the cultural point of view may in one instance originate from a "noble" motive, in another not. Ethical theorists class as "good" actions only those which are the outcome of good impulses; to the others they refuse recognition. But society, which is practical in its aims, is not on the whole troubled by this distinction; it is content if a man regulates his behaviour and actions by the precepts of civilization, and is little concerned with his motives.

We have learned that the *external compulsion* exercised on a human being by his upbringing and environment produces a further transformation towards good in his instinctual life—a further turning from egoism towards altruism. But this is not the regular or necessary effect of the external compulsion. Upbringing and environment not only offer benefits in the way of love, but also employ other kinds of incentive, namely, rewards and punishments. In this way their effect may turn out to be that a person who is subjected to their influence will choose to behave well in the cultural sense of the phrase, although no ennoblement of instinct, no transformation of egoistic into altruistic inclinations, has taken place in him. The result will, roughly speaking, be the same; only a particular concatenation of circumstances will reveal that one man always acts in a good way because his instinctual inclinations compel him to, and the other is good only in so far and for so long as such cultural behaviour is advantageous for his own selfish purposes. But superficial acquaintance with an individual will not enable us to distinguish between the two cases, and we are certainly misled by our optimism into grossly exaggerating the number of human beings who have been transformed in a cultural sense.

Civilized society, which demands good conduct and does not trouble itself about the instinctual basis of this conduct, has thus won over to obedience a great many people who are not in this following their own natures. Encouraged by this success, society has allowed itself to be misled into tightening the moral standard to the greatest possible degree, and it has thus forced its members into a yet greater estrangement from their instinctual disposition. They are consequently subject to an unceasing suppression of instinct, and the resulting tension betrays itself in the most remarkable phenomena of reaction and compensation. In the domain of sexuality, where such suppression is most difficult to carry out, the result is seen in the reactive phenomena of neurotic disorders. Elsewhere the pressure of civilization brings in its train no pathological results, it is true, but is shown in malformations of character, and in the perpetual readiness of the inhibited instincts to break through to satisfaction at any suitable opportunity. Anyone thus compelled to act continually in accordance with precepts which are not the expression of his instinctual inclinations, is living, psychologically speaking, beyond his means, and may objectively be described as a hypocrite, whether he is clearly aware of the incongruity or not. It is undeniable that our contemporary civilization favours the production of this form of hypocrisy to an extraordinary extent. One might venture to say that it is built up on such hypocrisy, and that it would have to submit to far-reaching modifications if people were to undertake to live in accordance with psychological truth. Thus there are very many more cultural hypocrites than truly civilized men—indeed, it is a debatable point whether a certain degree of cultural hypocrisy is not indispensable for the maintenance of civilization, because the susceptibility to culture which has hitherto been organized in the minds of present-day men would perhaps not prove sufficient for the task. On the other hand, the maintenance of civilization even on so dubious a basis offers the prospect of paving the way in each new generation for a more far-reaching transformation of instinct which shall be the vehicle of a better civilization.

We may already derive one consolation from this discussion: our mortification and our painful disillusionment on account of the uncivilized behaviour of our fellow-citizens of the world during this war were unjustified. They were based on an illusion to which we had given way. In reality our fellow-citizens have not sunk so low as we feared, because they had never risen so high as we believed. The fact that the collective individuals of mankind, the peoples and states, mutually abrogated their moral restraints naturally prompted these individual citizens to withdraw for a while from the constant pressure of civilization and to grant a temporary satisfaction to the instincts which they had been holding in check. This probably involved no breach in their relative morality within their own nations.

We may, however, obtain a deeper insight than this into the change brought about by the war in our former compatriots, and at the same time receive a warning against doing them an injustice. For the development of the mind shows a peculiarity which is present in no other developmental process. When a village grows into a town or a child into a man, the village and the child become lost in the town and the man. Memory alone can trace the old features in the new picture; and in fact the old materials or forms have been got rid of and replaced by new ones. It is otherwise with the development of the mind. Here one can describe the state of affairs, which has nothing to compare with it, only by saying that in this case every earlier stage of development persists alongside the later stage which has arisen from it; here succession also involves co-existence, although it is to the same materials that the whole series of transformations has applied. The earlier mental state may not have manifested itself for years, but none the less it is so far present that it may at any time again become the mode of expression of the forces in the mind, and indeed the only one, as though all later developments had been annulled or undone. This extraordinary plasticity of mental developments is not unrestricted as regards direction; it may be described as a special capacity for involution—for regression— since it may well happen that a later and higher stage of development, once abandoned, cannot be reached again. But the primitive stages can always be re-established; the primitive mind is, in the fullest meaning of the word, imperishable.

What are called mental diseases inevitably produce an impression in the layman that intellectual and mental life have been destroyed. In reality, the destruction only applies to later acquisitions and developments. The essence of mental disease lies in a return to earlier states of affective life and of functioning. An excellent example of the plasticity of mental life is afforded by the state of sleep, which is our goal every night. Since we have learnt to interpret even absurd and confused dreams, we know that whenever we go to sleep we throw off our hard-won morality like a garment, and put it on again next morning. This stripping of ourselves is not, of course, dangerous, because we are paralysed, condemned to inactivity, by the state of sleep. It is only dreams that can tell us about the regression of our emotional life to one of the earliest stages of development. For instance, it is noteworthy that all our dreams are governed by purely egoistic motives. One of my English friends put forward this thesis at a scientific meeting in America, whereupon a lady who was present remarked that that might be the case in Austria, but she could assert as regards herself and her friends that *they* were altruistic even in their dreams. My friend, although himself of English race, was obliged to contradict the lady emphatically on the ground of his personal experience in dream-analysis, and to declare that in their dreams highminded American ladies were quite as egoistic as the Austrians.

Thus the transformation of instinct, on which our susceptibility to culture is based, may also be permanently or temporarily undone by the impacts of life. The influences of war are undoubtedly among the forces that can bring about such involution; so we need not deny susceptibility to culture to all who are at the present time behaving in an uncivilized way, and we may anticipate that the ennoblement of their instincts will be restored in more peaceful times.

There is, however, another symptom in our fellow-citizens of the world which has perhaps astonished and shocked us no less than the descent from their ethical heights which has given us so much pain. What I have in mind is the want of insight shown by the best intellects, their obduracy, their inaccessibility to the most forcible arguments and their uncritical credulity towards the most disputable assertions. This indeed presents a lamentable picture, and I wish to say emphatically that in this I am by no means a blind partisan who finds all the intellectual shortcomings on one side. But this phenomenon is much easier to account for and much less disquieting than the one we have just considered. Students of human nature and philosophers have long ago taught us that we are mistaken in regarding our intelligence as an independent force and in overlooking its dependence on emotional life. Our intellect, they teach us, can function reliably only when it is removed from the influences of strong emotional impulses; otherwise it behaves merely as an instrument of the will and delivers the inference which the will requires. Thus, in their view, logical arguments are impotent against affective interests, and that is why disputes backed by reasons, which in Falstaff's phrase are "as plenty as blackberries," are so unfruitful in the world of interests. Psycho-analytic experience has, if possible, further confirmed this statement. It can show every day that the shrewdest people will all of a sudden behave without insight, like imbeciles, as soon as the necessary insight is confronted by an emotional resistance, but that they will completely regain their understanding once that resistance has been overcome. The logical bedazzlement which this war has conjured up in our fellow-citizens, many of them the best of their kind, is therefore a secondary phenomenon, a consequence of emotional excitement, and is bound, we may hope, to disappear with it.

Having in this way once more come to understand our fellow-citizens who are now alienated from us, we shall much more easily endure the disappointment which the nations, the collective individuals of mankind, have caused us, for the demands we make upon these should be far more modest. Perhaps they are recapitulating the course of individual development, and today still represent very primitive phases in organization and in the formation of higher unities. It is in agreement with this that the educative factor of an external compulsion towards morality, which we found was so effective in individuals, is as yet barely discernible in them. We had hoped, certainly, that the extensive community of interests established by commerce and production would constitute the germ of such a compulsion, but it would seem that nations still obey their passions far more readily than their interests. Their interests serve them, at most, as *rationalizations* for their passions; they put forward their interests in order to be able to give reasons for satisfying their passions. It is, to be sure, a mystery why the collective individuals should in fact despise, hate and detest one another—

every nation against every other—and even in times of peace. I cannot tell why that is so. It is just as though when it becomes a question of a number of people, not to say millions, all individual moral acquisitions are obliterated, and only the most primitive, the oldest, the crudest mental attitudes are left. It may be that only later stages in development will be able to make some change in this regrettable state of affairs. But a little more truthfulness and honesty on all sides—in the relations of men to one another and between them and their rulers—should also smooth the way for this transformation.

2. Our Attitude towards Death

The second factor to which I attribute our present sense of estrangement in this once lovely and congenial world is the disturbance that has taken place in the attitude which we have hitherto adopted towards death.

That attitude was far from straightforward. To anyone who listened to us we were of course prepared to maintain that death was the necessary outcome of life, that everyone owes nature a death and must expect to pay the debt—in short, that death was natural, undeniable and unavoidable. In reality, however, we were accustomed to behave as if it were otherwise. We showed an unmistakable tendency to put death on one side, to eliminate it from life. We tried to hush it up; indeed we even have a saying [in German]: "to think of something as though it were death." That is, as though it were our own death, of course. It is indeed impossible to imagine our own death; and whenever we attempt to do so we can perceive that we are in fact still present as spectators. Hence the psycho-analytic school could venture on the assertion that at bottom no one believes in his own death, or, to put the same thing in another way, that in the unconscious every one of us is convinced of his own immortality.

When it comes to someone else's death, the civilized man will carefully avoid speaking of such a possibility in the hearing of the person under sentence. Children alone disregard this restriction; they unashamedly threaten one another with the possibility of dying, and even go so far as to do the same thing to someone whom they love, as, for instance: "Dear Mummy, when you're dead I'll do this or that." The civilized adult can hardly even entertain the thought of another person's death without seeming to himself hard-hearted or wicked; unless, of course, as a doctor or lawyer or something of the kind, he has to deal with death professionally. Least of all will he allow himself to think of the other person's death if some gain to himself in freedom, property or position is bound up with it. This sensitiveness of ours does not, of course, prevent the occurrence of deaths; when one does happen, we are always deeply affected, and it is as though we were badly shaken in our expectations. Our habit is to lay stress on the fortuitous causation of the death—accident, disease, infection, advanced age; in this way we betray an effort to reduce death from a necessity to a chance event. A number of simultaneous deaths strikes us as something extremely terrible. Towards the actual person who has died we adopt a special attitude—something almost like admiration for someone who has accomplished a very difficult task. We suspend criticism of him, overlook his possible misdeeds, declare that *"de mortuis nil nisi bonum,"* and think it justifiable to set out all that is most favourable to his memory in the funeral oration and upon the tombstone. Consideration for the dead, who, after all, no longer need it, is more important to us than the truth, and certainly, for most of us, than consideration for the living.

The complement to this cultural and conventional attitude towards death is provided by our complete collapse when death has struck down someone whom we love—a parent or a partner in marriage, a brother or sister, a child or a close friend. Our hopes, our desires and our pleasures lie in the grave with him, we will not be consoled, we will not fill the lost one's place. We behave as if we were a kind of Asra, who die when those they love die.

But this attitude of ours towards death has a powerful effect on our lives. Life is impoverished, it loses in interest, when the highest stake in the game of living, life itself, may not be risked. It becomes as shallow and empty as, let us say, an American flirtation, in which it is understood from the first that nothing is to happen, as contrasted with a Continental love-affair in which both partners must constantly bear its serious consequences in mind. Our emotional ties, the unbearable intensity of our grief, make us disinclined to court danger for ourselves and for those who belong to us. We dare not contemplate a great many undertakings which are dangerous but in fact indispensable, such as attempts at artificial flight, expeditions to distant countries or experiments with explosive substances. We are paralysed by the thought of who is to take the son's place with his mother, the husband's with his wife, the father's with his children, if a disaster should occur. Thus the tendency to exclude death from our calculations in life brings in its train many other renunciations and exclusions. Yet the motto of the Hanseatic League ran: *"Navigare necesse est, vivere non necesse."* ("It is necessary to sail the seas, it is not necessary to live.")

It is an inevitable result of all this that we should seek in the world of fiction, in literature and in the theatre compensation for what has been lost in life. There we still find people who know how to die—who, indeed, even manage to kill someone else. There alone too the condition can be fulfilled which makes it possible for us to reconcile ourselves with death: namely, that behind all the vicissitudes of life we should still be able to preserve a life intact. For it is really too sad that in life it should be as it is in chess, where one false move may force us to resign the game, but with the difference that we can start no second game, no return-match. In the realm of fiction we find the plurality of lives which we need. We die with the hero with whom we have identified ourselves; yet we survive him, and are ready to die again just as safely with another hero.

It is evident that war is bound to sweep away this conventional treatment of death. Death will no longer be denied; we are forced to believe in it. People really die; and no longer one by one, but many, often tens of thousands, in a single day. And death is no longer a chance event. To be sure, it still seems a matter of chance whether a bullet hits this man or that; but a second bullet may well hit the survivor; and the accumulation of deaths puts an end to the impression of chance. Life has, indeed, become interesting again; it has recovered its full content.

Here a distinction should be made between two groups—those who themselves risk their lives in battle, and those who have stayed at home and have only to wait for the loss of one of their dear ones by wounds, disease or infection. It would be most interesting, no doubt, to study the changes in the psychology of the combatants, but I know too little about it. We must restrict ourselves to the second group, to which we ourselves belong. I have said already that in my opinion the bewilderment and the paralysis of capacity, from which we suffer, are essentially determined among other things by the circumstance that we are unable to maintain our former attitude towards death, and have not yet found a new one. It may assist us to do this if we direct our psychological enquiry towards two other relations to death—the one which we may ascribe to primaeval, prehistoric men, and the one which still exists in every one of us, but which conceals itself, invisible to consciousness, in the deeper strata of our mental life.

What the attitude of prehistoric man was towards death is, of course, only known to us by inferences and constructions, but I believe that these methods have furnished us with fairly trustworthy conclusions.

Primaeval man took up a very remarkable attitude towards death. It was far from consistent; it was indeed most contradictory. On the one hand, he took death seriously, recognized it as the termination of life and made use of it in that sense; on the other hand, he also denied death and reduced it to nothing. This contradiction arose from the fact that he took up radically different attitudes towards the death of other people, of strangers, of enemies, and towards his own. He had no objection to someone else's death; it meant the annihilation of someone he hated, and primitive man had no scruples against bringing it about. He was no doubt a very passionate creature and more cruel and more malignant than other animals. He liked to kill, and killed as a matter of course. The instinct which is said to restrain other animals from killing and devouring their own species need not be attributed to him.

Hence the primaeval history of mankind is filled with murder. Even today, the history of the world which our children learn at school is esssentially a series of murders of peoples. The obscure sense of guilt to which mankind has been subject since prehistoric times, and which in some religions has been condensed into the doctrine of primal guilt, of original sin, is probably the outcome of a blood-guilt incurred by prehistoric man. In my book *Totem and Taboo* (1912–13) I have, following clues given by Robertson Smith, Atkinson and Charles Darwin, tried to guess the nature of this primal guilt, and I believe, too, that the Christian doctrine of today enables us to deduce it. If the Son of God was obliged to sacrifice his life to redeem mankind from original sin, then by the law of talion, the requital of like by like, that sin must have been a killing, a murder. Nothing else could call for the sacrifice of a life for its expiation. And the original sin was an offence against God the Father, the primal crime of mankind must have been a parricide, the killing of the primal father of the primitive human horde, whose mnemic image was later transfigured into a deity.

His own death was certainly just as unimaginable and unreal for primaeval man as it is for any one of us today. But there was for him one case in which the two opposite attitudes towards death collided and came into conflict with each other; and this case became highly important and productive of far-reaching consequences. It occurred when primaeval man saw someone who belonged to him die—his wife, his child, his friend—whom he undoubtedly loved as we love ours, for love cannot be much younger than the lust to kill. Then, in his pain, he was forced to learn that one can die, too, oneself, and his whole being revolted against the admission; for each of these loved ones was, after all, a part of his own beloved self. But, on the other hand, deaths such as these pleased him as well, since in each of the loved persons there was also something of the stranger. The law of ambivalence of feeling, which to this day governs our emotional relations with those whom we love most, certainly had a very much wider validity in primaeval times. Thus these beloved dead had also been enemies and strangers who had aroused in him some degree of hostile feeling.

Philosophers have declared that the intellectual enigma presented to primaeval man by the picture of death forced him to reflection, and thus became the starting-point of all speculation. I believe that here the philosophers are thinking too philosophically, and giving too little consideration to the motives that were primarily operative. I should like therefore to limit and correct their assertion. In my view, primaeval man must have triumphed beside the body of his slain enemy, without being led to rack his brains about the enigma of life and death. What released the spirit of enquiry in man was not the intellectual enigma, and not every death, but the conflict of feeling at the death of loved yet alien and hated persons. Of this conflict of feeling psychology was the first offspring. Man could no longer keep death at a distance, for he had tasted it in his pain about the dead; but he was nevertheless unwilling to acknowledge it, for he could not conceive of himself as dead. So he devised a compromise: he conceded the fact of his own death as well, but denied it the significance of annihilation—a significance which he had had no motive for denying where the death of his enemy was concerned. It was beside the dead body of someone he loved that he invented spirits, and his sense of guilt at the satisfaction mingled with his sorrow turned these new-born spirits into evil demons that had to be dreaded. The [physical] changes brought about by death suggested to him the division of the individual into a body and a soul—originally several souls. In this way his train of thought ran parallel with the process of disintegration which sets in with death. His persisting memory of the dead became the basis for assuming other forms of existence and gave him the conception of a life continuing after apparent death.

These subsequent existences were at first no more than appendages to the existence which death had brought to a close—shadowy, empty of content, and valued at little until later times; they still bore the character of wretched makeshifts. We may recall the answer made to Odysseus by the soul of Achilles:

> "For of old, when thou wast alive, we Argives honoured thee even as the gods, and now that thou art here, thou rulest mightily over the dead. Wherefore grieve not at all that thou art dead, Achilles."
>
> So I spoke, and he straightway made answer and said: "Nay, seek not to speak soothingly to me of death, glorious Odysseus. I should choose, so I might live on earth, to serve as the hireling of another, of some portionless man whose livelihood was but small, rather than to be lord over all the dead that have perished."

Or in Heine's powerful and bitter parody:

> Der kleinste lebendige Philister
> Zu Stuckert am Neckar
> Viel glücklicher ist er
> Als ich, der Pelide, der tote Held,
> Der Schattenfürst in der Unterwelt.

It was only later that religions succeeded in representing this after-life as the more desirable, the truly valid one, and in reducing the life which is ended by death to a mere preparation. After this, it was no more than consistent to extend life backwards into the past, to form the notion of earlier existences, of the transmigration of souls and of reincarnation, all with the purpose of depriving death of its meaning as the termination of life. So early did the denial of death, which we have described [p. 168] as a "conventional and cultural attitude," have its origin.

What came into existence beside the dead body of the loved one was not only the doctrine of the soul, the belief in immortality and a powerful source of man's sense of guilt, but also the earliest ethical commandments. The first and most important prohibition made by the awakening conscience was: "Thou shalt not kill." It was acquired in relation to dead people who were loved, as a reaction against the satisfaction of the hatred hidden behind the grief for them; and it was gradually extended to strangers who were not loved, and finally even to enemies.

This final extension of the commandment is no longer experienced by civilized man. When the furious struggle of the present war has been decided, each one of the victorious fighters will return home joyfully to his wife and children, unchecked and undisturbed by thoughts of the enemies he has killed whether at close quarters or at long range. It is worthy of note that the primitive races which still survive in the world, and are undoubtedly closer than we are to primaeval man, act differently in this respect, or did until they came under the influence of our civilization. Savages—Australians, Bushmen, Tierra del Fuegans—are far from being remorseless murderers; when they return victorious from the war-path they may not set foot in their villages or touch their wives till they have atoned for the murders they committed in war by penances which are often long and tedious. It is easy, of course, to attribute this to their superstition: the savage still goes in fear of the avenging spirits of the slain. But the spirits of his slain enemy are nothing but the expression of his bad conscience about his blood-guilt; behind this superstition there lies concealed a vein of ethical sensitiveness which has been lost by us civilized men.

Pious souls, no doubt, who would like to believe that our nature is remote from any contact with what is evil and base, will not fail to use the early appearance and the urgency of the prohibition against murder as the basis for gratifying conclusions as to the strength of the ethical impulses which must have been implanted in us. Unfortunately this argument proves even more for the opposite view. So powerful a prohibition can only be directed against an equally powerful impulse. What no human soul desires stands in no need of prohibition; it is excluded automatically. The very emphasis laid on the commandment "Thou shalt not kill" makes it certain that we spring from an endless series of generations of murderers, who had the lust for killing in their blood, as, perhaps, we ourselves have today. Mankind's ethical strivings, whose strength and significance we need not in the least depreciate, were acquired in the course of man's history; since then they have become, though unfortunately only in a very variable amount, the inherited property of contemporary men.

Let us now leave primaeval man, and turn to the unconscious in our own mental life. Here we depend entirely upon the psycho-analytic method of investigation, the only one which reaches to such depths. What, we ask, is the attitude of our unconscious towards the problem of death? The answer must be: almost exactly the same as that of primaeval man. In this respect, as in many others, the man of prehistoric times survives unchanged in our unconscious. Our unconscious, then, does not believe in its own death; it behaves as if it were immortal. What we call our "unconscious"—the deepest strata of our minds, made up of instinctual impulses—knows nothing that is negative, and no negation; in it contradictories coincide. For that reason it does not know its own death, for to that we can give only a negative content. Thus there is nothing instinctual in us which responds to a belief in death. This may even be the secret of heroism. The rational grounds for heroism rest on a judgement that the subject's own life cannot be so precious as certain abstract and general goods. But more frequent, in my view, is the instinctive and impulsive heroism which knows no such reasons, and flouts danger in the spirit of Anzengruber's *Steinklopferhans:* "Nothing can happen to *me.*" Or else those reasons only serve to clear away the hesitations which might hold back the heroic reaction that corresponds to the unconscious. The fear of death, which dominates us oftener than we know, is on the other hand something secondary, and is usually the outcome of a sense of guilt.

On the other hand, for strangers and for enemies we do acknowledge death, and consign them to it quite as readily and unhesitatingly as did primaeval man. There is, it is true, a distinction here which will be pronounced decisive so far as real life is concerned. Our unconscious does not carry out the killing; it merely thinks it and wishes it. But it would be wrong so completely to undervalue this psychical reality as compared with factual reality. It is significant and momentous enough. In our unconscious impulses we daily and hourly get rid of anyone who stands in our way, of anyone who has offended or injured us. The expression "Devil take him!", which so often comes to people's lips in joking anger and which really means "Death take him!", is in our unconscious a serious and powerful death-wish. Indeed, our unconscious will murder even for trifles; like the ancient Athenian code of Draco, it knows no other punishment for crime than death. And this has a certain consistency, for every injury to our almighty and autocratic ego is at bottom a crime of *lèse-majesté.*

And so, if we are to be judged by our unconscious wishful impulses, we ourselves are, like primaeval man, a gang of murderers. It is fortunate that all these wishes do not possess the potency that was attributed to them in primaeval times; in the cross-fire of mutual curses mankind would long since have perished, the best and wisest of men and the loveliest and fairest of women with the rest.

Psycho-analysis finds as a rule no credence among laymen for assertions such as these. They reject them as calumnies which are confuted by conscious experience, and they adroitly overlook the faint indications by which even the unconscious is apt to betray itself to consciousness. It is therefore relevant to point out that many thinkers who could not have been influenced by psycho-analysis have quite definitely accused our unspoken thoughts of being ready, heedless of the prohibition against murder, to get rid of anything which stands in our way. From many examples of this I will choose one that has become famous:

In *Le Père Goriot,* Balzac alludes to a passage in the works of J. J. Rousseau where that author asks the reader what he would do if—without leaving Paris and of course without being discovered—he could kill, with great profit to himself, an old mandarin in Peking by a mere act of will. Rousseau implies that he would not give much for the life of that dignitary. *"Tuer son mandarin"* has become a proverbial phrase for this secret readiness, present even in modern man.

There are also a whole number of cynical jokes and anecdotes which reveal the same tendency—such, for instance, as the words attributed to a husband: "If one of us two dies, I shall move to Paris." Such cynical jokes would not be possible unless they contained an unacknowledged truth which could not be admitted if it were expressed seriously and without disguise. In jest—it is well known—one may even tell the truth.

Just as for primaeval man, so also for our unconscious, there is one case in which the two opposing attitudes towards death, the one which acknowledges it as the annihilation of life and the other which denies it as unreal, collide and come into conflict. This case is the same as in primal ages: the death, or the risk of death, of someone we love, a parent or a partner in marriage, a brother or sister, a child or a dear friend. These loved ones are on the one hand an inner possession, components of our own ego; but on the other hand they are partly strangers, even enemies. With the exception of only a very few situations, there adheres to the tenderest and most intimate of our love-relations a small portion of hostility which can excite an unconscious death-wish. But this conflict due to ambivalence does not now, as it did then, lead to the doctrine of the soul and ethics, but to neurosis, which affords us deep insight into normal mental life as well. How often have physicians who practise psycho-analysis had to deal with the symptom of an exaggerated worry over the well-being of relatives, or with entirely unfounded self-reproaches after the death of a loved person. The study of such phenomena has left them in no doubt about the extent and importance of unconscious death-wishes.

The layman feels an extraordinary horror at the possibility of such feelings, and takes this aversion as a legitimate ground for disbelief in the assertions of psycho-analysis. Mistakenly, I think. No depreciation of feelings of love is intended, and there is in fact none. It is indeed foreign to our intelligence as well as to our feelings thus to couple love and hate; but Nature, by making use of this pair of opposites, contrives to keep love ever vigilant and fresh, so as to guard it against the hate which lurks behind it. It might be said that we owe the fairest flowerings of our love to the reaction against the hostile impulse which we sense within us.

To sum up: our unconscious is just as inaccessible to the idea of our own death, just as murderously inclined towards strangers, just as divided (that is, ambivalent) towards those we love, as was primaeval man. But how far we have moved from this primal state in our conventional and cultural attitude towards death!

It is easy to see how war impinges on this dichotomy. It strips us of the later accretions of civilization, and lays bare the primal man in each of us. It compels us once more to be heroes who cannot believe in their own death; it stamps strangers as enemies, whose death is to be brought about or desired; it tells us to disregard the death of those we love. But war cannot be abolished; so long as the conditions of existence among nations are so different and their mutual repulsion so violent, there are bound to be wars. The question then arises: Is it not we who should give in, who should adapt ourselves to war? Should we not confess that in our civilized attitude towards death we are once again living psychologically beyond our means, and should we not rather turn back and recognize the truth? Would it not be better to give death the place in reality and in our thoughts which is its due, and to give a little more prominence to the unconscious attitude towards death which we have hitherto so carefully suppressed? This hardly seems an advance to higher achievement, but rather in some respects a backward step—a regression; but it has the advantage of taking the truth more into account, and of making life more tolerable for us once again. To tolerate life remains, after all, the first duty of all living beings. Illusion becomes valueless if it makes this harder for us.

We recall the old saying: *Si vis pacem, para bellum.* If you want to preserve peace, arm for war.

It would be in keeping with the times to alter it: *Si vis vitam, para mortem.* If you want to endure life, prepare yourself for death.

14. John Maynard Keynes, *The Economic Consequences of the Peace*

John Maynard Keynes (1883–1946) was educated at Eton and Cambridge, where he studied mathematics and economics. In 1908 he was appointed lecturer in economics at Cambridge, where he was also elected to a fellowship at King's College. In 1915 Keynes was named to a temporary position at the British Treasury and attended the Peace Conference at Paris in 1919 as the principal representative of the Treasury. Dissatisfied with the harsh, punitive terms of the treaty of Versailles against Germany, terms which he felt Germany could not possibly meet and which would seriously disrupt all of the European economies, Keynes resigned his official position and wrote a scathing denunciation of the economic aspects of the peace settlement in the book from which the selections below are reproduced. The book became a best-seller and played a significant part in shaping subsequent British attitudes towards Germany and the Versailles treaty in the 1920s and 1930s.

Thereafter Keynes resumed his position in economics at Cambridge University. His original and powerful mind made him one of the leading economists, perhaps the leading economist, of his time. His book, *The General Theory of Employment, Interest and Money,* first published in 1936, constituted a landmark in economic theory. Keynes's proposals during the Depression for using government intervention, and especially public works spending, to restore aggregate demand, to stimulate industrial recovery, and to expand employment became an influential model for public policy makers in both Europe and America after 1945. During World War II Keynes returned to government service and assumed a leading role in the financial negotiations between Britain and America during and immediately after the war.

The subject of Keynes's famous indictment, the treaty signed at Versailles in June 1919, imposed a series of draconian economic, territorial, and military requirements on Germany, including a prohibition of a possible annexation of Austria, the cession of Alsace-Lorraine to France and large parts of West Prussia and Posen to Poland, the confiscation of all German colonies, Allied occupation of the west bank of the Rhine for fifteen years, and the internationalization of the German rivers. Danzig was declared a free city with Poland responsible for its foreign affairs, while the Saar Basin was placed under international control for fifteen years, and France given ownership of its extensive coal mines. Germany was also forced to accept the famous Clause 231, which postulated sole German responsibility for the damages incurred by the Allies during the war, "as a consequence of the war imposed upon them by the aggression of Germany and her allies," and it was held responsible for paying huge reparations, the final amount of which was to be presented to the new German government by 1 May 1921. Severe restrictions were placed on German armed forces (the army limited to 100,000 regulars), and Germany lost much of its merchant marine fleet as well.

Although it also provided for the creation of a League of Nations (to which Germany was not admitted), the treaty seemed to most German political leaders to bear little resemblance to the famous Fourteen Points, which Woodrow Wilson had proposed to Congress on 8 January 1918 as a basis for the postwar settlement and on the basis of which the last Imperial German government, led by Prince Max of Baden, had appealed for peace on 3–4 October 1918.

Chapter 3. The Conference

In Chapters 4 and 5 I shall study in some detail the economic and financial provisions of the Treaty of Peace with Germany. But it will be easier to appreciate the true origin of many of these terms if we examine here some of the personal factors which influenced their preparation. In attempting this task, I touch, inevitably, questions of motive, on which spectators are liable to error and are not entitled to take on themselves the responsibilities of final judgment. Yet, if I seem in this chapter to assume sometimes the liberties which are habitual to historians, but which, in spite of the greater knowledge with which we speak, we generally hesitate to assume towards contemporaries, let the reader excuse me when he remembers how greatly, if it is to understand its destiny, the world needs light, even if it is partial and uncertain, on the complex struggle of human will and purpose, not yet finished, which, concentrated in the persons of four individuals in a manner never paralleled, made them, in the first months of 1919, the microcosm of mankind.

In those parts of the Treaty with which I am here concerned, the lead was taken by the French, in the sense that it was generally they who made in the first instance the most definite and the most extreme proposals. This was partly a matter of tactics. When the final result is expected to be a compromise, it is often prudent to start from an extreme position; and the French anticipated at the outset—like most other persons—a double process of compromise, first of all to suit the ideas of their allies and associates, and secondly in the course of the Peace Conference proper with the Germans themselves. These tactics were justified by the event. Clemenceau gained a reputation for moderation with his colleagues in Council by sometimes throwing over with an air of intellectual impartiality the more

From John Maynard Keynes, *The Economic Consequences of the Peace* (New York: Harcourt, Brace and Howe, 1920), pp. 27–54, 226–28; © 1920 by Harcourt Brace and Howe, Inc.; copyright renewed 1948 by Lydia Lopokova Keynes. Reprinted by permission of the publisher, The Royal Economic Society, and Macmillan, London and Basingstoke.

extreme proposals of his ministers; and much went through where the American and British critics were naturally a little ignorant of the true point at issue, or where too persistent criticism by France's allies put them in a position which they felt as invidious, of always appearing to take the enemy's part and to argue his case. Where, therefore, British and American interests were not seriously involved their criticism grew slack, and some provisions were thus passed which the French themselves did not take very seriously, and for which the eleventh-hour decision to allow no discussion with the Germans removed the opportunity of remedy.

But, apart from tactics, the French had a policy. Although Clemenceau might curtly abandon the claims of a Klotz or a Loucheur, or close his eyes with an air of fatigue when French interests were no longer involved in the discussion, he knew which points were vital, and these he abated little. In so far as the main economic lines of the Treaty represent an intellectual idea, it is the idea of France and of Clemenceau.

Clemenceau was by far the most eminent member of the Council of Four, and he had taken the measure of his colleagues. He alone both had an idea and had considered it in all its consequences. His age, his character, his wit, and his appearance joined to give him objectivity and a defined outline in an environment of confusion. One could not despise Clemenceau or dislike him, but only take a different view as to the nature of civilized man, or indulge, at least, a different hope.

The figure and bearing of Clemenceau are universally familiar. At the Council of Four he wore a square-tailed coat of very good, thick black broadcloth, and on his hands, which were never uncovered, gray suède gloves; his boots were of thick black leather, very good, but of a country style, and sometimes fastened in front, curiously, by a buckle instead of laces. His seat in the room in the President's house, where the regular meetings of the Council of Four were held (as distinguished from their private and unattended conferences in a smaller chamber below), was on a square brocaded chair in the middle of the semicircle facing the fireplace, with Signor Orlando on his left, the President next by the fireplace, and the Prime Minister opposite on the other side of the fireplace on his right. He carried no papers and no portfolio, and was unattended by any personal secretary, though several French ministers and officials appropriate to the particular matter in hand would be present round him. His walk, his hand, and his voice were not lacking in vigor, but he bore nevertheless, especially after the attempt upon him, the aspect of a very old man conserving his strength for important occasions. He spoke seldom, leaving the initial statement of the French case to his ministers or officials; he closed his eyes often and sat back in his chair with an impassive face of parchment, his gray gloved hands clasped in front of him. A short sentence, decisive or cynical, was generally sufficient, a question, an unqualified abandonment of his ministers, whose face would not be saved, or a display of obstinacy reinforced by a few words in a piquantly delivered English. But speech and passion were not lacking when they were wanted, and the sudden outburst of words, often followed by a fit of deep coughing from the chest, produced their impression rather by force and surprise than by persuasion.

Not infrequently Mr. Lloyd George, after delivering a speech in English, would, during the period of its interpretation into French, cross the hearthrug to the President to reinforce his case by some *ad hominem* argument in private conversation, or to sound the ground for a compromise— and this would sometimes be the signal for a general upheaval and disorder. The President's advisers would press round him, a moment later the British experts would dribble across to learn the result or see that all was well, and next the French would be there, a little suspicious lest the others were arranging something behind them, until all the room were on their feet and conversation was general in both languages. My last and most vivid impression is of such a scene—the President and the Prime Minister as the center of a surging mob and a babel of sound, a welter of eager, impromptu compromises and counter-compromises, all sound and fury signifying nothing, on what was an unreal question anyhow, the great issues of the morning's meeting forgotten and neglected; and Clemenceau silent and aloof on the outskirts—for nothing which touched the security of France was forward—throned, in his gray gloves, on the brocade chair, dry in soul and empty of hope, very old and tired, but surveying the scene with a cynical and almost impish air; and when at last silence was restored and the company had returned to their places, it was to discover that he had disappeared.

He felt about France what Pericles felt of Athens—unique value in her, nothing else mattering; but his theory of politics was Bismarck's. He had one illusion—France; and one disillusion—mankind, including Frenchmen, and his colleagues not least. His principles for the peace can be expressed simply. In the first place, he was a foremost believer in the view of German psychology that the German understands and can understand nothing but intimidation, that he is without generosity or remorse in negotiation, that there is no advantage he will not take of you, and no extent to which he will not demean himself for profit, that he is without honor, pride, or mercy. Therefore you must never negotiate with a German or conciliate him; you must dictate to him. On no other terms will he respect you, or will you prevent him from cheating you. But it is doubtful how far he thought these characteristics peculiar to Germany, or whether his candid view of some other nations was fundamentally different. His philosophy had, therefore, no place for "sentimentality" in international relations. Nations are real things, of whom you love one and feel for the rest indifference—or hatred. The glory of the nation you love is a desirable end,—but generally to be obtained at your neighbor's expense. The politics of power are inevitable, and there is nothing very new to learn about this war or the end it was fought for; England had destroyed, as in each preceding century, a trade rival; a mighty chapter had been closed in the secular struggle between the glories of Germany and of France. Prudence required some measure of lip service to the "ideals" of foolish Americans and hypocritical Englishmen; but it would be stupid to believe that there is much room in the world, as it really is, for such affairs as the League of Nations, or any sense in the principle of self-determination except as an ingenious formula for rearranging the balance of power in one's own interests.

These, however, are generalities. In tracing the practical details of the Peace which he thought necessary for the power and the security of France, we must go back to the historical causes which had operated during his lifetime. Before the Franco-German war the populations of France and Germany were approximately equal; but the coal and iron and shipping of Germany were in their infancy, and the wealth of France was greatly superior. Even after the loss of Alsace-Lorraine there was no great discrepancy between the real resources of the two countries. But in the intervening period the relative position had changed completely. By 1914 the population of Germany was nearly seventy per cent in excess of that of France; she had become one of the first manufacturing and trading nations of the world; her technical skill and her means for the production of future wealth were unequaled. France on the other hand had a stationary or declining population, and, relatively to others, had fallen seriously behind in wealth and in the power to produce it.

In spite, therefore, of France's victorious issue from the present struggle (with the aid, this time, of England and America), her future position remained precarious in the eyes of one who took the view that European civil war is to be regarded as a normal, or at least a recurrent, state of affairs for the future, and that the sort of conflicts between organized great powers which have occupied the past hundred years will also engage the next. According to this vision of the future, European history is to be a perpetual prize-fight, of which France has won this round, but of which this round is certainly not the last. From the belief that essentially the old order does not change, being based on human nature which is always the same, and from a consequent skepticism of all that class of doctrine which the League of Nations stands for, the policy of France and of Clemenceau followed logically. For a Peace of magnanimity or of fair and equal treatment, based on such "ideology" as the Fourteen Points of the President, could only have the effect of shortening the interval of Germany's recovery and hastening the day when she will once again hurl at France her greater numbers and her superior resources and technical skill. Hence the necessity of "guarantees"; and each guarantee that was taken, by increasing irritation and thus the probability of a subsequent *Revanche* by Germany, made necessary yet further provisions to crush. Thus, as soon as this view of the world is adopted and the other discarded, a demand for a Carthaginian Peace is inevitable, to the full extent of the momentary power to impose it. For Clemenceau made no pretense of considering himself bound by the Fourteen Points and left chiefly to others such concoctions as were necessary from time to time to save the scruples or the face of the President.

So far as possible, therefore, it was the policy of France to set the clock back and to undo what, since 1870, the progress of Germany had accomplished. By loss of territory and other measures her population was to be curtailed; but chiefly the economic system, upon which she depended for her new strength, the vast fabric built upon iron, coal, and transport must be destroyed. If France could seize, even in part, what Germany was compelled to drop, the inequality of strength between the two rivals for European hegemony might be remedied for many generations.

Hence sprang those cumulative provisions [in the treaty of Versailles— ED.] for the destruction of highly organized economic life. . . .

This is the policy of an old man, whose most vivid impressions and most lively imagination are of the past and not of the future. He sees the issue in terms of France and Germany, not of humanity and of European civilization struggling forwards to a new order. The war has bitten into his consciousness somewhat differently from ours, and he neither expects nor hopes that we are at the threshold of a new age.

It happens, however, that it is not only an ideal question that is at issue. My purpose in this book is to show that the Carthaginian Peace is not *practically* right or possible. Although the school of thought from which it springs is aware of the economic factor, it overlooks, nevertheless, the deeper economic tendencies which are to govern the future. The clock cannot be set back. You cannot restore Central Europe to 1870 without setting up such strains in the European structure and letting loose such human and spiritual forces as, pushing beyond frontiers and races, will overwhelm not only you and your "guarantees," but your institutions, and the existing order of your Society.

By what legerdemain was this policy substituted for the Fourteen Points, and how did the President come to accept it? The answer to these questions is difficult and depends on elements of character and psychology and on the subtle influence of surroundings, which are hard to detect and harder still to describe. But, if ever the action of a single individual matters, the collapse of the President has been one of the decisive moral events of history;

and I must make an attempt to explain it. What a place the President held in the hearts and hopes of the world when he sailed to us in the *George Washington!* What a great man came to Europe in those early days of our victory!

In November, 1918, the armies of Foch and the words of Wilson had brought us sudden escape from what was swallowing up all we cared for. The conditions seemed favorable beyond any expectation. The victory was so complete that fear need play no part in the settlement. The enemy had laid down his arms in reliance on a solemn compact as to the general character of the Peace, the terms of which seemed to assure a settlement of justice and magnanimity and a fair hope for a restoration of the broken current of life. To make assurance certain the President was coming himself to set the seal on his work.

When President Wilson left Washington he enjoyed a prestige and a moral influence throughout the world unequaled in history. His bold and measured words carried to the peoples of Europe above and beyond the voices of their own politicians. The enemy peoples trusted him to carry out the compact he had made with them; and the Allied peoples acknowledged him not as a victor only but almost as a prophet. In addition to this moral influence the realities of power were in his hands. The American armies were at the height of their numbers, discipline, and equipment. Europe was in complete dependence on the food supplies of the United States; and financially she was even more absolutely at their mercy. Europe not only already owed the United States more than she could pay; but only a large measure of further assistance could save her from starvation and bankruptcy. Never had a philosopher held such weapons wherewith to bind the princes of this world. How the crowds of the European capitals pressed about the carriage of the President! With what curiosity, anxiety, and hope we sought a glimpse of the features and bearing of the man of destiny who, coming from the West, was to bring healing to the wounds of the ancient parent of his civilization and lay for us the foundations of the future.

The disillusion was so complete, that some of those who had trusted most hardly dared speak of it. Could it be true? they asked of those who returned from Paris. Was the Treaty really as bad as it seemed? What had happened to the President? What weakness or what misfortune had led to so extraordinary, so unlooked-for a betrayal?

Yet the causes were very ordinary and human. The President was not a hero or a prophet; he was not even a philosopher; but a generously intentioned man, with many of the weaknesses of other human beings, and lacking that dominating intellectual equipment which would have been necessary to cope with the subtle and dangerous spellbinders whom a tremendous clash of forces and personalities had brought to the top as triumphant masters in the swift game of give and take, face to face in Council,—a game of which he had no experience at all.

We had indeed quite a wrong idea of the President. We knew him to be solitary and aloof, and believed him very strong-willed and obstinate. We did not figure him as a man of detail, but the clearness with which he had taken hold of certain main ideas would, we thought, in combination with his tenacity, enable him to sweep through cobwebs. Besides these qualities he would have the objectivity, the cultivation, and the wide knowledge of the student. The great distinction of language which had marked his famous Notes seemed to indicate a man of lofty and powerful imagination. His portraits indicated a fine presence and a commanding delivery. With all this he had attained and held with increasing authority the first position in a country where the arts of the politician are not neglected. All of which, without expecting the impossible, seemed a fine combination of qualities for the matter in hand.

The first impression of Mr. Wilson at close quarters was to impair some but not all of these illusions. His head and features were finely cut and exactly like his photographs, and the muscles of his neck and the carriage of his head were distinguished. But, like Odysseus, the President looked wiser when he was seated; and his hands, though capable and fairly strong, were wanting in sensitiveness and finesse. The first glance at the President suggested not only that, whatever else he might be, his temperament was not primarily that of the student or the scholar, but that he had not much even of that culture of the world which marks M. Clemenceau and Mr. Balfour as exquisitely cultivated gentlemen of their class and generation. But more serious than this, he was not only insensitive to his surroundings in the external sense, he was not sensitive to his environment at all. What chance could such a man have against Mr. Lloyd George's unerring, almost medium-like, sensibility to every one immediately round him? To see the British Prime Minister watching the company, with six or seven senses not available to ordinary men, judging character, motive, and subconscious impulse, perceiving what each was thinking and even what each was going to say next, and compounding with telepathic instinct the argument or appeal best suited to the vanity, weakness, or self-interest of his immediate auditor, was to realize that the poor President would be playing blind man's buff in that party. Never could a man have stepped into the parlor a more perfect and predestined victim to the finished accomplishments of the Prime Minister. The Old World was tough in wickedness anyhow; the Old World's heart of stone might blunt the sharpest blade of the bravest knight-errant. But this blind and deaf Don Quixote was entering a cavern where the swift and glittering blade was in the hands of the adversary.

But if the President was not the philosopher-king, what was he? After all he was a man who had spent much of his life at a University. He was by no means a business man or an ordinary party politician, but a man of force, personality, and importance. What, then, was his temperament?

The clue once found was illuminating. The President was like a Nonconformist minister, perhaps a Presbyterian. His thought and his temperament were essentially theological not intellectual, with all the strength and the weakness of that manner of thought, feeling, and expression. It is a type of which there are not now in England and Scotland such magnificent specimens as formerly; but this description, nevertheless, will give the ordinary Englishman the distinctest impression of the President.

With this picture of him in mind, we can return to the actual course of events. The President's program for the World, as set forth in his speeches and his Notes, had displayed a spirit and a purpose so admirable that the last desire of his sympathizers was to criticize details,—the details, they felt, were quite rightly not filled in at present, but would be in due course. It was commonly believed at the commencement of the Paris Conference that the President had thought out, with the aid of a large body of advisers, a comprehensive scheme not only for the League of Nations, but for the embodiment of the Fourteen Points in an actual Treaty of Peace. But in fact the President had thought out nothing; when it came to practice his ideas were nebulous and incomplete. He had no plan, no scheme, no constructive ideas whatever for clothing with the flesh of life the commandments which he had thundered from the White House. He could have preached a sermon on any of them or have addressed a stately prayer to the Almighty for their fulfilment; but he could not frame their concrete application to the actual state of Europe.

He not only had no proposals in detail, but he was in many respects, perhaps inevitably, ill-informed as to European conditions. And not only was he ill-informed—that was true of Mr. Lloyd George also—but his mind was slow and unadaptable. The President's slowness amongst the Europeans was noteworthy. He could not, all in a minute, take in what the rest were saying, size up the situation with a glance, frame a reply, and meet the case by a slight change of ground; and he was liable, therefore, to defeat by the mere swiftness, apprehension, and agility of a Lloyd George. There can seldom have been a statesman of the first rank more incompetent than the President in the agilities of the council chamber. A moment often arrives when substantial victory is yours if by some slight appearance of a concession you can save the face of the opposition or conciliate them by a restatement of your proposal helpful to them and not injurious to anything essential to yourself. The President was not equipped with this simple and usual artfulness. His mind was too slow and unresourceful to be ready with *any* alternatives. The President was capable of digging his toes in and refusing to budge, as he did over Fiume. But he had no other mode of defense, and it needed as a rule but little maneuvering by his opponents to prevent matters from coming to such a head until it was too late. By pleasantness and an appearance of conciliation, the President would be maneuvered off his ground, would miss the moment for digging his toes in, and, before he knew where he had been got to, it was too late. Besides, it is impossible month after month in intimate and ostensibly friendly converse between close associates, to be digging the toes in all the time. Victory would only have been possible to one who had always a sufficiently lively apprehension of the position as a whole to reserve his fire and know for certain the rare exact moments for decisive action. And for that the President was far too slow-minded and bewildered.

He did not remedy these defects by seeking aid from the collective wisdom of his lieutenants. He had gathered round him for the economic chapters of the Treaty a very able group of business men; but they were inexperienced in public affairs, and knew (with one or two exceptions) as little of Europe as he did, and they were only called in irregularly as he might need them for a particular purpose. Thus the aloofness which had been found effective in Washington was maintained, and the abnormal reserve of his nature did not allow near him any one who aspired to moral equality or the continuous exercise of influence. His fellow-plenipotentiaries were dummies; and even the trusted Colonel House, with vastly more knowledge of men and of Europe than the President, from whose sensitiveness the President's dullness had gained so much, fell into the background as time went on. All this was encouraged by his colleagues on the Council of Four, who, by the break-up of the Council of Ten, completed the isolation which the President's own temperament had initiated. Thus day after day and week after week, he allowed himself to be closeted, unsupported, unadvised, and alone, with men much sharper than himself, in situations of supreme difficulty, where he needed for success every description of resource, fertility, and knowledge. He allowed himself to be drugged by their atmosphere, to discuss on the basis of their plans and of their data, and to be led along their paths.

These and other various causes combined to produce the following situation. The reader must remember that the processes which are here compressed into a few pages took place slowly, gradually, insidiously, over a period of about five months.

As the President had thought nothing out, the Council was generally working on the basis of a French or British draft. He had to take up, therefore, a persistent attitude of obstruction, criticism, and negation, if the draft was to become at all in line with his own ideas and purpose. If he was met on some points with apparent generosity (for there was always a safe margin of quite preposterous suggestions which no one took seriously), it was difficult for him not to yield on others. Compromise was inevitable, and never to compromise on the essential, very difficult. Besides, he was soon made to appear to be taking the German part and laid himself open to the suggestion (to which he was foolishly and unfortunately sensitive) of being "pro-German."

After a display of much principle and dignity in the early days of the Council of Ten, he discovered that there were certain very important points in the program of his French, British, or Italian colleague, as the case might be, of which he was incapable of securing the surrender by the methods of secret diplomacy. What then was he to do in the last resort? He could let the Conference drag on an endless length by the exercise of sheer obstinacy. He could break it up and return to America in a rage with nothing settled. Or he could attempt an appeal to the world over the heads of the Conference. These were wretched alternatives, against each of which a great deal could be said. They were also very risky,—especially for a politician. The President's mistaken policy over the Congressional election had weakened his personal position in his own country, and it was by no means certain that the American public would support him in a position of intransigeancy. It would mean a campaign in which the issues would be clouded by every sort of personal and party consideration, and who could say if right would triumph in a struggle which would certainly not be decided on its merits? Besides, any open rupture with his colleagues would certainly bring upon his head the blind passions of "anti-German" resentment with which the public of all allied countries were still inspired. They would not listen to his arguments. They would not be cool enough to treat the issue as one of international morality or of the right governance of Europe. The cry would simply be that, for various sinister and selfish reasons, the President wished "to let the Hun off." The almost unanimous voice of the French and British Press could be anticipated. Thus, if he threw down the gage publicly he might be defeated. And if he were defeated, would not the final Peace be far worse than if he were to retain his prestige and endeavor to make it as good as the limiting conditions of European politics would allow him? But above all, if he were defeated, would he not lose the League of Nations? And was not this, after all, by far the most important issue for the future happiness of the world? The Treaty would be altered and softened by time. Much in it which now seemed so vital would become trifling, and much which was impracticable would for that very reason never happen. But the League, even in an imperfect form, was permanent; it was the first commencement of a new principle in the government of the world; Truth and Justice in international relations could not be established in a few months,—they must be born in due course by the slow gestation of the League. Clemenceau had been clever enough to let it be seen that he would swallow the League at a price.

At the crisis of his fortunes the President was a lonely man. Caught up in the toils of the Old World, he stood in great need of sympathy, of moral support, of the enthusiasm of masses. But buried in the Conference, stifled in the hot and poisoned atmosphere of Paris, no echo reached him from the outer world, and no throb of passion, sympathy, or encouragement from his silent constituents in all countries. He felt that the blaze of popularity which had greeted his arrival in Europe was already dimmed; the Paris Press jeered at him openly; his political opponents at home were taking advantage of his absence to create an atmosphere against him; England was cold, critical, and unresponsive. He had so formed his *entourage* that he did not receive through private channels the current of faith and enthusiasm of which the public sources seemed dammed up. He needed, but lacked, the added strength of collective faith. The German terror still overhung us, and even the sympathetic public was very cautious; the enemy must not be encouraged, our friends must be supported, this was not the time for discord or agitations, the President must be trusted to do his best. And in this drought the flower of the President's faith withered and dried up.

Thus it came to pass that the President countermanded the *George Washington,* which, in a moment of well-founded rage, he had ordered to be in readiness to carry him from the treacherous halls of Paris back to the seat of his authority, where he could have felt himself again. But as soon, alas, as he had taken the road of compromise, the defects, already indicated, of his temperament and of his equipment, were fatally apparent. He could take the high line; he could practise obstinacy; he could write Notes from Sinai or Olympus; he could remain unapproachable in the White House or even in the Council of Ten and be safe. But if he once stepped down to the intimate equality of the Four, the game was evidently up.

Now it was that what I have called his theological or Presbyterian temperament became dangerous. Having decided that some concessions were unavoidable, he might have sought by firmness and address and the use of the financial power of the United States to secure as much as he could of the substance, even at some sacrifice of the letter. But the President was not capable of so clear an understanding with himself as this implied. He was too conscientious. Although compromises were now necessary, he remained a man of principle and the Fourteen Points a contract absolutely binding upon him. He would do nothing that was not honorable; he would do nothing that was not just and right; he would do nothing that was contrary to his great profession of faith. Thus, without any abatement of the verbal inspiration of the Fourteen Points, they became a document for gloss and interpretation and for all the intellectual apparatus of self-deception, by which, I daresay, the President's forefathers had persuaded themselves that the course they thought it necessary to take was consistent with every syllable of the Pentateuch.

The President's attitude to his colleagues had now become: I want to meet you so far as I can; I see your difficulties and I should like to be able to agree to what you propose; but I can do nothing that is not just and right, and you must first of all show me that what you want does really fall within the words of the pronouncements which are binding on me. Then began the weaving of that web of sophistry and Jesuitical exegesis that was finally to clothe with insincerity the language and substance of the whole Treaty. The word was issued to the witches of all Paris:

> Fair is foul, and foul is fair,
> Hover through the fog and filthy air.

The subtlest sophisters and most hypocritical draftsmen were set to work, and produced many ingenious exercises which might have deceived for more than an hour a cleverer man than the President.

Thus instead of saying that German-Austria is prohibited from uniting with Germany except by leave of France (which would be inconsistent with the principle of self-determination), the Treaty, with delicate draftsmanship, states that "Germany acknowledges and will respect strictly the independence of Austria, within the frontiers which may be fixed in a Treaty between that State and the Principal Allied and Associated Powers; she agrees that this independence shall be inalienable, except with the consent of the Council of the League of Nations," which sounds, but is not, quite different. And who knows but that the President forgot that another part of the Treaty provides that for this purpose the Council of the League must be *unanimous*.

Instead of giving Danzig to Poland, the Treaty establishes Danzig as a "Free" City, but includes this "Free" City within the Polish Customs frontier, entrusts to Poland the control of the river and railway system, and provides that "the Polish Government shall undertake the conduct of the foreign relations of the Free City of Danzig as well as the diplomatic protection of citizens of that city when abroad."

In placing the river system of Germany under foreign control, the Treaty speaks of declaring international those "river systems which naturally provide more than one State with access to the sea, with or without transhipment from one vessel to another."

Such instances could be multiplied. The honest and intelligible purpose of French policy, to limit the population of Germany and weaken her economic system, is clothed, for the President's sake, in the august language of freedom and international equality.

But perhaps the most decisive moment, in the disintegration of the President's moral position and the clouding of his mind, was when at last, to the dismay of his advisers, he allowed himself to be persuaded that the expenditure of the Allied Governments on pensions and separation allowances could be fairly regarded as "damage done to the civilian population of the Allied and Associated Powers by German aggression by land, by sea, and from the air," in a sense in which the other expenses of the war could not be so regarded. It was a long theological struggle in which, after the rejection of many different arguments, the President finally capitulated before a masterpiece of the sophist's art.

At last the work was finished; and the President's conscience was still intact. In spite of everything, I believe that his temperament allowed him to leave Paris a really sincere man; and it is probable that to this day he is genuinely convinced that the Treaty contains practically nothing inconsistent with his former professions.

But the work was too complete, and to this was due the last tragic episode of the drama. The reply of Brockdorff-Rantzau inevitably took the line that Germany had laid down her arms on the basis of certain assurances, and that the Treaty in many particulars was not consistent with these assurances. But this was exactly what the President could not admit; in the sweat of solitary contemplation and with prayers to God he had done *nothing* that was not just and right; for the President to admit that the German reply had force in it was to destroy his self-respect and to disrupt the inner equipoise of his soul; and every instinct of his stubborn nature rose in self-protection. In the language of medical psychology, to suggest to the President that the Treaty was an abandonment of his professions was to touch on the raw a Freudian complex. It was a subject intolerable to discuss, and every subconscious instinct plotted to defeat its further exploration. . . .

Chapter 6. Europe after the Treaty

This chapter must be one of pessimism. The Treaty includes no provisions for the economic rehabilitation of Europe—nothing to make the defeated Central Empires into good neighbors, nothing to stabilize the new States of Europe, nothing to reclaim Russia; nor does it promote in any way a compact of economic solidarity amongst the Allies themselves; no arrangement was reached at Paris for restoring the disordered finances of France and Italy, or to adjust the systems of the Old World and the New.

The Council of Four paid no attention to these issues, being preoccupied with others—Clemenceau to crush the economic life of his enemy, Lloyd George to do a deal and bring home something which would pass muster for a week, the President to do nothing that was not just and right. It is an extraordinary fact that the fundamental economic problems of a Europe starving and disintegrating before their eyes, was the one question in which it was impossible to arouse the interest of the Four. Reparation was their main excursion into the economic field, and they settled it as a problem of theology, of politics, of electoral chicane, from every point of view except that of the economic future of the States whose destiny they were handling.

I leave, from this point onwards, Paris, the Conference, and the Treaty, briefly to consider the present situation of Europe, as the War and the Peace have made it; and it will no longer be part of my purpose to distinguish between the inevitable fruits of the War and the avoidable misfortunes of the Peace.

The essential facts of the situation, as I see them, are expressed simply. Europe consists of the densest aggregation of population in the history of the world. This population is accustomed to a relatively high standard of life, in which, even now, some sections of it anticipate improvement rather than deterioration. In relation to other continents Europe is not self-sufficient; in particular it cannot feed itself. Internally the population is not evenly distributed, but much of it is crowded into a relatively small number of dense industrial centers. This population secured for itself a livelihood before the war, without much margin of surplus, by means of a delicate and immensely complicated organization, of which the foundations were supported by coal, iron, transport, and an unbroken supply of imported food and raw materials from other continents. By the destruction of this organization and the interruption of the stream of supplies, a part of this population is deprived of its means of livelihood. Emigration is not open to the redundant surplus. For it would take years to transport them overseas, even, which is not the case, if countries could be found which were ready to receive them. The danger confronting us, therefore, is the rapid depression of the standard of life of the European populations to a point which will mean actual starvation for some (a point already reached in Russia and approximately reached in Austria). Men will not always die quietly. For starvation, which brings to some lethargy and a helpless despair, drives other temperaments to the nervous instability of hysteria and to a mad despair. And these in their distress may overturn the remnants of organization, and submerge civilization itself in their attempts to satisfy desperately the overwhelming needs of the individual. This is the danger against which all our resources and courage and idealism must now co-operate. . . .

3
Europe between the Wars

Extremists: Fascist Right and Communist Left

15. Adolf Hitler, *Mein Kampf*

Adolf Hitler (1889–1945) was the son of an Austrian customs official in Braunau, Upper Austria. As a boy he held the ambition to become an artist, and in 1907 he went to Vienna with hopes of entering the Academy of Fine Arts. He was refused admission and for the next five years eked out a lonely, miserable existence in the capital of the Austro-Hungarian Empire, working as a casual laborer, living in a hostel for homeless men, sitting long hours in cafes, and producing cheap drawings and watercolors to earn a living. During these years, Hitler later claimed, he acquired his convictions on anti-Semitism, anti-Marxism, and racist nationalism.

In order to escape service in the Austrian army Hitler moved to Munich in 1913. At the outbreak of the First World War Hitler joined a Bavarian regiment as a volunteer. After the war he returned to Munich; in 1919 he became a member and (from 1921) the leader of the "German Workers' Party" (since 1920 the "National Socialist German Workers' Party"). After his abortive putsch in November 1923, Hitler was sentenced to five years in prison at the fortress of Landsberg (he served less than nine months). The enforced leisure allowed him to begin an account of his early life and thoughts, the first volume of which was published in 1925 under the title *Mein Kampf*. This book articulated Hitler's fanatical ideas on anti-Semitism, racism, and anti-Marxist mass politics. Like early Nazi propaganda it also played upon German popular hatred of the postwar settlement, but it went beyond themes like the famous "Stab in the Back" legend of Germany's defeat to proffer a canon of expansive nationalism and social revolution in the aftermath of the Revolution of 1918/1919. *Mein Kampf* was thus, in rhetorical and thematic terms, as much a memoir of the anarchic rightism of the early 1920s as it was an anticipation of the horrors of the later 1930s.

The National Socialist party was banned in 1923, but reconstituted by Hitler in 1925. The party grew quickly during the economic and political crises of the late Weimar Republic (810,000 votes in the 1928 national elections, 6.4 million in 1930, 13.7 million in 1932). In 1928 it had 12 representatives in the German Reichstag; 107 in 1930; 230 in July 1932 (reduced to 196 in November). On 30 January 1933 Hitler was nominated Chancellor of Germany by President von Hindenburg. He quickly eliminated all other parties and instituted a regime of institutional and racial barbarism unparalleled in modern history, which was responsible by 1945 for the deaths of over 30 million people. After the collapse of the Third Reich, Hitler committed suicide in Berlin on 30 April 1945. The last words of his final Testament, written immediately before his death— urging "merciless struggle against the universal poisoner of all nations, international Jewry"—suggest both the fanaticism and the unspeakable cruelty of a man and a state poisoned by mass social hatred.

The following selections from *Mein Kampf* consist of (1) Hitler's description of his life in Vienna before 1914; (2) his comments on the nature and purpose of the State; and (3) his description of propaganda in modern political movements.

Vienna

What I knew about Social Democracy in my youth was precious little and highly erroneous.

Inwardly I was glad that the Social Democrats led in the struggle for universal and secret voting. Even then my understanding told me that this must lead to a weakening of the Hapsburg regime which I hated so much. In the conviction that the Danubian state could never be maintained without the sacrifice of its German character, but that even the price of a gradual Slavicization of the German elements would not in any way have guaranteed a really viable Empire because the ability of the Slavs to maintain a state had to be assessed as highly dubious, I welcomed every development

From Hitler, *Mein Kampf* (Munich: Zentralverlag der NSDAP, 1939), pp. 39–45, 53–55, 59–70, translated by William Kunze and Myron Brick for this volume; and *Mein Kampf*, translated by Ralph Manheim (Boston, Mass.: Houghton Mifflin, 1943), pp. 393–99, 407–12, 579–86; ©1943 and copyright renewed 1971 by Houghton Mifflin Company. Reprinted by permission of Houghton Mifflin Company and Century Hutchinson Limited.

that in my opinion would lead to the breakup of this impossible state which was condemning ten million people to the death of their Germanic character. The more the babble of different tongues ate into and decomposed the Parliament, the nearer the hour of the downfall of this Babylonian empire must come, and therewith also the hour of liberation for my Germanic-Austrian people. Only in this way, then, could union with the old Motherland come again.

Therefore I was not unsympathetic to this activity of Social Democracy. That they strove in the long run (as my simple soul was still stupid enough to believe) to raise the living conditions of the workers also seemed to me to speak for them rather than against them. What bothered me the most was their hostility toward the struggle for the preservation of German nationality, their deplorable illicit courtship of the favor of Slavic "comrades," who (for their part) readily accepted this wooing so long as it was tied to practical concessions, but who otherwise remained arrogantly and haughtily aloof, thus giving the importunate beggars their well-earned pay.

Thus, at the age of seventeen I scarcely knew the word "Marxism," while "Social Democracy" and socialism seemed to be identical terms. Here too the hand of Fate was required to open my eyes to this incredible national betrayal.

Until this time I had come to know the Social Democratic Party only as an onlooker at various mass demonstrations, without possessing so much as the slightest insight into the mentality of its followers or even into the essence of its teachings; now I came with a slap into sudden contact with the products of its education and world view. And what I might otherwise have realized only after decades, I now obtained in the course of a few months: an understanding of the pestilential whore, masking herself as social virtue and charitable love, from which, let us hope, mankind will free the earth as quickly as possible, since otherwise the earth could all too easily become rid of mankind instead.

My first encounter with Social Democrats took place when I was a construction worker.

From the beginning it was not very enjoyable. My clothing was still somewhat respectable, my speech was refined, and my manner was withdrawn. I was still so busy with my destiny that I was not able to concern myself much with my surroundings. I sought work so as not to starve, to obtain the possibility of a continuation, however gradual, of my education. Perhaps I would not have troubled myself at all about my new surroundings, if on the third or fourth day something had not happened that forced me at once to take a stand. I was called upon to join the union.

My knowledge of the trade union organization was then virtually nil. I would not have been able to prove either the expediency or the inexpediency of their existence. When it was explained to me that I had to join, I refused. I based my refusal on the ground that I did not understand the matter, but that under no circumstances would I permit myself to be forced into anything. Perhaps it was for the first of these reasons that they did not throw me out immediately. Possibly they hoped to convert me or to soften me up after a few days. At any rate they were basically fooling themselves. After a fortnight I could no longer have joined even if I had wanted to. In those fourteen days I came to know my surroundings so much better that no power on earth could have moved me to enlist in an organization whose supporters in the meantime had appeared to me in such an unfavorable light.

The first few days I was irritable.

At midday part of the workmen went to the nearby saloons while the others remained on the job site and consumed what was usually a very miserable lunch. These were the married men, whose wives brought them their midday soup in pitiable bowls. Toward the end of the week their number steadily increased; why, I understood only later. At this point they talked politics.

I drank my bottle of milk and ate my piece of bread somewhere off to the side and carefully studied my new surroundings or mulled over my wretched fate. Nevertheless, I heard more than enough; also, it often seemed to me that they inched closer to me intentionally, perhaps in order to lead me to take a stand. In any case, what I overheard was apt to infuriate me in the extreme. They rejected everything: the nation as an invention of the "capitalist"—how often I had to hear this word alone!—classes; the Fatherland as a device of the bourgeoisie for exploiting the workers; the authority of the law as a means for the suppression of the proletariat; the school as an institution for breeding slave material as well as slaveholders; religion as a means of stupefying people marked out for exploitation; morals as a sign of dumb sheeplike patience, etc. There was absolutely nothing that was not dragged through muck of a dreadful depth.

In the beginning I tried to keep silent. Finally it became impossible. I began to take a stand, began to contradict. But I had to realize that my efforts would be perfectly pointless so long as I did not have certain knowledge about the points in dispute, at the very least. Therefore I began to track down the sources from which they drew their alleged wisdom. Book after book, pamphlet after pamphlet now had its turn.

At work, however, the arguments often waxed hot. I quarreled, better informed day by day about their own theories than my opponents themselves, until one day those means were used which certainly win most easily over reason: terror and force. Some of the spokesmen for the opposition forced me to either leave the job site immediately or be thrown from the scaffolding. Since I was alone and resistance seemed pointless, I preferred to follow the first advice, one experience richer.

I left filled with disgust, but at the same time so affected that it would have been quite impossible for me to turn my back upon the whole thing. No: after the first rush of indignation, obstinacy regained the upper hand. I was firmly determined to get another construction job. I was strengthened in this decision by the privation which, several weeks later, after I had consumed what little I have saved from my wages, locked me in its heartless arms. I had to work whether I wanted to or not. And the game started over again, from the beginning, only to end as it had the first time.

I grappled then with my innermost soul: Are these still human beings, worthy of belonging to a great nation?

An agonizing question: because if it is answered with yes, then the struggle on behalf of a nationality is really no longer worth the trouble and sacrifice which the best of us have to bear for the sake of such dregs; but if the answer is no, then our nation is indeed poor in human beings.

With restless anxiety I saw, on such days of brooding and reflection, the masses of those who could be no longer counted as belonging to their own nation swell into a threatening army.

With what different feelings I now stared at the endless columns, four abreast, of a mass demonstration of Viennese workers that took place one day. For almost two hours I stood there and watched with bated breath the enormous human dragon's tail which slowly snaked past. In a state of anxious depression I finally left the square and wandered homeward. En route I caught sight of the "Workers Journal" [*Arbeiter-Zeitung*], the central organ of the old Austrian Social Democracy, in a tobacco shop. At a cheap popular café where I often went to read the papers it was also lying around. Until then I could not bring myself to look over that miserable rag for more than two minutes; its whole tone worked on me like spiritual vitriol. Under the depressing influence of the demonstration, an inner voice now drove me to buy the paper and read it thoroughly. That evening I did so, surmounting the sudden anger that rose up in me from time to time at this concentrated solution of lies.

More than from any theoretical literature, I was able from my daily reading of the Social Democratic press to study the inner character of this line of thinking.

What a contrast between the scintillating phrases about freedom, beauty, and dignity in the theoretical literature, the delusive light of a seemingly profound wisdom expressed in an irksome flock of lies, the repulsive humanitarian morality—all written down with the brazen effrontery of prophetic certainty—and the brutal daily press, which stops at no dirty trick, employs every means of libel and a truly girder-bending virtuosity for lying—all on behalf of this Gospel of the new humanity! The one is certainly for the simpletons from the middle class and, of course, also for the upper "intelligentsia," the other for the masses.

For me, plunging into the literature and press of this dogma and organization meant finding my own people again.

What at first appeared to me as an unbridgeable chasm now became the occasion for a greater love than ever before.

Only a fool could be aware of this monstrous work of poison and still damn the victim. The more independent I made myself in the next few years, increasing my distance from the matter, the more my insight into the inner reasons for the Social Democratic successes grew. Now I comprehended the significance of the brutal demands to subscribe only to Red newspapers, visit only Red meetings, read only Red books, etc. With plastic lucidity I saw before my eyes the unavoidable result of this dogma of intolerance.

The psyche of the masses is not receptive to half measures and weakness.

Just like the woman whose frame of mind is fixed less by the grounds of abstract reason than by an indefinable emotional yearning toward a strength that offers her completion, and who therefore prefers to bow to the strong man rather than dominate a weakling, the masses also love a sovereign more than a supplicant, and feel themselves inwardly more gratified by a dogma that suffers no other beside it, than by the grant of liberal freedom. For the most part, they hardly know what to do with the latter and, what is more, readily feel themselves abandoned. They are just as unconscious of the shamelessness of their spiritual terrorization as of the outrageous abuse of their human freedom, in no way suspecting the inner insanity of the entire doctrine. They see only the relentless strength and brutality of its purposeful expressions, to which they always bow in the end.

If Social Democracy is opposed by a doctrine of greater truthfulness but the same brutality of enforcement, the latter will conquer, if only after the heaviest fighting. . . .

The more I obtained insight into the outward nature of Social Democracy the greater my longing became to grasp the inner core of this doctrine.

The official party literature was of little use here. It is, insofar as it deals with economic questions, incorrect in its assertions and its proofs; insofar as political goals are attended to, it lies. In addition, inwardly I felt myself especially repelled by their newfangled hair-splitting manner of expression and style of presentation. With an enormous outpouring of words of uncertain content or unintelligible meaning, sentences are stammered together which are supposed to be as clever as they are in fact senseless. Only the decadence of our cosmopolitan bohemians allows them to feel cosily at

home in this labyrinth of reasoning, to cull an "inner experience" from the
dung of this literary dadaism, endorsed by the proverbial modesty of one
part of our people which always suspects the more profound wisdom is to
be found in what is to them personally the most incomprehensible.

But by weighing out the theoretical falsehood and absurdity of this doctrine with the truth of the phenomenon, gradually I gained a clear idea of
its inner will.

At such times I was seized by bleak presentiments and virulent fear. I
saw before me a doctrine consisting of egoism and hate that could follow
mathematical laws to victory, but which in doing so must also bring an end
to the human race.

I had learned to understand by that time the connection between this
doctrine of destruction and the nature of a people who until then had been
as good as unknown to me.

*A knowledge of Jewry alone offers the key to comprehending the inner
and, with that, the real designs of Social Democracy.*

Whoever knows this nation-race [Volk] has the veil of misconceptions
concerning their aim and meaning fall from his eyes, and from the mist
and fog of social catch-phrases there rises sneering the distorted face of
Marxism.

It is difficult today, if not impossible, for me to say when the word
"Jew" first gave me cause for particular thought. In the paternal household
during the lifetime of my father I cannot remember ever having heard the
word. I believe the old gentleman would have considered the particular emphasis on this term to be cultural backwardness. In the course of his life he
had arrived at more or less cosmopolitan views which had not only maintained themselves despite his rugged sense of nationalism, but which had
also colored my own views.

Nor did I find any inducement in school which could have led me to
change this adopted point of view.

In high school, to be sure, I became well acquainted with a Jewish
boy who was treated by all of us with circumspection, but only because we
did not especially trust his discretion, having learned from various experiences; yet I gave the matter no particular thought any more than the
others did.

Not until my fourteenth or fifteenth year did I come more frequently
across the word "Jew," partly in connection with political discussions. I
reacted with a mild aversion and could not resist an uncomfortable feeling
that always overcame me whenever denominational bickering occurred in
my presence.

But at that time I did not see the matter as a question of anything else.

Linz contained very few Jews. In the course of centuries their outward appearance had been Europeanized and had become humanized; yes, I even considered them to be Germans. The absurdity of this delusion was hardly clear to me because the only distinguishing feature I perceived was their alien religion. That they had, as I believed, been persecuted because of this, sometimes turned my antipathy against untoward remarks about them almost to disgust.

As yet I did not suspect at all the existence of an organized opposition to the Jews.

Then I came to Vienna. . . . [The transformation of my views on anti-Semitism] cost me the most inner spiritual struggles, and only after months of wrestling between understanding and sentiment did victory come down on the side of understanding. Two years later my sentiment had followed my understanding, from then on to be its most loyal guardian and monitor.

In the course of this bitter struggle between my spiritual upbringing and cold reason, the visual instruction of the Viennese streets had performed inestimable services. There came a time when I no longer ambled blindly through the vast city, as in the first days, but rather viewed not only the buildings but also the men with open eyes.

One time as I strolled in this way through the Inner City, I suddenly came upon an apparition in a long caftan and black hair locks.

Is this also a Jew? was my first thought.

Certainly they did not look this way in Linz. I studied the man secretly and charily, but the longer I stared into this strange face, searching it feature by feature, the more the first question transformed itself in my brain into another:

Is this also a German?

As always in such cases I now began to attempt to dispel my doubts through books. I bought for a few pennies the first anti-Semitic pamphlets of my life. Unfortunately they all started with the assumption that to a certain degree the reader was at least acquainted with or even comprehended the Jewish question. For the most part, the tone was such that doubt in the end always returned to me, in part due to the superficial and extraordinarily unscientific reasoning in support of the thesis.

I would then backslide again for weeks—indeed, once even for months.

The whole thing seemed to me so atrocious, the charge so excessive that, tormented by the fear of committing an injustice, I again became worried and uncertain.

To be sure, I could no longer very well doubt that the issue concerned itself not with Germans of a special denomination, but rather with a distinct nationality unto itself; for since I had begun to busy myself with this question, and first took notice of the Jews, Vienna appeared to me in a different light than previously. Wherever I went I now saw Jews, and the more of them I saw the more sharply my eyes segregated them from other men. The Inner City and the districts north of the Danube canal, in particular, swarmed with a people that no longer even superficially possessed any likeness to Germans.

But if I still might have doubted the matter, the vacillation was conclusively dispelled by the attitude of a portion of the Jews themselves.

A great movement among them, more than a little extensive in Vienna, advocated most sharply the acknowledgement of the national character of Jewry: Zionism.

To be sure, there was the appearance that only a portion of the Jews approved of this attitude, while the great majority condemned the arrangement, even inwardly disapproved. Upon closer inspection, however, this appearance dissipated into an evil mist of pretexts advanced for reasons of pure expediency, not to say lies. For the so-called Jews of liberal mentality did not reject the Zionists as non-Jews, but only as Jews with an unpractical, perhaps even dangerous manner of publicly declaring their Judaism.

Their inner solidarity didn't change itself a bit.

This apparent struggle between Zionistic and liberal Jews disgusted me in short order. It was false through and through, consequently mendacious and little suited to the ever maintained moral elevation and purity of this race of people.

On the whole, the moral and other cleanliness of this race of people was a point in itself. That the question here was of their lack of love for water one could see from outward appearances, unfortunately too often with your eyes shut. Later, the smell of these caftan-wearers often made me sick. Added to that, there was their unclean apparel and unheroic appearance.

All this could hardly produce a very charming impression; but it became repulsive when on top of their corporeal uncleanliness one suddenly discovered the blemished morality of this chosen people.

Nothing had made me so thoughtful in a brief time as my gradually increasing insight into the activity carried on by the Jews in certain areas.

Was there any form of shamelessness, then, any kind of filth, above all in cultural life, in which at least one Jew was not taking part?

As soon as one cut ever so carefully into such a tumor, one found, like the maggot in a rotting corpse, often totally blinded by the sudden light, a little Jew.

In my eyes, as I became acquainted with its activity in the press, in art, literature and theater, Judaism carried with it a heavy load. All the unctuous protestations were more or less useless then. It was enough to look at one of the advertising kiosks, to study the names of the intellectual producers of the ghastly concoctions for stage or screen which were hyped there, to harden yourself for a long time to come. This was pestilence, spiritual pestilence, worse than the Black Death of old, and with it they infected the nation. And what a multitude was engendered and propagated by this poisoning! Naturally, the lower the intellectual and moral level of one of these producers of art, the more boundless his fecundity, until such a fellow is like a centrifuge splashing his filth in the faces of other men. One should consider the infinitude of their numbers; one should bear in mind that for one Goethe, Nature easily dumps on the present generation ten thousand of these scribblers, who poison souls just like bacterial carriers of the worst kind.

It was dreadful, but not to be overlooked, that just the Jew seemed chosen by nature in superabundant numbers for this disgraceful calling.

Should their chosenness be sought for in this?

I began to check carefully the names of all the producers of these filthy products of public artistic life. The result was ever more unfavorable for my previous posture toward the Jews. Though feeling may resist a thousand times over, the understanding must draw its own conclusion.

The fact that nine-tenths of all the literary smut, artistic rubbish, and theatrical imbecility is to be ascribed to the account of one people, who amount to hardly one-hundredth of the inhabitants of the country, could not be easily denied; this was plainly the case.

I now began to check as well my beloved "world press" from this angle.

The more thoroughly I probed, the more the object of my former admiration shriveled. The style became ever more unbearable. I had to condemn the contents as inwardly shallow and superficial; the apparent objectivity of the presentation seemed to me now to be more lies than honest truth; the authors were again—Jews.

A thousand things that I had scarcely seen before impressed me now as noteworthy; still others which formerly gave me pause I learned to comprehend and understand.

I now saw the liberal convictions of these newspapers in a different light. Their refined tone when replying to some attacks, their deathly silence when replying to others, unmasked for me a trick as clever as it was underhanded; the press's radiantly written theater reviews were always directed toward a Jewish writer, and their hostile remarks were never aimed at anyone but a German. The faint taunting of Wilhelm II suggested their persistence, just like their praise for French culture and civilization. The trashy content of the short story bordered on indecency, and in the language I heard the sounds of an alien race; the disposition of the whole phenomenon was so obviously detrimental to German culture that it could only have been deliberate.

Yet who possessed such an interest?

Was this all mere chance?

So I gradually became uncertain.

My development was hastened, though, by insights which I gained in a succession of other proceedings. I refer to the general conception of customs and morals, which one could see flaunted and displayed quite openly by a great proportion of Jewry.

Here again the streets afforded at times a truly evil object lesson.

The relationship of Jewry to prostitution and even more to the white slave trade itself could be studied in Vienna as in no other west European city, perhaps excepting the seaports of southern France. If you went at night through the streets and alleys of Leopoldstadt, you witnessed at every step, whether you wanted to or not, proceedings which remained hidden from most of the German people until the war gave the soldiers on the eastern front the opportunity to see similar goings on—or, better put, forced them to see them.

When I thus for the first time recognized the Jew as the enterprising director of this scandalous trafficking in the scum of the city, as cold-hearted as he was shameless, a gentle shiver ran down my spine.

But then a flame flared up.

I no longer avoided consideration of the Jewish question; no, now I wanted to discuss it. But as I thus learned to seek out the Jew in all the branches of cultural and artistic life and in their various expressions, suddenly I came across him in a place where I would least have expected him.

As I recognized the Jew as leader of the Social Democracy, the scales began to fall from my eyes. Therewith a long spiritual struggle found its conclusion.

Already in my daily relations with my fellow workers I noticed the astonishing versatility with which they took different positions on the same question, at times within the space of a few days or even just a few hours. I could hardly understand how men who, when spoken to in private, always held reasonable views, suddenly lost them as soon as they came under the spell of the masses. Often it was enough to drive one mad. When I was convinced after long hours of argument that this time I had finally broken the ice or had thrown light upon some rigamarole and was heartily rejoicing at the success, to my dismay the next day I had to begin again from scratch; it had all been in vain. Like an eternal pendulum the insanity of their opinions seemed to swing back and forth again and again.

I could comprehend all this: that they were dissatisfied with their lot, that they condemned their Fate which often struck them so bitterly; that they hated their employers who seemed to them to be the hardhearted executors of that Fate; that they insulted the authorities who, in their eyes, had no feeling for their circumstances; that they demonstrated against food prices and marched on the street for their demands—all this could still at least be understood without regard for reason. But what had to remain inexplicable was the limitless hatred they exhibited toward their own nationality, defaming its greatness, dirtying its history, and dragging its great men into the gutter.

This fight against their own kind, their own nest, their own homeland was as absurd as it was incredible. It was unnatural.

One could cure them of this vice temporarily but only for a few days or at most a few weeks. If one met the supposed convert later, he had reverted to his old self.

The old unnatural state had him again in its possession.

I gradually came to know that the Social Democratic press was directed chiefly by Jews; in and of itself I ascribed no special significance to this fact since the situation at the other newspapers was exactly the same. One thing did perhaps strike me: not a single paper on whose staff there were Jews could truly be spoken of as national, along the lines of my education and interpretation.

I now overcame my scruples and tried to read the products of this kind of Marxist journalism, but my revulsion grew to unending proportions; I also tried now to get to know better the manufacturers of these collections of villainy.

Starting with the publisher, they were all Jews.

I took all the Social Democratic pamphlets I could get hold of and looked for the names of their authors: Jews. I noticed the names of almost all the leaders; far and away the largest part were also members of the "chosen people," whether they were Deputies in the Reichsrat or trade-union secretaries, the chairmen of the organizations or agitators in the streets. The same sinister picture always emerged. The names of the Austerlitzes, Davids, Adlers, Ellenbogens, etc., will forever remain in my memory.

One thing had become clear to me: the leadership of the party, with whose minor representatives I had for months waged the most vehement struggle, was almost exclusively in the hands of a foreign people; for I knew conclusively, to my inner joyful satisfaction, that the Jew was no German.

Only now did I first become thoroughly acquainted with the seducer of our nation.

One year of my stay in Vienna was already enough to bring me to the conviction that no worker could be so stubborn as not to succumb to better knowledge and better explanation. I slowly became an expert in their own dogma, and used this as a weapon in the battle for my inner belief.

Success almost always came down on my side.

The great masses could be saved, if only after the most difficult sacrifice of time and patience.

But a Jew could never be liberated from his views.

I was then still childish enough to want to make clear for them the insanity of their doctrine; in my small circle I talked until my tongue was sore and my throat was hoarse, thinking I must eventually succeed in persuading them of the perniciousness of their Marxian insanity; but all the more I only achieved the opposite. It seemed as though increasing insight into the devastating effect of Social-Democratic theories and their fulfillment only served to strengthen their resolution.

The more I quarreled with them, the better I became acquainted with their dialectic. First they counted upon the stupidity of their opponent, and then, when there was no other escape, they played dumb themselves. If all this was useless, then they didn't understand you correctly, or in the blink of an eye they jumped when challenged to another topic, advanced only truisms whose acceptance they immediately applied to fundamentally different matters, and then if again seized hold of, they side-stepped matters and pretended not to know anything in particular. Whenever one attacked one of these apostles, one's hand closed on a jelly-like slime; the slime oozed through one's fingers only to reassemble itself a moment later. If one struck a really annihilating blow so that he, having been observed by the audience, could do nothing else but agree, and if one believed that that was at least one step forward, then one's astonishment would be great the next day. The Jew knew not the least little bit from the day before, he vented his old nonsense again as though nothing at all had taken place, and, if angrily called to account, acted stunned, could remember absolutely nothing except the proven soundness of his assertions from the previous day.

At times I stood there dumbfounded.

You didn't know what to marvel at more: the dexterity of their tongues or the ingenuity of their lies.

Little by little I began to hate them.

All this had but one saving grace: that to the precise extent to which the identity of the real champions or at least the propagators of Social Democracy became clear to me, love for my own nation had to grow. Considering the devilish cleverness of these seducers, who could damn the unfortunate victims? How hard it was even for me to master the dialectical mendacity of this race! Yet how futile was this kind of success with people who twist the truth in their mouths, who flatly deny what was just said in order to claim it for themselves a moment later.

No. The more I became acquainted with the Jews, the more I had to forgive the worker.

In my eyes the heaviest guilt no longer belonged with him but with all those who found it not worth the trouble to have pity for him, to give the son of the nation his birthright with unrelenting justice, shoving the tempter and corrupter up against the wall.

Guided by the experience of daily life I now began to investigate the sources of Marxist doctrine itself. Its operation was clear to me in the particulars, its success presented itself daily to my attentive gaze, the consequences I was capable of drawing out with a little imagination. The only remaining question was whether the creators already had a notion of the consequences of their creation in its final form, or whether they were themselves the victims of an error.

Both were possible, I felt.

In one case, it was the duty of every thinking man to force himself to the front of this unfortunate movement, in order perhaps to prevent the worst from happening; in the other case, however, the erstwhile authors of this international disease must have been true devils, for only in the brain of a monster—not that of a man—could the plan of an organization take on sensible form whose activity must finally lead to the ruin of human culture and thus to the devastation of the world.

In this case only combat remains as the last means of salvation, combat with every weapon that the human spirit, understanding, and will can lay hold of, regardless to whom Fate tips the scale with her blessing.

Therefore I now began to familiarize myself with the founders of this dogma in order to study the basis of the movement. That I succeeded here more quickly than perhaps I originally considered possible was thanks to my newly won, though at that time hardly profound, awareness of the Jewish question. This knowledge alone permitted me the practical comparison of reality with the theoretical humbug of the founding apostles of Social Democracy, since it had taught me to understand the language of the Jewish race, who speak in order to hide or at least to mask their thoughts; their real objective therefore is not to be found in the lines themselves, but slumbers well hidden between them.

For me it was the time of the greatest inward upheaval that I had ever had to put myself through.

I went from weak cosmopolitan to fanatical anti-Semite.

Just once more—it was the last time—nerve-wrenching thoughts came to me in profound anxiety.

As I searchingly examined the activities of the Jewish race through long periods of human history, the disquieting question suddenly arose as to whether perhaps inexplicable Fate had not, for reasons that were unknown to us poor humans, with eternal and unalterable determination desired the final victory of this little people?

Should this race, who live eternally only for this world, be adjudged this world as a reward?

Do we have an objective right to fight for our own self-preservation, or is this right only subjectively grounded in us?

As I steeped myself in the teachings of Marxism, and so could subject the activities of the Jewish race to contemplation in peaceful lucidity, Fate itself gave me its answer.

The Jewish dogma of Marxism rejects the aristocratic principle of Nature and sets in the place of the everlasting prerogative of power and strength the mass of numbers and their dead weight. Therewith it denies the value of the individual in man, disputes the importance of nationality and race and with this deprives humanity of the prerequisite of its existence and its culture. As a basis for the universe, it would lead to the end of every order conceivable to man. And so, as in this greatest of all recognizable organisms the application of such a law could only result in chaos, on earth it could only bring about their own destruction for the inhabitants of this star.

If, with the aid of his Marxist faith, the Jew triumphs over the peoples of this world, then his crown will be the funeral wreath of the human race; then this planet will move through the ether empty of men as it did millions of years before.

Eternal Nature is relentless in taking vengeance for trespasses against her commandments.

So today I believe that I am acting in accordance with the almighty Creator: *by resisting the Jews, I am fighting for the work of the Lord.*

The State

For this glorious creative ability was given only to the Aryan, whether he bears it dormant within himself or gives it to awakening life, depending whether favorable circumstances permit this or an inhospitable Nature prevents it.

From this the following realization results:

The state is a means to an end. Its end lies in the preservation and advancement of a community of physically and psychically homogeneous creatures. This preservation itself comprises first of all existence as a race and thereby permits the free development of all the forces dormant in this race. Of them a part will always primarily serve the preservation of physical life, and only the remaining part the promotion of a further spiritual development. Actually the one always creates the precondition for the other.

States which do not serve this purpose are misbegotten, monstrosities in fact. The fact of their existence changes this no more than the success of a gang of bandits can justify robbery.

We National Socialists as champions of a new philosophy of life must never base ourselves on so-called "accepted facts"—and false ones at that. If we did, we would not be the champions of a new great idea, but the coolies of the present-day lie. We must distinguish in the sharpest way between the state as a vessel and the race as its content. This vessel has meaning only if it can preserve and protect the content; otherwise it is useless.

Thus, the highest purpose of a folkish state is concern for the preservation of those original racial elements which bestow culture and create the beauty and dignity of a higher mankind. We, as Aryans, can conceive of the state only as the living organism of a nationality which not only assures the preservation of this nationality, but by the development of its spiritual and ideal abilities leads it to the highest freedom.

But what they try to palm off on us as a state today is usually nothing but a monstrosity born of deepest human error, with untold misery as a consequence.

We National Socialists know that with this conception we stand as revolutionaries in the world of today and are also branded as such. But our thoughts and actions must in no way be determined by the approval or disapproval of our time, but by the binding obligation to a truth which we have recognized. Then we may be convinced that the higher insight of posterity will not only understand our actions of today, but will also confirm their correctness and exalt them.

From this, we National Socialists derive a standard for the evaluation of a state. This value will be relative from the standpoint of the individual nationality, absolute from that of humanity as such. This means, in other words:

The quality of a state cannot be evaluated according to the cultural level or the power of this state in the frame of the outside world, but solely and exclusively by the degree of this institution's virtue for the nationality involved in each special case.

A state can be designated as exemplary if it is not only compatible with the living conditions of the nationality it is intended to represent, but if in practice it keeps this nationality alive by its own very existence—quite regardless of the importance of this state formation within the framework of the outside world. For the function of the state is not to create abilities, but only to open the road for those forces which are present. *Thus, conversely, a state can be designated as bad if, despite a high cultural level, it dooms the bearer of this culture in his racial composition.* For thus it destroys to all intents and purposes the premise for the survival of this culture which it did not create, but which is the fruit of a culture-creating nationality safe-guarded by a living integration through the state. The state does not represent the content, but a form. *A people's cultural level at any time does not, therefore, provide a standard for measuring the quality of the state* in which it lives. It is easily understandable that a people highly endowed with culture offers a more valuable picture than a Negro tribe; nevertheless, the state organism of the former, viewed according to its fulfillment of purpose, can be inferior to that of the Negro. Though the best state and the best state form are not able to extract from a people abilities which are simply lacking and never did exist, a bad state is assuredly able to kill originally existing abilities by permitting or even promoting the destruction of the racial culture-bearer.

Hence our judgment concerning the quality of a state can primarily be determined only by the relative utility it possesses for a definite nationality, and in no event by the intrinsic importance attributable to it in the world.

This relative judgment can be passed quickly and easily, but the judgment concerning absolute value only with great difficulty, since this absolute judgment is no longer determined merely by the state, but by the quality and level of the nationality in question.

If, therefore, we speak of a higher mission of the state, we must not forget that the higher mission lies essentially in the nationality whose free development the state must merely make possible by the organic force of its being.

Hence, if we propound the question of how the state which we Germans need should be constituted, we must first clearly understand what kind of people it is to contain and what purpose it is to serve.

Our German nationality, unfortunately, is no longer based on a unified racial nucleus. The blending process of the various original components has advanced so far that we might speak of a new race. On the contrary, the poisonings of the blood which have befallen our people, especially since the Thirty Years' War, have led not only to a decomposition of our blood, but also of our soul. The open borders of our fatherland, the association with un-German foreign bodies along these frontier districts, but above all the strong and continuous influx of foreign blood into the interior of the Reich itself, due to its continuous renewal, leaves no time for an absolute blending. No new race is distilled out, the racial constituents remain side by side, with the result that, especially in critical moments in which otherwise a herd habitually gathers together, the German people scatters to all the four winds. Not only are the basic racial elements scattered territorially, but on a small scale within the same territory. Beside Nordic men Easterners, beside Easterners Dinarics, beside both of these Westerners, and mixtures in between. On the one hand, this is a great disadvantage: the

German people lack that sure herd instinct which is based on unity of the blood and, especially in moments of threatening danger, preserves nations from destruction in so far as all petty inner differences in such peoples vanish at once on such occasions and the solid front of a unified herd confronts the common enemy. This co-existence of unblended basic racial elements of the most varying kind accounts for what is termed *hyper-individualism* in Germany. In peaceful periods it may sometimes do good services, but taking all things together, it has robbed us of world domination. If the German people in its historic development had possessed that herd unity which other peoples enjoyed, the German Reich today would doubtless be mistress of the globe. World history would have taken a different course, and no one can distinguish whether in this way we would not have obtained what so many blinded pacifists today hope to gain by begging, whining, and whimpering: *a peace, supported not by the palm branches of tearful, pacifist female mourners, but based on the victorious sword of a master people, putting the world into the service of a higher culture.*

The fact of the non-existence of a nationality of unified blood has brought us untold misery. It has given capital cities to many small German potentates, but deprived the German people of the master's right.

Today our people are still suffering from this inner division; but what brought us misfortune in the past and present can be our blessing for the future. For detrimental as it was on the one hand that a complete blending of our original racial components did not take place, and that the formation of a unified national body was thus prevented, it was equally fortunate on the other hand that in this way at least a part of our best blood was preserved pure and escaped racial degeneration.

Assuredly, if there had been a complete blending of our original racial elements, a unified national body would have arisen; however, as every racial cross-breeding proves, it would have been endowed with a smaller cultural capacity than the highest of the original components originally possessed. This is the blessing of the absence of complete blending: that today in our German national body we still possess great unmixed stocks of Nordic-Germanic people whom we may consider the most precious treasure for our future. In the confused period of ignorance of all racial laws, when a man appeared to be simply a man, with full equality—clarity may have been lacking with regard to the different value of the various original elements. Today we know that a complete intermixture of the components of our people might, in consequence of the unity thus produced, have given us outward power, but that the highest goal of mankind would have been unattainable, since the sole bearer, whom Fate had clearly chosen for this completion, would have perished in the general racial porridge of the unified people.

But what, through none of our doing, a kind Fate prevented, we must today examine and evaluate from the standpoint of the knowledge we have now acquired.

Anyone who speaks of a mission of the German people on earth must know that it can exist only in the formation of a state which sees its highest task in the preservation and promotion of the most noble elements of our nationality, indeed of all mankind, which still remain intact.

Thus, for the first time the state achieves a lofty inner goal. Compared to the absurd catchword about safeguarding law and order, thus laying a peaceable groundwork for mutual swindles, the task of preserving and advancing the highest humanity, given to this earth by the benevolence of the Almighty, seems a truly high mission.

From a dead mechanism which only lays claim to existence for its own sake, there must be formed a living organism with the exclusive aim of serving a higher idea.

The German Reich as a state must embrace all Germans and has the task, not only of assembling and preserving the most valuable stocks of basic racial elements in this people, but slowly and surely of raising them to a dominant position.

Thus, a condition which is fundamentally one of paralysis is replaced by a period of struggle, but as everywhere and always in this world, here, too, the saying remains valid that "he who rests—rusts," and, furthermore, that victory lies eternally and exclusively in attack. The greater the goal we have in mind in our struggle, and the smaller the understanding of the broad masses for it may be at the moment, all the more gigantic, as the experience of world history shows, will be the success—and the significance of this success if the goal is correctly comprehended and the struggle is carried through with unswerving perseverance.

Of course it may be more soothing for many of our present official helmsmen of the state to work for the preservation of an *existing* condition than having to fight for a new one. They will find it much easier to regard the state as a mechanism which exists simply in order to keep itself alive, since in turn their lives "*belong to the state*"—as they are accustomed to put it. As though something which sprang from the nationality could logically serve anything else than the nationality or man could work for anything else than man. *Of course, as I have said before, it is easier to see in state authority the mere formal mechanism of an organization than the sovereign embodiment of a nationality's instinct of self-preservation on earth.* For in the one case the state, as well as state authority, is for these weak minds a purpose in itself, while in the other, it is only a mighty weapon in the service of the great, eternal life struggle for existence, a weapon to which everyone must submit because it is not formal and mechanical, but the expression of a common will for preserving life.

Hence, in the struggle for our new conception, which is entirely in keeping with the primal meaning of things, we shall find few fellow warriors in a society which not only is physically senile but, sad to say, usually, mentally as well. Only exceptions, old men with young hearts and fresh minds, will come to us from those classes, never those who see the ultimate meaning of their life task in the preservation of an existing condition.

We are confronted by the endless army, not so much of the deliberately bad as of the mentally lazy and indifferent, including those with a stake in the preservation of the present condition. But precisely in this apparent hopelessness of our gigantic struggle lies the greatness of our task and also the possibility of our success. The battle-cry which either scares away the small spirits at the very start, or soon makes them despair, will be the signal for the assemblage of real fighting natures. And this we must see clearly: *If in a people a certain amount of the highest energy and active force seems concentrated upon one goal and hence is definitively removed from the inertia of the broad masses, this small percentage has risen to be master over the entire number. World history is made by minorities when this minority of number embodies the majority of will and determination.*

What, therefore, may appear as a difficulty today is in reality the premise for our victory. Precisely in the greatness and the difficulties of our task lies the probability that only the best fighters will step forward to struggle for it. And in this selection lies the guaranty of success. . . .

If as the first task of the state in the service and for the welfare of its nationality we recognize the preservation, care, and development of the best racial elements, it is natural that this care must not only extend to the birth of every little national and racial comrade, but that it must educate the young offspring to become a valuable link in the chain of future reproduction.

And as in general the precondition for spiritual achievement lies in the racial quality of the human material at hand, education in particular must first of all consider and promote physical health; for taken in the mass, a healthy, forceful spirit will be found only in a healthy and forceful body. The fact that geniuses are sometimes physically not very fit, or actually sick, is no argument against this. Here we have to do with exceptions which—as everywhere—only confirm the rule. But if the mass of a people consists of physical degenerates, from this swamp a really great spirit will very seldom arise. In any case his activity will not meet with great success. The degenerate rabble will either not understand him at all, or it will be so weakened in will that it can no longer follow the lofty flight of such an eagle.

Realizing this, the folkish state must not adjust its entire educational work primarily to the inoculation of mere knowledge, but to the breeding of absolutely healthy bodies. The training of mental abilities is only secondary. And here again, first place must be taken by the development of character, especially the promotion of will-power and determination, combined with the training of joy in responsibility, and only in last place comes scientific schooling.

Here the folkish state must proceed from the assumption *that a man of little scientific education but physically healthy, with a good, firm character, imbued with the joy of determination and will-power, is more valuable for the national community than a clever weakling.* A people of scholars, if they are physically degenerate, weak-willed and cowardly pacifists, will not storm the heavens, indeed they will not even be able to safeguard their existence on this earth. In the hard struggle of destiny the man who knows least seldom succumbs, but always he who from his knowledge draws the weakest consequences and is most lamentable in transforming them into action. Here too, finally, a certain harmony must be present. *A decayed body is not made the least more aesthetic by a brilliant mind,* indeed the highest intellectual training could not be justified if its bearers were at the same time physically degenerate and crippled, weak-willed, wavering and cowardly individuals. What makes the Greek ideal of beauty a model is the wonderful combination of the most magnificent physical beauty with brilliant mind and noblest soul.

If Moltke's saying, "In the long run only the able man has luck," is anywhere applicable, it is surely to the relation between body and mind; the mind, too, if it is healthy, will as a rule and in the long run dwell only in the healthy body.

Physical training in the folkish state, therefore, is not an affair of the individual, and not even a matter which primarily regards the parents and only secondly or thirdly interests the community; it is a requirement for the self-preservation of the nationality, represented and protected by the state. Just as the state, as far as purely scientific education is concerned, even today interferes with the individual's right of self-determination and upholds the right of the totality toward him by subjecting the child to compulsory education without asking whether the parents want it or not—in far greater measure the folkish state must some day enforce its authority against the individual's ignorance or lack of understanding in questions regarding the preservation of the nationality. It must so organize its educational work that the young bodies are treated expediently in their earliest childhood and obtain the necessary steeling for later life. It must above all prevent the rearing of a generation of hothouse plants.

This work of care and education must begin with the young mother. Just as it became possible in the course of careful work over a period of decades to achieve antiseptic cleanliness in childbirth and reduce puerperal fever to a few cases, it must and will be possible, by a thorough training of nurses and mothers themselves, to achieve a treatment of the child in his first years that will serve as an excellent basis for future development.

The school as such in a folkish state must create infinitely more free time for physical training. It is not permissible to burden young brains with a ballast only a fraction of which they retain, as experience shows, not to mention the fact that as a rule it is unnecessary trifles that stick instead of essentials, since the young child cannot undertake a sensible sifting of the material that has been funneled into him. If today, even in the curriculum of the secondary schools, gymnastics gets barely two hours a week and participation in it is not even obligatory, but is left open to the individual, that is a gross incongruity compared to the purely mental training. Not a day should go by in which the young man does not receive one hour's physical training in the morning and one in the afternoon, covering every type of sport and gymnastics. And here one sport in particular must not be forgotten, which in the eyes of many "folkish" minded people is considered vulgar and undignified: boxing. It is incredible what false opinions are widespread in "educated" circles. It is regarded as natural and honorable that a young man should learn to fence and proceed to fight duels right and left, but if he boxes, it is supposed to be vulgar! Why? There is no sport that so much as this one promotes the spirit of attack, demands lightning decisions, and trains the body in steel dexterity. It is no more vulgar for two young men to fight out a difference of opinion with their fists than with a piece of whetted iron. It is not less noble if a man who has been attacked defends himself against his assailant with his fists, instead of running away and yelling for a policeman. But above all, the young, healthy body must also learn to suffer blows. Of course this may seem wild to the eyes of our present spiritual fighters. But it is not the function of the folkish state to breed a colony of peaceful aesthetes and physical degenerates. Not in the respectable shopkeeper or virtuous old maid does it see its ideal of humanity, but in the defiant embodiment of manly strength and in women who are able to bring men into the world.

And so sport does not exist only to make the individual strong, agile and bold; it should also toughen him and teach him to bear hardships.

If our entire intellectual upper crust had not been brought up so exclusively on upper-class etiquette; if instead they had learned boxing thoroughly, a German revolution of pimps, deserters, and such-like rabble would never have been possible; for what gave this revolution success was not the bold, courageous energy of the revolutionaries, but the cowardly, wretched indecision of those who led the state and were responsible for it.

The fact is that our whole intellectual leadership had received only "intellectual" education and hence could not help but be defenseless the moment not intellectual weapons but the crowbar went into action on the opposing side. All this was possible only because as a matter of principle especially our higher educational system did not train men, but officials, engineers, technicians, chemists, jurists, journalists, and to keep these intellectuals from dying out, professors.

Our intellectual leadership always performed brilliant feats, while our leadership in the matter of will-power usually remained beneath all criticism.

Certainly it will not be possible to turn a man of basically cowardly disposition into a courageous man by education, but just as certainly a man who in himself is not cowardly will be paralyzed in the development of his qualities if due to deficiencies in his education he is from the very start inferior to his neighbor in physical strength and dexterity. To what extent the conviction of physical ability promotes a man's sense of courage, even arouses his spirit of attack, can best be judged by the example of the army. Here, too, essentially, we have to deal not solely with heroes but with the broad average. But the superior training of the German soldier in peacetime inoculated the whole gigantic organism with that suggestive faith in its own superiority to an extent which even our foes had not considered possible. For the immortal offensive spirit and offensive courage achieved in the long months of midsummer and autumn 1914 by the forward-sweeping German armies was the result of that untiring training which in the long, long years of peace obtained the most incredible achievement often out of frail bodies, and thus cultivated that self-confidence which was not lost even in the terror of the greatest battles.

Particularly our German people which today lies broken and defenseless, exposed to the kicks of all the world, needs that suggestive force that lies in self-confidence. This self-confidence must be inculcated in the young national comrade from childhood on. His whole education and training must be so ordered as to give him the conviction that he is absolutely superior to others. Through his physical strength and dexterity, he must recover his faith in the invincibility of his whole people. For what formerly led the German army to victory was the sum of the confidence which each individual had in himself and all together in their leadership. What will raise the German people up again is confidence in the possibility of regaining its freedom. And this conviction can only be the final product of the same feeling in millions of individuals.

Here, too, we must not deceive ourselves:

Immense was the collapse of our people, and the exertion needed to end this misery some day will have to be just as immense. Anyone who thinks that our present bourgeois education for peace and order will give our people the strength some day to smash the present world order, which means our doom, and to hurl the links of our slavery into the face of our enemies, is bitterly mistaken. Only by super-abundance of national will-power, thirst for freedom, and highest passion, will we compensate for what we formerly lacked. . . .

Propaganda and Organization

In several respects the year 1921 had assumed a special significance for me and the movement.

After my entrance into the German Workers' Party, I at once took over the management of propaganda. I regarded this department as by far the most important. For the present, it was less important to rack one's brains over organizational questions than to transmit the idea itself to a larger number of people. Propaganda had to run far in advance of organization and provide it with the human material to be worked on. Moreover, I am an enemy of too rapid and too pedantic organizing. It usually produces nothing but a dead mechanism, seldom a living organization. For organization is a thing that owes its existence to organic life, organic development. Ideas which have gripped a certain number of people will always strive for a greater order, and a great value must be attributed to this inner molding. Here, too, we must reckon with the weakness of men, which leads the individual, at first at least, instinctively to resist a superior mind. If an organization is mechanically ordered from above, there exists a great danger that a once appointed leader, not yet accurately evaluated and perhaps none too capable, will from jealousy strive to prevent the rise of abler elements within the movement. The harm that arises in such a case can, especially in a young movement, be of catastrophic significance.

For this reason it is more expedient for a time to disseminate an idea by propaganda from a central point and then carefully to search and examine the gradually gathering human material for leading minds. Sometimes it will turn out that men inconspicuous in themselves must nevertheless be regarded as born leaders.

But it would be absolutely mistaken to regard a wealth of theoretical knowledge as characteristic proof for the qualities and abilities of a leader.

The opposite is often the case.

The great *theoreticians* are only in the rarest cases great *organizers,* since the greatness of the *theoretician* and *program-maker* lies primarily in the *recognition* and *establishment of abstractly correct laws,* while the *organizer* must primarily be a *psychologist.* He must take people as they are and must therefore know them. He must not overestimate them, any more than he must underestimate them in the mass. On the contrary, he must endeavor to take weakness and bestiality equally into account, in order, considering all factors, to create a formation which will be a living organism, imbued with strong and stable power, and thus suited to upholding an idea and paving the way for its success.

Even more seldom, however, is a great theoretician a great leader. Much more readily will an *agitator* be one, something which many who only work scientifically on the question do not want to hear. And yet that is understandable. An agitator who demonstrates the ability to transmit an idea to the broad masses must always be a psychologist, even if he were only a demagogue. Then he will still be more suited for leadership than the unworldly theoretician, who is ignorant of people. *For leading means: being able to move masses.* The gift of shaping ideas has nothing to do with ability as a leader. And it is quite useless to argue which is of greater importance, to set up ideals and aims for mankind, or to realize them. Here, as so often in life: one would be utterly meaningless without the other. The finest theoretical insight remains without purpose and value if the leader does not set the masses in motion toward it. And conversely, of what avail would be all the genius and energy of a leader, if the brilliant theoretician did not set up aims for the human struggle? However, the combination of theoretician, organizer, and leader in one person is the rarest thing that can be found on this earth; this combination makes the great man.

As I have already remarked, I devoted myself to propaganda in the first period of my activity in the movement. What it had to do was gradually to fill a small nucleus of men with the new doctrine, and so prepare the material which could later furnish the first elements of an organization.

When a movement harbors the purpose of tearing down a world and building another in its place, complete clarity must reign in the ranks of its own leadership with regard to the following principles:

Every movement will first have to sift the human material it wins into two large groups: supporters and members.

The function of propaganda is to attract supporters, the function of organization is to win members.

A supporter of a movement is one who declares himself to be in agreement with its aims, a member is one who fights for them.

The supporter is made amenable to the movement by propaganda. The member is induced by the organization to participate personally in the recruiting of new supporters, from whom in turn members can be developed.

Since being a supporter requires only a passive recognition of an idea, while membership demands active advocacy and defense, to ten supporters there will at most be one or two members.

Being a supporter is rooted only in understanding, membership in the courage personally to advocate and disseminate what has been understood.

Understanding in its passive form corresponds to the majority of man-

kind which is lazy and cowardly. Membership requires an activistic frame of mind and thus corresponds only to the minority of men.

Propaganda will consequently have to see that an idea wins supporters, while the organization must take the greatest care only to make the most valuable elements among the supporters into members. Propaganda does not, therefore, need to rack its brains with regard to the importance of every individual instructed by it, with regard to his ability, capacity, and understanding, or character, while the organization must carefully gather from the mass of these elements those which really make possible the victory of the movement.

Propaganda tries to force a doctrine on the whole people; the organization embraces within its scope only those who do not threaten on psychological grounds to become a brake on the further dissemination of the idea.

Propaganda works on the general public from the standpoint of an idea and makes them ripe for the victory of this idea, while the organization achieves victory by the persistent, organic, and militant union of those supporters who seem willing and able to carry on the fight for victory.

The victory of an idea will be possible the sooner, the more comprehensively propaganda has prepared people as a whole and the more exclusive, rigid, and firm the organization which carries out the fight in practice.

From this it results that the number of supporters cannot be too large, but that the number of members can more readily be too large than too small.

If propaganda has imbued a whole people with an idea, the organization can draw the consequences with a handful of men. Propaganda and organization, in other words, supporters and members thus stand in a certain mutual relation. The better the propaganda has worked, the smaller the organization can be; and the larger the number of supporters, the more modest the number of members can be; and vice versa: the poorer the propaganda is, the larger the organization must be, and the smaller the host of followers of a movement remains, the more extensive the number of its members must be, if it still hopes to count on any success at all.

The first task of propaganda is to win people for subsequent organization; the first task of organization is to win men for the continuation of propaganda. The second task of propaganda is the disruption of the existing state of affairs and the permeation of this state of affairs with the new doctrine, while the second task of organization must be the struggle for power, thus to achieve the final success of the doctrine.

The most striking success of a revolution based on a philosophy of life will always have been achieved when the new philosophy of life as far as possible has been taught to all men, and, if necessary, later forced upon them, while the organization of the idea, in other words, the movement, should embrace only as many as are absolutely required for occupying the nerve centers of the state in question.

This, in other words, means the following:

In every really great world-shaking movement, propaganda will first have to spread the idea of this movement. Thus, it will indefatigably attempt to make the new thought processes clear to the others, and therefore to draw them over to their own ground, or to make them uncertain of their previous conviction. Now, since the dissemination of an idea, that is, propaganda, must have a firm backbone, the doctrine will have to give itself a solid organization. The organization obtains its members from the general body of supporters won by propaganda. The latter will grow the more rapidly, the more intensively the propaganda is carried on, and the latter in turn can work better, the stronger and more powerful the organization is that stands behind it.

Hence it is the highest task of the organization to make sure that no inner disunities within the membership of the movement lead to a split and hence a weakening of the movement's work; further, that the spirit of determined attack does not die out, but is continuously renewed and reinforced. The number of members need not grow infinitely; on the contrary: since only a small fraction of mankind is by nature energetic and bold, a movement which endlessly enlarges its organization would inevitably be weakened some day as a result. *Organizations, in other words, membership figures, which grow beyond a certain level gradually lose their fighting power and are no longer capable of supporting or utilizing the propaganda of an idea resolutely and aggressively.*

The greater and more essentially revolutionary an idea is, the more activistic its membership will become, since the revolutionary force of a doctrine involves a danger for its supporters, which seems calculated to keep cowardly little shopkeepers away from it. They will privately regard themselves as supporters, but decline to make a public avowal of this by membership. *By virtue of this fact, the organization of a really revolutionary idea obtains as members only the most active among the supporters won over by propaganda.* And precisely in this activity of a movement's membership, guaranteed by natural selection, lies the premise for equally active future propaganda as well as a successful struggle for the realization of the idea.

The greatest danger that can threaten a movement is a membership which has grown abnormally as a result of too rapid successes. For, just as a movement is shunned by all cowardly and egotistic individuals, as long as it has to fight bitterly, these same people rush with equal alacrity to acquire membership when a success of the party has been made probable or already realized by developments.

To this it must be ascribed why many victorious movements, on the point of success, or, rather, the ultimate completion of their will, suddenly from inexplicable inner weakness, flag, stop fighting, and finally die out. In consequence of their first victory, so many inferior, unworthy, and worst of all cowardly, elements have entered their organization that these inferior people finally achieve predominance over the militants and then force the movement into the service of their own interests, lower it to the level of their own scanty heroism, and do nothing to complete the victory of the original idea. The fanatical zeal has been blurred, the fighting force paralyzed, or, as the bourgeois world correctly puts it in such cases: "Water has been mixed with the wine." And when that happens, the trees can no longer grow skyward.

It is, therefore, most necessary that a movement, for pure reasons of self-preservation, should, once it has begun to achieve success, immediately block enrollments and henceforth increase its organization only with extreme caution and after the most thorough scrutiny. Only in this way will it be able to preserve the core of the movement in unvitiated freshness and health. *It must see to it that, from this point on, this core alone shall exclusively lead the movement, that is, determine the propaganda which should lead to its universal recognition, and, in full possession of the power, undertake the actions which are necessary for the practical realization of its ideas.*

It must not only occupy all the important positions of the conquered territory with the basic core of the old movement, but also constitute the entire leadership. And this until the principles and doctrines of the party have become the foundation and content of the new state. Only then can the reins gradually be handed over to the special government of this state, born of its spirit. This, however, in turn occurs for the most part only in mutual struggle, since it is less a question of human insight than of the play and workings of forces which can perhaps be recognized from the first, but cannot forever be guided.

All great movements, whether of a religious or a political nature, must attribute their mighty successes only to the recognition and application of these principles, and all lasting successes in particular are not even thinkable without consideration of these laws. . . .

16. Benito Mussolini, *The Doctrine of Fascism*

Benito Mussolini (1883–1945) was born in a small village in northern
Italy, his father a blacksmith, his mother a schoolteacher. As a young man
he worked briefly as a schoolteacher himself. He early became a socialist
and lived for two years in Switzerland, where he attended lectures by
Vilfredo Pareto at Lausanne and read the works of Sorel, Nietzsche, and
Schopenhauer, all of whom influenced his later political visions. From
1912 to 1914 he was editor of *Avanti!* the newspaper of the Italian Socialist party. A neutralist at the beginning of World War I, he soon moved
to fervent interventionism, working for the entry of Italy into the war on
the side of the Allies. In November 1914 he was expelled from the Socialist party and founded his own paper, the *Il Popolo d'Italia* in Milan.
From 1915 to 1917 he served in the Italian army. In 1919 he founded the
Fasci di Combattimento, a revolutionary network of political cells appealing to ex-socialists, disgruntled war veterans, syndicalists, intellectuals, and petty bourgeois voters which gained a reputation for terrorism
and anti-Socialist propaganda. The maneuvering behind the Fascist
"March on Rome" in October 1922 forced King Victor Emmanuel III to
name Mussolini Prime Minister. In the following years Mussolini crushed
all opposition and from 1925 ruled Italy as authoritarian leader (*Duce*).
His dismissal from office in July 1943 brought the collapse of the Fascist
regime. He was arrested and placed in custody at a ski resort on the Gran
Sasso in the Apennines. Rescued by German commandos, he escaped to
Germany and reentered Italy in September 1943, a broken man. In late
April 1945 he was arrested by Italian partisans and executed with his
mistress, Clara Petacci, near Lake Como on April 28.

The essay printed below was first published in the *Enciclopedia Itali-
ana* in 1932.

(i) Fundamental Ideas

1. Like every sound political conception, Fascism is both practice and
thought; action in which a doctrine is immanent, and a doctrine which,
arising out of a given system of historical forces, remains embedded in
them and works there from within. Hence it has a form correlative to the
contingencies of place and time, but it has also a content of thought which

From *The Social and Political Doctrines of Contemporary Europe*, edited and translated
by Michael Oakeshott (Cambridge: At the University Press, 1947), pp. 164–79. Reprinted by
permission of the publisher.

raises it to a formula of truth in the higher level of the history of thought. In the world one does not act spiritually as a human will dominating other wills without a conception of the transient and particular reality under which it is necessary to act, and of the permanent and universal reality in which the first has its being and its life. In order to know men it is necessary to know man; and in order to know man it is necessary to know reality and its laws. There is no concept of the State which is not fundamentally a concept of life: philosophy or intuition, a system of ideas which develops logically or is gathered up into a vision or into a faith, but which is always, at least virtually, an organic conception of the world.

2. Thus Fascism could not be understood in many of its practical manifestations as a party organization, as a system of education, as a discipline, if it were not always looked at in the light of its whole way of conceiving life, a spiritualized way. The world seen through Fascism is not this material world which appears on the surface, in which man is an individual separated from all others and standing by himself, and in which he is governed by a natural law that makes him instinctively live a life of selfish and momentary pleasure. The man of Fascism is an individual who is nation and fatherland, which is a moral law, binding together individuals and the generations into a tradition and a mission, suppressing the instinct for a life enclosed within the brief round of pleasure in order to restore within duty a higher life free from the limits of time and space: a life in which the individual, through the denial of himself, through the sacrifice of his own private interests, through death itself, realizes that completely spiritual existence in which his value as a man lies.

3. Therefore it is a spiritualized conception, itself the result of the general reaction of modern times against the flabby materialistic positivism of the nineteenth century. Anti-positivistic, but positive: not sceptical, nor agnostic, nor pessimistic, nor passively optimistic, as are, in general, the doctrines (all negative) that put the centre of life outside man, who with his free will can and must create his own world. Fascism desires an active man, one engaged in activity with all his energies: it desires a man virilely conscious of the difficulties that exist in action and ready to face them. It conceives of life as a struggle, considering that it behoves man to conquer for himself that life truly worthy of him, creating first of all in himself the instrument (physical, moral, intellectual) in order to construct it. Thus for the single individual, thus for the nation, thus for humanity. Hence the high value of culture in all its forms (art, religion, science), and the enormous importance of education. Hence also the essential value of work, with which man conquers nature and creates the human world (economic, political, moral, intellectual).

4. This positive conception of life is clearly an ethical conception. It

covers the whole of reality, not merely the human activity which controls it. No action can be divorced from moral judgement; there is nothing in the world which can be deprived of the value which belongs to everything in its relation to moral ends. Life, therefore, as conceived by the Fascist, is serious, austere, religious: the whole of it is poised in a world supported by the moral and responsible forces of the spirit. The Fascist disdains the "comfortable" life.

5. Fascism is a religious conception in which man is seen in his immanent relationship with a superior law and with an objective Will that transcends the particular individual and raises him to conscious membership of a spiritual society. Whoever has seen in the religious politics of the Fascist regime nothing but mere opportunism has not understood that Fascism besides being a system of government is also, and above all, a system of thought.

6. Fascism is an historical conception, in which man is what he is only in so far as he works with the spiritual process in which he finds himself, in the family or social group, in the nation and in the history in which all nations collaborate. From this follows the great value of tradition, in memories, in language, in customs, in the standards of social life. Outside history man is nothing. Consequently Fascism is opposed to all the individualistic abstractions of a materialistic nature like those of the eighteenth century; and it is opposed to all Jacobin utopias and innovations. It does not consider that "happiness" is possible upon earth, as it appeared to be in the desire of the economic literature of the eighteenth century, and hence it rejects all teleological theories according to which mankind would reach a definitive stabilized condition at a certain period in history. This implies putting oneself outside history and life, which is a continual change and coming to be. Politically, Fascism wishes to be a realistic doctrine; practically, it aspires to solve only the problems which arise historically of themselves and that of themselves find or suggest their own solution. To act among men, as to act in the natural world, it is necessary to enter into the process of reality and to master the already operating forces.

7. Against individualism, the Fascist conception is for the State; and it is for the individual in so far as he coincides with the State, which is the conscience and universal will of man in his historical existence. It is opposed to classical Liberalism, which arose from the necessity of reacting against absolutism, and which brought its historical purpose to an end when the State was transformed into the conscience and will of the people. Liberalism denied the State in the interests of the particular individual; Fascism reaffirms the State as the true reality of the individual. And if liberty is to be the attribute of the real man, and not of that abstract puppet envisaged by individualistic Liberalism, Fascism is for liberty. And for the

only liberty which can be a real thing, the liberty of the State and of the individual within the State. Therefore, for the Fascist, everything is in the State, and nothing human or spiritual exists, much less has value, outside the State. In this sense Fascism is totalitarian, and the Fascist State, the synthesis and unity of all values, interprets, develops and gives strength to the whole life of the people.

8. Outside the State there can be neither individuals nor groups (political parties, associations, syndicates, classes). Therefore Fascism is opposed to Socialism, which confines the movement of history within the class struggle and ignores the unity of classes established in one economic and moral reality in the State; and analogously it is opposed to class syndicalism. Fascism recognizes the real exigencies for which the socialist and syndicalist movement arose, but while recognizing them wishes to bring them under the control of the State and give them a purpose within the corporative system of interests reconciled within the unity of the State.

9. Individuals form classes according to the similarity of their interests, they form syndicates according to differentiated economic activities within these interests; but they form first, and above all, the State, which is not to be thought of numerically as the sum-total of individuals forming the majority of a nation. And consequently Fascism is opposed to Democracy, which equates the nation to the majority, lowering it to the level of that majority; nevertheless it is the purest form of democracy if the nation is conceived, as it should be, qualitatively and not quantitatively, as the most powerful idea (most powerful because most moral, most coherent, most true) which acts within the nation as the conscience and the will of a few, even of One, which ideal tends to become active within the conscience and the will of all—that is to say, of all those who rightly constitute a nation by reason of nature, history or race, and have set out upon the same line of development and spiritual formation as one conscience and one sole will. Not a race, nor a geographically determined region, but as a community historically perpetuating itself, a multitude unified by a single idea, which is the will to existence and to power: consciousness of itself, personality.

10. This higher personality is truly the nation in so far as it is the State. It is not the nation that generates the State, as according to the old naturalistic concept which served as the basis of the political theories of the national States of the nineteenth century. Rather the nation is created by the State, which gives to the people, conscious of its own moral unity, a will and therefore an effective existence. The right of a nation to independence derives not from a literary and ideal consciousness of its own being, still less from a more or less unconscious and inert acceptance of a *de facto* situation, but from an active consciousness, from a political will in action and ready to demonstrate its own rights: that is to say, from a state already

coming into being. The State, in fact, as the universal ethical will, is the creator of right.

11. The nation as the State is an ethical reality which exists and lives in so far as it develops. To arrest its development is to kill it. Therefore the State is not only the authority which governs and gives the form of laws and the value of spiritual life to the wills of individuals, but it is also a power that makes its will felt abroad, making it known and respected, in other words, demonstrating the fact of its universality in all the necessary directions of its development. It is consequently organization and expansion, at least virtually. Thus it can be likened to the human will which knows no limits to its development and realizes itself in testing its own limitlessness.

12. The Fascist State, the highest and most powerful form of personality, is a force, but a spiritual force, which takes over all the forms of the moral and intellectual life of man. It cannot therefore confine itself simply to the functions of order and supervision as Liberalism desired. It is not simply a mechanism which limits the sphere of the supposed liberties of the individual. It is the form, the inner standard and the discipline of the whole person; it saturates the will as well as the intelligence. Its principle, the central inspiration of the human personality living in the civil community, pierces into the depths and makes its home in the heart of the man of action as well as of the thinker, of the artist as well as of the scientist: it is the soul of the soul.

13. Fascism, in short, is not only the giver of laws and the founder of institutions, but the educator and promoter of spiritual life. It wants to remake, not the forms of human life, but its content, man, character, faith. And to this end it requires discipline and authority that can enter into the spirits of men and there govern unopposed. Its sign, therefore, is the Lictors' rods, the symbol of unity, of strength and justice.

(ii) Political and Social Doctrine

1. When in the now distant March of 1919 I summoned to Milan, through the columns of the *Popolo d'Italia,* my surviving supporters who had followed me since the constitution of the Fasces of Revolutionary Action, founded in January 1915, there was no specific doctrinal plan in my mind. I had known and lived through only one doctrine, that of the Socialism of 1903–4 up to the winter of 1914, almost ten years. My experience in this had been that of a follower and of a leader, but not that of a theoretician. My doctrine, even in that period, had been a doctrine of action. An unequivocal Socialism, universally accepted, did not exist after 1905, when the Revisionist Movement began in Germany under Bernstein

and there was formed in opposition to that, in the see-saw of tendencies, an extreme revolutionary movement, which in Italy never emerged from the condition of mere words, whilst in Russian Socialism it was the prelude to Bolshevism. Reform, Revolution, Centralization—even the echoes of the terminology are now spent; whilst in the great river of Fascism are to be found the streams which had their source in Sorel, Peguy, in the Lagardelle of the *Mouvement Socialiste* and the groups of Italian Syndicalists, who between 1904 and 1914 brought a note of novelty into Italian Socialism, which by that time had been devitalized and drugged by fornication with Giolitti, in *Pagine Libere* of Olivetti, *La Lupa* of Orano and *Divenire Sociale* of Enrico Leone.

In 1919, at the end of the War, Socialism as a doctrine was already dead: it existed only as hatred, it had still only one possibility, especially in Italy, that of revenge against those who had wished for the War and who should be made to expiate it. The *Popolo d'Italia* expressed it in its sub-title— "The Newspaper of Combatants and Producers." The word "producers" was already the expression of a tendency. Fascism was not given out to the wet nurse of a doctrine elaborated beforehand round a table: it was born of the need for action; it was not a party, but in its first two years it was a movement against all parties. The name which I gave to the organization defined its characteristics. Nevertheless, whoever rereads, in the now crumpled pages of the time, the account of the constituent assembly of the *Fasci italiani di Combattimento* will not find a doctrine, but a series of suggestions, of anticipations, of admonitions, which when freed from the inevitable vein of contingency, were destined later, after a few years, to develop into a series of doctrinal attitudes which made of Fascism a self-sufficient political doctrine able to face all others, both past and present. "If the bourgeoisie," I said at that time, "thinks to find in us a lightning-conductor, it is mistaken. We must go forward in opposition to Labour. . . . We want to accustom the working classes to being under a leader, to convince them also that it is not easy to direct an industry or a commercial undertaking successfully. . . . We shall fight against technical and spiritual retrogression. . . . The successors of the present regime still being undecided, we must not be unwilling to fight for it. We must hasten; when the present regime is superseded, we must be the ones to take its place. The right of succession belongs to us because we pushed the country into the War and we led it to victory. The present method of political representation cannot be sufficient for us, we wish for a direct representation of individual interests. . . . It might be said against this programme that it is a return to the corporations. It doesn't matter! . . . I should like, nevertheless, the Assembly to accept the claims of national syndicalism from the point of view of economics. . . ."

Is it not surprising that from the first day in the Piazza San Sepolcro there should resound the word "Corporation" which was destined in the course of the revolution to signify one of the legislative and social creations at the base of the regime?

2. The years preceding the March on Rome were years during which the necessity of action did not tolerate enquiries or complete elaborations of doctrine. Battles were being fought in the cities and villages. There were discussions, but—and this is more sacred and important—there were deaths. People knew how to die. The doctrine—beautiful, well-formed, divided into chapters and paragraphs and surrounded by a commentary— might be missing; but there was present something more decisive to supplant it—Faith. Nevertheless, he who recalls the past with the aid of books, articles, votes in Parliament, the major and the minor speeches, he who knows how to investigate and weigh evidence, will find that the foundations of the doctrine were laid while the battle was raging. It was precisely in these years that Fascist thought armed itself, refined itself, moving towards one organization of its own. The problems of the individual and the State; the problems of authority and liberty; political and social problems and those more specifically national; the struggle against liberal, democratic, socialist, Masonic, demagogic doctrines was carried on at the same time as the "punitive expeditions." But since the "system" was lacking, adversaries ingenuously denied that Fascism had any power to make a doctrine of its own, while the doctrine rose up, even though tumultuously, at first under the aspect of a violent and dogmatic negation, as happens to all ideas that break new ground, then under the positive aspect of a constructive policy which, during the years 1926, 1927, 1928, was realized in the laws and institutions of the regime.

Fascism is to-day clearly defined not only as a regime but as a doctrine. And I mean by this that Fascism to-day, self-critical as well as critical of other movements, has an unequivocal point of view of its own, a criterion, and hence an aim, in face of all the material and intellectual problems which oppress the people of the world.

3. Above all, Fascism, in so far as it considers and observes the future and the development of humanity quite apart from the political considerations of the moment, believes neither in the possibility nor in the utility of perpetual peace. It thus repudiates the doctrine of Pacifism—born of a renunciation of the struggle and an act of cowardice in the face of sacrifice. War alone brings up to their highest tension all human energies and puts the stamp of nobility upon the peoples who have the courage to meet it. All other trials are substitutes, which never really put a man in front of himself in the alternative of life and death. A doctrine, therefore, which begins with a prejudice in favour of peace is foreign to Fascism; as are foreign to

the spirit of Fascism, even though acceptable by reason of the utility which they might have in given political situations, all internationalistic and socialistic systems which, as history proves, can be blown to the winds when emotional, idealistic and practical movements storm the hearts of peoples. Fascism carries over this anti-pacifist spirit even into the lives of individuals. The proud motto of the *Squadrista,* "Me ne frego," written on the bandages of a wound is an act of philosophy which is not only stoical, it is the epitome of a doctrine that is not only political: it is education for combat, the acceptance of the risks which it brings; it is a new way of life for Italy. Thus the Fascist accepts and loves life, he knows nothing of suicide and despises it; he looks on life as duty, ascent, conquest: life which must be noble and full: lived for oneself, but above all for those others near and far away, present and future.

4. The "demographic" policy of the regime follows from these premises. Even the Fascist does in fact love his neighbour, but this "neighbour" is not for him a vague and ill-defined concept; love for one's neighbour does not exclude necessary educational severities, and still less differentiations and distances. Fascism rejects universal concord, and, since it lives in the community of civilized peoples, it keeps them vigilantly and suspiciously before its eyes, it follows their states of mind and the changes in their interests and it does not let itself be deceived by temporary and fallacious appearances.

5. Such a conception of life makes Fascism the precise negation of that doctrine which formed the basis of the so-called Scientific or Marxian Socialism: the doctrine of historical Materialism, according to which the history of human civilizations can be explained only as the struggle of interest between the different social groups and as arising out of change in the means and instruments of production. That economic improvements—discoveries of raw materials, new methods of work, scientific inventions—should have an importance of their own, no one denies, but that they should suffice to explain human history to the exclusion of all other factors is absurd: Fascism believes, now and always, in holiness and in heroism, that is in acts in which no economic motive—remote or immediate—plays a part. With this negation of historical materialism, according to which men would be only by-products of history, who appear and disappear on the surface of the waves while in the depths the real directive forces are at work, there is also denied the immutable and irreparable "class struggle" which is the natural product of this economic conception of history, and above all it is denied that the class struggle can be the primary agent of social changes. Socialism, being thus wounded in these two primary tenets of its doctrine, nothing of it is left save the sentimental aspiration—old as humanity—towards a social order in which the sufferings and the pains of

the humblest folk could be alleviated. But here Fascism rejects the concept of an economic "happiness" which would be realized socialistically and almost automatically at a given moment of economic evolution by assuring to all a maximum prosperity. Fascism denies the possibility of the materialistic conception of "happiness" and leaves it to the economists of the first half of the eighteenth century; it denies, that is, the equation of prosperity with happiness, which would transform men into animals with one sole preoccupation: that of being well-fed and fat, degraded in consequence to a merely physical existence.

6. After Socialism, Fascism attacks the whole complex of democratic ideologies and rejects them both in their theoretical premises and in their applications or practical manifestations. Fascism denies that the majority, through the mere fact of being a majority, can rule human societies; it denies that this majority can govern by means of a periodical consultation; it affirms the irremediable, fruitful and beneficent inequality of men, who cannot be levelled by such a mechanical and extrinsic fact as universal suffrage. By democratic regimes we mean those in which from time to time the people is given the illusion of being sovereign, while true effective sovereignty lies in other, perhaps irresponsible and secret, forces. Democracy is a regime without a king, but with very many kings, perhaps more exclusive, tyrannical and violent than one king even though a tyrant. This explains why Fascism, although before 1922 for reasons of expediency it made a gesture of republicanism, renounced it before the March on Rome, convinced that the question of the political forms of a State is not pre-eminent to-day, and that studying past and present monarchies, past and present Republics, it becomes clear that monarchy and republic are not to be judged *sub specie aeternitatis,* but represent forms in which the political evolution, the history, the tradition, the psychology of a given country are manifested. Now Fascism overcomes the antithesis between monarchy and republic which retarded the movements of democracy, burdening the former with every defect and defending the latter as the regime of perfection. Now it has been seen that there are inherently reactionary and absolutistic republics, and monarchies that welcome the most daring political and social innovations.

7. "Reason, Science," said Renan (who was inspired before Fascism existed) in one of his philosophical Meditations, "are products of humanity, but to expect reason directly from the people and through the people is a chimera. It is not necessary for the existence of reason that everybody should know it. In any case, if such an initiation should be made, it would not be made by means of base democracy, which apparently must lead to the extinction of every difficult culture, and every higher discipline. The principle that society exists only for the prosperity and the liberty of the

individuals who compose it does not seem to conform with the plans of nature, plans in which the species alone is taken into consideration and the individual seems to be sacrificed. It is strongly to be feared lest the last word of democracy thus understood (I hasten to say that it can also be understood in other ways) would be a social state in which a degenerate mass would have no other care than to enjoy the ignoble pleasures of vulgar men."

Thus far Renan. Fascism rejects in democracy the absurd conventional lie of political equalitarianism clothed in the dress of collective irresponsibility and the myth of happiness and indefinite progress. But if democracy can be understood in other ways, that is, if democracy means not to relegate the people to the periphery of the State, then Fascism could be defined as an "organized, centralized, authoritarian democracy."

8. In face of Liberal doctrines, Fascism takes up an attitude of absolute opposition both in the field of politics and in that of economics. It is not necessary to exaggerate—merely for the purpose of present controversies—the importance of Liberalism in the past century, and to make of that which was one of the numerous doctrines sketched in that century a religion of humanity for all times, present and future. Liberalism flourished for no more than some fifteen years. It was born in 1830, as a reaction against the Holy Alliance that wished to drag Europe back to what it had been before 1789, and it had its year of splendour in 1848 when even Pius IX was a Liberal. Immediately afterwards the decay set in. If 1848 was a year of light and of poetry, 1849 was a year of darkness and of tragedy. The Republic of Rome was destroyed by another Republic, that of France. In the same year Marx launched the gospel of the religion of Socialism with the famous *Communist Manifesto*. In 1851 Napoleon III carried out his unliberal *coup d'état* and ruled over France until 1870, when he was dethroned by a popular revolt, but as a consequence of a military defeat which ranks among the most resounding that history can relate. The victor was Bismarck, who never knew the home of the religion of liberty or who were its prophets. It is symptomatic that a people of high culture like the Germans should have been completely ignorant of the religion of liberty during the whole of the nineteenth century. It was, there, no more than a parenthesis, represented by what has been called the "ridiculous Parliament of Frankfort" which lasted only a season. Germany has achieved her national unity outside the doctrines of Liberalism, against Liberalism, a doctrine which seems foreign to the German soul, a soul essentially monarchical, whilst Liberalism is the historical and logical beginning of anarchism. The stages of German unity are the three wars of 1864, 1866 and 1870, conducted by "Liberals" like Moltke and Bismarck. As for Italian unity, Liberalism has had in it a part absolutely inferior to the share of

Mazzini and of Garibaldi, who were not Liberals. Without the intervention of the unliberal Napoleon we should not have gained Lombardy, and without the help of the unliberal Bismarck at Sadowa and Sedan, very probably we should not have gained Venice in 1866; and in 1870 we should not have entered Rome. From 1870–1915 there occurs the period in which the very priests of the new creed had to confess the twilight of their religion: defeated as it was by decadence in literature, by activism in practice. Activism: that is to say, Nationalism, Futurism, Fascism. The "Liberal" century, after having accumulated an infinity of Gordian knots, tried to untie them by the hecatomb of the World War. Never before has any religion imposed such a cruel sacrifice. Were the gods of Liberalism thirsty for blood? Now Liberalism is about to close the doors of its deserted temples because the peoples feel that its agnosticism in economics, its indifferentism in politics and in morals, would lead, as they have led, the States to certain ruin. In this way one can understand why all the political experiences of the contemporary world are anti-Liberal, and it is supremely ridiculous to wish on that account to class them outside of history; as if history were a hunting ground reserved to Liberalism and its professors, as if Liberalism were the definitive and no longer surpassable message of civilization.

9. But the Fascist repudiations of Socialism, Democracy, Liberalism must not make one think that Fascism wishes to make the world return to what it was before 1789, the year which has been indicated as the year of the beginning of the liberal-democratic age. One does not go backwards. The Fascist doctrine has not chosen De Maistre as its prophet. Monarchical absolutism is a thing of the past and so also is every theocracy. So also feudal privileges and division into impenetrable and isolated castes have had their day. The theory of Fascist authority has nothing to do with the police State. A party that governs a nation in a totalitarian way is a new fact in history. References and comparisons are not possible. Fascism takes over from the ruins of Liberal Socialistic democratic doctrines those elements which still have a living value. It preserves those that can be called the established facts of history, it rejects all the rest, that is to say the idea of a doctrine which holds good for all times and all peoples. If it is admitted that the nineteenth century has been the century of Socialism, Liberalism and Democracy, it does not follow that the twentieth must also be the century of Liberalism, Socialism and Democracy. Political doctrines pass; peoples remain. It is to be expected that this century may be that of authority, a century of the "Right," a Fascist century. If the nineteenth was the century of the individual (Liberalism means individualism) it may be expected that this one may be the century of "collectivism" and therefore the century of the State. That a new doctrine should use the still vital elements of other doctrines is perfectly logical. No doctrine is born quite new,

shining, never before seen. No doctrine can boast of an absolute "originality." It is bound, even if only historically, to other doctrines that have been, and to develop into other doctrines that will be. Thus the scientific socialism of Marx is bound to the Utopian Socialism of the Fouriers, the Owens and the Saint-Simons; thus the Liberalism of the nineteenth century is connected with the whole "Enlightenment" of the eighteenth century. Thus the doctrines of democracy are bound to the *Encyclopédie*. Every doctrine tends to direct the activity of men towards a determined objective; but the activity of man reacts upon the doctrine, transforms it, adapts it to new necessities or transcends it. The doctrine itself, therefore, must be, not words, but an act of life. Hence, the pragmatic veins in Fascism, its will to power, its will to be, its attitude in the face of the fact of "violence" and of its own courage.

10. The keystone of Fascist doctrine is the conception of the State, of its essence, of its tasks, of its ends. For Fascism the State is an absolute before which individuals and groups are relative. Individuals and groups are "thinkable" in so far as they are within the State. The Liberal State does not direct the interplay and the material and spiritual development of the groups, but limits itself to registering the results; the Fascist State has a consciousness of its own, a will of its own, on this account it is called an "ethical" State. In 1929, at the first quinquennial assembly of the regime, I said: "For Fascism, the State is not the night-watchman who is concerned only with the personal security of the citizens; nor is it an organization for purely material ends, such as that of guaranteeing a certain degree of prosperity and a relatively peaceful social order, to achieve which a council of administration would be sufficient, nor is it a creation of mere politics with no contact with the material and complex reality of the lives of individuals and the life of peoples. The State, as conceived by Fascism and as it acts, is a spiritual and moral fact because it makes concrete the political, juridical, economic organization of the nation and such an organization is, in its origin and in its development, a manifestation of the spirit. The State is the guarantor of internal and external security, but it is also the guardian and the transmitter of the spirit of the people as it has been elaborated through the centuries in language, custom, faith. The State is not only present, it is also past, and above all future. It is the State which, transcending the brief limit of individual lives, represents the immanent conscience of the nation. The forms in which States express themselves change, but the necessity of the State remains. It is the State which educates citizens for civic virtue, makes them conscious of their mission, calls them to unity; harmonizes their interests in justice; hands on the achievements of thought in the sciences, the arts, in law, in human solidarity; it carries men from the elementary life of the tribe to the highest human expression of power which is

Empire; it entrusts to the ages the names of those who died for its integrity or in obedience to its laws; it puts forward as an example and recommends to the generations that are to come the leaders who increased its territory and the men of genius who gave it glory. When the sense of the State declines and the disintegrating and centrifugal tendencies of individuals and groups prevail, national societies move to their decline."

11. From 1929 up to the present day these doctrinal positions have been strengthened by the whole economico-political evolution of the world. It is the State alone that grows in size, in power. It is the State alone that can solve the dramatic contradictions of capitalism. What is called the crisis cannot be overcome except by the State, within the State. Where are the shades of the Jules Simons who, at the dawn of liberalism, proclaimed that "the State must strive to render itself unnecessary and to prepare for its demise"; of the MacCullochs who, in the second half of the last century, affirmed that the State must abstain from too much governing? And faced with the continual, necessary and inevitable interventions of the State in economic affairs what would the Englishman Bentham now say, according to whom industry should have asked of the State only to be left in peace? Or the German Humboldt, according to whom the "idle" State must be considered the best? It is true that the second generation of liberal economists was less extremist than the first, and already Smith himself opened, even though cautiously, the door to State intervention in economics. But when one says liberalism, one says the individual; when one says Fascism, one says the State. But the Fascist State is unique; it is an original creation. It is not reactionary, but revolutionary in that it anticipates the solutions of certain universal problems. These problems are no longer seen in the same light: in the sphere of politics they are removed from party rivalries, from the supreme power of parliament, from the irresponsibility of assemblies; in the sphere of economics they are removed from the sphere of the syndicates' activities—activities that were ever widening their scope and increasing their power both on the workers' side and on the employers'— removed from their struggles and their designs; in the moral sphere they are divorced from ideas of the need for order, discipline and obedience, and lifted into the plane of the moral commandments of the fatherland. Fascism desires the State to be strong, organic and at the same time founded on a wide popular basis. The Fascist State has also claimed for itself the field of economics and, through the corporative, social and educational institutions which it has created, the meaning of the State reaches out to and includes the farthest off-shoots; and within the State, framed in their respective organizations, there revolve all the political, economic and spiritual forces of the nation. A State founded on millions of individuals who recognize it, feel it, are ready to serve it, is not the tyrannical State of the medi-

eval lord. It has nothing in common with the absolutist States that existed either before or after 1789. In the Fascist State the individual is not suppressed, but rather multiplied, just as in a regiment a soldier is not weakened but multiplied by the number of his comrades. The Fascist State organizes the nation, but it leaves sufficient scope to individuals; it has limited useless or harmful liberties and has preserved those that are essential. It cannot be the individual who decides in this matter, but only the State.

12. The Fascist State does not remain indifferent to the fact of religion in general and to that particular positive religion which is Italian Catholicism. The State has no theology, but it has an ethic. In the Fascist State religion is looked upon as one of the deepest manifestations of the spirit; it is, therefore, not only respected, but defended and protected. The Fascist State does not create a "God" of its own, as Robespierre once, at the height of the Convention's foolishness, wished to do; nor does it vainly seek, like Bolshevism, to expel religion from the minds of men; Fascism respects the God of the ascetics, of the saints, of the heroes, and also God as seen and prayed to by the simple and primitive heart of the people.

13. The Fascist State is a will to power and to government. In it the tradition of Rome is an idea that has force. In the doctrine of Fascism Empire is not only a territorial, military or mercantile expression, but spiritual or moral. One can think of an empire, that is to say a nation that directly or indirectly leads other nations, without needing to conquer a single square kilometre of territory. For Fascism the tendency to Empire, that is to say, to the expansion of nations, is a manifestation of vitality; its opposite, staying at home, is a sign of decadence: peoples who rise or re-rise are imperialist, peoples who die are renunciatory. Fascism is the doctrine that is most fitted to represent the aims, the states of mind, of a people, like the Italian people, rising again after many centuries of abandonment or slavery to foreigners. But Empire calls for discipline, co-ordination of forces, duty and sacrifice; this explains many aspects of the practical working of the regime and the direction of many of the forces of the State and the necessary severity shown to those who would wish to oppose this spontaneous and destined impulse of the Italy of the twentieth century, to oppose it in the name of the superseded ideologies of the nineteenth, repudiated wherever great experiments of political and social transformation have been courageously attempted: especially where, as now, peoples thirst for authority, for leadership, for order. If every age has its own doctrine, it is apparent from a thousand signs that the doctrine of the present age is Fascism. That it is a doctrine of life is shown by the fact that it has resuscitated a faith. That this faith has conquered minds is proved by the fact that Fascism has had its dead and its martyrs.

Fascism henceforward has in the world the universality of all those doctrines which, by fulfilling themselves, have significance in the history of the human spirit.

17. Joseph Stalin, *The Foundations of Leninism*

Joseph Vissarionovich Dzhugashvili, better known by his assumed name of Stalin (1879–1953), began revolutionary activities in 1898, working in the socialist underground in Tiflis, in Russian Georgia, his native province. He adhered to the Bolshevik wing of the Russian Social-Democratic Party after the split of 1903. Arrested and exiled by the Czarist police on various occasions, he often managed to escape from detention and surveillance. After a new arrest in February 1913, however, he was exiled to Siberia until the outbreak of the Russian Revolution in March 1917. He then came to Petrograd where he became an active member of the Central Committee of the Bolshevik party. After the November revolution, he became Commissar of Nationalities. During the Civil War he acted as political commissar with the army defending Tsaritsyn, the future Stalingrad, from Cossack and White attack, and later participated in the Red invasion of Poland.

In 1922 Stalin became Secretary General of the Central Committee of the Communist Party; it was upon the power which this post gave him that his later rise turned. In spite of Lenin's misgivings, Stalin was able to build up a following among party officials, and in the struggle for control which followed Lenin's death in 1924, Stalin outmaneuvered all his rivals. By 1929 his primacy in the party and in the Soviet state was secure.

Lenin (whose original name was Vladimir Ilyich Ulyanov) was born in 1870 and died in January 1924. His older brother Alexander was hanged in 1887 for planning to assassinate Czar Alexander III. Lenin studied law on a private basis and was admitted to the Russian bar in 1892. He became an active Marxist in 1893; in 1895 he was arrested; and in 1897 he was exiled to Siberia for three years. In 1900 he left Russia and (with the exception of 1905–7) lived in exile until 1917. In 1903 he became the leader of the left wing of the Russian Social Democrats, in 1912 the head of the now independent Bolshevik party. He returned to Russia in April 1917. After the "October" (November) Revolution in 1917, he led the establishment of the Council of People's Commissars. As head of the new Soviet government and, more importantly, as supreme leader of the Communist party, Lenin changed fundamentally the course of modern history.

The *Foundations of Leninism* contains lectures delivered by Stalin at the Sverdlov University in Moscow in early April 1924. Coming shortly after Lenin's death, it provided a theoretically codified and catechistic underpinning for Stalin's attempt to become the primary ideological spokesman for the party. Reprinted here are selections from the sections on "Theory," on the "Dictatorship of the Proletariat," and on "Style in Work."

III. Theory

3. The Theory of the Proletarian Revolution

The Leninist theory of the proletarian revolution proceeds from three fundamental theses.

First Thesis: The domination of finance capital in the advanced capitalist countries; the issue of stocks and bonds as the principal operation of finance capital; the export of capital to the sources of raw materials, which is one of the foundations of imperialism; the omnipotence of a financial oligarchy, which is the result of the domination of finance capital—all this reveals the grossly parasitic character of monopolist capitalism, makes the yoke of the capitalist trusts and syndicates a hundred times more burdensome, quickens the revolt of the working class against the foundations of capitalism, and brings the masses to the proletarian revolution as their only salvation. (Cf. Lenin, *Imperialism, the Highest Stage of Capitalism.*)

Hence the first conclusion: intensification of the revolutionary crisis within the capitalist countries and growth of the elements of an explosion on the internal, proletarian front in the "mother countries."

Second Thesis: The increase in the export of capital to the colonies and dependent countries; the extension of "spheres of influence" and colonial possessions until they cover the whole globe; the transformation of capitalism into a *world system* of financial enslavement and colonial oppression of the vast majority of the population of the earth by a handful of "advanced" countries—all this has, on the one hand, converted the separate national economies and national territories into links in a single chain called world economy and, on the other hand, split the population of the globe into two camps: a handful of "advanced" capitalist countries which exploit and oppress vast colonies and dependencies, and the vast majority of colonial and dependent countries which are compelled to fight for their liberation from the imperialist yoke. (Cf. *Imperialism.*)

Hence the second conclusion: intensification of the revolutionary crisis in the colonial countries and growth of the elements of revolt against imperialism on the exernal, colonial front.

From Joseph Stalin, *Foundations of Leninism* (New York: International Publishers, 1939), pp. 33–39, 44–60, 125–27. Reprinted by permission of the publisher. Footnotes deleted.

Third Thesis: The monopolistic possession of "spheres of influence" and colonies; the uneven development of the different capitalist countries, leading to a frenzied struggle for the redivision of the world between the countries which have already seized territories and those claiming their "share"; imperialist wars as the only method of restoring the disturbed "equilibrium"—all this leads to the aggravation of the third front, the inter-capitalist front, which weakens imperialism and facilitates the amalgamation of the first two fronts against imperialism: the front of the revolutionary proletariat and the front of colonial emancipation. (Cf. *Imperialism.*)

Hence the third conclusion: that under imperialism wars cannot be averted, and that a coalition between the proletarian revolution in Europe and the colonial revolution in the East in a united world front of revolution against the world front of imperialism is inevitable.

Lenin combines all these conclusions into one general conclusion that "*imperialism is the eve of the socialist revolution.*" (*Selected Works,* Vol. V, p. 5.)

The very approach to the question of the proletarian revolution, of the character of the revolution, of its scope, of its depth, the scheme of the revolution in general, changes accordingly.

Formerly, the analysis of the conditions for the proletarian revolution was usually approached from the point of view of the economic state of individual countries. Now, this approach is no longer adequate. Now the matter must be approached from the point of view of the economic state of all or the majority of countries, from the point of view of the state of world economy; for individual countries and individual national economies have ceased to be self-sufficient units, have become links in a single chain called world economy; for the old "cultured" capitalism has evolved into imperialism, and imperialism is a world system of financial enslavement and colonial oppression of the vast majority of the population of the earth by a handful of "advanced" countries.

Formerly, it was the accepted thing to speak of the existence or absence of objective conditions for the proletarian revolution in individual countries, or, to be more precise, in one or another developed country. Now this point of view is no longer adequate. Now we must speak of the existence of objective conditions for the revolution in the entire system of world imperialist economy as an integral unit; the existence within this system of some countries that are not sufficiently developed industrially cannot serve as an insurmountable obstacle to the revolution, *if* the system as a whole, or, more correctly, *because* the system as a whole is already ripe for revolution.

Formerly, it was the accepted thing to speak of the proletarian revolution in one or another developed country as of something separate and self-sufficient, facing a separate national front of capital as its opposite. Now this point of view is no longer adequate. Now we must speak of the world proletarian revolution; for the separate national fronts of capital have become links in a single chain called the world front of imperialism, which must be opposed by a common front of the revolutionary movement in all countries.

Formerly, the proletarian revolution was regarded exclusively as the result of the internal development of a given country. Now this point of view is no longer adequate. Now the proletarian revolution must be regarded primarily as the result of the development of the contradictions within the world system of imperialism, as the result of the snapping of the chain of the imperialist world front in one country or another.

Where will the revolution begin? Where, in what country, can the front of capital be pierced first?

Where industry is more developed, where the proletariat constitutes the majority, where there is more culture, where there is more democracy—that was the reply usually given formerly.

No, objects the Leninist theory of revolution; *not necessarily where industry is more developed,* and so forth. The front of capital will be pierced where the chain of imperialism is weakest, for the proletarian revolution is the result of the breaking of the chain of the world imperialist front at its weakest link; and it may turn out that the country which has started the revolution, which has made a breach in the front of capital, is less developed in a capitalist sense than other, more developed, countries, which have, however, remained within the framework of capitalism.

In 1917 the chain of the imperialist world front proved to be weaker in Russia than in the other countries. It was there that the chain gave way and provided an outlet for the proletarian revolution. Why? Because in Russia a great popular revolution was unfolding, and at its head marched the revolutionary proletariat, which had such an important ally as the vast mass of the peasantry who were oppressed and exploited by the landlords. Because the revolution there was opposed by such a hideous representative of imperialism as tsarism, which lacked all moral prestige and was deservedly hated by the whole population. The chain proved to be weaker in Russia, although that country was less developed in a capitalist sense than, say, France or Germany, England or America.

Where will the chain break in the near future? Again, where it is weakest. It is not precluded that the chain may break, say, in India. Why? Because that country has a young, militant, revolutionary proletariat, which has such an ally as the national liberation movement—an undoubtedly powerful and undoubtedly important ally. Because there the revolution is opposed by such a well-known foe as foreign imperialism, which lacks all moral credit and is deservedly hated by the oppressed and exploited masses of India.

It is also quite possible that the chain will break in Germany. Why? Because the factors which are operating, say, in India are beginning to operate in Germany as well; but, of course, the enormous difference in the level of development between India and Germany cannot but leave its impress on the progress and outcome of a revolution in Germany.

That is why Lenin said that:

> "The West-European capitalist countries are accomplishing their development towards socialism not by the even 'ripening' of socialism, but by the exploitation of some countries by others, by the exploitation of the first of the countries to be vanquished in the imperialist war combined with the exploitation of the whole of the East. On the other hand, precisely as a result of the first imperialist war, the East has been finally drawn into the revolutionary movement, has been drawn into the common maelstrom of the world revolutionary movement." (*Selected Works,* Vol. IX, p. 399.)

Briefly, the chain of the imperialist front must, as a rule, give way where the links are weaker and, at all events, not necessarily where capitalism is more developed, where there is such and such a percentage of proletarians and such and such a percentage of peasants, and so on.

This is why in deciding the question of proletarian revolution statistical calculations of the percentage of the proletarian population in a given country lose the exceptional importance so eagerly attached to them by the pedants of the Second International, who have not understood imperialism and who fear revolution like the plague.

To proceed: the heroes of the Second International asserted (and continue to assert) that between the bourgeois-democratic revolution and the proletarian revolution there is a chasm, or at any rate a Chinese Wall, separating one from the other by a more or less protracted interval of time, during which the bourgeoisie, having come into power, develops capitalism, while the proletariat accumulates strength and prepares for the "decisive struggle" against capitalism. This interval is usually calculated to extend over many decades, if not longer. It need hardly be proved that this Chinese Wall "theory" is totally devoid of scientific meaning under the conditions of imperialism, that it is and can be only a means of concealing and camouflaging the counter-revolutionary aspirations of the bourgeoisie. It need hardly be proved that under the conditions of imperialism, which is pregnant with collisions and wars; under the conditions of the "eve of the socialist revolution," when "flourishing" capitalism is becoming "moribund" capitalism and the revolutionary movement is growing in all countries of the world; when imperialism is allying itself with all reactionary forces without exception, down to and including tsarism and serfdom, thus making imperative the coalition of all revolutionary forces, from the proletarian movement of the West to the national liberation movement of the East; when the overthrow of the survivals of the regime of feudal serfdom becomes impossible without a revolutionary struggle against imperialism—it need hardly be proved that the bourgeois-democratic revolution, in a more or less developed country, must under such circumstances verge upon the proletarian revolution, that the former must pass into the latter. The history of the revolution in Russia has provided palpable proof that this thesis is correct and incontrovertible. It was not without reason that Lenin, as far back as 1905, on the eve of the first Russian revolution, in his pamphlet *Two Tactics,* depicted the bourgeois-democratic revolution and the socialist revolution as two links in the same chain, as a single and integral picture of the sweep of the Russian revolution:

> *"The proletariat must carry to completion the democratic revolution, by allying to itself the mass of the peasantry in order to crush by force the resistance of the autocracy and to paralyse the instability of the bourgeoisie. The proletariat must accomplish the socialist revolution by allying to itself the mass of the semi-proletarian elements of the population in order to crush by force the resistance of the bourgeoisie and to paralyse the instability of the peasantry and the petty bourgeoisie.* Such are the tasks of the proletariat, which the new *Iskra*-ists always present so narrowly in their arguments and resolutions about the scope of the revolution." (*Selected Works,* Vol. III, pp. 110–11.)

. . .

To proceed. Formerly, the victory of the revolution in one country was considered impossible, on the assumption that it would require the combined action of the proletarians of all or at least of a majority of the advanced countries to achieve victory over the bourgeoisie. Now this point of view no longer accords with the facts. Now we must proceed from the possibility of such a victory, for the uneven and spasmodic character of the development of the various capitalist countries under the conditions of imperialism, the development, within imperialism, of catastrophic contradictions leading to inevitable wars, the growth of the revolutionary movement in all countries of the world—all this leads, not only to the possibility, but also to the necessity of the victory of the proletariat in individual countries. The history of the Russian revolution is direct proof of this. At the same time, however, it must be borne in mind that the overthrow of the bourgeoisie can be successfully accomplished only when certain absolutely necessary conditions exist, in the absence of which there can be even no question of the proletariat taking power.

Here is what Lenin says about these conditions in his pamphlet *"Left-Wing" Communism, an Infantile Disorder:*

"The fundamental law of revolution, which has been confirmed by all revolutions, and particularly by all three Russian revolutions in the twentieth century, consists in the following: it is not enough for revolution that the exploited and oppressed masses should understand the impossibility of living in the old way and demand changes; for revolution it is necessary that the exploiters should not be able to live and rule in the old way. Only when the 'lower classes' *do not want* the old way, and when the 'upper classes' *cannot carry on in the old way*— only then can revolution triumph. This truth may be expressed in other words: *Revolution is impossible without a nation-wide crisis (affecting both the exploited and the exploiters).* It follows that for revolution it is essential, first, that a majority of the workers (or at least a majority of the class conscious, thinking, politically active workers) should fully understand the necessity for revolution and be ready to sacrifice their lives for it; secondly, that the ruling classes should be passing through a governmental crisis which would draw even the most backward masses into politics . . . weaken the government and make it possible for the revolutionaries to overthrow it rapidly." (*Selected Works,* Vol. X, p. 127.)

But the overthrow of the power of the bourgeoisie and establishment of the power of the proletariat in one country still does not mean that the complete victory of socialism has been ensured. After consolidating its power and taking the peasantry in tow, the proletariat of the victorious country can and must build up a socialist society. But does this mean that it will thereby achieve the complete and final victory of socialism, i.e., does it mean that with the forces of only one country it can finally consolidate socialism and fully guarantee that country against intervention and, consequently, also against restoration? No, it does not. For this the victory of the revolution in at least several countries is needed. Therefore, the development and support of revolution in other countries is an essential task of the victorious revolution. Therefore, the revolution in the victorious country must regard itself not as a self-sufficient entity but as an aid, as a means of hastening the victory of the proletariat in other countries.

Lenin expressed this thought in a nutshell when he said that the task of the victorious revolution is to do "the utmost possible in one country *for* the development, support and awakening of the revolution *in all countries.*" (*Selected Works,* Vol. VII, p. 182.)

These, in general, are the characteristic features of Lenin's theory of proletarian revolution.

IV. The Dictatorship of the Proletariat

From this theme I take the three main questions: (1) the dictatorship of the proletariat as the instrument of the proletarian revolution; (2) the dictatorship of the proletariat as the domination of the proletariat over the bourgeoisie; (3) the Soviet power as the state form of the dictatorship of the proletariat.

1. The Dictatorship of the Proletariat as the Instrument of the Proletarian Revolution

The question of the proletarian dictatorship is above all a question of the main content of the proletarian revolution. The proletarian revolution, its movement, its scope and its achievements acquire flesh and blood only through the dictatorship of the proletariat. The dictatorship of the proletariat is the instrument of the proletarian revolution, its organ, its most important mainstay, brought into being for the purpose of, firstly, crushing the resistance of the overthrown exploiters and consolidating the achievements of the proletarian revolution, and, secondly, carrying the proletarian revolution to its completion, carrying the revolution to the complete victory of socialism. The revolution can vanquish the bourgeoisie, can overthrow its power, without the dictatorship of the proletariat. But the revolution will be unable to crush the resistance of the bourgeoisie, to maintain its victory and to push forward to the final victory of socialism unless, at a certain stage in its development, it creates a special organ in the form of the dictatorship of the proletariat as its principal mainstay.

"The fundamental question of revolution is the question of power." (Lenin.) Does this mean that all that is required is to assume power, to seize it? No, it does not mean that. The seizure of power is only the beginning. For many reasons the bourgeoisie that is overthrown in one country remains for a long time stronger than the proletariat which has overthrown it. Therefore, the whole point is to retain power, to consolidate it, to make it invincible. What is needed to attain this? To attain this it is necessary to carry out at least the three main tasks that confront the dictatorship of the proletariat "on the morrow" of victory:

(a) to break the resistance of the landlords and capitalists who have been overthrown and expropriated by the revolution, to liquidate every attempt on their part to restore the power of capital;

(b) to organize construction in such a way as to rally all the labouring people around the proletariat, and to carry on this work along the lines of preparing for the liquidation, the abolition of classes;

(c) to arm the revolution, to organize the army of the revolution for the struggle against foreign enemies, for the struggle against imperialism.

The dictatorship of the proletariat is needed to carry out, to fulfil these tasks.

"The transition from capitalism to communism," says Lenin, "represents an entire historical epoch. Until this epoch has terminated, the exploiters will inevitably cherish the hope of restoration, and this *hope* will be converted into *attempts* at restoration. And after their first serious defeat, the overthrown exploiters—who had not expected their overthrow, never believed it possible, never conceded the thought of it—will throw themselves with tenfold energy, with furious passion and hatred grown a hundredfold, into the battle for the recovery of their lost 'paradise,' on behalf of their families, who had been leading such a sweet and easy life and whom now the 'common herd' is condemning to ruin and destitution (or to 'common' work). . . . In the train of the capitalist exploiters will be found the broad masses of the petty bourgeoisie, with regard to whom the historical experience of every country for decades testifies that they vacillate and hesitate, one day marching behind the proletariat and the next day taking fright at the difficulties of the revolution; that they become panic-stricken at the first defeat or semi-defeat of the workers, grow nervous, run about aimlessly, snivel, and rush from one camp to the other." (*Selected Works,* Vol. VII, pp. 140–41.)

And the bourgeoisie has its grounds for making attempts at restoration, because for a long time after its overthrow it remains stronger than the proletariat which has overthrown it.

"If the exploiters are defeated in one country only," says Lenin, "and this, of course, is typical, since a simultaneous revolution in a number of countries is a rare exception, they *still* remain *stronger* than the exploited." (*Ibid.,* p. 140.)

Wherein lies the strength of the overthrown bourgeoisie?

Firstly, "in the strength of international capital, in the strength and durability of the international connections of the bourgeoisie." (Lenin, *Selected Works,* Vol. X, p. 60.)

Secondly, in the fact that:

"for a long time after the revolution the exploiters inevitably continue to enjoy a number of great practical advantages: they still have money (since it is impossible to abolish money all at once), some movable property—often fairly considerable; they still have various connections, habits of organization and management, knowledge of all the 'secrets' (customs, methods, means and possibilities) of management, superior education, close connections with the higher technical personnel (who live and think like the bourgeoisie), incomparably greater experience in the art of war (this is very important), and so on, and so forth." (Lenin, *Selected Works,* Vol. VII, p. 140.)

Thirdly,

"in the *force of habit,* in the strength of *small-scale production.* For unfortunately, there is still very, very much of small-scale production

left in the world, and small-scale production *engenders* capitalism and
the bourgeoisie continuously, daily, hourly, spontaneously, and on a
mass scale; . . ." for "the abolition of classes means not only driving
out the landlords and capitalists—that we accomplished with comparative ease; it means also *getting rid of the small commodity
producers,* and they *cannot be driven out,* they cannot be crushed, we
must live *in harmony* with them; they can (and must) be remoulded
and re-educated only by very prolonged, slow, cautious organizational
work." (Lenin, *Selected Works,* Vol. X, pp. 60, 83.)

That is why Lenin says:

"The dictatorship of the proletariat is a most determined and most
ruthless war waged by the new class against a *more powerful* enemy,
the bourgeoisie, whose resistance is increased *tenfold* by its overthrow"; that "the dictatorship of the proletariat is a persistent
struggle—sanguinary and bloodless, violent and peaceful, military
and economic, educational and administrative—against the forces and
traditions of the old society." (*Selected Works,* Vol. X, pp. 60, 84.)

It need hardly be proved that there is not the slightest possibility of
carrying out these tasks in a short period, of doing all this in a few years.
Therefore, the dictatorship of the proletariat, the transition from capitalism
to communism, must not be regarded as a fleeting period of "super-
revolutionary" acts and decrees, but as an entire historical era, replete with
civil wars and external conflicts, with persistent organizational work and
economic construction, with advances and retreats, victories and defeats.
This historical era is needed not only to create the economic and cultural
prerequisites for the complete victory of socialism, but also to enable the
proletariat, first, to educate itself and become steeled as a force capable of
governing the country, and, secondly, to re-educate and remould the petty-
bourgeois strata along such lines as will assure the organization of socialist
production.

Marx said to the workers:

"You will have to go through fifteen, twenty or fifty years of civil
wars and international conflicts, not only to change existing conditions, but also to change yourselves and to make yourselves capable of
wielding political power."

Continuing and developing Marx's idea still further, Lenin wrote that: It
will be necessary under the dictatorship of the proletariat to re-educate:

"millions of peasants and small proprietors and hundreds of thousands
of office employees, officials and bourgeois intellectuals," to subordinate "all these to the proletarian state and to proletarian leadership,"
to overcome "their bourgeois habits and traditions . . ." just as it will

be necessary "to re-educate—in a protracted struggle, on the basis of the dictatorship of the proletariat—the proletarians themselves, who do not abandon their petty-bourgeois prejudices at one stroke, by a miracle, at the behest of the Virgin Mary, at the behest of a slogan, resolution or decree, but only in the course of a long and difficult mass struggle against mass petty-bourgeois influences." (*Selected Works*, Vol. X, pp. 157, 156.)

2. The Dictatorship of the Proletariat as the Domination of the Proletariat over the Bourgeoisie

From the foregoing it is evident that the dictatorship of the proletariat is not a mere change of personalities in the government, a change of "cabinet," etc., leaving the old economic and political order intact. The Mensheviks and opportunists of all countries, who fear dictatorship like fire and in their fright substitute the concept "conquest of power" for the concept "dictatorship of the proletariat," usually reduce the meaning of "conquest of power" to a change of "cabinet," to the accession to power of a new ministry made up of people like Scheidemann and Noske, MacDonald and Henderson. It is hardly necessary to explain that these and similar cabinet changes have nothing in common with the dictatorship of the proletariat, with the conquest of real power by the real proletariat. The MacDonalds and Scheidemanns in power, while the old bourgeois order is allowed to remain, their so-called governments cannot be anything else than an apparatus serving the bourgeoisie, a screen to hide the ulcers of imperialism, a weapon in the hands of the bourgeoisie against the revolutionary movement of the oppressed and exploited masses. Capital needs such governments as a screen when it finds it inconvenient, unprofitable, difficult to oppress and exploit the masses without the aid of a screen. Of course, the appearance of such governments is a symptom that "over there" (i.e., in the capitalist camp) "all is not quiet at the Shipka Pass"; nevertheless, governments of this kind necessarily remain governments of capital in disguise. The government of a MacDonald or a Scheidemann is as far removed from the conquest of power by the proletariat as the sky from the earth. The dictatorship of the proletariat is not a mere change of government, but a new state, with new organs of power, both central and local; it is the state of the proletariat, which has arisen on the ruins of the old state, the state of the bourgeoisie.

The dictatorship of the proletariat arises not on the basis of the bourgeois order, but in the process of the breaking up of this order after the overthrow of the bourgeoisie, in the process of the expropriation of the landlords and capitalists, in the process of the socialization of the principal instruments and means of production, in the process of violent proletarian revolution. The dictatorship of the proletariat is a revolutionary power based on the use of force against the bourgeoisie.

The state is a machine in the hands of the ruling class for suppressing the resistance of its class enemies. *In this respect* the dictatorship of the proletariat does not differ essentially from the dictatorship of any other class, for the proletarian state is a machine for the suppression of the bourgeoisie. But there is one *substantial* difference. This difference consists in the fact that all hitherto existing class states have been dictatorships of an exploiting minority over the exploited majority, whereas the dictatorship of the proletariat is the dictatorship of the exploited majority over the exploiting minority.

Briefly: *the dictatorship of the proletariat is the rule—unrestricted by law and based on force—of the proletariat over the bourgeoisie, a rule enjoying the sympathy and support of the labouring and exploited masses.* (*The State and Revolution.*)

From this follow two main conclusions:

First conclusion: The dictatorship of the proletariat cannot be "complete" democracy, democracy for *all,* for the rich as well as for the poor; the dictatorship of the proletariat "must be a state that is democratic *in a new way—for* the proletarians and the propertyless in general—and dictatorial *in a new way—against* the bourgeoisie. . . ." (Lenin, *Selected Works,* Vol. VII, p. 34.) The talk of Kautsky and Co. about universal equality, about "pure" democracy, about "perfect" democracy, and the like, is but a bourgeois screen to conceal the indubitable fact that equality between exploited and exploiters is impossible. The theory of "pure" democracy is the theory of the upper stratum of the working class, which has been broken in and is being fed by the imperialist robbers. It was brought into being for the purpose of concealing the ulcers of capitalism, of touching up imperialism and lending it moral strength in the struggle against the exploited masses. Under capitalism there are no real "liberties" for the exploited, nor can there be, if for no other reason than that the premises, printing plants, paper supplies, etc., indispensable for the actual enjoyment of "liberties" are the privilege of the exploiters. Under capitalism the exploited masses do not, nor can they, really participate in the administration of the country, if for no other reason than that, even under the most democratic regime, governments, under the conditions of capitalism, are not set up by the people but by the Rothschilds and Stinneses, the Rockefellers and Morgans. Democracy under capitalism is *capitalist* democracy, the democracy of the exploiting minority, based on the restriction of the rights of the exploited majority and directed against this majority. Only under the dictatorship of the proletariat are real "liberties" for the exploited and real participation in the administration of the country by the proletarians and peasants possible. Under the dictatorship of the proletariat, democracy is *proletarian* democracy, the democracy of the exploited majority, based upon the restriction of the rights of the exploiting minority and directed against this minority.

Second conclusion: The dictatorship of the proletariat cannot arise as the result of the peaceful development of bourgeois society and of bourgeois democracy; it can arise only as the result of the smashing of the bourgeois state machine, the bourgeois army, the bourgeois bureaucratic machine, the bourgeois police.

In a preface to *The Communist Manifesto* Marx and Engels wrote, quoting from *The Civil War in France:*

> "The working class cannot simply lay hold of the ready-made state machine and wield it for its own purposes." (Marx, *Selected Works,* Vol. I, p. 190.)

In a letter to Kugelmann (1871) Marx wrote that the task of the proletarian revolution is

> "no longer as before, to transfer the bureaucratic military machine from one hand to another, but to *smash* it, and that is a preliminary condition for every real people's revolution on the Continent." (Marx, *Selected Works,* Vol. II, p. 528.)

Marx's qualifying phrase about the Continent gave the opportunists and Mensheviks of all countries a pretext for proclaiming that Marx had thus conceded the possibility of the peaceful evolution of bourgeois democracy into a proletarian democracy, at least in certain countries outside the European continent (England, America). Marx did in fact concede that possibility, and he had good grounds for conceding it in regard to England and America in the 'seventies of the last century, when monopoly capitalism and imperialism did not yet exist, and when these countries, owing to the special conditions of their development, had as yet no developed militarism and bureaucracy. That was the situation before the appearance of developed imperialism. But later, after a lapse of thirty or forty years, when the situation in these countries had radically changed, when imperialism had developed and had embraced all capitalist countries without exception, when militarism and bureaucracy had appeared in England and America also, when the special conditions for peaceful development in England and the United States had disappeared—then the qualification in regard to these countries necessarily could no longer hold good.

"Today," said Lenin, "in 1917, in the epoch of the first great imperialist war, this qualification made by Marx is no longer valid. Both England and America, the greatest and the last representatives—in the whole world—of Anglo-Saxon 'liberty,' in the sense that militarism and bureaucracy were absent, have slid down entirely into the all-European, filthy, bloody morass of military-bureaucratic institutions to which everything is subordinated and which trample everything underfoot. Today, both in England and in America, the 'preliminary condition for every real people's revolution' is the smashing, the *destruction* of the 'ready-made state machine' (brought in those countries, between 1914 and 1917, to general 'European' imperialist perfection)." (*Selected Works,* Vol. VII, p. 37.)

In other words, the law of violent proletarian revolution, the law of the smashing of the bourgeois state machine as a preliminary condition for such a revolution, is an inevitable law of the revolutionary movement in the imperialist countries of the world.

Of course, in the remote future, if the proletariat is victorious in the most important capitalist countries, and if the present capitalist encirclement is replaced by a socialist encirclement, a "peaceful" path of development is quite possible for certain capitalist countries, whose capitalists, in view of the "unfavourable" international situation, will consider it expedient "voluntarily" to make substantial concessions to the proletariat. But this supposition applies only to a remote and possible future. With regard to the immediate future, there is no ground whatsoever for this supposition.

Therefore, Lenin is right in saying:

"The proletarian revolution is impossible without the forcible destruction of the bourgeois state machine and the substitution for it of a *new one. . . .*" (*Selected Works,* Vol. VII, p. 124.)

3. The Soviet Power as the State Form of the Dictatorship of the Proletariat

The victory of the dictatorship of the proletariat signifies the suppression of the bourgeoisie, the smashing of the bourgeois state machine, and the substitution of proletarian democracy for bourgeois democracy. That is clear. But by means of what organizations can this colossal task be carried out? The old forms of organization of the proletariat, which grew up on the basis of bourgeois parliamentarism, are inadequate for this task—of that there can hardly be any doubt. What then, are the new forms of organization of the proletariat that are capable of serving as the grave-diggers of the bourgeois state machine, that are capable not only of smashing this machine, not only of substituting proletarian democracy for bourgeois democracy, but also of becoming the foundation of the proletarian state power?

This new form of organization of the proletariat is the Soviets.

Wherein lies the strength of the Soviets as compared with the old forms of organization?

In that the Soviets are the most *all-embracing* mass organizations of the proletariat, for they and they alone embrace all workers without exception.

In that the Soviets are the *only* mass organizations which embrace all the oppressed and exploited, workers and peasants, soldiers and sailors, and in which the vanguard of the masses, the proletariat, can, for this reason, most easily and most completely exercise its political leadership of the mass struggle.

In that the Soviets are the *most powerful organs* of the revolutionary struggle of the masses, of the political actions of the masses, of the insurrection of the masses—organs capable of breaking the omnipotence of finance capital and of its political appendages.

In that the Soviets are the *immediate* organizations of the masses themselves, i.e., they are *the most democratic* and therefore the most authoritative organizations of the masses, which facilitate to the utmost their participation in the work of building up the new state and in its administration, and which bring into full play the revolutionary energy, initiative and creative abilities of the masses in the struggle for the destruction of the old order, in the struggle for the new, proletarian order.

The Soviet power is the amalgamation and formation of the local Soviets into one common state organization, into the state organization of the proletariat as the vanguard of the oppressed and exploited masses and as the ruling class—their amalgamation into the republic of Soviets.

The essence of the Soviet power is contained in the fact that these organizations of a most pronounced mass character, these most revolutionary organizations of precisely those classes that were oppressed by the capitalists and landlords are now the *"permanent and sole* basis of the whole power of the state, of the whole state apparatus"; that

> "precisely those masses which even in the most democratic bourgeois republics, while being equal in law, have in fact been prevented by thousands of tricks and devices from taking part in political life and from enjoying democratic rights and liberties, are now drawn unfailingly into *constant* and, moreover, *decisive* participation in the democratic administration of the state." (Lenin, *Selected Works,* Vol. VII, p. 231.)

This is why the Soviet power is a *new form* of state organization, different in principle from the old bourgeois-democratic and parliamentary form, a *new type* of state, adapted not to the task of exploiting and oppressing the labouring masses, but to the task of completely emancipating them from all oppression and exploitation, to the tasks facing the dictatorship of the proletariat.

Lenin rightly says that with the appearance of the Soviet power "the era of bourgeois-democratic parliamentarism has come to an end, and a new chapter in world history—the era of proletarian dictatorship—has commenced."

What are the characteristic features of the Soviet power?

The Soviet power has a most pronounced mass character and is the most democratic state organization of all possible state organizations while classes continue to exist; for, being the arena of the bond and collaboration between the workers and the exploited peasants in their struggle against the exploiters, and basing itself in its work on this bond and on this collaboration, it represents, by virtue of this, the power of the majority of the population over the minority, it is the state of the majority, the expression of its dictatorship.

The Soviet power is the most internationalist of all state organizations in class society, for, since it destroys every kind of national oppression and rests on the collaboration of the labouring masses of the various nationalities, it facilitates, by virtue of this, the amalgamation of these masses into a single state union.

The Soviet power, by its very structure, facilitates the task of leading the oppressed and exploited masses for the vanguard of these masses—for the proletariat, as the most consolidated and most class-conscious core of the Soviets.

"The experience of all revolutions and of all movements of the oppressed classes, the experience of the world socialist movement teaches," says Lenin, "that the proletariat alone is able to unite and lead the scattered and backward strata of the toiling and exploited population." (*Selected Works,* Vol. VII, p. 232.)

The structure of the Soviet power facilitates the practical application of the lessons drawn from this experience.

The Soviet power, by combining the legislative and executive functions in a single state body and replacing territorial electoral constituencies by industrial units, factories and mills, thereby directly links the workers and the labouring masses in general with the apparatus of state administration, teaches them how to administer the country.

The Soviet power alone is capable of releasing the army from its subordination to bourgeois command and of converting it from the instrument of oppression of the people, which it is under the bourgeois order, into an instrument for the liberation of the people from the yoke of the bourgeoisie, both native and foreign.

"The Soviet organization of the state alone is capable of immediately and effectively smashing and finally destroying the old, *i.e.,* the bourgeois, bureaucratic and judicial apparatus." (*Ibid.*)

The Soviet form of state alone, by drawing the mass organizations of the toilers and exploited into constant and unrestricted participation in state administration, is capable of preparing the ground for the withering away of the state, which is one of the basic elements of the future stateless communist society.

The republic of Soviets is thus the political form, so long sought and finally discovered, within the framework of which the economic emancipation of the proletariat, the complete victory of socialism, is to be accomplished.

The Paris Commune was the embryo of this form; the Soviet power is its development and culmination.

That is why Lenin says:

> "The republic of Soviets of Workers', Soldiers', and Peasants' Deputies is not only the form of a higher type of democratic institution . . . but is the *only form* capable of securing the most painless transition to socialism." (*Selected Works,* Vol. VI, p. 447.)

IX. Style in Work

I am not referring to literary style. What I have in mind is style in work, that which is specific and peculiar in the practice of Leninism which creates the special type of Leninist worker. Leninism is a school of theory and practice which trains a special type of Party and state worker, creates a special Leninist style in work. What are the characteristic features of this style? What are its peculiarities?

It has two specific features: (a) the Russian revolutionary sweep and (b) American efficiency. The style of Leninism is a combination of these two specific features in Party and state work.

The Russian revolutionary sweep is an antidote to inertness, routine, conservatism, mental stagnation and slavish submission to ancestral traditions. The Russian revolutionary sweep is the life-giving force which stimulates thought, impels things forward, breaks the past and opens up perspectives. Without it no progress is possible. But there is every chance of it degenerating in practice into empty "revolutionary" Manilovism if it is not combined with American efficiency in work. Examples of this degeneration are only too numerous. Who does not know the disease of "revolutionary" improvisation and "revolutionary" plan concocting, which springs from the belief in the power of decrees to arrange everything and reform everything? A Russian writer, I. Ehrenbourg, in his story *The Percomman* (*The Perfect Communist Man*), has portrayed the type of "Bolshevik" afflicted with this "disease," who set himself the task of finding a formula for the ideally perfect man and . . . became "submerged" in this "work." Some gross exaggerations are spun into this story, but it certainly gives a correct likeness of the disease. But no one, I think, has so ruthlessly and bitterly ridiculed those afflicted with this disease as Lenin has done. Lenin stigmatised this morbid belief in improvisation and in concocting decrees as "Communist vanity."

> "Communist vanity," says Lenin, "is characteristic of a man who, while still a member of the Communist Party, not having yet been combed out of it, imagines that he can solve all his problems by issuing Communist decrees." (*Selected Works,* Vol. IX, p. 273.)

Lenin usually contrasted *hollow "revolutionary" phrase-mongering* with plain everyday work, thus emphasising that "revolutionary" improvisation is repugnant to the spirit and the letter of true Leninism.

> "Fewer pompous phrases, more plain *everyday work,*" says Lenin. "Less political fireworks and more attention to the simplest but vital . . . facts of Communist construction. . . ." (*Selected Works,* Vol. IX, pp. 440, 430.)

American efficiency, on the other hand, is an antidote to "revolutionary" Manilovism and fantastic improvisation. American efficiency is that indomitable force which neither knows nor recognizes obstacles; which with its business-like perseverance brushes aside all obstacles; which continues at a task once started until it is finished, even if it is a minor task; and without which serious constructive work is inconceivable. But American efficiency has every chance of degenerating into narrow and unprincipled commercialism if not combined with the Russian revolutionary sweep. Who has not heard of that disease of narrow practicality and unprincipled commercialism which has not infrequently caused certain "Bolsheviks" to degenerate and to abandon the cause of the revolution? We find a reflection of this peculiar disease in a story by B. Pilnyak, entitled *The Barren Year,* which depicts types of Russian "Bolsheviks" of strong will and practical determination, who "function" very "energetically," but without vision, without knowing "what it is all about," and who, therefore, stray from the path of revolutionary work. No one has been more incisive in his ridicule of this disease of narrow commercialism than Lenin. He branded it as "narrow-minded practicality" and "brainless commercialism." He usually contrasted it with vital revolutionary work and the necessity of having a revolutionary perspective in all our daily activities, thus emphasizing that this unprincipled commercialism is as repugnant to true Leninism as "revolutionary" improvisation.

The combination of the Russian revolutionary sweep with American efficiency is the essence of Leninism in Party and state work.

This combination alone produces the finished type of Leninist worker, the style of Leninism in work.

Democratic Politicians

18. Léon Blum, Speech at the Congress of Tours and the Matignon Agreement

Léon Blum (1872–1950), whose long political career began with the Dreyfusard agitation of the 1890s and spanned both world wars, was the leading French socialist of the first half of the twentieth century.

Born in Paris to an upper-middle-class Jewish commercial family, Blum in many ways epitomized the assimilated French Jew of the period. He was indifferent to religious observance, regarding himself as an heir of the Enlightenment tradition of rationalism and anticlericalism; yet he always retained his public identity as a Jew; and as a political figure he was frequently the butt of anti-Semitic attacks. Blum attended the Ecole Normale Supérieure, the hatchery of the French intellectual elite, and, something of an aesthete, initially gravitated towards a literary career. Only later did politics become his consuming passion.

Crucial to his political development was his close association with Jean Jaurès (vol. 8, document 46). Blum became a socialist in the Jaurèsian mold—that is, he stressed the complete compatibility of socialist commitment with republican patriotism; and he cultivated the persona of the intellectual in politics. But whereas Jaurès had been stocky and robust, careless about his clothing, and famous for his passionate, musical speaking style, Blum was tall, slender and refined, impeccably attired, and won over his audiences by the logical clarity and precision of his arguments.

Blum first entered government in August 1914 as assistant to the Socialist Minister of Public Works Marcel Sembat, who was responsible for providing the French military effort with transportation, food, and fuel. In 1919, Blum was elected deputy from Paris and quickly emerged as leader of the Socialist parliamentary group. In the wake of the Russian Revolution of 1917, the salient issue facing French Socialists was whether or not to affiliate with the Third International in Moscow. Although Blum initially took the Jaurèsian stance that the unity of the French Left was the highest priority, he could not reconcile his own conception of socialism with that of the Bolsheviks and, in the end, led the schismatic movement which resulted in the formation of separate French socialist and communist parties in 1920.

In 1936, the Socialist, Communist, and Radical parties joined in an electoral alliance called the Popular Front whose campaign slogan was "Peace, Bread, and Liberty" and whose aim was to combat the growing strength and proto-Fascist tendencies of the French Right. The victory of the Popular Front, coupled with the fact that the Socialists had won the largest number of seats in the new Chamber, made Blum Prime Minister; and for thirteen months he presided over a government whose policy was, he acknowledged, inspired by President Roosevelt's New Deal in the United States. Laws passed in 1936 provided for a forty-hour work week and a two-week paid vacation and placed collective bargaining on a firm legal footing. After the fall of France in 1940, Blum was imprisoned by the Vichy government and put on trial at Riom. The charge was that he had, through the labor and pacifist policies of the Popular Front, allowed French industrial production to decline and the French military to sink to a level of unpreparedness that had made possible the defeat at the hands of the Germans. Blum's eloquent and fearless testimony at Riom—the Popular Front was not, he said, "some monstrous excrescence in the history of this country" but had fortified the tradition of the French Revolution—was hailed by the Allies and gave hope to the French Resistance. Blum spent the duration of World War II in prison, first in France and then in the German concentration camps of Buchenwald and Dachau (where, like other prominent political figures, he was given special treatment because of his value as a hostage). He died in 1950.

The two documents below, each showing Blum in a pivotal historical role, illustrate the central belief that animated his politics: the continuity between French socialism and French republicanism. The first is his speech at the Socialist Party Congress at Tours in 1920, where Blum broke with the vast majority of party members, who had already indicated their intention to remake French socialism in the Bolshevik image and to submit to guidance from Moscow. The second document, the Matignon agreement, was Blum's solution to the epidemic of strikes (taking the new form of factory sit-ins) that threatened to paralyze France in the late spring of 1936, when Blum assumed the premiership.

Speech at the Socialist Party Congress at Tours, 27 December 1920

I ask the indulgence of the Congress for the thankless task with which my comrades have entrusted me. Before an assembly whose decision has already been made, whose will to join [the Third International] is firm and unshakable, I must defend a motion which concludes in a pure and simple refusal to join. And I must present the reasons which have led my friends and me to take this stance.

You know the position in which we were placed. The second International Congress held in Moscow last July had the visible appearance of a sort of constituent assembly. (Uproar)

My voice is naturally very weak. I am, moreover, very tired, like all of you, and it would be physically impossible for me to surmount, by the strength of my lungs, this tumult and these violent interruptions.

The second International Congress at Moscow had, then, to all appearances, the character of a sort of constituent assembly. In all areas, the doctrinal as well as the tactical, it formulated a set of complementary resolutions. The whole set forms a sort of architectural structure, entirely patterned after a single design, in which every part is related to every other. It is impossible to deny the power and even the majesty of it.

You are in the presence of a totality, of a doctrinal ensemble. Thus, the following question is posed: Do you or do you not accept this body of doctrine formulated by the Congress of the Communist International? And to accept—I hope there will be no divergence of opinion on this point—to accept means to accept with mind, heart, and will and with the intention of strictly conforming, in thought and action, to the new doctrine. Any other kind of adherence would be a comedy, unworthy of the Communist International and unworthy of the French party. You are in the presence of a totality. There is not even room to quibble over this or that detail. It is a question of looking at the unifying theme, the central idea. It doesn't much matter if your acceptance entails this or that reservation about a detail. There is no trickery or deception in that. But if you contest the doctrine in its essentials, you really have no right to accept with second thoughts or mental reservations, to say "I agree, but I only pay lip-service, with the conviction that this is nothing but a joke, and that tomorrow the party will continue to live and to act as it did yesterday." We are all agreed in rejecting such an interpretation. (Applause)

The Congress may believe this of us. With an effort at intellectual impartiality and honesty that no one here will deny, we faced the problem

From *L'Oeuvre de Léon Blum*, vol. 3, 1914–1928 (Paris: Editions Albin Michel, 1972), pp. 137–52, 154–60. Translated for this volume by Alan Kahan.

squarely and said to ourselves: "Studying the texts of the Communist International, its theses, its statutes"—and I will not dwell on the difficulties and really excessive slowness with which we were given each of the materials under discussion—"can we or can we not accept them?" For us to accept would really mean to accept in the strongest possible sense of the word.

We had the duty of making that textual examination. . . .

What is the result? It is twofold. First of all (and I believe there will be no disagreement about this), we are in the presence of something new. Some have tried to prove the contrary, and perhaps will try again. I remember the meeting of the Federation of the Seine when I was responding to Frossard, who had made the most ingenious and clever effort to combine the communist theses with the traditional principles of the Socialist Party. I tried to show him that those theses reflected a force, a will to construct something new, differing entirely from the essential tenets of the traditional socialism we had until then known and practiced. I remember that the most qualified delegates of the Third International supported me. "It's true," they said. "That is what we think; that is what we want. It is a new socialism that we want to create in our country and in the whole proletarian world."

That is what Lenin and Trotsky have said. It is what you yourselves said when returning from Russia. For example, Cachin,[1] in the last letter that he sent from Moscow, spoke of a break with the past. Trotsky, in the most recent document that the *Communist Bulletin* has published, said that it was a new party.

A DELEGATE: New, because it is after the war!

BLUM: Do not try to dispute it. You have the right to think that, to a world situation that appears entirely novel to you, there ought to correspond an entirely new conception of socialism. That idea of novelty does not frighten us. I can say that we have made efforts, sometimes ignored or misunderstood by the Party, to bring our socialist doctrine up to date. After the war we made a serious and fruitful effort at revision and readaptation, and we did it together in the April 1919 program.

But here it is not only a question of revision and readaptation. I am going to try to prove to you—it is the core of my argument—that this is a socialism new in every essential point: its conceptions of organization, of

---

1. L. O. Frossard and Marcel Cachin were the two delegates sent by the French Socialist party to Moscow in 1920, to attend the second congress of the Third International and to explore the terms of French affiliation with the Soviet communists. Lenin was supposed to have told them half-jokingly, "Here in Russia we shoot [socialist] reformists." The two men came back filled with enthusiasm for affiliation. "They have seized the flame," Frossard said of the Bolsheviks. "We are left with the ashes."—ED.

the relations between political and economic structure, of revolution, of the dictatorship of the proletariat.

It is a new socialism. In our opinion, it is based on ideas erroneous in themselves, and contrary to the basic and invariable principles of Marxist socialism. Furthermore, it is based on a sort of vast error of fact, which consists of generalizing to all international socialism certain ideas drawn from a local and particular experience, that of the Russian Revolution. It gives as a necessary and universal rule of action, for all international socialism, the experience of those who carried out and kept alive the Russian Revolution.

This is what we think: novelty on the one hand, and error on the other; error of fact, error of doctrine. I will go over the points I have indicated and, for each one, I will show you how the statements made in our motion [against joining the communist Third International] can be justified.

First, party organization. That organization born of the unity pact of 1905 [2] and of the practice and experience of a decade (I don't count the war years)—you know the essential principles on which it is based. A constitution having, above all, a popular character, in which, following the excellent formula of our statutes, the direction of our Party belongs to the Party itself. It is in the base of the Party itself, in the mass of militants and dues-payers, that the Party's collective will and thought are formed. That will and thought are transmitted from one level to another, from the Section to the Federation, from the Federation to the National Council, from the Council to the Congress.

A DELEGATE: And the parliamentary deputies?

BLUM: We will speak of them in their turn. I am not avoiding that question. The C.A.P. [3] and the parliamentary group are the two permanent organizations of the Party, its executive organs. During the intervals between National Councils and Congresses, they are responsible for applying decisions made by all of our active members, during the meetings of their section. Consequently there is everywhere the life of the people, everywhere liberty, everywhere a free atmosphere, everywhere popular supervision, everywhere responsibility.

2. The agreement which ended the longstanding fragmentation of French socialism, bringing most of its varieties, both moderate and revolutionary—including Guesdism, Blanquism, and the independent socialism of Jean Jaurès—into a single political party, the S.F.I.O. (Section française de l'internationale ouvrière), or French Section of the Workers' International. The new party was led and held together by Jaurès until his assassination in 1914.—ED.

3. The Commission administrative permanente, or C.A.P., was the executive committee of the French Socialist party, a body of some twenty or thirty members elected at each annual congress on a proportional basis to represent the so-called tendencies, or different strands of opinion, in the Party.—ED.

Some people speak of bosses. There were no bosses at all in the Socialist party. Supervision was exercised or can be exercised over those so-called bosses. It used to depend—and it still depends—on the members to invoke the relevant statutory regulations. A strong supervisory control is organized by them and depends only on their initiative. But in fact, in this Constitution, those so-called bosses are nothing but interpreters, representatives charged to give voice or practical form to the collective will and thought created at the base of the Party in the mass of its members. That is what the Constitution of the Party said.

The Party was a party of the largest possible recruitment, and for a simple reason—that, as Marx and Engels said in *The Communist Manifesto* (when speaking of the true Communist party, the Communist party of former times), socialism is not a party opposed to other parties. It is the entire working class. Its object is to assemble, by their common class interest, the workers of all countries.

When someone tells us, "Socialism had a period of recruitment, followed by another period in which recruitment is no longer pursued," that person controverts the essential idea of international socialism. Your vocation is to gather together all the proletarians of all countries. There is no other limit to the size of the Socialist party than the number of workers and wage-earners.

Our Party was therefore a party with as large a recruitment as possible. As such, it was a party of freedom of thought, for the two ideas are necessarily related. If you want to group all workers, all wage-earners, all the exploited in a single party, you can only unite them around simple and general slogans. You will say to them: "All those who want to work to change the economic system, all those who believe (for this is the foundation of Marxism) that there is an ineluctable connection between the development of capitalism on the one hand and that of socialism on the other—all of you are socialists. If you are with us in this task, your act of faith is completed. You are socialists." Within this credo, this essential affirmation, all varieties and shades of opinion are tolerated. . . .

Thus, when the Party set down in its statutes that freedom of discussion was to be complete, that the press was to be free, that was no vague democratic idea introduced into our socialist constitution. That was a rule drawn from the very essence of what the Socialist party ought to be. . . .

And the action of the Party? What form did it take? Popular education and public propaganda. The Socialist party, whose ultimate aspiration was to gather all workers under its flag, addressed itself to those workers by means of public recruitment and propaganda. It founded groups and opened them to all comers. It held meetings, ran electoral campaigns, and tried to influence the voters. That is what the Socialist party still is today, for a few hours more.

What is the new party that you want to create going to be like? Instead of a popular will formed at the base and rising by degrees, your regimen of centralization involves the subordination of each organ to the one which is hierarchically above it. It entails an executive committee at the top to which everyone is subordinated, a sort of military chain of command whose orders are formulated at the top and transmitted from one rank to another down to the mere members in their sections. The autonomy of groups and federations? That, the theses will tell you, is a heresy pure and simple and must be excluded from communist organization. . . .

Alongside public organization, underground organization. I want to return here to a charge that has been made against us. An error of translation in the documents, a sort of mirror-imaging of the words *legal* and *clandestine,* has made a certain number of comrades believe that we, the adversaries of the Third International, were, by the same token, also adversaries of illegal action.

Sembat replied to you yesterday on this point; I will not go back over it. There is not a single socialist who will let himself be imprisoned in legality. I said so in my electoral campaign, I will say so from the tribune of the Chamber at the first opportunity, I will say it everywhere it needs to be said. But legality is a thing . . .

PAUL FAURE: I didn't speak of illegal action, I spoke . . . (Noise, tumult)

A DELEGATE: I protest against the intervention of Paul Faure. (Commotion)

BLUM: I say that there is not the slightest relationship between illegal action, about which we are all, I repeat, in agreement, and secret organization, about which we are far from being in agreement. That these two ideas do not coincide, is proven by the fact that the French Party currently recognizes the justifiability of illegal action and still does not recognize secret organization.

What I want to show here is the organizational structure the communist theses are going to impose on you, on the one hand, subordination at all levels with an executive committee on top, and on the other hand, secret organizations.

A DELEGATE: Not necessarily. (Commotion)

BLUM: I won't cite chapter and verse here, but you will do me the justice of assuming that I wouldn't say anything that I couldn't support with texts. I say that you are required, by the theses and the statutes, to organize secret committees, and that the executive committee of the Third International even reserves the right to impose its own creation directly upon you if you show some weakness or slowness in complying with that requirement. There is yet another thing that the theses indicate, though needlessly. When a public and a secret organ exist side by side, to which does the real authority belong? By necessity, to the secret one. That is inevitable, and the theses recognize this necessity. Paul Faure has read you the texts. . . .

How will these organizations be formed? After this Congress is over, after you have named your public executive committee, are you going to proceed to name your secret committee? (Exclamations) Are you going to put the designation of its members to a vote?

Your hidden executive committee cannot, then, be born of the public deliberations of your Congress; it must have another origin. Its constitution must be given to you from outside. This means that in the party you want to make of us, the central power will belong to a secret committee designated—there is no other possible hypothesis—under the supervision of the executive committee of the International itself. The most important decisions in the life of the Party, by whom will they be made? By men whom you do not know.

I analyse texts, and I try to present them in their mutual relationships and as an ensemble.

A DELEGATE: Yes, with incomplete quotations.

BLUM: I simply say: Given the organization whose existence we cannot deny—it results from the letter and spirit of all the texts—it is really quite extraordinary that some people should speak to us of tyranny in the present Party: tyranny of bosses, tyranny of elected parliamentary deputies. I don't know what means the deputies employ today to exercise their tyranny, but at least you know who they are, and you can take their means away from them. From whom will you take them tomorrow? From anonymities, from unknown persons, from masks.

Party unity—we told you yesterday in terms that I hope you will not forget—was until today a synthesizing unity, a harmonic unity, a kind of resultant of all the forces and tendencies coming together to determine the common axis of action.

It is no longer that kind of unity that you seek, but rather uniformity, absolute homogeneity. You want in your party men ready, not merely to act together, but to make the commitment to think together. Your doctrine is fixed once and for all! *Ne varietur!* Whoever does not accept it does not enter your party; whoever no longer accepts it must leave. It is not from the viewpoint of particular persons that I wish to examine the question of exclusions! It matters little to me whether the dividing line is drawn here or there, whether this or that individual is retained. The texts have another importance. The goal is to constitute an entirely homogeneous party. That is logical, and it is that logic that I want to show you.

From the texts were inferred all the propensities that you are now familiar with. In the Moscow debates we foresaw—and one couldn't help foreseeing—the complete and radical purge of everything that has, up to the present, been the Socialist party. That is why we said: whoever will not accept the theses in their letter and their spirit will not enter the Communist party and the Third International. Whoever votes against joining and does not make his complete submission during the allowed period of delay, will be driven out of the Third International. That is why we foresee periodic purges; that is why proportional representation has been eliminated, and you are certainly right to get rid of proportional representation since it is not a kind of politics designed to give control of part of the government to this or that minority; it is the guarantee of freedom of thought within the Party. You are right to say that proportional representation no longer has any reason for existence! You are right to declare that the whole Party press, central or local, should be in the hands of pure communists and pure communist doctrine. You are certainly right to submit the works published by the Party to a kind of censorship. All that is logical. You want an entirely homogeneous party, a party in which there is no longer free thought, no longer different tendencies: you are therefore right to act as you have done. This results—I am going to prove it to you—from your revolutionary conception itself. But you will understand that envisioning that situation, considering it, making the comparison of what will be tomorrow with what was yesterday, we all had the same reaction of fright, of recoil, and that we said: is that the Party that we have known? No! The Party that we knew was the appeal to all workers, while the one they want to found is the creation of little disciplined vanguards, homogeneous, subjected to a strict structure of command—their numbers scarcely matter, you will find that in the theses—but all kept under control, and ready for prompt and decisive action.

Well, in that respect as in the others, we remain of the Party as it was yesterday, and we do not accept the new party that they want to make.

The trade union question proceeds from the same spirit of discipline and homogeneity, even to the detriment of numbers. (Interruption: No!)

Let me finish my thought. I don't want to go back over the history of the relations between trade unionism and socialism in France, although that would be interesting, I think, for many members. But let us leave that aside.

We had arrived painfully, and after many hesitations, at a conception which, all in all, had satisfied everyone in practice: autonomy for the two organizations; common goals, but with different means; and the possibility of common action for specific purposes.

In your conception of military homogeneity, and given your preoccupation with mobilizing the forces of attack for the destruction of capitalist society as quickly as possible, it was indispensable that you subject every working-class unit, syndicalist or political, to the same discipline. That is undeniably the spirit of the Moscow theses.

You have expressed one reservation in your motion. In order not to make

the task too difficult for your friends of the revolutionary syndicalist minority, you have come out against the direct, hierarchical connection of labor
organizations to political organizations. You have informed us that that
concession was only provisional. If you accept for the moment, until your
work is more advanced, the relative autonomy of labor movements won
over by your propaganda, you still have as of now the duty of affiliating
those groups with the Labor International of Moscow which, incontestably,
is nothing but a subsidiary, a branch of the Communist International itself.

None of you can dispute it. (Interruption: That's it exactly.) Since you
recognize it, that's enough for me.

I will show you the consequence of your dominant idea of substituting
for as large a group of free organizations as possible a lesser number of
homogeneous groups (for one sacrifices numbers to homogeneity), tightly
linked together and, in the final analysis, under the control of both the national central committee, and the executive committee of the Third International, to whose decisions you have all committed yourselves. That
executive committee . . . will have, in each country, its own bureau, subordinate to it alone. It will reserve to itself the right of constituting that
secret organization that has been thrust upon you. You see, it is a kind of
secret society, a sort of vast Carbonarism, something which is manifestly
conceived on the model of those secret societies which, I recognize, have
made revolutions in France, and must not be libeled. . . . (Interruption:
Well, then!)

I do not insult them; I recognize and remember them. Now comrades,
why this organization which deprives us of one of the elements which, until now, seemed the essential element of all revolutionary organizations:
numbers? Which sacrifices everything for discipline, homogeneity, and the
speed of mobilization?

For a very simple reason. This conception of organization corresponds
exactly to the conception of revolution at the very heart of communism.

As wearisome as such a theoretical argument may be, I ask your permission to go on with it a moment longer. A system of socialism is judged
above all by its conception of revolution. I do not want to repeat here a
statement that my friends and I have made so many times. We have had to
drum it into people's ears. However, I must protest one last time against the
polemical device which consists of proving that the adversaries of the
Third International are counterrevolutionaries and holding that the debate
for or against joining the Third International is in reality the debate between the revolutionary and the reformist conceptions. Nothing could be
further from the truth. . . .

Let me tell you that reformism, or, to speak more exactly, revisionism—
I prefer that word—has ceased to exist either in French or international

socialism since the Amsterdam Congress and the unity pact. The doctrine of the Party is a revolutionary doctrine. If that point eludes anyone, it is up to the members, to the Federations, to the Congress, to apply the sanctions that the regulations provide. But, for my part, I know in France, up to the present time, only one socialism, that which is defined by the statutes, mentioned on our cards, and which is a revolutionary socialism.

I add that, insofar as I am concerned, there are not two species of socialism, one revolutionary and the other not. I recognize only one socialism, revolutionary socialism, since socialism is a movement of ideas and actions that leads to the total transformation of the organization of property, and the revolution, by definition, is that transformation itself. Where, then, is the point of disagreement, the point of conflict between you and us? I am going to try to specify it.

Revolution means, for traditional French socialism, the transformation of an economic regime based on private property into one based on collective or common property. That transformation is itself the revolution, regardless of the means employed to reach that end.

Revolution means something more. It means that the passage from an order based on property to an essentially different economic regime will not be the result of a series of incremental reforms, of imperceptible modifications of capitalist society.

The advance of the revolution is parallel to the evolution of capitalist society. The transformation will therefore necessarily be prepared by imperceptible modifications of capitalist society. But the revolutionary idea means, in our and all opinions, I think, this: that despite this parallelism, the passage from the condition of property to another condition will not be made by gradual modifications and continual evolution, but that at a given moment, when you come down to the essential question, to the rule of property itself, whatever the changes and ameliorations previously obtained, a rupture of continuity will be necessary, an absolute, categorical change.

We mean still another thing by the word revolution: the break in continuity which is the start of the revolution itself has, as a necessary but insufficient condition, the conquest of political power. That is the very root of our doctrine. We socialists think that the revolutionary transformation of property can be accomplished only when we have conquered political power.

If a delegate to a socialist Congress, having the required five years of membership in the Party, contests statements like those I have just made, there is no further discussion possible.

A DELEGATE: You would get rid of all ambiguity by saying that, to your mind, it's not a matter of electoral conquest.

BLUM: I am asked to eliminate a point of misunderstanding. I'm going to do so. The conquest of political power, what does that mean? It means: taking control of the central authority, which is presently called the State, by any means, without legal or illegal means being excluded. That is the socialist idea.

THE PRESIDENT: Let Citizen Blum finish. Our comrade is tired. And it is very difficult to speak in this atmosphere.

BLUM: Neither international nor French socialism has ever limited the means that can be used to conquer political power. Lenin himself has admitted that in England political power could be conquered perfectly well by the ballot box. But there is no socialist, however moderate he may be, who has ever condemned himself to expecting political power to come only through an electoral success. On that point, there is no possible discussion. Our common slogan is the slogan of Guesde, that Bracke repeated to me a little while ago: By every means, including legal means.

But that said, where does the point of divergence appear? It appears in the revolutionary conception that I have just described for you, which Jaurès, Vaillant, and Guesde have always had to defend against two different deviations, and which has always made its way with difficulty between deviations to the right and left. The right-wing deviation is precisely the reformism of which I just spoke. The basis of the reformist thesis is that if not the whole social transformation, at least the most important advantages that it will provide for the working class can be obtained without the previous conquest of political power. That is the essence of reformism.

But there is a second error, which is, I am strongly obliged to say, at bottom anarchist. It consists in thinking that the conquest of political power is itself the final end, when it is in fact nothing but a means, that it is the goal, when it is nothing but the precondition, that it is the play, when it is nothing but the prologue. . . . For when you reason in that way, what is the only positive, certain result that you have in view? The destruction of the present governmental apparatus. When you fasten upon the seizure of power as your purpose, without being sure that it can result in social transformation, the sole positive goal of your effort is the destruction of what is called the bourgeois apparatus of government. An error that is anarchist in its origins and which, in my opinion, is at the root of communist doctrine.

I am making this argument now, not in order to embarrass some people or to serve others, but in order to bring the greatest possible clarity to the discussion of this group of doctrines which, for my own part, I have been studying for weeks with a mixture of scrupulousness and anxiety.

Open your Party card. What has the object of the Socialist party been up until now? The transformation of the economic system.

Open the statutes of the Communist International. Read the article in which the International defines its goal. What is it? The armed struggle against bourgeois power.

I am going to make an effort to explain your own doctrine, an effort for which you ought to be grateful to me. I want to show to what, in the ideas of Lenin and the authors of the theses, the new revolutionary idea corresponds. It comes from the idea, deeply anchored in the minds of the authors and constantly repeated, that it is impossible, before the conquest of political power, to carry out propaganda and worker's education effectively. Which means that the conquest of political power is not only, as we have always said, the condition of social transformation, but that it is the condition of the first efforts at organization and propaganda which ought later to lead to that transformation.

Lenin thinks that, inasmuch as the domination of the capitalist class over the working class will not be broken except by violence, all efforts to bring together, educate, and organize the working class will necessarily remain futile. Thus the imperative summons to seize power immediately, as quickly as possible, since it is on the conquest of power that, not only your final efforts, but your initial efforts depend.

But that position—pardon me for repeating this to those who have already heard it—I understand it when one is facing a proletariat like the Russian one and a country like Russia, where we hadn't made any generally effective propaganda efforts prior to the seizure of power. One can then imagine that, before everything, one must overthrow the bourgeois power in order that propaganda even become possible. But is the situation the same in our western countries? I refuse to concede that until the conquest of political power (which you will no doubt accomplish tomorrow) everything you do will be wasted effort, and there will not have been any socialist propaganda in that country. I refuse to tell myself that all the work of the past has been worthless, and that everything remains to be done. No, much has been done, and you have no right to deny it to yourselves and to disavow those efforts today.

Without getting lost in oratory, I want to carry out to the end the comparison between the two revolutionary conceptions: the one which sees in the transformation the end and in the conquest of political power the means; and that which, on the contrary, sees in the conquest of political power the end. Do you think that this has only a casuistic importance? That it divides only socialist professors with their mortarboards on? No, it is crucial in the sense that it leads to two absolutely different conceptions of organization and propaganda.

If you think that the revolution consists in transformation, then everything, even in the midst of bourgeois society, can prepare for that transformation and becomes revolutionary work. If that is the revolution, the daily effort of propaganda carried on by every Party member is the revolution advancing a little each day. . . .

And even reforms, of which Sembat spoke yesterday in terms which should have united the assembly, if they serve to increase and to consolidate the influence of the working class on capitalist society, if they give the working class more impetus and courage, if they sharpen its militant ardor, then reforms, construed in that sense, are revolutionary. And it is only in that sense that we have defended them and that we wish to continue to defend them.

But if, on the contrary, the only object is the promptest possible seizure of political power, then all that activity becomes in effect useless. When we discussed the electoral program two years ago, Loriot was already telling us: "I do not contest the value for socialism of reforms, in theory. But today, in fact, the situation is such, the revolutionary crisis is so close, that reforms . . ." (Interruptions and noise)

The Congress will understand that I can hardly follow a train of thought in the midst of such interruptions. . . . If the crisis is so close, and if that crisis is the revolution, then, in effect, the only things that have revolutionary value are those which prepare, as quickly as possible, for the conquest of political power. One then understands your whole concept of organization, for it was formed with that end in view, fashioned so that no occasion would be lost, so that the attacking troops would always be well under control, ready to obey at the first signal, each unit transmitting below the order it received from above.

I beg the Assembly's pardon, but you will recognize that there is a certain logical coherence to my remarks. They comprise a unity within my thought. I ask that you do not make my task still more awkward by interruptions which necessarily force me to stray from the line I have traced for myself.

This idea of the conquest of political power, where is it going to lead you? You know well, since numbers matter little to you, that you won't win political power with your communist vanguards alone. To the theory of organization that I have analyzed, you therefore add the tactic of relying on the masses, borrowing from the old remembered Blanquist doctrine,[4] for the line of descent is clear.

You think that, taking advantage of favorable circumstances, you'll be able to pull along behind your vanguards the noncommunist popular

4. Named for the frequently imprisoned and almost mythic activist Louis Auguste Blanqui (1805–81), Blanquism was a strand of French socialist thought and practice from the 1830s on. It represented a continuation of the French Revolutionary tradition of Babeuf and focused upon conspiratorial association for the purpose of overthrowing the existing government.—ED.

masses, who won't understand the exact goal of the movement, but who will be kept in a state of sufficiently intense passion by your propaganda. That's really your idea. What has Blanquism ever accomplished with that? Not much. In recent years, it hasn't even succeeded in taking a firehouse on the Boulevard de la Villette. . . . But it is the idea itself, without attempting to decide whether or not it can be realized in practice, it is the theoretical conception that I want to consider.

This tactic of relying on masses lacking in class consciousness, led, in ignorance of what they are about, by the vanguards, this tactic of conquering political power by a mighty surprise blow—we cannot accept it. We believe that it will lead the proletariat into the most tragic disillusionments. We believe that, in the present state of capitalist society, it would be madness to count on unorganized masses. We know, in France, what unorganized masses are, whom they march behind one day and whom the next. We know that the unorganized masses sided first with Boulanger and then with Clemenceau. . . . We think that all movements for the seizure of power that base themselves on instinctive passion, on the sheeplike violence of vast unorganized masses, have a very fragile foundation indeed and would be exposed to many dangerous reversals. We do not know with whom those masses you have captivated today would be tomorrow. We think that they have an almost singular lack of revolutionary stoicism. We think that on the first day material difficulties arise, the day when the meat or the milk arrives a little late, you perhaps won't find in them the sustained stoical will to sacrifice that the kind of movements you envisage require for success. And those who marched behind you the day before will, perhaps, on that day be the first to drive you to the wall.

No, it is not by means of unorganized masses trailing behind your communist vanguards that you'll have a chance to seize power. You have an opportunity to seize power in this country: do you know how? By vast workers' movements of an organized character, which suppose an education and abilities pushed as far as possible. You will not make a revolution with those who jump onto every bandwagon. You will make it with millions of organized workers, who know what they want, and how to get it, and are ready to accept the necessary suffering and sacrifices.

Your doctrine which despises recruitment from the outset, which fragments the unions, as if they were too powerful, your party has failed even before it has had its adventure.

I will show you now—for in my mind it's all connected—how it is that out of our disagreement about organization and the conception of revolution arises our disagreement about the idea of the dictatorship of the proletariat. . . .

We are partisans of the dictatorship of the proletariat. There, too, there's

no disagreement in principle. We so much support it that we've even put
the idea and theory of it into an electoral program. Thus we have fear neither of the word, nor of the thing.

I add that, for my part, I do not think that the dictatorship of the proletariat must retain a democratic form—even though Marx and, more recently, Morris Hilquist said so. I think it impossible, first of all, to conceive
in advance precisely what form such a dictatorship would take, for the essence of a dictatorship is the elimination of all previous forms and all constitutional prescriptions. Dictatorship is an arbitrary power given to one or
several men to take whatever measures a given situation demands. As a
result, it is impossible, and also completely contradictory, to determine in
advance what form the dictatorship of the proletariat will take.

Where then is the disagreement? Neither is it over the issue of whether
the dictatorship of the proletariat may be exercised by a Party. In fact, in
Russia the dictatorship is exercised not by the soviets, but by the Communist party itself. We've always thought in France that the future dictatorship
of the proletariat would be exercised by the groups of the Socialist party
itself becoming, by virtue of a fiction which we all accept, the representative of the whole proletariat. The difference comes, as I have told you,
from our divergence in opinion over organization and the conception of
revolution. Dictatorship exercised by the Party, yes, but by a Party organized like ours, and not like yours.

Dictatorship exercised by a Party based on the popular will and popular
liberty, on the will of the masses, in sum, an impersonal dictatorship of the
proletariat. But not a dictatorship exercised by a centralized party, where
all authority rises from one level to the next and ends up by being concentrated in the hands of a secret Committee. . . .

Just as the dictatorship should be impersonal, it should be, we hold,
temporary, provisional. . . . But if, on the contrary, one sees the conquest
of power as a goal, if one imagines (in opposition to the whole Marxist
conception of history) that it is the only method for preparing that transformation, that neither capitalist evolution nor our own work of propaganda
could have any effect, if as a result too wide a gap and an almost infinite
period of time must be inserted between taking power as the precondition,
and revolutionary transformation as the goal, then we cease to be in agreement. Then we say to you that your dictatorship is no longer a temporary
dictatorship which will permit you to put the finishing touches on your society. It is a stable system of government, almost normal to your way of
thinking, under whose shelter you want to carry out the whole project.

That's the Moscow system. Moscow doesn't think that the conditions for
a total revolutionary transformation have in the slightest been realized in

Russia. It counts on the dictatorship of the proletariat to bring about a sort of forced maturation, independently of the country's previous state of economic development. I repeat to you, the dictatorship of the proletariat is then no longer a kind of necessary expedient to which all movements for the seizure of power have recourse the day after they succeed. It is, to your way of thinking, a system of government created once and for all. So true is this that, for the first time in socialist history, you conceive of terrorism not merely as a last-ditch effort, not merely as an extreme measure for the public safety imposed on you by bourgeois resistance, not merely as a vital necessity for the revolution, but as a means of government.

A DELEGATE: Can you give us a single citation in support of what you're saying?

BLUM: Before arriving at my conclusion, I would like to present you with one last observation, even though it doesn't seem essential from the doctrinal point of view. I would like to say a few words about a question which we have voluntarily addressed in our motion: the question of national defense.

A DELEGATE: The *Marseillaise,* then.

BLUM: The motion of the Third International, to my great regret, is silent on this point, and it's not mentioned very explicitly in the texts. I want to say a few very brief words on the subject, very clear and, if necessary, very harsh.

What do those who wrote and those who will vote for this motion have in mind? We don't deny that the establishment of international socialism in the world is the sole means of preventing war. We also don't deny—I said so to Vaillant-Couturier, when telling him how much Raymond Lefebvre's speech at Strasbourg had moved me—we also don't deny that international socialism, having been taught the bloodiest of lessons, must today consider as its paramount and its life-and-death task, the choice and the preparation of all means for stopping future wars. But that said, we affirm that even under a capitalist regime, international duty and national duty can coexist in a socialist conscience.

A DELEGATE: On the condition that everyone has one.

BLUM: Cachin expressed himself on this matter this morning in a way that was, in my opinion, completely ambiguous. That ambiguity is also found in the response that he made to Trotsky and which appears in the documents published by the Party. Trotsky had asked him if henceforth, in the event of war, the French Socialist party would vote for or against war credits. Cachin dodged the question. He responded: "In the present state of things, the danger of war could come only from an imperialist French policy and, under those conditions, we would certainly refuse the credits."

It's not a question of the present state of things. One dodges the question by sheltering oneself thus in an isolated bit of time and space. The question remains. . . .

Cachin's response does not trouble or embarrass us in any way. None of us has ever said that the duty of national defense was absolute and unconditional. But we said that the refusal, the abstention from national defense, was also not an absolute and unconditional duty for socialists.

Nevertheless you must state your views on this point, because a question like that shouldn't be eluded with tricks or omissions. We don't want to practice deceit in anything. In our motion, we have voluntarily posed the problem. We have affirmed something, and we affirm it still: there are circumstances when, even under a capitalist regime, the duty of national defense exists for socialists. I do not want to go into the heart of the matter.

A DELEGATE: Be explicit.

BLUM: No. I don't want to struggle with a thought which is at bottom Tolstoyan or neo-Christian rather than socialist.

A DELEGATE: Give some hypothetical situations.

BLUM: It's very simple: the situation of a clear aggression, the attack of whatever nation . . . (Many movements, noise, shouts: Down with war! The delegates sing the International. Tumult)

THE PRESIDENT: Pressemane has the floor with the permission of comrade Blum.

NUMEROUS VOICES: No! No! (Uproar)

BLUM: I have stayed a few minutes too long at the tribune. I thank you for the attention you have given me. The last words that I spoke elicited from you sentiments which, I hope, you will express in your motion, for it is still silent on that point. (Applause, cries, tumult)

That said, I will hasten to conclude and to get down from the rostrum. On the questions of organization, of revolutionary conception, of the relations between political and trade union organization, on the questions of the dictatorship of the proletariat, of national defense, I could also say on the sentimental residue of communist doctrine—on all these points, there is formal opposition and contradiction between what socialism has been until now and what communism will be in the future.

It is no longer, as has been inaccurately stated, a question of discipline. Each of us is faced with a question of conscience at once individual and collective. Confronted with an entirely new situation, such as you have desired, one must look it in the face and say: I can, or I cannot. This must be said without holding anything back, without second thoughts, without evasion, without mental reservations, without anything that would be unworthy of either side.

I ask you a very simple question. Do you believe that, if it had been possible for me to join the Communist International after your vote, I would have waited until your vote to do so? If I could have made myself do it tomorrow, do you think that I would not have done it yesterday? Do you believe that I wouldn't have wished to save my Party from these weeks and months of discussions and controversy?

If I had had a few objections about details, I would have kept them silent, hidden within myself. I would have tried to have this act, whose solemnity we all feel, accomplished insofar as possible with unanimity among us. If I had been able to make myself do this, I repeat, I would have done it the first day, the moment Frossard and Cachin returned from Russia, the moment Frossard personally asked me to. I could not do it.

Do you believe that a majority vote is going to change my conscience? Because so many voices have pronounced for and so many against, do you believe that my state of mind and heart vis-à-vis a problem like this one could be transformed? Do you believe that numbers have that virtue? Surely not! None of you can think so.

There is only one thing that could change our decision—that the Communist International itself change; that we be presented with something other than what is offered us at present, something which is not opposed to what we have preserved and wish to preserve.

I know very well that certain among you who are with us at heart enter the Communist International with the hidden motive of changing it from within, of transforming it once they have penetrated it. But I think that is pure illusion. You are faced with something too powerful, too coherent, too stable for you even to dream of modifying it.

I also believe that that is not a very noble attitude. One enters, or one does not enter. One joins because one wants to, or one does not join. One joins or does not join because one's ideas are in adherence or are not.

Nor do I, I can say to you with Sembat, nor do I want to make an emotional scene. I have only been involved with the public life of the Party on two occasions separated by fifteen years. I entered its public life in 1904–5 to work for unity, and I returned to it in 1917, at a moment when that unity seemed threatened. I have returned now only for that reason.

When it is suggested that we are motivated by envy, pride, jealousy, attachment to tradition, when such feelings are attributed to us in the face of such a formidable event which could have such immeasurable consequences, we are wronged in a way that is gratuitous and very unwarranted.

Throughout this debate people have spoken again and again of bosses whose usurped authority must be destroyed once and for all. I don't know if I am a boss in the Socialist party; it doesn't make any difference to me. I know that I occupy a post which carries with it a responsibility.

I have often thought of the old joke: "I am their leader, I have to follow them." In a party like the Socialist party, that joke contains a great deal of truth and, personally, I have never denied it. I know that in a party with a large membership, popular in essence like ours is, the leaders are only loud voices to speak in the name of the mass, they are nothing but hands to act more directly in the name of the crowd.

All the same, they have a right; they have a duty. They are the servants of the collective will. But they have the right to try to recognize and to interpret that will. They have the right to ask themselves if what they see before them is only a random flux of eddies straying towards the banks, or if it is the true, underlying current, slow and majestic, that flows down the river.

And then they retain, despite everything, an individual conscience. And there are moments when they have the right and the duty to say to themselves: "Can I follow, or can I not?"

That is where we have arrived today. A majority vote, I repeat, will not alter a cry of conscience so strong within us that it drowns out the concern for unity that has always been our guide.

We are convinced that at this moment, there is a more urgent question than whether socialism will remain united or not. It is the question of whether socialism will survive or not.

We are convinced, to the very depth of our being, that while you go running after adventure, someone must remain to guard the old house.

It is the very life of socialism that we are profoundly aware of preserving at this moment with all our strength.

And, since it is perhaps the last occasion for me to say it to you, I would like to ask from you something which is of grave importance in my eyes. Can we truly, both sides, make a supreme commitment to this? Tomorrow, we will be divided, perhaps, as men who understand the interests and duties of socialism differently. Or will we be divided as enemies?

Are we going to pass our time in front of the bourgeoisie treating one another as traitors and renegades, madmen and criminals? Will we not give one another credit for acting in good faith? I ask: Is there anyone here who believes that I am not a socialist?

In this hour, which is, for all of us, an hour of tragic anxiety, let us not add that to our sorrows and fears. Let us know how to abstain from words which wound and lacerate, from hurtful acts, from everything that would be fratricidal struggle.

I say this to you because it is without doubt the last time I will address many of you and because it must, however, be said. Let all of us, though we are separated, remain socialists. Despite everything, let us remain brothers, brothers separated by a quarrel which is cruel but which is, nonetheless, a family quarrel, and whom a common hearth may someday reunite.

The Matignon Agreement (June 7, 1936)

Article 1—The employers' delegation agrees to the immediate establishment of collective agreements of labor.

Article 2—These agreements must include especially the following Articles 3 to 5.

Article 3—As all citizens are under obligation to observe the law the employers recognize the freedom of opinion and the right of workers to join freely and belong to an occupational *syndicat* constituted in accordance with Book 3 of the Labor Code.

The employers undertake not to take into account whether or not a worker belongs to a *syndicat* in making their decisions about taking him on, or organizing or distributing work, or measures of discipline or dismissal.

If one of the contracting parties challenges the grounds for the dismissal of a worker as being in violation of the above-mentioned right, both parties will endeavor to establish the facts and to find an equitable solution for all disputes.

This intervention does not limit the right of the parties to obtain before the courts damages for injury to their interests. Exercise of the right to have a *syndicat* must not lead to contravention of the law.

Article 4—Actual wages paid to all workers on the date of May 25, 1936, will, from the day when work is resumed, be readjusted according to a diminishing scale, starting with a rise of 15 per cent for the lowest paid and amounting to a rise of 7 per cent for the highest-paid workers.

The total wages bill for any company must in no case be increased by more than 12 per cent; the increases already given since the above-mentioned date will be counted toward the readjustments defined above. But increases in excess of these readjustments will remain the right of the beneficiaries.

Negotiations for determining minimum wages by collective agreements, according to regions and by categories, which shall be begun at once, must deal in particular with the necessary readjustment of abnormally low wages.

The employers' delegation undertakes to proceed with any necessary readjustments to maintain a normal relationship between salaries and wages.

Article 5—Except in special cases already provided for by law, every factory employing more than ten workers, after agreement with the *syndicat* organizations or, in their absence, with the interested parties, will

From *France: Empire and Republic, 1850–1940*, edited by David Thomson (New York: Harper & Row, 1968), pp. 177–79.

have two (titular) or several (titular and deputy) shop stewards, according to the importance of the factory. These shop stewards are entitled to lay before the management any individual claims that have not been satisfied directly and which have to do with application of the laws, decrees and regulations of the Labor Code, wage scales and measures of hygiene and safety.

All working men and women over eighteen shall have a vote, provided that they have at the time of the election been in the factory for more than three months and have not been deprived of their civil rights.

Those eligible for election shall be electors as defined above, of French nationality and aged at least twenty-five, who have worked in the factory for at least one year, but this time must be shortened if the number of candidates would be reduced to five.

Workers who themselves or whose wives keep a retail store, no matter of what kind, cannot be candidates.

Article 6—The employers' delegation undertakes that no sanctions will be taken against strike actions.

Article 7—The confederal workers' delegation will ask workers on strike to decide to resume work as soon as the managements have accepted the general agreement now made, and as soon as negotiations for its application have been begun between the managements and the staffs of the factories.

Paris, June 7, 1936
President of the Council (Prime Minister): Léon Blum

For the C.G.T.:⁵ Léon Jouhaux, René Belin, B. Frachon, Semat,
H. Cordier, Milan.

For the C.G.P.F.: Duchemin, Dalbouze, Richemont, Lambert-Ribot.

19. Gustav Stresemann, Two Views of Locarno

Gustav Stresemann (1878–1929) was a prominent German nationalist politician who, as leader of the National Liberal party, had supported a program of extreme annexationism during the First World War. Initially he opposed the revolution and held hopes for a restoration of the monarchy. He also opposed the treaty of Versailles and had contempt for the League of Nations. But after 1919 he came to accept the new republic

---

5. The C.G.T. (Confédération générale de Travail) is the confederation of French labor unions. The Communist unions seceded after World War I but rejoined in 1936. The C.G.P.F. (Confédération générale de la Production française, after 1936 du Patronat français) is the confederation of French employers' associations.—ED.

and in August 1923 was appointed Chancellor and Foreign Minister, holding the latter post under nine different cabinets until his death in 1929.
As a *Vernunftrepublikaner* after 1923—one who supported the Weimar
Republic for reasons of practical utility and realism rather than moral
conviction—Stresemann sought to revise the unfavorable terms of the
treaty of Versailles, particularly the burden of reparations, the limits on
German armaments, and the occupation of the Rhineland. He also hoped
to end Germany's diplomatic isolation while preventing the establishment
of a permanent Anglo-Belgian-French guarantee pact. By accepting the
Dawes Plan in 1924 Stresemann sought to reengage American investment
to rebuild Germany's industrial power and to end the French occupation
of the Ruhr.

The initial effect of Locarno was to usher in an era of temporary calm
Along with Aristide Briand and Austen Chamberlain, Stresemann was
a principal architect of the treaties of Locarno, agreed upon in October
1925. Their principal component was a Treaty of Mutual Guarantee (sometimes referred to as the Rhineland Pact), a regional security agreement
which ensured nonaggression among France, Belgium, and Germany, and
guaranteed the post-1918 Franco-German and Belgo-German frontiers.
This agreement was signed by Germany, France, and Belgium, and by
Great Britain and Italy as guarantors. Further, Locarno set in place arbitration treaties between Germany and Poland and Germany and Czechoslovakia, as well as between Germany and Belgium and Germany and
France. Concurrently, France concluded with Poland and Czechoslovakia
treaties for mutual assistance in the event of aggression by Germany. The
treaty did not provide an explicit German agreement to refrain from military action in the east, nor did Germany guarantee its eastern borders.

The initial effect of Locarno was to usher in an era of temporary calm
in European foreign affairs (characterized by the contemporary phrase
"spirit of Locarno"). Germany was admitted to the League of Nations,
and accorded a permanent seat on its Council. Locarno's reaffirmation of
the European polity proved short-lived, however, as political and economic chaos enveloped Germany after 1929 and as the League's collective security system collapsed in the early 1930s.

A critical problem with Locarno involved the motives which inspired
Stresemann and his collaborators to sponsor the treaties, and their long-
term expectations for German foreign policy. The following documents—an exchange of letters written confidentially between the former German Crown Prince and Stresemann in 1925 and a public talk
given to the Nobel Peace assembly in Oslo, 29 June 1927 (Stresemann
was awarded the prize for 1926, but formally accepted it in 1927)—
suggest the range of positions which Stresemann offered in defense of
Locarno. They also illuminate, if only indirectly, the difficulties which

"Republican" statesmen encountered both in demonstrating and reinforc-ing the legitimacy of the Weimar Republic. A politician who generated immense domestic as well as foreign controversy, Stresemann was, ac-cording to his American biographer, Henry Ashby Turner, "a pragmatic conservative" whose goals "remained the same as those of most Germans who could be termed, in the broadest sense of the word, conservatives: the restoration of the country's power and prosperity and the preservation of as much of the prerevolutionary social and economic order as was possible. But in contrast to most of his conservative compatriots, he was, as a pragmatist, willing to be flexible about the political means of achiev-ing these goals." [1]

Exchange between Crown Prince Wilhelm and Gustav Stresemann on Locarno, August–September 1925

Crown Prince Wilhelm to Gustav Stresemann, 28 August 1925

Dear Herr Minister,

I am very grateful to you for sending to me the book you had promised. I found it very interesting. It was for me a great pleasure to have seen you again at Cecilienhof after so long a time, and to have been able to discuss with you so many different questions which concern our fatherland.

I am following with lively interest in the newspapers the development of the matter of the Security Pact. You know that I have always felt that I could express my opinions frankly to you, and accordingly, I would not want to let this opportunity pass by without telling you once again what grave apprehensions I would have if we allowed ourselves to join the League of Nations without favorable guarantees. It may be that now and then we could, by our presence in the League of Nations, achieve minor political successes. But I fear that on big questions affecting our fatherland, we might still be outvoted by the other side, and that we would then forfeit our freedom of action. At the moment we are still in the favorable position of being able to opt either for the East or the West. In this respect we hold the balance, so to speak.

All those peoples who wish to free themselves from the yoke of the En-tente see us as their natural allies at the present time (look at Morocco, the

1. Henry Ashby Turner, *Stresemann and the Politics of the Weimar Republic* (Princeton, 1963), pp. 263–64.

From the *Gustav Stresemann Nachlass,* U.S. National Archives Microfilm, roll no. 3168, frames 159787–88, 159871–75. Translated for this volume by John W. Boyer.

Druse rebellion, the movement for independence in China, the many portents in India and Egypt).

This favorable situation would be transformed at one blow into its opposite, if we were now to enter into a firm commitment with the Western Powers.

I beg you, dear Dr. Stresemann, not to regard my apprehensions as presumptuous, for you know with what deep concern I follow the future of our fatherland, and how convinced I am of the necessity of exploiting every opportunity in the field of foreign affairs, in order that slowly but surely we win back for Germany her rightful place in the assembly of nations.

I have just returned from Upper Austria, where the idea of the *Anschluss* is extraordinarily animated. Here indeed one observes an inevitable development.

It would very much interest me, if, time permitting, you would briefly comment on my remarks.

With warmest greetings, I remain,

Yours faithfully,
Wilhelm

Gustav Stresemann to Crown Prince Wilhelm, 7 September 1925

I am very much obliged to Your Royal Highness for the comments in your letter of August 28. I am happy that the small booklet, about which I spoke with Your Royal Highness, has found your interest. Permit me also to send you from Berlin a journal in which Dr. Hans Schumann has published a discussion of the Security Pact, which to a great extent touches upon the complex of questions which you raised in your letter. His exposition is based on intensive discussions with me and in this respect reproduces my own opinions.

In regard to the question of Germany's entry into the League of Nations, I would like to make the following comments:

German foreign policy has, in my opinion, three great assignments in the immediately foreseeable future:

First, the solution of the reparations question in a way tolerable for Germany and the guarantee of peace, which is the precondition for the re-establishment of our strength.

Second, I would include the protection of ethnic Germans living abroad, those ten to twelve million of our kindred who now live in foreign lands under a foreign yoke.

The third great task is the revision of our Eastern boundaries: the recovery of Danzig, the Polish corridor, and a correction of the frontier in Upper Silesia.

In the background lies the *Anschluss* with Austria, although it is very clear to me that this union will not only bring advantages to Germany, but also greatly complicate the problem of the German *Reich* (strengthening of the Catholic influence, Bavaria plus Austria against Prussia, predominance of the clerical and socialist parties in German Austria).

If we wish to achieve these goals, we must concentrate on these tasks. Hence the Security Pact, which should at one and the same time guarantee peace for us and bind England as well as Italy as guarantors of our western border, if Mussolini goes along. On the other hand the Security Pact involves the renunciation by Germany of martial conflict with France for the recovery of Alsace-Lorraine, a renunciation, however, which is only theoretical inasmuch as no possibility of war with France now exists. The burdens of reparations, which the Dawes Plan has imposed on us, will probably be intolerable already by 1927. At that point, we must ask for a new conference to establish a new assessment of German economic potential, a right that, according to the Versailles Treaty, is available to us at any time. If we compare the 2.5 billion which is the maximum sum we have to pay (in my opinion we cannot pay more than 1.75 billion) with the average of over 4 billion which the other side has to pay in interest on their war debt, then we must reflect that our opponents face at least as great a tax burden as we.

Our concern for the ethnic Germans living abroad argues in favor of our joining the League of Nations. I might even point to the remarks of Kramář, which are reprinted in the above-mentioned journal. Also the Saar, and even the politicians there who are farthest on the right, are in favor of entry into the League. In Geneva we will be the spokesmen for the whole German cultural community, because all Germans everywhere will see in us their bulwark and protector. The misgivings that we would be outvoted in the League of Nations are based on the false assumption that in the Council of the League, which has the real power, decisions are taken by majority vote. The decisions of the Council must be passed unanimously. Germany is guaranteed a permanent seat on the Council. If we were now on the League Council, Poland would not have achieved its way on the issue of the postal service in Danzig, because an objection by the German representative would suffice to reject this demand. Poland, Czechoslovakia, Yugoslavia, and Rumania, who are all bound by international treaties to look after their ethnic minorities (and that means especially their German minorities), will not be able to disregard so reprehensibly their obligations if they know that Germany can bring all these shortcomings before the League. Add to that all the questions which lie so close to the German heart, for example the questions of war guilt, of general disarmament, Danzig, the Saar territory, etc. These matters fall under the jurisdiction of the League of Nations, and in the hands of a skillful speaker at a plenary session of the League can become very unpleasant for the Entente.

France is not at all delighted by the idea of Germany's entrance into the League, while England wants it, in order to offer resistance to France's hitherto paramount influence in the League.

The question of opting between East and West does not ensue from our entrance into the League of Nations. Indeed, one can only choose, if one has military power behind one. Unfortunately we lack such power. We can neither become England's continental spearhead, as some believe, nor can we get involved in a German-Russian alliance. I warn against the uto-pia of coquetting with Bolshevism. When the Russians are in Berlin, the Red flag will soon wave over the Castle, and in Russia, where they are hoping for world revolution, there will be great satisfaction in having bol-shevized Europe up to the Elbe, while the rest of Germany will be served up as fodder to the French. That we are otherwise completely ready to come to an understanding on a different basis with the Russian state (in whose evolutionary development I believe), and that we are absolutely not selling ourselves to the West by our entrance into the League, is a fact which I would be happy to discuss further with Your Royal Highness when an occasion offers itself. I believe our joining the League will in no way harm the great movement which is now mobilizing the primitive peoples against the colonial rule of the great powers. The most important problem, in the context of the first question of German foreign policy I mentioned above, is the liberation of German territory from foreign occupation. We must first get the strangler's hands off our neck. Therefore, as Metternich said of Austria after 1809, German policy for the time being will have to consist of "finessing things" [2] and in side-stepping big decisions.

I beg Your Royal Highness to allow me to limit myself to these brief suggestions, and I might also ask you kindly to view this letter itself— which I deliberately have not signed, in the event that it were to fall into foreign hands, even by mistake—in light of the fact that I am naturally forced to exercise great restraint in my remarks. If Your Royal Highness would like to give me the opportunity to discuss in a quiet conversation these questions, which will soon demand a decision, I shall be happy to place myself at your disposal.

I would also like to have a small pamphlet, *Die Sendung des Prinzen Wilhelm,* sent from Berlin to Oels. I ask you to consider it most kindly from the point of view of the methods which Stein and Hardenberg once had to use, in order to be able to save the Prussian state.

I beg most humbly to reciprocate the friendly greetings of Your Royal Highness.

2. "finassieren." Stresemann may have adapted the word from Heinrich Ritter von Srbik, *Metternich: Der Staatsmann und der Mensch* (2 vols., Munich, 1925), 1: 114.—ED.

Germany Gropes toward Peace

It is a great honor for me to address you today. I would like to begin by expressing my heartfelt thanks for the great distinction which the Nobel Committee has conferred upon me. I would also add my warm gratitude for the cordial welcome you have extended to me. I know that this honor has a special character, since it is awarded not for scientific and theoretical research, but for practical politics. It is not awarded to an individual country nor to a representative of an individual country. It reflects, rather, the common policy of all those countries who are traveling along the same road. And thus, in the case of Germany too, it is not awarded for the work of a single individual. As a confirmed individualist I certainly do not wish to underrate the influence of the individual, for the masses do not lead the individual; rather, in the individual is vested the capacity to lead the masses. But when great ideas and the vital affairs of a nation are at stake, then the individual needs the suppport of the spiritual leaders of the nation.

During the past few years I have led a sometimes hard battle for German foreign policy. I am thus, perhaps, particularly well placed to answer the questions so often raised about Germany's frame of mind. The attitude abroad concerning our state of mind vacillates among approval, skepticism, criticism, and hostility. Let me identify and discuss with you the leading trends in politics and thought in the new Germany, insofar as they have emerged in the historically short time since the war.

I must begin by saying something about the old Germany. That Germany, too, suffered from superficial judgment, because appearances and reality were not always kept apart in people's minds. True, it still preserved the spirit of paternalism imparted to it by Frederick William I,[3] but it was a paternalism administered with an iron loyalty and sense of duty to the state and the people. It had an officialdom disparaged in other countries as a bureaucracy that knew only one ideal: service to the state. This old Germany was partly defeated in its conflict with the progressive ideas of socialism, for it had given the people nothing that could serve as a successful alternative to socialism. It was, however, a land of social and political progress far less given to the philosophy of laissez-faire than some other countries with other forms of government. It was a land of barracks, a land of universal military conscription, and a land of strong sympathy for the military; but it was also a land of technology, of chemistry, and in general

From Gustav Stresemann, "The New Germany," in *Nobel Lectures. Peace 1926–1950*, vol. 2, edited by Frederick W. Haberman (New York and Amsterdam: Elsevier Publishers, 1972), pp. 8–22. Reprinted by permission of the publisher. Some footnotes deleted.

3. Frederick William I (1688–1740), king of Prussia (1713–40).

of the most up-to-date research. The old and the new struggled for control. Whoever writes its history must not merely look at the surface of things but rather look into its depths.

This was the country in which most of us who today occupy responsible positions in Germany spent the greater part of our lives. Just as the child is father to the man, so the impressions of one's youth remain the most vivid in manhood. Just as a child respects his father even when he perceives his weaknesses and faults, so a German will not despise the old Germany which was once a symbol of greatness to him. The idea in the British saying, "England, with all thy faults, I love thee still," [4] applies also to all that was creditable and worthy in the old Germany. Just as the British subject loves England despite her faults, so we must insist that all Germans who were part of the old Germany and helped shape her, recognize the greatness and worthiness of present-day Germany.

As a result of the World War, this old Germany collapsed. It collapsed in its constitution, in its social order, in its economic structure. Its thinking and feeling changed. No one can say that this transformation is yet complete. It is a process which will continue through generations. But just as haste and restlessness are typical of our present-day life, so change also takes place more rapidly than before. This applies to change in the relationships between nations as it does to change within an individual nation.

The purpose of the Nobel Foundation is the furthering of peace. The intention of the man who created it was to counter the natural forces which his own genius had released with the restraining powers of the human spirit. Is the recent development of the German people such as to justify the award being given here for a policy aimed at peace? One may well say that the question is answered by the very existence of the German policy of reconciliation and peace, for this policy would have been impossible had it not been in accord with the deepest desire of the German people, the desire for peaceful international cooperation in justice and freedom.

Here we encounter two conflicting concepts with which we must come to grips in our time: the idea of national solidarity and the idea of international cooperation. The superficial view is that the intellectual, spiritual, and emotional faculties of a nation are bounded by geographic, linguistic, and ethnic barriers. To contrast national solidarity and international cooperation as two opposites seems foolish to me. As Germany's representative in Geneva,[5] I tried to discuss this particular point. I expressed the

4. From *The Task* (1785), Book II, l. 206, by William Cowper (1731–1800).

5. Stresemann was a delegate to the League of Nations from the time of Germany's entry in September of 1926 to 1929. Some of the ideas referred to here were among those advanced in Stresemann's first speech to the League.

belief that it cannot have been intended in the divine plan that man's noblest abilities should be working in opposition to one another. I tried to make the point that the man who cultivates to the highest degree the qualities inherent in his national culture will gain insight into universal knowledge and feeling which transcend the limitations of his own heritage; and he will create works which, like cathedrals, although built upon the soil of his native land, will soar into the heaven of all mankind. A Shakespeare could have arisen only on English soil. In the same way, your great dramatists and poets express the nature and essence of the Norwegian people, but they also express that which is universally valid for all mankind. Dante can be understood only within the context of Italian thought, and *Faust* would be unthinkable if divorced from its German background; but both are part of our common cultural heritage. They break the bonds which bind them to their own nations, yet they are great only because their inspiration is so firmly rooted in their own countries. National culture can act as a bridge, instead of an obstacle, to mutual spiritual and intellectual understanding. The great men of a nation reach out to all mankind. They are unifying, not divisive; internationally conciliating and still great nationally. The French Minister Herriot[6] expressed this well at the international music festival at Frankfurt am Main when he said, "A worker for internationalism must first have a sense of nationalism." He also said, "To work effectively for peace, a man must first know peace within himself." Here we face the great question that each nation asks the others, "Do you really mean it when you talk of cooperation? What are you really thinking? Can I look into the depths of your soul and find out if you really want to work and build with me?" This is the question which Germany has been asked so often that I would like to discuss it here in some detail.

If one seeks to analyze experiences and reactions to the first postwar years, I hope one may say without being accused of bias that it is easier for the victor than for the vanquished to advocate peace. For the victor peace means the preservation of the position of power which he has secured. For the vanquished it means resigning himself to the position left to him. To walk behind others on a road you are traveling together, to give precedence to others without envy—this is painful for an individual and painful for a nation. But to believe that the work of half a century has brought one to the summit, and then to plunge down from that summit—that is even more painful to the human soul. The psychology of a people who have experienced this is not so easy to understand and not so easy to alter as many believe.

6. Edouard Herriot (1872–1957), leader of the French Radical Socialists, several times premier of France.

This was the problem facing the new Germany. The way which led to those events, referred to by your chairman when he mentioned Locarno and Geneva and spoke of Germany's admission to the League of Nations, was not made easy for Germany. The courtesy which most becomes a victor was denied to Germany for a long time. Germany had to assume superhuman reparations which the people would never have borne had there not existed an ageless legacy of service to the state. Historians still often see the end of the war as meaning nothing more for Germany than lost territories, lost participation in colonization, and lost assets for the state and individuals. They frequently overlook the most serious loss that Germany suffered. This was, in my view, that the intellectual and professional middle class, which traditionally upheld the idea of service to the state, paid for its total devotion to the state during the war with the total loss of its own wealth, and with its consequent reduction to the level of the proletariat. Its money became worthless when the state, which had issued it, refused to redeem it at face value.[7] To what extent demanding this sacrifice from an entire generation as a service to the state was legitimate is a matter of controversy which concerns laymen and legislators alike and one which has not yet been resolved. But all that has taken place in Germany since the war must be looked at in the light of the mood of this completely uprooted class. As a consequence of the terms of the Treaty of Versailles, the officer corps of the old army became part of this class, as did that part of the younger generation who, in the old Germany, would have become officers or civil servants. Theirs was an economic uprooting. But there was a mental and political uprooting, as well, of all those who had a deep loyalty to the five-hundred-year-old tradition of the monarchy and who were now without a solid foundation for their thinking and emotions. They all had shared in the rise and fall of Germany's fortunes during the war, but not one had expected this disaster. They did not want to break with the old because they did not know how to find their way in this changed Germany. As so often happens in history, their difficulties were increased by the overzealousness of those who promoted their innovations too rashly, instead of combining to a certain extent the old with the new.

Downtrodden and humiliated, beggars who had once been leaders, these people in their pessimism became the sharpest critics of unjustified attacks from without and of lack of respect for tradition at home. Furthermore, developments after the downfall of the leading class—and here I am

7. Because of a number of factors—among them, reparation payments, the flight of German capital abroad, the obstacles to the revival of German foreign trade—Germany was faced with a budgetary deficit which it met by issuing currency; in the resulting inflation the mark dropped in value from 4.2 to the dollar to 4,200,000,000,000 to the dollar.

speaking not of the nobility or the great landowners, but of the middle classes who saw the fruits of a lifetime of work vanish and who had to start from scratch to earn a bare livelihood—the developments after their downfall led to the convulsion of the whole social structure of the old Germany. Then came a further political shock: the invasion of the Ruhr.[8] Once again the feeling of being pillaged and plundered flared up in intense resistance. But this feeling now began to differentiate between those nations which apparently wanted to continue the conflict with Germany and those which held that a legal justification for the invasion did not exist. Voices were heard from the United States of America which made it clear that America wanted a peaceful and united Europe as a basis for mutual cooperation. Then came the conference in London about the Dawes Plan.[9] Statesmen took the place of the economists and the bankers, and as MacDonald[10] was leaving Downing Street one day during this time, he said that the words of the old Scottish song, "Should auld acquaintance be forgot?" were going through his mind.

For the first time, the wounded German people saw their representatives not merely as objects of legislation by others, but as participants in common negotiations; and they heard from Herriot's own lips the promise to evacuate the Ruhr. In the passionate struggle between the pessimists who could not believe in the possibility of a change in world outlook and those who were deliberately starting on a new road, the latter triumphed. From the beginning they had had a few supporters, but these were now augmented by the members of the working class. This group, no less patriotic than any other in Germany, had revived old connections in the hope of finding among their political and trade union comrades, men to work for their ideal of cooperation between nations.

Briand[11] succeeded Herriot as French minister of foreign affairs and implemented the pledge to evacuate the Ruhr. Then, with the note of February 9, 1925, German initiative inaugurated the policy of Locarno.[12] It would be quite untrue to suggest that from the first moment the Locarno policy met with joyful and enthusiastic approval. Distrust abroad delayed a

8. On January 11, 1923, by French and Belgian troops; they withdrew on July 31, 1925.

9. Named for Charles G. Dawes, co-recipient of the Nobel Peace Prize for 1925, the plan was put into effect on September 1, 1924; by its terms Germany received an international loan, payment of reparations was adjusted according to Germany's capacity to pay, German finances were stabilized with the reorganization of the Reichsbank under Allied supervision.

10. (James) Ramsay MacDonald (1866–1937), a founder of the British Labour Party, prime minister of Great Britain (1924; 1929–35).

11. Aristide Briand (1862–1932), Nobel Peace co-laureate for 1926.

12. This note, jointly issued by Chancellor Luther and Foreign Minister Stresemann, stated that Germany would accept a pact which guaranteed the Rhine frontier.

prompt response to the German move. It was met at home with misrepresentation; in what was really the beginning of an active policy, some saw weak resignation and the politics of renunciation. Our opponents introduced new questions into the debate to test the sincerity of Germany's desire for peace. Entry into the League of Nations was made a condition for putting the Locarno Treaties into effect. What a change that was! In 1919 Germany had tried to join the League of Nations and was rejected by shortsighted and undiscerning people. Now its entry was desired. The League, founded as an association of victors, was seeking cooperation and reconciliation with the most powerful of its World War opponents. Here too, strong feelings had to be overcome, for in Germany's view the right to self-determination had not always been recognized in the League's decisions concerning the fate of former German territories. At last, after many ups and downs of trust and distrust, agreement on the treaties was reached. Then, in March, 1926, petty maneuvering and petty jealousy once again made it impossible for Germany to join the League. But at the same time, however, came the well-known decision of the former Allies to negotiate as if Germany belonged to the League, even though she had not been officially admitted.

In September, Germany was admitted to the League of Nations. On that occasion Mr. Briand said in a speech, which was heard in all parts of the world, that the era of cannons and machine guns must end. He uttered words which should endure for the rest of this century, declaring that the two great nations, the German and the French, had won so many laurels from each other on the battlefields of war that the future should see them contending only for the great idealistic goals of mankind.[13]

No one who witnessed these events in Geneva is ever likely to forget them.

The history of nations shows that words are not always immediately followed by action. History uses a unit of measure for time that is different from that of the lifespan of the individual, whereas man is only too ready to measure the evolution of history by his own yardstick. In the period that followed we climbed to the heights and fell to the depths; we saw our budding confidence nipped by the frosts of suspicion and war psychosis; and even now, instead of unanimous support for peace from all the people of the world, we can observe a crisis of faith in its whole development.

13. In the course of his remarks to the Assembly on September 10, 1926, Briand said: ". . . our nations need give no further proof of their strength or of their heroism. Both nations have shown their prowess on the battlefield, and both have reaped an ample harvest of military glory. Henceforth they may seek laurels in other fields." (League of Nations, *Official Journal*, Special Supplement No. 44, p. 53.)

These were the first developments leading toward mutual understanding and coexistence on the part of former antagonists. But they were not always progressive. I have deliberately tried to give an honest account without glossing over the first breakdown and the ups and downs of the struggle. Nothing in the reporting of a nation's history could so mislead the younger generation as to represent great events in such a way that they appear to have happened as a matter of course. Nothing is more misleading to the youth of a nation than to state the outcome immediately after the beginning as if nothing could have taken place in between. Mankind advances only through struggle. The life of the individual is a continuous combat with errors and obstacles, and no victory is more satisfying than the one achieved against opposition. The life of man is not a level plane on which he moves ahead at will unopposed. A man should not end his days as a pessimist just because his short span of years has not brought fulfillment of his ideals. The complete realization of the ideal would remove the life-force which drives each of us forward, for human life would lose its meaning if there were nothing left for man to envision and strive for. Therefore, in this account of the difficulties, I do not address myself to the pessimists; I want to turn to those who ask why we have not made greater progress. I want to show them that in such times it is unreasonable to suppose that universal distrust and outdated attitudes will give way at one stroke to a new enlightenment.

Since these developments were not without periods of regression, because the intense hopes were followed by disappointment, Germany's development was also not without fluctuation. The feelings and emotions of an individualistic people like the Germans cannot easily be reduced to a common denominator. Nevertheless, it can be said today, and it has been demonstrated by recent debates in the Reichstag, that the overwhelming majority of the German people are united in a desire for peace and reconciliation.

I do not refer here to the extreme feelings of the Left and Right. A people that has experienced all that the Germans have been through, naturally offers fertile soil for the extremists. The ballast in the center of the German ship which saved it from heavy rolling in the past, that valuable and steady middle class group, no longer exists. The uprooted saw their hope in a complete reversal of affairs. It was at this time that the great tide of Bolshevism broke over Germany, appearing on the left as Communism and on the right as National Socialism. That a nation, whose currency had collapsed, whose social and economic reorganization had been as ruthless as ours—that this nation, which had to learn to live in an entirely new situation, has been able to master Bolshevism of the Right and of the Left, shows the healthiness of its spirit, the zeal of its industriousness, and the victory of realpolitik over the imaginary and illusory.

A German statesman of the postwar period has said that Napoleon's maxim that "politics is our destiny" is no longer valid. He thought he could equate our destiny with economics. I cannot agree, but I will admit that the policies of nations and groups have perhaps never been as greatly influenced by economic tendencies and developments as they are at present. And so I begin with economics, not because economics is of first importance, but because the inborn drive of the Germans to work, to create, and to rebuild, has been so apparent in this past decade. We did not, in accordance with the doctrine of laissez-faire, bring all welfare programs to a halt. Indeed, we tried in every way to reduce unemployment and its consequences. It may be that some individual initiative has been stifled by this far-reaching social concern on the part of the state; but taken overall, this policy points in the right direction. In the new Germany, the working class, regardless of the type of political representation they were subject to, has been won over to empire and state. In spite of the criticism which has so often been directed at the allegedly predominating influence of this class, I want to stress that the resulting fusion of the whole nation with the state is to be valued more highly than the one-sidedness or insufficiency of the legislation that brought this about is to be disparaged. Today a whole nation shares responsibility for the state and its future. In cities and communities throughout the country absolute opposition and negativism have been stopped. In previous centuries the king could truthfully say that he was the first servant of the state. But today all members of society are servants of the state.

No change in the balance of political parties can alter the general determination that no class should be excluded from contributing to and sharing responsibility for the state. This determination has provided a strong defense against extremists, a common interest in the rebuilding of the state, and a basis for the consolidation and preservation of national unity. The German people were united in their will to protect this unity against all attacks from within and without. They were stronger in adversity than in prosperity.

The fusion of these groups which were once fundamentally antagonistic to the state was in contrast during the first few years to the aversion held by many intellectuals and powerful industrialists for the new state, an aversion sustained by their disregard of important intangible drives in the national spirit. These negative attitudes, aversions, and enmities are today confined to a few groups of extreme rightist radicals. The winning over of those who in former times had been against the state was followed by the winning over of those who at first felt compelled to reject the new state and the new form of government. Here too, the events and politics of the day cannot obscure the historical fact that a working cooperation has been achieved. I cite for example Germany's most industrialized province, the province in which socialism can look back on its longest tradition, the former kingdom and present free state of Saxony where a ministry is functioning in which Socialists and Nationalists are working together. The urge to get things done will in the long run prove stronger than party loyalty. Today the differences of opinion are no longer confined by the boundaries of parties and factions; they run right across the individual parties themselves. In the end, all differences of opinion were conquered by the conviction that all hands were needed for rebuilding and that the children and grandchildren who will one day look back on our time will award the palm of approval only to those who did not stand aside in these difficult days, but who offered their help to rebuild the house which had collapsed.

True, the conflict between old and new has not yet been resolved. How could it be, even in a whole decade?

But the idea of an irreconcilable struggle between the old Germany and the new was confronted by the concept of a synthesis of old and new. Nobody in Germany is fighting for the reestablishment of the past. Its weaknesses and faults are obvious. What many do wish to have recognized in the new Germany is respect for what was great and worthy in the old. All events are linked with personalities that become their symbols. For the German people, this synthesis of old and new is embodied in the person of their president. He came as the successor to the first president of the Reich, who rose from the opposition and with great tact, political wisdom, and patriotism, smoothed the road from chaos to order and from order to reconstruction. In President von Hindenburg,[14] elected by the people, the nation sees a unity which transcends parties and a personality which commands respect, reverence, and affection. Raised in the traditions of the old monarchy he now fulfills his duties to the young republic during the most difficult and trying times. The President of the Reich personifies the idea of national unity. On the occasion of his eightieth birthday which will soon be here, all will join to show that for the overwhelming majority the concept of Germany itself comes before loyalty to political parties and ideologies. . . .

The concept of active cooperation has taken the place of opposition to the new form of government and of dreamy resignation entranced with the

---

14. Paul von Hindenburg (1847–1934), German field marshal and commander of the armies of the Central Powers (1916–18); president of Germany (1925–1934).

beauty of times past. Therefore, not only the present but also the future will have this republican Germany to reckon with.

The form of government is not, however, the decisive factor in the life of nations; it does not generate the philosophies of socialism or nationalism. Indeed, it may be asked in the sphere of economics, for instance, whether the party system does not give greater influence to capitalism than other forms of government accord it. The German economy, even because of its ties and because of the structure of postwar Europe, was among the first to break through national frontiers and find the path toward international involvement. The trend toward formation of large business combines which is taking place all over the world does not in itself, as I see it, make for progress for mankind as a whole. I regret that this is leading to the decline in the number of independent businessmen. It was the risk-taking initiative of these independent small businessmen that first caused our economy to thrive.

But there is no point in indulging in wishful thinking about the past. The changes were brought about by the World War and its repercussions. The war tore Europe from its previous position and transformed it into a continent bleeding from many wounds and left impoverished—not only in Germany—valuable segments of the population. "Where iron grows in the mountain shafts, the masters of the Earth arise." [15] Europe is no longer the main source of the world's war materials, and we can no longer delude ourselves that Europe is the leader of the world. For this reason the peoples of Europe are drawing closer together to protect themselves against conquest and inundation. And inasmuch as economics has an effect on politics, this drawing together, even though it might be questionable from the standpoint of economics, does constitute progress toward international understanding and peace. Even though the psychology of this process, which involves billions, causes sociologists to have reason for misgiving, the process is still an asset to mutual understanding among the nations. . . .

It was a turning point in European history when the Germans initiated the policy which led by way of Locarno to Geneva. Just read what Mr. Briand said about the significance of this German decision. Along this road, Germany has experienced numerous and profound disappointments. This is not the place to discuss them in detail. I do not think of Locarno only in terms of its consequences for Germany. Locarno means much more to me. It is the achievement of lasting peace on the Rhine, guaranteed by the formal renunciation of force by the two great neighboring nations and also by the commitment of other states to come to the aid of the victim of

15. Friedrich von Schiller, *The Bride of Messina,* Act I, ll. 226–27.

an act of aggression in violation of this treaty. *Treuga Dei,* the peace of God, shall reign where for centuries bloody wars have raged. It can and it ought to be the basis for a general cooperative effort among these nations to spread peace wherever their material power and moral influence reach. The overwhelming majority of the German people support these aims. The youth of Germany can be won over to the same cause. Youth sees its ideal of individual physical and spiritual achievement in the peaceful competition of the Olympic Games and, I hope, in technical and intellectual development as well.

Those who strive for these ideals, however, cannot succeed in the long run when, years after the war, foreign bayonets remain unsheathed in a nation which, although defeated, rejects revenge and asks only for peace. The policy of Locarno is incompatible with policies of distrust, violence, and oppression. Locarno is the policy of understanding and free will. It is the policy of faith in a new future and, in contrast to the policies of the past, it must become the policy of the future. Germany faces this future with a stable nation which has been based upon hard work, upon an economy which will give increasing millions income and security in our cramped territory, and upon a vital spirit which strives for peace in accordance with the philosophies of Kant and Fichte.[16]

If I understand you correctly, it was your people—a people that, having lived in peace for a hundred years, wished to endorse these ideas by means of the awards of the Nobel Committee—who decided that the men of Locarno should receive recognition for their efforts. In this you have remained true to the great ideals of your country. You have used your long period of peace for creative work in widely differing fields of science and research. You have sent men to the far corners of the earth who, with Faustian striving, have wanted to enlarge human understanding to the ultimate. You have opened your sympathetic hearts to the nations that suffered during the postwar period and to the people expelled from their native soil, all victims of the war and its aftermath. Thus you have combined love of your own country with love of your fellowmen, national pride with international action.

Today, in the capital of your country, I am happy to be allowed to express my thanks for the honor which you have shown us. With my thanks I link the hope that the ideals on which this honor is based may become the

---

16. Immanuel Kant (1724–1804); his "categorical imperative" of moral conduct may be briefly stated in this way: *Act in such a way in any given instance as if the principle governing the act were to become a universal principle.* Johann Gottlieb Fichte (1762–1814), German philospher and political leader; he based his ethical idealism on Kantian doctrine.

common property of dissenting nations. That great German who perhaps more than any other extended his influence beyond his own national boundaries said of his own times: "We belong to a generation struggling out of the darkness into the light." [17] May his words be true of our own times.

The Problem of Appeasement: Introduction

No strategy in the history of European international affairs in the twentieth century had more disastrous consequences, and yet none was more intellectually fascinating and revealing of popular mentalities toward war and peace than Neville Chamberlain's policy of appeasement toward Hitler in 1938–39. A recent historian, following Anthony Eden, has distinguished between two broad meanings of the term—appeasement as "making peace by inducing agreement" and as "making peace by offering concessions." [1] Although Chamberlain may have conceived of his policies in the former sense (he viewed Munich as an example of the ability of the *system* of European powers to settle its differences without either American or Russian intervention), many contemporaries, and certainly Hitler and Mussolini, viewed them in the latter meaning. Not only were appeasement's contemporary advocates quickly proven wrong—the policy died an ignominious death with the brutal Nazi occupation of Bohemia and Moravia in March 1939—but the term assumed a remarkable life of its own, becoming a weapon of opprobrium and calumny in the hands of American Cold Warriors and Vietnam policymakers in the 1950s and 1960s.

Yet in 1938 appeasement connoted a policy which enjoyed vast, indeed immense, popularity. When Chamberlain returned to England on 30 September 1938 bearing the Munich Agreement—by which, under the threat of imminent German invasion, Britain and France agreed to the cession to the Third Reich of the predominantly German (Sudeten) areas of Czechoslovakia—he received a hero's welcome, with glowing accolades in the press and genuine, almost hysterical affection from the crowds lining the streets of London. Equally important, Chamberlain returned with the sincere belief that he had accomplished an act of the highest

17. From Goethe; see Vol. 14, p. 697, of the Artemis-Gedenk edition of *Schriften zur Literatur,* Kurze Anzeigen III.

1. Roy Douglas, "Chamberlain and Appeasement," in *The Fascist Challenge and the Policy of Appeasement,* ed. Wolfgang J. Mommsen and Lothar Kettenacker (London, 1983), p. 79.

moral valor and strategic rationality, one which justified the tragic, but (in his mind) necessary and inevitable sacrifice of Czechoslovak territory. In turn the ambivalence, indeed, often the uneasiness, of appeasement's major opponents suggests the great complexity of events and decisions which led to the simple, yet ultimately perverse, idea of appeasing the dictators in hopes of preserving world peace.

Neville Chamberlain (1869–1940) was the son of Joseph Chamberlain and the half-brother of Austen Chamberlain, the British signatory of the Treaty of Locarno. A Conservative M.P. since 1918, Chamberlain held various Cabinet posts before succeeding Stanley Baldwin as Prime Minister in May 1937. His support of appeasement must be seen in the context of the unsteady course of French foreign policy in the later 1930s (it is perhaps an unanswerable question whether Chamberlain's equivocal and half-hearted assurances in 1938 that Britain might be forced to support France in the event the latter went to war in defense of Czechoslovakia were too little or too much for the French) and in light of his record of support for the modernization of the Royal Air Force.

Winston Churchill (1874–1965), one of the great political figures of the twentieth century, held various cabinet posts (Board of Trade, Home Office, Admiralty, Munitions, War, Colonies) under the Liberal cabinets of Asquith and Lloyd George between 1908 and 1922. He reentered politics as a Conservative in 1924 and served as Chancellor of the Exchequer from 1924 to 1929, but broke with the Tories in the early 1930s over policy toward India. The 1930s were years of frustrating political isolation for Churchill as he endured both Labour scorn and Tory mistrust. Immediately after the outbreak of the Second World War Churchill joined Chamberlain's war government as First Lord of the Admiralty. In May 1940, in the aftermath of the military fiasco in Norway and on the eve of the Nazi onslaught on France, Churchill succeeded Chamberlain as Prime Minister. A figure who joined homeric arete with rhetorical eloquence (although as a historian of his own times, not always objectivity), Churchill was among those most responsible for the survival of Britain in the desperate months of 1940 and for the achievement of ultimate victory.

The selections below, taken from the debate in the House of Commons on the Munich Crisis, consist of Chamberlain's opening and closing speeches in defense of the agreement, given on 3 and 6 October 1938, and Churchill's attack on the Government, given on 5 October.

A Brief Chronology of the Munich Crisis

20 February 1938: Hitler spoke in the Reichstag, promising protection to the millions of Germans in states neighboring to Germany.

11–12 March 1938: The *Anschluss* of Austria to Germany.

20 May 1938: General Wilhelm Keitel completed a new version of the draft operational directive for a military occupation of Czechoslovakia (Case Green), for Hitler's consideration. This order, with modifications, was issued on 30 May and included an introductory statement that "it is my unalterable decision to smash Czechoslovakia by military action in the near future."

In late May 1938 the Czechs mobilized part of their reserve forces and occupied their frontier districts, fearing possible German invasion. A diplomatic crisis ensued.

Throughout the summer and early autumn of 1938 negotiations were conducted between local Sudeten German leaders and the Czech government over the Germans' demands. The latter were contained in the "Fourteen Points" issued on 7 June, which provided extraordinary concessions of autonomy to Germans residing within the Czechoslovak state.

Also during the summer German military preparations for a surprise attack on Czechoslovakia continued. General Ludwig Beck, who opposed Hitler's plans for aggression, resigned as Chief of the General Staff on 18 August 1938.

7 September 1938: The Czech government presented the Sudeten Germans with a program of significant concessions—the so-called Fourth Plan—which met most of their demands. Sudeten reaction was uncertain, and negotiations broke down over a petty incident of violence between a German politician and a Czech policeman.

12 September 1938: In a vituperative speech given at the Nazi Party Congress at Nuremberg Hitler demanded the right of self-determination for the Sudeten Germans and declared that "if these tortured creatures cannot obtain justice and assistance by themselves they will get both from us."

Between 12 September and 15 September popular demonstrations and acts of violence perpetrated by Sudeten Nazis, led by Konrad Henlein, shocked world public opinion. The Czech government declared martial law in five Sudeten districts on 13 September. On 15 September Henlein fled across the German border.

15 September 1938: Chamberlain met Hitler at Berchtesgaden in an effort to prevent an escalation of the conflict into war. Hitler demanded the annexation of the Sudeten districts to Germany, on the basis of national self-determination.

16 September 1938: The Czech government outlawed the activities of the Sudeten German Party.

18 September 1938: Representatives of Britain and France met in London to draft the "Anglo-French Proposals," which would provide for the transfer to Germany of Sudeten districts where more than 50 percent of the population was German.

21 September 1938: The Czech government yielded to pressure from London and Paris, indicating its readiness to agree to a transfer of Sudeten territory in an orderly manner, as provided for by the Proposals.

22–23 September 1938: Chamberlain again visited Hitler, this time in Bad Godesberg, where Hitler rejected the Anglo-French plan and made even more drastic demands, including the immediate cession of Czech border districts by 1 October 1938. Evacuated territories were to be handed over to the Germans with all military installations intact.

23–28 September 1938: Following the diplomatic disaster at Bad Godesberg, a major European crisis ensued. Having mobilized its army, the Czech government rejected Hitler's Bad Godesberg memorandum. Upon the intervention of Mussolini, Hitler agreed on 28 September to Chamberlain's suggestion for a final international conference to settle the Sudeten question.

29–30 September 1938: The four-power Munich Conference, excluding the Czechs, gave Hitler most of what he had demanded at Bad Godesberg.

Within a month of the Munich Conference, Hitler ordered German army leaders to be prepared for the eventual occupation of the rest of Czechoslovakia.

14–16 March 1939: Bohemia and Moravia were occupied by German military forces and were declared a German "protectorate." Slovakia declared its independence and became a puppet state under National Socialist hegemony. Czech losses after Munich in population amounted to over four million (in a state of fifteen million people). Losses in military defense installations and economic resources were immense, making the new "state" a truncated, miserable creature on the stage of European affairs. As Williamson Murray has recently observed of Munich, "The economic results were catastrophic. Czechoslovakia lost 27 percent of her heavy industry, 32 percent of her lumber industry, 30 percent of her chemicals, and 53 percent of her paper industry. . . . The continued existence of the Czech state depended on an active, pro-German policy." [2]

20. Neville Chamberlain, Speech on the Munich Crisis

The Prime Minister: . . . When the House met last Wednesday, we were all under the shadow of a great and imminent menace. War, in a form more stark and terrible than ever before, seemed to be staring us in the face. Before I sat down, a message had come which gave us new hope that peace might yet be saved, and today, only a few days after, we all meet in joy and thankfulness that the prayers of millions have been answered, and a cloud of anxiety has been lifted from our hearts. Upon the Members of the Cabinet the strain of the responsibility of these last few weeks has been almost overwhelming. Some of us, I have no doubt, will carry the mark of it for the rest of our days. Necessarily, the weight fell heavier upon some shoulders than others. While all bore their part, I would like here and now to pay an especial tribute of gratitude and praise to the man upon whom fell the first brunt of those decisions which had to be taken day by day, almost hour by hour. The calmness, patience, and wisdom of the Foreign Secretary, and his lofty conception of his duty, not only to this country but to all humanity, were an example to us all, and sustained us all through the trials through which we have been passing.

Before I come to describe the Agreement which was signed at Munich in the small hours of Friday morning last, I would like to remind the House of two things which I think it is very essential not to forget when those

2. Williamson Murray, *The Change in the European Balance of Power, 1938–1939* (Princeton, 1984), p. 265.

From *Parliamentary Debates. Fifth Series. Volume 339. House of Commons Official Report* (London, 1938), pp. 41–50.

terms are being considered. The first is this: We did not go there to decide whether the predominantly German areas in the Sudetenland should be passed over to the German Reich. That had been decided already. Czechoslovakia had accepted the Anglo-French proposals. What we had to consider was the method, the conditions and the time of the transfer of the territory. The second point to remember is that time was one of the essential factors. All the elements were present on the spot for the outbreak of a conflict which might have precipitated the catastrophe. We had populations inflamed to a high degree; we had extremists on both sides ready to work up and provoke incidents; we had considerable quantities of arms which were by no means confined to regularly organised forces. Therefore, it was essential that we should quickly reach a conclusion, so that this painful and difficult operation of transfer might be carried out at the earliest possible moment and concluded as soon as was consistent with orderly procedure, in order that we might avoid the possibility of something that might have rendered all our attempts at peaceful solution useless.

The House will remember that when I last addressed them I gave them some account of the Godesberg Memorandum, with the terms of which I think they are familiar. They will recollect also that I myself at Godesberg expressed frankly my view that the terms were such as were likely to shock public opinion generally in the world and to bring their prompt rejection by the Czechoslovak Government. Those views were confirmed by the results, and the immediate and unqualified rejection of that Memorandum by the Czechoslovak Government was communicated to us at once by them. What I think the House will desire to take into consideration first, this afternoon, is what is the difference between those unacceptable terms and the terms which were included in the Agreement signed at Munich, because on the difference between those two documents will depend the judgment as to whether we were successful in what we set out to do, namely, to find an orderly instead of a violent method of carrying out an agreed decision.

I say, first of all, that the Godesberg Memorandum, although it was cast in the form of proposals, was in fact an ultimatum, with a time limit of six days. On the other hand, the Munich Agreement reverts to the Anglo-French plan, the plan referred to in the Preamble, though not in express terms, and it lays down the conditions for the application, on the responsibility of the four Powers and under international supervision, of the main principle of that Memorandum. Again, under the Munich Agreement evacuation of the territory which is to be occupied by German military forces and its occupation by those forces is to be carried out in five clearly defined stages between 1st October and 10th October, instead of having to be completed in one operation by 1st October. Thirdly, the line up to which

German troops will enter into occupation is no longer the line as laid down in the map which was attached to the Godesberg Memorandum. It is a line which is to be fixed by an International Commission. On that Commission both Germany and Czechoslovakia are represented. I take the fourth point. Under the Godesberg Memorandum the areas on the Czech side of this German line laid down in the map which were to be submitted to a plebiscite were laid down on that map by Germany, whereas those on the German side of the line were left undefined. Under the Munich Agreement all plebiscite areas are to be defined by the International Commission. The criterion is to be the predominantly German character of the area, the interpretation of that phrase being left to the Commission. I am bound to say that the German line, the line laid down in the map, did take in a number of areas which could not be called predominantly German in character.

Then, Sir, it will be remembered that, according to the Godesberg Memorandum, the occupation of plebiscite areas by German and Czech troops respectively was to be up to the time of the plebiscite. They were then to be withdrawn while the plebiscite was being held. Under the Munich Agreement these plebiscite areas are to be occupied at once by an international force. The Godesberg Memorandum did not indicate on what kind of areas the vote would be based. Accordingly, there were fears entertained on the side of the Czechs that large areas might be selected, which would operate to the disadvantage of the Czechoslovaks. In the Munich arrangement it is stated that the plebiscite is to be based on the conditions of the Saar plebiscite, and that indicates that the vote is to be taken by small administrative areas. Under the Munich arrangement the Czech Government, while it is bound to carry out the evacuation of the territories without damaging existing installations, is not placed under the objectionable conditions of the appendix to the Godesberg Memorandum, to which much exception was taken, in that it was provided that no foodstuffs, cattle or raw material were to be removed. Under the Godesberg Memorandum the detailed arrangements for the evacuation were to be settled by Germans and Czechs alone, and I think there were many who thought that such an arrangement did not give the Czechs much chance of making their voices heard. Well, Sir, under the Munich Agreement the conditions of evacuation are to be laid down in detail by the International Commission.

Again, the Munich arrangement includes certain very valuable provisions which found no place at all in the Godesberg Memorandum, such as the Article regarding the right of option: that is option to leave the territory and pass into Czech territory, provisions for facilitating the transfer of populations, the supplementary declaration which provides that all other questions arising out of the transfer of territory are to be referred to the International Commission, and, finally, the one which gives the Czechs the period of four weeks for the release of the Sudeten Germans from the army and the police, and for the release of Sudeten German political prisoners instead of demanding that those things should be done by 1st October—

Miss Wilkinson: What about the kidnapped Czechs?

The Prime Minister: The joint guarantee, which is given under the Munich Agreement to the Czechoslovak State and by the Governments of United Kingdom and France against unprovoked aggressions upon their boundaries, gives to the Czechs an essential counterpart which was not to be found in the Godesberg Memorandum, and it will not be unnoted that Germany will also undertake to give a guarantee on the question of Polish and Hungarian minorities being settled. Finally, there is a declaration by the Four Powers that if the problems of the Polish and Hungarian minorities in Czechoslovakia are not settled within three months by agreement be-tween the respective Governments, another meeting of the Four Powers will be held to consider them—[Interruption]. I think that every fair-minded, every serious-minded man who takes into consideration the modi-fications which I have described—modifications of the Memorandum—must agree that they are of very considerable extent and that they are all in the same direction. To those who dislike an ultimatum, but who were anxious for a reasonable and orderly procedure, every one of those modi-fications is a step in the right direction. It is no longer an ultimatum, but it is a method which is carried out largely under the supervision of an in-ternational body.

Before giving a verdict upon this arrangement, we should do well to avoid describing it as a personal or a national triumph for anyone. The real triumph is that it has shown that representatives of four great Powers can find it possible to agree on a way of carrying out a difficult and delicate operation by discussion instead of by force of arms, and thereby they have averted a catastrophe which would have ended civilisation as we have known it. The relief that our escape from this great peril of war has, I think, everywhere been mingled in this country with a profound feeling of sympathy—[Hon. Members: "Shame."] I have nothing to be ashamed of. Let those who have, hang their heads. We must feel profound sympathy for a small and gallant nation in the hour of their national grief and loss.

Mr. Bellenger: It is an insult to say it.

The Prime Minister: I say in the name of this House and of the people of this country that Czechoslovakia has earned our admiration and respect for her restraint, for her dignity, for her magnificent discipline in face of such a trial as few nations have ever been called upon to meet. General Syrovy said the other night in his broadcast:

The Government could have decided to stand up against overpowering forces, but it might have meant the death of millions.

The army, whose courage no man has ever questioned, has obeyed the order of their President, as they would equally have obeyed him if he had told them to march into the trenches. It is my hope, and my belief, that under the new system of guarantees, the new Czechoslovakia will find a greater security than she has ever enjoyed in the past. We must recognise that she has been put in a position where she has got to reconstruct her whole economy, and that in doing that she must encounter difficulties, which it would be practically impossible for her to solve alone. We have received from the Czechoslovak Government, through their Minister in London, an appeal to help them to raise a loan of £30,000,000 by a British Government guarantee. I believe that the House will feel with the Government that that is an appeal which should meet with a sympathetic and even a generous response. . . .

I pass from that subject, and I would like to say a few words in respect of the various other participants, besides ourselves, in the Munich Agreement. After everything that has been said about the German Chancellor today and in the past, I do feel that the House ought to recognise the difficulty for a man in that position to take back such emphatic declarations as he had already made amidst the enthusiastic cheers of his supporters, and to recognise that in consenting, even though it were only at the last moment, to discuss with the representatives of other Powers those things which he had declared he had already decided once for all, was a real and a substantial contribution on his part. With regard to Signor Mussolini, his contribution was certainly notable and perhaps decisive. It was on his suggestion that the final stages of mobilisation were postponed for 24 hours to give us an opportunity of discussing the situation, and I wish to say that at the Conference itself both he and the Italian Foreign Secretary, Count Ciano, were most helpful in the discussions. It was they who, very early in the proceedings, produced the Memorandum which M. Daladier and I were able to accept as a basis of discussion. I think that Europe and the world have reason to be grateful to the head of the Italian Government for his work in contributing to a peaceful solution.

M. Daladier had in some respects the most difficult task of all four of us, because of the special relations uniting his country and Czechoslovakia, and I should like to say that his courage, his readiness to take responsibility, his pertinacity and his unfailing good humour were invaluable throughout the whole of our discussions. There is one other Power which was not represented at the Conference and which nevertheless we felt to be exercising a constantly increasing influence. I refer, of course, to the United States of America. Those messages of President Roosevelt, so firmly and yet so persuasively framed, showed how the voice of the most powerful nation in the world could make itself heard across 3,000 miles of ocean and sway the minds of men in Europe.

In my view the strongest force of all, one which grew and took fresh shapes and forms every day was the force not of any one individual, but was that unmistakable sense of unanimity among the peoples of the world that war somehow must be averted. The peoples of the British Empire were at one with those of Germany, of France and of Italy, and their anxiety, their intense desire for peace, pervaded the whole atmosphere of the conference, and I believe that that, and not threats, made possible the concessions that were made. I know the House will want to hear what I am sure it does not doubt, that throughout these discussions the Dominions, the Governments of the Dominions, have been kept in the closest touch with the march of events by telegraph and by personal contact, and I would like to say how greatly I was encouraged on each of the journeys I made to Germany by the knowledge that I went with the good wishes of the Governments of the Dominions. They shared all our anxieties and all our hopes. They rejoiced with us that peace was preserved, and with us they look forward to further efforts to consolidate what has been done.

Ever since I assumed my present office my main purpose has been to work for the pacification of Europe, for the removal of those suspicions and those animosities which have so long poisoned the air. The path which leads to appeasement is long and bristles with obstacles. The question of Czechoslovakia is the latest and perhaps the most dangerous. Now that we have got past it, I feel that it may be possible to make further progress along the road to sanity.

My right hon. Friend has alluded in somewhat bitter terms to my conversation last Friday morning with Herr Hitler. I do not know why that conversation should give rise to suspicion, still less to criticism. I entered into no pact. I made no new commitments. There is no secret understanding. Our conversation was hostile to no other nation. The objects of that conversation, for which I asked, was to try to extend a little further the personal contact which I had established with Herr Hitler and which I believe to be essential in modern diplomacy. We had a friendly and entirely non-committal conversation, carried on, on my part, largely with a view to seeing whether there could be points in common between the head of a democratic Government and the ruler of a totalitarian State. . . .

I believe there are many who will feel with me that . . . a declaration, signed by the German Chancellor and myself, is something more than a pious expression of opinion. In our relations with other countries everything depends upon there being sincerity and good will on both sides. I believe that there is sincerity and good will on both sides in this declaration. That is why to me its significance goes far beyond its actual words. If there is one lesson which we should learn from the events of these last weeks it is this, that lasting peace is not to be obtained by sitting still and waiting for it to come. It requires active, positive efforts to achieve it. No doubt I shall have plenty of critics who will say that I am guilty of facile optimism, and that I should disbelieve every word that is uttered by rulers of other great States in Europe. I am too much of a realist to believe that we are going to achieve our paradise in a day. We have only laid the foundations of peace. The superstructure is not even begun.

For a long period now we have been engaged in this country in a great programme of rearmament, which is daily increasing in pace and in volume. Let no one think that because we have signed this agreement between these four Powers at Munich we can afford to relax our efforts in regard to that programme at this moment. Disarmament on the part of this country can never be unilateral again. We have tried that once, and we very nearly brought ourselves to disaster. If disarmament is to come it must come by steps, and it must come by the agreement and the active co-operation of other countries. Until we know that we have obtained that co-operation and until we have agreed upon the actual steps to be taken, we here must remain on guard. . . .

21. Winston Churchill, Speech on the Munich Crisis

Mr. Churchill: If I do not begin this afternoon by paying the usual, and indeed almost invariable, tributes to the Prime Minister for his handling of this crisis, it is certainly not from any lack of personal regard. We have always, over a great many years, had very pleasant relations, and I have deeply understood from personal experiences of my own in a similar crisis the stress and strain he has had to bear; but I am sure it is much better to say exactly what we think about public affairs, and this is certainly not the time when it is worth anyone's while to court political popularity. We had a shining example of firmness of character from the late First Lord of the Admiralty two days ago. He showed that firmness of character which is utterly unmoved by currents of opinion, however swift and violent they may be. My hon. Friend the Member for South-West Hull (Mr. Law), to whose compulsive speech the House listened on Monday—which I had not the good fortune to hear, but which I read, and which I am assured by all who heard it revived the memory of his famous father, so cherished in this House, and made us feel that his gifts did not die with him—was quite right in reminding us that the Prime Minister has himself throughout his conduct of these matters shown a robust indifference to cheers or boos and to the alternations of criticism and applause. If that be so, such qualities

From *Parliamentary Debates. Fifth Series. Volume 339. House of Commons Official Report* (London, 1938), pp. 359–73.

and elevation of mind should make it possible for the most severe expressions of honest opinion to be interchanged in this House without rupturing personal relations, and for all points of view to receive the fullest possible expression.

Having thus fortified myself by the example of others, I will proceed to emulate them. I will, therefore, begin by saying the most unpopular and most unwelcome thing. I will begin by saying what everybody would like to ignore or forget but which must nevertheless be stated, namely, that we have sustained a total and unmitigated defeat, and that France has suffered even more than we have.

Viscountess Astor: Nonsense.

Mr. Churchill: When the Noble Lady cries "Nonsense," she could not have heard the Chancellor of the Exchequer admit in his illuminating and comprehensive speech just now that Herr Hitler had gained in this particular leap forward in substance all he set out to gain. The utmost my right hon. Friend the Prime Minister has been able to secure by all his immense exertions, by all the great efforts and mobilisation which took place in this country, and by all the anguish and strain through which we have passed in this country, the utmost he has been able to gain—[Hon. Members: "Is peace."] I thought I might be allowed to make that point in its due place, and I propose to deal with it. The utmost he has been able to gain for Czechoslovakia and in the matters which were in dispute has been that the German dictator, instead of snatching his victuals from the table, has been content to have them served to him course by course.

The Chancellor of the Exchequer said it was the first time Herr Hitler had been made to retract—I think that was the word—in any degree. We really must not waste time, after all this long Debate, upon the difference between the positions reached at Berchtesgaden, at Godesberg and at Munich. They can be very simply epitomised, if the House will permit me to vary the metaphor. £1 was demanded at the pistol's point. When it was given, £2 were demanded at the pistol's point. Finally, the dictator consented to take £1 17s. 6d. and the rest in promises of good will for the future.

Now I come to the point, which was mentioned to me just now from some quarters of the House, about the saving of peace. No one has been a more resolute and uncompromising struggler for peace than the Prime Minister. Everyone knows that. Never has there been such intense and undaunted determination to maintain and to secure peace. That is quite true. Nevertheless, I am not quite clear why there was so much danger of Great Britain or France being involved in a war with Germany at this juncture if, in fact, they were ready all along to sacrifice Czechoslovakia. The terms which the Prime Minister brought back with him—I quite agree at the last moment; everything had got off the rails and nothing but his intervention could have saved the peace, but I am talking of the events of the summer—could easily have been agreed, I believe, through the ordinary diplomatic channels at any time during the summer. And I will say this, that I believe the Czechs, left to themselves and told they were going to get no help from the Western Powers, would have been able to make better terms than they have got—they could hardly have worse—after all this tremendous perturbation.

There never can be any absolute certainty that there will be a fight if one side is determined that it will give way completely. When one reads the Munich terms, when one sees what is happening in Czechoslovakia from hour to hour, when one is sure, I will not say of Parliamentary approval but of Parliamentary acquiescence, when the Chancellor of the Exchequer makes a speech which at any rate tries to put in a very powerful and persuasive manner the fact that, after all, it was inevitable and indeed righteous—right—when we saw all this, and everyone on this side of the House, including many Members of the Conservative Party who are supposed to be vigilant and careful guardians of the national interest, it is quite clear that nothing vitally affecting us was at stake, it seems to me that one must ask, What was all the trouble and fuss about?

The resolve was taken by the British and the French Governments. Let me say that it is very important to realise that it is by no means a question which the British Government only have had to decide. I very much admire the manner in which, in the House, all references of a recriminatory nature have been repressed, but it must be realised that this resolve did not emanate particularly from one or other of the Governments but was a resolve for which both must share in common the responsibility. When this resolve was taken and the course was followed—you may say it was wise or unwise, prudent or short-sighted—once it had been decided not to make the defence of Czechoslovakia a matter of war, then there was really no reason, if the matter had been handled during the summer in the ordinary way, to call into being all this formidable apparatus of crisis. I think that point should be considered.

We are asked to vote for this Motion which has been put upon the Paper, and it is certainly a Motion couched in very uncontroversial terms, as, indeed, is the Amendment moved from the Opposition side. I cannot myself express my agreement with the steps which have been taken, and as the Chancellor of the Exchequer has put his side of the case with so much ability I will attempt, if I may be permitted, to put the case from a different angle. I have always held the view that the maintenance of peace depends upon the accumulation of deterrents against the aggressor, coupled with a sincere effort to redress grievances. Herr Hitler's victory, like so many of the famous struggles that have governed the fate of the world, was won upon the narrowest of margins. After the seizure of Austria in March we faced this problem in our Debates. I ventured to appeal to the Government to go a little further than the Prime Minister went, and to give a pledge that in conjunction with France and other Powers they would guarantee the security of Czechoslovakia while the Sudeten-Deutsch question was being examined either by a League of Nations Commission or some other impartial body, and I still believe that if that course had been followed events would not have fallen into this disastrous state. I agree very much with my right hon. Friend the Member for Sparkbrook (Mr. Amery) when he said on that occasion—I cannot remember his actual words—"Do one thing or the other; either say you will disinterest yourself in the matter altogether or take the step of giving a guarantee which will have the greatest chance of securing protection for that country."

France and Great Britain together, especially if they had maintained a close contact with Russia, which certainly was not done, would have been able in those days in the summer, when they had the prestige, to influence many of the smaller States of Europe, and I believe they could have determined the attitude of Poland. Such a combination, prepared at a time when the German dictator was not deeply and irrevocably committed to his new adventure, would, I believe, have given strength to all those forces in Germany which resisted this departure, this new design. They were varying forces, those of a military character which declared that Germany was not ready to undertake a world war, and all that mass of moderate opinion and popular opinion which dreaded war, and some elements of which still have some influence upon the German Government. Such action would have given strength to all that intense desire for peace which the helpless German masses share with their British and French fellow men, and which, as we have been reminded, found a passionate and rarely permitted vent in the joyous manifestations with which the Prime Minister was acclaimed in Munich.

All these forces, added to the other deterrents which combinations of Powers, great and small, ready to stand firm upon the front of law and for the ordered remedy of grievances, would have formed, might well have been effective. Of course you cannot say for certain that they would. *[Interruption.]* I try to argue fairly with the House. At the same time I do not think it is fair to charge those who wished to see this course followed, and followed consistently and resolutely, with having wished for an immediate war. Between submission and immediate war there was this third alternative, which gave a hope not only of peace but of justice. It is quite true that such a policy in order to succeed demanded that Britain should declare straight out and a long time beforehand that she would, with others, join to defend Czechoslovakia against an unprovoked aggression. His Majesty's Government refused to give that guarantee when it would have saved the situation, yet in the end they gave it when it was too late, and now, for the future, they renew it when they have not the slightest power to make it good.

All is over. Silent, mournful, abandoned, broken, Czechoslovakia recedes into the darkness. She has suffered in every respect by her association with the Western democracies and with the League of Nations, of which she has always been an obedient servant. She has suffered in particular from her association with France, under whose guidance and policy she has been actuated for so long. The very measures taken by His Majesty's Government in the Anglo-French Agreement to give her the best chance possible, namely, the 50 per cent. clean cut in certain districts instead of a plebiscite, have turned to her detriment, because there is to be a plebiscite too in wide areas, and those other Powers who had claims have also come down upon the helpless victim. Those municipal elections upon whose voting the basis is taken for the 50 per cent. cut were held on issues which had nothing to do with joining Germany. When I saw Herr Henlein over here he assured me that was not the desire of his people. Positive statements were made that it was only a question of home rule, of having a position of their own in the Czechoslovakian State. No one has a right to say that the plebiscite which is to be taken in areas under Saar conditions, and the clean-cut of the 50 per cent. areas—that those two operations together amount in the slightest degree to a verdict of self-determination. It is a fraud and a farce to invoke that name.

We in this country, as in other Liberal and democratic countries, have a perfect right to exalt the principle of self-determination, but it comes ill out of the mouths of those in totalitarian States who deny even the smallest element of toleration to every section and creed within their bounds. But, however you put it, this particular block of land, this mass of human beings to be handed over, has never expressed the desire to go into the Nazi rule. I do not believe that even now—if their opinion could be asked, they would exercise such an option.

What is the remaining position of Czechoslovakia? Not only are they politically mutilated, but, economically and financially, they are in complete confusion. Their banking, their railway arrangements, are severed and broken, their industries are curtailed, and the movement of their population is most cruel. The Sudeten miners, who are all Czechs and whose families have lived in that area for centuries, must now flee into an area where there are hardly any mines left for them to work. It is a tragedy which has occurred. I did not like to hear the Minister of Transport yesterday talking about Humpty Dumpty. It was the Minister of Transport who was saying that it was a case of Humpty Dumpty that could never be put together again. There must always be the most profound regret and a sense of vexation in British hearts at the treatment and the misfortunes which have overcome the Czechoslovakian Republic. They have not ended here. At any moment there may be a hitch in the programme. At any moment there may be an order for Herr Goebbels to start again his propaganda of calumny and lies; at any moment an incident may be provoked, and now that the fortress line is given away what is there to stop the will of the conqueror? *[Interruption.]* It is too serious a subject to treat lightly. Obviously, we are not in a position to give them the slightest help at the present time, except what everyone is glad to know has been done, the financial aid which the Government have promptly produced.

I venture to think that in future the Czechoslovak State cannot be maintained as an independent entity. You will find that in a period of time which may be measured by years, but may be measured only by months, Czechoslovakia will be engulfed in the Nazi régime. Perhaps they may join it in despair or in revenge. At any rate, that story is over and told. But we cannot consider the abandonment and ruin of Czechoslovakia in the light only of what happened only last month. It is the most grievous consequence which we have yet experienced of what we have done and of what we have left undone in the last five years—five years of futile good intention, five years of eager search for the line of least resistance, five years of uninterrupted retreat of British power, five years of neglect of our air defences. Those are the features which I stand here to declare and which marked an improvident stewardship for which Great Britain and France have dearly to pay. We have been reduced in those five years from a position of security so overwhelming and so unchallengeable that we never cared to think about it. We have been reduced from a position where the very word "war" was considered one which would be used only by persons qualifying for a lunatic asylum. We have been reduced from a position of safety and power—power to do good, power to be generous to a beaten foe, power to make terms with Germany, power to give her proper redress for her grievances, power to stop her arming if we chose, power to take any step in strength or mercy or justice which we thought right—reduced in five years from a position safe and unchallenged to where we stand now.

When I think of the fair hopes of a long peace which still lay before Europe at the beginning of 1933 when Herr Hitler first obtained power, and of all the opportunities of arresting the growth of the Nazi power which have been thrown away, when I think of the immense combinations and resources which have been neglected or squandered, I cannot believe that a parallel exists in the whole course of history. So far as this country is concerned the responsibility must rest with those who have the undisputed control of our political affairs. They neither prevented Germany from re-arming, nor did they rearm ourselves in time. They quarrelled with Italy without saving Ethiopia. They exploited and discredited the vast institution of the League of Nations and they neglected to make alliances and combinations which might have repaired previous errors, and thus they left us in the hour of trial without adequate national defence or effective international security. . . .

I have ventured to express those views in justifying myself for not being able to support the Motion which is moved tonight, but I recognise that this great matter of Czechoslovakia, and of British and French duty there, has passed into history. New developments may come along, but we are not here to decide whether any of those steps should be taken or not. They have been taken. They have been taken by those who had a right to take them because they bore the highest executive responsibility under the Crown. Whatever we may think of it, we must regard those steps as belonging to the category of affairs which are settled beyond recall. The past is no more, and one can only draw comfort if one feels that one has done one's best to advise rightly and wisely and in good time. I, therefore, turn to the future, and to our situation as it is today. Here, again, I am sure I shall have to say something which will not be at all welcome.

We are in the presence of a disaster of the first magnitude which has befallen Great Britain and France. Do not let us blind ourselves to that. It must now be accepted that all the countries of Central and Eastern Europe will make the best terms they can with the triumphant Nazi Power. The system of alliances in Central Europe upon which France has relied for her safety has been swept away, and I can see no means by which it can be reconstituted. The road down the Danube Valley to the Black Sea, the resources of corn and oil, the road which leads as far as Turkey, has been opened. In fact, if not in form, it seems to me that all those countries of Middle Europe, all those Danubian countries, will, one after another, be drawn into this vast system of power politics—not only power military politics but power economic politics—radiating from Berlin, and I believe this can be achieved quite smoothly and swiftly and will not necessarily entail the firing of a single shot. . . .

. . . You will see, day after day, week after week, entire alienation of those regions. Many of those countries, in fear of the rise of the Nazi Power, have already got politicians, Ministers, Governments, who were pro-German, but there was always an enormous popular movement in Poland, Rumania, Bulgaria and Yugoslavia which looked to the Western democracies and loathed the idea of having this arbitrary rule of the totalitarian system thrust upon them, and hoped that a stand would be made. All that has gone by the board. We are talking about countries which are a long

way off and of which, as the Prime Minister might say, we know nothing. *[Interruption.]* The noble Lady says that that very harmless allusion is—
   Viscountess Astor: Rude.

   Mr. Churchill: She must very recently have been receiving her finishing course in manners. What will be the position, I want to know, of France and England this year and the year afterwards? What will be the position of that Western front of which we are in full authority the guarantors? The German army at the present time is more numerous than that of France, though not nearly so matured or perfected. Next year it will grow much larger, and its maturity will be more complete. Relieved from all anxiety in the East, and having secured resources which will greatly diminish, if not entirely remove, the deterrent of a naval blockade, the rulers of Nazi Germany will have a free choice open to them in what direction they will turn their eyes. If the Nazi dictator should choose to look westward, as he may, bitterly will France and England regret the loss of that fine army of ancient Bohemia which was estimated last week to require not fewer than 30 German divisions for its destruction.

   Can we blind ourselves to the great change which has taken place in the military situation, and to the dangers we have to meet? We are in process, I believe, of adding, in four years, four battalions to the British Army. No fewer than two have already been completed. Here at least 30 divisions which must now be taken into consideration upon the French front, besides the 12 that were captured when Austria was engulfed. Many people, no doubt, honestly believe that they are only giving away the interests of Czechoslovakia, whereas I fear we shall find that we have deeply compromised, and perhaps fatally endangered, the safety and even the independence of Great Britain and France. This is not merely a question of giving up the German colonies, as I am sure we shall be asked to do. Nor is it a question only of losing influence in Europe. It goes far deeper than that. You have to consider the character of the Nazi movement and the rule which it implies. The Prime Minister desires to see cordial relations between this country and Germany. There is no difficulty at all in having cordial relations with the German people. Our hearts go out to them. But they have no power. You must have diplomatic and correct relations, but there can never be friendship between the British democracy and the Nazi Power, that Power which spurns Christian ethics, which cheers its onward course by a barbarous paganism, which vaunts the spirit of aggression and conquest, which derives strength and perverted pleasure from persecution, and uses, as we have seen, with pitiless brutality the threat of murderous force. That Power cannot ever be the trusted friend of the British democracy.

   What I find unendurable is the sense of our country falling into the power, into the orbit and influence of Nazi Germany, and of our existence becoming dependent upon their good will or pleasure. It is to prevent that that I have tried my best to urge the maintenance of every bulwark of defence—first the timely creation of an Air Force superior to anything within striking distance of our shores; secondly, the gathering together of the collective strength of many nations; and thirdly, the making of alliances and military conventions, all within the Covenant, in order to gather together forces at any rate to restrain the onward movement of this Power. It has all been in vain. Every position has been successively undermined and abandoned on specious and plausible excuses. We do not want to be led upon the high road to becoming a satellite of the German Nazi system of European domination. In a very few years, perhaps in a very few months, we shall be confronted with demands with which we shall no doubt be invited to comply. Those demands may affect the surrender of territory or the surrender of liberty. I foresee and foretell that the policy of submission will carry with it restrictions upon the freedom of speech and debate in Parliament, on public platforms, and discussions in the Press, for it will be said—indeed, I hear it said sometimes now—that we cannot allow the Nazi system of dictatorship to be criticised by ordinary, common English politicians. Then, with a Press under control, in part direct but more potently indirect, with every organ of public opinion doped and chloroformed into acquiescence, we shall be conducted along further stages of our journey. . . .

I have been casting about to see how measures can be taken to protect us from this advance of the Nazi Power, and to secure those forms of life which are so dear to us. What is the sole method that is open? The sole method that is open is for us to regain our old island independence by acquiring that supremacy in the air which we were promised, that security in our air defences which we were assured we had, and thus to make ourselves an island once again. That, in all this grim outlook, shines out as the overwhelming fact. An effort at rearmament the like of which has not been seen ought to be made forthwith, and all the resources of this country and all its united strength should be bent to that task. I was very glad to see that Lord Baldwin yesterday in the House of Lords said that he would mobilise industry tomorrow. But I think it would have been much better if Lord Baldwin has said that 2½ years ago, when everyone demanded a Ministry of Supply. I will venture to say to hon. Gentlemen sitting here behind the Government Bench, hon. Friends of mine, whom I thank for the patience with which they have listened to what I have to say, that they have some responsibility for all this too, because, if they had given one tithe of the cheers they have lavished upon this transaction of Czechoslovakia to the small band of Members who were endeavouring to get timely rearmament set in motion, we should not now be in the position in which we are.

Hon. Gentlemen opposite, and hon. Members on the Liberal benches, are not entitled to throw these stones. I remember for two years having to face, not only the Government's deprecation, but their stern disapproval. Lord Baldwin has now given the signal, tardy though it may be; let us at least obey it.

After all, there are no secrets now about what happened in the air and in the mobilisation of our anti-aircraft defences. . . . Who pretends now that there is air parity with Germany? Who pretends now that our anti-aircraft defences were adequately manned or armed? We know that the German General Staff are well informed upon these subjects, but the House of Commons has hitherto not taken seriously its duty of requiring to assure itself on these matters. . . .

I do not grudge our loyal, brave people, who were ready to do their duty no matter what the cost, who never flinched under the strain of last week— I do not grudge them the natural, spontaneous outburst of joy and relief when they learned that the hard ordeal would no longer be required of them at the moment; but they should know the truth. They should know that there has been gross neglect and deficiency in our defences; they should know that we have sustained a defeat without a war, the consequences of which will travel far with us along our road; they should know that we have passed an awful milestone in our history, when the whole equilibrium of Europe has been deranged, and that the terrible words have for the time being been pronounced against the Western democracies:

Thou art weighed in the balance and found wanting.

And do not suppose that this is the end. This is only the beginning of the reckoning. This is only the first sip, the first foretaste of a bitter cup which will be proffered to us year by year unless by a supreme recovery of moral health and martial vigour, we arise again and take our stand for freedom as in the olden time.

22. Neville Chamberlain, Reply to His Critics

The Prime Minister: . . . I do not remember a Debate in which there were so many allusions to a single Minister, some of them complimentary—for which I am sincerely grateful—and some of them which could not be described by that name. I have been charged with cowardice, with weakness, with presumption, and with stupidity. I have been accused of bringing the country to the edge of war, and I have been denied the merit of having snatched it back to safety.

From *Parliamentary Debates. Fifth Series. Volume 339. House of Commons Official Report* (London, 1938), pp. 544–52.

It seems to me that some of those who threw these accusations across the Floor of the House have very quickly forgotten the conditions of last week, and the thoughts and the emotions which then filled our minds and hearts. Anybody who had been through what I had to go through day after day, face to face with the thought that in the last resort it would have been I, and I alone, who would have to say that yes or no which would decide the fate of millions of my countrymen, of their wives, of their families—a man who had been through that could not readily forget. For that reason alone, I am not yet in a mood to try to see what I can do by way of retort. When a man gets to my age and fills my position, I think he tends to feel that criticism, even abuse, matters little to him if his conscience approves of his actions. Looking back on the events, I feel convinced that by my action—I seek no credit for my action; I think it is only what anyone in my position would have felt it his duty to do—I say, by my action I did avert war. I feel equally sure that I was right in doing so.

War today—this has been said before, and I say it again—is a different thing not only in degree, but in kind from what it used to be. We no longer think of war as it was in the days of Marlborough or the days of Napoleon or even in the days of 1914. When war starts today, in the very first hour, before any professional soldier, sailor or airman has been touched, it will strike the workman, the clerk, the man-in-the-street or in the 'bus, and his wife and children in their homes. As I listened I could not help being moved, as I am sure everybody was who heard the hon. Member for Bridgeton (Mr. Maxton) when he began to paint the picture which he himself had seen and realised what it would mean in war—people burrowing underground, trying to escape from poison gas, knowing that at any hour of the day or night death or mutilation was ready to come upon them. Remembering that the dread of what might happen to them or to those dear to them might remain with fathers and mothers for year after year—when you think of these things you cannot ask people to accept a prospect of that kind; you cannot force them into a position that they have got to accept it; unless you feel yourself, and can make them feel, that the cause for which they are going to fight is a vital cause—a cause that transcends all the human values, a cause to which you can point, if some day you win the victory, and say, "That cause is safe."

Since I first went to Berchtesgaden more than 20,000 letters and telegrams have come to No. 10, Downing Street. Of course, I have only been able to look at a tiny fraction of them, but I have seen enough to know that the people who wrote did not feel that they had such a cause for which to fight, if they were asked to go to war in order that the Sudeten Germans might not join the Reich. That is how they are feeling. That is my answer to those who say that we should have told Germany weeks ago that, if her army crossed the border of Czechoslovakia, we should be at war with her.

We had no treaty obligations and no legal obligations to Czechoslovakia and if we had said that, we feel that we should have received no support from the people of this country.

There is something else which I fancy hon. Members are a little too apt to forget. They often speak of the British Empire. Do they always remember how deeply and how vitally the great self-governing nations of the British Empire are affected by the issues of peace and war? You may say that we are the country that is directly affected in such a case as that which we are considering, but must not the very loyalty of the Dominions to the Empire, their consciousness of their sympathy, make them feel that where the mother country stands they would wish to stand, too. They have a right to be brought into consultation before we take a step which may have incalculable consequences for them. Although it is not for me to speak for them, I say that it would have been difficult to convince them that we should have been justified in giving such an assurance as has been suggested.

I am told that if you were not prepared to put the issue of peace and war out of the hands of this country and into someone else's hands in that way, you should have told Czechoslovakia long ago that in no circumstances would you help her and that she had better make the best terms she could with the Sudetens or with Germany. Was the issue as simple as that? Consider France, who was under Treaty obligations to Czechoslovakia to go to her assistance by virtue of her Treaty. Were we to say that we would not go to the assistance of France if in consequence she became involved in conflict with Germany? If so, we should have been false to our own obligations. Therefore, it would not have been enough for us to tell Czechoslovakia that we would have nothing to do with her and that she must make the best terms she could. It would have been necessary for France also to say that. Is anybody prepared to suggest that France, who was bound by solemn treaty to give aid and assistance to Czechoslovakia if she was the subject of unprovoked aggression, should repudiate this obligation beforehand? I would not have cared to have been the one who made such a suggestion to a French Minister.

It was impossible for us to take either of these courses, either to say that we would stand by Czechoslovakia if she were attacked, or to say that in no circumstances would we be involved if she were attacked and other countries were involved. What we did do, and it was the only course we could take, was twofold. We advised the Czech Government repeatedly to come to terms with the Sudeten Germans, and when Germany mobilised we uttered no threats, but we did utter a warning. We warned her again and again that if as a consequence of her obligations France was engaged in active hostilities against Germany we were bound to support her. When we were convinced, as we became convinced, that nothing any longer would keep the Sudetenland within the Czechoslovakian State, we urged the Czech Government as strongly as we could to agree to the cession of territory, and to agree promptly. The Czech Government, through the wisdom and courage of President Beneš, accepted the advice of the French Government and ourselves. It was a hard decision for anyone who loved his country to take, but to accuse us of having by that advice betrayed the Czechoslovakian State is simply preposterous. What we did was to save her from annihilation and give her a chance of new life as a new State, which involves the loss of territory and fortifications, but may perhaps enable her to enjoy in the future and develop a national existence under a neutrality and security comparable to that which we see in Switzerland today. Therefore, I think the Government deserve the approval of this House for their conduct of affairs in this recent crisis which has saved Czechoslovakia from destruction and Europe from Armageddon.

That is all I want to say of the past. I come to the present and the future. . . .

As regards future policy, it seems to me that there are really only two possible alternatives. One of them is to base yourself upon the view that any sort of friendly relations, or possible relations, shall I say, with totalitarian States are impossible, that the assurances which have been given to me personally are worthless, that they have sinister designs and that they are bent upon the domination of Europe and the gradual destruction of democracies. Of course, on that hypothesis, war has got to come, and that is the view—a perfectly intelligible view—of a certain number of hon. and right hon. Gentlemen in this House. I am not sure that it is not the view of some Members of the party opposite. [An HON. MEMBER: "Yes."] Not all of them. They certainly have never put it in so many words, but it is illustrated by the observations of the hon. Member for Derby (Mr. Noel-Baker), who spoke this afternoon, and who had examined the Agreement signed by the German Chancellor and myself, which he described as a pact designed by Herr Hitler to induce us to relinquish our present obligations. That shows how far prejudice can carry a man. The Agreement, as anyone can see, is not a pact at all. So far as the question of "never going to war again" is concerned, it is not even an expression of the opinion of the two who signed the paper, except that it is their opinion of the desire of their respective peoples. I do not know whether the hon. Member will believe me or attribute to me also sinister designs when I tell him that it was a document not drawn up by Herr Hitler but by the humble individual who now addresses this House.

If the view which I have been describing is the one to be taken, I think we must inevitably proceed to the next stage—that war is coming, broadly speaking the democracies against the totalitarian States—that certainly we must arm ourselves to the teeth, that clearly we must make military alliances with any other Powers whom we can get to work with us, and that we must hope that we shall be allowed to start the war at the moment that suits us and not at the moment that suits the other side. That is what some right hon. and hon. Gentlemen call collective security. Some hon. Members opposite will walk into any trap if it is only baited with a familiar catchword and they do it when this system is called collective security. But that is not the collective security we are thinking of or did think of when talking about the system of the League of Nations. That was a sort of universal collective security in which all nations were to take their part. This plan may give you security; it certainly is not collective in any sense. It appears to me to contain all the things which the party opposite used to denounce before the War—entangling alliances, balance of power and power politics. If I reject it, as I do, it is not because I give it a label; it is because, to my mind, it is a policy of utter despair.

If that is hon. Members' conviction, there is no future hope for civilisation or for any of the things that make life worth living. Does the experience of the Great War and of the years that followed it give us reasonable hope that if some new war started that would end war any more than the last one did? No. I do not believe that war is inevitable. Someone put into my hand a remark made by the great Pitt about 1787, when he said:

> To suppose that any nation can be unalterably the enemy of another is weak and childish and has its foundations neither in the experience of nations nor in the history of man.

It seems to me that the strongest argument against the inevitability of war is to be found in something that everyone has recognised or that has been recognised in every part of the House. That is the universal aversion from war of the people, their hatred of the notion of starting to kill one another again. This morning I received a letter not written to me, but written to a friend by a German professor. I cannot give his name, because I have not asked whether I might do so. I think it is typical of feeling in Germany, because I have heard the same from many other sources. I would like to repeat to the House one or two phrases from it. He writes:

> "Never again." That is the main idea, not only among the professors, but also among the students who did not share the experience of 1914, but heard enough about it. That is the idea of the rich and of the poor and even of the army themselves. As an officer of the Reserve I know what I am speaking about.

Later in the letter he says:

> Now peace has been secured, and not only for the moment. Now the end of the period of changes and treaties of 1918 can be foreseen and we all hope that a new era will begin in Anglo-German relations.

What is the alternative to this bleak and barren policy of the inevitability of war? In my view it is that we should seek by all means in our power to avoid war, by analysing possible causes, by trying to remove them, by discussion in a spirit of collaboration and good will. I cannot believe that such a programme would be rejected by the people of this country, even if it does mean the establishment of personal contact with dictators, and of talks man to man on the basis that each, while maintaining his own ideas of the internal government of his country, is willing to allow that other systems may suit better other peoples. The party opposite surely have the same idea in mind even if they put it in a different way. They want a world conference. Well, I have had some experience of conferences, and one thing I do feel certain of is that it is better to have no conference at all than a conference which is a failure. The corollary to that is that before you enter a conference you must have laid out very clearly the lines on which you are going to proceed, if you are at least to have in front of you a reasonable prospect that you may obtain success. I am not saying that a conference would not have its place in due course. But I say it is no use to call a conference of the world, including these totalitarian Powers, until you are sure that they are going to attend, and not only that they are going to attend, but that they are going to attend with the intention of aiding you in the policy on which you have set your heart.

I am told that the policy which I have tried to describe is inconsistent with the continuance, and much more inconsistent with the acceleration of our present programme of arms. I am asked how I can reconcile an appeal to the country to support the continuance of this programme with the words which I used when I came back from Munich the other day and spoke of my belief that we might have peace for our time. I hope hon. Members will not be disposed to read into words used in a moment of some emotion, after a long and exhausting day, after I had driven through miles of excited, enthusiastic, cheering people—I hope they will not read into those words more than they were intended to convey. I do indeed believe that we may yet secure peace for our time, but I never meant to suggest that we should do that by disarmament, until we can induce others to disarm too. Our past experience has shown us only too clearly that weakness in armed strength means weakness in diplomacy, and if we want to secure a lasting peace, I realise that diplomacy cannot be effective unless the consciousness exists, not here alone, but elsewhere, that behind the diplomacy is the strength to give effect to it.

One good thing, at any rate, has come out of this emergency through which we have passed. It has thrown a vivid light upon our preparations for defence, on their strength and on their weakness. I should not think we were doing our duty if we had not already ordered that a prompt and thorough inquiry should be made to cover the whole of our preparations, military and civil, in order to see, in the light of what has happened during these hectic days, what further steps may be necessary to make good our deficiencies in the shortest possible time. There have been references in the course of the Debate to other measures which hon. Members have suggested should be taken. I would not like to commit myself now, until I have had a little time for reflection, as to what further it may seem good to ask the nation to do, but I think nobody could fail to have been impressed by the fact that the emergency brought out that the whole of the people of this country, whatever their occupation, whatever their class, whatever their station, were ready to do their duty, however disagreeable, however hard, however dangerous it may have been.

I cannot help feeling that if, after all, war had come upon us, the people of this country would have lost their spiritual faith altogether. As it turned out the other way, I think we have all seen something like a new spiritual revival, and I know that everywhere there is a strong desire among the people to record their readiness to serve their country, wherever or however their services could be most useful. I would like to take advantage of that strong feeling if it is possible, and although I must frankly say that at this moment I do not myself clearly see my way to any particular scheme, yet I want also to say that I am ready to consider any suggestion that may be made to me, in a very sympathetic spirit.

Finally, I would like to repeat what my right hon. Friend the Chancellor of the Exchequer said yesterday in his great speech. Our policy of appeasement does not mean that we are going to seek new friends at the expense of old ones, or, indeed, at the expense of any other nations at all. I do not think that at any time there has been a more complete identity of views between the French Government and ourselves than there is at the present time. Their objective is the same as ours—to obtain the collaboration of all nations, not excluding the totalitarian States, in building up a lasting peace for Europe. . . .

23. Arnold Toynbee, Lord Rothermere, and Winston Churchill: Three Views of Appeasement

Arnold Joseph Toynbee (1889–1975) was a distinguished English historian whose twelve-volume work, *A Study of History* (1934–61), presented a magisterial, if hotly debated, interpretation of the emergence, growth, and decline of world civilizations. Toynbee was educated at Balliol College, Oxford, where he was appointed a fellow and tutor in 1912. In 1915 he joined the Foreign Office in the Political Intelligence Department, and served as a member of the British delegation at the Paris Peace conference in 1919. In 1925 Toynbee was appointed research professor at the University of London and director of studies at the Royal Institute of International Affairs (Chatham House), the latter founded in 1920 with the support of Lionel Curtis, Alfred Zimmern, and other members of the Round Table circle (see above, document 8).

Harold Sidney Harmsworth, the first Viscount Rothermere (1868–1940), was among the most influential newspaper proprietors and opinion-makers of early and mid twentieth-century Britain. Together with his older brother, Alfred (later Lord Northcliffe), he gained control of the *Evening News* in 1894 and founded the immensely popular *Daily Mail* in 1896.

Arnold Toynbee to Quincy Wright

Ganthorpe
Terrington
York

14th October 1938
Dear Wright,[1]
It is rather odd for me to find myself putting up a defense for Chamberlain, but I am convinced that he had no Machiavellian plans and wasn't thinking of Fascism v. Communism, or anything like that. The simplest explanation is the complete one. He was thinking about avoiding being

From *Quincy Wright Papers*, Addendum I, Box 26, University of Chicago Library. Reprinted by permission of Lawrence Toynbee.

1. Quincy Wright (1890–1970) was an American political scientist and authority on international law. The author of *A Study of War*, Wright served from 1923 until 1956 as professor of political science and law at the University of Chicago.—ED.

bombed here and now, and it was because he did avoid that that he carried the country with him.

This is an explanation of his policy, not a defense of it. For the price has been Hitler's predominance in Europe; this will put it in his power to bomb us much more intensively a bit later; so, if the Chamberlain policy is to be carried through, it means being prepared for concessions *without limit*.

Are the British people now prepared for that? I simply don't know. But what one can foresee is that, next time, they will be faced with a choice between staggering concessions and fighting a war in which, this time, we shall be faced with hopeless odds.

What is the next chapter? A struggle for world power between the Triangle and North America? And what will be the role of France and England? Shall we be neutrals or battlefields? (You know my theory about the centres of civilisation in one chapter becoming the battlefields in the next: e.g. Lombardy and Flanders; is it our turn now?)

It is probably impossible to convey what the imminent expectation of being intensively bombed feels like in a small and densely populated country like this. I couldn't have conveyed it to myself if I hadn't experienced it in London the week before last (we were expecting 30,000 casualties a night in London, and on the Wednesday morning we believed ourselves, I believe correctly, to be within three hours of the zero hour). It was just like facing the end of the world. In a few minutes the clock was going to stop, and life, as we had known it, was coming to an end. This prospect of the horrible destruction of all that is meant to one by "England" and "Europe" was much worse than the mere personal prospect that one's family and oneself would very soon be blown to bits. It was, in fact, a vary harrowing experience. Seven or eight million people in London went through it. What is going to be the political effect? It is bound to be a very great one, which will deeply affect the history of the world—and there, for the moment, I must leave it.

Yours sincerely,
Arnold J. Toynbee

Lord Rothermere to Winston S. Churchill

15 October 1938
My dear Winston,

I urge you to go slow in regard to your Constituency. Neville Chamberlain's reputation will be undimmed so long as he is Prime Minister and

From *Winston S. Churchill*. Vol. 5, *Companion Documents. Part 3,* "The Coming of the War 1936–39," edited by Martin Gilbert (Boston: Houghton Mifflin, 1983), p. 1216; ©1981 any member of his Party who challenges that fact may suffer a complete eclipse.

The public is so terrified of being bombed that they will support anyone who keeps them out of war. I always knew they had no desire to stand up to the Dictators and I always knew that when there was a sharp issue of peace or war ninety-five per cent of the electors would rally to the peace policy however humiliating such a policy might be.

I do hope you will soft pedal on the whole position. If you were not in the House it would be a national loss.

I don't trust the Epping electorate[2] because Epping is on one of the routes by which enemy aeroplanes will approach London.

Ward Price[3] was very downright last evening in asserting this point of view. I entirely agree with him.

Yours always,
Rothermere

Winston S. Churchill: draft[4]

We shall hear in succeeding generations a lot of talk about the pacific virtues we displayed; how we exhausted every expedient; how we flaunted a magnificent patience; how we never lost our heads or were carried away by fear or excitement; how we turned the second cheek to the smiter seven times or more.

Some historians will urge that admiration should be given to a Government of honourable high-minded men who bore provocation with exemplary forbearance and piled up to their credit all the Christian virtues, especially those which command electioneering popularity; but who when their patience was at length worn out by repeated injury and peril turned upon their aggressor with their backs to the wall.

I hope it will also be written how hard all this was upon the ordinary

---

by C. & T. Publications. Reprinted by permission of Curtis Brown Ltd., on behalf of C. & T. Publications. Footnote deleted.

2. Epping was Churchill's constituency in the House of Commons.—ED.

3. George Ward Price (1886–1961) was an English journalist who served as a special foreign correspondent for the *Daily Mail* in the interwar years.—ED.

From *Winston S. Churchill.* Vol. 5, *Companion Documents. Part 3,* "The Coming of the War 1936–39," edited by Martin Gilbert (Boston: Houghton Mifflin, 1983), p. 1623; ©1981 by C. & T. Publications. Reprinted by permission of Curtis Brown Ltd., on behalf of C. & T. Publications.

4. Churchill wrote this passage in 1946 or 1947, for the first volume of his war memoirs, but deleted it before publication.

common folk who fill the casualty lists of world wars. Under representative
Government and Parliamentary institutions, they confide their safety to the
Ministers and the Prime Minister of the day. They have just cause of com-
plaint if their guides or rulers so mismanage their affairs that in the end
they are thrust into the worst of wars with the worst of chances.

Intellectuals and Cultural Critics

24. Antonio Gramsci, *The Prison Notebooks*

One of the most subtle and original Marxist theoreticians of the twentieth
century, Antonio Gramsci was born in 1891 into a large petty bourgeois
family on the island of Sardinia, the most remote and impoverished region of Italy. A university education in the city of Turin brought him into
contact with a highly organized working-class movement and prompted
him to join the Socialist party. Employed as a party journalist, Gramsci
greeted the Bolshevik Revolution of 1917 with enthusiasm, interpreting it
in "heretical" fashion as proof that the supposedly iron laws of historical
materialism were in fact malleable, that the course of history was not
simply determined by economic conditions but could be shaped by human will. He had, in effect, injected a dose of Italian idealism (his men-
tors here were Benedetto Croce and Giovanni Gentile) into a Marxism
which he believed had become contaminated by the admixture of late
nineteenth-century positivism. Although Marx's 1844 manuscripts, the
products of his most Hegelian phase, had not yet been rediscovered,
Gramsci was attempting to restore to Marx an idealist component which
he had inferred, correctly, was there.

After the end of the First World War, Gramsci and some classmates
founded *Ordine Nuovo* (The New Order), a periodical devoted to radi-
calizing the Socialist party. When the latter split at Livorno in January
1921—a schism analogous to that of the French Socialist party at Tours
the previous year (see document 18)—Gramsci became one of the leaders
of the newly formed Italian Communist party. He spent the next two
years in Moscow as party liaison to the Third International.

In 1926, the Fascist government of Italy put Gramsci in jail in order,
the public prosecutor said, "to stop that brain from working for twenty
years." But even in the inhuman conditions of Mussolini's prisons, "that

brain" refused to stop. Gramsci filled thirty-two notebooks—some three thousand manuscript pages—with writing on a vast range of political and philosophical subjects. His chronically frail health undermined by ill treatment, he died in Rome in 1937, a short time after his commuted prison term ended. His prison notebooks (*Quaderni del carcere*) thus form the bulk of his literary legacy. Composed of fragments, usually a paragraph or two in length, they are raw material rather than a finished work; and published excerpts from them, like the one below, are usually an editor's compilation of fragments on a related topic. Such texts clearly present the reader with more than the usual problems of interpretation.

In the following selection from the *Notebooks,* Gramsci disputes the orthodox Marxist conception of the intellectual as a merely passive, super-structural reflection of the dynamic, economic base of society. His theory of intellectuals is a key element in his rendition of Marxism, which ascribes to human consciousness a critical measure of autonomy.

The Intellectuals

The Formation of the Intellectuals

Are intellectuals an autonomous and independent social group, or does every social group have its own particular specialised category of intellectuals? The problem is a complex one, because of the variety of forms assumed to date by the real historical process of formation of the different categories of intellectuals.

The most important of these forms are two:

1. Every social group, coming into existence on the original terrain of an essential function in the world of economic production, creates together with itself, organically, one or more strata of intellectuals which give it homogeneity and an awareness of its own function not only in the economic but also in the social and political fields. The capitalist entrepreneur creates alongside himself the industrial technician, the specialist in political economy, the organisers of a new culture, or a new legal system, etc. It should be noted that the entrepreneur himself represents a higher level of social elaboration, already characterised by a certain directive [*dirigente*] and technical (i.e. intellectual) capacity: he must have a certain technical capacity, not only in the limited sphere of his activity and initiative but in other spheres as well, at least in those which are closest to economic pro-

From Antonio Gramsci, *Selections of the Prison Notebooks,* edited and translated by Quintin Hoare and Geoffrey Nowell Smith (New York: International Publishers, 1971), pp. 5–23. Reprinted by permission of the publisher. Footnotes omitted.

duction. He must be an organiser of masses of men; he must be an organiser of the "confidence" of investors in his business, of the customers for his product, etc.

If not all entrepreneurs, at least an *élite* amongst them must have the capacity to be an organiser of society in general, including all its complex organism of services, right up to the state organism, because of the need to create the conditions most favourable to the expansion of their own class; or at the least they must possess the capacity to choose the deputies (specialised employees) to whom to entrust this activity of organising the general system of relationships external to the business itself. It can be observed that the "organic" intellectuals which every new class creates alongside itself and elaborates in the course of its development, are for the most part "specialisations" of partial aspects of the primitive activity of the new social type which the new class has brought into prominence.

Even feudal lords were possessors of a particular technical capacity, military capacity, and it is precisely from the moment at which the aristocracy loses its monopoly of technico-military capacity that the crisis of feudalism begins. But the formation of intellectuals in the feudal world and in the preceding classical world is a question to be examined separately: this formation and elaboration follows ways and means which must be studied concretely. Thus it is to be noted that the mass of the peasantry, although it performs an essential function in the world of production, does not elaborate its own "organic" intellectuals, nor does it "assimilate" any stratum of "traditional" intellectuals, although it is from the peasantry that other social groups draw many of their intellectuals and a high proportion of traditional intellectuals are of peasant origin.

2. However, every "essential" social group which emerges into history out of the preceding economic structure, and as an expression of a development of this structure, has found (at least in all of history up to the present) categories of intellectuals already in existence and which seemed indeed to represent an historical continuity uninterrupted even by the most complicated and radical changes in political and social forms.

The most typical of these categories of intellectuals is that of the ecclesiastics, who for a long time (for a whole phase of history, which is partly characterised by this very monopoly) held a monopoly of a number of important services: religious ideology, that is the philosophy and science of the age, together with schools, education, morality, justice, charity, good works, etc. The category of ecclesiastics can be considered the category of intellectuals organically bound to the landed aristocracy. It had equal status juridically with the aristocracy, with which it shared the exercise of feudal ownership of land, and the use of state privileges connected with property. But the monopoly held by the ecclesiastics in the superstructural field was not exercised without a struggle or without limitations, and hence there took place the birth, in various forms (to be gone into and studied concretely), of other categories, favoured and enabled to expand by the growing strength of the central power of the monarch, right up to absolutism. Thus we find the formation of the *noblesse de robe,* with its own privileges, a stratum of administrators, etc., scholars and scientists, theorists, non-ecclesiastical philosophers, etc.

Since these various categories of traditional intellectuals experience through an *"esprit de corps"* their uninterrupted historical continuity and their special qualification, they thus put themselves forward as autonomous and independent of the dominant social group. This self-assessment is not without consequences in the ideological and political field, consequences of wide-ranging import. The whole of idealist philosophy can easily be connected with this position assumed by the social complex of intellectuals and can be defined as the expression of that social utopia by which the intellectuals think of themselves as "independent," autonomous, endowed with a character of their own, etc.

One should note however that if the Pope and the leading hierarchy of the Church consider themselves more linked to Christ and to the apostles than they are to senators Agnelli and Benni, the same does not hold for Gentile and Croce, for example: Croce in particular feels himself closely linked to Aristotle and Plato, but he does not conceal, on the other hand, his links with senators Agnelli and Benni, and it is precisely here that one can discern the most significant character of Croce's philosophy.

What are the "maximum" limits of acceptance of the term "intellectual"? Can one find a unitary criterion to characterise equally all the diverse and disparate activities of intellectuals and to distinguish these at the same time and in an essential way from the activities of other social groupings? The most widespread error of method seems to me that of having looked for this criterion of distinction in the intrinsic nature of intellectual activities, rather than in the ensemble of the system of relations in which these activities (and therefore the intellectual groups who personify them) have their place within the general complex of social relations. Indeed the worker or proletarian, for example, is not specifically characterised by his manual or instrumental work, but by performing this work in specific conditions and in specific social relations (apart from the consideration that purely physical labour does not exist and that even Taylor's phrase of "trained gorilla" is a metaphor to indicate a limit in a certain direction: in any physical work, even the most degraded and mechanical, there exists a minimum of technical qualification, that is, a minimum of creative intellectual activity). And we have already observed that the entrepreneur, by virtue of his very function, must have to some degree a certain number of qualifications of an intellectual nature although his part in society is determined not by these, but by the general social relations which specifically characterise the position of the entrepreneur within industry.

All men are intellectuals, one could therefore say: but not all men have in society the function of intellectuals.

When one distinguishes between intellectuals and non-intellectuals, one is referring in reality only to the immediate social function of the professional category of the intellectuals, that is, one has in mind the direction in which their specific professional activity is weighted, whether towards intellectual elaboration or towards muscular-nervous effort. This means that, although one can speak of intellectuals, one cannot speak of non-intellectuals, because non-intellectuals do not exist. But even the relationship between efforts of intellectual-cerebral elaboration and muscular-nervous effort is not always the same, so that there are varying degrees of specific intellectual activity. There is no human activity from which every form of intellectual participation can be excluded: *homo faber* cannot be separated from *homo sapiens*. Each man, finally, outside his professional activity, carries on some form of intellectual activity, that is, he is a "philosopher," an artist, a man of taste, he participates in a particular conception of the world, has a conscious line of moral conduct, and therefore contributes to sustain a conception of the world or to modify it, that is, to bring into being new modes of thought.

The problem of creating a new stratum of intellectuals consists therefore in the critical elaboration of the intellectual activity that exists in everyone at a certain degree of development, modifying its relationship with the muscular-nervous effort towards a new equilibrium, and ensuring that the muscular-nervous effort itself, in so far as it is an element of a general practical activity, which is perpetually innovating the physical and social world, becomes the foundation of a new and integral conception of the world. The traditional and vulgarised type of the intellectual is given by the man of letters, the philosopher, the artist. Therefore journalists, who claim to be men of letters, philosophers, artists, also regard themselves as the "true" intellectuals. In the modern world, technical education, closely bound to industrial labour even at the most primitive and unqualified level, must form the basis of the new type of intellectual.

On this basis the weekly *Ordine Nuovo* worked to develop certain forms of new intellectualism and to determine its new concepts, and this was not the least of the reasons for its success, since such a conception corresponded to latent aspirations and conformed to the development of the real forms of life. The mode of being of the new intellectual can no longer consist in eloquence, which is an exterior and momentary mover of feelings and passions, but in active participation in practical life, as constructor, organiser, "permanent persuader" and not just a simple orator (but superior at the same time to the abstract mathematical spirit); from technique-as-work one proceeds to technique-as-science and to the humanistic conception of history, without which one remains "specialised" and does not become "directive" (specialised and political).

Thus there are historically formed specialised categories for the exercise of the intellectual function. They are formed in connection with all social groups, but especially in connection with the more important, and they undergo more extensive and complex elaboration in connection with the dominant social group. One of the most important characteristics of any group that is developing towards dominance is its struggle to assimilate and to conquer "ideologically" the traditional intellectuals, but this assimilation and conquest is made quicker and more efficacious the more the group in question succeeds in simultaneously elaborating its own organic intellectuals.

The enormous development of activity and organisation of education in the broad sense in the societies that emerged from the medieval world is an index of the importance assumed in the modern world by intellectual functions and categories. Parallel with the attempt to deepen and to broaden the "intellectuality" of each individual, there has also been an attempt to multiply and narrow the various specialisations. This can be seen from educational institutions at all levels, up to and including the organisms that exist to promote so-called "high culture" in all fields of science and technology.

School is the instrument through which intellectuals of various levels are elaborated. The complexity of the intellectual function in different states can be measured objectively by the number and gradation of specialised schools: the more extensive the "area" covered by education and the more numerous the "vertical" "levels" of schooling, the more complex is the cultural world, the civilisation, of a particular state. A point of comparison can be found in the sphere of industrial technology: the industrialisation of a country can be measured by how well equipped it is in the production of machines with which to produce machines, and in the manufacture of ever more accurate instruments for making both machines and further instruments for making machines, etc. The country which is best equipped in the construction of instruments for experimental scientific laboratories and in the construction of instruments with which to test the first instruments, can be regarded as the most complex in the technical-industrial field, with the highest level of civilisation, etc. The same applies to the preparation of intellectuals and to the schools dedicated to this preparation; schools and institutes of high culture can be assimilated to each other. In this field also, quantity cannot be separated from quality. To the most refined technical-cultural specialisation there cannot but correspond the maximum possible diffusion of primary education and the maximum care taken to expand the middle grades numerically as much as possible. Naturally this need to provide the widest base possible for the selection and elaboration of the top intellectual qualifications—i.e. to give a democratic structure to high culture and top-level technology—is not without its disadvantages: it creates the possibility of vast crises of unemployment for the middle intellectual strata, and in all modern societies this actually takes place.

It is worth noting that the elaboration of intellectual strata in concrete reality does not take place on the terrain of abstract democracy but in accordance with very concrete traditional historical processes. Strata have grown up which traditionally "produce" intellectuals and these strata coincide with those which have specialised in "saving," i.e. the petty and middle landed bourgeoisie and certain strata of the petty and middle urban bourgeoisie. The varying distribution of different types of school (classical and professional) over the "economic" territory and the varying aspirations of different categories within these strata determine, or give form to, the production of various branches of intellectual specialisation. Thus in Italy the rural bourgeoisie produces in particular state functionaries and professional people, whereas the urban bourgeoisie produces technicians for industry. Consequently it is largely northern Italy which produces technicians and the South which produces functionaries and professional men.

The relationship between the intellectuals and the world of production is not as direct as it is with the fundamental social groups but is, in varying degrees, "mediated" by the whole fabric of society and by the complex of superstructures, of which the intellectuals are, precisely, the "functionaries." It should be possible both to measure the "organic quality" [*organicità*] of the various intellectual strata and their degree of connection with a fundamental social group, and to establish a gradation of their functions and of the superstructures from the bottom to the top (from the structural base upwards). What we can do, for the moment, is to fix two major superstructural "levels": the one that can be called "civil society," that is the ensemble of organisms commonly called "private," and that of "political society" or "the State." These two levels correspond on the one hand to the function of "hegemony" which the dominant group exercises throughout society and on the other hand to that of "direct domination" or command exercised through the State and "juridical" government. The functions in question are precisely organisational and connective. The intellectuals are the dominant group's "deputies" exercising the subaltern functions of social hegemony and political government. These comprise:

1. The "spontaneous" consent given by the great masses of the population to the general direction imposed on social life by the dominant fundamental group; this consent is "historically" caused by the prestige (and consequent confidence) which the dominant group enjoys because of its position and function in the world of production.

2. The apparatus of state coercive power which "legally" enforces discipline on those groups who do not "consent" either actively or passively. This apparatus is, however, constituted for the whole of society in anticipation of moments of crisis of command and direction when spontaneous consent has failed.

This way of posing the problem has as a result a considerable extension of the concept of intellectual, but it is the only way which enables one to reach a concrete approximation of reality. It also clashes with preconceptions of caste. The function of organising social hegemony and state domination certainly gives rise to a particular division of labour and therefore to a whole hierarchy of qualifications in some of which there is no apparent attribution of directive or organisational functions. For example, in the apparatus of social and state direction there exist a whole series of jobs of a manual and instrumental character (non-executive work, agents rather than officials or functionaries). It is obvious that such a distinction has to be made just as it is obvious that other distinctions have to be made as well. Indeed, intellectual activity must also be distinguished in terms of its intrinsic characteristics, according to levels which in moments of extreme opposition represent a real qualitative difference—at the highest level would be the creators of the various sciences, philosophy, art, etc., at the lowest the most humble "administrators" and divulgators of pre-existing, traditional, accumulated intellectual wealth.

In the modern world the category of intellectuals, understood in this sense, has undergone an unprecedented expansion. The democratic-bureaucratic system has given rise to a great mass of functions which are not all justified by the social necessities of production, though they are justified by the political necessities of the dominant fundamental group. Hence Loria's conception of the unproductive "worker" (but unproductive in relation to whom and to what mode of production?), a conception which could in part be justified if one takes account of the fact that these masses exploit their position to take for themselves a large cut out of the national income. Mass formation has standardised individuals both psychologically and in terms of individual qualification and has produced the same phenomena as with other standardised masses: competition which makes necessary organisations for the defence of professions, unemployment, overproduction in the schools, emigration, etc.

The Different Position of Urban and Rural-Type Intellectuals

Intellectuals of the urban type have grown up along with industry and are linked to its fortunes. Their function can be compared to that of subaltern officers in the army. They have no autonomous initiative in elaborating plans for construction. Their job is to articulate the relationship between the entrepreneur and the instrumental mass and to carry out the immediate execution of the production plan decided by the industrial general staff, controlling the elementary stages of work. On the whole the average urban intellectuals are very standardised, while the top urban intellectuals are more and more identified with the industrial general staff itself.

Intellectuals of the rural type are for the most part "traditional," that is they are linked to the social mass of country people and the town (particularly small-town) petite bourgeoisie, not as yet elaborated and set in motion by the capitalist system. This type of intellectual brings into contact the peasant masses with the local and state administration (lawyers, notaries, etc.). Because of this activity they have an important politico-social function, since professional mediation is difficult to separate from political. Furthermore: in the countryside the intellectual (priest, lawyer, notary, teacher, doctor, etc.), has on the whole a higher or at least a different living standard from that of the average peasant and consequently represents a social model for the peasant to look to in his aspiration to escape from or improve his condition. The peasant always thinks that at least one of his sons could become an intellectual (especially a priest), thus becoming a gentleman and raising the social level of the family by facilitating its economic life through the connections which he is bound to acquire with the rest of the gentry. The peasant's attitude towards the intellectual is double and appears contradictory. He respects the social position of the intellectuals and in general that of state employees, but sometimes affects contempt for it, which means that his admiration is mingled with instinctive elements of envy and impassioned anger. One can understand nothing of the collective life of the peasantry and of the germs and ferments of development which exist within it, if one does not take into consideration and examine concretely and in depth this effective subordination to the intellectuals. Every organic development of the peasant masses, up to a certain point, is linked to and depends on movements among the intellectuals.

With the urban intellectuals it is another matter. Factory technicians do not exercise any political function over the instrumental masses, or at least this is a phase that has been superseded. Sometimes, rather, the contrary takes place, and the instrumental masses, at least in the person of their own organic intellectuals, exercise a political influence on the technicians.

The central point of the question remains the distinction between intellectuals as an organic category of every fundamental social group and intellectuals as a traditional category. From this distinction there flow a whole series of problems and possible questions for historical research.

The most interesting problem is that which, when studied from this point of view, relates to the modern political party, its real origins, its developments and the forms which it takes. What is the character of the political party in relation to the problem of the intellectuals? Some distinctions must be made:

1. The political party for some social groups is nothing other than their specific way of elaborating their own category of organic intellectuals directly in the political and philosophical field and not just in the field of productive technique. These intellectuals are formed in this way and cannot indeed be formed in any other way, given the general character and the conditions of formation, life and development of the social group.

2. The political party, for all groups, is precisely the mechanism which carries out in civil society the same function as the State carries out, more synthetically and over a larger scale, in political society. In other words it is responsible for welding together the organic intellectuals of a given group—the dominant one—and the traditional intellectuals. The party carries out this function in strict dependence on its basic function, which is that of elaborating its own component parts—those elements of a social group which has been born and developed as an "economic" group—and of turning them into qualified political intellectuals, leaders [*dirigenti*] and organisers of all the activities and functions inherent in the organic development of an integral society, both civil and political. Indeed it can be said that within its field the political party accomplishes its function more completely and organically than the State does within its admittedly far larger field. An intellectual who joins the political party of a particular social group is merged with the organic intellectuals of the group itself, and is linked tightly with the group. This takes place through participation in the life of the State only to a limited degree and often not at all. Indeed it happens that many intellectuals think that they *are* the State, a belief which, given the magnitude of the category, occasionally has important consequences and leads to unpleasant complications for the fundamental economic group which *really* is the State.

That all members of a political party should be regarded as intellectuals is an affirmation that can easily lend itself to mockery and caricature. But if one thinks about it nothing could be more exact. There are of course distinctions of level to be made. A party might have a greater or lesser proportion of members in the higher grades or in the lower, but this is not the point. What matters is the function, which is directive and organisational, i.e. educative, i.e. intellectual. A tradesman does not join a political party in order to do business, nor an industrialist in order to produce more at lower cost, nor a peasant to learn new methods of cultivation, even if some aspects of these demands of the tradesman, the industrialist or the peasant can find satisfaction in the party.

For these purposes, within limits, there exists the professional association, in which the economic-corporate activity of the tradesman, industrialist or peasant is most suitably promoted. In the political party the elements of an economic social group get beyond that moment of their historical development and become agents of more general activities of a national and international character. This function of a political party should emerge even more clearly from a concrete historical analysis of how both organic and traditional categories of intellectuals have developed in the context of different national histories and in that of the development of the various major social groups within each nation, particularly those groups whose economic activity has been largely instrumental.

The formation of traditional intellectuals is the most interesting problem historically. It is undoubtedly connected with slavery in the classical world and with the position of freed men of Greek or Oriental origin in the social organisation of the Roman Empire.

> *Note.* The change in the condition of the social position of the intellectuals in Rome between Republican and Imperial times (a change from an aristocratic-corporate to a democratic-bureaucratic régime) is due to Caesar, who granted citizenship to doctors and to masters of liberal arts so that they would be more willing to live in Rome and so that others should be persuaded to come there. (*"Omnesque medicinam Romae professos et liberalium artium doctores, quo libentius et ipsi urbem incolerent et coeteri appeterent civitate donavit."* Suetonius, *Life of Caesar,* XLII.) Caesar therefore proposed: 1. to establish in Rome those intellectuals who were already there, thus creating a permanent category of intellectuals, since without their permanent residence there no cultural organisation could be created; and 2. to attract to Rome the best intellectuals from all over the Roman Empire, thus promoting centralisation on a massive scale. In this way there came into being the category of "imperial" intellectuals in Rome which was to be continued by the Catholic clergy and to leave so many traces in the history of Italian intellectuals, such as their characteristic "cosmopolitanism," up to the eighteenth century.

This not only social but national and racial separation between large masses of intellectuals and the dominant class of the Roman Empire is repeated after the fall of the Empire in the division between Germanic warriors and intellectuals of romanised origin, successors of the category of freedmen. Interweaved with this phenomenon are the birth and development of Catholicism and of the ecclesiastical organisation which for many centuries absorbs the major part of intellectual activities and exercises a monopoly of cultural direction with penal sanctions against anyone who attempted to oppose or even evade the monopoly. In Italy we can observe the phenomenon, whose intensity varies from period to period, of the cosmopolitan function of the intellectuals of the peninsula. I shall now turn to the differences which are instantly apparent in the development of the intellectuals in a number of the more important countries, with the proviso that these observations require to be controlled and examined in more depth.

As far as Italy is concerned the central fact is precisely the international or cosmopolitan function of its intellectuals, which is both cause and effect of the state of disintegration in which the peninsula remained from the fall of the Roman Empire up to 1870.

France offers the example of an accomplished form of harmonious development of the energies of the nation and of the intellectual categories in particular. When in 1789 a new social grouping makes its political appearance on the historical stage, it is already completely equipped for all its social functions and can therefore struggle for total dominion of the nation. It does not have to make any essential compromises with the old classes but instead can subordinate them to its own ends. The first intellectual cells of the new type are born along with their first economic counterparts. Even ecclesiastical organisation is influenced (gallicanism, precocious struggles between Church and State). This massive intellectual construction explains the function of culture in France in the eighteenth and nineteenth centuries. It was a function of international and cosmopolitan outward radiation and of imperialistic and hegemonic expansion in an organic fashion, very different therefore from the Italian experience, which was founded on scattered personal migration and did not react on the national base to potentiate it but on the contrary contributed to rendering the constitution of a solid national base impossible.

In England the development is very different from France. The new social grouping that grew up on the basis of modern industrialism shows a remarkable economic-corporate development but advances only gropingly in the intellectual-political field. There is a very extensive category of organic intellectuals—those, that is, who come into existence on the same industrial terrain as the economic group—but in the higher sphere we find that the old land-owning class preserves its position of virtual monopoly. It loses its economic supremacy but maintains for a long time a politico-intellectual supremacy and is assimilated as "traditional intellectuals" and as directive [*dirigente*] group by the new group in power. The old land-owning aristocracy is joined to the industrialists by a kind of suture which is precisely that which in other countries unites the traditional intellectuals with the new dominant classes.

The English phenomenon appears also in Germany, but complicated by other historical and traditional elements. Germany, like Italy, was the seat of an universalistic and supranational institution and ideology, the Holy Roman Empire of the German Nation, and provided a certain number of personnel for the mediaeval cosmopolis, impoverishing its own internal energies and arousing struggles which distracted from problems of national organisation and perpetuated the territorial disintegration of the Middle Ages. Industrial development took place within a semi-feudal integument that persisted up to November 1918, and the *Junkers* preserved a politico-intellectual supremacy considerably greater even than that of the corresponding group in England. They were the traditional intellectuals of the German industrialists, but retained special privileges and a strong consciousness of being an independent social group, based on the fact that they held considerable economic power over the land, which was more "productive" than in England. The Prussian *Junkers* resemble a priestly-military caste, with a virtual monopoly of directive-organisational functions in political society, but possessing at the same time an economic base of its own and so not exclusively dependent on the liberality of the dominant economic group. Furthermore, unlike the English landowning aristocracy, the *Junkers* constituted the officer class of a large standing army, which gave them solid organisational cadres favouring the preservation of an *esprit de corps* and of their political monopoly.

In Russia various features: the political and economico-commercial organisation was created by the Normans (Varangians), and religious organisation by the Byzantine Greeks. In a later period the Germans and the French brought to Russia the European experience and gave a first consistent skeleton to the protoplasm of Russian history. National forces were inert, passive and receptive, but perhaps precisely for this reason they assimilated completely the foreign influences and the foreigners themselves, Russifying them. In the more recent historical period we find the opposite phenomenon. An *élite* consisting of some of the most active, energetic, enterprising and disciplined members of the society emigrates abroad and assimilates the culture and historical experiences of the most advanced countries of the West, without however losing the most essential characteristics of its own nationality, that is to say without breaking its sentimental and historical links with its own people. Having thus performed its intellectual apprenticeship it returns to its own country and compels the people to an enforced awakening, skipping historical stages in the process. The difference between this *élite* and that imported from Germany (by Peter the Great, for example) lies in its essentially national-popular character. It could not be assimilated by the inert passivity of the Russian people, because it was itself an energetic reaction of Russia to her own historical inertia.

On another terrain, and in very different conditions of time and place, the Russian phenomenon can be compared to the birth of the American nation (in the United States). The Anglo-Saxon immigrants are themselves an intellectual, but more especially a moral, *élite*. I am talking, naturally, of the first immigrants, the pioneers, protagonists of the political and religious struggles in England, defeated but not humiliated or laid low in their country of origin. They import into America, together with themselves, apart from moral energy and energy of the will, a certain level of civilisation, a certain stage of European historical evolution, which, when transplanted by such men into the virgin soil of America, continues to develop the forces implicit in its nature but with an incomparably more rapid rhythm than in Old Europe, where there exists a whole series of checks (moral, intellectual, political, economic, incorporated in specific sections of the population, relics of past régimes which refuse to die out) which generate opposition to speedy progress and give to every initiative the equilibrium of mediocrity, diluting it in time and in space.

One can note, in the case of the United States, the absence to a considerable degree of traditional intellectuals, and consequently a different equilibrium among the intellectuals in general. There has been a massive development, on top of an industrial base, of the whole range of modern superstructures. The necessity of an equilibrium is determined, not by the need to fuse together the organic intellectuals with the traditional, but by the need to fuse together in a single national crucible with a unitary culture the different forms of culture imported by immigrants of differing national origins. The lack of a vast sedimentation of traditional intellectuals such as one finds in countries of ancient civilisation explains, at least in part, both the existence of only two major political parties, which could in fact easily be reduced to one only (contrast this with the case of France, and not only in the post-war period when the multiplication of parties became a general phenomenon), and at the opposite extreme the enormous proliferation of religious sects.

One further phenomenon in the United States is worth studying, and that is the formation of a surprising number of negro intellectuals who absorb American culture and technology. It is worth bearing in mind the indirect influence that these negro intellectuals could exercise on the backward masses in Africa, and indeed direct influence if one or other of these hypotheses were ever to be verified: 1. that American expansionism should use American negroes as its agents in the conquest of the African market and the extension of American civilisation (something of the kind has already happened, but I don't know to what extent); 2. that the struggle for the unification of the American people should intensify in such a way as to provoke a negro exodus and the return to Africa of the most independent and energetic intellectual elements, the ones, in other words, who would be least inclined to submit to some possible future legislation that was even more humiliating than are the present widespread social customs. This development would give rise to two fundamental questions: 1. linguistic: whether English could become the educated language of Africa, bringing unity in the place of the existing swarm of dialects? 2. whether this intellectual stratum could have sufficient assimilating and organising capacity to give a "national" character to the present primitive sentiment of being a despised race, thus giving the African continent a mythic function as the common fatherland of all the negro peoples? It seems to me that, for the moment, American negroes have a national and racial spirit which is negative rather than positive, one which is a product of the struggle carried on by the whites in order to isolate and depress them. But was not this the case with the Jews up to and throughout the eighteenth century? Liberia, already Americanised and with English as its official language, could become the Zion of American negroes, with a tendency to set itself up as an African Piedmont.

In considering the question of the intellectuals in Central and South America, one should, I think, bear in mind certain fundamental conditions. No vast category of traditional intellectuals exists in Central or South America either, but the question does not present itself in the same terms as with the United States. What in fact we find at the root of development of these countries are the patterns of Spanish and Portuguese civilisation of the sixteenth and seventeenth century, characterised by the effects of the Counter Reformation and by military parasitism. The change-resistant crystallisations which survive to this day in these countries are the clergy and a military caste, two categories of traditional intellectuals fossilised in a form inherited from the European mother country. The industrial base is very restricted, and has not developed complicated superstructures. The majority of intellectuals are of the rural type, and, since the latifundium is dominant, with a lot of property in the hands of the Church, these intellectuals are linked with the clergy and the big landowners. National composition is very unbalanced even among the white population and is further complicated by the great masses of Indians who in some countries form the majority of the inhabitants. It can be said that in these regions of the American continent there still exists a situation of the *Kulturkampf* and of the Dreyfus trial, that is to say a situation in which the secular and bourgeois element has not yet reached the stage of being able to subordinate clerical and militaristic influence and interests to the secular politics of the modern State. It thus comes about that Free Masonry and forms of cultural organisation like the "positivist Church" are very influential in the opposition to Jesuitism. Most recent events (November 1930), from the *Kulturkampf* of Calles in Mexico to the military-popular insurrections in Argentina, Brazil, Peru, Chile and Bolivia, demonstrate the accuracy of these observations.

Further types of formation of the categories of intellectuals and of their relationship with national forces can be found in India, China and Japan. In Japan we have a formation of the English and German type, that is an industrial civilisation that develops within a feudal-bureaucratic integument with unmistakable features of its own.

In China there is the phenomenon of the script, an expression of the complete separation between the intellectuals and the people. In both India and China the enormous gap separating intellectuals and people is manifested also in the religious field. The problem of different beliefs and of different ways of conceiving and practising the same religion among the various strata of society, but particularly as between clergy, intellectuals and people, needs to be studied in general, since it occurs everywhere to a certain degree; but it is in the countries of East Asia that it reaches its most extreme form. In Protestant countries the difference is relatively slight (the proliferation of sects is connected with the need for a perfect suture between intellectuals and people, with the result that all the crudity of the effective conceptions of the popular masses is reproduced in the higher organisational sphere). It is more noteworthy in Catholic countries, but its extent varies. It is less in the Catholic parts of Germany and in France; rather greater in Italy, particularly in the South and in the islands; and very great indeed in the Iberian peninsula and in the countries of Latin America. The phenomenon increases in scale in the Orthodox countries where it becomes necessary to speak of three degrees of the same religion: that of the higher clergy and the monks, that of the secular clergy and that of the people. It reaches a level of absurdity in East Asia, where the religion of the people often has nothing whatever to do with that of books, although the two are called by the same name.

25. Julien Benda, *The Betrayal of the Intellectuals*

Julien Benda (1867–1956) was a French critic and essayist who devoted his life to defending classical and rationalist traditions against all forms of romanticism, especially against the intuitionism of the French philosopher Henri Bergson. Among his better-known works were a defense of Dreyfus, *Dialogues à Byzance* (1900); *Le Bergsonisme* (1912), a vitriolic attack on Bergson that won Benda fame and enemies; *Belphégor* (1918), an equally contemptuous attack on modern art; *Les Amorandes* (1922), a novel showing how sentiments destroy the intellect; *La Trahison des clercs* (the betrayal of the intellectuals) (1927); and *La grande épreuve des démocraties* (the great trial of the democracies) (1942), a trenchant, though unoriginal, analysis of modern liberal democracy.

The Betrayal of the Intellectuals was Benda's most famous work, and it was vehemently attacked from all sides. The issue—whether an intellectual ought to become involved in pragmatic political causes—arose again with particular force during the French Resistance. It might be noted, however, that Benda did not advise the intellectual to withdraw into an ivory tower, but simply to battle for the universal interests of humanity as his reason instructed him, and not for what Benda considered to be the particularistic passions of a class or a nation.

Today this desire inspires not only the moralist, but another kind of "clerk" who speaks from much higher ground. I am referring to that teaching of modern metaphysics which exhorts man to feel comparatively little esteem for the truly thinking portion of himself and to honour the active and *willing* part of himself with all his devotion. The theory of knowledge from which humanity has taken its values during the past half century assigns a secondary rank to the mind which proceeds by clear and distinct ideas, by categories, by words, and places in the highest rank the mind which succeeds in liberating itself from these intellectual habits and in becoming conscious of itself insofar as it is a "pure tendency," a "pure will," a "pure activity." Philosophy which formerly raised man to feel conscious of himself because he was a thinking being and to say, "I think, therefore I am," now raises him to say, "I am, therefore I think, I think, therefore I am not" (unless he takes thought into consideration only in that humble region where it is confused with action). Formerly philosophy taught him that his soul is divine insofar as it resembles the soul of Pythagoras linking up concepts; now she informs him that his soul is divine insofar as it resembles that of the small chicken breaking its eggshell. From his loftiest pulpit the modern "clerk" assures man that he is great in proportion as he is practical.

During fifty years, especially in France (see Barrès and Bourget) a whole literature has assiduously proclaimed the superiority of instinct, the unconscious, intuition, the will (in the German sense, i.e. as opposed to the intelligence) and has proclaimed it in the name of the practical spirit, because the instinct and not the intelligence knows what we ought to do— as individuals, as a nation, as a class—to secure our own advantage. These

From Julien Benda, *The Betrayal of the Intellectuals,* translated by Richard Aldington (Boston, Mass.: Beacon Press, 1955), pp. 119–23, 126–32, 134–39, 142–43; ©1928, 1955 by William Morrow and Co., Inc. Reprinted by permission of the publisher and Routledge & Kegan Paul. Footnotes omitted.

writers have eagerly expatiated on the example of the insect whose "instinct" (it appears) teaches it to strike its prey precisely in the spot which will paralyse it without killing it, so that its offspring may feed on the living prey and develop better. Other teachers denounce this "barbarous" extolling of instinct in the name of "the French tradition" and preach "the superiority of the intelligence"; but they preach it because in their opinion it is the intelligence which shows us the actions required by our interests, i.e. from exactly the same passion for the practical. This brings us to one of the most remarkable and certainly the most novel forms of this preaching of the practical by the modern "clerks."

I mean that teaching according to which *intellectual activity is worthy of esteem to the extent that it is practical and to that extent alone.* It may be said that since the Greeks the predominant attitude of thinkers towards intellectual activity was to glorify it insofar as (like aesthetic activity) it finds its satisfaction in itself, apart from any attention to the advantages it may procure. Most thinkers would have agreed with Plato's famous hymn to geometry, where that discipline is venerated more than all others because for him it represents the type of speculative thought which brings in nothing material; and with Renan's verdict which declares that the man who loves science for its fruits commits the worst of blasphemies against that divinity. By this standard of values the "clerks" put before the laymen the spectacle of a class of men for whom the value of life lies in its disinterestedness, and they acted as a check on—or at least shamed—the laymen's practical passions. The modern "clerks" have violently torn up this charter. They proclaim that intellectual functions are only respectable to the extent that they are bound up with the pursuit of a concrete advantage, and that the intelligence which takes no interest in its objects is a contemptible activity. They teach that the superior form of the intelligence is that which thrusts its roots into "the vital urge," occupied in discovering what is most valuable in securing our existence. In historical science especially, they honour the intelligence which labours under the guidance of political interests, and they are completely disdainful of all efforts towards "objectivity." Elsewhere they assert that the intelligence to be venerated is that which limits its activities within the bounds of national interests and social order, while the intelligence which allows itself to be guided by the desire for truth alone, apart from any concern with the demands of society, is merely a "savage and brutal" activity, which "dishonours the highest of human faculties." Let me also point out their devotion to the doctrine (Bergson, Sorel) which says that science has a purely utilitarian origin—the necessity of man to dominate matter, "knowledge is adaptation"; and their scorn for the beautiful Greek conception which made science bloom from the desire to play, the perfect type of disinterested activity. And then they teach men that to accept an error which is of service to them (the "myth") is an undertaking which does them honour, while it is shameful to admit a truth which harms them. In other words, as Nietzsche, Barrès, and Sorel plainly put it, sensibility to truth in itself apart from any practical aim is a somewhat contemptible form of mind. Here the modern "clerk" positively displays genius in his defence of the material, since the material has nothing to do with the truth, or rather to speak more truly—has no worse enemy. . . .

For half a century, such has been the attitude of men whose function is to thwart the realism of nations, and who have laboured to excite it with all their power and with complete decision of purpose. For this reason I dare to call this attitude "The Great Betrayal." If I look for its causes, I see profound causes which forbid me to look upon this movement as a mere fashion, to which the contrary movement might succeed tomorrow.

One of the principal causes is that the modern world has made the "clerk" into a citizen, subject to all the responsibilities of a citizen, and consequently to despise lay passions is far more difficult for him than for his predecessors. If he is reproached for not looking upon national quarrels with the noble serenity of Descartes and Goethe, the "clerk" may well retort that his nation claps a soldier's pack on his back if she is insulted, and crushes him with taxes even if she is victorious. If shame is cried upon him because he does not rise superior to social hatreds, he will point out that the day of enlightened patronage is over, that today he has to earn his living, and that it is not his fault if he is eager to support the class which takes a pleasure in his productions. No doubt this explanation is not valid for the true "clerk," who submits to the laws of his State without allowing them to injure his soul. He renders unto Caesar the things that are Caesar's, i.e. his life perhaps, but nothing more. The true "clerk" is Vauvenargues, Lamarck, Fresnel, who never imbibed national patriotism although they perfectly performed their patriotic duty; he is Spinoza, Schiller, Baudelaire, César Franck, who were never diverted from single-hearted adoration of the Beautiful and the Divine by the necessity of earning their daily bread. But such "clerks" are inevitably rare. So much contempt for suffering is not the law of human nature even among the "clerks"; the law is that the living creature condemned to struggle for life turns to practical passions, and thence to the sanctifying of those passions. The "clerk's" new faith is to a great extent a result of the social conditions imposed upon him, and the real evil to deplore is perhaps not so much the "great betrayal" of the "clerks" as the disappearance of the "clerks," the impossibility of leading the life of a "clerk" in the world of today. One of the gravest responsibilities of the modern State is that it has not maintained (but could it do so?) a class of men exempt from civic duties, men whose sole function is to maintain non-practical values. Renan's prophecy is verified; he foretold the inevitable degradation of a society where every member was forced to discharge worldly tasks, although Renan himself was the very type of those whom such servitude would never have prevented—in the phrase of one of his peers—"from breathing only in the direction of Heaven."

It would be very unjust to explain the existence of national passion in the modern "clerk" by self-interest alone. This is also to be explained, and in a more simple manner, by the love, the impulse which naturally inspires every man to love the group from which he derives, more than the other groups which share the earth. There again, it may be argued that the "clerk's" new faith is caused by the changes of the nineteenth century, which by giving national groups a consistency hitherto unknown furnishes food to a passion which in many countries before that period could have been little more than potential. Obviously, attachment to the world of the spirit alone was easier for those who were capable of it when there were no nations to love. And, in fact, it is most suggestive to notice that the true appearance of the "clerk" coincides with the fall of the Roman Empire, i.e. with the time when the great nation collapsed and the little nations had not yet come into existence. It is equally suggestive to notice that the age of the great lovers of spiritual things, the age of Thomas Aquinas, Roger Bacon, Galilei, Erasmus, was the age when most of Europe was in a state of chaos and the nations were unknown; that the regions where pure speculation endured longest seem to be Germany and Italy, i.e. the regions which were the last to be nationalized; and practically ceased to produce pure speculation from the moment when they became nations. Of course, here again the vicissitudes of the world of sense do not affect the true "clerk." The misfortunes of their country, and even its triumphs, did not prevent Einstein and Nietzsche from feeling no passion but the passion for thought. When Jules Lemaître exclaimed that the wound of Sedan made him lose his reason, Renan replied that he perfectly retained his, and that a true priest of the mind could only be wounded in other than earthly *interests*.

In the cases I have just mentioned, the "clerk's" devotion to his nation or class is sincere, whether it is from interest or from love. I admit I think this sincerity is infrequent. The practice of the life of the spirit seems to me to lead inevitably to universalism, to the feeling of the eternal, to a lack of vigour in the belief in worldly conventions. The sincerity of national passion especially, in men of letters particularly, seems to me to assume the virtue of naiveté, which everyone will admit is not characteristic of this body of men, apart from their own self-esteem. It will also be hard to convince me that the motives of their public attitudes in artists are such simple things as the desire to live and to eat. I therefore seek—and find—other reasons for the realism of the modern "clerk," and these, although less natural, are none the less profound. They seem to me particularly valid for men of letters, especially in France, the country where the attitude of writers in the past half century differs most from that of their fathers.

First of all, I see the interests of their careers. It is an obvious fact that during the past two centuries most of the men of letters who have attained wide fame in France assumed a political attitude—for instance, Voltaire, Diderot, Chateaubriand, Lamartine, Victor Hugo, Anatole France, Barrès. With some of them, real fame dates from the moment when they assumed that attitude. This law has not escaped the attention of their descendants, and it may be said today that every French writer who desires wide fame (which means every writer endowed with the real temperament of a man of letters) also desires inevitably to play a political part. This desire may arise from other motives. For instance, in Barrès and d'Annunzio, from the desire "to act," to be something more than "men at a desk," to lead a life like that of the "heroes" and not like that of "scribes"; or, more ingenuously, as no doubt happened with Renan when he stood as a Parliamentary candidate, from the idea that he could perform a public service. Let me add that the modern writer's desire to be a political man is excused by the fact that the position is to some extent offered him by public opinion, whereas the compatriots of Racine and La Bruyère would have laughed in their faces if they had thought of publishing their views on the advisability of the war with Holland or the legality of Chambres de réunion. There again, it was easier to be a true "clerk" in the past than today.

These observations explain why the contemporary French writer so frequently desires to assume a political attitude, but they do not explain why this attitude is so inevitably in support of arbitrary authority. Liberalism is also a political attitude; and the least which can be said is that the modern French "clerk" has very seldom adopted it in the past twenty years. Another factor comes in here. That is the practical writer's desire to please the bourgeoisie, who are the creators of fame and the source of honours. It may even be argued that for this sort of writer the necessity to treat the passions of this class with deference is greater than ever, if I may judge by the fate of those who in recent times have dared to defy them, i.e. Zola, Romain Rolland. Now, the bourgeoisie of today, terrified by the progress of the opposing class, solely anxious to retain the privileges which are left them, feel nothing but aversion from liberal dogmas; and the man of letters who displays any political flag is bound to wave the flag of "Order" if he wishes to obtain favours. The case of Barrès is particularly instructive from this point of view. He began as a great intellectual sceptic, and his material star waxed a hundredfold greater, at least in his own country, on the day when he made himself the apostle of "necessary prejudices." This sort of thing makes me believe that the present political fashion of French writers is going to last a long time. A phenomenon which is caused by the uneasiness of the French bourgeoisie does not seem likely to disappear quickly. . . .

To come back to the modern writer and the causes for his political attitude—I shall add that he is not only in the service of a bourgeoisie which is in a state of anxiety, but that he himself has become more and more of a bourgeois, endowed with all the social position and respect which belong to that caste. The Bohemian man of letters has practically disappeared, at least among those who engage public interest. Consequently, he has more and more come to possess the bourgeois form of soul, one of whose most conspicuous characteristics is an affectation of the political feelings of the aristocracy—an attachment to systems of arbitrary authority, to military and priestly institutions, a scorn for societies founded upon justice, upon civic equality, a cult for the past, etc. . . . How many writers in France during the past fifty years, men whose names are on everyone's lips, obviously think they are ennobling themselves by expressing disgust for democratic institutions! In the same way I explain the adoption by many of them of harshness and cruelty, which they think are also attributes of the souls of the nobility.

The reasons I have just mentioned for the new political attitude of men of letters arise from the changes in their social status. Those I am about to mention arise from changes in the structure of their minds, in their literary desires, in their aesthetic cults, in their morality. These reasons seem to me even more worthy of the historian's attentions than those which have gone before.

First of all, we have their Romanticism, taking that word to mean the desire which arose in the writers of the nineteenth century (but which has become greatly perfected in the last thirty years) to treat themes which lend themselves in a literary manner to striking attitudes. About 1890 the men of letters, especially in France and Italy, realized with astonishing astuteness that the doctrines of arbitrary authority, discipline, tradition, contempt for the spirit of liberty, assertion of the morality of war and slavery, were opportunities for haughty and rigid poses infinitely more likely to strike the imagination of simple souls than the sentimentalities of Liberalism and Humanitarianism. And as a matter of fact, the so-called reactionary doctrines do lend themselves to a pessimistic and contemptuous Romanticism which makes a far deeper impression on the common herd than enthusiastic and optimistic Romanticism. . . .

There is another transformation of the literary soul in men of letters, wherein I think I see a cause of their new political creed. This is, that recently the only one of their faculties they venerate is their artistic sensibility, on which to some extent they base all their judgments. Until the last thirty years it may be said that men of letters, at least in Latin Europe, disciples in this of the Greeks, were determined in their judgments—even their literary judgments—far more by their sensibility to reason than by their artistic sensibility, whereof moreover they were scarcely conscious as something distinct from the former. . . . This great change affected their political attitudes. Obviously, as soon as we think things are good only insofar as they content our artistic needs, the only good political systems are those of arbitrary authority. Artistic sensibility is far more gratified by a system which tends to the realization of force and grandeur than by a system which tends to the establishment of justice, for the characteristic of artistic sensibility is the love of concrete realities and the repugnance for abstract conceptions and conceptions of pure reason, the model of which is the idea of justice. Artistic sensibility is especially flattered by the spectacle of a mass of units which are subordinated to each other up to the final head who dominates them all, whereas the spectacle of a democracy, which is a mass of units *where no one is first,* deprives this sensibility of one of its fundamental needs. Add to this that every doctrine which honours Man in the universal, in what is common to all men, is a personal injury to the artist, whose characteristic (at least since Romanticism) is precisely to set himself up as an exceptional being. Add also the sovereignty the artist now attributes to his desires and their satisfaction (the "rights of genius") and, consequently, his natural hatred for systems which limit each person's liberty of action by that of others. . . .

This attitude also seems to me to result from the decline of the study of classical literature in the formation of their minds. The humanities, as the word implies, have always taught the cult of humanity in its universal aspect, at least since the time of the Portico. The decline of Graeco-Roman culture in Barrès and his literary generation, in comparison with that of Taine, Renan, Hugo, Michelet, even Anatole France and Bourget, is undeniable. Still less will it be denied that this decline is considerably more noticeable in Barrès's successors. However, this decline does not prevent these writers from extolling classical studies, but they do not do this with the idea of reviving the cult for what is human in its universal aspect, but on the contrary to strengthen the "French" mind, or at least the "Latin" mind, in the grasp of its own roots, in consciousness of itself as distinct from other minds. . . .

Let me recapitulate the causes for this change in the "clerks": The imposition of political interests on all men without any exception; the growth of consistency in matters apt to feed realist passions; the desire and the possibility for men of letters to play a political part; the need in the interests of their own fame for them to play the game of a class which is daily becoming more anxious; the increasing tendency of the "clerks" to become bourgeois and to take on the vanities of that class; the perfecting of their

Romanticism; the decline of their knowledge of antiquity and of their intellectual discipline. It will be seen that these causes arise from certain phenomena which are most profoundly and generally characteristic of the present age. The political realism of the "clerks," far from being a superficial fact due to the caprice of an order of men, seems to me bound up with the very essence of the modern world.

26. Simone Weil, *Letters on the Factory* and *Metaxu*

The brief career of Simone Weil (1909–43) represents a singular response to the political urgency of the 1930s and the opening years of the war.

Born in Paris into an upper-middle-class assimilated Jewish family, Weil distinguished herself early at the educational institutions, including the Ecole Normale Supérieure, which typically form France's intellectuals. She gravitated to left-wing politics as a student but, while apparently considering herself a communist, never joined the Communist party. The years of her first assignments as philosophy instructor at *lycées* in a variety of provincial towns coincided with the arrival of the Depression in France, and Weil became deeply immersed in trade unionism.

By 1934, Weil's activism began to lose its explicitly political character and to take on a quality of devoted secular saintliness that was to become her most characteristic stance. She felt a principled need for self-deprivation as a way of identifying with and honoring the suffering that had always been the lot of the lowest in society and that in her own day was borne primarily by the proletariat. Taking a year's leave of absence from teaching, she worked as an unskilled laborer in several factories in the Paris region, including an electrical company, an iron foundry, and the Renault automobile plant—work for which her frail health made her particularly unsuited. She used her first-hand knowledge of the factory in her book *La Condition ouvrière*. In 1940 Weil left Paris for the unoccupied zone in the south of France where she harvested grapes and developed her spirituality under the guidance of Father Perrin, a Dominican priest. She stopped short of baptism into the Catholic Church, just as she had earlier stopped short of membership in the Communist party.

In 1942, Weil arrived in London to volunteer her services to the French Resistance. She had hoped to be sent on a dangerous mission and was bitterly disappointed to find that her assignment was intellectual work. While in London she wrote her most famous book, *The Need for Roots,* addressed to her compatriots in occupied France and intended to reaffirm their will to regain control over their country. At the same time, her sense of personal accountability intensified boundlessly. Believing herself entitled only to an amount of food equal to the rations of the French civilian population, she ate little. Then, falling ill, she felt uneasy about eating at all, for she was contributing nothing to the British war effort. In 1943 at the age of thirty-four, Weil died in a nursing home in Kent of a lung ailment complicated by voluntary malnutrition. Her character, as the American critic Elizabeth Hardwick has written, was one of "spectacular, in many ways exemplary abnormality."[1]

The first selection below is a letter written by Weil, during her year of factory labor, to Mme Albertine Thévenon, the wife of a prominent trade unionist in the industrial town of St. Etienne. The second letter was written by Weil the following year, when she had returned to teaching but participated in activities at a local factory and corresponded with its manager, Monsieur B.; appended to the letter is the article by Weil which Monsieur B. refused to publish in the factory newspaper. The final selection comes from the notebooks Weil kept in the early 1940s at the time of her near-conversion to Catholicism. Combining her wide learning with her newfound religiosity, she seems to have subsumed the political in the transcendental.

To Mme Albertine Thévenon, January 1935

Dear Albertine,

I am obliged to rest because of a slight illness (a touch of inflammation of the ear—nothing serious) so I seize the opportunity for a little talk with you. In a normal working week it is difficult to make any effort beyond what I am compelled to make. But that's not the only reason I haven't written; it's also the number of things there are to tell and the impossibility of telling the essential. Perhaps later on I shall find the right words, but at present it seems to me that I should need a new language to convey what needs to be said. Although this experience is in many ways what I expected it to be, there is also an abysmal difference: it is reality and no longer imagination. It is not that it has changed one or the other of my ideas (on the contrary, it has confirmed many of them), but infinitely more—it has changed my whole view of things, even my very feeling about life. I shall

---

1. Elizabeth Hardwick, "Simone Weil," in *Bartleby in Manhattan and Other Essays* (New York, 1983), p. 158.

From Simone Weil, *Seventy Letters*, translated and edited by Richard Rees (London: Oxford University Press, 1965), pp. 14–17, 23–30. Reprinted by permission of Editions Gallimard.

know joy again in the future, but there is a certain lightness of heart which, it seems to me, will never again be possible. But that's enough about it: to try to express the inexpressible is to degrade it.

As regards the things that can be expressed, I have learnt quite a lot about the organization of a firm. It is inhuman; work broken down into small processes, and paid by the piece; relations between different units of the firm and different work processes organized in a purely bureaucratic way. One's attention has nothing worthy to engage it, but on the contrary is constrained to fix itself, second by second, upon the same trivial problem, with only such variants as speeding up your output from 6 minutes to 5 for 50 pieces, or something of that sort. Thank heaven, there are manual skills to be acquired, which from time to time lends some interest to this pursuit of speed. But what I ask myself is how can all this be humanized; because if the separate processes were not paid by the piece the boredom they engender would inhibit attention and slow down the work considerably, and produce a lot of spoiled pieces. And if the processes were not subdivided. . . . But I have no time to go into all this by letter. Only when I think that the great Bolshevik leaders proposed to create a *free* working class and that doubtless none of them—certainly not Trotsky, and I don't think Lenin either—had even set foot inside a factory, so that they hadn't the faintest idea of the real conditions which make servitude or freedom for the workers—well, politics appears to me a sinister farce.

I must point out that all I have said refers to unskilled labour. About skilled labour I have almost everything still to learn. It will come, I hope.

To speak frankly, for me this life is pretty hard. And the more so because my headaches have not been obliging enough to withdraw so as to make things easier—and working among machines with a headache is painful. It is only on Saturday afternoon and Sunday that I can breathe, and find myself again, and recover the ability to turn over a few thoughts in my head. In a general way, the temptation to give up thinking altogether is the most difficult one to resist in a life like this: one feels so clearly that it is the only way to stop suffering! First of all, to stop suffering morally. Because the situation itself automatically banishes rebellious feelings: to work with irritation would be to work badly and so condemn oneself to starvation; and leaving aside the work, there is no person to be a target for one's irritation. One dare not be insolent to the foremen and, moreover, they very often don't even make one want to be. So one is left with no possible feeling about one's own fate except sadness. And thus one is tempted to cease, purely and simply, from being conscious of anything except the sordid daily round of life. And physically too it is a great temptation to lapse into semi-somnolence outside working hours. I have the greatest respect for workmen who manage to educate themselves. It is true they are usually tough; but all the same it must require a lot of stamina. And it is becoming more and more unusual with the advance of rationalization. I wonder if it is the same with skilled workers.

I am sticking it, in spite of everything. And I don't for one moment regret having embarked on the experience. Quite the contrary, I am infinitely thankful whenever I think of it. But curiously enough I don't often think of it. My capacity for adaptation is almost unlimited, so that I am able to forget that I am a "qualified lecturer" on tour in the working class, and to live my present life as though I had always been destined for it (which is true enough in a sense), and as though it would last for ever and was imposed on me by ineluctable necessity instead of my own free choice.

But I promise you that when I can't stick it any longer I'll go and rest somewhere—perhaps with you. . . .

I perceive I haven't said anything about my fellow workers. It will be for another time. But once again, it is hard to express. . . . They are nice, very nice. But as for real fraternity, I have hardly felt any. With one exception: the storekeeper in the tool-shop, a skilled worker and extremely competent, whom I appeal to whenever I am in despair over a job which I cannot manage properly, because he is a hundred times nicer and more intelligent than the machine-setters (who are not skilled workers). There is a lot of jealousy among the women—who are indeed obliged by the organization of the factory to compete with one another. I only know 3 or 4 who are entirely sympathetic. As for the men, some of them seem to be very nice types. But there aren't many of them in the shop where I work, apart from the machine-setters, who are not real comrades. I hope to be moved to another shop after a time, so as to enlarge my experience. . . .

Well, au revoir. Write soon.

S.W.

To Monsieur B., Bourges, 13 January 1936

Monsieur,

I cannot say I was surprised by your reply. I hoped for a different one, but without counting on it too much.

I won't try to defend the article which you have refused. If you were a Catholic I could not resist the temptation to show that its spirit, which shocked you, is purely and simply the Christian spirit; I don't think it would be difficult. But there are no grounds for using that argument with you. And anyway I don't want to argue. You are the boss and cannot be called to account for your decisions.

I only want to say that I deliberately and with intention developed the "tendency" which you found unacceptable. You told me—I repeat your own words—that it is very difficult to raise the workers. The first principle of education is that in order to "raise" anyone, whether infant or adult, one must begin by raising him in his own eyes. And this is a hundred times truer still when the chief obstacle to his development is the humiliating conditions of his life.

For me, this fact is the point of departure for any useful action affecting the mass of people, and especially the factory workers. And I understand, of course, that it is precisely this point of departure that you don't admit. In the hope of bringing you to do so, and because you control the fate of eight hundred workmen, I forced myself to tell you without reticence the feelings which my own experience had impressed on me. It was a painful effort to tell you some of those things which one can hardly bear to tell one's equals and which it is intolerable to speak of to a superior. It seemed to me that you were touched. But no doubt it was a mistake to hope that an hour's interview can counteract the pressure of daily routine. To put themselves in the place of those who obey is not easy for those who command.

In my eyes, the essential point of my collaboration in your paper was this: that my experience last year may perhaps enable me to write in such a way as to alleviate a little the weight of humiliations which life inflicts every day upon the workers at R., as upon the workers in all modern factories. That is not the only purpose but it is, I am convinced, the essential condition for widening their horizon. Nothing is more paralysing to thought than the sense of inferiority which is necessarily induced by the daily assault of poverty, subordination, and dependence. The first thing to be done for them is to help them to recover or retain, as the case may be, their sense of dignity. I know too well how difficult it is, in such conditions, to retain that sense, and how precious any moral support can be. I hoped with all my heart that by collaborating in your paper I might be able to give a little support of this kind to the workers at R.

I don't think you have a clear idea of exactly what class feeling is. In my opinion, it can hardly be stimulated by mere words, whether spoken or written. It is determined by actual conditions of life. What stimulates it is the infliction of humiliation and suffering, and the fact of subordination; but it is continually repressed by the inexorable daily pressure of need, and often to the point where, in the weaker characters, it turns into servility. Apart from exceptional moments which, I think, can neither be induced nor prevented, nor even foreseen, the pressure of need is always more than strong enough to maintain order; for the relations of power are all too obvious. But from the point of view of the moral health of the workers, the continual repression of class feeling—which to some extent is always secretly smouldering—is almost everywhere being carried much too far. To give an occasional outlet to this feeling—without demagogy, of course—

would not be to excite it but on the contrary to soften its bitterness. For the unfortunate, their social inferiority is infinitely harder to bear for the reason that they see it everywhere treated as something that goes without saying.

Above all, I don't see how an article like mine could have a bad effect when published in your own paper. In any other paper an article of that kind might just conceivably seem to be setting the poor against the rich, the rank and file against the leaders; but, appearing in a paper controlled by you, such an article can only give the workers the feeling that an approach is being made to them, that someone is trying to understand them. I think they would be grateful to you. I am convinced that if the workers at R. could find in your paper articles really conceived for them, in which their susceptibilities were scrupulously respected (for the unfortunate have keen susceptibilities, though mute), and which concentrated upon whatever can raise them in their own eyes, nothing but good would come of it, from every point of view.

On the other hand, what might exacerbate class feeling is the use of unfortunate expressions which by an effect of unconscious cruelty emphasize implicitly the social inferiority of the readers. There are many such unfortunate expressions in previous numbers of your paper. I will point them out if you like at our next meeting. Perhaps no one can possess tact in dealing with these people when he has been too long in a position too different from theirs.

Apart from all this, however, the reasons you give for rejecting my two suggestions may well be perfectly sound. And anyway it is a relatively minor question.

Thank you for sending the last numbers of the paper.

If you are still disposed to take me on as a worker, I won't come to see you at R., for the reason I gave. But I have grounds for thinking that your views have changed. To be successful, an arrangement of the kind requires a very high degree of mutual confidence and understanding.

If you are no longer disposed to take me on, or if Monsieur M. is against it, I will certainly come to R., since you are good enough to authorize it, as soon as I have time. I will let you know in advance.

Sincerely yours,
S. Weil

An Appeal to the Workers at R.

Dear unknown friends who are toiling in the R. workshops, I have an appeal to make to you. I want to ask you to collaborate in *Entre Nous*.

We don't want any more work, you'll say; we have enough on our plates already.

Of course you are right. Nevertheless I am asking you, please, to take pen and paper and say something about your work.

Don't protest. I know quite well: at the end of eight hours you're fed up, you've had it right up to there—to use two expressions which have the merit of saying forcibly what they mean. All you ask is not to have to think about the factory until tomorrow morning. It is a perfectly natural state of mind, which it is right to indulge. In that state of mind, the best thing is to relax: talk with friends, read something light, have a drink and a card game, play with the children.

But aren't there also some days when you find it oppressive never to be able to say what you feel but always to keep it to yourself? It is to those who know that oppressive feeling that my appeal is made. Perhaps some of you have never felt it. But when you do feel it you really suffer.

In the factory, all you have to do is to obey orders, and produce work which conforms to prescribed standards, and collect your money on pay-day according to the piece-rates in force. But in addition to this you are men—you toil and suffer, and also have moments of happiness, and perhaps a pleasant hour or so; sometimes everything goes quite nicely, at other times the work is a painful effort; some of the time you are interested, at other times bored. But nobody around you can pay attention to all that; and you can't even let it make any difference to yourself. All you are asked for is work, all you get is the rate.

All this becomes depressing sometimes, doesn't it? One feels like a mere machine for turning out parts of stoves.

But such are the conditions of work in industry. It is nobody's fault. Perhaps some of you can adapt to it all quite easily. It depends on one's temperament. But there are people who find that sort of thing hard to take; and for people of that type the state of affairs is really too unpleasant.

I would like *Entre Nous* to be used for an attempt to improve the situation a bit, if you will consent to help me.

This is what I ask you to do. If it happens some evening, or some Sunday, that you suddenly feel you don't want to go on bottling up your feelings for ever, take a pen and some paper. Don't try for fine-sounding phrases. Use the first words that come. And say what you feel about your work.

Say if the work makes you suffer. Describe the suffering, moral as well as physical. Say if there are times when you can't bear it; if there are times when the monotony of the work sickens you; if you hate being always driven by the need to work fast; if you hate being always at the orders of the overseers.

And say also if you sometimes enjoy the work and feel pride in labour accomplished. And if you manage to take an interest in your job, and if there are days when you have the pleasant feeling of working fast and earning good money. Or if you are sometimes able to work for hours like a machine, almost unconsciously, thinking of other things and losing your-self in pleasant dreams. Or if you sometimes feel glad to have nothing to do except carry out the work you are given, without having to worry your head.

Say, in a general way, if you find time goes slowly in the factory or if it seems to fly. Perhaps it's different on different days. If so, try to decide exactly what makes the difference. Say if you are full of beans when you come to work, or if you start every morning with the thought: "Roll on, Saturday!" Say if you're cheerful when you clock out, or if you're dead beat, worn out, stunned by the day's work.

And finally, say if you feel sustained in the factory by the cheerful feel-ing that you are among comrades, or if on the contrary you feel lonely.

Above all, say whatever comes into your mind, whatever is weighing on your heart.

And when you've finished writing, there's no need whatever to sign it. Try rather to do it so that no one can guess who you are.

Or even, since there may still be a risk, take a further precaution if you care to. Instead of sending what you write to *Entre Nous,* send it to me. I will copy your articles out again for *Entre Nous,* in such a way that nobody can be recognized in them. I will cut one article into several pieces, and sometimes put together pieces from different articles. As for any impru-dent words, I will fix it so that no one can even tell from which workshop they come. And if there are any remarks which I feel it would be dangerous for you to publish even with all these precautions, I will leave them out. You can be sure I will be very careful. I know what the position of a worker in a factory is. I wouldn't for anything in the world be responsible for bring-ing trouble on any of you.

In this way you will be able to express yourselves freely, without need-ing to be careful what you say. You don't know me, but you feel, do you not, that my only wish is to be of use to you and that for nothing in the world would I bring harm on you? I have no connexion with the manufacture of stoves. My only interest is in the physical and moral well-being of those who manufacture them.

Be quite sincere. Don't minimize or exaggerate anything, whether good or bad. I believe you will find a certain relief in speaking the unadulterated truth.

Your comrades will read you. If they feel the same as you they will be glad to see in print some things which they may have felt in their hearts but been unable to express; or perhaps some things which they could have ex-pressed but forced themselves not to. If they feel differently, they will write to explain what they do feel. Either way, you will get to know more about one another. This can only make for more comradeship, which is already a great gain.

The managers will also read you. Perhaps they won't always like what they read. That doesn't matter. It will do them no harm to hear some unpleasant truths.

They will understand you better after reading you. Very often a manager who is at bottom a good man appears hard, simply because he doesn't understand. Human nature is like that. Men never know how to see things from one another's point of view.

Perhaps they will find ways of remedying, at least partially, some of the troubles you have described. These managers of yours show a great deal of ingenuity in manufacturing stoves; who knows if they mightn't also show it in organizing more humane conditions of work? They certainly don't lack goodwill. The best proof of that is the appearance of these lines in *Entre Nous*.

Unfortunately, their goodwill does not suffice. The difficulties are enormous. To begin with, the ruthless law of profit weighs upon the managers as it does upon you; it weighs with inhuman force upon the whole life of industry. One can't get round it. So long as it exists, one can only submit. All one can do in the meantime is to attempt to get round difficulties by ingenuity, trying to find the most humane organization that is compatible with a given rate of profit.

But this is the big snag: you are the ones who suffer the burden of the industrial régime, but it is not you who can solve or even state the problems of organization. That is the responsibility of the managers. And the managers, like all men, see things from their own point of view, and not from yours. They don't really know how you live. They know nothing of your thoughts. Even those of them who were once workmen themselves have forgotten a great deal.

By the scheme I am proposing you might perhaps be able to make them understand what at present they don't; and you could do it without risk or loss of self-respect. And perhaps they in turn will make use of *Entre Nous* to reply. Perhaps they will explain the inevitable difficulties which the organization of industry imposes on them.

Large-scale industry is what it is. The least one can say is that it imposes harsh living conditions. But neither you nor the employers will be able to change it in the near future.

In the circumstances, this would be the ideal solution, as I see it. The managers should understand exactly what is the life of the men they employ as hands. And their chief concern should be, not to be always trying to increase profit to the maximum, but to organize the most humane conditions of work that are compatible with whatever rate of profit is essential for the factory's existence.

The workers, on the other hand, should know and understand the necessities which control the factory's existence and their life in it. They would then be in a position to judge and appreciate the managers' goodwill. They would lose the sense of being always at the mercy of arbitrary commands, and the inevitable hardships would perhaps become less bitter to endure.

Needless to say, this ideal is unrealizable. Day-to-day preoccupations weigh much too heavily on both sides. Moreover, the relation of chief to subordinate is one which does not facilitate mutual understanding. One never fully understands the people one gives orders to. One never fully understands the people from whom one gets them.

Nevertheless, it may be possible to approach a little nearer to this ideal. It depends on you now to make the attempt. Even if your little articles don't lead to any serious practical improvements, you will always have had the satisfaction of saying for once what you really think.

So that's agreed, isn't it? I hope I shall soon receive a great many articles.

I cannot end without sincerest thanks to M. B. for having been willing to publish this appeal.

Metaxu

All created things refuse to be for me as ends. Such is God's extreme mercy toward me. And that very thing is what constitutes evil. Evil is the form which God's mercy takes in this world.

This world is the closed door. It is a barrier. And at the same time it is the way through.

Two prisoners whose cells adjoin communicate with each other by knocking on the wall. The wall is the thing which separates them but it is also their means of communication. It is the same with us and God. Every separation is a link.

By putting all our desire for good into a thing, we make that thing a condition of our existence. But we do not, on that account, make of it a good. Merely to exist is not enough for us.

The essence of created things is to be intermediaries. They are intermediaries leading from one to the other, and there is no end to this. They are intermediaries leading to God. We have to experience them as such.

From Simone Weil, *Gravity and Grace* (New York: G. P. Putnam's Sons, 1952), pp. 200–203; ©1952, 1980 by G. P. Putnam's Sons. Reprinted by permission of the Putnam Publishing Group and Routledge & Kegan Paul.

The bridges of the Greeks. We have inherited them but we do not know how to use them. We thought they were intended to have houses built upon them. We have erected skyscrapers on them to which we ceaselessly add stories. We no longer know that they are bridges, things made so that we may pass along them, and that by passing along them we go toward God.

Only he who loves God with a supernatural love can look upon means simply as means.

Power (and money, power's master key) is a means at its purest. For that very reason it is the supreme end for all those who have not understood.

This world, the realm of necessity, offers us absolutely nothing except means. Our will is forever sent from one means to another like a billiard ball.

All our desires are contradictory, like the desire for food. I want the person I love to love me. If, however, he is totally devoted to me he does not exist any longer and I cease to love him. And as long as he is not totally devoted to me he does not love me enough. Hunger and repletion.

Desire is evil and illusory, yet without desire we should not seek for that which is truly absolute, truly boundless. We have to have experienced it. Misery of those beings from whom fatigue takes away that supplementary energy which is the source of desire.

Misery also of those who are blinded by desire.

We have to fix our desire to the axis of the poles.

What is it a sacrilege to destroy? Not that which is base, for that is of no importance. Not that which is high, for, even should we want to, we cannot touch that. The *metaxu*. The *metaxu* form the region of good and evil.

No human being should be deprived of his *metaxu*, that is to say of those relative and mixed blessings (home, country, traditions, culture, etc.) which warm and nourish the soul and without which, short of saint-hood, a *human* life is not possible.

The true earthly blessings are *metaxu*. We can respect those of others only in so far as we regard those we ourselves possess as *metaxu*. This implies that we are already making our way toward the point where it is possible to do without them. For example, if we are to respect foreign countries, we must make of our own country not an idol, but a stepping-stone toward God.

All the faculties being freely exercised without becoming mixed, starting from a single, unique principle. It is the microcosm, the imitation of the world. Christ according to St. Thomas. The just man of the *Republic*. When Plato speaks of specialization he speaks of the specialization of man's faculties and not of the specialization of men; the same applies to hierarchy. The temporal having no meaning except by and for the spiritual, but not being mixed with the spiritual. Leading to it by nostalgia, by reaching beyond itself. It is the temporal seen as a bridge, a *metaxu*. It is the Greek and Provençal vocation.

Civilization of the Greeks. No adoration of force. The temporal was only a bridge. Among the states of the soul they did not seek intensity, but purity.

27. Arthur Koestler, *The God That Failed*

Arthur Koestler (1905–83) was born in Budapest of a Hungarian father and Austrian mother. He moved with his family to Vienna in 1919, where he was educated at the *Technische Hochschule*. In 1927 he was employed by the Ullstein newspaper chain in Berlin as a reporter to cover Near Eastern affairs. Eventually Koestler was named foreign editor of the *Berliner Zeitung am Mittag*.

Koestler joined the German Communist party in 1931. He left Berlin for Moscow in the summer of 1932, six months before Hitler came to power. After a year in Russia as an expatriate journalist and "guest" of Soviet literary authorities, Koestler joined the German Communist emigre community in Paris, whose leader was Willi Münzenburg. During 1936 Koestler worked as a pro-Republican journalist covering the Spanish civil war. Captured by nationalist forces and condemned to death, he was saved in May 1937 in a prisoner exchange sponsored by the International Red Cross. The experience, described in his *Spanish Testament* (1938), ultimately led him to abandon communism. His internment had convinced him "that man is a reality, mankind an abstraction; that men cannot be treated as units in operations of political arithmetic because they behave like the symbols for zero and the infinite, which dislocate all mathematical operations; that the end justifies the means only within very narrow limits; that ethics is not a function of social utility, and charity not a petty bourgeois sentiment but the gravitational force which keeps civilization in its orbit."[1]

1. Richard Crossman, ed., *The God That Failed* (New York, 1949), p. 68.

In October 1939 Koestler was imprisoned by French authorities, but was eventually released and joined the Foreign Legion in May 1940. He escaped to England after the fall of France. During World War II he worked at the British Ministry of Information and became a naturalized British citizen. Koestler's books, especially *Darkness at Noon* (1940), *Arrival and Departure* (1943), and *The Yogi and the Commissar* (1945), express his disillusionment with totalitarianism while offering insightful discussions of the conflict between morality and expediency and between means and ends in modern politics. Koestler's work also presents a commentary on the delusions of Communism's supporters in the 1930s and 1940s, many of whom, despairing of liberal democracy and Western values, sought refuge in Communism as a last bastion against fascist tyranny.

In the autobiographical commentary below, Koestler describes his experiences in joining the German Communist party. The essay was originally published in Richard Crossman's *The God That Failed*, a book which, according to Crossman, tried to explore "the state of mind of the Communist convert, and the atmosphere of the period—from 1917 to 1939—when conversion was so common." [2]

A faith is not acquired by reasoning. One does not fall in love with a woman, or enter the womb of a church, as a result of logical persuasion. Reason may defend an act of faith—but only after the act has been committed, and the man committed to the act. Persuasion may play a part in a man's conversion; but only the part of bringing to its full and conscious climax a process which has been maturing in regions where no persuasion can penetrate. A faith is not acquired; it grows like a tree. Its crown points to the sky; its roots grow downward into the past and are nourished by the dark sap of the ancestral humus.

From the psychologist's point of view, there is little difference between a revolutionary and a traditionalist faith. All true faith is uncompromising, radical, purist; hence the true traditionalist is always a revolutionary zealot in conflict with pharisaian society, with the lukewarm corrupters of the creed. And vice-versa: the revolutionary's Utopia, which in appearance represents a complete break with the past, is always modeled on some image of the lost Paradise, of a legendary Golden Age. The classless Communist society, according to Marx and Engels, was to be a revival, at the end of the

2. Ibid., p. 2.

From *The God That Failed*, edited by Richard Crossman (New York: Harper & Brothers, 1949), pp. 15–21, 41–55; ©1949 by Richard Crossman. Reprinted by permission of Harper & Row, Publishers, Inc., and A. D. Peters & Co. Ltd.

dialectical spiral, of the primitive Communist society which stood at its beginning. Thus all true faith involves a revolt against the believer's social environment, and the projection into the future of an ideal derived from the remote past. All Utopias are fed from the sources of mythology; the social engineer's blueprints are merely revised editions of the ancient text.

Devotion to pure Utopia, and revolt against a polluted society, are thus the two poles which provide the tension of all militant creeds. To ask which of the two makes the current flow—attraction by the ideal or repulsion by the social environment—is to ask the old question about the hen and the egg. To the psychiatrist, both the craving for Utopia and the rebellion against the status quo are symptoms of social maladjustment. To the social reformer, both are symptoms of a healthy rational attitude. The psychiatrist is apt to forget that smooth adjustment to a deformed society creates deformed individuals. The reformer is equally apt to forget that hatred, even of the objectively hateful, does not produce that charity and justice on which a utopian society must be based.

Thus each of the two attitudes, the sociologist's and the psychologist's, reflects a half-truth. It is true that the case-history of most revolutionaries and reformers reveals a neurotic conflict with family or society. But this only proves, to paraphrase Marx, that a moribund society creates its own morbid gravediggers.

It is also true that in the face of revolting injustice the only honorable attitude is to revolt, and to leave introspection for better times. But if we survey history and compare the lofty aims, in the name of which revolutions were started, and the sorry end to which they came, we see again and again how a polluted civilization pollutes its own revolutionary offspring.

Fitting the two half-truths—the sociologist's and the psychologist's—together, we conclude that if on the one hand oversensitivity to social injustice and obsessional craving for Utopia are signs of neurotic maladjustment, society may, on the other hand, reach a state of decay where the neurotic rebel causes more joy in heaven than the sane executive who orders pigs to be drowned under the eyes of starving men. This in fact was the state of our civilization when, in December, 1931, at the age of twenty-six, I joined the Communist Party of Germany.

I became converted because I was ripe for it and lived in a disintegrating society thirsting for faith. But the day when I was given my Party card was merely the climax of a development which had started long before I had read about the drowned pigs or heard the names of Marx and Lenin. Its roots reach back into childhood; and though each of us, comrades of the Pink Decade, had individual roots with different twists in them, we are products of, by and large, the same generation and cultural climate. It is this unity underlying diversity which makes me hope that my story is worth telling.

I was born in 1905 in Budapest; we lived there till 1919, when we moved to Vienna. Until the First World War we were comfortably off, a typical Continental middle-middle-class family: my father was the Hungarian representative of some old-established British and German textile manufacturers. In September, 1914, this form of existence, like so many others, came to an abrupt end; my father never found his feet again. He embarked on a number of ventures which became the more fantastic the more he lost self-confidence in a changed world. He opened a factory for radioactive soap; he backed several crank-inventions (everlasting electric bulbs, self-heating bed bricks and the like); and finally lost the remains of his capital in the Austrian inflation of the early 'twenties. I left home at twenty-one, and from that day became the only financial support of my parents.

At the age of nine, when our middle-class idyl collapsed, I had suddenly become conscious of the economic Facts of Life. As an only child, I continued to be pampered by my parents; but, well aware of the family crisis, and torn by pity for my father, who was of a generous and somewhat child-like disposition, I suffered a pang of guilt whenever they bought me books or toys. This continued later on, when every suit I bought for myself meant so much less to send home. Simultaneously, I developed a strong dislike of the obviously rich; not because they could afford to buy things (envy plays a much smaller part in social conflict than is generally assumed) but because they were able to do so without a guilty conscience. Thus I projected a personal predicament onto the structure of society at large.

It was certainly a tortuous way of acquiring a social conscience. But precisely because of the intimate nature of the conflict, the faith which grew out of it became an equally intimate part of my self. It did not, for some years, crystallize into a political creed; at first it took the form of a mawkishly sentimental attitude. Every contact with people poorer than myself was unbearable—the boy at school who had no gloves and red chilblains on his fingers, the former traveling salesman of my father's reduced to cadging occasional meals—all of them were additions to the load of guilt on my back. The analyst would have no difficulty in showing that the roots of this guilt-complex go deeper than the crisis in our household budget; but if he were to dig even deeper, piercing through the individual layers of the case, he would strike the archetypal pattern which has produced millions of particular variations on the same theme—"Woe, for they chant to the sound of harps and anoint themselves, but are not grieved for the affliction of the people."

Thus sensitized by a personal conflict, I was ripe for the shock of learning that wheat was burned, fruit artificially spoiled and pigs were drowned in the depression years to keep prices up and enable fat capitalists to chant to the sound of harps, while Europe trembled under the torn boots of hunger-marchers and my father hid his frayed cuffs under the table. The frayed cuffs and drowned pigs blended into one emotional explosion, as the fuse of the archetype was touched off. We sang the "Internationale," but the words might as well have been the older ones: "Woe to the shepherds who feed themselves, but feed not their flocks."

In other respects, too, the story is more typical than it seems. A considerable proportion of the middle classes in central Europe was, like ourselves, ruined by the inflation of the 'twenties. It was the beginning of Europe's decline. This disintegration of the middle strata of society started the fatal process of polarization which continues to this day. The pauperized bourgeois became rebels of the Right or Left; Schickelgrüber and Djugashwili shared about equally the benefits of the social migration. Those who refused to admit that they had become déclassé, who clung to the empty shell of gentility, joined the Nazis and found comfort in blaming their fate on Versailles and the Jews. Many did not even have that consolation; they lived on pointlessly, like a great black swarm of tired winterflies crawling over the dim windows of Europe, members of a class displaced by history.

The other half turned Left, thus confirming the prophecy of the "Communist Manifesto":

> Entire sections of the ruling classes are . . . precipitated into the proletariat, or are at least threatened in their conditions of existence. They . . . supply the proletariat with fresh elements of enlightenment and progress.

That "fresh element of enlightenment," I discovered to my delight, was I. As long as I had been nearly starving, I had regarded myself as a temporarily displaced offspring of the bourgeoisie. In 1931, when at last I had achieved a comfortable income, I found that it was time to join the ranks of the proletariat. But the irony of this sequence only occurred to me in retrospect.

> The bourgeois family will vanish as a matter of course with the vanishing of Capital. . . . The bourgeois claptrap about the family and education, about the haloed correlation of parent and child, becomes all the more disgusting the more, by the action of modern industry, all family ties among the proletarians are torn asunder. . . .

Thus the "Communist Manifesto." Every page of Marx, and even more of Engels, brought a new revelation, and an intellectual delight which I had only experienced once before, at my first contact with Freud. Torn from its context, the above passage sounds ridiculous; as part of a closed system which made social philosophy fall into a lucid and comprehensive pattern, the demonstration of the historical relativity of institutions and ideals—of family, class, patriotism, bourgeois morality, sexual taboos—had the intoxicating effect of a sudden liberation from the rusty chains with which a pre-1914 middle-class childhood had cluttered one's mind. Today, when Marxist philosophy has degenerated into a Byzantine cult and virtually every single tenet of the Marxist program has become twisted round into its opposite, it is difficult to recapture that mood of emotional fervor and intellectual bliss.

I was ripe to be converted, as a result of my personal case-history; thousands of other members of the intelligentsia and the middle classes of my generation were ripe for it, by virtue of other personal case-histories; but, however much these differed from case to case, they had a common denominator: the rapid disintegration of moral values, of the pre-1914 pattern of life in postwar Europe, and the simultaneous lure of the new revelation which had come from the East.

I joined the Party (which to this day remains "the" Party for all of us who once belonged to it) in 1931, at the beginning of that short-lived period of optimism, of that abortive spiritual renaissance, later known as the Pink Decade. The stars of that treacherous dawn were Barbusse, Romain Rolland, Gide and Malraux in France; Piscator, Becher, Renn, Brecht, Eisler, Säghers in Germany; Auden, Isherwood, Spender in England; Dos Passos, Upton Sinclair, Steinbeck in the United States. (Of course, not all of them were members of the Communist Party.) The cultural atmosphere was saturated with Progressive Writers' congresses, experimental theaters, committees for peace and against Fascism, societies for cultural relations with the USSR, Russian films and avant-garde magazines. It looked indeed as if the Western world, convulsed by the aftermath of war, scourged by inflation, depression, unemployment and the absence of a faith to live for, was at last going to

> Clear from the head the masses of impressive rubbish;
> Rally the lost and trembling forces of the will,
> Gather them up and let them loose upon the earth,
> Till they construct at last a human justice.

Auden

The new star of Bethlehem had risen in the East; and for a modest sum, Intourist was prepared to allow you a short and well-focused glimpse of the Promised Land. . . .

[Koestler describes his work at the Ullstein publishing firm in Berlin, as well as his initial involvement with the German Communist party, which he joined in December 1931. He lost his job in 1932.]

Having lost my job, I was at last free from all fetters of the bourgeois world. The lump sum which Ullstein's paid me I sent to my parents; it was enough to keep them going for two or three years, and thus free me from my obligation until after the victorious revolution and the dawn of the New Era. I retained, however, two hundred marks (about ten pounds or fifty dollars), to pay my fare to Soviet Russia if and when the Party gave me permission to emigrate. I gave up my flat in the expensive district of Neu Westend, and moved into an apartment house on Bonner Platz; it was mainly inhabited by penniless artists of radical views, and was known as the "Red Block." My three months there were the happiest time in my seven years as a member of the Party.

Now that I had lost my usefulness to the Apparat, there was no longer any objection to my joining a cell and leading the full life of a regular Party member. In actual fact, Edgar[3] had given me permission to join the cell of the Red Block, under my cover-name Ivan Steinberg, some time before I was fired by the Ullsteins. It had been a kind of reward for being a good boy and dictating those long reports to Paula. I then still lived in Neu Westend, miles away from Bonner Platz; so it was assumed that if I joined the Red Block cell nobody would guess the identity of Comrade Ivan Steinberg. It was one of the incredibly crass blunders of the Machiavellian Apparat; for, the Red Block being an artists' and writers' colony, the first time I turned up in the cell and was laconically introduced as "a new member—Comrade Ivan," half a dozen familiar faces grinned in welcome.

Having left Ullstein's, I no longer had any reason to keep my Party membership secret. In the Red Block I threw myself body and soul into the fraternal life of the cell. It had about twenty members and met regularly once or twice a week. Like all other Party cells, it was led by a "triangle": *Pol.-Leiter* ("political leader"), *Org.-Leiter* ("administrative organizer") and *Agit-Prop* (the member responsible for "agitation and propaganda"). Our *Pol.-Leiter* was Alfred Kantorowicz, now editor of a Soviet-sponsored literary magazine in Berlin. He was then about thirty, tall, gaunt, squinting, a free-lance critic and essayist and prospective author of the Novel of Our Time, which never saw the light. But he was an exceptionally warmhearted comrade and a self-sacrificing friend, and he had both dignity and a rich sense of humor; his only shortcoming was lack of moral courage. We remained friends all through the Paris emigré years; when I broke with the Party, he was the only one who did not spit at me. Now he is a literary

3. Edgar was the cover name for Koestler's liaison with the Communist party organization in Berlin.—ED.

bigwig under the Soviets—may his innocence and compliance protect him from ever getting caught in the snares of counter-revolutionary formalisms, bourgeois cosmopolitanism, neo-Kantian banditism, or just liberal depravity.

Our *Org.-Leiter* was Max Schröder, also a literateur who lived on the reputation he had earned with several remarkable poems published at the age of nineteen, that is to say fifteen years earlier. But he too was a good egg, the lovable type of Munich bohemian, who had found in his devotion to the Party a compensation for his literary, sexual, pecuniary, and other frustrations. The job of *Agitprop* fell to me soon after I had joined the cell; some of the leaflets and broadsheets I produced had, I still believe, a truly Jacobin pathos. Among other members of our cell I remember Dr. Wilhelm Reich, Founder and Director of the *Sex-Pol.* (Institute for Sexual Politics). He was a Freudian Marxist; inspired by Malinowski, he had just published a book called *The Function of the Orgasm,* in which he expounded the theory that the sexual frustration of the Proletariat caused a thwarting of its political consciousness; only through a full, uninhibited release of the sexual urge could the working-class realize its revolutionary potentialities and historic mission; the whole thing was less cock-eyed than it sounds. After the victory of Hitler, Reich published a brilliant psychological study of the Nazi mentality, which the Party condemned; he broke with Communism and is now director of a scientific research institute in the U.S.A. We also had two actors from an avant-garde theater called "The Mouse Trap"; several girls with vaguely intellectual ambitions; an insurance agent; young Ernst, son of our local fruit vendor, and several working men.

Half the activities of the cell were legal, half illegal. All our meetings started with a political lecture which was delivered either by the *Pol.-Leiter* after he had been briefed at the Party's District HQ, or by an instructor from Headquarters itself. The purpose of the lecture was to lay down the political line on the various questions of the day. During that fateful spring and summer of 1932, a series of elections took place which shook the country like a succession of earthquakes—the Presidential elections, two Reichstag elections, and an election for the Prussian Diet; all in all four red-hot election campaigns within eight months in a country on the verge of civil war. We participated in the campaigns by door-to-door canvassing, distributing Party literature and turning out leaflets of our own. The canvassing was the most arduous part of it; it was mostly done on Sunday mornings, when people were supposed to be at home. You rang the doorbell, wedged your foot between door and post and offered your pamphlets and leaflets, with a genial invitation to engage in a political discussion on the spot. In short, we sold the World Revolution like vacuum cleaners. Reactions were mostly unfriendly, rarely aggressive. I often had the door banged in my face but never a fight. However, we avoided ringing the bells of known Nazis. And the Nazis in and round our block were mostly known to us, just as we were all known to the Nazis, through our rival nets of cells and *Blockwarts*. The whole of Germany, town and countryside, was covered by those two elaborate and fine-meshed dragnets. I still believe that, without the wild jerks from Moscow which kept entangling our nets and tearing them from our hands, we would have had a fair chance to win. The idea, the readiness for sacrifice, the support of the masses were all there.

We lost the fight, because we were not fishermen, as we thought, but bait dangling from a hook. We did not realize this, because our brains had been reconditioned to accept any absurd line of action ordered from above as our innermost wish and conviction. We had refused to nominate a joint candidate with the Socialists for the Presidency, and when the Socialists backed Hindenburg as the lesser evil against Hitler, we nominated Thälmann though he had no chance whatsoever—except, maybe, to split off enough proletarian votes to bring Hitler immediately into power. Our instructor gave us a lecture proving that there was no such thing as a "lesser evil," that it was a philosophical, strategical and tactical fallacy; a Trotskyite, diversionist, liquidatorial and counter-revolutionary conception. Henceforth we had only pity and spite for those who as much as mentioned the ominous term; and, moreover, we were convinced that we had always been convinced that it was an invention of the devil. How could anybody fail to see that to have both legs amputated was better than trying to save one, and that the correct revolutionary policy was to kick the crippled Republic's crutches away? Faith is a wondrous thing; it is not only capable of moving mountains, but also of making you believe that a herring is a race horse.

Not only our thinking, but also our vocabulary was reconditioned. Certain words were taboo—for instance "lesser evil" or "spontaneous"; the latter because "spontaneous" manifestations of the revolutionary class-consciousness were part of Trotsky's theory of the Permanent Revolution. Other words and turns of phrase became favorite stock-in-trade. I mean not only the obvious words of Communist jargon like "the toiling masses"; but words like "concrete" or "sectarian" ("You must put your question into a more concrete form, Comrade"; "you are adopting a Left-sectarian attitude, Comrade"); and even such abstruse words as "herostratic." In one of his works Lenin had mentioned Herostratus, the Greek who burnt down a temple because he could think of no other way of achieving fame. Accordingly, one often heard and read phrases like "the criminally herostratic madness of the counter-revolutionary wreckers of the heroic efforts of the toiling masses in the Fatherland of the Proletariat to achieve the second Five Year Plan in four years."

According to their vocabulary and favorite clichés, you could smell out at once people with Trotskyite, Reformist, Brandlerite, Blanquist and other deviations. And vice versa, Communists betrayed themselves by their vocabulary to the police, and later to the Gestapo. I know of one girl whom the Gestapo had picked up almost at random, without any evidence against her, and who was caught out on the word "concrete." The Gestapo Commissar had listened to her with boredom, half-convinced that his underlings had blundered in arresting her—until she used the fatal word for the second time. The Commissar pricked his ears. "Where did you pick up that expression?" he asked. The girl, until that moment quite self-possessed, became rattled, and once rattled she was lost.

Our literary, artistic and musical tastes were similarly reconditioned. Lenin had said somewhere that he had learned more about France from Balzac's novels than from all history books put together. Accordingly, Balzac was the greatest of all times, whereas other novelists of the past merely reflected "the distorted values of the decaying society which had produced them." On the Art Front the guiding principle of the period was Revolutionary Dynamism. A picture without a smoking factory chimney or a tractor in it was escapist; on the other hand, the slogan "dynamism" left sufficient scope for cubist, expressionist, and other experimental styles. This changed a few years later when Revolutionary Dynamism was superseded by Socialist Realism; henceforth everything modern and experimental became branded as "bourgeois formalism" expressing "the putrid corruption of capitalist decay." In both music and drama, the chorus was regarded at that time as the highest form of expression, because it reflected a collective, as opposed to a bourgeois-individualistic, approach. As individual *personae* could not be altogether abolished on the stage, they had to be stylized, typified, depersonalized (Meyerhold, Piscator, Brecht, Auden-Isherwood-Spender). Psychology became greatly simplified: there were two recognized emotive impulses: class solidarity and the sexual urge. The rest was "bourgeois metaphysics"; or, like ambition and the lust for power, "products of competitive capitalist economy."

As for the "sexual urge," though it was officially sanctioned, we were in something of a quandary about it. Monogamy, and the whole institution of the family, were a product of the economic system; they bred individualism, hypocrisy, an escapist attitude to the class struggle and were altogether to be rejected; bourgeois matrimony was merely a form of prostitution sanctioned by society. But promiscuity was equally a Bad Thing. It had flourished in the Party, both in Russia and abroad, until Lenin made his famous pronouncement against the Glass of Water Theory (that is, against the popular maxim that the sexual act was of no more consequence than the quenching of thirst by a glass of water). Hence bourgeois morality was a

Bad Thing. But promiscuity was an equally Bad Thing, and the only correct, concrete attitude towards the sexual urge was Proletarian Morality. This consisted in getting married, being faithful to one's spouse, and producing proletarian babies. But then, was this not the same thing as bourgeois morality?—The question, Comrade, shows that you are thinking in mechanistic, not in dialectical, terms. What is the difference between a gun in the hands of a policeman and a gun in the hands of a member of the revolutionary working class? The difference between a gun in the hands of a policeman and in the hands of a member of the revolutionary working class is that the policeman is a lackey of the ruling class and his gun an instrument of oppression, whereas the same gun in the hands of a member of the revolutionary working class is an instrument of the liberation of the oppressed masses. Now the same is true of the difference between so-called bourgeois "morality" and Proletarian Morality. The institution of marriage which in capitalist society is an aspect of bourgeois decay, is dialectically transformed in its function in a healthy proletarian society. Have you understood, Comrade, or shall I repeat my answer in more concrete terms?

Repetitiveness of diction, the catechism technique of asking a rhetorical question and repeating the full question in the answer; the use of stereotyped adjectives and the dismissal of an attitude or fact by the simple expedient of putting words in inverted commas and giving them an ironic inflection (the "revolutionary" past of Trotsky, the "humanistic" bleatings of the "liberal" press, etc.); all these were essential parts of a style, of which Josef Djugashwili is the uncontested master, and which through its very tedium produced a dull, hypnotic effect. Two hours of this dialectical tom-tom and you didn't know whether you were a boy or a girl, and were ready to believe either as soon as the rejected alternative appeared in inverted commas. You were also ready to believe that the Socialists were: (a) your main enemies, (b) your natural allies; that socialist and capitalist countries: (a) could live peacefully side by side, and (b) could not live peacefully side by side; and that when Engels had written that Socialism in One Country was impossible, he had meant the exact opposite. You further learned to prove, by the method of chain-deduction, that anybody who disagreed with you was an agent of Fascism, because: (a) by his disagreeing with your line he endangered the unity of the Party; (b) by endangering the unity of the Party he improved the chances of a Fascist victory; hence (c) he acted objectively as an agent of Fascism even if subjectively he happened to have his kidneys smashed to pulp by the Fascists in Dachau. Generally speaking, words like "agent of," "Democracy," "Freedom," etc. meant something quite different in Party usage from what they meant in general usage; and as, furthermore, even their Party meaning changed with each shift of the line, our polemical methods became rather like the croquet game of the Queen of Hearts, in which the hoops moved about the field and the balls were live hedgehogs. With this difference, that when a player missed his turn and the Queen shouted "Off with his head," the order was executed in earnest. To survive, we all had to become virtuosos of Wonderland croquet.

A special feature of Party life at that period was the cult of the proletarian and abuse of the intelligentsia. It was the obsession, the smarting complex of all Communist intellectuals of middle-class origin. We were in the Movement on sufferance, not by right; this was rubbed into our consciousness night and day. We had to be tolerated because Lenin had said so, and because Russia could not do without the doctors, engineers and scientists of the pre-revolutionary intelligentsia, and without the hated foreign specialists. But we were no more trusted or respected than the category of "Useful Jews" in the Third Reich who were allowed to survive and were given distinctive armlets so that they should not by mistake be pushed into a gas-chamber before their span of usefulness expired. The "Aryans" in the Party were the Proletarians, and the social origin of parents and grandparents was as weighty a factor both when applying for membership and during the biannual routine purges as Aryan descent was with the Nazis. The ideal Proletarians were the Russian factory workers, and the élite among the latter were those of the Putilov Works in Leningrad and of the oil fields in Baku. In all books which we read or wrote, the ideal proletarian was always broad-shouldered, with an open face and simple features; he was fully class-conscious, his sexual urge was kept well under control; he was strong and silent, warmhearted but ruthless when necessary, had big feet, horny hands and a deep baritone voice to sing revolutionary songs with. Proletarians who were not Communists were not real proletarians—they belonged either to the Lumpen-Proletariat or to the Workers' Aristocracy. No movement can exist without a heroic archetype; Comrade Ivan Ivanovich of the Putilov Works was our Buffalo Bill.

A member of the intelligentsia could never become a real proletarian, but his duty was to become as nearly one as he could. Some tried to achieve this by forsaking neckties, by wearing polo sweaters and black fingernails. This, however, was discouraged: it was imposture and snobbery. The correct way was never to write, say, and above all never to think, anything which could not be understood by the dustman. We cast off our intellectual baggage like passengers on a ship seized by panic, until it became reduced to the strictly necessary minimum of stock-phrases, dialectical clichés and Marxist quotations, which constitute the international jargon of Djugashwilese. To have shared the doubtful privilege of a bourgeois education, to be able to see several aspects of a problem and not only one, became a permanent cause of self-reproach. We craved to become single-

and simple-minded. Intellectual self-castration was a small price to pay for achieving some likeness to Comrade Ivan Ivanovich.

To come back to life in the cell. The meetings, as I have said, started with one, sometimes two, political lectures which laid down the line. This was followed by discussion, but discussion of a peculiar kind. It is a basic rule of Communist discipline that, once the Party has decided to adopt a certain line regarding a given problem, all criticism of that decision becomes deviationist sabotage. In theory, discussion is permissible prior to the decision. But as all decisions are imposed from above, out of the blue, without consulting any representative body of the rank and file, the latter is deprived of any influence on policy and even of the chance of expressing an opinion on it; while at the same time the leadership is deprived of the means of gauging the mood of the masses. One of the slogans of the German Party said: "The front-line is no place for discussions." Another said: "Wherever a Communist happens to be, he is always in the front-line."

So our discussions always showed a complete unanimity of opinion, and the form they took was that one member of the cell after another got up and recited approving variations in Djugashwilese on the theme set by the lecturer. But "recited" is probably not the proper word here. We groped painfully in our minds not only to find justifications for the line laid down, but also to find traces of former thoughts which would prove to ourselves that we had always held the required opinion. In this operation we mostly succeeded. I may have been somewhat bewildered when we were told by the instructor that the Party's main slogan in the coming elections to the Prussian Diet was to be not the seven million German unemployed, or the threats of the Brownshirts, but "the defense of the Chinese proletariat against the aggression of the Japanese pirates." But if I was bewildered, I no longer remember it. I do, however, remember writing a sincere and eloquent election leaflet, which proved just why events in Shanghai were more important to the German working class than events in Berlin; and the pat on the shoulder I received for it from District HQ still makes me feel good—I can't help it.

The proletarian members of the cell ususally sat through the lecture with a sleepy expression; they listened, with eyelids slit in mistrust, to the intellectuals expounding the reasons for their agreement; then, after some nudging, one of them would get up and repeat, in a deliberately awkward manner and with an air of defiance, the main slogans from the Inspector's speech without bothering to change the words. He would be listened to in solemn silence, sit down amidst a murmur of approval, and the instructor, winding up the proceedings, would point out that of all the speakers Comrade X had formulated the problem in the happiest and most concrete terms.

As I mentioned before, the summer of 1932 was a period of transition; the Party was preparing to go underground and accordingly regrouping its *cadres*. We might be outlawed overnight; everything had to be ready for this emergency. The moment we were forced into illegality all Party cells would cease to function and would be superseded by a new, nation-wide structure, the "Groups of Five." The cells, whose membership ranged from ten to thirty comrades, were too large for underground work and offered easy opportunities for *agents provocateurs* and informers. The breaking up of the *cadres* into Groups of Five meant organizational de-centralization and a corresponding diminution of risks. Only the leader of the Group was to know the identity and addresses of the other four; and he alone had contact with the next higher level of the Party hierarchy. If he was arrested, he could only betray the four individuals in his Group, and his contact man.

So, while the cell still continued to function, each member was secretly allotted to a Group of Five, the idea being that none of the Groups should know the composition of any other. In fact, as we were all neighbors in the Block, we each knew which Group was secretly meeting in whose flat; and on the night of the burning of the Reichstag, when Göring dealt his death blow to the Communist Party, the Groups scattered and the whole elaborate structure collapsed all over the Reich. We had marveled at the conspir-atorial ingenuity of our leaders, and, though all of us had read works on the technique of insurrection and civil warfare, our critical faculties had be-come so numbed that none of us realized the catastrophic implications of the scheme. To prepare for a long underground existence in small de-centralized groups meant that our leaders accepted the victory of Nazism as inevitable. And the breaking up of the *cadres* into small units indicated that the Party would offer no open, armed resistance to the ascent of Hitler to power, but was preparing for sporadic small-scale action instead.

But we, the rank and file, knew nothing of this. During that long, sti-fling summer of 1932 we fought our ding-dong battles with the Nazis. Hardly a day passed without one or two dead in Berlin. The main battle-fields were the *Bierstuben,* the smoky little taverns of the working-class districts. Some of these served as meeting-places for the Nazis, some as meeting-places (*Verkehrslokale*) for us. To enter the wrong pub was to ven-ture into the enemy lines. From time to time the Nazis would shoot up one of our *Verkehrslokale.* It was done in the classic Chicago tradition: a gang of SA men would drive slowly past the tavern, firing through the glass-panes, then vanish at breakneck speed. We had far fewer motorcars than the Nazis, and retaliation was mostly carried out in cars either stolen or borrowed from sympathizers. The men who did these jobs were members of the RFB, the League of Communist War Veterans. My car was some-times borrowed by comrades whom I had never seen before, and returned a few hours later with no questions asked and no explanations offered. It was a tiny, red, open Fiat car, model 509, most unsuitable for such purposes; but nobody else in our cell had one. It was the last relic of my bourgeois past; now it served as a vehicle for the Proletarian Revolution. I spent half my time driving it round on various errands: transporting pamphlets and leaflets, shadowing certain Nazi cars whose numbers had been indicated to us, and acting as a security escort. Once I had to transport the equipment of a complete hand printing press from a railway station to a cellar under a greengrocer's shop.

The RFB men who came to fetch the car for their guerrilla expedition were sometimes rather sinister types from the Berlin underworld. They came, announced by a telephone call or verbal message from District HQ, but the same men rarely turned up twice. Sometimes, on missions of a more harmless nature, I was ordered myself to act as driver. We would drive slowly past a number of Nazi pubs to watch the goings-on, or patrol a pub of our own when one of our informers in the Nazi camp warned us of an impending attack. This latter kind of mission was unpleasant; we would park, with headlights turned off and engine running, in the proximity of the pub; and at the approach of a car I would hear the click of the safety catch on my passengers' guns, accompanied by the gentle advice "to keep my block well down." But I never saw it come to any actual shooting.

Once the RFB men who came to fetch the car disguised themselves in my flat before starting out. They stuck on mustaches, put on glasses, dark jackets and bowler hats. I watched them from the window driving off—four stately, bowler-hatted gents in the ridiculous little red car, looking like a party in a funeral procession. They came back four hours later, changed back to normal, and made off with a silent handshake. My instructions, in case the number of the car was taken by the police during some action, were to say that it had been stolen and that I had found it again in a deserted street.

From time to time a rumor got around that the Nazis were going to attack our Red Block as they had attacked other notorious Communist agglomerations before. Then we were alerted and some RFB men turned up to mount guard. One critical night about thirty of us kept vigil in my tiny flat, armed with guns, lead pipes and leather batons. It happened to be the night when Ernst, a friend of mine, arrived from Vienna to stay for a few days. He was a young scientist with a shy, gentle manner and a razor-sharp mind. The flat was dim with cigarette smoke; men were sitting or sleeping all over the place—on the beds, on the floor, under the kitchen sink, amid lead pipes, beer glasses and batons. When my turn came to patrol the street, I took Ernst with me. "What is all this romantic brigandage about?" he asked me. I explained to him. "I know, I know," he said, "but what do

you think you are doing with your life?" "I am helping to prepare the Revolution," I said cheerfully. "It doesn't look like it," he said. "Why?" "I don't
know," he said doubtfully. "I know of course nothing about how revolutions
are done. But the whole scene upstairs looked to me like a huddle of strag-
glers from a beaten army."

He was right; we thought of ourselves as the vanguard of the Revolution,
and were the rearguard of the disintegrating workers' movement. A few
weeks later von Papen staged his *coup d'état:* one lieutenant and eight men
chased the Socialist government of Prussia from office. The Socialist Party,
with its eight million followers, did nothing. The Socialist-controlled
Trade Unions did not even call a protest strike. Only we, the Communists,
who a year earlier had joined hands with the Nazis against the same Prussian government and who kept repeating that the Socialists were the main
enemy of the working class—we now called for an immediate general
strike. The call fell on deaf ears in the whole of Germany. Our verbiage
had lost all real meaning for the masses, like inflated currency. And so we
lost the battle against Hitler before it was joined. After July 20, 1932, it
was evident to all but ourselves that the KPD, strongest among the Communist Parties in Europe, was a castrated giant whose brag and bluster
only served to cover its lost virility.

The day after the abortive General Strike, the Party Press affirmed that
it had been a resounding victory: by calling for the strike in the face of
Socialist inaction, our Party had definitely unmasked the treachery of the
Social Fascist leaders.

A few months later everything was over. Years of conspiratorial training
and preparation for the emergency proved within a few hours totally useless. The giant was swept off his feet and collapsed like a Carnival monster. Thälmann, leader of the Party, and the majority of his lieutenants were
found in their carefully prepared hide-outs and arrested within the first few
days. The Central Committee emigrated. The long night descended over
Germany; today, seventeen years later, it has not yet ended.

With Hitler in power, Thälmann in jail, thousands of Party members
murdered and tens of thousands in concentration camps, the Comintern at
last awoke to its responsibilities. The Party tribunals abroad and the
GPU *Collegia* in the USSR sat in merciless judgment over "the enemy
within"—the bandits and agents of Fascism who murmured against the
official line, according to which the Socialist Party was the Enemy No. 1 of
the German working class, and the Communist Party had suffered no defeat, but merely carried out a strategic retreat. . . .

28. André Breton, *What Is Surrealism?*

The work of André Breton is inseparable from the movement called surrealism, which probably exercised the greatest single influence on the
cultural climate of France during the interwar years.

The son of a Norman shopkeeper, Breton was born in 1896. At the
start of World War I, he was a medical student with a special interest in
mental diseases. Thus when the movement called Dada, founded by the
Rumanian poet Tristan Tzara in Zurich in 1916, arrived in Paris in 1919,
Breton joined eagerly. For Dada exalted the unconscious, which had been
systematically studied by Freud and others in the clinical context with
which Breton was already familiar; and it used the unconscious as the
basis for criticizing bourgeois civilization and its misguided enshrinement
of the value of rationality. At their "provocation-performances," the
Dadaists might read a newspaper to the deafening accompaniment of bells
and rattles and call it a poem, or even pelt their audience with raw beef.
By 1922, Breton had grown tired of the nihilism of Dada, and with
friends he created surrealism as a schismatic movement.

Like its parent movement, surrealism was implacably hostile to bourgeois rationality and championed the revitalizing power of unconscious
mental processes. But unlike Dada, it sought to be constructive and to
put something in the place of the bourgeois civilization it abhorred. In the
selection below, written in 1934, Breton recounts the evolution of the
movement from its inception through its increasing politicization and involvement with the Communist Party in the 1930s.

At the beginning of the war of 1870 (he was to die four months later,
aged twenty-four), the author of the *Chants de Maldoror* and of *Poésies,*
Isidore Ducasse, better known by the name of Comte de Lautréamont,
whose thought has been of the very greatest help and encouragement to my
friends and myself throughout the fifteen years during which we have succeeded in carrying on a common activity, made the following remark,
among many others which were to electrify us fifty years later: "At the hour
in which I write, new tremors are running through the intellectual atmosphere; it is only a matter of having the courage to face them." 1868–75: it
is impossible, looking back upon the past, to perceive an epoch so *poetically* rich, so victorious, so revolutionary and so charged with distant

From André Breton, *What Is Surrealism?*, translated by David Gascoyne (London: Faber
& Faber, 1936), pp. 44–71, 82–83, 86–90. Reprinted by permission of Faber & Faber Ltd.

meaning as that which stretches from the separate publication of the *Premier Chant de Maldoror* to the insertion in a letter to Ernest Delahaye of Rimbaud's last poem, *Rêve,* which has not so far been included in his *Complete Works.* It is not an idle hope to wish to see the works of Lautréamont and Rimbaud restored to their correct historical background: the coming and the immediate results of the war of 1870. Other and analogous cataclysms could not have failed to rise out of that military and social cataclysm whose final episode was to be the atrocious crushing of the Paris Commune; the last in date caught many of us at the very age when Lautréamont and Rimbaud found themselves thrown into the preceding one, and by way of revenge has had as its consequence—and this is the new and important fact—the triumph of the Bolshevik Revolution.

I should say that to people socially and politically uneducated as we then were—we who, on the one hand, came for the most part from the petite-bourgeoisie, and on the other, were all by vocation possessed with the desire to intervene upon the artistic plane—the days of October, which only the passing of the years and the subsequent appearance of a large number of works within the reach of all were fully to illumine, could not there and then have appeared to turn so decisive a page in history. We were, I repeat, ill-prepared and ill-informed. Above all, we were exclusively preoccupied with a campaign of systematic refusal, exasperated by the conditions under which, in such an age, we were forced to live. But our refusal did not stop there; it was insatiable and knew no bounds. Apart from the incredible stupidity of the arguments which attempted to legitimize our participation in an enterprise such as the war, whose issue left us completely indifferent, this refusal was directed—and having been brought up in such a school, we are not capable of *changing* so much that is no longer so directed—against the whole series of intellectual, moral and social obligations that continually and from all sides weigh down upon man and crush him. Intellectually, it was vulgar rationalism and chop logic that more than anything else formed the causes of our horror and our destructive impulse; morally, it was all duties: religious, civic and of the family; socially, it was work (did not Rimbaud say: "Jamais je ne travaillerai, ô flots de feu!" and also: "La main à plume vaut la main à charrue. Quel siècle à mains! Je n'aurai jamais ma main!"). The more I think about it, the more certain I become that nothing was to our minds worth saving, unless it was . . . unless it was, at last, "l'amour la poésie," to take the bright and trembling title of one of Paul Eluard's books, "l'amour la poésie," considered as inseparable in their essence and as the sole good. Between the negation of this good, a negation brought to its climax by the war, and its full and total affirmation ("Poetry should be made by all, not one"), the field was not, to our minds, open to anything but a Revolution truly extended into all domains, improbably radical, to the highest degree impractical and tragically destroying within itself the whole time the feeling that it brought with it both of desirability and of absurdity. Many of you, no doubt, would put this down to a certain youthful exaltation and to the general savagery of the time; I must, however, insist on this attitude, common to particular men and manifesting itself at periods nearly half a century distant from one another. I should affirm that in ignorance of this attitude one could form no idea of what surrealism really stands for. This attitude alone can account, and very sufficiently at that, for all the excesses that may be attributed to us but which cannot be deplored unless one gratuitously supposes that we could have started from any other point. The ill-sounding remarks that are imputed to us, the so-called inconsiderate attacks, the insults, the quarrels, the scandals—all the things that we are so much reproached with—turned up on the same road as the surrealist poems. From the very beginning, the surrealist attitude has had that in common with Lautréamont and Rimbaud which once and for all binds our lot to theirs, and that is wartime *defeatism*.

I am not afraid to say that this *defeatism* seems to me more relevant than ever. "New tremors are running through the intellectual atmosphere; it is only a matter of having the courage to face them." They are, in fact, *always* running through the intellectual atmosphere: the problem of their propagation and interpretation remains the same and, as far as we are concerned, remains to be solved. But, paraphrasing Lautréamont, I cannot refrain from adding that at the hour in which I speak, old and mortal shivers are trying to substitute themselves for those which are the very shivers of knowledge and of life. They come to announce a frightful disease, a disease inevitably followed by the deprivation of all rights; it is only a matter of having the courage to face them also. This disease is called fascism.

Let us be careful today not to underestimate the peril: the shadow has greatly advanced over Europe recently. Hitler, Dolfuss and Mussolini have either drowned in blood or subjected to corporal humiliation everything that formed the effort of generations straining towards a more tolerable and more worthy form of existence. In capitalist society, hypocrisy and cynicism have now lost all sense of proportion and are becoming more outrageous every day. Without making exaggerated sacrifices to humanitarianism, which always involves impossible reconciliations and truces to the advantage of the stronger, I should say that in this atmosphere, thought cannot consider the exterior world without an immediate shudder. Everything we know about fascism shows that it is precisely the homologation of this state of affairs, aggravated to its furthest point by the lasting resignation that it seeks to obtain from those who suffer. Is not the evident role of fascism to re-establish for the time being the tottering supremacy of finance-capital? Such a role is of itself sufficient to make it worthy of all our hatred; we continue to consider this feigned resignation as one of the greatest evils that can possibly be inflicted upon beings of our kind, and those who would inflict it deserve, in our opinion, to be beaten like dogs. Yet it is impossible to conceal the fact that this immense danger is there, lurking at our doors, that it has made its appearance within our walls, and that it would be pure byzantinism to dispute too long, as in Germany, over the choice of the barrier to be set up against it, when all the while, *under several aspects,* it is creeping nearer and nearer to us. During the course of taking various steps with a view to contributing, in so far as I am capable, to the organization in Paris of the anti-fascist struggle, I have noticed that already a certain doubt has crept into the intellectual circles of the left as to the possibility of successfully combating fascism, a doubt which has unfortunately infected even those elements whom one might have thought it possible to rely on and who had come to the fore in this struggle. Some of them have even begun to make excuses for the loss of the battle already. Such dispositions seem to me to be so dismaying that I should not care to be speaking here without first having made clear my position in relation to them, or without anticipating a whole series of remarks that are to follow, affirming that today, more than ever before, *the liberation of the mind,* the express aim of surrealism, demands as primary condition, in the opinion of the surrealists, *the liberation of man,* which implies that we must struggle with our fetters with all the energy of despair; that today more than ever before the surrealists entirely rely for the bringing about of the liberation of man upon the proletarian Revolution.

I now feel free to turn to the object of this pamphlet, which is to attempt to explain what surrealism is. A certain immediate ambiguity contained in the word surrealism, is, in fact, capable of leading one to suppose that it designates I know not what transcendental attitude, while, on the contrary it expresses—and always has expressed for us—a desire to deepen the foundations of the real, to bring about an ever clearer and at the same time ever more passionate consciousness of the world perceived by the senses. The whole evolution of surrealism, from its origins to the present day, which I am about to retrace, shows that our unceasing wish, growing more and more urgent from day to day, has been at all costs to avoid considering a system of thought as a refuge, to pursue our investigations with eyes wide open to their outside consequences, and to assure ourselves that the results of these investigations would be capable of facing the *breath of the street.* At the limits, for many years past—or more exactly, since the conclusion of what one may term the purely *intuitive* epoch of surrealism (1919– 25)—at the limits, I say, we have attempted to present interior reality and exterior reality as two elements in process of unification, of finally becoming *one.* This final unification is the supreme aim of surrealism: interior reality and exterior reality being, in the present form of society, in contradiction (and in this contradiction we see the very cause of man's unhappiness, but also the source of his movement), we have assigned to ourselves the task of confronting these two realities with one another on every possible occasion, of refusing to allow the preeminence of the one over the other, yet not of acting on the one and on the other *both at once,* for that would be to suppose that they are less apart from one another than they are (and I believe that those who pretend they are acting on both simultaneously are either deceiving us or are a prey to a disquieting illusion); of acting on these two realities not both at once, then, but one after the other, in a systematic manner, allowing us to observe their reciprocal attraction and interpenetration and to give to this interplay of forces all the extension necessary for the trend of these two adjoining realities to become one and the same thing.

As I have just mentioned in passing, I consider that one can distinguish two epochs in the surrealist movement, of equal duration, from its origins (1919, year of the publication of the *Champs Magnétiques*) until today: a purely *intuitive* epoch, and a *reasoning* epoch. The first can summarily be characterized by the belief expressed during this time in the allpowerfulness of thought, considered capable of freeing itself by means of its own resources. This belief witnesses to a prevailing view that I look upon today as being extremely mistaken, the view that *thought is supreme over matter.* The definition of surrealism that has passed into the dictionary, a definition taken from the *Manifesto* of 1924, takes account only of this entirely idealist disposition and (for voluntary reasons of simplification and amplification destined to influence in my mind the future of this definition) does so in terms that suggest that I deceived myself at the time in advocating the use of an automatic thought not only removed from all control exercised by the reason but also disengaged from *"all aesthetic or moral preoccupations."* It should at least have been said: *conscious* aesthetic or moral preoccupations. During the period under review, in the absence, of course, of all seriously discouraging exterior events, surrealist activity remained strictly confined to its first theoretical premises, continuing all the while to be the vehicle of that total "non-conformism" which, as we have seen, was the binding feature in the coming together of those who took part in it, and the cause, during the first few years after the war, of an uninterrupted series of adhesions. No coherent political or social attitude, however, made its appearance until 1925, that is to say (and it is important to stress this), until the outbreak of the Moroccan war,[1] which, re-arousing

1. The French military effort to put down an anticolonialist uprising of the North Moroccan tribe called the Riffs led by Abd-el-Krim. Unlike most French intellectuals of the day, the Surrealists opposed the Third Republic's use of repressive force in Morocco and found that the French Communist party shared their view.—ED.

in us our particular hostility to the way armed conflicts affect man, abruptly placed before us the necessity of making a public protest. This protest, which, under the title *La Révolution d'Abord et Toujours* (October 1925), joined the names of the surrealists proper to those of thirty other intellectuals, was undoubtedly rather confused ideologically; it none the less marked the breaking away from a whole way of thinking; it none the less created a precedent that was to determine the whole future direction of the movement. Surrealist activity, faced with a brutal, revolting, *unthinkable* fact, was forced to ask itself what were its proper resources and to determine their *limits;* it was forced to adopt a precise attitude, exterior to itself, in order to continue to face whatever exceeded these limits. Surrealist activity at this moment entered into its *reasoning* phase. It suddenly experienced the necessity of crossing over the gap that separates absolute idealism from dialectical materialism. This necessity made its appearance in so urgent a manner that we had to consider the problem in the clearest possible light, with the result that for some months we devoted our entire attention to the means of bringing about this change of front once and for all. If I do not today feel any retrospective embarrassment in explaining this change, that is because it seems to me quite natural that surrealist thought, before coming to rest in dialectical materialism and insisting, as today, on the *supremacy of matter over mind,* should have been condemned to pass, in a few years, through the whole historic development of modern thought. It came *normally* to Marx through Hegel, just as it came *normally* to Hegel through Berkeley and Hume. These latter influences offer a certain particularity in that, contrary to certain poetic influences undergone in the same way, and accommodated to those of the French materialists of the eighteenth century, they yielded a residuum of *practical action*. To try and hide these influences would be contrary to my desire to show that surrealism has not been drawn up as an abstract system, that is to say, safeguarded against all contradictions. It is also my desire to show how surrealist activity, driven, as I have said, to ask itself what were its proper resources, had in some way or another to *reflect upon itself* its realization, in 1925, of its relative insufficiency; how surrealist activity had to cease being content with the results (automatic texts, the recital of dreams, improvised speeches, spontaneous poems, drawings and actions) which it had originally planned; and how it came to consider these first results as being simply so much *material,* starting from which the problem of knowledge inevitably arose again under quite a new form.

As a *living* movement, that is to say a movement undergoing a constant process of becoming and, what is more, solidly relying on concrete facts, surrealism has brought together and is still bringing together diverse temperaments individually obeying or resisting a variety of bents. The determinant of their enduring or short-lived adherence is not to be considered as a blind concession to an inert stock of ideas held in common, but as a continuous sequence of acts which, propelling the doer to more or less distant points, forces him for each fresh start to return to the same starting-line. These exercises not being without peril, one man may break a limb or—for which there is no precedent—his head, another may peaceably submerge himself in a quagmire or report himself dying of fatigue. Unable as yet to treat itself to an ambulance, surrealism simply leaves these individuals by the wayside. Those who continue in the ranks are aware of course of the casualties left behind them. But what of it? The essential is always to look ahead, to remain sure that one has not forfeited the burning desire for beauty, truth and justice, toilingly to go onward towards the discovery, one by one, of *fresh landscapes,* and to continue doing so indefinitely and without coercion to the end, that others may afterwards travel the same spiritual road, *unhindered and in all security.* Penetration, to be sure, has not been as deep as one would have wished. Poetically speaking, a few wild, or shall we say charming, beasts whose cries fill the air and bar access to a domain as yet only surmised, are still far from being exorcized. But for all that, the piercing of the thicket would have proceeded less tortuously, and those who are doing the pioneering would have acquitted themselves with unabating tenacity in the service of the cause, if, between the beginning and the end of the spectacle which they provide for themselves and would be glad to provide for others, a change had not taken place.

In 193(6), more than ever before, surrealism owes it to itself to defend the postulate of the necessity of change. It is amusing, indeed, to see how the more spiteful and silly of our adversaries affect to triumph whenever they stumble on some old statement we may have made and which now sounds more or less discordantly in the midst of others intended to render comprehensible our present conduct. This insidious manoeuvre, which is calculated to cast a doubt on our good faith, or at least on the genuineness of our principles, can easily be defeated. The development of surrealism throughout the decade of its existence is, we take it, a function of the unrolling of historical realities as these may be speeded up between the period of relief which follows the conclusion of a peace and the fresh outbreak of war. It is also a function of the process of seeking after new values in order to confirm or invalidate existing ones. The fact that certain of the first participants in surrealist activity have thrown in the sponge and have been discarded has brought about the retiring from circulation of some ways of thinking and the putting into circulation of others in which there were implicit certain general dissents on the one hand and certain general assents on the other. Hence it is that this activity has been fashioned by events. At the present moment, contrary to current biased rumour according to which surrealism itself is supposed, in its cruelty of disposition, to have sacrificed nearly all the blood first vivifying it, it is heartening to be able to point out that it has never ceased to avail itself of the perfect teamwork of René Crevel, Paul Eluard, Max Ernst, Benjamin Péret, Man Ray, Tristan Tzara, and the present writer, all of whom can attest that from the inception of the movement—which is also the date of our own enlistment in it—until now, the initial principle of their covenant has never been violated. If there have occurred differences on some points, it was essentially within the rhythmic scope of the integral whole, in itself a least disputable element of objective value. The others, they whom we no longer meet, can they say as much? They cannot, for the simple reason that since they separated from us they have been incapable of achieving a single concerted action that had any definite form of its own, and they have confined themselves, instead, to a reaction against surrealism with the greatest wastage to themselves—a fate always overtaking those who go back on their past. The history of their apostasy and denials will ultimately be read into the great limbo of human failings, without profit to any observer—ideal yesterday, but real today— who, called upon to make a pronouncement, will decide whether they or ourselves have brought the more appreciable efforts to bear upon a rational solution of the many problems surrealism has propounded.

Although there can be no question here of going through the history of the surrealist movement—its history has been told many a time and sometimes told fairly well; moreover, I prefer to pass on as quickly as possible to the exposition of its present attitude—I think I ought briefly to recall, for the benefit of those of you who were unaware of the fact, that there is no doubt that before the surrealist movement properly so called, there existed among the promoters of the movement and others who later rallied round it, very active, not merely dissenting but also antagonistic dispositions which, between 1915 and 1920, were willing to align themselves under the signboard of *Dada*. Post-war disorder, a state of mind essentially anarchic that guided that cycle's many manifestations, a deliberate refusal to judge— for lack, it was said, of criteria—the actual qualifications of individuals, and, perhaps, in the last analysis, a certain spirit of negation which was making itself conspicuous, had brought about a dissolution of the group as yet inchoate, one might say, by reason of its dispersed and heterogeneous character, a group whose germinating force has nevertheless been decisive and, by the general consent of present-day critics, has greatly influenced the course of ideas. It may be proper before passing rapidly—as I must— over this period, to apportion by far the handsomest share to Marcel Duchamp (canvases and glass objects still to be seen in New York), to Francis Picabia (reviews "291" and "391"), Jacques Vaché (*Lettres de Guerre*) and Tristan Tzara (*Twenty-five Poems, Dada Manifesto* 1918).

Strangely enough, it was round a discovery of language that there was seeking to organize itself in 1920 what—as yet on a basis of confidential exchange—assumed the name of *surrealism,* a word fallen from the lips of Apollinaire, which we had diverted from the rather general and very confusing connotation he had given it. What was at first no more than a new method of poetic writing broke away after several years from the much too general theses which had come to be expounded in the *Surrealist Manifesto—Soluble Fish,* 1924, the *Second Manifesto* adding others to them, whereby the whole was raised to a vaster ideological plane; and so there had to be revision.

In an article, "Enter the Mediums," published in *Littérature,* 1922, reprinted in *Les Pas Perdus,* 1924, and subsequently in the *Surrealist Manifesto,* I explained the circumstance that had originally put us, my friends and myself, on the track of the surrealist activity we still follow and for which we are hopeful of gaining ever more numerous new adherents in order to extend it further than we have so far succeeded in doing. It reads:

> It was in 1919, in complete solitude and at the approach of sleep, that my attention was arrested by sentences more or less complete, which became perceptible to my mind without my being able to discover (even by very meticulous analysis) any possible previous volitional effort. One evening in particular, as I was about to fall asleep, I became aware of a sentence articulated clearly to a point excluding all possibility of alteration and stripped of all quality of vocal sound; a curious sort of sentence which came to me bearing—in sober truth—not a trace of any relation whatever to any incidents I may at that time have been involved in; an insistent sentence, it seemed to me, a sentence I might say, that *knocked at the window.* I was prepared to pay no further attention to it when the organic character of the sentence detained me. I was really bewildered. Unfortunately, I am unable to remember the exact sentence at this distance, but it ran approximately like this: "A man is cut in half by the window." What made it plainer was the fact that it was accompanied by a feeble visual representation of a man in the process of walking, but cloven, at half his height, by a window perpendicular to the axis of his body. Definitely, there was the form, re-erected against space, of a man leaning out of a window. But the window following the man's locomotion, I understood that I was dealing with an image of great rarity. Instantly the idea came to me to use it as material for poetic construction. I had no sooner invested it with that quality, than it had given place to a succession of all but intermittent sentences which left me no less astonished, but in a state, I would say, of extreme detachment.
>
> Preoccupied as I still was at that time with Freud, and familiar with his methods of investigation, which I had practised occasionally upon

the sick during the War, I resolved to obtain from myself what one seeks to obtain from patients, namely a monologue poured out as rapidly as possible, over which the subject's critical faculty has no control—the subject himself throwing reticence to the winds—and which as much as possible represents *spoken thought*. It seemed and still seems to me that the speed of thought is no greater than that of words, and hence does not exceed the flow of either tongue or pen. It was in such circumstances that, together with Philippe Soupault, whom I had told about my first ideas on the subject, I began to cover sheets of paper with writing, feeling a praiseworthy contempt for whatever the literary result might be. Ease of achievement brought about the rest. By the end of the first day of the experiment we were able to read to one another about fifty pages obtained in this manner and to compare the results we had achieved. The likeness was on the whole striking. There were similar faults of construction, the same hesitant manner, and also, in both cases, an illusion of extraordinary verve, much emotion, a considerable assortment of images of a quality such as we should never have been able to obtain in the normal way of writing, a very special sense of the picturesque, and, here and there, a few pieces of out and out buffoonery. The only differences which our two texts presented appeared to me to be due essentially to our respective temperaments, Soupault's being less static than mine, and, if he will allow me to make this slight criticism, to his having scattered about at the top of certain pages—doubtlessly in a spirit of mystification— various words under the guise of titles. I must give him credit, on the other hand, for having always forcibly opposed the least correction of any passage that did not seem to me to be quite the thing. In that he was most certainly right.

It is of course difficult in these cases to appreciate at their just value the various elements in the result obtained; one may even say that it is entirely impossible to appreciate them at a first reading. To you who may be writing them, these elements are, in appearance, *as strange as to anyone else,* and you are yourself naturally distrustful of them. Poetically speaking, they are distinguished chiefly by a very high degree of *immediate absurdity,* the peculiar quality of that absurdity being, on close examination, their yielding to whatever is most admissible and legitimate in the world: divulgation of a given number of facts and properties on the whole not less objectionable than the others.

The word "surrealism" having thereupon become descriptive of the *generalizable* undertaking to which we had devoted ourselves, I thought it indispensable, in 1924, to define this word once and for all:

SURREALISM, n. Pure psychic automatism, by which it is intended to express, verbally, in writing, or by other means, the real process of thought. Thought's dictation, in the absence of all con-

trol exercised by the reason and outside all aesthetic or moral preoccupations.

ENCYCL. *Philos.* Surrealism rests in the belief in the superior reality of certain forms of association neglected heretofore; in the omnipotence of the dream and in the disinterested play of thought. It
tends definitely to do away with all other psychic mechanisms and to
substitute itself for them in the solution of the principal problems of
life. Have professed *absolute surrealism:* Messrs. Aragon, Baron,
Boiffard, Breton, Carrive, Crevel, Delteil, Desnos, Eluard, Gérard,
Limbour, Malkine, Morise, Naville, Noll, Péret, Picon, Soupault,
Vitrac.

These till now appear to be the only ones. . . . Were one to consider their output only superficially, a goodly number of poets might
well have passsed for surrealists, beginning with Dante and Shakespeare at his best. *In the course of many attempts I have made towards an analysis of what, under false pretences, is called genius, I
have found nothing that could in the end be attributed to any other
process than this.*

There followed an enumeration that will gain, I think, by being clearly
set out thus:

. . . Heraclitus is surrealist in dialectic. . . .
Swift is surrealist in malice.
Sade is surrealist in sadism. . . .
Baudelaire is surrealist in morals.
Rimbaud is surrealist in life and elsewhere. . . .
Carroll is surrealist in nonsense. . . .
Picasso is surrealist in cubism. . . .
Etc.

They were not always surrealists—on this I insist—in the sense
that one can disentangle in each of them a number of preconceived
notions to which—very naïvely!—they clung. And they clung to them
so because they had not heard the *surrealist voice,* the voice that exhorts on the eve of death and in the roaring storm, and because they
were unwilling to dedicate themselves to the task of no more than
orchestrating the score replete with marvellous things. They were
proud instruments; hence the sounds they produced were not always
harmonious sounds.

We, on the contrary, who have not given ourselves to processes of
filtering, who through the medium of our work have been content to be
the silent receptacles of so many echoes, modest *registering machines*
that are not hypnotized by the pattern that they trace, we are perhaps
serving a yet much nobler cause. So we honestly give back the talent
lent to us. You may talk of the "talent" of this yard of platinum, of this
mirror, of this door and of this sky, if you wish.

We have no talent. . . .

The *Manifesto* also contained a certain number of practical recipes, entitled: "Secrets of the Magic Surrealist Art," such as the following:

Written Surrealist Composition or First and Last Draft.
Having settled down in some spot most conducive to the mind's concentration upon itself, order writing material to be brought to you. Let your state of mind be as passive and receptive as possible. Forget your genius, talents, as well as the genius and talents of others. Repeat to yourself that literature is pretty well the sorriest road that leads to everywhere. Write quickly without any previously chosen subject, quickly enough not to dwell on, and not to be tempted to read over, what you have written. The first sentence will come of itself; and this is self-evidently true, because there is never a moment but some sentence alien to our conscious thought clamours for outward expression. It is rather difficult to speak of the sentence to follow, since it doubtless comes in for a share of our conscious activity and so the other sentences, if it is conceded that the writing of the first sentence must have involved even a minimum of consciousness. But that should in the long run matter little, because therein precisely lies the greatest interest in the surrealist exercise. Punctuation of course necessarily hinders the stream of absolute continuity which preoccupies us. But you should particularly distrust the prompting whisper. If through a fault ever so trifling there is a forewarning of silence to come, a fault, let us say, of inattention, break off unhesitatingly the line that has become too lucid. After the word whose origin seems suspect you should place a letter, any letter, *l* for example, always the letter *l,* and restore the arbitrary flux by making that letter the initial of the word to follow.

. . .

I believe that the real interest of that book—there was no lack of people who were good enough to concede interest, for which no particular credit is due to me because I have no more than given expression to sentiments shared with friends, present and former—rests only subordinately on the formula above given. It is rather confirmatory of a *turn of thought* which, for good or ill, is peculiarly distinctive of our time. The defence originally attempted of that turn of thought still seems valid to me in what follows:

We still live under the reign of logic, but the methods of logic are applied nowadays only to the resolution of problems of secondary interest. The absolute rationalism which is still the fashion does not permit consideration of any facts but those strictly relevant to our experience. Logical ends, on the other hand, escape us. Needless to say that even experience has had limits assigned to it. It revolves in a cage from which it becomes more and more difficult to release it. Even experience is dependent on immediate utility, and common sense is its keeper. Under colour of civilization, under pretext of progress, all that rightly or wrongly may be regarded as fantasy or superstition has been banished from the mind, all uncustomary searching after truth has been proscribed. It is only by what must seem sheer luck that there has recently been brought to light an aspect of mental life—to my belief by far the most important—with which it was supposed that we no longer had any concern. All credit for these discoveries must go to Freud. Based on these discoveries a current of opinion is forming that will enable the explorer of the human mind to continue his investigations, justified as he will be in taking into account more than mere summary realities. The imagination is perhaps on the point of reclaiming its rights. If the depths of our minds harbour strange forces capable of increasing those on the surface, or of successfully contending with them, then it is all in our interest to canalize them, to canalize them first in order to submit them later, if necessary, to the control of the reason. The analysts themselves have nothing to lose by such a proceeding. But it should be observed that there are no means designed *a priori* for the bringing about of such an enterprise, that until the coming of the new order it might just as well be considered the affair of poets and scientists, and that its success will not depend on the more or less capricious means that will be employed. . . .

Interesting in a different way from the future of surrealist *technics* (theatrical, philosophical, scientific, critical) appears to me the application of surrealism to action. Whatever reservations I might be inclined to make with regard to responsibility in general, I should quite particularly like to know how the first misdemeanours whose surrealist character is indubitable will be *judged*. When surrealist methods extend from writing to action, there will certainly arise the need of a new morality to take the place of the current one, the cause of all our woes.

The *Manifesto of Surrealism* has improved on the Rimbaud principle that the poet must turn *seer*. Man in general is going to be summoned to manifest through life those *new sentiments* which the gift of vision will so suddenly have placed within his reach. . . .

. . .

Surrealism then was securing expression in all its purity and force. The freedom it possesses is a perfect freedom in the sense that it recognizes no limitations exterior to itself. As it was said on the cover of the first issue of *La Révolution Surréaliste,* "it will be necessary to draw up a new declaration of the Rights of Man." The concept of surreality, concerning which quarrels have been sought with us repeatedly and which it was attempted to turn into a metaphysical or mystic rope to be placed afterwards round our necks, lends itself no longer to misconstruction, nowhere does it declare itself opposed to the need of transforming the world which henceforth will more and more definitely yield to it.

As I said in the *Manifesto:*

> I believe in the future transmutation of those two seemingly contradictory states, dream and reality, into a sort of absolute reality, of surreality, so to speak. I am looking forward to its consummation, certain that I shall never share in it, but death would matter little to me could I but taste the joy it will yield ultimately.

. . .

After years of endeavour and perplexities, when a variety of opinions had disputed amongst themselves the direction of the craft in which a number of persons of unequal ability and varying powers of resistance had originally embarked together, the surrealist idea recovered in the *Second Manifesto* all the brilliancy of which events had vainly conspired to despoil it. It should be emphasized that the *First Manifesto* of 1924 did no more than sum up the conclusions we had drawn during what one may call the *heroic epoch* of surrealism, which stretches from 1919 to 1923. The concerted elaboration of the first automatic texts and our excited reading of them, the first results obtained by Max Ernst in the domain of "collage" and of painting, the practice of surrealist "speaking" during the hypnotic experiments introduced among us by René Crevel and repeated every evening for over a year, uncontrovertibly mark the decisive stages of surrealist exploration during this first phase. After that, up till the taking into account of the social aspect of the problem round about 1925 (though not formally sanctioned until 1930), surrealism began to find itself a prey to characteristic wranglings. These wranglings account very clearly for the expulsion-orders and tickets-of-leave which, as we went along, we had to deal out to certain of our companions of the first and second hour. Some people have quite gratuitously concluded from this that we are apt to overestimate *personal questions.* During the last ten years, surrealism has almost unceasingly been obliged to defend itself against deviations to the right and to the left. On the one hand we have had to struggle against the will of those who would maintain surrealism on a purely speculative level and treasonably transfer it on to an artistic and literary plane (Artaud, Desnos, Ribemont-Dessaignes, Vitrac) at the cost of all the hope for subversion we have placed in it; on the other, against the will of those who would place it on a purely practical basis, available at any moment to be sacrificed to an ill-conceived political militancy (Naville, Aragon)—at the cost, this time, of what constitutes the originality and reality of its researches, at the cost of the autonomous risk that it has to run. Agitated though it was, the epoch that separates the two *Manifestos* was none the less a rich one, since it saw the publication of so many works in which the vital principles of surrealism were amply accounted for. . . .

It should be pointed out that in a number of declarations in *La Révolution et les Intellectuels. Que peuvent faire les surréalistes?* (1926), [Pierre Naville] demonstrated the utter vanity of intellectual bickerings in the face of the human exploitation which results from the wage-earning system. These declarations gave rise amongst us to considerable anxiety and, attempting for the first time to justify surrealism's social implications, I desired to put an end to it in *Légitime Défense*. This pamphlet set out to demonstrate that there is no fundamental antinomy in the basis of surrealist thought. In reality, we are faced with two problems, one of which is the problem raised, at the beginning of the twentieth century, by the discovery of the relations between the conscious and the unconscious. That was how the problem chose to present itself to us. We were the first to apply to its resolution a particular method, which we have not ceased to consider both the most suitable and the most likely to be brought to perfection; there is no reason why we should renounce it. The other problem we are faced with is that of the social action we should pursue. We consider that this action has its own method in dialectical materialism, and we can all the less afford to ignore this action since, I repeat, we hold the liberation of man to be the *sine qua non* condition of the *liberation of the mind,* and we can expect this liberation of man to result only from the proletarian Revolution. These two problems are essentially distinct and we deplore their becoming confused by not remaining so. There is good reason, then, to take up a stand against all attempts to weld them together and, more especially, against the urge to abandon all such researches as ours in order to devote ourselves to the poetry and art of propaganda. Surrealism, which has been the object of brutal and repeated summonses in this respect, now feels the need of making some kind of counter-attack. Let me recall the fact that its very definition holds that it must escape, in its written manifestations, or any others, from all *control* exercised by the reason. Apart from the puerility of wishing to bring a supposedly Marxist control to bear on the immediate aspect of such manifestations, this control cannot be envisaged in *principle*. And how ill-boding does this distrust seem, coming as it does from men who declare themselves Marxists, that is to say possessed not only of a strict line in revolutionary matters, but also of a marvellously open mind and an insatiable curiosity!

This brings us to the eve of the *Second Manifesto*. These objections had to be put an end to, and for that purpose it was indispensable that we should proceed to liquidate certain individualist elements amongst us, more or less openly hostile to one another, whose intentions did not, in the final analysis, appear as irreproachable, nor their motives as disinterested, as might have been desired. An important part of the work was devoted to a statement of the reasons which moved surrealism to dispense for the future with certain collaborators. It was attempted, on the same occasion, to complete the specific method of creation proposed six years earlier, and thoroughly to tidy up surrealist ideas. . . .

From 1930 until today the history of surrealism is that of successful efforts to restore to it its proper *becoming* by gradually removing from it every trace both of political opportunism and of artistic opportunism. The review *La Révolution Surréaliste* (12 issues) has been succeeded by another, *Le Surréalisme au Service de la Révolution* (6 issues). Owing particularly to influences brought to bear by new elements, surrealist experimenting, which had for too long been erratic, has been unreservedly resumed; its perspectives and its aims have been made perfectly clear; I may say that it has not ceased to be carried on in a continuous and enthusiastic manner. This experimenting has regained momentum under the master-impulse given to it by Salvador Dali, whose exceptional interior "boiling" has been for surrealism, during the whole of this period, an invaluable ferment. As Guy Mangeot has very rightly pointed out in his *History of Surrealism* . . . Dali has endowed surrealism with an instrument of primary importance, in particular the paranoiac-critical method, which has immediately shown itself capable of being applied with equal success to painting, poetry, the cinema, to the construction of typical surrealist objects, to fashions, to sculpture and even, if necessary, to all manner of exegesis.

He first announced his convictions to us in *La Femme Visible* (1930):

I believe the moment is at hand when, by a paranoiac and active advance of the mind, it will be possible (simultaneously with automatism and other passive states) to systematize confusion and thus to help to discredit completely the world of reality.

In order to cut short all possible misunderstandings, it should perhaps be said: "immediate" reality.

Paranoia uses the external world in order to assert its dominating idea and has the disturbing characteristic of making others accept this idea's reality. The reality of the external world is used for illustration and proof, and so comes to serve the reality of our mind.

. . .

Surrealism, starting fifteen years ago with a discovery that seemed only to involve poetic language, has spread like wildfire, on pursuing its course, not only in art but in life. It has provoked new states of consciousness and overthrown the walls beyond which it was immemorially supposed to be impossible to see; it has—as is being more and more generally recognized—modified the sensibility, and taken a decisive step towards the unification of the personality, which it found threatened by an ever more profound dissociation. Without attempting to judge what direction it will ultimately take, for the lands it fertilizes as it flows are those of surprise itself, I should like to draw your attention to the fact that its most recent advance is producing a *fundamental crisis of the "object."* It is essentially upon the *object* that surrealism has thrown most light in recent years. Only the very close examination of the many recent speculations to which the *object* has publicly given rise (the oneiric object, the object functioning symbolically, the real and virtual object, the moving but silent object, the phantom object, the discovered object, etc.), can give one a proper grasp of the experiments that surrealism is engaged in now. In order to continue to understand the movement, it is indispensable to focus one's attention on this point.

I must crave your indulgence for speaking so technically, *from the inside.* But there could be no question of concealing any aspect of the persuasions to which surrealism has been and is still exposed. I say that there exists a lyrical element that conditions *for one part* the psychological and moral structure of human society, that has conditioned it at all times and that will continue to condition it. This lyrical element has until now, even though in spite of them, remained the fact and *the sole fact* of specialists. In the state of extreme tension to which class antagonisms have led the society to which we belong and which we tend with all our strength to reject, it is natural and it is *fated* that this solicitation should continue, that it should assume for us a thousand faces, imploring, tempting and eager by turns. It is not within our power, it would be unworthy of our historic role to give way to this solicitation. By surrealism we intend to account for nothing less than the manner in which it is possible today to make use of the magnificent and overwhelming *spiritual legacy* that has been handed down to us. We have accepted this legacy from the past, and surrealism can well say that the use to which it has been put has been to turn it to the routing of capitalist society. I consider that for that purpose it was and is still necessary for us to stand where we are, to beware against breaking the thread of our researches and to continue these researches, not as literary men and artists, certainly, but rather as chemists and the various other kinds of technicians. To pass on to the poetry and art called (doubtless in anticipation) *proletarian:* No. The forces we have been able to bring together and which for fifteen years we have never found lacking, have arrived at a particular point of application: the question is not to know whether this point of application is the best, but simply to point out that the application of our forces at this point has given us up to an activity that has proved itself valuable and fruitful on the plane on which it was undertaken, and has also been of a kind to engage us more and more on the revolutionary plane. What it is essential to realize is that no other activity could have produced such rich results, nor could any other similar activity have been so effective in combating the present form of society. On that point we have history on our side.

A comrade, Claude Cahun, in a striking pamphlet published recently: *Les Paris Sont Ouverts,* a pamphlet that attempts to predict the future of poetry by taking account both of its own laws and of the social bases of its existence, takes Aragon to task for the lack of rigour in his present position (I do not think anyone can contest the fact that Aragon's poetry has perceptibly weakened since he abandoned surrealism and undertook to place himself *directly* at the service of the proletarian cause, which leads one to suppose that such an undertaking has defeated him and is proportionately more or less unfavourable to the Revolution). . . . It is of particular interest that the author of *Les Paris Sont Ouverts* has taken the opportunity of expressing himself from the "historic" point of view. His appreciation is as follows:

> The most revolutionary experiment in poetry under the capitalist regime having been incontestably, for France and perhaps for Europe, the Dadaist-surrealist experiment, in that it has tended to destroy all the myths about art that for centuries have permitted the ideologic as well as economic exploitation of painting, sculpture, literature, etc. (e.g. the *frottages* of Max Ernst, which, among other things, have been able to upset the scale of values of art-critics and experts, values based chiefly on technical perfection, personal touch and the lastingness of the materials employed), this experiment can and should serve the cause of the liberation of the proletariat. It is only when the proletariat has become aware of the myths on which capitalist culture depends, when they have become aware of what these myths and this culture mean for them and have destroyed them, that they will be able to pass on to their own proper development. The positive lesson of this negating experiment, that is to say its transfusion among the proletariat, constitutes the only valid revolutionary poetic propaganda.

Surrealism could not ask for anything better. Once the cause of the movement is understood, there is perhaps some hope that, on the plane of revolutionary militantism proper, our turbulence, our small capacity for adaptation, until now, to the necessary rules of a party (which certain people have thought proper to call our "blanquism"), may be excused us. It is only too certain that an activity such as ours, owing to its particularization, cannot be pursued within the limits of any one of the existing revolutionary organizations: it would be forced to come to a halt on the very threshold of that organization. If we are agreed that such an activity has above all tended to *detach* the intellectual creator from the illusions with which bourgeois society has sought to surround him, I for my part can only see in that tendency a further reason for continuing our activity.

None the less, the right that we demand and our desire to make use of it depend, as I said at the beginning, on our remaining able to continue our investigations without having to reckon, as for the last few months we have had to do, with a sudden attack from the forces of criminal imbecility. Let it be clearly understood that for us, surrealists, the interests of thought cannot cease to go hand in hand with the interests of the working class, and that all attacks on liberty, all fetters on the emancipation of the working class and all armed attacks on it cannot fail to be considered by us as attacks on thought likewise. I repeat, the danger is far from having been removed. The surrealists cannot be accused of having been slow to recognize the fact, since, on the very next day after the first fascist *coup* in France, it was they amongst the intellectual circles who had the honour of taking the initiative in sending out an *Appel à la lutte,* which appeared on February 10th, 1934, furnished with twenty-four signatures.[2] You may rest assured, comrades, that they will not confine themselves, that already they have not confined themselves, to this single act.

29. Virginia Woolf, *A Room of One's Own*

Virginia Woolf (1882–1941), one of the foremost English novelists of the twentieth century, was born into that English intellectual aristocracy which dated back to the early nineteenth-century Evangelicals (vol. 8, introduction to document 25): her father, Leslie Stephen, edited the monumental *Dictionary of National Biography;* her uncle James Fitz-james Stephen attempted in his *Liberty, Equality, Fraternity* (1873) to refute J. S. Mill's *On Liberty.* A frail and lonely child, especially after her mother's death in 1895, Virginia Stephen was educated at home, having the full run of her father's library and meeting his many literary friends.

She and her husband Leonard Woolf belonged to the Bloomsbury circle, a coterie including E. M. Forster, J. M. Keynes (see document 14), and Lytton Strachey which was named after the district in London

---

2. During the night of 6 February 1934, the powerful antiparliamentary leagues of the French Right fought with Paris police in what looked like an attempt at a coup d'état to overthrow the French Republic. The episode mobilized French Communists—as well as Socialists and Radicals (i.e., middle-class democrats)—to speak out and demonstrate against the threat of fascism at home.—ED.

where its members lived. Bloomsbury was known for its championing of the avant-garde. It sponsored, for example, the first English exhibition of the French Postimpressionist painters in 1910; beginning in 1924, the Woolfs' Hogarth Press published all of the works of Sigmund Freud in English translation. Virginia Woolf's own novels, of which *Jacob's Room* (1922), *Mrs. Dalloway* (1925), and *To the Lighthouse* (1927) are generally regarded as the most important, turned away from a narrative of action to a representation of the stream of consciousness, or interior monologue, of the characters. In this endeavor, Woolf was influenced to some degree by Freud's conceptualization of the mind and more particularly by the French philosopher Henri Bergson's notion of time as "pure duration."

An intensely private person, Woolf lived largely in the society of her husband, relatives, and close friends. It was not in her character to join clamorous public movements; yet some of her essays espoused views that can only be called feminist. Among these is *A Room of One's Own* (1929), a rumination on the paucity of woman writers throughout history. While most of Woolf's argument here is of a general nature, the specific historical background of the essay comes through in her discussion of the question of gender in fascist literature.

Chapter One

But, you may say, we asked you to speak about women and fiction—what has that got to do with a room of one's own? I will try to explain. When you asked me to speak about women and fiction I sat down on the banks of a river and began to wonder what the words meant. They might mean simply a few remarks about Fanny Burney; a few more about Jane Austen; a tribute to the Brontës and a sketch of Haworth Parsonage under snow; some witticisms if possible about Miss Mitford; a respectful allusion to George Eliot; a reference to Mrs. Gaskell and one would have done. But at second sight the words seemed not so simple. The title women and fiction might mean, and you may have meant it to mean, women and what they are like; or it might mean women and the fiction that they write; or it might mean women and the fiction that is written about them; or it might mean that somehow all three are inextricably mixed together and you want me to con-

From Virginia Woolf, *A Room of One's Own* (New York: Harcourt, Brace & World, 1929), pp. 3–6, 71–75, 80–84, 88–92, 165–74, 176–82; ©1929 by Harcourt, Brace & World, Inc.; renewed 1957 by Leonard Woolf. Reprinted by permission of the publisher, the author's estate, and the Hogarth Press.

sider them in that light. But when I began to consider the subject in this last way, which seemed the most interesting, I soon saw that it had one fatal drawback. I should never be able to come to a conclusion. I should never be able to fulfil what is, I understand, the first duty of a lecturer—to hand you after an hour's discourse a nugget of pure truth to wrap up between the pages of your notebooks and keep on the mantelpiece for ever. All I could do was to offer you an opinion upon one minor point—a woman must have money and a room of her own if she is to write fiction; and that, as you will see, leaves the great problem of the true nature of woman and the true nature of fiction unsolved. I have shirked the duty of coming to a conclusion upon these two questions—women and fiction remain, so far as I am concerned, unsolved problems. But in order to make some amends I am going to do what I can to show you how I arrived at this opinion about the room and the money. I am going to develop in your presence as fully and freely as I can the train of thought which led me to think this. Perhaps if I lay bare the ideas, the prejudices, that lie behind this statement you will find that they have some bearing upon women and some upon fiction. At any rate, when a subject is highly controversial—and any question about sex is that—one cannot hope to tell the truth. One can only show how one came to hold whatever opinion one does hold. One can only give one's audience the chance of drawing their own conclusions as they observe the limitations, the prejudices, the idiosyncrasies of the speaker. Fiction here is likely to contain more truth than fact. Therefore I propose, making use of all the liberties and licences of a novelist, to tell you the story of the two days that preceded my coming here—how, bowed down by the weight of the subject which you have laid upon my shoulders, I pondered it, and made it work in and out of my daily life. I need not say that what I am about to describe has no existence; Oxbridge is an invention; so is Fernham; "I" is only a convenient term for somebody who has no real being. Lies will flow from my lips, but there may perhaps be some truth mixed up with them; it is for you to seek out this truth and to decide whether any part of it is worth keeping. If not, you will of course throw the whole of it into the wastepaper basket and forget all about it.

Here then was I (call me Mary Beton, Mary Seton, Mary Carmichael or by any name you please—it is not a matter of any importance) sitting on the banks of a river a week or two ago in fine October weather, lost in thought. . . .

Chapter Three

It was disappointing not to have brought back in the evening some important statement, some authentic fact. Women are poorer than men because—this or that. Perhaps now it would be better to give up seeking for the truth, and receiving on one's head an avalanche of opinion hot as lava, discoloured as dish-water. It would be better to draw the curtains; to shut out distractions; to light the lamp; to narrow the enquiry and to ask the historian, who records not opinions but facts, to describe under what conditions women lived, not throughout the ages, but in England, say in the time of Elizabeth.

For it is a perennial puzzle why no woman wrote a word of that extraordinary literature when every other man, it seemed, was capable of song or sonnet. What were the conditions in which women lived, I asked myself; for fiction, imaginative work that is, is not dropped like a pebble upon the ground, as science may be; fiction is like a spider's web, attached ever so lightly perhaps, but still attached to life at all four corners. . . .

I went, therefore, to the shelf where the histories stand and took down one of the latest, Professor Trevelyan's *History of England*. Once more I looked up Women, found "position of," and turned to the pages indicated. "Wife-beating," I read, "was a recognised right of man, and was practised without shame by high as well as low. . . . Similarly," the historian goes on, "the daughter who refused to marry the gentleman of her parents' choice was liable to be locked up, beaten and flung about the room, without any shock being inflicted on public opinion. Marriage was not an affair of personal affection, but of family avarice, particularly in the 'chivalrous' upper classes. . . . Betrothal often took place while one or both of the parties was in the cradle, and marriage when they were scarcely out of the nurses' charge." That was about 1470, soon after Chaucer's time. The next reference to the position of women is some two hundred years later, in the time of the Stuarts. "It was still the exception for women of the upper and middle class to choose their own husbands, and when the husband had been assigned, he was lord and master, so far at least as law and custom could make him. Yet even so," Professor Trevelyan concludes, "neither Shakespeare's women nor those of authentic seventeenth-century memoirs, like the Verneys and the Hutchinsons, seem wanting in personality and character." Certainly, if we consider it, Cleopatra must have had a way with her; Lady Macbeth, one would suppose, had a will of her own; Rosalind, one might conclude, was an attractive girl. Professor Trevelyan is speaking no more than the truth when he remarks that Shakespeare's women do not seem wanting in personality and character. Not being a historian, one might go even further and say that women have burnt like beacons in all the works of all the poets from the beginning of time—Clytemnestra, Antigone, Cleopatra, Lady Macbeth, Phèdre, Cressida, Rosalind, Desdemona, the Duchess of Malfi, among the dramatists; then among the prose writers: Millamant, Clarissa, Becky Sharp, Anna Karenine, Emma Bovary,

Madame de Guermantes—the names flock to mind, nor do they recall women "lacking in personality and character." Indeed, if woman had no existence save in the fiction written by men, one would imagine her a person of the utmost importance; very various; heroic and mean; splendid and sordid; infinitely beautiful and hideous in the extreme; as great as a man, some think even greater. But this is woman in fiction. In fact, as Professor Trevelyan points out, she was locked up, beaten and flung about the room.

A very queer, composite being thus emerges. Imaginatively she is of the highest importance; practically she is completely insignificant. She pervades poetry from cover to cover; she is all but absent from history. She dominates the lives of kings and conquerors in fiction; in fact she was the slave of any boy whose parents forced a ring upon her finger. Some of the most inspired words, some of the most profound thoughts in literature fall from her lips; in real life she could hardly read, could scarcely spell, and was the property of her husband. . . .

. . . I could not help thinking, as I looked at the works of Shakespeare on the shelf, that . . . it would have been impossible, completely and entirely, for any woman to have written the plays of Shakespeare in the age of Shakespeare. Let me imagine, since facts are so hard to come by, what would have happened had Shakespeare had a wonderfully gifted sister, called Judith, let us say. Shakespeare himself went, very probably—his mother was an heiress—to the grammar school, where he may have learnt Latin—Ovid, Virgil and Horace—and the elements of grammar and logic. He was, it is well known, a wild boy who poached rabbits, perhaps shot a deer, and had, rather sooner than he should have done, to marry a woman in the neighbourhood, who bore him a child rather quicker than was right. That escapade sent him to seek his fortune in London. He had, it seemed, a taste for the theatre; he began by holding horses at the stage door. Very soon he got work in the theatre, became a successful actor, and lived at the hub of the universe, meeting everybody, knowing everybody, practising his art on the boards, exercising his wits in the streets, and even getting access to the palace of the queen. Meanwhile his extraordinarily gifted sister, let us suppose, remained at home. She was as adventurous, as imaginative, as agog to see the world as he was. But she was not sent to school. She had no chance of learning grammar and logic, let alone of reading Horace and Virgil. She picked up a book now and then, one of her brother's perhaps, and read a few pages. But then her parents came in and told her to mend the stockings or mind the stew and not moon about with books and papers. They would have spoken sharply but kindly, for they were substantial people who knew the conditions of life for a woman and loved their daughter—indeed, more likely than not she was the apple of her father's eye. Perhaps she scribbled some pages up in an apple loft on the sly, but was careful to hide them or set fire to them. Soon, however, before she was out of her teens, she was to be betrothed to the son of a neighbouring wool-stapler. She cried out that marriage was hateful to her, and for that she was severely beaten by her father. Then he ceased to scold her. He begged her instead not to hurt him, not to shame him in this matter of her marriage. He would give her a chain of beads or a fine petticoat, he said; and there were tears in his eyes. How could she disobey him? How could she break his heart? The force of her own gift alone drove her to it. She made up a small parcel of her belongings, let herself down by a rope one summer's night and took the road to London. She was not seventeen. The birds that sang in the hedge were not more musical than she was. She had the quickest fancy, a gift like her brother's, for the tune of words. Like him, she had a taste for the theatre. She stood at the stage door; she wanted to act, she said. Men laughed in her face. The manager—a fat, loose-lipped man—guffawed. He bellowed something about poodles dancing and women acting—no woman, he said, could possibly be an actress. He hinted—you can imagine what. She could get no training in her craft. Could she even seek her dinner in a tavern or roam the streets at midnight? Yet her genius was for fiction and lusted to feed abundantly upon the lives of men and women and the study of their ways. At last—for she was very young, oddly like Shake-speare the poet in her face, with the same grey eyes and rounded brows—at last Nick Greene the actor-manager took pity on her; she found herself with child by that gentleman and so—who shall measure the heat and violence of the poet's heart when caught and tangled in a woman's body?—killed herself one winter's night and lies buried at some cross-roads where the omnibuses now stop outside the Elephant and Castle.

That, more or less, is how the story would run, I think, if a woman in Shakespeare's day had had Shakespeare's genius. . . . But what is the state of mind that is most propitious to the act of creation, I asked? Can one come by any notion of the state that furthers and makes possible that strange activity? . . . Shakespeare himself said nothing about it. We only know casually and by chance that he "never blotted a line." Nothing indeed was ever said by the artist himself about his state of mind until the eigh-teenth century perhaps. Rousseau perhaps began it. At any rate, by the nineteenth century self-consciousness had developed so far that it was the habit for men of letters to describe their minds in confessions and auto-biographies. Their lives also were written, and their letters were printed after their deaths. Thus, though we do not know what Shakespeare went through when he wrote *Lear,* we do know what Carlyle went through when he wrote the *French Revolution;* what Flaubert went through when he wrote *Madame Bovary;* what Keats was going through when he tried to write poetry against the coming of death and the indifference of the world.

And one gathers from this enormous modern literature of confession and self-analysis that to write a work of genius is almost always a feat of prodigious difficulty. Everything is against the likelihood that it will come from the writer's mind whole and entire. Generally material circumstances are against it. Dogs will bark; people will interrupt; money must be made; health will break down. Further, accentuating all these difficulties and making them harder to bear is the world's notorious indifference. It does not ask people to write poems and novels and histories; it does not need them. It does not care whether Flaubert finds the right word or whether Carlyle scrupulously verifies this or that fact. Naturally, it will not pay for what it does not want. And so the writer, Keats, Flaubert, Carlyle, suffers, especially in the creative years of youth, every form of distraction and discouragement. A curse, a cry of agony, rises from those books of analysis and confession. "Mighty poets in their misery dead"—that is the burden of their song. If anything comes through in spite of all this, it is a miracle, and probably no book is born entire and uncrippled as it was conceived.

But for women, I thought, looking at the empty shelves, these difficulties were infinitely more formidable. In the first place, to have a room of her own, let alone a quiet room or a sound-proof room, was out of the question, unless her parents were exceptionally rich or very noble, even up to the beginning of the nineteenth century. Since her pin money, which depended on the good will of her father, was only enough to keep her clothed, she was debarred from such alleviations as came even to Keats or Tennyson or Carlyle, all poor men, from a walking tour, a little journey to France, from the separate lodging which, even if it were miserable enough, sheltered them from the claims and tyrannies of their families. Such material difficulties were formidable; but much worse were the immaterial. The indifference of the world which Keats and Flaubert and other men of genius have found so hard to bear was in her case not indifference but hostility. The world did not say to her as it said to them, Write if you choose; it makes no difference to me. The world said with a guffaw, Write? What's the good of your writing? Here the psychologists of Newnham and Girton might come to our help, I thought, looking again at the blank spaces on the shelves. For surely it is time that the effect of discouragement upon the mind of the artist should be measured, as I have seen a dairy company measure the effect of ordinary milk and Grade A milk upon the body of the rat. They set two rats in cages side by side, and of the two one was furtive, timid and small, and the other was glossy, bold and big. Now what food do we feed women as artists upon? . . .

Chapter Six

Next day the light of the October morning was falling in dusty shafts through the uncurtained windows, and the hum of traffic rose from the street. London then was winding itself up again; the factory was astir; the machines were beginning. It was tempting, after all this reading, to look out of the window and see what London was doing on the morning of the twenty-sixth of October 1928. . . . Here came an errand-boy; here a woman with a dog on a lead. The fascination of the London street is that no two people are ever alike; each seems bound on some private affair of his own. There were the business-like, with their little bags; there were the drifters rattling sticks upon area railings; there were affable characters to whom the streets serve for clubroom, hailing men in carts and giving information without being asked for it. . . .

At this moment, as so often happens in London, there was a complete lull and suspension of traffic. Nothing came down the street; nobody passed. A single leaf detached itself from the plane tree at the end of the street, and in that pause and suspension fell. Somehow it was like a signal falling, a signal pointing to a force in things which one had overlooked. It seemed to point to a river, which flowed past, invisibly, round the corner, down the street, and took people and eddied them along, as the stream at Oxbridge had taken the undergraduate in his boat and the dead leaves. Now it was bringing from one side of the street to the other diagonally a girl in patent leather boots, and then a young man in a maroon overcoat; it was also bringing a taxi-cab; and it brought all three together at a point directly beneath my window; where the taxi stopped; and the girl and the young man stopped; and they got into the taxi; and then the cab glided off as if it were swept on by the current elsewhere.

The sight was ordinary enough; what was strange was the rhythmical order with which my imagination had invested it; and the fact that the ordinary sight of two people getting into a cab had the power to communicate something of their own seeming satisfaction. The sight of two people coming down the street and meeting at the corner seems to ease the mind of some strain, I thought, watching the taxi turn and make off. Perhaps to think, as I had been thinking these two days, of one sex as distinct from the other is an effort. It interferes with the unity of the mind. Now that effort had ceased and that unity had been restored by seeing two people come together and get into a taxi-cab. The mind is certainly a very mysterious organ, I reflected, drawing my head in from the window, about which nothing whatever is known, though we depend upon it so completely. Why do I feel that there are severances and oppositions in the mind, as there are strains from obvious causes on the body? What does one mean by "the unity of the mind," I pondered, for clearly the mind has so great a power of concentrating at any point at any moment that it seems to have no single state of being. It can separate itself from the people in the street, for example, and think of itself as apart from them, at an upper window looking down on them. Or it can think with other people spontaneously, as, for instance, in a crowd waiting to hear some piece of news read out. It can think back through its fathers or through its mothers, as I have said that a woman writing thinks back through her mothers. Again if one is a woman one is often surprised by a sudden splitting off of consciousness, say in walking down Whitehall, when from being the natural inheritor of that civilisation, she becomes, on the contrary, outside of it, alien and critical. Clearly the mind is always altering its focus, and bringing the world into different perspectives. But some of these states of mind seem, even if adopted spontaneously, to be less comfortable than others. In order to keep oneself continuing in them one is unconsciously holding something back, and gradually the repression becomes an effort. But there may be some state of mind in which one could continue without effort because nothing is required to be held back. And this perhaps, I thought, coming in from the window, is one of them. For certainly when I saw the couple get into the taxi-cab the mind felt as if, after being divided, it had come together again in a natural fusion. The obvious reason would be that it is natural for the sexes to cooperate. One has a profound, if irrational, instinct in favour of the theory that the union of man and woman makes for the greatest satisfaction, the most complete happiness. But the sight of the two people getting into the taxi and the satisfaction it gave me made me also ask whether there are two sexes in the mind corresponding to the two sexes in the body, and whether they also require to be united in order to get complete satisfaction and happiness? And I went on amateurishly to sketch a plan of the soul so that in each of us two powers preside, one male, one female; and in the man's brain, the man predominates over the woman, and in the woman's brain, the woman predominates over the man. The normal and comfortable state of being is that when the two live in harmony together, spiritually cooperating. If one is a man, still the woman part of the brain must have effect; and a woman also must have intercourse with the man in her. Coleridge perhaps meant this when he said that a great mind is androgynous. It is when this fusion takes place that the mind is fully fertilised and uses all its faculties. Perhaps a mind that is purely masculine cannot create, any more than a mind that is purely feminine, I thought. But it would be well to test what one meant by man-womanly, and conversely by woman-manly, by pausing and looking at a book or two.

Coleridge certainly did not mean, when he said that a great mind is androgynous, that it is a mind that has any special sympathy with women; a mind that takes up their cause or devotes itself to their interpretation. Perhaps the androgynous mind is less apt to make these distinctions than the single-sexed mind. He meant, perhaps, that the androgynous mind is resonant and porous; that it transmits emotion without impediment; that it is naturally creative, incandescent and undivided. In fact one goes back to Shakespeare's mind as the type of the androgynous, of the man-womanly mind, though it would be impossible to say what Shakespeare thought of women. And if it be true that it is one of the tokens of the fully developed mind that it does not think specially or separately of sex, how much harder it is to attain that condition now than ever before. Here I came to the books by living writers, and there paused and wondered if this fact were not at the root of something that had long puzzled me. No age can ever have been as stridently sex-conscious as our own; those innumerable books by men about women in the British Museum are a proof of it. The Suffrage campaign was no doubt to blame. It must have roused in men an extraordinary desire for self-assertion; it must have made them lay an emphasis upon their own sex and its characteristics which they would not have troubled to think about had they not been challenged. And when one is challenged, even by a few women in black bonnets, one retaliates, if one has never been challenged before, rather excessively. That perhaps accounts for some of the characteristics that I remember to have found here, I thought, taking down a new novel by Mr. A, who is in the prime of life and very well thought of, apparently, by the reviewers. I opened it. Indeed, it was delightful to read a man's writing again. It was so direct, so straightforward after the writing of women. It indicated such freedom of mind, such liberty of person, such confidence in himself. One had a sense of physical well-being in the presence of this well-nourished, well-educated, free mind, which had never been thwarted or opposed, but had had full liberty from birth to stretch itself in whatever way it liked. All this was admirable. But after reading a chapter or two a shadow seemed to lie across the page. It was a straight dark bar, a shadow shaped something like the letter "I." One began dodging this way and that to catch a glimpse of the landscape behind it. Whether that was indeed a tree or a woman walking I was not quite sure. Back one was always hailed to the letter "I." One began to be tired of "I." Not but what this "I" was a most respectable "I"; honest and logical; as hard as a nut, and polished for centuries by good teaching and good feeding. I respect and admire that "I" from the bottom of my heart. But—here I turned a page or two, looking for something or other—the worst of it is that in the shadow of the letter "I" all is shapeless as mist. Is that a tree? No, it is a woman. But . . . she has not a bone in her body, I thought, watching Phoebe, for that was her name, coming across the beach. Then Alan got up and the shadow of Alan at once obliterated Phoebe. For Alan had views and Phoebe was quenched in the flood of his views. And then Alan, I thought, has passions; and here I turned page after page very fast, feeling that the crisis was approaching, and so it was. It took place on the beach under the sun. It was done very openly. It was done very vigorously. Nothing could have been more indecent. But . . . I had said "but" too often. One cannot go on saying "but." One must finish the sentence somehow, I rebuked myself. Shall I finish it, "But—I am bored!" But why was I bored? Partly because of the dominance of the letter "I" and the aridity, which, like the giant beech tree, it casts within its shade. Nothing will grow there. And partly for some more obscure reason. There seemed to be some obstacle, some impediment in Mr. A's mind which blocked the fountain of creative energy and shored it within narrow limits. . . .

What, then, it amounts to, if this theory of the two sides of the mind holds good, is that virility has now become self-conscious—men, that is to say, are now writing only with the male side of their brains. It is a mistake for a woman to read them, for she will inevitably look for something that she will not find. It is the power of suggestion that one most misses, I thought, taking Mr. B the critic in my hand and reading, very carefully and very dutifully, his remarks upon the art of poetry. Very able they were, acute and full of learning; but the trouble was, that his feelings no longer communicated; his mind seemed separated into different chambers; not a sound carried from one to the other. Thus, when one takes a sentence of Mr. B into the mind it falls plump to the ground—dead; but when one takes a sentence of Coleridge into the mind, it explodes and gives birth to all kinds of other ideas, and that is the only sort of writing of which one can say that it has the secret of perpetual life.

But whatever the reason may be, it is a fact that one must deplore. For it means—here I had come to rows of books by Mr. Galsworthy and Mr. Kipling—that some of the finest works of our greatest living writers fall upon deaf ears. Do what she will a woman cannot find in them that fountain of perpetual life which the critics assure her is there. It is not only that they celebrate male virtues, enforce male values and describe the world of men; it is that the emotion with which these books are permeated is to a woman incomprehensible. It is coming, it is gathering, it is about to burst on one's head, one begins saying long before the end. That picture will fall on old Jolyon's head; he will die of the shock; the old clerk will speak over him two or three obituary words; and all the swans on the Thames will simultaneously burst out singing. But one will rush away before that happens and hide in the gooseberry bushes, for the emotion which is so deep, so subtle, so symbolical to a man moves a woman to wonder. So with Mr. Kipling's officers who turn their backs; and his Sowers who sow the Seed; and his Men who are alone with their Work; and the Flag—one blushes at all these capital letters as if one had been caught eavesdropping at some purely masculine orgy. The fact is that neither Mr. Galsworthy nor Mr.

Kipling has a spark of the woman in him. Thus all their qualities seem to a woman, if one may generalise, crude and immature. They lack suggestive power. And when a book lacks suggestive power, however hard it hits the surface of the mind it cannot penetrate within.

And in that restless mood in which one takes books out and puts them back again without looking at them I began to envisage an age to come of pure, of self-assertive virility, such as the letters of professors (take Sir Walter Raleigh's letters, for instance) seem to forebode, and the rulers of Italy have already brought into being. For one can hardly fail to be impressed in Rome by the sense of unmitigated masculinity; and whatever the value of unmitigated masculinity upon the state, one may question the effect of it upon the art of poetry. At any rate, according to the newspapers, there is a certain anxiety about fiction in Italy. There has been a meeting of academicians whose object it is "to develop the Italian novel." "Men famous by birth, or in finance, industry or the Fascist corporations" came together the other day and discussed the matter, and a telegram was sent to the Duce expressing the hope "that the Fascist era would soon give birth to a poet worthy of it." We may all join in that pious hope, but it is doubtful whether poetry can come out of an incubator. Poetry ought to have a mother as well as a father. The Fascist poem, one may fear, will be a horrid little abortion such as one sees in a glass jar in the museum of some county town. Such monsters never live long, it is said; one has never seen a prodigy of that sort cropping grass in a field. Two heads on one body do not make for length of life.

However, the blame for all this, if one is anxious to lay blame, rests no more upon one sex than upon the other. All seducers and reformers are responsible. . . . All who have brought about a state of sex-consciousness are to blame, and it is they who drive me, when I want to stretch my faculties on a book, to seek it in that happy age . . . when the writer used both sides of his mind equally. One must turn back to Shakespeare then, for Shakespeare was androgynous; and so was Keats and Sterne and Cowper and Lamb and Coleridge. Shelley perhaps was sexless. Milton and Ben Jonson had a dash too much of the male in them. So had Wordsworth and Tolstoi. In our time Proust was wholly androgynous, if not perhaps a little too much of a woman. But that failing is too rare for one to complain of it, since without some mixture of the kind the intellect seems to predominate and the other faculties of the mind harden and become barren. However, I consoled myself with the reflection that this is perhaps a passing phase; much of what I have said in obedience to my promise to give you the course of my thoughts will seem out of date; much of what flames in my eyes will seem dubious to you who have not yet come of age.

Even so, the very first sentence that I would write here, I said, crossing over the the writing-table and taking up the page headed Women and Fiction, is that it is fatal for any one who writes to think of their sex. It is fatal to be a man or woman pure and simple; one must be woman-manly or man-womanly. It is fatal for a woman to lay the least stress on any grievance; to plead even with justice any cause; in any way to speak consciously as a woman. And fatal is no figure of speech; for anything written with that conscious bias is doomed to death. It ceases to be fertilised. Brilliant and effective, powerful and masterly, as it may appear for a day or two, it must wither at nightfall; it cannot grow in the minds of others. Some collaboration has to take place in the mind between the woman and the man before the act of creation can be accomplished. Some marriage of opposites has to be consummated. The whole of the mind must lie wide open if we are to get the sense that the writer is communicating his experience with perfect fullness. There must be freedom and there must be peace. Not a wheel must grate, not a light glimmer. The curtains must be close drawn. The writer, I thought, once his experience is over, must lie back and let his mind celebrate its nuptials in darkness. . . .

30. Walter Gropius, On the Bauhaus

While the Weimar Republic failed to bring about the far-reaching social changes it initially sought, it did succeed in revolutionizing German cultural life. Modernist tendencies in art and literature, which had been systematically discouraged by the ministers of education of the Second Reich, were now supported by the government, and an exhilarating atmosphere of artistic and intellectual experimentation became a defining feature of the Weimar era. The architect Walter Gropius was one of the cultural innovators whose work thrived in this environment.

Born in Berlin in 1883, Gropius had since boyhood been determined to become an architect. "Creation and love of beauty appeared to me the bases of human happiness," he wrote in an autobiographical sketch; and the ugliness of the modern city, contrasted to the visual harmony of the preindustrial town, repelled him. Immediately after World War I, he was appointed director of both a school of applied arts and an academy of fine arts in Saxony. The next year, he boldly merged the two and opened in the city of Weimar the Bauhaus, an institution which would subsequently always be linked with his name. The merger represented a deliberate democratization of culture, in that fine art had traditionally been regarded as hierarchically superior to crafts. A democratic spirit guided the work at the school, too, in that the stated ideal of the Bauhaus was a form of collaboration among artists which would not sacrifice the personal modes of expression of any of the collaborators. The school attracted architects, painters, printmakers, and craftsmen, including Marcel Breuer, Wassily Kandinsky, Paul Klee, and Lyonel Feininger. It sought to create a "total art" in which form followed from function. Each design problem was to be tackled afresh: Gropius stressed that, despite an obvious preference for clean, geometric lines, there was no "modern style," in the sense of a fixed canon of formal elements. Students were to refrain from imitating his own solutions to particular problems of architectural design, just as they were to refrain from imitating the styles of the past.

Almost from the start, the Bauhaus met with hostility from right-wing critics who regarded its artistic modernism as "degenerate." In 1925, in search of a more congenial political climate, Gropius moved the Bauhaus to Dessau; in 1932, he moved it to Berlin. In 1934, feeling the oppressive weight of nazism, Gropius emigrated, coming to the United States in 1937, where he held a chair at Harvard's Graduate School of Design until 1952. He continued to pursue the Bauhaus experiment, influencing American architecture and design to an extent aptly summed up in the title of Tom Wolfe's 1981 essay, "From Bauhaus to Our House."

The first selection below, a statement of the principles of the Bauhaus, was written in 1935. The second selection is an occasional piece—an article written by Gropius for a Weimar newspaper in April 1924—which reflects the intensely political nature of the contemporary German response to the Bauhaus. The piece was written shortly after the Landtag elections had given a majority to the rightist parties, with the result that attacks against the Bauhaus in the Thuringian parliament grew more severe. Finding himself unprotected by the Minister of Culture, Gropius took his case directly to the public.

The New Architecture and the Bauhaus

Can the real nature and significance of the New Architecture be conveyed in words? If I am to attempt to answer this question it must needs be in the form of an analysis of my own work, my own thoughts and discoveries. I hope, therefore, that a short account of my personal evolution as an architect will enable the reader to discern its basic characteristics for himself.

A breach has been made with the past, which allows us to envisage a new aspect of architecture corresponding to the technical civilization of the

From Walter Gropius, *The New Architecture and the Bauhaus*, translated by P. Morton Shand (London: Faber & Faber, 1965), pp. 19–20, 23–26, 29–30, 33–34, 37–40, 43–44, 47–48, 51–54, 57–58, 61–62, 65–66. Reprinted by permission of Faber & Faber Ltd.

age we live in; the morphology of dead styles has been destroyed; and we are returning to honesty of thought and feeling. The general public, formerly profoundly indifferent to everything to do with building, has been shaken out of its torpor; personal interest in architecture as something that concerns every one of us in our daily lives has been very widely aroused; and the broad lines of its future development are already clearly discernible. It is now becoming widely recognized that although the outward forms of the New Architecture differ fundamentally in an organic sense from those of the old, they are not the personal whims of a handful of architects avid for innovation at all cost, but simply the inevitable logical product of the intellectual, social and technical conditions of our age. A quarter of a century's earnest and pregnant struggle preceded their eventual emergence.

But the development of the New Architecture encountered serious obstacles at a very early stage of its development. Conflicting theories and the dogmas enunciated in architects' personal manifestos all helped to confuse the main issue. Technical difficulties were accentuated by the general economic decline that followed the war. Worst of all, "modern" architecture became fashionable in several countries; with the result that formalistic imitation and snobbery distorted the fundamental truth and simplicity on which this renascence was based.

That is why the movement must be purged from within if its original aims are to be saved from the strait-jacket of materialism and false slogans inspired by plagiarism or misconception. Catch phrases like "functionalism" (*die neue Sachlichkeit*) and "fitness for purpose = beauty" have had the effect of deflecting appreciation of the New Architecture into external channels or making it purely one-sided. This is reflected in a very general ignorance of the true motives of its founders: an ignorance that impels superficial minds, who do not perceive that the New Architecture is a bridge uniting opposite poles of thought, to relegate it to a single circumscribed province of design.

For instance rationalization, which many people imagine to be its cardinal principle, is really only its purifying agency. The liberation of architecture from a welter of ornament, the emphasis on its structural functions, and the concentration on concise and economical solutions, represent the purely material side of that formalizing process on which the *practical* value of the New Architecture depends. The other, the aesthetic satisfaction of the human soul, is just as important as the material. Both find their counterpart in that unity which is life itself. What is far more important than this structural economy and its functional emphasis is the intellectual achievement which has made possible a new spatial vision. For whereas building is merely a matter of methods and materials, architecture implies the mastery of space.

For the last century the transition from manual to machine production has so preoccupied humanity that, instead of pressing forward to tackle the new problems of design postulated by this unprecedented transformation, we have remained content to borrow our styles from antiquity and perpetuate historical prototypes in decoration.

That state of affairs is over at last. A new conception of building, based on realities, has emerged; and with it has come a new conception of space. These changes, and the superior technical resources we can now command as a direct result of them, are embodied in the very different appearance of the already numerous examples of the New Architecture.

Just think of all that modern technique has contributed to this decisive phase in the renascence of architecture, and the rapidity of its development!

Our fresh technical resources have furthered the disintegration of solid masses of masonry into slender piers, with consequent far-reaching economies in bulk, space, weight, and haulage. New synthetic substances—steel, concrete, glass—are actively superseding the traditional raw materials of construction. Their rigidity and molecular density have made it possible to erect wide-spanned and all but transparent structures for which the skill of previous ages was manifestly inadequate. This enormous saving in structural volume was an architectural revolution in itself.

One of the outstanding achievements of the new constructional technique has been the abolition of the separating function of the wall. Instead of making the walls the element of support, as in a brick-built house, our new space-saving construction transfers the whole load of the structure to a steel or concrete framework. Thus the role of the walls becomes restricted to that of mere screens stretched between the upright columns of this framework to keep out rain, cold, and noise. In order to save weight and bulk still further, these non-supporting and now merely partitioning walls are made of lightweight pumice-concrete, breeze, or other reliable synthetic materials, in the form of hollow blocks or thin slabs. Systematic technical improvements in steel and concrete, and nicer and nicer calculation of their tensile and compressive strength, are steadily reducing the area occupied by supporting members. This, in turn, naturally leads to a progressively bolder (i.e. wider) opening up of the wall surfaces, which allows rooms to be much better lit. It is, therefore only logical that the old type of window—a hole that had to be hollowed out of the full thickness of a supporting wall—should be giving place more and more to the continuous horizontal casement, subdivided by thin steel mullions, characteristic of the New Architecture. And as a direct result of the growing preponderance of voids over solids, glass is assuming an ever greater structural importance. Its sparkling insubstantiality, and the way it seems to float between wall and wall imponderably as the air, adds a note of gaiety to our modern homes.

In the same way the flat roof is superseding the old penthouse roof with its tiled or slated gables. For its advantages are obvious: (1) light normally shaped top-floor rooms instead of poky attics, darkened by dormers and sloping ceilings, with their almost unutilizable corners; (2) the avoidance of timber rafters, so often the cause of fires; (3) the possibility of turning the top of the house to practical account as a sun loggia, open-air gymnasium, or children's playground; (4) simpler structural provision for subsequent additions, whether as extra stories or new wings; (5) elimination of unnecessary surfaces presented to the action of wind and weather, and therefore less need for repairs; (6) suppression of hanging gutters, external rain-pipes, etc., that often erode rapidly. With the development of air transport the architect will have to pay as much attention to the bird's-eye perspective of his houses as to their elevations. The utilization of flat roofs as "grounds" offers us a means of re-acclimatizing nature amidst the stony deserts of our great towns; for the plots from which she has been evicted to make room for buildings can be given back to her up aloft. Seen from the skies, the leafy house-tops of the cities of the future will look like endless chains of hanging gardens. But the primary advantage of the flat roof is that it renders possible a much freer kind of interior planning.

Standardization

The elementary impulse of all national economy proceeds from the desire to meet the needs of the community at less cost and effort by the improvement of its productive organizations. This has led progressively to mechanization, specialized division of labour, and rationalization: seemingly irrevocable steps in industrial evolution which have the same implications for building as for every other branch of organized production. Were mechanization an end in itself it would be an unmitigated calamity, robbing life of half its fulness and variety by stunting men and women into sub-human, robot-like automatons. (Here we touch the deeper causality of the dogged resistance of the old civilization of handicrafts to the new world-order of the machine.) But in the last resort mechanization can have only one object: to abolish the individual's physical toil of providing himself with the necessities of existence in order that hand and brain may be set free for some higher order of activity.

Our age has initiated a rationalization of industry based on the kind of working partnership between manual and mechanical production we call standardization which is already having direct repercussions on building.

There can be no doubt that the systematic application of standardization to housing would effect enormous economies—so enormous, indeed, that it is impossible to estimate their extent at present.

Standardization is not an impediment to the development of civilization, but, on the contrary, one of its immediate prerequisites. A standard may be defined as that simplified practical exemplar of anything in general use which embodies a fusion of the best of its anterior forms—a fusion preceded by the elimination of the personal content of their designers and all otherwise ungeneric or non-essential features. Such an impersonal standard is called a "norm," a word derived from a carpenter's square.

The fear that individuality will be crushed out by the growing "tyranny" of standardization is the sort of myth which cannot sustain the briefest examination. In all great epochs of history the existence of standards—that is the conscious adoption of type-forms—has been the criterion of a polite and well-ordered society; for it is a commonplace that repetition of the same things for the same purposes exercises a settling and civilizing influence on men's minds.

As the basic cellular unit of that larger unit the street, the dwelling-house represents a typical group-organism. The uniformity of the cells whose multiplication by streets forms the still larger unit of the city therefore calls for formal expression. Diversity in their sizes provides the necessary modicum of variation, which in turn promotes natural competition between dissimilar types developing side by side. The most admired cities of the past are conclusive proof that the reiteration of "typical" (i.e. typified) buildings notably enhances civic dignity and coherence. As a maturer and more final model than any of the individual prototypes merged in it, an accepted standard is always a formal common denominator of a whole period. The unification of architectural components would have the salutary effect of imparting that homogeneous character to our towns which is the distinguishing mark of a superior urban culture. A prudent limitation of variety to a few standard types of buildings increases their quality and decreases their cost; thereby raising the social level of the population as a whole. Proper respect for tradition will find a truer echo in these than in the miscellaneous solutions of an often arbitrary and aloof individualism because the greater communal utility of the former embodies a deeper architectural significance. The concentration of essential qualities in standard types presupposes methods of unprecedented industrial potentiality, which entail capital outlay on a scale that can only be justified by mass-production.

Rationalization

Building, hitherto an essentially manual trade, is already in course of transformation into an organized industry. More and more work that used to be done on the scaffolding is now carried out under factory conditions far away from the site. The dislocation which the seasonal character of building operations causes employers and employed alike—as, indeed, the community at large—is being gradually overcome. Continuous activity throughout the year will soon become the rule instead of the exception.

And just as fabricated materials have been evolved which are superior to natural ones in accuracy and uniformity, so modern practice in house construction is increasingly approximating to the successive stages of a manufacturing process. We are approaching a state of technical proficiency when it will become possible to rationalize buildings and mass-produce them in factories by resolving their structure into a number of component parts. Like boxes of toy bricks, these will be assembled in various formal compositions in a dry state: which means that building will definitely cease to be dependent on the weather. Ready-made houses of solid fireproof construction, that can be delivered fully equipped from stock, will ultimately become one of the principal products of industry. Before this is practicable, however, every part of the house—floor-beams, wall-slabs, windows, doors, staircases, and fittings—will have to be normed. The repetition of standardized parts, and the use of identical materials in different buildings, will have the same sort of coordinating and sobering effect on the aspect of our towns as uniformity of type in modern attire has in social life. But that will in no sense restrict the architect's freedom of design. For although every house and block of flats will bear the unmistakable impress of our age, there will always remain, as in the clothes we wear, sufficient scope for the individual to find expression for his own personality. The net result should be a happy architectonic combination of maximum standardization and maximum variety. Since 1910 I have consistently advocated pre-fabrication of houses in numerous articles and lectures; besides which I have undertaken a number of practical experiments in this field of research in conjunction with important industrial concerns.

Dry assembly offers the best prospects because (to take only one of its advantages) moisture in one form or another is the principal obstacle to economy in masonry or brick construction (mortar joints). Moisture is the direct cause of most of the weaknesses of the old methods of building. It leads to badly fitting joints, warping and staining, unforeseen piecework, and serious loss of time and money through delays in drying. By eliminating this factor, and so assuring the perfect interlocking of all component parts, the pre-fabricated house makes it possible to guarantee a fixed price and a definite period of construction. Moreover the use of reliable modern materials enables the stability and insulation of a building to be increased and its weight and bulk decreased. A pre-fabricated house can be loaded on to a couple of lorries at the factory—walls, floors, roof, fittings and all—

conveyed to the site, and put together in next to no time regardless of the season of the year.

The outstanding concomitant advantages of rationalized construction are superior economy and an enhanced standard of living. Many of the things that are regarded as luxuries today will be standard fitments in the homes of tomorrow.

So much for technique!—But what about beauty?

The New Architecture throws open its walls like curtains to admit a plenitude of fresh air, daylight and sunshine. Instead of anchoring buildings ponderously into the ground with massive foundations, it poises them lightly, yet firmly, upon the face of the earth; and bodies itself forth, not in stylistic imitation or ornamental frippery, but in those simple and sharply modelled designs in which every part merges naturally into the comprehensive volume of the whole. Thus its aesthetic meets our material and psychological requirements alike.

For unless we choose to regard the satisfaction of those conditions which can alone animate, and so humanize, a room—spatial harmony, repose, proportion—as an ideal of some higher order, architecture cannot be limited to the fulfilment of its structural function.

We have had enough and to spare of the arbitrary reproduction of historic styles. In the progress of our advance from the vagaries of mere architectural caprice to the dictates of structural logic, we have learned to seek concrete expression of the life of our epoch in clear and crisply simplified forms.

Having briefly surveyed what the New Architecture has already achieved, and outlined the probable course of its development in the near future, I will turn back to my own part in its genesis. In 1908, when I finished my preliminary training and embarked on my career as an architect with Peter Behrens, the prevalent conceptions of architecture and architectural education were still entirely dominated by the academic stylisticism of the classical "Orders." It was Behrens who first introduced me to logical and systematical coordination in the handling of architectural problems. In the course of my active association with the important schemes on which he was then engaged, and frequent discussions with him and other prominent members of the *Deutscher Werkbund,* my own ideas began to crystallize as to what the essential nature of building ought to be. I became obsessed by the conviction that modern constructional technique could not be denied expression in architecture, and that that expression demanded the use of unprecedented forms. Dynamic as was the stimulus of Behrens's masterly teaching, I could not contain my growing impatience to start on my own account. In 1910 I set up in independent practice. Shortly afterwards I was commissioned to design the *Faguswerke* at Alfeld-an-der-Leine in conjunction with the late Adolf Meyer. This factory, and the buildings entrusted to me for the Cologne *Werkbund* Exhibition of 1914, clearly manifested the essential characteristics of my later work.

The full consciousness of my responsibility in advancing ideas based on my own reflections only came home to me as a result of the war, in which these theoretical premises first took definite shape. After that violent interruption, which kept me, like most of my fellow-architects, from work for four years, every thinking man felt the necessity for an intellectual change of front. Each in his own particular sphere of activity aspired to help in bridging the disastrous gulf between reality and idealism. It was then that the immensity of the mission of the architects of my own generation first dawned on me. I saw that an architect cannot hope to realize his ideas unless he can influence the industry of his country sufficiently for a new school of design to arise as a result; and unless that school succeeds in acquiring authoritative significance. I saw, too, that to make this possible would require a whole staff of collaborators and assistants: men who would work, not automatically as an orchestra obeys its conductor's baton, but independently, although in close cooperation, to further a common cause.

The Bauhaus

This idea of the fundamental unity underlying all branches of design was my guiding inspiration in founding the original *Bauhaus*. During the war I had been summoned to an audience with the Grand Duke of Sachsen-Weimar-Eisenach to discuss my taking over the Weimar School of Arts and Crafts (*Grossherzogliche Kunstgewerbeschule*) from the distinguished Belgian architect, Henri Van de Velde, who had himself suggested that I should be his successor. Having asked for, and been accorded, full powers in regard to reorganization I assumed control of the Weimar School of Arts and Crafts, and also of the Weimar Academy of Fine Art (*Grossherzogliche Hochschule für Bildende Kunst*), in the spring of 1919. As a first step towards the realization of a much wider plan—in which my primary aim was that the principle of training the individual's natural capacities to grasp life as a whole, a single cosmic entity, should form the basis of instruction throughout the school instead of in only one or two arbitrarily "specialized" classes—I amalgamated these institutions into a *Hochschule für Gestaltung*, or High School for Design, under the name of *Das Staatliche Bauhaus Weimar*.

In carrying out this scheme I tried to solve the ticklish problem of combining imaginative design and technical proficiency. That meant finding a new and hitherto non-existent type of collaborator who could be moulded into being equally proficient in both. As a safeguard against any recrudescence of the old dilettante handicraft spirit I made every pupil (including the architectural students) bind himself to complete his full legal term of apprenticeship in a formal letter of engagement registered with the local trades council. I insisted on manual instruction, not as an end in itself, or with any idea of turning it to incidental account by actually producing handicrafts, but as providing a good all-round training for hand and eye, and being a practical first step in mastering industrial processes.

The *Bauhaus* workshops were really laboratories for working out practical new designs for present-day articles and improving models for mass-production. To create type-forms that would meet all technical, aesthetic and commercial demands required a picked staff. It needed a body of men of wide general culture as thoroughly versed in the practical and mechanical sides of design as in its theoretical and formal laws. Although most parts of these prototype models had naturally to be made by hand, their constructors were bound to be intimately acquainted with factory methods of production and assembly, which differ radically from the practices of handicraft. It is to its intrinsic particularity that each different type of machine owes the "genuine stamp" and "individual beauty" of its products. Senseless imitation of hand-made goods by machinery infallibly bears the mark of a makeshift substitute. The *Bauhaus* represented a school of thought which believes that the difference between industry and handicraft is due, far less to the different nature of the tools employed in each, than to subdivision of labour in the one and undivided control by a single workman in the other. Handicrafts and industry may be regarded as opposite poles that are gradually approaching each other. The former have already begun to change their traditional nature. In the future the field of handicrafts will be found to lie mainly in the preparatory stages of evolving experimental new type-forms for mass-production.

There will, of course, always be talented craftsmen who can turn out individual designs and find a market for them. The *Bauhaus,* however, deliberately concentrated primarily on what has now become a work of paramount urgency: to avert mankind's enslavement by the machine by giving its products a content of reality and significance, and so saving the home from mechanistic anarchy. This meant evolving goods specifically designed for mass-production. Our object was to eliminate every drawback of the machine without sacrificing any one of its real advantages. We aimed at realizing standards of excellence, not creating transient novelties.

When the *Bauhaus* was four years old, and all the essentials of its organization had been definitely established, it could already look back on initial achievements that had commanded widepread attention in Germany and abroad. It was then that I decided to set forth my views. These had naturally developed considerably in the light of experience, but they had not undergone any substantial change as a result. The pages which follow are abstracted from this essay, which was published in 1923 under the title of *Idee und Aufbau des Staatlichen Bauhauses* (The Conception and Realization of the Bauhaus).

The art of building is contingent on the coordinated team-work of a band of active collaborators whose orchestral cooperation symbolizes the cooperative organism we call society. Architecture and design in a general sense are consequently matters of paramount concern to the nation at large. There is a widespread heresy that art is just a useless luxury. This is one of our fatal legacies from a generation which arbitrarily elevated some of its branches above the rest as the "Fine Arts," and in so doing robbed all of their basic identity and common life. The typical embodiment of the *l'art pour l'art* mentality, and its chosen instrument, was "the Academy." By depriving handicrafts and industry of the informing services of the artist the academies drained them of their vitality, and brought about the artist's complete isolation from the community. Art is not one of those things that may be imparted. Whether a design be the outcome of knack or creative impulse depends on individual propensity. But if what we call art cannot be taught or learnt, a thorough knowledge of its principles and of sureness of hand can be. Both are as necessary for the artist of genius as for the ordinary artisan.

What actually happened was that the academies turned out an "artistic proletariat" foredoomed to semi-starvation. Lulled by false hopes of the rewards of genius, this soon numerous class was brought up to the "professions" of architect, painter, sculptor, etc., without the requisite training to give it an independent artistic volition and to enable it to find its feet in the struggle for existence. Thus such skill as it acquired was of that amateurish studio-bred order which is innocent of realities like technical progress and commercial demand. The besetting vice of the academy schools was that they were obsessed by that rare "biological" sport, the commanding genius; and forgot that their business was to teach drawing and painting to hundreds and hundreds of minor talents, barely one in a thousand of whom could be expected to have the makings of a real architect or painter. In the vast majority of cases this hopelessly one-sided instruction condemned its pupils to the lifelong practice of a purely sterile art. Had these hapless drones been given a proper practical training they could have become useful members of society.

The rise of the academies spelt the gradual decay of the spontaneous traditional art that had permeated the life of the whole people. All that remained was a "Salon Art," entirely remote from everyday life, which by the middle of the XIXth Century had petered out into mere exercises in individual virtuosity. It was then that a revolt began. Ruskin and Morris strove to find a means of reuniting the world of art with the world of work. Towards the end of the century their lead was followed by Van de Velde, Olbrich, Behrens and others on the Continent. This movement which started with the building of the "Artists' Colony" at Darmstadt and culminated in the founding of the *Deutscher Werkbund* in Munich, led to the establishment of *Kunstgewerbeschulen* in the principal German towns. These were intended to give the rising generation of artists a practical training for handicrafts and industry. But the academic spirit was too firmly implanted for that "practical training" to be more than a dilettante smattering. The *project* and the "composition" still held pride of place in their curricula. The first attempts to get away from the old unreal art-for-art's sake attitude failed because they were not planned on a sufficiently wide front and did not go deep enough to touch the root of the evil.

Notwithstanding, commerce, and more particularly industry, began to look towards the artist. There was a genuine ambition to supplement efficiency by beauty of shape and finish: things which the working technician was not in a position to supply. So manufacturers bought "artistic designs." But these paper aids proved broken reeds. The artist was a man "remote from the world," at once too unpractical and too unfamiliar with technical requirements to be able to assimilate his conceptions of form to the processes of manufacture. On the other hand the business man and the technician lacked sufficient foresight to realize that the combination of form, efficiency and economy they desired could only be obtained by recognizing painstaking cooperation with a responsible artist as part of the routine of production. Since the kind of designer to fill this gap was non-existent, the future training of artistic talent clearly demanded a thorough practical grounding under factory conditions combined with sound theoretical instruction in the laws of design.

Thus the *Bauhaus* was inaugurated with the specific object of realizing a modern architectonic art, which, like human nature, should be all-embracing in its scope. Within that sovereign federative union all the different "arts" (with the various manifestations and tendencies of each)— every branch of design, every form of technique—could be coordinated and find their appointed place. Our ultimate goal, therefore, was the composite but inseparable work of art, the great building, in which the old dividing-line between monumental and decorative elements would have disappeared forever.

The quality of a man's creative work depends on a proper balance of his faculties. It is not enough to train one or other of these, since all alike need to be developed. That is why manual and mental instruction in design were given simultaneously.

The Staatliche Bauhaus and the Thuringian Landtag

On April 12 [1924], the faction of the German Völkische [later known as Nazi] group in the Thuringian Landtag put the following "Small Question" to the state government:

"According to §1 of the Bauhaus statutes the training of the Bauhaus students provides for the completion of their apprenticeship with an examination for a journeyman's certificate to be taken before the Handwerkskammer (Apprenticeship Board).

"According to our information the teaching staff of the Staatliche Bauhaus consists of 19 Masters under whose direction approximately 15 students have completed the Bauhaus training in the period of four and a half years of the existence of the Bauhaus. These students passed their journeyman's examination before the Handwerkskammer, but only five of them are said to be still active in the Bauhaus.

"Our questions are:

"1. Is it true that this glaring disproportion between teaching staff and the number of trained journeymen exists at the Bauhaus, and does the government think the big expenditure required by the Bauhaus budget is justified by the ridiculous number of Bauhaus journeymen?

"2. Is it true that the government has not taken any steps so far to phase out such an unprofitable institution as the Bauhaus, despite pleas from various sides demanding such action and despite the fact that before April 1 of this year there would have been an opportunity to start such action by terminating the contracts of a number of Bauhaus Masters?

"3. Is it true that doubts have been raised about the moral qualities of the Director of the Bauhaus, Gropius, and does the government have any evidence to justify such accusations?"

In reply to this "Small Question," the Director of the Staatliche Bauhaus, Walter Gropius, issues the following statement:

"The question put to the state government on April 12, by the faction of the Völkische parties in the Thuringian Landtag and directed against the Staatliche Bauhaus and against me as its Director evidences a deplorable lack of information and understanding of the acknowledged cultural work of this Institute and its leading personalities. The incomprehensible looseness in regard to the information gathered for the question and the superficial view of the work of the Bauhaus which it expresses makes it incumbent upon the Bauhaus to furnish a strong reply.

"To Point 1: The Bauhaus is not a trade school. The crafts are a means

From Hans M. Wingler, *The Bauhaus: Weimar Dessau Berlin Chicago*, translated by Wolfgang Jabs and Basil Gilbert and edited by Joseph Stein (Cambridge, Mass.: MIT Press, 1969), pp. 84–86; English adaptation ©1969 by the Massachusetts Institute of Technology. Reprinted by permission of the publisher.

of training students within the comprehensive artistic and professional education which the Bauhaus offers. Therefore the mere number of journeyman's certificates issued is not the determining factor by which to judge the institution, but rather that accomplishment of the Bauhaus which has been acknowledged by a wide section of the public and by numerous experts in the field. Yet, in spite of the fact that because of the reconstruction of the workshops regular training of apprentices started essentially only as late as 1921—hence just three years ago—the numerical results, contrary to the assertion of the inquiry, are as follows:

"a) 23 (not 15) apprentices at the Bauhaus received their public journeyman's certificates from the Handwerkskammer. (Of that number 12—not 5—journeymen are still at the Bauhaus.) Furthermore, an additional 6 apprentices of the Bauhaus are presently taking their journeyman's examination before the Handwerkskammer. 11 students who joined the Bauhaus as journeymen (6 of them as heads of workshops) have earned their Master's certificates from the Handwerkskammer.

"b) 28 apprentices, aside from those counted under "a," have reached journeyman's status in those workshops for which the Handwerkskammer does not issue public certificates (the weaving workshop, the glass-painting workshop, and the stage workshop). (12 of these are still at the Bauhaus.) . . .

"f) A total of 526 students have been enrolled at the Bauhaus since October 1919. A larger number of them completed the preliminary course only. Numerous apprentices had to discontinue their training in the middle of their course of studies at the Bauhaus and often even shortly before their journeyman's examination because of their financial plight during the time of inflation. But the majority of these students found employment on the open market because of the valuable knowledge they had acquired at the Bauhaus; they passed their journeyman's examinations elsewhere. . . .

"The budget allowances for this dual institute (formerly the Grand-Ducal Saxon Academy of Arts and the Grand-Ducal Saxon School of Arts and Crafts) have been demonstrably lower than those of most of the corresponding single institutes in the country. Side by side with the school activity, the production activity, which was established by the state, has even yielded a surplus of 30,292 gold marks in capital goods and cash, based on a conservative estimate and after deduction of all state allowances and loans.

"This was possible despite exceptional local and general obstacles which were overcome only by the most resolute devotion on the part of the Bauhaus members. Since the success of this year's Leipzig Spring Fair (contracts amounting to approximately 12,900 gold marks) the possibility of economic self-sufficiency has greatly increased.

"The actual results of the Bauhaus—the first successful attempt of a basic training for journeymen, the exhibition of 1923, and the artistic, economic, and educational achievements—represent a unique cultural accomplishment unprecedented in Germany, particularly since the entire institute had to be rebuilt during a time of general decline. We look back upon this accomplishment with pride.

"To Point 2: According to the resolution of the Thuringian State Ministry of July 1923, the contracts of the Masters at the Staatliche Bauhaus were extended until March 31, 1925. Therefore, there could not have been a termination of contracts on April 1 of this year.

"To Point 3: Of the teaching staff at the Bauhaus, which at the moment consists of 16 permanent Masters, including the Director and the business manager, and 2 part-time teachers, two Masters are foreigners: the world-renowned Russian painter Kandinsky, who has spent most of his life in Germany and has written his books in German, and the distinguished Hungarian painter Moholy-Nagy. The painter Feininger, who is equally well known all over the world, was born in America but is of German descent and since the war has been without a nationality. The German students in the Bauhaus consider it an honor to profit from the encouragement of these artists who are renowned in the entire cultural world. The fact that these irreplaceable men are being attacked on account of their non-German origin is a disgrace for our German culture, which is greatly enriched by contact with them. The German Bauhaus is proud of them.

"To Point 4: Since no objective points of attack could be found, the inquiry falls back on the method of publicly casting suspicion upon my person. Cause for this question to the government was the disgraceful slander that was brought forth against myself and the Bauhaus more than a year ago by a number of former employees who had been dismissed without notice. These libelous statements, having been carried to the state government and other public offices, have been officially investigated upon my request and been rejected as "unfounded," "irresponsible," and "dishonorable" by the Ministry of Education. Retribution for these insults through public legal action is about to be concluded. Stemming from the same sources was the public attack in the Landtag in 1923 against me and the Bauhaus, which was subsequently dismissed by the Landtag.

"In view of the facts here stated, the entire question posed to the government on April 12 collapses. For the past four and a half years the Staatliche Bauhaus has been hampered in its important work by ignorance and malicious slander of the most humiliating kind. When now even public representatives are beginning to believe these false machinations, then the Bauhaus has to protest very strongly against such derogation, particularly at a moment when distinguished experts all over the country in important publications of all persuasions welcome the constructive work of the Bauhaus as an essential cultural factor in the development of an "intellectual Germany," and when, based on the achievements that have become known up to now, these men urgently demand its patronage by the state.

"Gropius, Director of the Staatliche Bauhaus."

31. Walter Benjamin, *The Work of Art in the Age of Mechanical Reproduction*

Once regarded by only a few close friends as among the most original critical and analytic minds of his time, Walter Benjamin (1892–1940) has, since the mid-1950s, achieved a posthumous fame which has made that assessment a widely shared one.

Born in Berlin into a family of well-to-do Jews, Benjamin prepared for an academic career. But his thesis on the origin of German tragedy proved too strange and obscure to satisfy his examiners at the University of Frankfurt and, thus barred from the professoriate, he became instead a freelance man of letters, eking out a living as a translator and journalist. Benjamin was affiliated with the Frankfurt School, the group which founded the Institute for Social Research in 1923 in order to develop Marxist theory in an atmosphere free of the pressures of party politics and whose collective project of Critical Theory came to include the amalgamation of Freudian and Marxist ideas. Benjamin's affiliation with the School was, however, a rather loose and often troubled one; and despite many entreaties and his own difficult situation after the Nazi rise to power, he would not follow the School when it changed its location to New York City in 1934, explaining that he considered himself the "last European." Indeed, Benjamin seems to have shied away from complete affiliation with any group: in the mid-1920s he was on the verge of joining the Communist party but never became a member; he flirted seriously with Zionism throughout his life but would neither make the decision to go to Palestine nor rule it out as a possibility. It is telling that his love of Paris, which dated from his first boyhood visit, was based upon his perception of the French capital as a home for the homeless.

Benjamin spent the last seven years of his life in Paris as a political refugee. His situation there became perilous after the fall of France in 1940—the Gestapo confiscated his apartment—and he finally accepted aid from his friends at the Institute for Social Research in the form of an emergency visa to the United States. Lacking a French exit visa, he was forced to go on foot through the Pyrenees to a point on the Spanish border known to be unguarded by the French police. He arrived there only to learn that Spain had just closed the border and that he was to retrace his steps and return to France the next day. That night Benjamin, knowing that return to France was likely to mean deportation to Germany, took his own life.

Most of Benjamin's writing, like that of his close friend and fellow Frankfurt School member Theodor Adorno, concerned culture and aesthetics. Benjamin produced important critical essays on Proust and Baudelaire (both of whom he had translated into German), Goethe, Kafka, and Brecht, as well as portions of a never-completed magnum opus to be called "Paris, Capital of the Nineteenth Century." The essay below, "The Work of Art in the Age of Mechanical Reproduction," was first published in 1936 and is a study of the interrelation of art, technology, and mass society. The concept of the "aura" used by Benjamin here had been developed by the Frankfurt School. The essay concludes with Benjamin's reconceptualization of fascism in terms of the role it accords to art.

Preface

When Marx undertook his critique of the capitalistic mode of production, this mode was in its infancy. Marx directed his efforts in such a way as to give them prognostic value. He went back to the basic conditions underlying capitalistic production and through his presentation showed what could be expected of capitalism in the future. The result was that one could expect it not only to exploit the proletariat with increasing intensity, but ultimately to create conditions which would make it possible to abolish capitalism itself.

The transformation of the superstructure, which takes place far more slowly than that of the substructure, has taken more than half a century to manifest in all areas of culture the change in the conditions of production. Only today can it be indicated what form this has taken. Certain prognostic requirements should be met by these statements. However, theses about the art of the proletariat after its assumption of power or about the art of a classless society would have less bearing on these demands than theses about the developmental tendencies of art under present conditions of production. Their dialectic is no less noticeable in the superstructure than in the economy. It would therefore be wrong to underestimate the value of such theses as a weapon. They brush aside a number of outmoded con-

From Walter Benjamin, *Illuminations*, edited by Hannah Arendt and translated by Harry Zohn (New York: Harcourt, Brace & World, 1968), pp. 217–251; ©1955 by Suhrkamp Verlag, Frankfurt a.M.; English translation ©1968 by Harcourt, Brace & World, Inc. Reprinted by permission of Harcourt Brace Jovanovich, Inc., and Jonathan Cape Limited. Footnotes omitted.

cepts, such as creativity and genius, eternal value and mystery—concepts whose uncontrolled (and at present almost uncontrollable) application would lead to a processing of data in the Fascist sense. The concepts which are introduced into the theory of art in what follows differ from the more familiar terms in that they are completely useless for the purposes of Fascism. They are, on the other hand, useful for the formulation of revolutionary demands in the politics of art.

1

In principle a work of art has always been reproducible. Man-made artifacts could always be imitated by men. Replicas were made by pupils in practice of their craft, by masters for diffusing their works, and, finally, by third parties in the pursuit of gain. Mechanical reproduction of a work of art, however, represents something new. Historically, it advanced intermittently and in leaps at long intervals, but with accelerated intensity. The Greeks knew only two procedures of technically reproducing works of art: founding and stamping. Bronzes, terra cottas, and coins were the only art works which they could produce in quantity. All others were unique and could not be mechanically reproduced. With the woodcut graphic art became mechanically reproducible for the first time, long before script became reproducible by print. The enormous changes which printing, the mechanical reproduction of writing, has brought about in literature are a familiar story. However, within the phenomenon which we are here examining from the perspective of world history, print is merely a special, though particularly important, case. During the Middle Ages engraving and etching were added to the woodcut; at the beginning of the nineteenth century lithography made its appearance.

   With lithography the technique of reproduction reached an essentially new stage. This much more direct process was distinguished by the tracing of the design on a stone rather than its incision on a block of wood or its etching on a copperplate and permitted graphic art for the first time to put its products on the market, not only in large numbers as hitherto, but also in daily changing forms. Lithography enabled graphic art to illustrate everyday life, and it began to keep pace with printing. But only a few decades after its invention, lithography was surpassed by photography. For the first time in the process of pictorial reproduction, photography freed the hand of the most important artistic functions which henceforth devolved only upon the eye looking into a lens. Since the eye perceives more swiftly than the hand can draw, the process of pictorial reproduction was accelerated so enormously that it could keep pace with speech. A film operator shooting a scene in the studio captures the images at the speed of an actor's speech. Just as lithography virtually implied the illustrated newspaper, so did photography foreshadow the sound film. The technical reproduction of sound was tackled at the end of the last century. These convergent endeavors made predictable a situation which Paul Valéry pointed up in this sentence: "Just as water, gas, and electricity are brought into our houses from far off to satisfy our needs in response to a minimal effort, so we shall be supplied with visual or auditory images, which will appear and disappear at a simple movement of the hand, hardly more than a sign." Around 1900 technical reproduction had reached a standard that not only permitted it to reproduce all transmitted works of art and thus to cause the most profound change in their impact upon the public; it also had captured a place of its own among the artistic processes. For the study of this standard nothing is more revealing than the nature of the repercussions that these two different manifestations—the reproduction of works of art and the art of the film—have had on art in its traditional form.

2

Even the most perfect reproduction of a work of art is lacking in one element: its presence in time and space, its unique existence at the place where it happens to be. This unique existence of the work of art determined the history to which it was subject throughout the time of its existence. This includes the changes which it may have suffered in physical condition over the years as well as the various changes in its ownership. The traces of the first can be revealed only by chemical or physical analyses which it is impossible to perform on a reproduction; changes of ownership are subject to a tradition which must be traced from the situation of the original.

The presence of the original is the prerequisite to the concept of authenticity. Chemical analyses of the patina of a bronze can help to establish this, as does the proof that a given manuscript of the Middle Ages stems from an archive of the fifteenth century. The whole sphere of authenticity is outside technical—and, of course, not only technical—reproducibility. Confronted with its manual reproduction, which was usually branded as a forgery, the original preserved all its authority; not so *vis à vis* technical reproduction. The reason is twofold. First, process reproduction is more independent of the original than manual reproduction. For example, in photography, process reproduction can bring out those aspects of the original that are unattainable to the naked eye yet accessible to the lens, which is adjustable and chooses its angle at will. And photographic reproduction, with the aid of certain processes, such as enlargement or slow motion, can capture images which escape natural vision. Secondly, technical reproduction can put the copy of the original into situations which would be out of reach for the original itself. Above all, it enables the original to meet the beholder halfway, be it in the form of a photograph or a phonograph record. The cathedral leaves its locale to be received in the studio of a lover of art; the choral production, performed in an auditorium or in the open air, resounds in the drawing room.

The situations into which the product of mechanical reproduction can be brought may not touch the actual work of art, yet the quality of its presence is always depreciated. This holds not only for the art work but also, for instance, for a landscape which passes in review before the spectator in a movie. In the case of the art object, a most sensitive nucleus—namely, its authenticity—is interfered with whereas no natural object is vulnerable on that score. The authenticity of a thing is the essence of all that is transmissible from its beginning, ranging from its substantive duration to its testimony to the history which it has experienced. Since the historical testimony rests on the authenticity, the former, too, is jeopardized by reproduction when substantive duration ceases to matter. And what is really jeopardized when the historical testimony is affected is the authority of the object.

One might subsume the eliminated element in the term "aura" and go on to say: that which withers in the age of mechanical reproduction is the aura of the work of art. This is a symptomatic process whose significance points beyond the realm of art. One might generalize by saying: the technique of reproduction detaches the reproduced object from the domain of tradition. By making many reproductions it substitutes a plurality of copies for a unique existence. And in permitting the reproduction to meet the beholder or listener in his own particular situation, it reactivates the object reproduced. These two processes lead to a tremendous shattering of tradition which is the obverse of the contemporary crisis and renewal of mankind. Both processes are intimately connected with the contemporary mass movements. Their most powerful agent is the film. Its social significance, particularly in its most positive form, is inconceivable without its destructive, cathartic aspect, that is, the liquidation of the traditional value of the cultural heritage. This phenomenon is most palpable in the great historical films. It extends to ever new positions. In 1927 Abel Gance exclaimed enthusiastically: "Shakespeare, Rembrandt, Beethoven will make films . . . all legends, all mythologies and all myths, all founders of religion, and the very religions . . . await their exposed resurrection, and the heroes crowd each other at the gate." Presumably without intending it, he issued an invitation to a far-reaching liquidation.

3

During long periods of history, the mode of human sense perception changes with humanity's entire mode of existence. The manner in which human sense perception is organized, the medium in which it is accomplished, is determined not only by nature but by historical circumstances as well. The fifth century, with its great shifts of population, saw the birth of the late Roman art industry and the Vienna Genesis, and there developed not only an art different from that of antiquity but also a new kind of perception. The scholars of the Viennese school, Riegl and Wickhoff, who resisted the weight of classical tradition under which these later art forms had been buried, were the first to draw conclusions from them concerning the organization of perception at the time. However far-reaching their insight, these scholars limited themselves to showing the significant, formal hallmark which characterized perception in late Roman times. They did not attempt—and, perhaps, saw no way—to show the social transformations expressed by these changes of perception. The conditions for an analogous insight are more favorable in the present. And if changes in the medium of contemporary perception can be comprehended as decay of the aura, it is possible to show its social causes.

The concept of aura which was proposed above with reference to historical objects may usefully be illustrated with reference to the aura of natural ones. We define the aura of the latter as the unique phenomenon of a distance, however close it may be. If, while resting on a summer afternoon, you follow with your eyes a mountain range on the horizon or a branch which casts its shadow over you, you experience the aura of those mountains, of that branch. This image makes it easy to comprehend the social bases of the contemporary decay of the aura. It rests on two circumstances, both of which are related to the increasing significance of the masses in contemporary life. Namely, the desire of contemporary masses to bring things "closer" spatially and humanly, which is just as ardent as their bent toward overcoming the uniqueness of every reality by accepting its reproduction. Every day the urge grows stronger to get hold of an object at very close range by way of its likeness, its reproduction. Unmistakably, reproduction as offered by picture magazines and newsreels differs from the image seen by the unarmed eye. Uniqueness and permanence are as closely linked in the latter as are transitoriness and reproducibility in the former. To pry an object from its shell, to destroy its aura, is the mark of a perception whose "sense of the universal equality of things" has increased to such a degree that it extracts it even from a unique object by means of reproduction. Thus is manifested in the field of perception what in the theoretical sphere is noticeable in the increasing importance of statistics.

The adjustment of reality to the masses and of the masses to reality is a process of unlimited scope, as much for thinking as for perception.

4

The uniqueness of a work of art is inseparable from its being imbedded in the fabric of tradition. This tradition itself is thoroughly alive and extremely changeable. An ancient statue of Venus, for example, stood in a different traditional context with the Greeks, who made it an object of veneration, than with the clerics of the Middle Ages, who viewed it as an ominous idol. Both of them, however, were equally confronted with its uniqueness, that is, its aura. Originally the contextual integration of art in tradition found its expression in the cult. We know that the earliest art works originated in the service of a ritual—first the magical, then the religious kind. It is significant that the existence of the work of art with reference to its aura is never entirely separated from its ritual function. In other words, the unique value of the "authentic" work of art has its basis in ritual, the location of its original use value. This ritualistic basis, however remote, is still recognizable as secularized ritual even in the most profane forms of the cult of beauty. The secular cult of beauty, developed during the Renaissance and prevailing for three centuries, clearly showed that ritualistic basis in its decline and the first deep crisis which befell it. With the advent of the first truly revolutionary means of reproduction, photography, simultaneously with the rise of socialism, art sensed the approaching crisis which has become evident a century later. At the time, art reacted with the doctrine of *l'art pour l'art,* that is, with a theology of art. This gave rise to what might be called a negative theology in the form of the idea of "pure" art, which not only denied any social function of art but also any categorizing by subject matter. (In poetry, Mallarmé was the first to take this position.)

An analysis of art in the age of mechanical reproduction must do justice to these relationships, for they lead us to an all-important insight: for the first time in world history, mechanical reproduction emancipates the work of art from its parasitical dependence on ritual. To an ever greater degree the work of art reproduced becomes the work of art designed for reproducibility. From a photographic negative, for example, one can make any number of prints; to ask for the "authentic" print makes no sense. But the instant the criterion of authenticity ceases to be applicable to artistic production, the total function of art is reversed. Instead of being based on ritual, it begins to be based on another practice—politics.

5

Works of art are received and valued on different planes. Two polar types stand out: with one, the accent is on the cult value; with the other, on the exhibition value of the work. Artistic production begins with ceremonial objects destined to serve in a cult. One may assume that what mattered was their existence, not their being on view. The elk portrayed by the man of the Stone Age on the walls of his cave was an instrument of magic. He did expose it to his fellow men, but in the main it was meant for the spirits. Today the cult value would seem to demand that the work of art remain hidden. Certain statues of gods are accessible only to the priest in the cella; certain Madonnas remain covered nearly all year round; certain sculptures on medieval cathedrals are invisible to the spectator on ground level. With the emanicipation of the various art practices from ritual go increasing opportunities for the exhibition of their products. It is easier to exhibit a portrait bust that can be sent here and there than to exhibit the statue of a divinity that has its fixed place in the interior of a temple. The same holds for the painting as against the mosaic or fresco that preceded it. And even though the public presentability of a mass originally may have been just as great as that of a symphony, the latter originated at the moment when its public presentability promised to surpass that of the mass.

With the different methods of technical reproduction of a work of art, its fitness for exhibition increased to such an extent that the quantitative shift between its two poles turned into a qualitative transformation of its nature. This is comparable to the situation of the work of art in prehistoric times when, by the absolute emphasis on its cult value, it was, first and foremost, an instrument of magic. Only later did it come to be recognized as a work of art. In the same way today, by the absolute emphasis on its exhibition value the work of art becomes a creation with entirely new functions, among which the one we are conscious of, the artistic function, later may be recognized as incidental. This much is certain: today photography and the film are the most serviceable exemplifications of this new function.

6

In photography, exhibition value begins to displace cult value all along the line. But cult value does not give way without resistance. It retires into an ultimate retrenchment: the human countenance. It is no accident that the portrait was the focal point of early photography. The cult of remembrance of loved ones, absent or dead, offers a last refuge for the cult value of the picture. For the last time the aura emanates from the early photographs in the fleeting expression of a human face. This is what constitutes their melancholy, incomparable beauty. But as man withdraws from the photographic image, the exhibition value for the first time shows its superiority to the ritual value. To have pinpointed this new stage constitutes the incomparable significance of Atget, who, around 1900, took photographs of deserted Paris streets. It has quite justly been said of him that he photographed them like scenes of crime. The scene of a crime, too, is deserted; it is photographed for the purpose of establishing evidence. With Atget, photographs become standard evidence for historical occurrences, and acquire a hidden political significance. They demand a specific kind of approach; free-floating contemplation is not appropriate to them. They stir the viewer; he feels challenged by them in a new way. At the same time picture magazines begin to put up signposts for him, right ones or wrong ones, no matter. For the first time, captions have become obligatory. And it is clear that they have an altogether different character than the title of a painting. The directives which the captions give to those looking at pictures in illustrated magazines soon become even more explicit and more imperative in the film where the meaning of each single picture appears to be prescribed by the sequence of all preceding ones.

7

The nineteenth-century dispute as to the artistic value of painting versus photography today seems devious and confused. This does not diminish its importance, however; if anything, it underlines it. The dispute was in fact the symptom of a historical transformation the universal impact of which was not realized by either of the rivals. When the age of mechanical reproduction separated art from its basis in cult, the semblance of its autonomy disappeared forever. The resulting change in the function of art transcended the perspective of the century; for a long time it even escaped that of the twentieth century, which experienced the development of the film.

Earlier much futile thought had been devoted to the question of whether photography is an art. The primary question—whether the very invention of photography had not transformed the entire nature of art—was not raised. Soon the film theoreticians asked the same ill-considered question with regard to the film. But the difficulties which photography caused traditional aesthetics were mere child's play as compared to those raised by the film. Whence the insensitive and forced character of early theories of the film. Abel Gance, for instance, compares the film with hieroglyphs: "Here, by a remarkable regression, we have come back to the level of expression of the Egyptians. . . . Pictorial language has not yet matured because our eyes have not yet adjusted to it. There is as yet insufficient respect for, insufficient cult of, what it expresses." Or, in the words of Séverin-

Mars: "What art has been granted a dream more poetical and more real at the same time! Approached in this fashion the film might represent an incomparable means of expression. Only the most high-minded persons, in the most perfect and mysterious moments of their lives, should be allowed to enter its ambience." Alexandre Arnoux concludes his fantasy about the silent film with the question: "Do not all the bold descriptions we have given amount to the definition of prayer?" It is instructive to note how their desire to class the film among the "arts" forces these theoreticians to read ritual elements into it—with a striking lack of discretion. Yet when these speculations were published, films like *L'Opinion publique* and *The Gold Rush* had already appeared. This, however, did not keep Abel Gance from adducing hieroglyphs for purposes of comparison, nor Séverin-Mars from speaking of the film as one might speak of paintings by Fra Angelico. Characteristically, even today ultrareactionary authors give the film a similar contextual significance—if not an outright sacred one, then at least a supernatural one. Commenting on Max Reinhardt's film version of *A Midsummer Night's Dream,* Werfel states that undoubtedly it was the sterile copying of the exterior world with its streets, interiors, railroad stations, restaurants, motorcars, and beaches which until now had obstructed the elevation of the film to the realm of art. "The film has not yet realized its true meaning, its real possibilities . . . these consist in its unique faculty to express by natural means and with incomparable persuasiveness all that is fairylike, marvelous, supernatural."

8

The artistic performance of a stage actor is definitely presented to the public by the actor in person; that of the screen actor, however, is presented by a camera, with a twofold consequence. The camera that presents the performance of the film actor to the public need not respect the performance as an integral whole. Guided by the cameraman, the camera continually changes its position with respect to the performance. The sequence of positional views which the editor composes from the material supplied him constitutes the completed film. It comprises certain factors of movement which are in reality those of the camera, not to mention special camera angles, close-ups, etc. Hence, the performance of the actor is subjected to a series of optical tests. This is the first consequence of the fact that the actor's performance is presented by means of a camera. Also, the film actor lacks the opportunity of the stage actor to adjust to the audience during his performance, since he does not present his performance to the audience in person. This permits the audience to take the position of a critic, without experiencing any personal contact with the actor. The audience's identification with the actor is really an identification with the camera. Consequently the audience takes the position of the camera; its approach is that of testing. This is not the approach to which cult values may be exposed.

9

For the film, what matters primarily is that the actor represents himself to the public before the camera, rather than representing someone else. One of the first to sense the actor's metamorphosis by this form of testing was Pirandello. Though his remarks on the subject in his novel *Si Gira* were limited to the negative aspects of the question and to the silent film only, this hardly impairs their validity. For in this respect, the sound film did not change anything essential. What matters is that the part is acted not for an audience but for a mechanical contrivance—in the case of the sound film, for two of them. "The film actor," wrote Pirandello, "feels as if in exile—exiled not only from the stage but also from himself. With a vague sense of discomfort he feels inexplicable emptiness: his body loses its corporeality, it evaporates, it is deprived of reality, life, voice, and the noises caused by his moving about, in order to be changed into a mute image, flickering an instant on the screen, then vanishing into silence. . . . The projector will play with his shadow before the public, and he himself must be content to play before the camera." The situation might also be characterized as follows: for the first time—and this is the effect of the film—man has to operate with his whole living person, yet forgoing its aura. For aura is tied to his presence; there can be no replica of it. The aura which, on the stage, emanates from Macbeth, cannot be separated for the spectators from that of the actor. However, the singularity of the shot in the studio is that the camera is substituted for the public. Consequently, the aura that envelops the actor vanishes, and with it the aura of the figure he portrays.

It is not surprising that it should be a dramatist such as Pirandello who, in characterizing the film, inadvertently touches on the very crisis in which we see the theater. Any thorough study proves that there is indeed no greater contrast than that of the stage play to a work of art that is completely subject to or, like the film, founded in, mechanical reproduction. Experts have long recognized that in the film "the greatest effects are almost always obtained by 'acting' as little as possible. . . ." In 1932 Rudolf Arnheim saw "the latest trend . . . in treating the actor as a stage prop chosen for its characteristics and . . . inserted at the proper place." With this idea something else is closely connected. The stage actor identifies himself with the character of his role. The film actor very often is denied this opportunity. His creation is by no means all of a piece; it is composed of many separate performances. Besides certain fortuitous considerations, such as cost of studio, availability of fellow players, décor, etc., there are elementary necessities of equipment that split the actor's work into a series of mountable episodes. In particular, lighting and its installation require the presentation of an event that, on the screen, unfolds as a rapid and unified scene, in a sequence of separate shootings which may take hours at the studio; not to mention more obvious montage. Thus a jump from the window can be shot in the studio as a jump from a scaffold, and the ensuing flight, if need be, can be shot weeks later when outdoor scenes are taken. Far more paradoxical cases can easily be construed. Let us assume that an actor is supposed to be startled by a knock at the door. If his reaction is not satisfactory, the director can resort to an expedient: when the actor happens to be at the studio again he has a shot fired behind him without his being forewarned of it. The frightened reaction can be shot now and be cut into the screen version. Nothing more strikingly shows that art has left the realm of the "beautiful semblance" which, so far, had been taken to be the only sphere where art could thrive.

10

The feeling of strangeness that overcomes the actor before the camera, as Pirandello describes it, is basically of the same kind as the estrangement felt before one's own image in the mirror. But now the reflected image has become separable, transportable. And where is it transported? Before the public. Never for a moment does the screen actor cease to be conscious of this fact. While facing the camera he knows that ultimately he will face the public, the consumers who constitute the market. This market, where he offers not only his labor but also his whole self, his heart and soul, is beyond his reach. During the shooting he has as little contact with it as any article made in a factory. This may contribute to that oppression, that new anxiety which, according to Pirandello, grips the actor before the camera. The film responds to the shriveling of the aura with an artificial build-up of the "personality" outside the studio. The cult of the movie star, fostered by the money of the film industry, preserves not the unique aura of the person but the "spell of the personality," the phony spell of a commodity. So long as the movie-makers' capital sets the fashion, as a rule no other revolutionary merit can be accredited to today's film than the promotion of a revolutionary criticism of traditional concepts of art. We do not deny that in some cases today's films can also promote revolutionary criticism of social conditions, even of the distribution of property. However, our present study is no more specifically concerned with this than is the film production of Western Europe.

It is inherent in the technique of the film as well as that of sports that everybody who witnesses its accomplishments is somewhat of an expert. This is obvious to anyone listening to a group of newspaper boys leaning on their bicycles and discussing the outcome of a bicycle race. It is not for nothing that newspaper publishers arrange races for their delivery boys. These arouse great interest among the participants, for the victor has an opportunity to rise from delivery boy to professional racer. Similarly, the newsreel offers everyone the opportunity to rise from passer-by to movie extra. In this way any man might even find himself part of a work of art, as witness Vertoff's *Three Songs About Lenin* or Ivens' *Borinage*. Any man today can lay claim to being filmed. This claim can best be elucidated by a comparative look at the historical situation of contemporary literature.

For centuries a small number of writers were confronted by many thousands of readers. This changed toward the end of the last century. With the increasing extension of the press, which kept placing new political, religious, scientific, professional, and local organs before the readers, an increasing number of readers became writers—at first, occasional ones. It began with the daily press opening to its readers space for "letters to the editor." And today there is hardly a gainfully employed European who could not, in principle, find an opportunity to publish somewhere or other comments on his work, grievances, documentary reports, or that sort of thing. Thus, the distinction between author and public is about to lose its basic character. The difference becomes merely functional; it may vary from case to case. At any moment the reader is ready to turn into a writer. As expert, which he had to become willy-nilly in an extremely specialized work process, even if only in some minor respect, the reader gains access to authorship. In the Soviet Union work itself is given a voice. To present it verbally is part of a man's ability to perform the work. Literary license is now founded on polytechnic rather than specialized training and thus becomes common property.

All this can easily be applied to the film, where transitions that in literature took centuries have come about in a decade. In cinematic practice, particularly in Russia, this change-over has partially become established reality. Some of the players whom we meet in Russian films are not actors in our sense but people who portray *themselves*—and primarily in their own work processes. In Western Europe the capitalistic exploitation of the film denies consideration to modern man's legitimate claim to being reproduced. Under these circumstances the film industry is trying hard to spur the interest of the masses through illusion-promoting spectacles and dubious speculations.

11

The shooting of a film, especially of a sound film, affords a spectacle unimaginable anywhere at any time before this. It presents a process in which it is impossible to assign to a spectator a viewpoint which would exclude from the actual scene such extraneous accessories as camera equipment, lighting machinery, staff assistants, etc.—unless his eye were on a line parallel with the lens. This circumstance, more than any other, renders superficial and insignificant any possible similarity between a scene in the studio and one on the stage. In the theater one is well aware of the place from which the play cannot immediately be detected as illusionary. There is no such place for the movie scene that is being shot. Its illusionary nature is that of the second degree, the result of cutting. That is to say, in the studio the mechanical equipment has penetrated so deeply into reality that its pure aspect freed from the foreign substance of equipment is the result of a special procedure, namely, the shooting by the specially adjusted camera and the mounting of the shot together with other similar ones. The equipment-free aspect of reality here has become the height of artifice; the sight of immediate reality has become an orchid in the land of technology.

Even more revealing is the comparison of these circumstances, which differ so much from those of the theater, with the situation in painting. Here the question is: How does the cameraman compare with the painter? To answer this we take recourse to an analogy with a surgical operation. The surgeon represents the polar opposite of the magician. The magician heals a sick person by the laying on of hands; the surgeon cuts into the patient's body. The magician maintains the natural distance between the patient and himself; though he reduces it very slightly by the laying on of hands, he greatly increases it by virtue of his authority. The surgeon does exactly the reverse; he greatly diminishes the distance between himself and the patient by penetrating into the patient's body, and increases it but little by the caution with which his hand moves among the organs. In short, in contrast to the magician—who is still hidden in the medical practitioner—the surgeon at the decisive moment abstains from facing the patient man to man; rather, it is through the operation that he penetrates into him.

Magician and surgeon compare to painter and cameraman. The painter maintains in his work a natural distance from reality, the cameraman penetrates deeply into its web. There is a tremendous difference between the pictures they obtain. That of the painter is a total one, that of the cameraman consists of multiple fragments which are assembled under a new law. Thus, for contemporary man the representation of reality by the film is incomparably more significant than that of the painter, since it offers, precisely because of the thoroughgoing permeation of reality with mechanical equipment, an aspect of reality which is free of all equipment. And that is what one is entitled to ask from a work of art.

12

Mechanical reproduction of art changes the reaction of the masses toward art. The reactionary attitude toward a Picasso painting changes into the progressive reaction toward a Chaplin movie. The progressive reaction is characterized by the direct, intimate fusion of visual and emotional enjoyment with the orientation of the expert. Such fusion is of great social significance. The greater the decrease in the social significance of an art form, the sharper the distinction between criticism and enjoyment by the public. The conventional is uncritically enjoyed, and the truly new is criticized with aversion. With regard to the screen, the critical and the receptive attitudes of the public coincide. The decisive reason for this is that individual reactions are predetermined by the mass audience response they are about to produce, and this is nowhere more pronounced than in the film. The moment these responses become manifest they control each other. Again, the comparison with painting is fruitful. A painting has always had an excellent chance to be viewed by one person or by a few. The simultaneous contemplation of paintings by a large public, such as developed in the nineteenth century, is an early symptom of the crisis of painting, a crisis which was by no means occasioned exclusively by photography but rather in a relatively independent manner by the appeal of art works to the masses.

Painting simply is in no position to present an object for simultaneous collective experience, as it was possible for architecture at all times, for the epic poem in the past, and for the movie today. Although this circumstance in itself should not lead one to conclusions about the social role of painting, it does constitute a serious threat as soon as painting, under special conditions and, as it were, against its nature, is confronted directly by the masses. In the churches and monasteries of the Middle Ages and at the princely courts up to the end of the eighteenth century, a collective reception of paintings did not occur simultaneously, but by graduated and hierarchized mediation. The change that has come about is an expression of the particular conflict in which painting was implicated by the mechanical reproducibility of paintings. Although paintings began to be publicly exhibited in galleries and salons, there was no way for the masses to organize and control themselves in their reception. Thus the same public which responds in a progressive manner toward a grotesque film is bound to respond in a reactionary manner to surrealism.

13

The characteristics of the film lie not only in the manner in which man presents himself to mechanical equipment but also in the manner in which, by means of this apparatus, man can represent his environment. A glance at occupational psychology illustrates the testing capacity of the equipment. Psychoanalysis illustrates it in a different perspective. The film has enriched our field of perception with methods which can be illustrated by those of Freudian theory. Fifty years ago, a slip of the tongue passed more or less unnoticed. Only exceptionally may such a slip have revealed dimensions of depth in a conversation which had seemed to be taking its course on the surface. Since the *Psychopathology of Everyday Life* things have changed. This book isolated and made analyzable things which had heretofore floated along unnoticed in the broad stream of perception. For the entire spectrum of optical, and now also acoustical, perception the film has brought about a similar deepening of apperception. It is only an obverse of this fact that behavior items shown in a movie can be analyzed much more precisely and from more points of view than those presented on paintings or on the stage. As compared with painting, filmed behavior lends itself more readily to analysis because of its incomparably more precise statements of the situation. In comparison with the stage scene, the filmed behavior item lends itself more readily to analysis because it can be isolated more easily. This circumstance derives its chief importance from its tendency to promote the mutual penetration of art and science. Actually, of a screened behavior item which is neatly brought out in a certain situation, like a muscle of a body, it is difficult to say which is more fascinating, its artistic value or its value for science. To demonstrate the identity of the artistic and scientific uses of photography which heretofore usually were separated will be one of the revolutionary functions of the film.

By close-ups of the things around us, by focusing on hidden details of familiar objects, by exploring commonplace milieus under the ingenious guidance of the camera, the film, on the one hand, extends our comprehension of the necessities which rule our lives; on the other hand, it manages to assure us of an immense and unexpected field of action. Our taverns and our metropolitan streets, our offices and furnished rooms, our railroad stations and our factories appeared to have us locked up hopelessly. Then came the film and burst this prison-world asunder by the dynamite of the tenth of a second, so that now, in the midst of its far-flung ruins and debris, we calmly and adventurously go traveling. With the close-up, space expands; with slow motion, movement is extended. The enlargement of a snapshot does not simply render more precise what in any case was visible, though unclear: it reveals entirely new structural formations of the subject.

So, too, slow motion not only presents familiar qualities of movement but reveals in them entirely unknown ones "which, far from looking like retarded rapid movements, give the effect of singularly gliding, floating, supernatural motions." Evidently a different nature opens itself to the camera than opens to the naked eye—if only because an unconsciously penetrated space is substituted for a space consciously explored by man. Even if one has a general knowledge of the way people walk, one knows nothing of a person's posture during the fractional second of a stride. The act of reaching for a lighter or a spoon is familiar routine, yet we hardly know what really goes on between hand and metal, not to mention how this fluctuates with our moods. Here the camera intervenes with the resources of its lowerings and liftings, its interruptions and isolations, its extensions and accelerations, its enlargements and reductions. The camera introduces us to unconscious optics as does psychoanalysis to unconscious impulses.

14

One of the foremost tasks of art has always been the creation of a demand which could be fully satisfied only later. The history of every art form shows critical epochs in which a certain art form aspires to effects which could be fully obtained only with a changed technical standard, that is to say, in a new art form. The extravagances and crudities of art which thus appear, particularly in the so-called decadent epochs, actually arise from the nucleus of its richest historical energies. In recent years, such barbarisms were abundant in Dadaism. It is only now that its impulse becomes discernible: Dadaism attempted to create by pictorial—and literary—means the effects which the public today seeks in the film.

Every fundamentally new, pioneering creation of demands will carry beyond its goal. Dadaism did so to the extent that it sacrificed the market values which are so characteristic of the film in favor of higher ambitions—though of course it was not conscious of such intentions as here described. The Dadaists attached much less importance to the sales value of their work than to its uselessness for contemplative immersion. The studied degradation of their material was not the least of their means to achieve this uselessness. Their poems are "word salad" containing obscenities and every imaginable waste product of language. The same is true of their paintings, on which they mounted buttons and tickets. What they intended and achieved was a relentless destruction of the aura of their creations, which they branded as reproductions with the very means of production. Before a painting of Arp's or a poem by August Stramm it is impossible to take time for contemplation and evaluation as one would before a canvas of Derain's or a poem by Rilke. In the decline of middle-class society, contemplation became a school for asocial behavior; it was countered by distraction as a variant of social conduct. Dadaistic activities actually assured a rather vehement distraction by making works of art the center of scandal. One requirement was foremost: to outrage the public.

From an alluring appearance or persuasive structure of sound the work of art of the Dadaists became an instrument of ballistics. It hit the spectator like a bullet, it happened to him, thus acquiring a tactile quality. It promoted a demand for the film, the distracting element of which is also primarily tactile, being based on changes of place and focus which periodically assail the spectator. Let us compare the screen on which a film unfolds with the canvas of a painting. The painting invites the spectator to contemplation; before it the spectator can abandon himself to his associations. Before the movie frame he cannot do so. No sooner has his eye grasped a scene than it is already changed. It cannot be arrested. Duhamel, who detests the film and knows nothing of its significance, though something of its structure, notes this circumstance as follows: "I can no longer think what I want to think. My thoughts have been replaced by moving images." The spectators' process of association in view of these images is indeed interrupted by their constant, sudden change. This constitutes the shock effect of the film, which, like all shocks, should be cushioned by heightened presence of mind. By means of its technical structure, the film has taken the physical shock effect out of the wrappers in which Dadaism had, as it were, kept it inside the moral shock effect.

15

The mass is a matrix from which all traditional behavior toward works of art issues today in a new form. Quantity has been transmuted into quality. The greatly increased mass of participants has produced a change in the mode of participation. The fact that the new mode of participation first appeared in a disreputable form must not confuse the spectator. Yet some people have launched spirited attacks against precisely this superficial aspect. Among these, Duhamel has expressed himself in the most radical manner. What he objects to most is the kind of participation which the movie elicits from the masses. Duhamel calls the movie "a pastime for helots, a diversion for uneducated, wretched, worn-out creatures who are consumed by their worries . . . , a spectacle which requires no concentration and presupposes no intelligence . . . , which kindles no light in the heart and awakens no hope other than the ridiculous one of someday becoming a 'star' in Los Angeles." Clearly, this is at bottom the same ancient lament that the masses seek distraction whereas art demands concentration from the spectator. That is a commonplace. The question remains whether it provides a platform for the analysis of the film. A closer look is needed here. Distraction and concentration form polar opposites which may be stated as follows: A man who concentrates before a work of art is absorbed by it. He enters into this work of art the way legend tells of the Chinese painter when he viewed his finished painting. In contrast, the distracted mass absorbs the work of art. This is most obvious with regard to buildings. Architecture has always represented the prototype of a work of art the reception of which is consummated by a collectivity in a state of distraction. The laws of its reception are most instructive.

Buildings have been man's companions since primeval times. Many art forms have developed and perished. Tragedy begins with the Greeks, is extinguished with them, and after centuries its "rules" only are revived. The epic poem, which had its origin in the youth of nations, expires in Europe at the end of the Renaissance. Panel painting is a creation of the Middle Ages, and nothing guarantees its uninterrupted existence. But the human need for shelter is lasting. Architecture has never been idle. Its history is more ancient than that of any other art, and its claim to being a living force has significance in every attempt to comprehend the relationship of the masses to art. Buildings are appropriated in a twofold manner: by use and by perception—or rather, by touch and sight. Such appropriation cannot be understood in terms of the attentive concentration of a tourist before a famous building. On the tactile side there is no counterpart to contemplation on the optical side. Tactile appropriation is accomplished not so much by attention as by habit. As regards architecture, habit determines to a large extent even optical reception. The latter, too, occurs much less through rapt attention than by noticing the object in incidental fashion. This mode of appropriation, developed with reference to architecture, in certain circumstances acquires canonical value. For the tasks which face the human apparatus of perception at the turning points of history cannot be solved by optical means, that is, by contemplation, alone. They are mastered gradually by habit, under the guidance of tactile appropriation.

The distracted person, too, can form habits. More, the ability to master certain tasks in a state of distraction proves that their solution has become a matter of habit. Distraction as provided by art presents a covert control of the extent to which new tasks have become soluble by apperception. Since, moreover, individuals are tempted to avoid such tasks, art will tackle the most difficult and most important ones where it is able to mobilize the masses. Today it does so in the film. Reception in a state of distraction, which is increasing noticeably in all fields of art and is symptomatic of profound changes in apperception, finds in the film its true means of exercise. The film with its shock effect meets this mode of reception halfway. The film makes the cult value recede into the background not only by putting the public in the position of the critic, but also by the fact that at the movies this position requires no attention. The public is an examiner, but an absent-minded one.

Epilogue

The growing proletarianization of modern man and the increasing formation of masses are two aspects of the same process. Fascism attempts to organize the newly created proletarian masses without affecting the property structure which the masses strive to eliminate. Fascism sees its salvation in giving these masses not their right, but instead a chance to express themselves. The masses have a right to change property relations; Fascism seeks to give them an expression while preserving property. The logical result of Fascism is the introduction of aesthetics into political life. The violation of the masses, whom Fascism, with its *Führer* cult, forces to their knees, has its counterpart in the violation of an apparatus which is pressed into the production of ritual values.

All efforts to render politics aesthetic culminate in one thing: war. War and war only can set a goal for mass movements on the largest scale while respecting the traditional property system. This is the political formula for the situation. The technological formula may be stated as follows: Only war makes it possible to mobilize all of today's technical resources while maintaining the property system. It goes without saying that the Fascist apotheosis of war does not employ such arguments. Still, Marinetti says in his manifesto on the Ethiopian colonial war: "For twenty-seven years we Futurists have rebelled against the branding of war as antiaesthetic. . . . Accordingly we state: . . . War is beautiful because it establishes man's dominion over the subjugated machinery by means of gas masks, terrifying megaphones, flame throwers, and small tanks. War is beautiful because it initiates the dreamt-of metalization of the human body. War is beautiful because it enriches a flowering meadow with the fiery orchids of machine guns. War is beautiful because it combines the gunfire, the cannonades, the cease-fire, the scents, and the stench of putrefaction into a symphony. War is beautiful because it creates new architecture, like that of the big tanks, the geometrical formation flights, the smoke spirals from burning villages, and many others. . . . Poets and artists of Futurism! . . . remember these principles of an aesthetics of war so that your struggle for a new literature and a new graphic art . . . may be illumined by them!"

This manifesto has the virtue of clarity. Its formulations deserve to be accepted by dialecticians. To the latter, the aesthetics of today's war appears as follows: If the natural utilization of productive forces is impeded by the property system, the increase in technical devices, in speed, and in the sources of energy will press for an unnatural utilization, and this is found in war. The destructiveness of war furnishes proof that society has not been mature enough to incorporate technology as its organ, that technology has not been sufficiently developed to cope with the elemental forces of society. The horrible features of imperialistic warfare are attributable to the discrepancy between the tremendous means of production and their inadequate utilization in the process of production—in other words, to unemployment and the lack of markets. Imperialistic war is a rebellion of technology which collects, in the form of "human material," the claims to which society has denied its natural material. Instead of draining rivers, society directs a human stream into a bed of trenches; instead of dropping seeds from airplanes, it drops incendiary bombs over cities; and through gas warfare the aura is abolished in a new way.

"*Fiat ars—pereat mundus*," says Fascism, and, as Marinetti admits, expects war to supply the artistic gratification of a sense perception that has been changed by technology. This is evidently the consummation of "*l'art pour l'art.*" Mankind, which in Homer's time was an object of contemplation for the Olympian gods, now is one for itself. Its self-alienation has reached such a degree that it can experience its own destruction as an aesthetic pleasure of the first order. This is the situation of politics which Fascism is rendering aesthetic. Communism responds by politicizing art.

Custodians of the Liberal Conscience: Two Views from Vienna

32. Friedrich von Hayek, *The Road to Serfdom*

Friedrich August von Hayek (born 1899) was born into a Viennese family of some intellectual distinction. He received a doctor of law degree from the University of Vienna in 1921 and then obtained a position in an Austrian government office which handled the settlement of prewar debts. At this time Hayek adhered to moderate socialist ideas and was quite impressed by the writings of Walther Rathenau (see document 10). Under the influence of one of his superiors at work (Ludwig von Mises, who was a leading Viennese economist and a severe critic of socialism), however, Hayek made a sudden and permanent turn toward traditional liberal doctrines.

In 1923 Hayek received a doctorate in economics and political science and set off for America for further studies. After his return to Vienna he collaborated with Mises in the founding of the Austrian Institute for Business Cycle Research, which he then directed from 1927 to 1931. In 1931 he emigrated to Britain and became professor of economics at the London School of Economics. There followed a spectacular rise to prominence and then an equally spectacular loss of influence as Hayek dueled with J. M. Keynes over the nature of the Great Depression and the proper course for dealing with it. By the end of the 1930s the focus of Hayek's attention began to turn toward social and political philosophy, one of his first major efforts being his tract *The Road to Serfdom* (1944), from which the following passages are taken.

Hayek represents a powerful tradition of Liberal thought within the political culture of Central Europe, namely, the Austrian School of Economics, founded by Carl Menger, Eugen von Böhm-Bawerk, and Friedrich von Wieser. In the writings of its younger exponents like Mises and Hayek in the 1920s and 1930s, the Austrian School opposed the social interventionist doctrines of interwar Socialist parties like the Austro-Marxists. During the late 1940s the work of Hayek was influential among the Freiburg circle of neo-liberal economists and social theorists (led by Walter Eucken). Out of this circle (as well as from the work of Alfred Müller-Armack) emerged some of the theoretical assumptions which underpinned the political concept of the "Social Market economy" made famous by Ludwig Erhard in western Germany in the late 1940s and 1950s (see below, document 38).

In 1950 Hayek joined the Committee on Social Thought at the University of Chicago, where he remained until 1962. From 1962 to 1968 he was professor of economics at the University of Freiburg and from 1969 to 1977 held a similar position at the University of Salzburg. In 1974 Hayek was awarded the Nobel Prize for Economic Science.

The Abandoned Road

When the course of civilization takes an unexpected turn—when, instead of the continuous progress which we have come to expect, we find ourselves threatened by evils associated by us with past ages of barbarism—

From Friedrich A. Hayek, *The Road to Serfdom* (Chicago: University of Chicago Press; London: Routledge & Kegan Paul, 1944), pp. 10–23, 210–15; ©1944 by The University of Chicago Press. Reprinted by permission of the publishers. Footnotes omitted.

we naturally blame anything but ourselves. Have we not all striven according to our best lights, and have not many of our finest minds incessantly worked to make this a better world? Have not all our efforts and hopes been directed toward greater freedom, justice, and prosperity? If the outcome is so different from our aims—if, instead of freedom and prosperity, bondage and misery stare us in the face—is it not clear that sinister forces must have foiled our intentions, that we are the victims of some evil power which must be conquered before we can resume the road to better things? However much we may differ when we name the culprit—whether it is the wicked capitalist or the vicious spirit of a particular nation, the stupidity of our elders, or a social system not yet, although we have struggled against it for half a century, fully overthrown—we all are, or at least were until recently, certain of one thing: that the leading ideas which during the last generation have become common to most people of good will and have determined the major changes in our social life cannot have been wrong. We are ready to accept almost any explanation of the present crisis of our civilization except one: that the present state of the world may be the result of genuine error on our own part and that the pursuit of some of our most cherished ideals has apparently produced results utterly different from those which we expected.

While all our energies are directed to bring this war to a victorious conclusion, it is sometimes difficult to remember that even before the war the values for which we are now fighting were threatened here and destroyed elsewhere. Though for the time being the different ideals are represented by hostile nations fighting for their existence, we must not forget that this conflict has grown out of a struggle of ideas within what, not so long ago, was a common European civilization and that the tendencies which have culminated in the creation of the totalitarian systems were not confined to the countries which have succumbed to them. Though the first task must now be to win the war, to win it will only gain us another opportunity to face the basic problems and to find a way of averting the fate which has overtaken kindred civilizations.

Now, it is somewhat difficult to think of Germany and Italy, or of Russia, not as different worlds but as products of a development of thought in which we have shared; it is, at least so far as our enemies are concerned, easier and more comforting to think that they are entirely different from us and that what happened there cannot happen here. Yet the history of these countries in the years before the rise of the totalitarian system showed few features with which we are not familiar. The external conflict is a result of a transformation of European thought in which others have moved so much faster as to bring them into irreconcilable conflict with our ideals, but which has not left us unaffected.

That a change of ideas and the force of human will have made the world what it is now, though men did not foresee the results, and that no spontaneous change in the facts obliged us thus to adapt our thought is perhaps particularly difficult for the Anglo-Saxon nations to see, just because in this development they have, fortunately for them, lagged behind most of the European peoples. We still think of the ideals which guide us, and have guided us for the past generation, as ideals only to be realized in the future and are not aware how far in the last twenty-five years they have already transformed not only the world but also our own countries. We still believe that until quite recently we were governed by what are vaguely called nineteenth-century ideas or the principle of laissez faire. Compared with some other countries, and from the point of view of those impatient to speed up the change, there may be some justification for such belief. But although until 1931 England and America had followed only slowly on the path on which others had led, even by then they had moved so far that only those whose memory goes back to the years before the last war know what a liberal world has been like.

The crucial point of which our people are still so little aware is, however, not merely the magnitude of the changes which have taken place during the last generation but the fact that they mean a complete change in the direction of the evolution of our ideas and social order. For at least twenty-five years before the specter of totalitarianism became a real threat, we had progressively been moving away from the basic ideas on which Western civilization has been built. That this movement on which we have entered with such high hopes and ambitions should have brought us face to face with the totalitarian horror has come as a profound shock to this generation, which still refuses to connect the two facts. Yet this development merely confirms the warnings of the fathers of the liberal philosophy which we still profess. We have progressively abandoned that freedom in economic affairs without which personal and political freedom has never existed in the past. Although we had been warned by some of the greatest political thinkers of the nineteenth century, by De Tocqueville and Lord Acton, that socialism means slavery, we have steadily moved in the direction of socialism. And now that we have seen a new form of slavery arise before our eyes, we have so completely forgotten the warning that it scarcely occurs to us that the two things may be connected.

How sharp a break not only with the recent past but with the whole evolution of Western civilization the modern trend toward socialism means becomes clear if we consider it not merely against the background of the nineteenth century but in a longer historical perspective. We are rapidly abandoning not the views merely of Cobden and Bright, of Adam Smith and Hume, or even of Locke and Milton, but one of the salient characteristics of Western civilization as it has grown from the foundations laid by Christianity and the Greeks and Romans. Not merely nineteenth- and eighteenth-century liberalism, but the basic individualism inherited by us from Erasmus and Montaigne, from Cicero and Tacitus, Pericles and Thucydides, is progressively relinquished.

The Nazi leader who described the National Socialist revolution as a counter-Renaissance spoke more truly than he probably knew. It was the decisive step in the destruction of that civilization which modern man had built up from the age of the Renaissance and which was, above all, an individualist civilization. Individualism has a bad name today, and the term has come to be connected with egotism and selfishness. But the individualism of which we speak in contrast to socialism and all other forms of collectivism has no necessary connection with these. Only gradually in the course of this book shall we be able to make clear the contrast between the two opposing principles. But the essential features of that individualism which, from elements provided by Christianity and the philosophy of classical antiquity, was first fully developed during the Renaissance and has since grown and spread into what we know as Western civilization—are the respect for the individual man *qua* man, that is, the recognition of his own views and tastes as supreme in his own sphere, however narrowly that may be circumscribed, and the belief that it is desirable that men should develop their own individual gifts and bents. "Freedom" and "liberty" are now words so worn with use and abuse that one must hesitate to employ them to express the ideals for which they stood during that period. "Tolerance" is, perhaps, the only word which still preserves the full meaning of the principle which during the whole of this period was in the ascendant and which only in recent times has again been in decline, to disappear completely with the rise of the totalitarian state.

The gradual transformation of a rigidly organized hierarchic system into one where men could at least attempt to shape their own life, where man gained the opportunity of knowing and choosing between different forms of life, is closely associated with the growth of commerce. From the commercial cities of northern Italy the new view of life spread with commerce to the west and north, through France and the southwest of Germany to the Low Countries and the British Isles, taking firm root wherever there was no despotic political power to stifle it. In the Low Countries and Britain it for a long time enjoyed its fullest development and for the first time had an opportunity to grow freely and to become the foundation of the social and political life of these countries. And it was from there that in the late seventeenth and eighteenth centuries it again began to spread in a more fully developed form to the West and East, to the New World and to the center of the European continent, where devastating wars and political oppression had largely submerged the earlier beginnings of a similar growth.

During the whole of this modern period of European history the general direction of social development was one of freeing the individual from the ties which had bound him to the customary or prescribed ways in the pursuit of his ordinary activities. The conscious realization that the spontaneous and uncontrolled efforts of individuals were capable of producing a complex order of economic activities could come only after this development had made some progress. The subsequent elaboration of a consistent argument in favor of economic freedom was the outcome of a free growth of economic activity which had been the undesigned and unforeseen by-product of political freedom.

Perhaps the greatest result of the unchaining of individual energies was the marvelous growth of science which followed the march of individual liberty from Italy to England and beyond. That the inventive faculty of man had been no less in earlier periods is shown by the many highly ingenious automatic toys and other mechanical contrivances constructed while industrial technique still remained stationary and by the development in some industries which, like mining or watchmaking, were not subject to restrictive controls. But the few attempts toward a more extended industrial use of mechanical inventions, some extraordinarily advanced, were promptly suppressed, and the desire for knowledge was stifled, so long as the dominant views were held to be binding for all: the beliefs of the great majority on what was right and proper were allowed to bar the way of the individual innovator. Only since industrial freedom opened the path to the free use of new knowledge, only since everything could be tried—if somebody could be found to back it at his own risk—and, it should be added, as often as not from outside the authorities officially intrusted with the cultivation of learning, has science made the great strides which in the last hundred and fifty years have changed the face of the world.

As is so often true, the nature of our civilization has been seen more clearly by its enemies than by most of its friends: "the perennial Western malady, the revolt of the individual against the species," as that nineteenth-century totalitarian, Auguste Comte, has described it, was indeed the force which built our civilization. What the nineteenth century added to the individualism of the preceding period was merely to make all classes conscious of freedom, to develop systematically and continuously what had grown in a haphazard and patchy manner, and to spread it from England and Holland over most of the European continent.

The result of this growth surpassed all expectations. Wherever the barriers to the free exercise of human ingenuity were removed, man became rapidly able to satisfy ever widening ranges of desire. And while the rising standard soon led to the discovery of very dark spots in society, spots which men were no longer willing to tolerate, there was probably no class that did not substantially benefit from the general advance. We cannot do justice to this astonishing growth if we measure it by our present standards, which themselves result from this growth and now make many defects obvious. To appreciate what it meant to those who took part in it, we must measure it by the hopes and wishes men held when it began: and there can be no doubt that its success surpassed man's wildest dreams, that by the beginning of the twentieth century the workingman in the Western world had reached a degree of material comfort, security, and personal independence which a hundred years before had seemed scarcely possible.

What in the future will probably appear the most significant and far-reaching effect of this success is the new sense of power over their own fate, the belief in the unbounded possibilities of improving their own lot, which the success already achieved created among men. With the success grew ambition—and man had every right to be ambitious. What had been an inspiring promise seemed no longer enough, the rate of progress far too slow; and the principles which had made this progress possible in the past came to be regarded more as obstacles to speedier progress, impatiently to be brushed away, than as the conditions for the preservation and development of what had already been achieved.

There is nothing in the basic principles of liberalism to make it a stationary creed; there are no hard-and-fast rules fixed once and for all. The fundamental principle that in the ordering of our affairs we should make as much use as possible of the spontaneous forces of society, and resort as little as possible to coercion, is capable of an infinite variety of applications. There is, in particular, all the difference between deliberately creating a system within which competition will work as beneficially as possible and passively accepting institutions as they are. Probably nothing has done so much harm to the liberal cause as the wooden insistence of some liberals on certain rough rules of thumb, above all the principle of laissez faire. Yet, in a sense, this was necessary and unavoidable. Against the innumerable interests which could show that particular measures would confer immediate and obvious benefits on some, while the harm they caused was much more indirect and difficult to see, nothing short of some hard-and-fast rule would have been effective. And since a strong presumption in favor of industrial liberty had undoubtedly been established, the temptation to present it as a rule which knew no exceptions was too strong always to be resisted.

But, with this attitude taken by many popularizers of the liberal doctrine, it was almost inevitable that, once their position was penetrated at some points, it should soon collapse as a whole. The position was further weakened by the inevitably slow progress of a policy which aimed at a gradual improvement of the institutional framework of a free society. This progress depended on the growth of our understanding of the social forces and the conditions most favorable to their working in a desirable manner. Since the task was to assist, and where necessary to supplement, their operation, the first requisite was to understand them. The attitude of the liberal toward society is like that of the gardener who tends a plant and, in order to create the conditions most favorable to its growth, must know as much as possible about its structure and the way it functions.

No sensible person should have doubted that the crude rules in which the principles of economic policy of the nineteenth century were expressed were only a beginning—that we had yet much to learn and that there were still immense possibilities of advancement on the lines on which we had moved. But this advance could come only as we gained increasing intellectual mastery of the forces of which we had to make use. There were many obvious tasks, such as our handling of the monetary system and the prevention or control of monopoly, and an even greater number of less obvious but hardly less important tasks to be undertaken in other fields, where there could be no doubt that the governments possessed enormous powers for good and evil; and there was every reason to expect that, with a better understanding of the problems, we should some day be able to use these powers successfully.

But while the progress toward what is commonly called "positive" action was necessarily slow, and while for the immediate improvement liberalism had to rely largely on the gradual increase of wealth which freedom brought about, it had constantly to fight proposals which threatened this progress. It came to be regarded as a "negative" creed because it could offer to particular individuals little more than a share in the common progress—a progress which came to be taken more and more for granted and was no longer recognized as the result of the policy of freedom. It might even be said that the very success of liberalism became the cause of its decline. Because of the success already achieved, man became increasingly unwilling to tolerate the evils still with him which now appeared both unbearable and unnecessary.

Because of the growing impatience with the slow advance of liberal policy, the just irritation with those who used liberal phraseology in defense of antisocial privileges, and the boundless ambition seemingly justified by the material improvements already achieved, it came to pass that toward the turn of the century the belief in the basic tenets of liberalism was more and more relinquished. What had been achieved came to be regarded as a secure and imperishable possession, acquired once and for all. The eyes of the people became fixed on the new demands, the rapid satisfaction of which seemed to be barred by the adherence to the old principles. It became more and more widely accepted that further advance could be expected not along the old lines within the general framework which had made past progress possible but only by a complete remodeling of society. It was no longer a question of adding to or improving the existing machinery but of completely scrapping and replacing it. And, as the hope of the new generation came to be centered on something completely new, interest in and understanding of the functioning of the existing society rapidly declined; and, with the decline of the understanding of the way in which the free system worked, our awareness of what depended on its existence also decreased.

This is not the place to discuss how this change in outlook was fostered by the uncritical transfer to the problems of society of habits of thought engendered by the preoccupation with technological problems, the habits of thought of the natural scientist and the engineer, and how these at the same time tended to discredit the results of the past study of society which did not conform to their prejudices and to impose ideals of organization on a sphere to which they are not appropriate. All we are here concerned to show is how completely, though gradually and by almost imperceptible steps, our attitude toward society has changed. What at every stage of this process of change had appeared a difference of degree only has in its cumulative effect already brought about a fundamental difference between the older liberal attitude toward society and the present approach to social problems. The change amounts to a complete reversal of the trend we have sketched, an entire abandonment of the individualist tradition which has created Western civilization.

According to the views now dominant, the question is no longer how we can make the best use of the spontaneous forces found in a free society. We have in effect undertaken to dispense with the forces which produced unforeseen results and to replace the impersonal and anonymous mechanism of the market by collective and "conscious" direction of all social forces to deliberately chosen goals. The difference cannot be better illustrated than by the extreme position taken in a widely acclaimed book on whose program of so-called "planning for freedom" we shall have to comment yet more than once. "We have never had to set up and direct," writes Dr. Karl Mannheim, "the entire system of nature as we are forced to do today with society. . . . Mankind is tending more and more to regulate the whole of its social life, although it has never attempted to create a second nature."

It is significant that this change in the trend of ideas has coincided with a reversal of the direction in which ideas have traveled in space. For over two hundred years English ideas had been spreading eastward. The rule of freedom which had been achieved in England seemed destined to spread throughout the world. By about 1870 the reign of these ideas had probably reached its easternmost expansion. From then onward it began to retreat, and a different set of ideas, not really new but very old, began to advance from the East. England lost her intellectual leadership in the political and social sphere and became an importer of ideas. For the next sixty years Germany became the center from which the ideas destined to govern the world in the twentieth century spread east and west. Whether it was Hegel or Marx, List or Schmoller, Sombart or Mannheim, whether it was socialism in its more radical form or merely "organization" or "planning" of a less radical kind, German ideas were everywhere readily imported and German institutions imitated.

Although most of the new ideas, and particularly socialism, did not originate in Germany, it was in Germany that they were perfected and during the last quarter of the nineteenth and the first quarter of the twentieth century that they reached their fullest development. It is now often forgotten how very considerable was the lead which Germany had during this period in the development of the theory and practice of socialism; that a generation before socialism became a serious issue in this country, Germany had a large socialist party in her parliament and that until not very long ago the doctrinal development of socialism was almost entirely carried on in Germany and Austria, so that even today Russian discussion largely carries on where the Germans left off. Most English and American socialists are still unaware that the majority of the problems they begin to discover were thoroughly discussed by German socialists long ago.

The intellectual influence which German thinkers were able to exercise during this period on the whole world was supported not merely by the great material progress of Germany but even more by the extraordinary reputation which German thinkers and scientists had earned during the preceding hundred years when Germany had once more become an integral and even leading member of the common European civilization. But it soon served to assist the spreading from Germany of ideas directed against the foundations of that civilization. The Germans themselves—or at least those among them who spread these ideas—were fully aware of the conflict: what had been the common heritage of European civilization became to them, long before the Nazis, "Western" civilization—where "Western" was no longer used in the old sense of Occident but had come to mean west of the Rhine. "Western" in this sense was liberalism and democracy, capitalism and individualism, free trade and any form of internationalism or love of peace.

But in spite of the ill-concealed contempt of an ever increasing number of Germans for those "shallow" Western ideals, or perhaps because of it, the people of the West continued to import German ideas and were even induced to believe that their own former convictions had merely been rationalizations of selfish interests, that free trade was a doctrine invented to further British interests, and that the political ideals of England and America were hopelessly outmoded and a thing to be ashamed of. . . .

Material Conditions and Ideal Ends

. . . People who admit that present political trends constitute a serious threat to our economic prospects, and through their economic effects endanger much higher values, are yet likely to deceive themselves that we are making material sacrifices to gain ideal ends. It is, however, more than doubtful whether a fifty years' approach toward collectivism has raised our moral standards, or whether the change has not rather been in the opposite direction. Though we are in the habit of priding ourselves on our more sensitive social conscience, it is by no means clear that this is justified by the practice of our individual conduct. On the negative side, in its indignation about the inequities of the existing social order, our generation probably surpasses most of its predecessors. But the effect of that movement on our positive standards in the proper field of morals, individual conduct, and on the seriousness with which we uphold moral principles against the expediencies and exigencies of social machinery, is a very different matter.

Issues in this field have become so confused that it is necessary to go back to fundamentals. What our generation is in danger of forgetting is not only that morals are of necessity a phenomenon of individual conduct but also that they can exist only in the sphere in which the individual is free to decide for himself and is called upon voluntarily to sacrifice personal advantage to the observance of a moral rule. Outside the sphere of individual responsibility there is neither goodness nor badness, neither opportunity for moral merit nor the chance of proving one's conviction by sacrificing one's desires to what one thinks right. Only where we ourselves are responsible for our own interests and are free to sacrifice them has our decision moral value. We are neither entitled to be unselfish at someone else's expense nor is there any merit in being unselfish if we have no choice. The members of a society who in all respects are *made* to do the good thing have no title to praise. As Milton said: "If every action which is good or evil in a man of ripe years were under pittance and prescription and compulsion, what were virtue but a name, what praise should then be due to well-doing, what gramercy to be sober, just, or continent?"

Freedom to order our own conduct in the sphere where material circumstances force a choice upon us, and responsibility for the arrangement of our own life according to our own conscience, is the air in which alone moral sense grows and in which moral values are daily re-created in the free decision of the individual. Responsibility, not to a superior, but to one's conscience, the awareness of a duty not exacted by compulsion, the necessity to decide which of the things one values are to be sacrificed to others, and to bear the consequences of one's own decision, are the very essence of any morals which deserve the name.

That in this sphere of individual conduct the effect of collectivism has been almost entirely destructive is both inevitable and undeniable. A movement whose main promise is the relief from responsibility cannot but be antimoral in its effect, however lofty the ideals to which it owes its birth. Can there be much doubt that the feeling of personal obligation to remedy inequities, where our individual power permits, has been weakened rather than strengthened, that both the willingness to bear responsibility and the consciousness that it is our own individual duty to know how to choose have been perceptibly impaired? There is all the difference between demanding that a desirable state of affairs should be brought about by the authorities, or even being willing to submit provided everyone else is made to do the same, and the readiness to do what one thinks right one's self at the sacrifice of one's own desires and perhaps in the face of hostile public opinion. There is much to suggest that we have in fact become more tolerant toward particular abuses and much more indifferent to inequities in individual cases, since we have fixed our eyes on an entirely different system in which the state will set everything right. It may even be, as has been suggested, that the passion for collective action is a way in which we now without compunction collectively indulge in that selfishness which as individuals we had learned a little to restrain.

It is true that the virtues which are less esteemed and practiced now— independence, self-reliance, and the willingness to bear risks, the readiness to back one's own conviction against a majority, and the willingness to voluntary co-operation with one's neighbors—are essentially those on which the working of an individualist society rests. Collectivism has nothing to put in their place, and in so far as it already has destroyed them it has left a void filled by nothing but the demand for obedience and the compulsion of the individual to do what is collectively decided to be good. The periodical election of representatives, to which the moral choice of the individual tends to be more and more reduced, is not an occasion on which his moral values are tested or where he has constantly to reassert and prove the order of his values and to testify to the sincerity of his profession by the sacrifice of those of his values he rates lower to those he puts higher.

As the rules of conduct evolved by individuals are the source from which collective political action derives what moral standards it possesses, it would indeed be surprising if the relaxation of the standards of individual conduct were accompanied by a raising of the standards of social action. That there have been great changes is clear. Every generation, of course, puts some values higher and some lower than its predecessors. Which, however, are the aims which take a lower place now, which are the values which we are now warned may have to give way if they come into conflict with others? Which kind of values figure less prominently in the picture of the future held out to us by the popular writers and speakers than they did in the dreams and hopes of our fathers?

It is certainly not material comfort, certainly not a rise in our standard of living or the assurance of a certain status in society which ranks lower. Is there a popular writer or speaker who dares to suggest to the masses that they might have to make sacrifices of their material prospects for the enhancement of an ideal end? Is it not, in fact, entirely the other way round? Are not the things which we are more and more frequently taught to regard as "nineteenth-century illusions" all moral values—liberty and independence, truth and intellectual honesty, peace and democracy, and the respect for the individual *qua* man instead of merely as the member of an organized group?

What are the fixed poles now which are regarded as sacrosanct, which no reformer dare touch, since they are treated as the immutable boundaries which must be respected in any plan for the future? They are no longer the liberty of the individual, his freedom of movement, and scarcely that of speech. They are the protected standards of this or that group, their "right" to exclude others from providing their fellowmen with what they need. Discrimination between members and nonmembers of closed groups, not to speak of nationals of different countries, is accepted more and more as a matter of course; injustices inflicted on individuals by government action in the interest of a group are disregarded with an indifference hardly distinguishable from callousness; and the grossest violations of the most elementary rights of the individual, such as are involved in the compulsory transfer of populations, are more and more often countenanced even by supposed liberals.

All this surely indicates that our moral sense has been blunted rather than sharpened. When we are reminded, as more and more frequently happens, that one cannot make omelettes without breaking eggs, the eggs which are broken are almost all of the kind which a generation or two ago were regarded as the essential bases of civilized life. And what atrocities committed by powers with whose professed principles they sympathize have not been readily condoned by many of our so-called "liberals"?

33. Paul Lazarsfeld, Marie Jahoda, and Hans Zeisel, *Marienthal: The Sociography of an Unemployed Community*

The impact of the Depression in Europe in the early 1930s can be measured by various macroeconomic indices, but it can also be gauged by sociological portraits of individual communities, such as that undertaken by a team of young Austrian social scientists in a small town in Lower Austria in 1930. Paul Lazarsfeld, Marie Jahoda, and Hans Zeisel were young intellectuals trained at the University of Vienna who were also active members of the Austrian Socialist movement. Under the auspices of Lazarsfeld's Economic-Psychological Research Center and with the encouragement of the leader of the Austrian Socialist party, Otto Bauer (who first suggested the subject to them), they conducted a remarkable investigation of the fate of a small industrial community—Marienthal—in the aftermath of the closing of a local textile factory. The textile factory was the principal source of employment for most of the adult population. Upon the collapse of the factory three-fourths of the 478 families in Marienthal were forced on relief, a condition fraught with long-term uncertainty and short-term deprivation.

The Marienthal study presented a moving portrait of the despair and anguish of families thrust into dire economic distress, which led to what Lazarsfeld later called the "breakdown of a social personality structure." The authors' scientific work on the consequences of unemployment was influenced by their moral concern for the value of labor in a just society and by their belief in the responsibility of the state to ensure both social justice and economic security. But it was also impelled by their (and the Austrian Socialist party's) fear about the negative political consequences of unemployment on the working class. In both senses they were true representatives of Austro-Marxism, a distinguished form of Central European socialism, which combined a belief in social transformationalism with a dedication to democratic humanism, while rejecting Bolshevist doctrines about the dictatorship of the proletariat.

The extraordinary concern among European socialists after 1945 for developing strategies for "full employment" within the welfare state cannot be understood without reference to the intellectual commitments implicit in *Marienthal*. The work of Lazarsfeld's institute also formed an interesting empirical sociological counterpoint to the more heavily theoretical orientation of the Institute for Social Research at the University of Frankfurt under Max Horkheimer, although both assembled young intellectuals with profound loyalties to Central European Marxism.

Lazarsfeld, Jahoda, and Zeisel left Austria in the 1930s for distin-

guished careers in Britain and America. Paul Lazarsfeld became professor of sociology at Columbia University; Marie Jahoda, professor of
social psychology at the University of Sussex; and Hans Zeisel, like his
fellow Viennese Friedrich von Hayek and Bruno Bettelheim (documents
32 and 35), joined the faculty of the University of Chicago.

The account printed below is taken from the concluding chapters of
Marienthal.

Chapter 7: The Meaning of Time

Anyone who knows how tenaciously the working class has fought for more
leisure ever since it began to fight for its rights might think that even amid
the misery of unemployment, men would still benefit from having unlimited free time. On examination this leisure proves to be a tragic gift. Cut
off from their work and deprived of contact with the outside world, the
workers of Marienthal have lost the material and moral incentives to make
use of their time. Now that they are no longer under any pressure, they
undertake nothing new and drift gradually out of an ordered existence into
one that is undisciplined and empty. Looking back over any period of this
free time, they are unable to recall anything worth mentioning.

For hours on end, the men stand around in the street, alone or in small
groups, leaning against the wall of a house or the parapet of the bridge.
When a vehicle drives through the village they turn their heads slightly;
several of them smoke pipes. They carry on leisurely conversations for
which they have unlimited time. Nothing is urgent anymore; they have forgotten how to hurry.

Toward noon, when the traffic in Marienthal reaches its modest peak,
the movements of the people in the roughly three-hundred meters stretch of
the village's main street presented the following picture, when we counted
for (for one hundred of them) the number of times they stopped on their
way:

Stops on Main Street	Men	Women	Total
3 or more	39	3	42
2	7	2	9
1	16	15	31
0	6	12	18
Total	68	32	100

From Marie Jahoda, Paul Lazarsfeld, and Hans Zeisel, *Marienthal: The Sociography of
an Unemployed Community* (Chicago: Aldine Atherton, 1971), pp. 66–70, 77–98. Reprinted
by permission of Hans Zeisel.

Almost two-thirds of the men interrupted their walk at least twice; only one out of every ten walked to his destination without stopping. The women presented a strikingly different picture: only about one-sixth of them stopped on two or more occasions. As we shall see later, they have considerably less time on their hands. . . .

Time in Marienthal has a dual nature: it is different for men and women. For the men, the division of the days into hours has long since lost all meaning. Of one hundred men, eighty-eight were not wearing a watch and only thirty-one of these had a watch at home. Getting up, the midday meal, going to bed, are the only remaining points of reference. In between, time elapses without anyone really knowing what has taken place. The time sheets reveal this in a most graphic manner. A thirty-three year old unemployed man provided the following time sheet for a single day:

A.M.

6–7	Getting up.
7–8	Wake the boys because they have to go to school.
8–9	When they have gone, I go down to the shed to get wood and water.
9–10	When I get back up to the house my wife always asks me what she ought to cook; to avoid the question I go off into the field.
10–11	In the meantime midday comes around.
11–12	Empty.

P.M.

12–1	We eat at one o'clock; the children don't come home from school until then.
1–2	After the meal I take a look at the newspaper.
2–3	Go out.
3–4	Go to Treer's (the shopkeeper's).
4–5	Watch trees being cut down in the park; a pity about the park.
5–6	Go home.
6–7	Then it's time for the evening meal—noodles and semolina pudding.
7–8	Go to bed.

Compare this with the time sheet drawn up by a Viennese metalworker, still employed:

A.M.

6–7	Get up, wash, have breakfast.
7–8	Take the streetcar to the factory, read the newspaper on the way. Start work at 7:30.
8–12	Factory.

P.M.

12–1	Half an hour's lunch break. Stay at work and eat a packed lunch.
1–4	Factory.
4–5	Take the streetcar home, finish reading the paper, have a wash, then tea.
5–6	Lie on the sofa and talk to my wife about various things.
6–7	Fetch the children from the playground.
7–8	Evening meal.
8–9	Political party meeting.
9–10	Empty.
10–11	Go home, go to bed.

For an unemployed man the day lasts 13½ hours, for a worker, 17 hours. The few leisure hours the employed worker enjoys after his eight-hour shift are carefully disposed of and incomparably richer and more active than the many hours forced upon the man out of work. Waking the children certainly does not take up a whole hour. Treer's shop (where he spends 3:00–4:00 P.M.) is only three minutes from where this man lives, and the distance from the park to his home which he covers in the hour between 5:00–6:00 P.M. is about 300 yards. What happens in the intervals? . . .

It is always the same: when he fills out his time sheet, the unemployed worker can recall only a few "events." Between the three reference points of getting up, eating, and going to bed lie intervals of inactivity hard to describe for an observer and apparently also difficult to describe for the man himself. He merely knows that "in the meantime midday comes round." And it is when he attempts to describe this "in the meantime" that the curious entries on the time sheet occur; activities that cannot take more than five minutes are supposed to fill an entire hour. This manner of filling up the time sheet does not stem from a low level of intelligence among these workers; the much more difficult task of keeping household accounts was competently handled. An unemployed man is simply no longer capable of giving an account of everything he has done in the course of the day. Apart from the already mentioned main reference points, the only other activities that can be named and listed are the few that still retain some significance: washing the boys, feeding the rabbits. . . .

. . . [L]ooking at the village as a whole, we noticed a change in the general rhythm of time. Sundays and holidays have lost much of their significance. The librarian, for instance, reports that although book borrowing used to be particularly heavy on Sundays and holidays in Marienthal as everywhere else, this periodic increase is now scarcely perceptible. The biweekly payments of unemployment relief dictate the rhythm of the community; they have taken over the role of Sunday and the end of the month.

Only the children still show considerable adherence to the weekly cycle, and this is partially communicated to the rest of the family.

The seasons of the year, on the other hand, make themselves felt more strongly. The end of the need for lighting and heating, the relief afforded by the produce of the garden allotment, and the possibility of occasional work on the land have attained a significance that they did not normally have in the household of an industrial worker.

So both the general pattern of life and that of the individual show that the people of Marienthal have gone back to a more primitive, less differentiated experience of time. The new circumstances do not fit any longer an established time schedule. A life that is poorer in demands and activities has gradually begun to develop on a timetable that is correspondingly poor.

Chapter 8: Fading Resilience

We have described the state of affairs in Marienthal at the time we were there. But even if the people with their altered sense of time scarcely notice its progress any longer, the months go by and the foundations on which their life still rests are crumbling gradually and irresistibly away. The question is, how long can this life continue?

Since we have seen only the present, one brief moment of history as it were, we have no direct answer. Yet it is this long-term development that poses the real question that constantly forced itself upon us in Marienthal. We are, of course, unable to foretell the future itself, but we did perceive some dynamic symptoms already present in the cross-sectional view of the community that was open to us.

First, however, we shall take another brief look at the past. It appears that the closing of the factory in 1929 produced a definite shock effect. All at once life was completely altered. At the beginning, the women were reduced to panic. How were they to manage the housekeeping money? Who can keep house with an income suddenly reduced to one-quarter of its former size? Many a woman who today has learned how to manage her relief money, had, at the beginning of unemployment, run up debt after debt. . . .

At first, the men thought it would be intolerable to sit around at home merely looking on. We remember the man who sent off 130 applications for jobs in the early months of unemployment. This year he has not written a single one; now he is more worried about the amount of money spent on postage. By now conditions have become much worse; supplies are exhausted, clothes are worn out, the relief payments have been further reduced, and for many people all assistance has expired. Nevertheless, everyone's first reactions were more desperate and irrational. . . .

As time went by, the shock effect began to ebb. Life, as we saw earlier, has reached stability on a somewhat higher level than the first weeks of unemployment allowed people to expect. But the crucial question is: will it *remain* stable?

Let us see which of our data can contribute to an answer. To begin with, economic conditions are constantly changing, and changing for the worse. This is a direct consequence of the unemployment relief laws. After a certain time, unemployment payments are superseded by emergency relief, which in turn is gradually reduced, and can eventually be stopped altogether. But reduced relief payments are only one cause of the deteriorating economic situation. The process is significantly accelerated by the wear and tear on all personal belongings. There is no allowance for their replacement or even for their repair in the carefully balanced budget of a Marienthal household. The moment will finally come when shoes and clothes, repeatedly mended, finally reach the stage where they can no longer be repaired. Crockery breaks and cannot be replaced. A case of illness will plunge a whole family into debt.

That wear and tear did not raise greater havoc earlier is due to the fact that people had unusually large stocks of materials, especially textiles, which they used to get from the factory for next to nothing. Even now, many families still have some odd pieces of material from which something can be sewn when the need arises. The children's clothes suffered most, of course, and where no more material was available, the parents would take some of their own clothing that was still wearable and decent and have it cut down into coats and other clothing for the youngsters. . . .

In all three families for which we have detailed data, the children were better provided with clothes than the adults. The women have a ready explanation: it is the children who first benefit from any charity action (public or private). Furthermore, adult clothes can be converted into children's, but not the other way around; and finally it is the children who are cared for most. . . .

As economic conditions deteriorate, how will the attitude of the people of Marienthal change? It will be useful to refer back here to the four categories into which we divided the population according to their basic attitude. Following is the average income per consumer unit in each of these four attitude categories:

		Schillings per Month
Unbroken		34
Resigned		30
In despair	} Broken	25
Apathetic		19

This table is not only significant for the connection it establishes between a family's attitudes and its economic situation; it also allows us to foresee at approximately what point the deterioration of income will push a family into the next lower category. In Chapter 4, we summarized the basic differences between these four attitude groups, and we know already that this difference of approximately five schillings a month means the difference between being still able to use sugar or having to cook with saccharine, between having the children's shoes repaired or keeping the children at home, between occasionally having a cigarette or having to pick up butts on the street. But this difference means also the difference between being unbroken, resigned, in despair, or apathetic. . . .

Thus economic deterioration carries with it an almost calculable change in the prevailing mood. This fact is intensified by the concomitant decline in health. There seems to be a close relationship between income and health, as became clear when the medical examination records of the school children were related to the economic condition of their families. In the following table, the health of the children is rated from good to poor:

Children's Health Rating	Per Cent of Fathers Still Working
Good	38
Average	9
Poor	0

Of the fathers of the children still in good health, 38 per cent were still at work; of the fathers of the children with a "poor" rating, all had lost their jobs. This is an instance of how unemployment undermines the powers of physical resistance. . . .

One of the questions of major import for the future of the unemployed individual is how unemployment affects his personal relationships. We have already seen how political passions subsided[1] and how personal animosity increased, and we have seen also evidence of touching helpfulness, especially toward children.

---

1. Earlier in the study the authors had found that "the people are very much aware of the decline in political activity. The functionaries of all parties agree that political hostilities among the inhabitants have abated considerably since the period of unemployment began." They also noted that "this fact, which so curiously contradicts everything that is happening in Germany [in 1932], probably derives from the peculiarly uniform and hence unifying situation in Marienthal. Everyone, whatever his political affiliation, bears the same lot. However, it is also possible that peculiarities in the Austrian national temperament play their part." The authors were not certain what the long-range implications of such passivity might be: "It is not possible to foresee whether this tendency toward moderation of the traditional political differences will be upset by new political developments, for instance, by the growth of the recently-founded local branch of the National Socialist Party." *Marienthal*, p. 41.—ED.

Our knowledge about the effect of unemployment on relationships within the family came primarily from our conversations with the women. We are aware that this source by itself does not give the whole picture, since their remarks are often engendered by isolated incidents in the family. The evidence would have been better if we ourselves had observed family life over a long period of time; this, however, was not possible. Nevertheless, there is merit to those isolated reports, precisely because they select the incidents that stick in the women's minds as worth reporting. We shall draw no conclusions but simply point to possibilities.

In some cases, unemployment improved the relationship between husband and wife; for example, in one family mentioned earlier, the new situation forced the husband to give up drink. Often, too, where the wife used to feel neglected by her husband, his presence at home is now a source of satisfaction. . . .

On the other hand, in some marriages that had developed quite normally before, the new pressures created nervous tension and occasional quarrels. The best example of this was found in the diary that one unemployed worker kept conscientiously from the beginning of his unemployment. It showed how new and unfamiliar tensions and minor conflicts darkened the relationship between the man and his wife without, however, ever really destroying their basic understanding. Both spoke of one another with the greatest respect and affection when talking to a third party. Here is an entry made not many weeks after the onset of unemployment:

> Going into the forest with Martha [his wife] to collect some wood. The best, the only real friend one has in life is a good wife.

A few days later:

> Martha, that most faithful life companion, has just accomplished a feat worth recommending to all for imitation; she has managed to prepare an evening meal for three adults and four children for only sixty-five groschen.

A few weeks later:

> I am condemned to silence but Martha is beginning to waver. Today was pay day; after settling our debts at the shop we simply did not have a penny left. Icy silence at home, petty things disrupt the harmony. She did not say good night.

A few days later:

> What strangers we are to each other; we are getting visibly harder. Is it my fault that times are bad, do I have to take all the blame in silence???

Family 178 provides an example of the same development. The wife wrote:

> We sometimes have quarrels at home these days, but only minor ones, mainly when the boys go on wild hikes and ruin their shoes.

Finally there are cases where family relationships are seriously impaired as a result of unemployment. Yet a closer examination might reveal that these marriages were not exactly happy to begin with. A tense situation might have decisively deteriorated under the pressure of privation. One woman said:

> He had always been fairly quarrelsome, even during the old days at the factory, but his colleagues liked him and simply looked the other way when they saw him fly into a temper. Now things are worse, of course, because he takes it all out on the family.

Another woman:

> I often quarrel with my husband because he does not care about a thing any longer and is never at home. Before unemployment it was not so bad because the factory provided a distraction.

A third woman related how her husband used to drink and get on badly with her, adding:

> Hardship has made our rows more frequent because our nerves are on edge and we have so little patience left.

On the whole, it seems, improvements in the relationship between husband and wife as a result of unemployment are definitely exceptional. Generally, in happy marriages minor quarrels appear to occur more frequently than before. In marriages that were already unsettled, difficulties have become more acute. Tendencies already latent in a marriage are thus intensified by external circumstances.

Relationships between parents and children were illuminated during consultation hours of the Parent's Guidance Service that we incorporated into the medical consultations. We did not get the impression that Marienthal had more problem children than other communities, and this was confirmed by the school teachers. The typical complaints were more about the children ruining their shoes by playing soccer, and the like. Both from our consulting hours and our direct observations we had the impression that parental authority has not suffered in any way. The family continues to perform its educational function as well or as poorly as it did before unemployment began. Thus personal relations proved to be more resilient than relationships toward work or social institutions.

We are approaching the end of our report. We were able to survey quite precisely the material resources available to the people of Marienthal and the manner in which they disposed of them. We saw how economic pressures have slowly but relentlessly increased. We have traced their effects and the ways in which the unemployed confronted them. Their demands on life are continually declining; the circle of events and institutions in which they still participate keeps contracting. Whatever energy is left is concentrated on preserving this narrowing sphere of existence.

We found a characteristic indication of this process of contraction in the way people's sense of time became disrupted, losing its value as an ordering influence on the passing of the day. Only personal relationships seemed to remain essentially intact. We have distinguished four basic attitudes: the predominant one is *resignation;* a more active one we named *unbroken;* and two deteriorated forms we called *in despair* and *apathetic.* As we look back at these two forms, it now appears that they are probably but two different stages of a process of psychological deterioration that runs parallel to the narrowing of economic resources and the wear and tear on personal belongings. At the end of this process lies ruin and despair.

In the following passage we describe our impressions from a visit to a family typical of the last stage before catastrophe, which was as far as our investigation of Marienthal took us:

> We arrived on a Sunday to find the family in no way prepared for our visit. On entering, the following scene presented itself. The father was sitting on a low stool with a pile of worn-out children's shoes in front of him that he was trying to mend with roofing felt. The children were sitting together motionless on a box, in stockinged feet, waiting for their shoes to be finished. The father explained with embarrassment, "You see, this is my Sunday job. On Sundays I have to patch the shoes up a bit so that the children can go off to school again on Monday." He held up the completely dilapidated shoes of the eldest boy. "I just don't know what I can do with these. On holidays he can't go out of the house any more."
>
> We took stock of the household. It was extremely clean and seemed well cared for: the mother's and children's clothes were spotless. The father, it is true, was wearing a completely worn out shirt and a heavily patched pair of trousers. In drawing up the family's inventory we found that this was all he possessed. His jackets and other trousers and his overcoat had long since been converted into coats and trousers for the children. He said, "I don't have to go out, but the children must go to school." The remainder of this reduced set of possessions was found to be in excellent order. The children's shirts were held together with tape, and their summer dresses were wrapped up in an old table cloth and well preserved. Obviously every article had its assigned place. Everywhere—on the wall, in the cupboard, on the chest of

drawers—there were cartons of wooden boxes with possessions neatly arranged inside. Most of them had their contents inscribed. A keyboard with a variety of keys hung next to the door, each carrying a tag to show the lock it was for.

The youngest child caught our attention. His face was feverish and puffy and swollen around the nose. He breathed heavily with his mouth open. The mother explained: "He always has a cold. He ought to have his tonsils and adenoids out, but we can't afford the trip to the hospital. He would have to be brought back as well, and that means two trips. Perhaps when spring comes." We learned that another one of the children had spent a long time in a Viennese hospital with pleurisy and had only recently returned home, loaded with presents from the doctors and nurses. The girl had come back with a complete set of clothes, some of which by now had been passed on to her youngest sister. Another child was having three midday meals a week at a neighbor's house.

The father told us that things had been going terribly badly these last few days. All they had been able to buy was bread, and not enough of that. The children kept coming into the kitchen asking for another piece; they were always hungry. His wife sat in the kitchen crying. So he decided to go to see the village clerk, who gave him a bag of flour left over from the *Winter Help Drive*. He also received an advance of three schillings on his next payment of unemployment relief. Otherwise they would not have had a mouthful to eat that Sunday.

But how things will continue, we cannot foresee, even assuming that no unexpected changes occur in the external situation. Two developments are possible. As conditions deteriorate, forces may emerge in the community ushering in totally new events, such as revolt or migration. It is, however, also possible that the feeling of solidarity that binds the people of Marienthal together in the face of adversity will one day dissolve, leaving each individual to scramble after his own salvation.

Events of the first type are entirely out of our range of prediction. But as to the second, we can make some contribution to a question that could become important. How does an individual's life history affect his powers of resistance during unemployment? What connection is there between past experience and present attitude?

Working from sixty-two detailed life histories, we have made comparisons between behavior in earlier times and behavior during unemployment, and we shall summarize our findings here.

We begin with the life histories of a married couple whose present attitude we would characterize as resigned. Their household is running smoothly, and the wife is quiet and pleasant, a good mother who takes pride in her housekeeping. The husband has reduced his standard of living to a considerable extent. He does not go to the tavern any longer; occasionally he goes to the Workmen's Club. He has no plans for the future, but still keeps looking around for work.

J. T., the husband, was born in 1876 in Moravia, one of ten children of whom only he and his brother are still alive. He spent eight years at the school in Grammat-Neusiedl, where his favorite subject was drawing. He wanted to become a carpenter but could not get a job, so he had to go into the weaving mill, where he stayed for three years. Weaving, however, did not interest him, and he went to Mitterndorf. In 1894 the factory burned down and for four months he was engaged in its rebuilding, laying concrete. At that time his brother had already emigrated. He was envious and wanted to be off too. The opportunity arrived when a carpenter who was about to emigrate offered to take him with him, but he decided he could not leave his mother alone. So he never did get away and still envies his brother's experience abroad.

He then came to Marienthal, helped to build the engine house and worked his way up from there to become first a helper in the spinning mill and then an assistant in the machine maintenance department. As a young man he liked to go out a lot; there was a group of ten or twelve fellows who would go out together and have fun. He never read anything other than newspapers, and was not interested in sport. From 1914 to 1916 he worked in the engine shop; when the mill closed down he worked in the cannery in nearby Bruck. When they saw that he was the only man in the factory who knew anything about machines, he was given the good post of chief mechanic. In 1919 he was out of work for a short time, then found a job in the sugar refinery. Four months later he went to Mitterndorf to work in the warehouse that belonged to the timber yard; after a few weeks, when his interest in machinery was noticed, he was moved to the central heating unit.

There he stayed four months and then returned to the Marienthal factory, where he worked on the turbines until 1920. When the spinning mill started up he worked there as a mechanic until 1928. Machines had always been his chief interest. He was very proud that this knowledge, which he had picked up all by himself, without any books, had always got him better jobs.

In 1900 he married, just before the birth of his first child. He had known his wife for four years after meeting her at a dance; it had been a very good marriage. Now he had four children, aged twenty-eight, twenty-six, seventeen, and fourteen. The fourteen year old is to learn whatever he likes; the main thing is to learn something. Last year his mother took him to a shop in Vienna and the manager then and there wanted to take him on as an apprentice. She had to promise to send the boy back as soon as he finished school. The father hoped something would come of it. He himself, since unemployment started, had had three months work at the river regulation project, four months building the school, and five months in Mannersdorf. He still kept riding about on his bicycle looking for work. He had no plans for the future; that was something for the younger generation.

He earned some extra money disinfecting premises contaminated by infectious diseases. In the past he used to pay frequent visits to the tavern; he was earning good money then, but now he could not afford it any longer. Most of his free time is now spent at home, in the vegetable garden or looking after the rabbits; now and then he goes to the Workmen's Club. The happiest time of his life were the years before his marriage; he didn't have a care in the world then, just had to pay for his keep and could spend the rest of his money the way he wanted. The worst time is the present because there is no money around. Things had been bad during the war too; there had been money enough but nothing to eat. Now it is worse, because the food is here and he cannot buy it.

F. T., the wife, was born in 1883 in Moravia, one of nine children. She came to Marienthal at the age of seven. Her father had been an unskilled laborer. She went to school until she was fourteen; an outstanding student, she would have liked to learn sewing but was unable to as she had to go straight to work in the factory. She stayed until 1912 when she had to leave because her lungs were affected, and has never been back to work since. She married when she was eighteen. Her husband had been married to her sister who died in childbirth after a year. They were married soon thereafter. He was ten years older than she; they always got on very well together and never quarreled. He gave her all his money, didn't drink or gamble and was helpful.

They had seven children, of whom four were still alive. Two had died young, the third at the age of nine because the doctor had given him the wrong treatment. Things are much more difficult now that her husband is out of work. It is hard to make the money last and she has to make nearly all their clothes, even the elder boys'. She needs sixty schillings for two weeks for food and coal, and then there is the milk and meat on Sundays. If any money is left, it goes to the cobbler. During the summer, the eldest son, a painter and decorator, is helping out. Then she can occasionally buy something, such as a pair of shoes or new trousers. She had never bought anything on installments; that was one worry she wasn't going to have.

Her happiest time had been the first years of her marriage, until about 1912. Their earnings had been highest in those days. Then she had fallen ill and had to take care of herself. The worst time had been the war years; there was no money and nothing but *ersatz* (substitute) food. She was worried about one of the boys: he had only ten weeks to go to qualify as a hairdresser when he started having fits of some sort and had been sent home. She would be happy if she could find some apprenticeship for him so that he could get qualified. As a girl she had liked dancing but now she is too old for that sort of thing. She still enjoys going to the movie or the theater when there is anything on.

Some measure of resignation or lack of initiative can be found in the husband's earlier life; for example, he always wanted to go abroad but had never done so. He still envies his brother for having realized that ambition. Also, his lack of interest in reading and sports is a symptom of his resigned attitude to life.

His sickly wife, too, who already as a very young girl put up with renouncing the career she most wanted, early revealed traits of resignation. Perhaps her marriage to her late sister's husband also betrayed a limited degree of self-assertiveness. Her former life, like her present, was characterized by a restricted range and a certain easily satisfied contentment.

This basic attitude continued largely unchanged. What was formerly a quiet, unpretentious, simple life remained the same during unemployment, on a reduced level.

An entirely different case is presented in the life history of a thirty-four year old unemployed man who was now reduced to complete despair.

F. W. was born in 1897 in Marienthal. His father was a bricklayer. The son went to school from the age of six to fourteen. He was a rather mischievous lad and had no favorite subject, but he got on well with the teacher because he respected him. At fourteen, he entered the factory to learn his trade in the print works and stayed there two years. Then his father moved to Neufeld because of a quarrel with his colleagues in the shop. He was to be bumped by a worker, many years his junior, and was too proud to take the demotion. Nobody thought of asking him to stay on in his job, although he would have liked to very much.

In Neufeld, the whole family again went to work in the factory; in the beginning F. W. did unskilled labor, then rose to be a machine operator, not paid any longer by the hour but by the week. He was very happy, fitted in very well, and gave up his free time to catch up on his educaton. In 1915 he was drafted. He could have gotten an exemption but turned it down and went. He regretted it after a few weeks. First he went to Vienna for training and then to the Italian front, where he caught malaria which he never got rid of; he is still somewhat an invalid. In 1917 he was put into a hospital and stayed there until the collapse of the Empire.

Then he returned to Neufeld for two years. His parents supported him, refusing to let him go back to the factory because he was too weak; his elder brother had been killed in the war. From 1920 to 1925 he worked on a construction job in Zwillingsdorf. When the job was finished, he returned to Marienthal, doing some unskilled work in the factory. He soon managed to get an office job in the print works. He was very satisfied with it, except that it did not pay much.

In 1922 he married. His wife, who was a year older, came from Ebenfurth. They have two sons, aged two and seven. The whole family is undernourished. Even during the war things were better than they are now. His aim had always been to work his way up, wherever he started. He always put all his efforts behind his work and could turn his hand to anything. If he was given the chance to start, he was sure to work his way up. He is the man who during the first year of unemployment, sent off 130 applications for jobs without receiving a single answer. He has not yet earned a single groschen to supplement his unemployment relief.

Now all hope is gone. He wishes so very much to live by his own earning. His wife, who had never been out to work, is now a complete wreck, especially her nerves; she is always ill and moody. He has no hope left and just lives from one day to the next without knowing why. The will to resist is lost.

In the factory he got his hand in at the difficult office work and was doing well. Even as a young man he wanted to go into a cotton print works. He had been happy there. He would very much like to go to Vienna, if only so that the children could learn something. He would like to let his eldest boy study; if his own plans for a better education had fallen through, at least his children were to have it better but it is not possible.

This man had always made particularly high demands on life. He has been ambitious and hard working, always eager to work his way up. Even his free time was spent on educating himself and—this was decisive—his ambitions were always realized, despite his physical debility. The way in which he transferred his plans for his own life to his children was characteristic.

Then unemployment came. At first he still had enough confidence in his own ability to hope that he would find employment elsewhere. When all his applications remained unanswered, he began to grasp the hopelessness of his situation: there was no more room for his ambition, his desire to assert himself and find acknowledgement. This crushing setback broke his self-confidence. The collapse was complete; he even stopped looking for work. His wife, ill and highstrung, runs the household impeccably. At our visit, we were struck by the contrast between his desperate mood and his pleasant, comfortable home. We were told that he used to be an active official in the Christian Socialist Party: now he has given that up too.

We found in our files a number of similar cases, people whose power of resistance, after gradually deteriorating, suffered a sudden collapse. This usually occurred with men whose earlier life had been characterized by ambition and high expectations.

However, those who had been particularly well-off in the past were apt to develop a different reaction to unemployment, as in the following example:

Frau J. K. was born in 1890 in Erlach near Pitten. Her father had been an active member of the Social Democratic Party and consequently had been forced to continually change his place of work. Before reaching the age of six she lived in six different places. The family moving ended in Marienthal, where the political circumstances were quite favorable. The father worked here as a weaver. She was one of five children, enjoyed school very much and learned well without having any preference for a particular subject. She wanted to become a dressmaker, but the other children were still small and she could not leave. She entered the factory as a messenger girl and worked there until 1914. She liked to go out, was passionately fond of dancing, and frequently went to the theater or the movies in Vienna.

She married in 1910; her husband also worked in the factory. It was a very good marriage; she never had a moment's unhappiness. After her second child she stayed at home and thought she would devote herself to her children. When the war came, her husband enlisted; in 1917 he was killed. At that point the children were one and a half, three, and seven years old. She had to go back to earning a living and began in the cannery. Then she worked for a time for the railway in Mitterndorf, returned to Marienthal in 1920 and worked there until 1929. She now draws thirty-nine schillings relief money.

All her sons have made good. The oldest is a gardener in Marchegg, earning forty-four schillings a week. But he is not giving her anything; he is saving up for a motor bike. The second son works in Vienna, earns forty schillings a week, has part of his clothing provided by the firm he works for, and he sends her thirty schillings a week. She still has to support the youngest boy, who is apprenticed in Vienna. She always made all the children's clothes. The youngest was musical; she let him have music lessons, and even when things were at their worst, she paid seven schillings a month for a music teacher.

She has never lost her cheerfulness, and, although "an old girl" by now, still likes to dance. After the war she began to take an active part in the Social Democratic movement, first working in its Women's Section and later in its Child Welfare organization, where she is on the committee. Since the committee had to let the theater go, she now runs the nursery school one afternoon a week. Her hardest time had been between 1916 and 1918, and then last year up to August. During the war things had been bad because her husband had been killed and she was left alone with three children. The situation did not improve until 1918 when, working in the cannery, she was able to get food more easily. Last year had been bad because she had been completely dependent on her sons. She had not been starving, but didn't like depriving the boys.

Her best time was the present because she could see that her children had got somewhere. They all were devoted to her, took her to the movies in Vienna, and looked after her generally. She divides her money so that what she receives from her son, together with the unemployment relief, is spent on food; her pension of fifty schillings a month goes on clothes. When no clothes are needed, one eats a little better. She is already buying things for the boys without their knowing it. She likes to think that when one of them gets married he will have something put by.

. . .

On the whole, those who had been particularly well-off in the past either held out for an especially long time or broke down especially quickly. For those who held out especially long, it was hard to determine how much was due to economic advantage and how much to adaptability, since both factors were almost always jointly operative, and had been there before the onset of unemployment. One woman, for example, declared that she had no trouble with clothes because she had been so well provided with them when she was married; today, ten years later, she is still well equipped. And she proudly informed us that she never had to go out to work. In this group of successful people was a man who in the past had led a very unsettled and adventurous life, supporting himself in first one place then another without ever really being in a bad way, even though at times not too well off. He treats his present fate as just another of those adventures which he has always managed to cope with in one way or another. These people seem to have both economic and spiritual resources to fall back on.

On the other hand, the people who had been well off in the past but now put up particularly poor resistance are above all characterized by their complete lack of adaptability. Their life broke because they could neither grasp nor bear the enormous difference between past and present. Some of them give the impression that, because of some early developed mental posture, the original shock effect lasted a particularly long time. Eventually the shock will recede and give way to resignation. With others, however, the feeling of being the victims of an unexpected and undeserved catastrophe is so strong that they show not the faintest sign of coming to terms with their predicament. They seem to be heading for individual disaster long before the village as a whole reaches that point. It may well be that this is the psychological condition which, in a large city, culminates in suicide or a similar catastrophic reaction.

People who had been particularly bad off in the past, now either belong again to the broken families or, consoled by the fact that everyone is in the same miserable plight, have joined the class of the resigned. There is, for instance, the man who years ago was sent to prison because of various illegal dealings while holding a public office. Since then he has lost almost all contact with the other inhabitants of the village. He and his family live in relative isolation and extreme poverty. As a result of his run-in with the law, the family was already in a bad way economically before the factory was closed. In this and similar cases there is no reason for a change in the general attitude to life. The same is true for the family in which the father, an alcoholic, is maltreating and beating his wife and children. For this family, too, the situation has not been essentially altered by unemployment, and consequently their attitude has not changed either.

In some cases, however, where extreme poverty formerly prevailed and (judging from the father's life-history) the family always belonged to the broken group, unemployment brought a certain relaxation. For example, there is the mother of three children who lost her husband soon after they were married. Since early youth she has been comparing her own life with that of others in her age group and now clearly finds this comparison less unfavorable. The double burden of household and factory has been lifted from her; she draws relief money, but most important, now her life is much like that of any other woman in the village. Our files contain a number of such cases.

Finally, there are those who in the past led normal working lives with no particular distinguishing features; they are to be found in all three attitude categories. Just which one depends in each case on such factors as age, income, and character traits, but our rough analysis of the past was not sufficient to disclose such differentiating constellations.

Thus we have endeavored, here at the end, to put before the reader a living picture of some of these people with whom we have had such close contact for a few months. This brings us to the limit of our inquiry and also of our method, aimed as it is at the general and typical. We entered Marienthal as scientists; we leave it with only one desire: that the tragic opportunity for such an inquiry may not recur in our time.

4
Europe at Point Zero: The Reconstruction of Order after the Second World War

34. W. H. Auden, *Voltaire at Ferney*

Born in York and educated at Oxford, Wystan Hugh Auden (1907–73) came to the attention of the British public in the 1930s as part of a group of promising young poets which included Christopher Isherwood, C. Day Lewis, Louis MacNeice, and Stephen Spender. All the members of the group—which Samuel Hynes has called (in a book of that title) *The Auden Generation*—had come to maturity in the period between the wars and all were strongly oriented towards leftist politics. Auden himself, who did a stint as an ambulance driver for the republicans during the Spanish Civil War, drew on the theories of both Marx and Freud in diagnosing the ills that beset his country during the Great Depression. In the early 1940s, Auden emigrated to the United States, becoming an American citizen in 1946. This geographical relocation was paralleled by an even more profound shift in attitude: Auden's abandonment of Marxism for Anglo-Catholicism.

In the mid 1930s, Auden developed a concept of "parable-art," which he opposed, on the one hand, to "escape-art" and, on the other, to propaganda. While the propagandist endeavors to persuade his audience to a particular course of action, the parabolic poet teaches, extending the reader's knowledge and awareness to a point where rational and moral choice becomes possible and where the need for action may appear urgent. Written in 1940, "Voltaire at Ferney" [1] exemplifies Auden's notion of a socially and politically engaged art. It offers an oblique comment on the European Enlightenment tradition from the vantage point of the opening phase of the Second World War.

---

1. Ferney was Voltaire's estate near Geneva, where he spent most of his declining years.

Almost happy now, he looked at his estate.
An exile making watches glanced up as he passed,
And went on working; where a hospital was rising fast
A joiner touched his cap; an agent came to tell
Some of the trees he'd planned were progressing well.
The white alps glittered. It was summer. He was very great.

Far off in Paris, where his enemies
Whispered that he was wicked, in an upright chair
A blind old woman[2] longed for death and letters. He would write
"Nothing is better than life." But was it? Yes, the fight
Against the false and the unfair
Was always worth it. So was gardening. Civilize.

Cajoling, scolding, scheming, cleverest of them all,
He'd led the other children in a holy war
Against the infamous grownups; and, like a child, been sly
And humble when there was occasion for
The two-faced answer or the plain protective lie,
But patient like a peasant waited for their fall.

And never doubted, like D'Alembert, he would win:
Only Pascal was a great enemy, the rest
Were rats already poisoned; there was much, though, to be done,
And only himself to count upon.
Dear Diderot was dull but did his best;
Rousseau, he'd always known, would blubber and give in.

So, like a sentinel, he could not sleep. The night was full of wrong,
Earthquakes[3] and executions. Soon he would be dead,
And still all over Europe stood the horrible nurses
Itching to boil their children. Only his verses
Perhaps could stop them: He must go on working. Overhead
The uncomplaining stars composed their lucid song.

From *The Collected Poetry of W. H. Auden,* edited by Edward Mendelson (New York: Random House, 1945), pp. 1625–26; © 1940 and renewed 1968 by W. H. Auden. Reprinted by permission of Random House, Inc., and Faber and Faber, Ltd.

2. The Marquise Marie du Deffand (1697–1780), who went blind in 1753, corresponded with Voltaire and other famous men of letters.—ED.

3. The Lisbon earthquake of 1755 killed 30,000 people and destroyed two-thirds of the city. It became a subject for philosophic ruminations about God's providence.—ED.

35. Bruno Bettelheim, *The Experience of the Concentration Camps*

The concentration camps and extermination camps of the Third Reich have come to symbolize the depravity of Nazism and, in a larger sense, the potential for radical evil which exists in all human beings and the fragility of what Westerners have called with self-congratulation since the second half of the eighteenth century, "civilization."

Hitler established the concentration camps when he came to power in 1933 primarily as places for the detention of political enemies of the regime: communists, socialists, some clerical resisters. From 1938 until the last weeks of World War II, the camps were in a constant state of expansion—and their character was fundamentally altered—as new categories of inmates, hated in and of themselves, became their principal focus: Jews, gypsies, Jehovah's Witnesses, homosexuals. The concentration camps extracted labor from these inmates, but this utilitarian aim was generally undermined by another and more pressing aim: the slow but systematic wearing down of the bodies and psyches of the prisoners.

With the German victory in Poland and the euphoria aroused by the German invasion of the Soviet Union, Nazi policy towards the Jews, in particular, took a grandiose turn. Control over Eastern Europe and the western portions of the Soviet Union would mean control over the world's largest Jewish populations and would make feasible the Nazi dream of ridding the world of Jews. Whereas the fall of France in 1940 had prompted only a tentative scheme to deport world Jewry to the French island colony of Madagascar, making it a kind of super-ghetto, by late 1941 the memoranda of Nazi officials began to speak of the "final solution" to the "Jewish problem," codewords for extermination. At that date, extermination centers were already being built in Poland at Belzec, Sobibor, and Treblinka; and at Chelmno, mobile vans were being used to kill inmates by carbon monoxide poisoning. The combination labor-extermination center at Auschwitz, also in Poland, came somewhat later. Equipped with the new Zyklon B Gas, superior in lethal power to carbon monoxide, Auschwitz was, at its peak, able to exterminate twelve thousand daily. The exact toll of those who died either swiftly in the extermination camps or by slow degrees in the concentration camps is disputed: there were between five and six million Jews, about 200,000 gypsies. Auschwitz alone accounted for four million deaths.

While the camps were a wartime phenomenon, they were primarily a postwar issue, for it was only after 1945 that the full horror of their operations became widely and publicly known. If efficient production had been the dominant motif of European history in the nineteenth-century age of industrialization, by some demonic reversal, efficient destruction had come to seem the dominant motif of the twentieth century. As Hannah Arendt observed in *The Origins of Totalitarianism* (1951), of two, qualitatively different innovations in the technology of destruction that had taken place during the Second World War, "a victory of the concentration-camp system would mean the same inexorable doom for human beings" as the use of nuclear weapons "would mean the doom of the human race." [1]

The document below, a deposition before United States government officials in July 1945, describes the way the regimen at the concentration camps sought to eradicate the human being even while letting the human organism live. Its author Bruno Bettelheim was born in Vienna in 1903 and had just finished a doctorate in psychology and philosophy at the University of Vienna when he was arrested by the Nazis and incarcerated in the concentration camps at Dachau and Buchenwald (both in Germany) from 1938 to 1939. He then emigrated to the United States and became a naturalized citizen in 1944. Bettelheim developed the observations sketched out in this deposition in an article, "Mass Behavior in Extreme Situations," which became required reading for U.S. military government officers in Europe. He subsequently examined his camp experience in greater detail in *The Informed Heart: Autonomy in a Mass Age* (1960). From 1944 to 1973, Bettelheim was head of the Orthogenic School at the University of Chicago where, as a psychologist working within the Freudian canon broadly construed, he pioneered a mode of therapy for emotionally disturbed children, writing many books on aspects of child development.

---

1. I was born in Vienna, Austria and lived there up until the annexation of Austria by the Germans in March, 1938. My education was obtained at the Progressive-Real-Gymnasium at Vienna and the University of Vienna where I received a Ph.D. degree in psychology and philosophy in 1938. For a period of approximately twelve years prior thereto I had conducted research work in psychology and education. I was also interested in a business which I inherited from my father. This business, a joint stock com-

1. Hannah Arendt, *The Origins of Totalitarianism* (Cleveland and New York, 1958 ed.), p. 443.

From Office of U.S. Chief Counsel for Prosecution of Axis Criminality, *Nazi Conspiracy and Aggression,* vol. 7 (Washington, D.C.: U.S. Government Printing Office, 1946), Document L-73, pp. 818–39.

pany by the name of Bettelheim and Schnitzer, was engaged in lumber and saw mill operations in Austria.

2. My political affiliations were with the Social Democratic Party which stood for the independence of Austria. The tenets of this party were diametrically opposed to the Nazi viewpoint and principles.

3. Immediately following the occupation of Austria on or about March 12, 1938, it became apparent to me that I would not be permitted to live in peace in Austria. My wife and I left Vienna on or about 12 or 13 of March and were stopped at the Czechoslovakian-Hungarian border that night. The next day we undertook to leave Vienna by train, and while my wife was permitted to proceed, I was detained by the police, ordered to remain in Vienna, and my passport was taken away from me. Within the next day or two the police searched my home. I was extensively questioned but not taken into custody, the police stating that it did not appear that I had violated any of the laws of Austria. Three or four weeks later I was taken into custody by the Austrian police and for three days questioned about my political activities. At the conclusion of the questioning the police officer who was in charge of the investigation dictated a statement to the effect that there appeared to be no basis whatever for any legal action against me. Thereupon I was released. Two weeks later I was taken into custody and imprisoned. It was stated to me that my confinement was the result of orders issued by the Gestapo in Berlin. I spent three days in jail in Vienna after which I was transferred to the concentration camp at Dachau early in May, 1938. I spent approximately four months in Dachau after which I was transferred to the concentration camp at Buchenwald. Meanwhile my wife had proceeded to the United States. I was released from Buchenwald in April 1939. My release was effected through the aid of some influential friends of mine in America who were able to enlist the assistance of the State Department of the United States.

4. Upon my release I came to the United States. In November, 1939 I was appointed Research Associate of the Progressive Education Association at the University of Chicago. Since then I have been connected with this University. At present I am Assistant Professor of Education and Principal of the University's Orthogenic School.

5. My period of confinement in the concentration camp at Dachau and Buchenwald afforded an opportunity to conduct investigations, collect data, and make certain observations concerning the effect on the personality and behavior of individuals who have spent several years in such institutions. The motives which prompted me to make such a study are adverted to below. It is not the purpose of this statement to recount once more the horror story of the German concentration camp. That story has been repeatedly and adequately documented, particularly in recent months fol-

lowing the fall of Germany. Accordingly, this statement does not emphasize individual acts of terror but is limited to the sociological significance of the concentration camp; viz., an examination and appraisal of the concentration camp as a means of producing psychological changes in the prisoners. On the basis of my previous experience with Gestapo methods and my observation of the deteriorating changes which occurred in the prisoners during the process of their adaptation to the camp situation, I was enabled to reach certain conclusions as to the results which the Gestapo sought to achieve by means of the camps. These conclusions are stated below.

6. In the concentration camp the Gestapo developed methods for subjecting not only free men, but also the most ardent foes of the Nazi system, to a process of disintegration from their position as autonomous individuals. This process was attained by means of exposing them to extreme experiences. During the course of my confinement my study of this subject embraced an investigation and examination of what occurred in the prisoners from the moment they had their first experience with the Gestapo up to the time when the process of adaptation to the camp situation was practically concluded.

7. *Reasons for making studies.* While my former training and psychological interests were of material assistance to me in collecting the data and conducting the necessary investigations I did not analyze my own behavior and that of my fellow prisoners in order to add to pure scientific research. On the contrary, the study of these behaviors was a mechanism developed by me in order that I might have some intellectual interests and in this way be better equipped to endure life in the camp. It was developed by me to forestall a complete disintegration of my character and personality. I may add that I felt that without an activity which could force me to remain continuously critical of the Gestapo methods I would not be able to defend successfully the integrity of my personality against the impact of the Gestapo methods. The need for a strong defense against the influence which the camp was exercising on me became apparent during my first few days of confinement. I observed that I was behaving differently from the way I used to. I may add that I am convinced that I would have been unable to make these observations without the strict and continuous self-observation which my years of psycho-analytical training taught me. . . .

13. The process of adaptation to the camp situation can be broken down into three different stages. The main event of the first stage is the transportation to the camp and the first experiences in it. The next stage is characterized by a slow process of changing the prisoner's life and personality. It occurs step by step continuously. The last stage is the final adaptation to the camp situation. These three stages will be analyzed below:

14. *The transportation into the camp and the first experiences in it.* After having spent several days in prison, the prisoners were brought into the camp. During this transportation they were exposed to constant tortures of various kinds. Corporal punishment consisting of whipping, kicking, slapping intermingled with shooting and wounding with the bayonet, alternated with tortures the obvious goal of which was extreme exhaustion. For instance, the prisoners were forced to stare for hours into glaring lights, to kneel for hours, and so on. From time to time a prisoner got killed; no prisoner was permitted to take care of his or another's wounds. These tortures alternated with efforts on the part of the guards to force the prisoners to hit one another, and to defile what the guards considered the prisoners' most cherished values. For instance, the prisoners were forced to curse their God, to accuse themselves of vile actions, accuse their wives of adultery and of prostitution. This continued for hours and was repeated at various times.

15. The purpose of the tortures was to break the resistance of the prisoners, and to assure the guards that they were really superior to them. This can be seen from the fact that the longer the tortures lasted, the less violent they became. The guards became slowly less excited, and at the end even talked with the prisoners. As soon as a new guard took over, he started with new acts of terror, although not as violent as in the beginning, and he eased up sooner than his predecessor. Sometimes prisoners who had already spent time in camp were brought back with a group of new prisoners. These old prisoners were not tortured if they could furnish evidence that they had already been in the camp. That these tortures were planned can be seen from the fact that during my transportation into the camp after several prisoners had died and many had been wounded in tortures lasting for 12 hours, the command, "Stop mistreating the prisoners," came and from this moment on the prisoners were left in peace till they arrived in the camp when another group of guards took over and started anew to take advantage of them.

16. Most of the prisoners became so exhausted that they were only partly conscious of what happened. In general, prisoners remembered the details and did not mind talking about them, but they did not like to talk about what they had felt and thought during the time of torture. The few who volunteered information made vague statements which sounded like devious rationalizations, invented for the purpose of justifying that they had endured treatment injurious to their self-respect without trying to fight back. The few who had tried to fight back could not be interviewed; they were dead.

17. I can vividly recall my extreme weariness, resulting from a bayonet wound which I had received early in the course of transportation and from

a heavy blow on the head. Both injuries led to the loss of a considerable amount of blood, and made me groggy. Nevertheless I wondered that the guards really tortured prisoners in the way it had been described in books on the concentration camps; that the Gestapo was so simple-minded as either to enjoy forcing prisoners to defile themselves or to expect to break their resistance in this way. I wondered that the guards were lacking in fantasy when selecting the means to torture the prisoners; that their sadism was without imagination. I was rather amused by the repeated statement that guards do not shoot the prisoners but kill them by beating them to death because a bullet costs six pfennigs, and the prisoners are not worth even so much. Obviously the idea that these men, most of them formerly influential persons, were not worth such a trifle impressed the guards considerably. It was clear that these tortures followed a deliberate and purposeful plan. This is evidenced by the fact that the railroad coaches in which prisoners were transported were equipped with unusually strong light bulbs. The prisoners were forced to stare for hours at these lights which created in them a condition analogous to a state of hypnotism. These circumstances contributed to creating a condition which may best be described as a state of "depersonalization." It seemed as if I had become convinced that these horrible and degrading experiences somehow did not happen to "me" as a subject but to "me" as an object. This experience was corroborated by the statements of other prisoners.

18. All the thoughts and emotions which I had during the transportation were extremely detached. It was as if I watched things happening in which I only vaguely participated. Later I learned that many prisoners had developed this same feeling of detachment, as if what happened really did not matter to oneself. It was strangely mixed with a conviction that "this cannot be true, such things just do not happen." Not only during the transportation, but all through the time spent in camp, the prisoners had to convince themselves that this was real, was really happening, and not just a nightmare. They were never wholly successful.

19. There were good indications that most guards embraced a similar attitude, although for different reasons. They tortured the prisoners partly because they enjoyed demonstrating their superiority, partly because their superiors expected it of them. But, having been educated in a world which rejected brutality, they felt uneasy about what they were doing. It seems that they, too, had an emotional attitude toward their acts of brutality which might be described as a feeling of unreality. After having been guards in the camp for some time, they got accustomed to inhuman behavior, they became "conditioned" to it; it then became part of their "real" life.

20. To summarize: During the transportation the prisoners were exposed to physical and mental tortures, the purpose of which seemed to be

to break any ability to resist the Gestapo. They seemed, moreover, to serve the purpose of overcoming the Gestapo members' fear of the prisoners who were more intelligent and belonged usually to a higher social group. During the transportation the prisoners developed a state of detachment, feeling as if what happened did not really happen to them as persons. Thus, transportation into the camp was instrumental in bringing about the alienation of the prisoner from his normal personality.

21. It seems that camp experiences which remained within the normal frame of reference of a prisoner's life experience were dealt with by means of the normal psychological mechanisms. Once the experience transcended this frame of reference, the normal mechanisms seemed no longer able to deal adequately with it and new psychological mechanisms were needed. The experience during the transportation was one of those transcending the normal frame of reference and the reaction to it may be described as "unforgettable, but unreal."

22. Attitudes similar to those developed toward the transportation could be observed in other extreme situations. On a terribly cold winter night when a snow storm was blowing, all prisoners were punished by being forced to stand at attention without overcoats—they never wore any—for hours. This, after having worked for more than 12 hours in the open and having received hardly any food. The reason for this punishment was that two prisoners had tried to escape. On such occasions all prisoners were always punished very severely, so that in the future they would give away any secret they had learned, because otherwise they would have to suffer. The idea was that every prisoner ought to feel responsible for any act committed by any other prisoner. This was in line with the principle of the Gestapo to force the prisoners to feel and act as a group, and not as individuals. They were threatened with having to stand all through the night. After about 20 prisoners had died from exposure the discipline broke down. The threats of the guards became ineffective. To be exposed to the weather was a terrible torture; to see one's friends die without being able to help, and to stand a good chance of dying, created a situation similar to the transportation, except that the prisoners had by now more experience with the Gestapo. Open resistance was impossible, as impossible as it was to do anything definite to safeguard oneself. A feeling of utter indifference swept the prisoners. They did not care whether the guards shot them; they were indifferent to acts of torture committed by the guards. The guards had no longer any authority, the spell of fear and death was broken. It was again as if what happened did not "really" happen to oneself. There was again the split between the "me" to whom it happened, and the "me" who really did not care and was just an interested but detached observer. Unfortunate as the situation was, they felt free from fear and therefore were actually happier than at most other times during their camp experiences.

23. After more than 80 prisoners had died, and several hundred had their extremities so badly frozen that they had later to be amputated, the prisoners were permitted to return to the barracks. They were completely exhausted, but did not experience that feeling of happiness which some of them had expected. They felt relieved that the torture was over, but felt at the same time that they no longer were free from fear and no longer could strongly rely on mutual help. Each prisoner as an individual was now comparatively safer, but he had lost the safety originating in being a member of a unified group. This event was again freely discussed, in a detached way, and again the discussion was restricted to facts; the prisoners' emotions and thoughts during this night were hardly ever mentioned. The event itself and its details were not forgotten, but no particular emotions were attached to them; nor did they appear in dreams.

24. The psychological reactions to events which were somewhat more within the sphere of the normally comprehensible were decidedly different from those to extreme events. It seems that prisoners dealt with less extreme events in the same way as if they had happened outside of the camp. For example, if a prisoner's punishment was not of an unusual kind, he seemed ashamed of it, he tried not to speak about it. A slap in one's face was embarrassing, and not to be discussed. One hated individual guards who had kicked one, or slapped one, or verbally abused one much more than the guard who really had wounded one seriously. In the latter case one eventually hated the Gestapo as much, but not so much the individual inflicting the punishment. Obviously this differentiation was unreasonable, but it seemed to be inescapable. One felt deeper and more violent aggressions against particular Gestapo members who had committed minor vile acts than one felt against those who had acted in a much more terrible fashion.

25. It seems that all experiences which might have happened during the prisoner's "normal" life history provoked a "normal" reaction. Prisoners seemed for instance, particularly sensitive to punishments similar to those which a parent might inflict on his child. To punish a child was within their "normal" frame of reference, but that they should become the object of the punishment destroyed their adult frame of reference. So they reacted to it not in an adult, but in a childish way—with embarrassment and shame, with violent, impotent, and unmanageable emotions directed, not against the system, but against the person inflicting the punishment.

26. Resentment by prisoners of minor vile acts on the part of the guards more than extreme experiences is explained as follows: When a prisoner was cursed, slapped, pushed around "like a child" and if he was, like a child, unable to defend himself, this revived in him behavior patterns and psychological mechanisms which he had developed when a child. Like a child he was unable to see his treatment in the general context of the behav-

ior of the Gestapo. The degradation of the prisoner by means of being treated like a child took place not only in his mind, but in the minds of his fellow prisoners, too.

Differences in Attitudes of Old and New Prisoners

27. As time went on the difference in the reaction to minor and major sufferings slowly seemed to disappear. This change in reaction was only one of many differences between old and new prisoners. A few others ought to be mentioned. In the following discussion I refer to the term "new prisoners" to those who had not spent more than one year in the camp; "old" prisoners are those who have spent at least three years in the camp.

28. The main concern of the new prisoners seemed to be to remain intact as a personality and to return to the outer world the same persons who had left it; all their emotional efforts were directed towards this goal. Old prisoners seemed mainly concerned with the problem of how to live as well as possible within the camp. Once they had reached this attitude, everything that happened to them, even the worst atrocity, was "real" to them. No longer was there a split between one to whom things happened and the one who observed them. Once this stage was reached of taking everything that happened in the camp as "real," there was every indication that the prisoners who had reached it were afraid of returning to the outer world. They did not admit it directly, but from their talk it was clear that they hardly believed they would ever return to this outer world because they felt that only a cataclysmic event—a world war and world revolution—could free them; and even then they doubted that they would be able to adapt to this new life. They seemed aware of what had happened to them while growing older in the camp. They realized that they had adapted themselves to the life in the camp and that this process was coexistent with a basic change in their personality.

29. The most drastic demonstration of this realization was provided by the case of a formerly very prominent radical German politician. He declared that according to his experience nobody could live in the camp longer than five years without changing his attitudes so radically that he no longer could be considered the same person he used to be. He asserted that he did not see any point in continuing to live once his real life consisted in being a prisoner in a concentration camp, that he could not endure developing those attitudes and behaviors he saw developing in all old prisoners. He therefore had decided to commit suicide on the sixth anniversary of his being brought into the camp. His fellow prisoners tried to watch him carefully on this day, but nevertheless he succeeded. . . .

31. The new prisoners consistently accused their families of betraying

and cheating them. They would weep over a letter telling of the efforts in regard to their property which had been sold without their permission. They would swear at their families which "obviously" considered them "already dead." Even the smallest change in their former private world attained tremendous importance.

32. The violent reaction against changes in their families was the counterpart of the prisoners' realization that they were changing. What enraged them was probably not only the fact of the change, but the change in standing within the family which it implied. Their families had been dependent on them for decisions, and now they were the ones to be dependent. That created in them a feeling of dependency. The only chance they saw for becoming again the head of the family was that the family structure remain untouched despite their absence. Also they knew the attitudes of most persons toward those who have spent time in prisons of any kind.

33. Old prisoners did not like to be reminded of their families and former friends. When they spoke about them, it was in a very detached way. They liked to receive letters, but it was not very important to them. It has been mentioned that they had some realization of how difficult it might be for them to find their way back, but there was another contributing factor, namely, the prisoners' hatred of all those living outside of the camp, who "enjoyed life as if we were not rotting away."

34. This outside world which continued to live as if nothing had happened was in the minds of the prisoners represented by those whom they used to know, namely, by their relatives and friends. But even this hatred was very subdued in the old prisoners. It seemed that, as much as they had forgotten to love their kin, they had lost the ability to hate them. They had learned to direct a great amount of aggression against themselves so as not to get into too many conflicts with the Gestapo, while the new prisoners still directed their aggression against the outer world, and—when not supervised—against the Gestapo. Since the old prisoners did not show much emotion either way, they were unable to feel strongly about anybody.

35. Old prisoners did not like to mention their former social status or their former activities, whereas new prisoners were rather boastful about them. New prisoners seemed to try to back their self-esteem by letting others know how important they had been, with the very obvious implication that they still were important. Old prisoners seemed to have accepted their state of dejection, and to compare it with their former splendor—and anything was magnificent when compared with the situation in which they found themselves—was probably too depressing.

36. Closely connected with the prisoners' beliefs about, and attitudes toward, their families were their beliefs and hopes concerning their life after release from camp. Here the prisoners embarked a great deal on indi-

vidual and group daydreams. There was a marked difference between the daydreams of the new and the old prisoners. The longer the time a prisoner had spent in camp, the less true to reality were his daydreams. They were convinced that they would emerge as the future leaders of Germany at least, if not of the world. This was the least to which their sufferings entitled them. These grandiose expectations were coexistent with great vagueness as to their future private lives. In their daydreams they were certain to emerge as the future secretaries of state, but they were less certain whether they would continue to live with their wives and children. Part of these daydreams may be explained by the fact that they seemed to feel that only a high public position could help them to regain their standing within their families.

37. The hopes and expectations of the new prisoners about their future lives were much more true to reality. Despite their open ambivalence about their families, they never doubted that they were going to continue to live with them just where they had left off. They hoped to continue their public and professional lives in the same way as they used to live them.

38. Most of the adaptations to the camp situation mentioned so far were more or less individual. The changes discussed below, namely, the *regression to infantile behavior,* was a mass phenomenon. Whereas the prisoners did not interfere with another's daydreams or with his attitudes to his family, they asserted their power as a group over those prisoners who objected to deviations from normal adult behavior. They accused those who would not develop a childlike dependency on the guards as threatening the security of the group, an accusation which was not without foundation, since the Gestapo always punished the group for the misbehavior of individual members. This regression into childlike behavior was, therefore even more inescapable than other types of behavior imposed on the individual by the impact of the conditions in the camp.

39. The prisoners developed types of behavior which are characteristic of infancy or early youth. Some of these behaviors developed slowly, others were immediately imposed on the prisoners and developed only in intensity as time went on. Some of these more or less infantile behaviors have already been discussed, such as ambivalence to one's family, despondency, finding satisfaction in irrealistic daydreaming rather than in action.

40. I am convinced that these behavior patterns were deliberately produced by the Gestapo. I mentioned that during the transportation the prisoners were tortured in a way in which a cruel and domineering father might torture a helpless child; here I should add that the prisoners were also debased by techniques which went much further into childhood situations. They were forced to soil themselves. In the camp the defecation was strictly regulated; it was one of the most important daily events, discussed

in great detail. During the day the prisoners who wanted to defecate had to obtain the permission of the guard. It seemed as if the education to cleanliness would be once more repeated. It seemed to give pleasure to the guards to hold the power of granting or withholding the permission to visit the latrines. (Toilets were mostly not available.) This pleasure of the guards found its counterpart in the pleasure the prisoners derived from visiting the latrines, because there they usually could rest for a moment, secure from the whips of the overseers and guards. They were not always so secure, because sometimes enterprising young guards enjoyed interfering with the prisoners even at these moments.

41. The prisoners were forced to say "thou" to one another, which in Germany is indiscriminately used only among small children. They were not permitted to address one another with the many titles to which middle- and upper-class Germans are accustomed. On the other hand, they had to address the guards in the most deferential manner giving them all their titles. . . .

44. All changes produced by living in the camp seemed to force the prisoners back into childhood attitudes and behaviors and they became in this way more or less willing tools of the Gestapo.

45. *The final adjustment to the life in the camp.* A prisoner had reached the final stage of adjustment to the camp situation when he had changed his personality so as to accept as his own the values of the Gestapo. A few examples may illustrate how this acceptance expressed itself.

46. The prisoners found themselves in an impossible situation due to the steady interference with their privacy on the part of the guards and other prisoners. So a great amount of aggression accumulated. In the new prisoners it vented itself in the way it might have done in the world outside the camp. But slowly prisoners accepted, as expression of their verbal aggressions, terms which definitely did not originate in their previous vocabularies, but were taken over from the very different vocabulary of the Gestapo. From copying the verbal aggressions of the Gestapo to copying their form of bodily aggressions was one more step, but it took several years to make this step. It was not unusual to find old prisoners, when in charge of others, behaving worse than the Gestapo, in some cases because they were trying to win favor with the Gestapo in this way, but more often because they considered this the best way to behave toward prisoners in the camp.

47. Practically all prisoners who had spent a long time in the camp took over the Gestapo's attitude toward the so-called unfit prisoners. Newcomers presented the old prisoners with difficult problems. Their complaints about the unbearable life in camp added new strain to the life in the barracks, so did their inability to adjust to it. Bad behavior in the labor gang endangered

the whole group. So a newcomer who did not stand up well under the strain tended to become a liability for the other prisoners. Moreover, weaklings were those most apt eventually to turn traitors. Weaklings usually died during the first weeks in the camp anyway, so it seemed as well to get rid of them sooner. So old prisoners were sometimes instrumental in getting rid of the unfit, in this way making a feature of Gestapo ideology a feature of their own behavior. This was one of the many situations in which old prisoners demonstrated toughness and molded their way of treating other prisoners according to the example set by the Gestapo. That this was really a taking-over of Gestapo attitudes can be seen from the treatment of traitors. Self-protection asked for their elimination, but the way in which they were tortured for days and slowly killed was taken over from the Gestapo.

48. Old prisoners who seemed to have a tendency to identify themselves with the Gestapo did so not only in respect to aggressive behavior. They would try to arrogate to themselves old pieces of Gestapo uniforms. If that was not possible, they tried to sew and mend their uniforms so that they would resemble those of the guards. The length to which prisoners would go in these efforts seemed unbelievable, particularly since the Gestapo punished them for their efforts to copy Gestapo uniforms. When asked why they did it they admitted that they loved to look like one of the guards.

49. The identification with the Gestapo did not stop with the copying of their outer appearance and behavior. Old prisoners accepted their goals and values, too, even when they seemed opposed to their own interests. It was appalling to see how far formerly even politically well-educated prisoners would go in this identification. At one time American and English newspapers were full of stories about the cruelties committed in the camps. The Gestapo punished the prisoners for the appearance of these stories true to their policy of punishing the group for whatever a member or a former member did, and the stories must have originated in reports of former prisoners. In discussions of this event old prisoners would insist that it is not the business of foreign correspondents or newspapers to bother with German institutions and expressed their hatred of the journalists who tried to help them. I asked more than one hundred old political prisoners the following question: "If I am lucky and reach foreign soil, should I tell the story of the camp and arouse the interest of the cultured world?" I found only two who made the unqualified statement that everyone escaping Germany ought to fight the Nazis to the best of his abilities. All others were hoping for a German revolution, but did not like the idea of interference on the part of a foreign power. . . .

52. Often the Gestapo would enforce nonsensical rules, originating in the whims of one of the guards. They were usually forgotten as soon as formulated, but there were always some old prisoners who would continue

to follow these rules and try to enforce them on others long after the Gestapo had forgotten about them. Once, for instance, a guard on inspecting the prisoners' apparel found that the shoes of some of them were dirty on the inside. He ordered all prisoners to wash their shoes inside and out with water and soap. The heavy shoes treated this way became hard as stone. The order was never repeated, and many prisoners did not even execute it when given. Nevertheless there were some old prisoners who not only continued to wash the inside of their shoes every day but cursed all others who did not do so as negligent and dirty. These prisoners firmly believed that the rules set down by the Gestapo were desirable standards of human behavior, at least in the camp situation.

53. Other problems in which most old prisoners made their peace with the values of the Gestapo included the race problem, although race discrimination had been alien to their scheme of values before they were brought into the camp. They accepted as true the claim that Germany needed more space ("Lebensraum"), but added "as long as there does not exist a world federation," they believed in the superiority of the German race. It should be emphasized that this was not the result of propaganda on the side of the Gestapo. The Gestapo made no such efforts and insisted in its statements that it was not interested in how the prisoners felt as long as they were full of fear of the Gestapo. Moreover, the Gestapo insisted that it would prevent them from expressing their feelings anyway. . . .

Conclusions

55. Based upon my knowledge of the Gestapo, and my confinement in Dachau and Buchenwald for one year, which furnished the personal experience and laboratory for the foregoing observations, I have reached certain conclusions as to the Nazi reasons for setting up the concentration camps and the results which they sought to achieve by conducting such camps in the manner which I have described. The conclusions are as follows:

(a) To spread terror among the rest of the population by using the prisoners as hostages for good behaviour, and by demonstrating what happens to those who oppose the Nazi rules.

(b) To provide the Gestapo members with a training ground in which they were so educated as to lose all human emotions and attitudes, and learn the most effective ways of breaking resistance in a defenseless civilian population.

(c) To provide the Gestapo with an experimental laboratory in which to study the effective means for breaking civilian resistance, the minimum food, hygienic, and medical requirements needed to keep prisoners alive and able to perform hard labor when the threat of punishment takes the place of all other normal incentives, and the influence on performance if no time is allowed for anything but hard labor and if the prisoners are separated from their families.

(d) To break the prisoners as individuals and to change them into docile masses from which no individual or group act of resistance could arise.

56. Some additional comment on these conclusions is indicated. With respect to (a) above—the spreading of terror among the rest of the people— that objective does not appear to have been an original purpose of the concentration camp device. When the concentration camps were first established the Nazis detained in them their more prominent foes. Pretty soon there were no more prominent enemies available, because they were either dead, in the jails, the camps, or had emigrated. Still, an institution was needed to threaten the opponents of the system. Too many Germans became dissatisfied with the system. To imprison all of them would have interrupted the functioning of the industrial production, the upholding of which was a paramount goal of the Nazis. So if a group of the population got fed up with the Nazi regime, a selected few members of this group would be brought into the concentration camp. If lawyers became restless, a few hundred lawyers were sent to the camp, the same happened to physicians when the medical profession seemed rebellious, etc. The Gestapo called such group punishments "actions" and this new system was first used during 1937–38, when Germany was first preparing to embark on the annexation of foreign countries. During the first of these "actions" only the leaders of the opposition group were punished. That led to the feeling that just to belong to a rebellious group was not dangerous, since only the leaders were threatened. Soon the Gestapo revised its system, and selected the persons to be punished so that they represented a cross-section through the different strata of the group. This new procedure had not only the advantage of spreading terror among all members of the group, but made it possible to punish and destroy the group without necessarily touching the leader if that was for some reason inopportune. Though prisoners were never told exactly why they were imprisoned, those imprisoned as representatives of a group came to know about it. Prisoners were interviewed by the Gestapo to gain information about their relatives and friends. During those interviews prisoners sometimes complained that they were imprisoned while more prominent foes of the Nazis were at liberty. They were told that it was just their bad luck that they had to suffer as members of a group, but if their fate did not teach the group to behave better, they would get a chance to meet them all in the camp.

57. Moreover, the Gestapo saw to it that the rest of the population learned of these "actions" through the newspapers. For purposes of intimi-

dation not all news about the terror of the concentration camps was suppressed. Newspapers were permitted to reprint foreign reports on the concentration camps. The fact that the tortures were planned not only for breaking down the prisoners' ability to resist, but also for intimidating the rest of the population was demonstrated at the beginning of my experience with the Gestapo. When boarding the train for Dachau the SS men butchered several prisoners on an exposed platform. Hundreds of spectators viewed this incident from the windows of adjacent houses.

58. I learned from fellow prisoners how they were used as hostages. They had learned from letters that their release had been promised to their relatives if both prisoner and relatives would behave better, would be more loyal Nazis. The release was again and again postponed with the explanation that some relative was not a "good" Nazi.

59. A further example of (b) above, namely, the concentration camp as a training ground for Gestapo members in which they are so educated as to lose all human emotions, was afforded by the studied arrogance of Gestapo personnel in the presence of prisoners. The Gestapo considered, or pretended to consider, the prisoners the scum of the earth. They insisted that none of them was any better than the others. One of the reasons for this attitude was probably to impress the young guards who received their training in the camp that they were superior to even the most outstanding prisoner and to demonstrate to them that the former foes of the Nazis were now subdued and not worthy of any special attention. If a formerly prominent prisoner had been treated better, the simple guard would have thought that he is still influential; if he had been treated worse, they might have thought that he is still dangerous. This was in line with the desire to impress the guards that even a slight degree of opposition against the Nazi system led to the destruction of the person who dared to oppose, and that the degree of opposition made no difference in this respect.

60. The fact that these young SS men were not only permitted but encouraged to use former secretaries of state, generals, university professors as their slaves taught them not only to disrespect superiority, but to become convinced of their being "supermen."

61. Tortures were, moreover, such common occurrences in the camp that they no longer evoked any reaction in the guards. To kick and whip prisoners became to them a nearly automatic response. If a prisoner passed a guard he expected to be hit or kicked, since this seemed to be the "conditioned" response of these fledgling "supermen." Finally their daily contact with the undernourished prisoners accustomed them to feel no pity with a starving population.

62. An example of the use of the camp as a laboratory for experimentation in minimum food requirements (conclusion (c) above) were frequent

changes in food rations. Bread rations were increased and decreased. On some days no food was distributed, on other days no food other than bread. This was particularly true in Buchenwald where the prisoners' weight was regularly checked.

63. To recapitulate, it is apparent that the concentration camp had an importance reaching far beyond its being a place where the Gestapo took revenge on its enemies. It was the main training ground for young Gestapo soldiers who were planning to rule and police Germany and all conquered nations; it was the Gestapo's laboratory where it developed methods for changing free and upright citizens not only into grumbling slaves, but into serfs who in many respects accepted their masters' values. The "old" prisoners still thought that they were following their own life goals and values, whereas in reality they accepted the Nazis' values as their own.

64. Moreover, what happened in an extreme fashion to the prisoners who spent several years in the concentration camp happened in less exaggerated form to the inhabitants of the big concentration camp which was formerly greater Germany. The system seemed too strong for an individual to break its hold over his emotional life, particularly if he found himself within a group which had more or less accepted the Nazi system. It seemed easier to resist the pressure of the Gestapo and the Nazis if one functioned as an individual; the Gestapo seemed to know that and therefore insisted on forcing all individuals into groups which they supervised. Some of the methods used for that purpose were the hostage system and the punishment of the whole group for whatever a member of it did; not permitting anybody to deviate in his behavior from the group norm, whatever this norm may be; discouraging solitary activities of any kind, etc. The main goal of the efforts seemed to be to produce in the subjects childlike attitudes and childlike dependency on the will of the leaders. Thus, it was very difficult, if not impossible, for individuals to resist the slow process of personality disintegration produced by the unrelenting pressure of the Gestapo and Nazi system.

36. Jean-Paul Sartre, *Existentialism Is a Humanism*

More than any other twentieth-century figure, Jean-Paul Sartre exemplifies the modern French propensity to turn certain intellectuals into national moral leaders. Sartre's assumption of that latter position took place in the immediately postwar era and with specific reference to the Resistance, the underground organization which fought against Pétain's Vichy regime and its policy of collaboration with the Nazi occupying power. Sartre had joined the Resistance early, upon his release from nine months as a German war prisoner, and he would later explicate his main intellectual creation, the philosophy of existentialism, by pointing to the kind of intrinsically insoluble moral dilemma that the Resistance had posed for many Frenchmen.

Born in Paris in 1905, Sartre studied classical French philosophy at the Ecole Normale Supérieure. Hearing of the new German philosophical movement called phenomenology, he is reported to have turned pale with excitement; and he spent the 1933–34 academic year in Berlin studying the works of its masters, Edmund Husserl and Martin Heidegger. Sartre first adumbrated his existentialist philosophy, which drew upon German phenomenology as well as the work of the nineteenth-century Danish philosopher Søren Kierkegaard, in a novella called *Nausea* (1938). He spelled it out in detail in the 700-page treatise *Being and Nothingness* (1943) and presented an aspect of it in *No Exit,* the first play to be performed in Paris after the liberation of 1944. In the 1940s and 1950s, existentialism enjoyed an enormous vogue in France, its stark postulates (anguish, abandonment, despair) meshing well with the national mood of defeat, its concepts of choice and responsibility pointing a way forward.

Sartre continued to write prolifically for the next three decades, and his intellectual odyssey was something of a national event, eagerly followed by his countrymen. In 1960 appeared his *Critique of Dialectical Reason,* fusing existentialism with Marxism. In 1971 came *The Family Idiot,* his biography of the novelist Flaubert, in which the insights of psychoanalysis were added to existential Marxism and brought to bear upon an individual life. But Sartre's special stature always remained rooted in his role in France's wartime experience. At his death in 1980, crowds of people of all ages flooded the streets of Paris to pay him homage.

The selection below, *Existentialism Is a Humanism,* was delivered as a lecture in 1945 and published the next year. In it, Sartre offers both a defense of and a general introduction to his philosophy. The immediate postwar context of the lecture is evident.

My purpose here is to offer a defence of existentialism against several reproaches that have been laid against it.

First, it has been reproached as an invitation to people to dwell in quietism of despair. For if every way to a solution is barred, one would have to regard any action in this world as entirely ineffective, and one would arrive finally at a contemplative philosophy. Moreover, since con-

From Jean-Paul Sartre, *Existentialism and Humanism,* translated by Philip Mairet (London: Methuen, 1948), pp. 222–23, 287–311. Reprinted by permission of the publisher.

templation is a luxury, this would be only another bourgeois philosophy. This is, especially, the reproach made by the Communists.

From another quarter we are reproached for having underlined all that is ignominious in the human situation, for depicting what is mean, sordid or base to the neglect of certain things that possess charm and beauty and belong to the brighter side of human nature: for example, according to the Catholic critic, Mlle. Mercier, we forget how an infant smiles. Both from this side and from the other we are also reproached for leaving out of account the solidarity of mankind and considering man in isolation. And this, say the Communists, is because we base our doctrine upon pure subjectivity—upon the Cartesian "I think": which is the moment in which solitary man attains to himself; a position from which it is impossible to regain solidarity with other men who exist outside of the self. The *ego* cannot reach them through the *cogito*.

From the Christian side, we are reproached as people who deny the reality and seriousness of human affairs. For since we ignore the commandments of God and all values prescribed as eternal, nothing remains but what is strictly voluntary. Everyone can do what he likes, and will be incapable, from such a point of view, of condemning either the point of view or the action of anyone else.

It is to these various reproaches that I shall endeavor to reply today; that is why I have entitled this brief exposition "Existentialism is a Humanism." Many may be surprised at the mention of humanism in this connection, but we shall try to see in what sense we understand it. In any case, we can begin by saying that existentialism, in our sense of the word, is a doctrine that does render human life possible; a doctrine, also, which affirms that every truth and every action imply both an environment and a human subjectivity. The essential charge laid against us is, of course, that of overemphasis upon the evil side of human life. I have lately been told of a lady who, whenever she lets slip a vulgar expression in a moment of nervousness, excuses herself by exclaiming, "I believe I am becoming an existentialist." So it appears that ugliness is being identified with existentialism. That is why some people say we are "naturalistic," and if we are, it is strange to see how much we scandalize and horrify them, for no one seems to be much frightened or humiliated nowadays by what is properly called naturalism. Those who can quite well keep down a novel by Zola such as *La Terre* are sickened as soon as they read an existentialist novel. Those who appeal to the wisdom of the people—which is a sad wisdom— find ours sadder still. And yet, what could be more disillusioned than such sayings as "Charity begins at home" or "Promote a rogue and he'll sue you for damage, knock him down and he'll do you homage"? We all know how many common sayings can be quoted to this effect, and they all mean much the same—that you must not oppose the powers-that-be; that you must not fight against superior force; must not meddle in matters that are above your station. Or that any action not in accordance with some tradition is mere romanticism; or that any undertaking which has not the support of proven experience is foredoomed to frustration; and that since experience has shown men to be invariably inclined to evil, there must be firm rules to restrain them, otherwise we shall have anarchy. It is, however, the people who are forever mouthing these dismal proverbs and, whenever they are told of some more or less repulsive action, say "How like human nature!"—it is these very people, always harping upon realism, who complain that existentialism is too gloomy a view of things. Indeed their excessive protests make me suspect that what is annoying them is not so much our pessimism, but, much more likely, our optimism. For at bottom, what is alarming in the doctrine that I am about to try to explain to you is—is it not?—that it confronts man with a possibility of choice. To verify this, let us review the whole question upon the strictly philosophic level. What, then, is this that we call existentialism?

Most of those who are making use of this word would be highly confused if required to explain its meaning. For since it has become fashionable, people cheerfully declare that this musician or that painter is "existentialist." A columnist in *Clartés* signs himself "The Existentialist," and, indeed, the word is now so loosely applied to so many things that it no longer means anything at all. It would appear that, for the lack of any novel doctrine such as that of surrealism, all those who are eager to join in the latest scandal or movement now seize upon this philosophy in which, however, they can find nothing to their purpose. For in truth this is of all teachings the least scandalous and the most austere: it is intended strictly for technicians and philosophers. All the same, it can easily be defined.

The question is only complicated because there are two kinds of existentialists. There are, on the one hand, the Christians, amongst whom I shall name Jaspers and Gabriel Marcel, both professed Catholics; and on the other the existential atheists, amongst whom we must place Heidegger as well as the French existentialists and myself. What they have in common is simply the fact that they believe that *existence* comes before *essence*—or, if you will, that we must begin from the subjective. What exactly do we mean by that?

If one considers an article of manufacture—as, for example, a book or a paper-knife—one sees that it has been made by an artisan who had a conception of it; and he has paid attention, equally, to the conception of a paper-knife and to the pre-existent technique of production which is a part of that conception and is, at bottom, a formula. Thus the paper-knife is at the same time an article producible in a certain manner and one which, on the other hand, serves a definite purpose, for one cannot suppose that a man would produce a paper-knife without knowing what it was for. Let us say, then, of the paper-knife that its essence—that is to say the sum of the formulae and the qualities which made its production and its definition possible—precedes its existence. The presence of such-and-such a paper-knife or book is thus determined before my eyes. Here, then, we are viewing the world from a technical standpoint, and we can say that production precedes existence.

When we think of God as the creator, we are thinking of him, most of the time, as a supernal artisan. Whatever doctrine we may be considering, whether it be a doctrine like that of Descartes, or of Leibnitz himself, we always imply that the will follows, more or less, from the understanding or at least accompanies it, so that when God creates he knows precisely what he is creating. Thus, the conception of man in the mind of God is comparable to that of the paper-knife in the mind of the artisan: God makes man according to a procedure and a conception, exactly as the artisan manufactures a paper-knife, following a definition and a formula. Thus each individual man is the realization of a certain conception which dwells in the divine understanding. In the philosophic atheism of the eighteenth century, the notion of God is suppressed, but not, for all that, the idea that essence is prior to existence; something of that idea we still find everywhere, in Diderot, in Voltaire and even in Kant. Man possesses a human nature; that "human nature," which is the conception of human being, is found in every man; which means that each man is a particular example of a universal conception, the conception of Man. In Kant, this universality goes so far that the wild man of the woods, man in the state of nature and the bourgeois are all contained in the same definition and have the same fundamental qualities. Here again, the essence of man precedes that historic existence which we confront in experience.

Atheistic existentialism, of which I am a representative, declares with greater consistency that if God does not exist there is at least one being whose existence comes before its essence, a being which exists before it can be defined by any conception of it. That being is man or, as Heidegger has it, the human reality. What do we mean by saying that existence precedes essence? We mean that man first of all exists, encounters himself, surges up in the world—and defines himself afterwards. If man as the existentialist sees him is not definable, it is because to begin with he is nothing. He will not be anything until later, and then he will be what he makes of himself. Thus, there is no human nature, because there is no God to have a conception of it. Man simply is. Not that he is simply what he conceives himself to be, but he is what he wills, and as he conceives himself after already existing—as he wills to be after that leap towards existence. Man is nothing else but that which he makes of himself. That is the first principle of existentialism. And this is what people call its "subjectivity," using the word as a reproach against us. But what do we mean to say by this, but that man is of a greater dignity than a stone or a table? For we mean to say that man primarily exists—that man is, before all else, something which propels itself towards a future and is aware that it is doing so. Man is, indeed, a project which possesses a subjective life, instead of being a kind of moss, or a fungus or a cauliflower. Before that projection of the self nothing exists; not even in the heaven of intelligence: man will only attain existence when he is what he purposes to be. Not, however, what he may wish to be. For what we usually understand by wishing or willing is a conscious decision taken—much more often than not—after we have made ourselves what we are. I may wish to join a party, to write a book or to marry—but in such a case what is usually called my will is probably a manifestation of a prior and more spontaneous decision. If, however, it is true that existence is prior to essence, man is responsible for what he is. Thus, the first effect of existentialism is that it puts every man in possession of himself as he is, and places the entire responsibility for his existence squarely upon his own shoulders. And, when we say that man is responsible for himself, we do not mean that he is responsible only for his own individuality, but that he is responsible for all men. The word "subjectivism" is to be understood in two senses, and our adversaries play upon only one of them. Subjectivism means, on the one hand, the freedom of the individual subject and, on the other, that man cannot pass beyond human subjectivity. It is the latter which is the deeper meaning of existentialism. When we say that man chooses himself, we do mean that every one of us must choose himself; but by that we also mean that in choosing for himself he chooses for all men. For in effect, of all the actions a man may take in order to create himself as he wills to be, there is not one which is not creative, at the same time, of an image of man such as he believes he ought to be. To choose between this or that is at the same time to affirm the value of that which is chosen; for we are unable ever to choose the worse. What we choose is always the better; and nothing can be better for us unless it is better for all. If, moreover, existence precedes essence and we will to exist at the same time as we fashion our image, that image is valid for all and for the entire epoch in which we find ourselves. Our responsibility is thus much greater than we had supposed, for it concerns mankind as a whole. If I am a worker, for instance, I may choose to join a Christian rather than a Communist trade union. And if, by that membership, I choose to signify that resignation is, after all, the attitude that best becomes a man, that man's kingdom is not upon this earth, I do not commit myself alone to that view. Resignation is my will for everyone, and my action is, in consequence, a commitment on behalf of all mankind. Or if, to take a more personal case, I decide to marry and to have children, even though this decision proceeds simply from my situation, from my passion or my desire, I am thereby committing not only myself, but humanity as a whole, to the practice of monogamy. I am thus responsible for myself and for all men, and I am creating a certain image of man as I would have him to be. In fashioning myself I fashion man.

This may enable us to understand what is meant by such terms—perhaps a little grandiloquent—as anguish, abandonment and despair. As you will soon see, it is very simple. First, what do we mean by anguish? The existentialist frankly states that man is in anguish. His meaning is as follows—When a man commits himself to anything, fully realizing that he is not only choosing what he will be, but is thereby at the same time a legislator deciding for the whole of mankind—in such a moment a man cannot escape from the sense of complete and profound responsibility. There are many, indeed, who show no such anxiety. But we affirm that they are merely disguising their anguish or are in flight from it. Certainly, many people think that in what they are doing they commit no one but themselves to anything: and if you ask them, "What would happen if everyone did so?" they shrug their shoulders and reply, "Everyone does not do so." But in truth, one ought always to ask oneself what would happen if eveyone did as one is doing; nor can one escape from that disturbing thought except by a kind of self-deception. The man who lies in self-excuse, by saying "Everyone will not do it" must be ill at ease in his conscience, for the act of lying implies the universal value which it denies. By its very disguise his anguish reveals itself. This is the anguish that Kierkegaard called "the anguish of Abraham." You know the story: An angel commanded Abraham to sacrifice his son: and obedience was obligatory, if it really was an angel who had appeared and said, "Thou, Abraham, shalt sacrifice thy son." But anyone in such a case would wonder, first, whether it was indeed an angel and secondly, whether I am really Abraham. Where are the proofs? A certain mad woman who suffered from hallucinations said that people were telephoning to her, and giving her orders. The doctor asked, "But who is it that speaks to you?" She replied: "He says it is God." And what, indeed, could prove to her that it was God? If an angel appears to me, what is the proof that it is an angel; or, if I hear voices, who can prove that they proceed from heaven and not from hell, or from my own subconsciousness or some pathological condition? Who can prove that they are really addressed to me?

Who, then, can prove that I am the proper person to impose, by my own choice, my conception of man upon mankind? I shall never find any proof whatever; there will be no sign to convince me of it. If a voice speaks to me, it is still I myself who must decide whether the voice is or is not that of an angel. If I regard a certain course of action as good, it is only I who choose to say that it is good and not bad. There is nothing to show that I am Abraham: nevertheless I also am obliged at every instant to perform actions which are examples. Everything happens to every man as though the whole human race had its eyes fixed upon what he is doing and regulated its conduct accordingly. So every man ought to say, "Am I really a man who has the right to act in such a manner that humanity regulates itself by what I do." If a man does not say that, he is dissembling his anguish. Clearly, the anguish with which we are concerned here is not one that could lead to quietism or inaction. It is anguish pure and simple, of the kind well known to all those who have borne responsibilities. When, for instance, a military leader takes upon himself the responsibility for an attack and sends a number of men to their death, he chooses to do it and at bottom he alone chooses. No doubt he acts under a higher command, but its orders, which are more general, require interpretation by him and upon that interpretation depends the life of ten, fourteen or twenty men. In making the decision, he cannot but feel a certain anguish. All leaders know that anguish. It does not prevent their acting, on the contrary it is the very condition of their action, for the action presupposes that there is a plurality of possibilities, and in choosing one of these, they realize that it has value only because it is chosen. Now it is anguish of that kind which existentialism describes, and moreover, as we shall see, makes explicit through direct responsibility towards other men who are concerned. Far from being a screen which could separate us from action, it is a condition of action itself.

And when we speak of "abandonment"—a favorite word of Heidegger—we only mean to say that God does not exist, and that it is necessary to draw the consequences of his absence right to the end. The existentialist is strongly opposed to a certain type of secular moralism which seeks to suppress God at the least possible expense. Towards 1880, when the French professors endeavored to formulate a secular morality, they said something like this:—God is a useless and costly hypothesis, so we will do without it. However, if we are to have morality, a society and a law-abiding world, it is essential that certain values should be taken seriously; they must have an *à priori* existence ascribed to them. It must be considered obligatory *à priori* to be honest, not to lie, not to beat one's wife, to bring up children and so forth; so we are going to do a little work on this subject, which will enable us to show that these values exist all the same, inscribed in an intelligible heaven although, of course, there is no God. In other words—and this is, I believe, the purport of all that we in France call radicalism—nothing will be changed if God does not exist; we shall rediscover the same norms of honesty, progress and humanity, and we shall have disposed of God as an out-of-date hypothesis which will die away quietly of itself. The existentialist, on the contrary, finds it extremely embarrassing that God does not exist, for there disappears with Him all possibility of finding values in an intelligible heaven. There can no longer be any good *à priori,* since there is no infinite and perfect consciousness to think it. It is nowhere written that "the good" exists, that one must be honest or must not lie, since we are now upon the plane where there are only men. Dostoevsky once wrote "If God did not exist, everything would be permitted"; and that, for existentialism, is the starting point. Everything is indeed permitted if God does not exist, and man is in consequence forlorn, for he cannot find anything to depend upon either within or outside himself. He discovers forthwith, that he is without excuse. For if indeed existence precedes essence, one will never be able to explain one's action by reference to a given and specific human nature; in other words, there is no determinism—man is free, man *is* freedom. Nor, on the other hand, if God does not exist, are we provided with any values or commands that could legitimize our behavior. Thus we have neither behind us, nor before us in a luminous realm of values, any means of justification or excuse. We are left alone, without excuse. That is what I mean when I say that man is condemned to be free. Condemned, because he did not create himself, yet is nevertheless at liberty, and from the moment that he is thrown into this world he is responsible for everything he does. The existentialist does not believe in the power of passion. He will never regard a grand passion as a destructive torrent upon which a man is swept into certain actions as by fate, and which, therefore, is an excuse for them. He thinks that man is responsible for his passion. Neither will an existentialist think that a man can find help through some sign being vouchsafed upon earth for his orientation: for he thinks that the man himself interprets the sign as he chooses. He thinks that every man, without any support or help whatever, is condemned at every instant to invent man. As Ponge has written in a very fine article, "Man is the future of man." That is exactly true. Only, if one took this to mean that the future is laid up in Heaven, that God knows what it is, it would be false, for then it would no longer even be a future. If, however, it means that, whatever man may now appear to be, there is a future to be fashioned, a virgin future that awaits him—then it is a true saying. But in the present one is forsaken.

As an example by which you may the better understand this state of abandonment, I will refer to the case of a pupil of mine, who sought me out in the following circumstances. His father was quarrelling with his mother and was also inclined to be a "collaborator"; his elder brother had been killed in the German offensive of 1940 and this young man, with a sentiment somewhat primitive but generous, burned to avenge him. His mother was living alone with him, deeply afflicted by the semi-treason of his father and by the death of her eldest son, and her one consolation was in this young man. But he, at this moment, had the choice between going to England to join the Free French Forces or of staying near his mother and helping her to live. He fully realized that this woman lived only for him and that his disappearance—or perhaps his death—would plunge her into despair. He also realized that, concretely and in fact, every action he performed on his mother's behalf would be sure of effect in the sense of aiding her to live, whereas anything he did in order to go and fight would be an ambiguous action which might vanish like water into sand and serve no purpose. For instance, to set out for England he would have to wait indefinitely in a Spanish camp on the way through Spain; or, on arriving in England or in Algiers he might be put into an office to fill up forms. Consequently, he found himself confronted by two very different modes of action; the one concrete, immediate, but directed towards only one individual; and the other an action addressed to an end infinitely greater, a national collectivity, but for that very reason ambiguous—and it might be frustrated on the way. At the same time, he was hesitating between two kinds of morality; on the one side the morality of sympathy, of personal devotion and, on the other side, a morality of wider scope but of more debatable validity. He had to choose between those two. What could help him to choose? Could the Christian doctrine? No. Christian doctrine says: Act with charity, love your neighbour, deny yourself for others, choose the way which is hardest, and so forth. But which is the harder road? To whom does one owe the more brotherly love, the patriot or the mother? Which is the more useful aim, the general one of fighting in and for the whole community, or the precise aim of helping one particular person to live? Who can give an answer to that *à priori?* No one. Nor is it given in any ethical scripture. The Kantian ethic says, Never regard another as a means, but always as an end. Very well; if I remain with my mother, I shall be regarding her as the end and not as a means: but by the same token I am in danger of treating as means those who are fighting on my behalf; and the converse is also true, that if I go to the aid of the combatants I shall be treating them as the end at the risk of treating my mother as a means.

If values are uncertain, if they are still too abstract to determine the particular, concrete case under consideration, nothing remains but to trust in our instincts. That is what this young man tried to do; and when I saw him he said, "In the end, it is feeling that counts; the direction in which it is really pushing me is the one I ought to choose. If I feel that I love my mother enough to sacrifice everything else for her—my will to be avenged, all my longings for action and adventure—then I stay with her. If, on the contrary, I feel that my love for her is not enough, I go." But how does one estimate the strength of a feeling? The value of his feeling for his mother was determined precisely by the fact that he was standing by her. I may say that I love a certain friend enough to sacrifice such or such a sum of money for him, but I cannot prove that unless I have done it. I may say, "I love my mother enough to remain with her," if actually I have remained with her. I can only estimate the strength of this affection if I have performed an action by which it is defined and ratified. But if I then appeal to this affection to justify my action, I find myself drawn into a vicious circle.

Moreover, as Gide has very well said, a sentiment which is play-acting and one which is vital are two things that are hardly distinguishable one from another. To decide that I love my mother by staying beside her, and to play a comedy the upshot of which is that I do so—these are nearly the same thing. In other words, feeling is formed by the deeds that one does; therefore I cannot consult it as a guide to action. And that is to say that I can neither seek within myself for an authentic impulse to action, nor can I expect, from some ethic, formulae that will enable me to act. You may say that the youth did, at least, go to a professor to ask for advice. But if you seek counsel—from a priest, for example—you have selected that priest; and at bottom you already knew, more or less, what he would advise. In other words, to choose an adviser is nevertheless to commit oneself by that choice. If you are a Christian, you will say, Consult a priest; but there are collaborationists, priests who are resisters and priests who wait for the tide to turn: which will you choose? Had this young man chosen a priest of the resistance, or one of the collaboration, he would have decided beforehand the kind of advice he was to receive. Similarly, in coming to me, he knew what advice I should give him, and I had but one reply to make. You are free, therefore choose—that is to say, invent. No rule of general morality can show you what you ought to do: no signs are vouchsafed in this world. The Catholics will reply, "Oh, but they are!" Very well; still, it is I myself, in every case, who have to interpret the signs. While I was imprisoned, I made the acquaintance of a somewhat remarkable man, a Jesuit, who had become a member of that order in the following manner. In his life he had suffered a succession of rather severe setbacks. His father had died when he was a child, leaving him in poverty, and he had been awarded a free scholarship in a religious institution, where he had been made continually to feel that he was accepted for charity's sake, and, in consequence, he had been denied several of those distinctions and honours which gratify children. Later, about the age of eighteen, he came to grief in a sentimental affair; and finally, at twenty-two—this was a trifle in itself, but it was the last drop that overflowed his cup—he failed in his military examination. This young man, then, could regard himself as a total failure: it was a sign—but a sign of what? He might have taken refuge in bitterness or despair. But he took it—very cleverly for him—as a sign that he was not intended for secular successes, and that only the attainments of religion, those of sanctity and of faith, were accessible to him. He interpreted his record as a message from God, and became a member of the Order. Who can doubt but that this decision as to the meaning of the sign was his, and his alone? One could have drawn quite different conclusions from such a series of reverses—as, for example, that he had better become a carpenter or a revolutionary. For the decipherment of the sign, however, he bears the entire responsibility. That is what "abandonment" implies, that we ourselves decide our being. And with this abandonment goes anguish.

As for "despair," the meaning of this expression is extremely simple. It merely means that we limit ourselves to a reliance upon that which is within our wills, or within the sum of the probabilities which render our action feasible. Whenever one wills anything, there are always these elements of probability. If I am counting upon a visit from a friend, who may be coming by train or by tram, I presuppose that the train will arrive at the appointed time, or that the tram will not be derailed. I remain in the realm of possibilities; but one does not rely upon any possibilities beyond those that are strictly concerned in one's action. Beyond the point at which the possibilities under consideration cease to affect my action, I ought to disinterest myself. For there is no God and no prevenient design, which can adapt the world and all its possibilities to my will. When Descartes said, "Conquer yourself rather than the world," what he meant was, at bottom, the same—that we should act without hope.

Marxists, to whom I have said this, have answered: "Your action is limited, obviously, by your death; but you can rely upon the help of others. That is, you can count both upon what the others are doing to help you elsewhere, as in China and in Russia, and upon what they will do later, after your death, to take up your action and carry it forward to its final accomplishment which will be the revolution. Moreover you must rely upon this; not to do so is immoral." To this I rejoin, first, that I shall always count upon my comrades-in-arms in the struggle, in so far as they are committed, as I am, to a definite, common cause; and in the unity of a party or a group which I can more or less control—that is, in which I am enrolled as a militant and whose movements at every moment are known to me. In that respect, to rely upon the unity and the will of the party is exactly like my reckoning that the train will run on time or that the tram will not be derailed. But I cannot count upon men whom I do not know, I cannot base my confidence upon human goodness or upon man's interest in the good of society, seeing that man is free and that there is no human nature which I can take as foundational. I do not know where the Russian revolution will lead. I can admire it and take it as an example in so far as it is evident, today, that the proletariat plays a part in Russia which it has attained in no other nation. But I cannot affirm that this will necessarily lead to the triumph of the proletariat: I must confine myself to what I can see. Nor can I be sure that comrades-in-arms will take up my work after my death and carry it to the maximum perfection, seeing that those men are free agents and will freely decide, tomorrow, what man is then to be. Tomorrow, after my death, some men may decide to establish Fascism, and the others may be so cowardly or so slack as to let them do so. If so, Fascism will then be the truth of man, and so much the worse for us. In reality, things will be such as men have decided they shall be. Does that mean that I should abandon myself to quietism? No. First I ought to commit myself and then act upon my commitment, according to the time-honored formula that "one need not hope in order to undertake one's work." Nor does this mean that I should not belong to a party, but only that I should be without illusion and that I should do what I can. For instance, if I ask myself "Will the social ideal as such, ever become a reality?" I cannot tell, I only know that whatever may be in my power to make it so, I shall do; beyond that, I can count upon nothing.

Quietism is the attitude of people who say, "Let others do what I cannot do." The doctrine I am presenting before you is precisely the opposite of this, since it declares that there is no reality except in action. It goes further, indeed, and adds, "Man is nothing else but what he purposes, he exists only in so far as he realizes himself, he is therefore nothing else but the sum of his actions, nothing else but what his life is." Hence we can well understand why some people are horrified by our teaching. For many have but one resource to sustain them in their misery, and that is to think, "Circumstances have been against me, I was worthy to be something much better than I have been. I admit I have never had a great love or a great friendship; but that is because I never met a man or a woman who were worthy of it; if I have not written any very good books, it is because I had not the leisure to do so; or, if I have had no children to whom I could devote myself it is because I did not find the man I could have lived with. So there remains within me a wide range of abilities, inclinations and potentialities, unused but perfectly viable, which endow me with a worthiness that could never be inferred from the mere history of my actions." But in reality and for the existentialist, there is no love apart from the deeds of love; no potentiality of love other than that which is manifested in loving; there is no genius other than that which is expressed in works of art. The genius of Proust is the totality of the works of Proust; the genius of Racine is the series of his tragedies, outside of which there is nothing. Why should we attribute to Racine the capacity to write yet another tragedy when that is precisely what he did not write? In life, a man commits himself, draws his own portrait and there is nothing but that portrait. No doubt this thought may seem comfortless to one who has not made a success of his life. On the other hand, it puts everyone in a position to understand that reality alone is reliable; that dreams, expectations and hopes serve to define a man only as deceptive dreams, abortive hopes, expectations unfulfilled; that is to say, they define him negatively, not positively. Nevertheless, when one says, "You are nothing else but what you live," it does not imply that an artist is to be judged solely by his works of art, for a thousand other things contribute no less to his definition as a man. What we mean to say is that a man is no other than a series of undertakings, that he is the sum, the organization, the set of relations that constitute these undertakings.

In the light of all this, what people reproach us with is not, after all, our pessimism, but the sternness of our optimism. If people condemn our works of fiction, in which we describe characters that are base, weak, cowardly and sometimes even frankly evil, it is not only because those characters are base, weak, cowardly or evil. For suppose that, like Zola, we showed that the behavior of these characters was caused by their heredity, or by the action of their environment upon them, or by determining factors, psychic or organic. People would be reassured, they would say, "You see, that is what we are like, no one can do anything about it." But the existentialist, when he portrays a coward, shows him as responsible for his cowardice. He is not like that on account of a cowardly heart or lungs or cerebrum, he has not become like that through his physiological organism; he is like that because he has made himself into a coward by his actions. There is no such thing as a cowardly temperament. There are nervous temperaments; there is what is called impoverished blood, and there are also rich temperaments. But the man whose blood is poor is not a coward for all that, for what produces cowardice is the act of giving up or giving way; and a temperament is not an action. A coward is defined by the deed that he has done. What people feel obscurely, and with horror, is that the coward as we present him is guilty of being a coward. What people would prefer would be to be born either a coward or a hero. One of the charges most often laid against the *Chemins de la Liberté* is something like this—"But, after all, these people being so base, how can you make them into heroes?" That objection is really rather comic, for it implies that people are born heroes: and that is, at bottom, what such people would like to think. If you are born cowards, you can be quite content, you can do nothing about it and you will be cowards all your lives whatever you do; and if you are born heroes you can again be quite content; you will be heroes all your lives eating and drinking heroically. Whereas the existentialist says that the coward makes himself cowardly, the hero makes himself heroic; and that there is always a possibility for the coward to give up cowardice and for the hero to stop being a hero. What counts is the total commitment, and it is not by a particular case or particular action that you are committed altogether.

We have now, I think, dealt with a certain number of the reproaches against existentialism. You have seen that it cannot be regarded as a philosophy of quietism since it defines man by his action; nor as a pessimistic description of man, for no doctrine is more optimistic, the destiny of man is placed within himself. Nor is it an attempt to discourage man from action since it tells him that there is no hope except in his action, and that the one thing which permits him to have life is the deed. Upon this level therefore, what we are considering is an ethic of action and self-commitment. However, we are still reproached, upon these few data, for confining man within his individual subjectivity. There again people badly misunderstand us.

Our point of departure is, indeed, the subjectivity of the individual, and that for strictly philosophic reasons. It is not because we are bourgeois, but because we seek to base our teaching upon the truth, and not upon a collection of fine theories, full of hope but lacking real foundations. And at the point of departure there cannot be any other truth than this, *I think, therefore I am,* which is the absolute truth of consciousness as it attains to itself. Every theory which begins with man, outside of this moment of self-attainment, is a theory which thereby suppresses the truth, for outside of the Cartesian *cogito,* all objects are no more than probable, and any doctrine of probabilities which is not attached to a truth will crumble into nothing. In order to define the probable one must possess the true. Before there can be any truth whatever, then, there must be an absolute truth, and there is such a truth which is simple, easily attained and within the reach of everybody; it consists in one's immediate sense of one's self.

In the second place, this theory alone is compatible with the dignity of man, it is the only one which does not make man into an object. All kinds of materialism lead one to treat every man including oneself as an object— that is, as a set of pre-determined reactions, in no way different from the patterns of qualities and phenomena which constitute a table, or a chair or a stone. Our aim is precisely to establish the human kingdom as a pattern of values in distinction from the material world. But the subjectivity which we thus postulate as the standard of truth is no narrowly individual subjectivism, for as we have demonstrated, it is not only one's own self that one discovers in the *cogito,* but those of others too. Contrary to the philosophy of Descartes, contrary to that of Kant, when we say "I think" we are attaining to ourselves in the presence of the other, and we are just as certain of the other as we are of ourselves. Thus the man who discovers himself directly in the *cogito* also discovers all the others, and discovers them as the condition of his own existence. He recognizes that he cannot be anything (in the sense in which one says one is spiritual, or that one is wicked or jealous) unless others recognize him as such. I cannot obtain any truth whatsoever about myself, except through the mediation of another. The other is indispensable to my existence, and equally so to any knowledge I can have of myself. Under these conditions, the intimate discovery of myself is at the same time the revelation of the other as a freedom which confronts mine, and which cannot think or will without doing so either for or against me. Thus, at once, we find ourselves in a world which is, let us say, that of "inter-subjectivity." It is in this world that man has to decide what he is and what others are.

Furthermore, although it is impossible to find in each and every man a universal essence that can be called human nature, there is nevertheless a human universality of *condition*. It is not by chance that the thinkers of today are so much more ready to speak of the condition than of the nature of man. By his condition they understand, with more or less clarity, all the *limitations* which *à priori* define man's fundamental situation in the universe. His historical situations are variable: man may be born a slave in a pagan society, or may be a feudal baron, or a proletarian. But what never vary are the necessities of being in the world, of having to labor and to die there. These limitations are neither subjective nor objective, or rather there is both a subjective and an objective aspect of them. Objective, because we meet with them everywhere and they are everywhere recognizable: and subjective because they are *lived* and are nothing if man does not live them—if, that is to say, he does not freely determine himself and his existence in relation to them. And, diverse though man's purposes may be, at least none of them is wholly foreign to me, since every human purpose presents itself as an attempt either to surpass these limitations, or to widen them, or else to deny or to accommodate oneself to them. Consequently every purpose, however individual it may be, is of universal value. Every purpose, even that of a Chinese, an Indian or a Negro, can be understood by a European. To say it can be understood, means that the European of 1945 may be striving out of a certain situation towards the same limitations in the same way, and that he may reconceive in himself the purpose of the Chinese, of the Indian or the African. In every purpose there is universality, in this sense that every purpose is comprehensible to every man. Not that this or that purpose defines man for ever, but that it may be entertained again and again. There is always some way of understanding an idiot, a child, a primitive man or a foreigner if one has sufficient information. In this sense we may say that there is a human universality, but it is not something given; it is being perpetually made. I make this universality in choosing myself; I also make it by understanding the purpose of any other man, of what ever epoch. This absoluteness of the act of choice does not alter the relativity of each epoch.

What is at the very heart and center of existentialism, is the absolute character of the free commitment, by which every man realizes himself in realizing a type of humanity—a commitment always understandable, to no matter whom in no matter what epoch—and its bearing upon the relativity of the cultural pattern which may result from such absolute commitment. One must observe equally the relativity of Cartesianism and the absolute character of the Cartesian commitment. In this sense you may say, if you like, that every one of us makes the absolute by breathing, by eating, by sleeping or by behaving in any fashion whatsoever. There is no difference between free being—being as self-committal, as existence choosing its essence—and absolute being. And there is no difference whatever between being as an absolute, temporarily localized—that is, localized in history—and universally intelligible being.

This does not completely refute the charge of subjectivism. Indeed that objection appears in several other forms, of which the first is as follows. People say to us, "Then it does not matter what you do," and they say this in various ways. First they tax us with anarchy; then they say, "You cannot judge others, for there is no reason for preferring one purpose to another"; finally, they may say, "Everything being merely voluntary in this choice of yours, you give away with one hand what you pretend to gain with the other." These three are not very serious objections. As to the first, to say that it does not matter what you choose is not correct. In one sense choice is possible, but what is not possible is not to choose. I can always choose, but I must know that if I do not choose, that is still a choice. This, although it may appear merely formal, is of great importance as a limit to fantasy and caprice. For, when I confront a real situation—for example, that I am a sexual being, able to have relations with a being of the other sex and able to have children—I am obliged to choose my attitude to it, and in every respect I bear the responsibility of the choice which, in committing myself, also commits the whole of humanity. Even if my choice is determined by no *à priori* value whatever, it can have nothing to do with caprice: and if anyone thinks that this is only Gide's theory of the *acte gratuit* over again, he has failed to see the enormous difference between this theory and that of Gide. Gide does not know what a situation is, his "act" is one of pure caprice. In our view, on the contrary, man finds himself in an organized situation in which he is himself involved: his choice involves mankind in its entirety, and he cannot avoid choosing. Either he must remain single, or he must marry without having children, or he must marry and have children. In any case, and whichever he may choose, it is impossible for him, in respect of this situation, not to take complete responsibility. Doubtless he chooses without reference to any pre-established values, but it is unjust to tax him with caprice. Rather let us say that the moral choice is comparable to the construction of a work of art.

But here I must at once digress to make it quite clear that we are not propounding an aesthetic morality, for our adversaries are disingenuous enough to reproach us even with that. I mention the work of art only by way of comparison. That being understood, does anyone reproach an artist, when he paints a picture, for not following rules established à priori? Does one ever ask what is the picture that he ought to paint? As everyone knows, there is no pre-defined picture for him to make; the artist applies himself to the composition of a picture, and the picture that ought to be made is precisely that which he will have made. As everyone knows, there are no aesthetic values à priori, but there are values which will appear in due course in the coherence of the picture, in the relation between the will to create and the finished work. No one can tell what the painting of tomorrow will be like; one cannot judge a painting until it is done. What has that to do with morality? We are in the same creative situation. We never speak of a work of art as irresponsible; when we are discussing a canvas by Picasso, we understand very well that the composition became what it is at the time when he was painting it, and that his works are part and parcel of his entire life.

It is the same upon the plane of morality. There is this in common between art and morality, that in both we have to do with creation and invention. We cannot decide à priori what it is that should be done. I think it was made sufficiently clear to you in the case of that student who came to see me, that to whatever ethical system he might appeal, the Kantian or any other, he could find no sort of guidance whatever; he was obliged to invent the law for himself. Certainly we cannot say that this man, in choosing to remain with his mother—that is, in taking sentiment, personal devotion and concrete charity as his moral foundations—would be making an irresponsible choice, nor could we do so if he preferred the sacrifice of going away to England. Man makes himself; he is not found ready-made; he makes himself by the choice of his morality, and he cannot but choose a morality, such is the pressure of circumstances upon him. We define man only in relation to his commitments; it is therefore absurd to reproach us for irresponsibility in our choice.

In the second place, people say to us, "You are unable to judge others." This is true in one sense and false in another. It is true in this sense, that whenever a man chooses his purpose and his commitment in all clearness and in all sincerity, whatever that purpose may be, it is impossible for him to prefer another. It is true in the sense that we do not believe in progress. Progress implies amelioration; but man is always the same, facing a situation which is always changing, and choice remains always a choice in the situation. The moral problem has not changed since the time when it was a choice between slavery and anti-slavery—from the time of the war of Secession, for example, until the present moment when one chooses between the M.R.P. [*Mouvement Républicain Populaire*] and the Communists.

We can judge, nevertheless, for, as I have said, one chooses in view of others, and in view of others one chooses himself. One can judge, first— and perhaps this is not a judgment of value, but it is a logical judgment— that in certain cases choice is founded upon an error, and in others upon the truth. One can judge a man by saying that he deceives himself. Since we have defined the situation of man as one of free choice, without excuse and without help, any man who takes refuge behind the excuse of his passions, or by inventing some deterministic doctrine, is a self-deceiver. One may object: "But why should he not choose to deceive himself?" I reply that it is not for me to judge him morally, but I define his self-deception as an error. Here one cannot avoid pronouncing a judgment of truth. The self-deception is evidently a falsehood, because it is a dissimulation of man's complete liberty of commitment. Upon this same level, I say that it is also a self-deception if I choose to declare that certain values are incumbent upon me; I am in contradiction with myself if I will these values and at the same time say that they impose themselves upon me. If anyone says to me, "And what if I wish to deceive myself?" I answer, "There is no reason why you should not, but I declare that you are doing so, and that the attitude of strict consistency alone is that of good faith." Furthermore, I can pronounce a moral judgment. For I declare that freedom, in respect of concrete circumstances, can have no other end and aim but itself; and when once a man has seen that values depend upon himself, in that state of forsakenness he can will only one thing, and that is freedom as the foundation of all values. That does not mean that he wills it in the abstract: it simply means that the actions of men of good faith have, as their ultimate significance, the quest of freedom itself as such. A man who belongs to some communist or revolutionary society wills certain concrete ends, which imply the will to freedom, but that freedom is willed in community. We will freedom for freedom's sake, in and through particular circumstances. And in thus willing freedom, we discover that it depends entirely upon the freedom of others and that the freedom of others depends upon our own. Obviously, freedom as the definition of a man does not depend upon others, but as soon as there is a commitment, I am obliged to will the liberty of others at the same time as my own. I cannot make liberty my aim unless I make that of others equally my aim. Consequently, when I recognize, as entirely authentic, that man is a being whose existence precedes his essence, and that he is a free being who cannot, in any circumstances, but will his freedom, at the same time I realize that I cannot not will the freedom of others. Thus, in the name of that will to freedom which is implied in freedom itself, I can form judgments upon those who seek to hide from themselves the wholly voluntary nature of their existence and its complete freedom. Those who hide from this total freedom, in a guise of solemnity or with deterministic excuses, I shall call cowards. Others, who try to show that their existence is necessary, when it is merely an accident of the appearance of the human race on earth—I shall call scum. But neither cowards nor scum can be identified except upon the plane of strict authenticity. Thus, although the content of morality is variable, a certain form of this morality is universal. Kant declared that freedom is a will both to itself and to the freedom of others. Agreed: but he thinks that the formal and the universal suffice for the constitution of a morality. We think, on the contrary, that principles that are too abstract break down when we come to defining action. To take once again the case of that student; by what authority, in the name of what golden rule of morality, do you think he could have decided, in perfect peace of mind, either to abandon his mother or to remain with her? There are no means of judging. The content is always concrete, and therefore unpredictable; it has always to be invented. The one thing that counts, is to know whether the invention is made in the name of freedom.

Let us, for example, examine the two following cases, and you will see how far they are similar in spite of their difference. Let us take *The Mill on the Floss*. We find here a certain young woman, Maggie Tulliver, who is an incarnation of the value of passion and is aware of it. She is in love with a young man, Stephen, who is engaged to another, an insignificant young woman. This Maggie Tulliver, instead of heedlessly seeking her own happiness, chooses in the name of human solidarity to sacrifice herself and to give up the man she loves. On the other hand, La Sanseverina in Stendhal's *Chartreuse de Parme*, believing that it is passion which endows man with his real value, would have declared that a grand passion justifies its sacrifices, and must be preferred to the banality of such conjugal love as would unite Stephen to the little goose he was engaged to marry. It is the latter that she would have chosen to sacrifice in realizing her own happiness, and, as Stendhal shows, she would also sacrifice herself upon the plane of passion if life made that demand upon her. Here we are facing two clearly opposed moralities; but I claim that they are equivalent, seeing that in both cases the overruling aim is freedom. You can imagine two attitudes exactly similar in effect, in that one girl might prefer, in resignation, to give up her lover while the other preferred, in fulfillment of sexual desire, to ignore the prior engagement of the man she loved; and, externally, these two cases might appear the same as the two we have just cited, while being in fact entirely different. The attitude of La Sanseverina is much nearer to that of Maggie Tulliver than to one of careless greed. One can choose anything, but only if it is upon the plane of free commitment.

The third objection, stated by saying, "You take with one hand what you give with the other," means, at bottom, "Your values are not serious, since you choose them yourselves." To that I can only say that I am very sorry that it should be so; but if I have excluded God the Father, there must be somebody to invent values. We have to take things as they are. And moreover, to say that we invent values means neither more nor less than this; that there is no sense in life à priori. Life is nothing until it is lived; but it is yours to make sense of, and the value of it is nothing else but the sense that you choose. Therefore, you can see that there is a possibility of creating a human community. I have been reproached for suggesting that existentialism is a form of humanism: people have said to me, "But you have written in your Nausée that the humanists are wrong, you have even ridiculed a certain type of humanism, why do you now go back upon that?" In reality, the word humanism has two very different meanings. One may understand by humanism a theory which upholds man as the end-in-itself and as the supreme value. Humanism in this sense appears, for instance, in Cocteau's story Round the World in 80 Hours, in which one of the characters declares, because he is flying over mountains in an airplane, "Man is magnificent!" This signifies that although I, personally, have not built airplanes I have the benefit of those particular inventions and that I personally, being a man, can consider myself responsible for, and honored by, achievements that are peculiar to some men. It is to assume that we can ascribe value to man according to the most distinguished deeds of certain men. That kind of humanism is absurd, for only the dog or the horse would be in a position to pronounce a general judgment upon man and declare that he is magnificent, which they have never been such fools as to do—at least, not as far as I know. But neither is it admissible that a man should pronounce judgment upon Man. Existentialism dispenses with any judgment of this sort: an existentialist will never take man as the end, since man is still to be determined. And we have no right to believe that humanity is something to which we could set up a cult, after the manner of Auguste Comte. The cult of humanity ends in Comtian humanism, shut-in upon itself, and—this must be said—in Fascism. We do not want a humanism like that.

But there is another sense of the word, of which the fundamental meaning is this: Man is all the time outside of himself: it is in projecting and losing himself beyond himself that he makes man to exist; and, on the other hand, it is by pursuing transcendent aims that he himself is able to exist. Since man is thus self-surpassing, and can grasp objects only in relation to his self-surpassing, he is himself the heart and center of his transcendence.

There is no other universe except the human universe, the universe of human subjectivity. This relation of transcendence as constitutive of man (not in the sense that God is transcendent, but in the sense of self-surpassing) with subjectivity (in such a sense that man is not shut up in himself but forever present in a human universe)—it is this that we call existential humanism. This is humanism, because we remind man that there is no legislator but himself; that he himself, thus abandoned, must decide for himself; also because we show that it is not by turning back upon himself, but always by seeking, beyond himself, an aim which is one of liberation or of some particular realization, that man can realize himself as truly human.

You can see from these few reflections that nothing could be more unjust than the objections people raise against us. Existentialism is nothing else but an attempt to draw the full conclusions from a consistently atheistic position. Its intention is not in the least that of plunging men into despair. And if by despair one means—as the Christians do—any attitude of unbelief, the despair of the existentialists is something different. Existentialism is not atheist in the sense that it would exhaust itself in demonstrations of the non-existence of God. It declares, rather, that even if God existed that would make no difference from its point of view. Not that we believe God does exist, but we think that the real problem is not that of His existence; what man needs is to find himself again and to understand that nothing can save him from himself, not even a valid proof of the existence of God. In this sense existentialism is optimistic. It is a doctrine of action, and it is only by self-deception, by confusing their own despair with ours that Christians can describe us as without hope.

37. Sir William Beveridge, *New Britain*

The son of a British civil servant in India, William Henry Beveridge (1879–1963) was educated at Charterhouse and Balliol College, Oxford. Rather than pursue a career in the law, as his father had hoped, Beveridge followed the advice of Edward Caird, Master of Balliol, who advised his students that "when you have learnt all that Oxford can teach you, go and discover why, with so much wealth in Britain, there continues to be so much poverty, and how poverty can be cured." Beveridge took Caird at his word and developed an early interest in the problems of the poor, particularly relief for the unemployed, through his social work as subwarden of the London settlement, Toynbee Hall. Even before World War I Beveridge felt that state intervention was necessary to reorganize industrial and old-age insurance systems for the general benefit. His book on *Unemployment. A Problem of Industry* (1909) established him as a bril-

liant critic of contemporary social welfare and labor institutions in late
Edwardian England.

Beveridge sought to implement his thinking by numerous writings, by
teaching both at the London School of Economics (of which he was director from 1919 to 1937) and at Oxford, and by holding several social
service posts in the British government. However, Beveridge's outstanding achievement came during World War II. After he had put in a frustrating term of service in Ernest Bevin's Ministry of Labour, the British
government asked Beveridge in June 1941 to chair a committee of officials who would examine the widespread anomalies in the social insurance system and other welfare services which had evolved since 1900. As
José Harris has observed, "Beveridge was correct in believing that his
new appointment was not seen by the government as an important one,
and certainly not as the prelude to a massive programme of social reconstruction."[1] Beveridge seized the initiative, however, and developed a
comprehensive report which far exceeded the original mandate of his
committee. In December 1942 the *Social Insurance and Allied Services—
Report by Sir William Beveridge* was issued. The *Report* recommended
an ambitious program of social planning for postwar Britain: a comprehensive national health system; policies for sustaining employment in
peacetime; allowances for families with two or more children; and a
comprehensive system of social insurance, with benefits guaranteed by
statutory right.

Coming during a war which—like World War I—generated forms of
state intervention which many thought should be extended into peacetime
society, the *Report* was a plan that was not soon forgotten. It was vigorously discussed during the remainder of the war, generating intense
controversy among members of the Coalition Government, the political
parties, and the unions. Although politically a Liberal (and not a La-
bourite), Beveridge's belief in liberal individualism was cast in light of
his dedication to social justice. Not surprisingly, when he read Friedrich
von Hayek's *The Road to Serfdom* in 1944 he remarked that "Professor
Hayek . . . is not I think a man who understands British mentality. . . .
I did not find his book in the least convincing."[2]

After 1945 the new Labour government enacted a major program of
legislation—the Family Allowances Act of 1945, the National Insurance
and National Health Service Acts of 1946, and the National Assistance
Act of 1948—which fulfilled some of Beveridge's goals. Beveridge's assumptions that social planning might (or should) lead to rational human

---

1. José Harris, *William Beveridge: A Biography* (Oxford, 1977), p. 382.
2. Quoted in ibid., pp. 440–41.

control and that material redistribution might produce social justice remain a problem for the 1980s, just as they were for the 1940s. His biographer, José Harris, has noted that

> Beveridge's commitment to planning must be set against his spirited defence of personal freedom and against his emphasis on voluntarism and on the crucial role of a wide variety of intermediate organizations. Whether such a mixture of planning and pluralism is in fact feasible—without simply underwriting inequality and privilege—is still a matter for continuing political debate. In this respect Beveridge's attempt to harness state action to individual diversity touches upon one of the most fundamental problems of modern politics—namely, how far the so-called "liberal freedoms" are compatible with a context of highly collectivized social and economic control.[3]

The following, an address Beveridge presented at Oxford University on 6 December 1942, suggests the basic values informing the report on social insurance.

Though I am the author of a Report on Social Insurance and Allied Services, I am not today going to speak in any detail at all about that Report, and not indeed mainly about that Report. For that there are two reasons. One reason is that I am the author. I have just spilt about one hundred and ten thousand words into print on Social Insurance and Allied Services. There's really a good deal more than this number of words—there are about another fifty thousand of Appendix. I have a feeling that I ought to sit back for a time and let the other fellows have a say before I say more upon this subject. But the real reason, the second and greater reason why I have taken for my subject today New Britain rather than my Report, is that there are so many larger and more difficult problems to solve in the peace and after the war than this particular problem to which my Report is devoted. I shall be able to show that in a moment.

I have taken as my text for my address, the words "New Britain." I believe those two words are as good a short motto as one can find for all that one wants to do in postwar reconstruction. Most people want something new after the war. Very few of us want something utterly unlike the Britain that we have known and loved. Some people normally put the emphasis on *New* Britain. Others, generally a little older, put the emphasis on New *Britain*. Some people put the emphasis one way if they have got up rather bad-

3. Ibid., p. 475.

From William H. Beveridge, *The Pillars of Security and Other War-Time Essays and Addresses* (London: George Allen & Unwin, 1943), pp. 80–96. Reprinted by permission of the publisher.

tempered in the morning or haven't been doing very well, and they put the emphasis the other way when they've had a successful day. Some people shift the emphasis from time to time, and as they shift the emphasis they shift votes and power between the political parties, between those parties which are emphasizing change and those which are emphasizing the keeping of Britain. New Britain sums up the common desires of all of us today, of those who emphasize the *New* and those who emphasize the *Britain*.

New Britain as a motto for post-war aims has other implications also. It means that, in planning the world after the war, we in Britain should look first to putting our own house in order and dealing with things which are within our power, before we try to put the whole world in order, before we advise other countries how they should manage their colour problem or their colonial problem or any other problem; that we should put our house in order and make the kind of world in which our own people should live. That does not mean of course that Britain should have no concern with the rest of the world. For three hundred years Britain has been an important power and, on the whole, a power for good in the world and will go on being that in the future. I shall come back to international problems before I finish today.

Freedom from Five Giant Evils

But in the first instance I am concerned with asking—What kind of Britain do we want at home? In what shall New Britain differ most definitely from the old Britain that we have known? I phrase that difference to myself— I've said this before—chiefly by saying that New Britain should be free, as free as is humanly possible, of the five giant evils, of Want, of Disease, of Ignorance, of Squalor and of Idleness.

Freedom from Want is the aim of the Report on Social Insurance and Allied Services which I have just made to the Government and which they have just published. That Report is now before Government, Parliament and the nation, and, because I want to talk of other things chiefly, I shall say relatively little about it here today. I'll only say this: that all the proposals that I have made are part of a policy of a national minimum of income. You can't abolish Want unless you make sure that everybody willing to work, everybody subject to occasional accidents and misfortunes that interrupt his earning, has at all times, for all his responsibilities, the income necessary to meet those responsibilities. Abolition of Want means a national minimum and that national minimum mustn't be and can't be simply a minimum wage when a man is working—when he's earning, because there are times when men cannot work and cannot earn: when they are unemployed (there must always be some unemployment in a changing society), when they are sick, when they are old, when they are damaged by accident, when the bread-winner dies. If you want to abolish Want you must provide a minimum income as of right, without any question of other means, a minimum income as of right to meet those inevitable interruptions of earnings. That, in a sentence, is the point of all those many words which I've written about the Social Insurance Scheme in my Report. It's a means of taking some of the national income—the income of all the men and women of this country, when they are earning—and keeping it for the times when some of them cannot earn.

But social insurance alone, giving an income to people when their earning power is interrupted, will not abolish Want, because it will not always provide the necessary income for all urgent needs. It will not do that nor will a minimum wage do it. It's no use, for instance, to lay down a minimum wage and say this is the minimum wage, enough for a man and wife and two children or three children, because there will be some families with four and five and six children—and unless there are many families with large numbers of children, the British race will not continue. We haven't now anything like enough children being born to keep our race in being. If you want to abolish Want, you must add to your minimum wage legislation, and to your social insurance for interruption of earnings—you must add children's allowances. That is part of my scheme: children's allowances paid both when the responsible parent is earning and when the responsible parent is not earning. You must add also provision for those expenses which come when children are being born, at maternity; that is part of the Social Insurance Scheme.

Prevention of Want the First Step

Well now, that's all I'm going to say about this scheme of my Report. You must conceive of it as an attempt to secure freedom from Want, by seeing that everyone at all times, in virtue of contributions made by him, and as of right without any means tests, has the minimum income necessary to meet his responsibilities. If when you say freedom from Want you mean it, and don't just mean a pious platitude, you will have to adopt, not necessarily my precise scheme, but something like this scheme, something that does all the things that this scheme does. If you can find another way of doing them, I don't mind. But something like it is needed if you want freedom from Want. And that is the basis of all our post-war reconstruction—the first step to take.

But it is only the first step. Let me come on to those other giant evils that I have named. One is Disease. Well, Disease is also, to some extent, dealt with in my Report, because my Report proposes that there shall be a comprehensive medical service covering every kind of treatment at home and in hospital—dental, ophthalmic, general, specialist, consultant, nursing services, everything—covering that without a charge at the time of treatment, in virtue of a contribution made and included in the weekly contribution which the Social Insurance Scheme proposes. We can't of course abolish all Disease, but here again the principle of the national minimum applies. We ought to regard it as part of the national minimum for every citizen that he should be as well as science applied to the prevention and cure of Disease can make him. That is the medical side of my proposals and of the national minimum.

In regard to the giant Disease my Report says something. It provides the money or shows where you can get the money for dealing with this problem by a comprehensive medical service. But it doesn't go into the method of how you should organize the medical service, how you should control and finance voluntary hospitals, how you should pay and employ doctors. That's a very big problem of organization which had to be left out of my Report because I couldn't have written it by this Christmas if I'd had to deal with it. It will have to be tackled afterwards. You may say that my Report deals with the whole of the problem of freedom from Want, and about half of the problem of Disease.

Dealing with Ignorance

I come now to those three other evils: Ignorance, Squalor, Idleness. Dealing with Ignorance means, of course, the development of education. It means more and better schools. It means giving greater opportunity— greater equality of education—to all children, irrespective of their class or family circumstances. It means that for two reasons: first, that no community can afford to waste any of its talent; second, and this is an equally good human reason, that any wasted talent is a source of unhappiness. The people who are being employed below their capacity are the unhappy ones, and we want to abolish that cause of unhappiness as well as use their talents.

But dealing with Ignorance isn't only—I'm not sure that it's even mainly—a question regarding young people. All of us old people are very ignorant of many things which we ought to know. I believe that adult education on a greatly extended scale is almost as important as, if not more important than, more education of the young. There are really many things that you learn better when you are older, when you are out in the world. And I hope we shan't concentrate on just pumping more education into the young. We should insist on pumping more knowledge of the world at large, of politics, of history, of economics and all the rest of it, into our adult citizens.

To lay plans for our educational development is the third of our tasks. I have no time today to say much about this task. The main thing I would say is that the proper timing of our educational measures is essential. Look at what the position is going to be immediately after this war, in which we haven't been educating the necessary teachers; they've been fighting or doing urgent war work. We shall find an acute shortage of teachers. Frankly, I don't want to see an enormous mass of additional pupils brought into schools until we are certain that we can teach them better, until we have enough teachers and good enough teachers, to do not merely as well as we've been doing before, but better. The main problem at the moment is to make certain that we're going to have good teaching and enough teachers after the war. That's all I would say about that third task of dealing with Ignorance.

Dealing with Squalor

I come to my fourth giant—Squalor. What do I mean by Squalor? I mean the bad living conditions which arise from the fact that we do not plan our towns or our countryside, how cities shall grow, where our factories shall be placed, where our houses shall be placed. We do not have proper planning of the use of the land for the people to work in and to live in. Apart from that I mean that we haven't now anything like enough houses or good enough houses. Dealing with Squalor means planning town and country-side and having many more and better houses. We've had a number of Reports dealing with various sides of this question of planning the location of industry and planning the use of land. We've had the Barlow Report just before the war, or at the beginning of the war, and the Scott Report and the Uthwatt Report—and they have been of great value in showing some of the problems. But I think it's clear that we haven't yet in this country strong enough machinery to secure the proper distribution of industry and population over our country. Exactly what we ought to do, I don't know. This is a point on which I begin to raise questions rather than to answer them. It's very difficult to say what powers you need to determine how land shall be used, and when you begin to exercise that power, you get into very difficult questions of rights of property and value and compensation for inter-ference with the use of land, and so on and so on. Beyond that, if you're going to deal with Squalor, you've got a problem of regulating your trans-port facilities. Finally, we're going to have an immense task of reorganizing the whole of the building trade, so that it is equal to the heavy task that is going to fall upon it after the war. Here is a very difficult problem which we haven't, I think, yet even begun to get down to seriously—I don't mean we haven't done something. Many enquiries are being made, but there is a great unconquered evil of Squalor in our towns and countryside which we must learn to conquer.

I come now to the fifth of the evils from which I wish to see the country free, and we must all wish to see the country free—and that is the giant evil of Idleness, that is to say, of mass-unemployment. I don't believe that we need aim at getting rid of all unemployment in this country any more than we can get rid of all disease. A certain amount of unemployment can be properly dealt with by unemployment insurance, by giving a man an income while he is doing nothing. But to give a man an income while he is doing nothing—not for a few weeks or even a few months, but for years and years—is an entire misuse of the whole idea of unemployment insurance.

Prevention of Mass-Unemployment Vital

Somehow or other to prevent recurrence of mass-unemployment prolonged for years and years, such as we experienced between the first World War and the present World War, is the most important, the most difficult and most urgent of all the tasks which we have to consider today. It's the most important in itself, because unless we can avoid mass-unemployment, all else that we can do is futile. If we can avoid mass-unemployment, there's going to be no difficulty at all about paying for my scheme of social insurance in my Report and for all other essential social reforms. But if we cannot avoid mass-unemployment, if we have a large part of the people doing nothing, then we may not be able to afford it, or we may not be able to afford it in a way in which we really keep the people from Want. We may pay them so much in money, but there will not be enough goods being produced for that money, and they will not be out of Want. It's most important in itself, this abolition of mass-unemployment or prevention of mass-unemployment. It is also the most important of all the tasks psychologically, because everyone of us knows that the anxiety that is at the back of most people's minds in this country today is a fear of going back to something like what happened between the two wars.

That fear is the disturbing anxiety of all those who in the war have given up their former work, whether to go into the Forces or to do any other kind of work: they don't know what they're coming back to. Most important of all reconstruction problems on the home front is this task of dealing with mass-unemployment. It is also perhaps the most difficult. I do not know—and being an academic person I'm not going to say I know before I think I know—I know I do not now know just how to solve the problem of maintaining productive employment after the war. All I can say is that I refuse to believe that it is insoluble. When people tell me that we cannot abolish unemployment, I say that we have abolished unemployment twice in my lifetime—in the last war and in this war. I don't know how far it is absolutely true, but it is very nearly true, that in Russia they have abolished unemployment or at least they have no scheme of unemployment insurance. Now, I simply do not believe that it is impossible to abolish unemployment in Britain, but I do not yet know exactly how it ought to be done, and I don't know whether anybody yet knows how it ought to be done.

That is why I call this problem perhaps the most difficult. It is very difficult. It is at the same time extremely urgent, because if we are to maintain employment after the war, to find a use for all our labour—to change over the people who are now making the munitions of war into making what will be equally wanted—the munitions of peace and all that we need in peace—we must make the plans for that now: it's no good waiting until after the war to make the plans. Preparing to prevent Idleness is an urgent task.

Finally, this task may prove to be the most controversial. It does raise directly the question of how much further the State may need to enter into the economic sphere: of how much further in the direction either of Socialism or of planning or of something of that sort, we may need to go: of what are to be the relations between the State and private enterprise in the future. That, unfortunately, is one of the issues which are apt to divide political parties, as most of the other problems I have mentioned do not divide them. There's no party question at all about dealing with Want by social insurance; all parties would accept the principle of a national minimum and accept the principle of securing it by social insurance. There's no party question about Ignorance, about more education, or about dealing with Disease. There are difficult party questions with regard to ownership of land and the rights of property in dealing with Squalor, but they are not central to the problem. But when you come to this last problem of all—the maintaining of productive employment—you get into a region in which the policy of the country and the sentiment of the country aren't yet settled and agreed. That's why it is so necessary to discuss that problem, to see if by discussion we cannot reach agreement. In this Britain of ours, we are in fact all so sufficiently near to one another, that by discussion we can get to agreement on most things; discussion of this problem of maintaining productive employment is one of our most urgent duties today.

All Five Tasks Essential

From this review of the five evils whose absence or diminution should distinguish New Britain from the old, you will see why I spoke of the relative unimportance of social insurance. I don't under-estimate the value of the need for a minimum income for all times. But to provide that is only one of the five tasks and it's the easiest, because we're all agreed in principle and we're very nearly agreed on the methods. Until all the other tasks are taken in hand, I shall, for my part, put the emphasis on "new" and say that I want a *new* Britain rather than a new *Britain*. I shall want to see change, and you, I think, will all want to see change, until all five problems are dealt with seriously.

Three Strategic Principles

How should we approach those five tasks? I've no full answer to that question today. First of all I should have to study for many months and then talk for a month if I was to attempt to give full answers to all these questions. I am only going to lay down three general principles that today seem to me important in approaching the solution of these post-war problems; they are the three strategic principles of our campaign to win New Britain. The first principle is that whatever else we do there are certain essential British liberties which we must preserve. There are certain things which if we destroy, I should say we were not in New Britain, but in new somewhere else. Those—to me—essential British liberties include freedom of worship, freedom of speech, writing, study and teaching, freedom of association and making of new parties of every kind, freedom of choice of occupation, and freedom of spending a personal income. Without these freedoms Britain to me would not be Britain and I would go somewhere else, however new it was.

Having said that I go to the second principle. Subject to any limits set by the need to preserve these essential liberties, we ought to be prepared to use the powers of the State so far as may be necessary without any limit whatever, in order to abolish those five giant evils. Those freedoms I have named are essential, but no established interests are essential, no particular methods of production are essential. All these must, if necessary, be sacrificed to secure destruction of those five giants.

The third general principle is that if the power of the State is to be used in new fields for new purposes one must be prepared if necessary to make changes in the machinery of Government. Those are my three general principles for planning the campaign against the five giants. First, certain liberties are essential and must be preserved in any case. Second, subject to preservation of these liberties one must be prepared to use the powers of the State so far as necessary. Third, one must be prepared to change the machinery of Government so far as necessary for the performance of new tasks.

Let me make it clear that saying that the machinery of Government must be changed if necessary doesn't mean changing everything—making changes which aren't necessary. So saying that certain liberties are essential and must be kept at all costs doesn't mean that nothing else need be kept or will be kept. I don't want unnecessary change—change for the sake of change. Thus, though I do not regard any particular political device as essential, provided that I am sure of those essential liberties, I also do not believe that there is any need for changing the major part of our political institutions. When I name five or six essential liberties, I don't mean that they're the only things that will survive from the old Britain into the new. Many things will survive, and for my part I hope that the present Parliamentary system, with parties and the power to form new parties, with something of the present relation between Government and Parliament, and of members representing citizens in general will continue. In relation to Parliament, I'm inclined to be rather conservative, to say New *Britain,* rather than to try new forms of election, such as the indirect or Soviet system or representation of particular functions or interests, like councils of industry. I don't believe that we need any other type of assembly, other than this old British Parliament that we have known. We often amuse ourselves by saying rude things about Parliament and its members, but Parliament today gives the one absolutely essential condition of democracy.

The Essential Condition of Democracy

The essential part of democracy to me is not that I should spend a lot of time in governing myself, for I have many more amusing things to do. But I want to be quite certain that I can change the person who governs me without having to shoot him. That is the essence of Democracy, that you can have a peaceful change of governors without shooting. To me a country is not a Democracy, whatever else it may be and whatever other virtues it may have, if you cannot change the Government by a perfectly peaceful method of putting your cross on a piece of paper. Well, Parliament gives us that every five years, and that is all I want from Parliament really, though it can do a lot of other things as well.

But saying that Parliament should continue, doesn't mean that we want no change of Government machinery. If, for instance, we want to maintain employment in this country, one thing we have to do is to make a design of how all the productive resources of a country—all the men and the women and the factories and the skill in it—can be used after the war in meeting needs which we know will exist. That is what is called national planning, making a design as to how these resources could be used so as to produce the things that we need. Well, now it is quite certain that there is not now in this country any part of the existing machine of government capable of making such a design. The body that I look to to make such a design is what I call an Economic General Staff, somebody to plan our economic life—to make a plan for economic readjustment after the war—just as a military general staff plans a campaign. How the plan is to be carried out—whether it's to be carried out by the State or by private enterprise—is another question. The first step is that somebody has to make the plan. There is no one now to make the plan, and we want what I call an Economic General Staff to do it.

Apart from that special requirement of an Economic General Staff to plan our economic campaign, if the State is going to do a great many more things in the economic sphere, and I'm fairly sure it will have to do a great many more things in the economic sphere, we want—not necessarily better people than the present Civil Servants—but different types of people and different types of training and different types of organization. I think it's essential that all those who press for extension of the State's activity should realize that this means changing the machinery of the State to some extent.

A Positive Moral Aim

So far I have defined New Britain rather negatively by naming five evils which should be destroyed. You may ask whether I can't find a positive aim. Is there no moral purpose for the British community, and for the British individual?

Well, I think one can name it as a positive aim for the British community, that it should take the task of reconciling this security which we have not had in the past, with retention of the individual liberty and responsibility which we have had in the past, but which are threatened in some countries in the name of security. For the individual we can't find a moral aim as it is found in Germany, by subordinating the individual to the State, and by raising the State to Godhead. The essence of Britain, old and new, is that the individual is more than the State, and is the object for which the State exists. There must be as many separate aims as there are separate lives in the State. But perhaps a single common purpose may be found for all by saying that in every individual life there should be the ideal—what some people would call the sense of a Divine vocation—the ideal of doing something in his daily life which is not for his personal gain, or even for the personal gain of his own family—something which is done consciously by him as a member of a community, as a member of his local community, as a member of the nation, as a member of the brotherhood of man.

One of the weaknesses of many reformers in the past is that they have not taken account sufficiently of the immense feeling of patriotism in the British people, of that loving pride which we have in our country. It's often been said that the worker has no country. That has never been true of British workers and never will be. We have a loving pride in our country. It is in serving our country that most of us can find that aim outside our personal gain which we need in our lives—in peace as in war. . . .

Finding Agreement by Discussion

I've tried to put before you the magnitude and the difficulty of the problems that face us. To do so is not to suggest that they're insoluble. I've done so in the hope of helping to prepare the way for a solution by discussion. I'm an academic person: I don't find it easy to speak with certainty unless I feel sure, and I do not know yet with certainty, what is the remedy for those evils of Squalor and Idleness. But being an academic person means also being one who believes in the persuasive power of reason. As an academic person who lives by selling reason, I believe that in this eminently reasonable British community, sufficient discussion always leads ultimately to agreement.

One of the reasons why after winning the last war we lost all its fruits, was that during the war itself, there wasn't sufficient general discussion or forming of public opinion as to what should happen after. We all thought rather vaguely of going back to the good old days. This time we all know we can't go back to the old days because they weren't good enough, with their mass unemployment and economic wars and breeding of new military wars. We must go forward to something better than the old days. The reception that has been given to my Report shows that the people of this country are intensely interested and rightly interested now in making up their minds by discussion as to what should happen after the war to get a New Britain better than the old Britain. That is an admirable sign; what is most needed is informed discussion of all the problems that I've put before you.

38. Ludwig Erhard, *Economic Policy as a Component of Social Policy*

Ludwig Erhard (1897–1977) was the principal architect of the strategy for economic reconstruction pursued in western Germany following the nadir of 1945/46. Trained as an economist at the University of Frankfurt, Erhard was a director of an economic research institute in Nuremberg until he resigned after refusing to join the Nazi "German Labor Front" in 1942. In 1943–44 Erhard drafted a memorandum on the economic reconstruction of postwar Germany which anticipated many of his later policy decisions after the war. In May 1945 the American military occupation authorities in Bavaria appointed Erhard an advisor to assist in the reorganization of Bavarian industry. He soon became minister of economics in the Bavarian state government, eventually serving as the Director for Economic Administration for the joint British-American economic Bizone in 1948–49. Here Erhard was among those most responsible for the success of the 1948 currency reforms and the abolition of price controls which spurred West German economic recovery. In September 1949 Erhard became the first economics minister of the new Federal Republic of Germany, in the Christian Democratic / Free Democratic cabinet headed by Konrad Adenauer.

In the midst of the Korean boom and with the resources of the Marshall Plan, Erhard set about implementing his vision of a "Social Market" economic policy. This concept may have been indebted to the theoretical work of German Neo-Liberals like Alfred Müller-Armack and Walter Eucken, who insisted upon the technical, as well as moral, failings of planned economies; but as Wolfgang Benz has noted, it required a popular pragmatist like Erhard to "carry the quintessence of the theoretical opinions of the Neo-Liberal School into practice."[1] Erhard defended this vision of a new economic order for postwar Germany which articulated ardent neo-liberal beliefs in the value of private investment and market competition, but which also accepted a strong state and its institutions of social security. Following his Social Market prescriptions, Erhard presided over the so-called *Wirtschaftswunder* ("economic miracle") which by the late 1950s gave the Federal Republic the strongest economy on the European continent. Along with other leading Christian Democratic politicians, Erhard accepted the idea of European integration, although he resented French attempts to use the EEC to protect their economy. In 1963, following Adenauer's retirement, Erhard was named Chancellor of the Federal Republic, a position he held until 1966.

The speech below was delivered at the national party congress of the Christian Democratic Union in Karlsruhe, on 28 April 1960.

---

1. Wolfgang Benz, *Von der Besatzungsherrschaft zur Bundesrepublik* (Frankfurt, 1984), p. 125.

Any statement of economic policy, if it is to further the dynamic expansion of our national and social life, must be constantly under review in order to link past, present and future together in one smooth and unbroken harmony. This means that the guiding principles of economic policy not only leave their mark on society but are also shaped and altered by it. The echo that economic policy finds in the minds of a nation will resound all the more if that policy succeeds not merely in fulfilling its more immediate aims but also in giving a convincing answer to contemporary spiritual problems. This does not, of course, mean that it should adapt itself to every passing whim, romantic dream or unrealistic demand of this or that group. Truth is not so variable that it can, like fashion, respond to any and every mood, any more than the laws of logic can be dissociated from their inherent necessity.

Ever since the days of the currency reform the policy of the Social Market Economy has revolved round the central idea of combining personal freedom, growing prosperity and social security within the framework of a free, competitive economy and of bringing nations together by means of a policy of universal plain-dealing.

Who still remembers today the bottomless despair we once felt and have since shaken off? Elementary supply and production problems, unemployment, refugees, the need to restore an efficient commodity and capital market, to create fresh confidence in our new currency and to make the Federal Republic part of a renascent world economy—these were the practical problems which had to be solved if we were not to become a prey to shortages, want and hardship. Today even the opponents of the Social Market Economy no longer deny that it succeeded to an astonishing extent in providing our people once again with a soundly-based livelihood. The CDU/CSU has no need to feel ashamed of the fruits of its policy. This is something that the faint-hearted, even in our own ranks, might bear in mind when they are beset by resentment, disquiet or uncertainty.

It is not in our nature to allow pleasure or pride in work well done to degenerate into vain complacency or even to give rise to the belief that our work is done. But we are not prepared to accept criticism at any price from those who, lacking imagination and original ideas, steal the patent of the Social Market Economy and try to sell this second-hand product as if it were their own. This in itself should dispel quite a few doubts about the rightness of our economic policy, for it means that our political opponents cannot make any headway in the country today unless they renounce their

From Ludwig Erhard, *The Economics of Success,* translated by J. A. Arengo-Jones and D. J. S. Thomson (London: Thames & Hudson, 1963), pp. 275–92. Originally published as *Deutsche Wirtschaftspolitik,* ©1962 by Econ Verlag GmbH, Düsseldorf.

old traditions and ideologies and resign themselves to the sort of liberal system we are advocating. . . .

While we have no sympathy with the debased views of those whose cynical egoism leaves no room for social considerations, we are also vehemently opposed to those destructive elements that revel in their enjoyment of material gain and adopt a heartless, snobbish attitude towards what they mockingly refer to as the "economic miracle" or the "children of the economic miracle." They give the people stones instead of bread. We are, on the other hand, ready to welcome anyone who takes life seriously and who, even if he finds much to criticize, is anxious to find something better, to experiment and to help.

I hope you will not take it amiss, however, if I say that I find many criticisms and many judgments highly contradictory. When there were acute shortages and conditions were at their worst I kept hearing people say that a free market economy was no way to solve our problems, and when I contradicted them the reply I usually got was hate and scorn; now we are told that the liberal economic principle is only really equipped to deal with shortages, whereas prosperity and abundance call for quite different principles. "Common sense becomes nonsense, charity a plague."

No, what we must do is carry our inner convictions to the logical conclusion and remain true to our ideas. During the past twelve years questions of supply and employment have been uppermost, particularly in relation to an industrial state which is functioning in a confined area, but there have been many indications, such as the increase in personal savings, that the Social Market Economy, as it develops further, will succeed in mastering the problems created by the rise in incomes and property.

No truly sincere person can deny, after the experiences of the past twelve years, that anything we have not so far achieved is in process of achievement, and that any further progress we make in the economic field will, in the first instance, benefit the broad mass of the people. . . . [I]t is also worth pointing out that the obvious success of a free economic and social system in Germany has produced a more and more pronounced trend towards market economy methods in other parts of the free world. One can, indeed, say that the basic pattern, which Alfred Müller-Armack and Wilhelm Röpke were largely instrumental in creating, has so far proved itself as to be generally accepted today as the prototype of a worldwide system of free trading.

What then is lacking? Why is it that, for all the achievements and the almost grandiose triumphs of the Social Market Economy, people are still not entirely content and society is not entirely satisfied? How is one to explain the fact that, despite security of employment and growing production in a steadily expanding economy, people are still not satisfied? The prevailing and all too obvious unrest in our democratic society is alarming. When times were bad it was barely noticeable, whereas today it is quite apparent and, as an endemic weakness of any free society, seems hard to counteract. Where perfectly understandable differences of opinion emerge they meet head-on in an atmosphere overcharged with emotion, and we have not found any routine method of keeping such clashes within bounds. If storms blow up through lack of proportion and restraint we are certainly justified in recalling all that has already been achieved and, where it seems advisable, in making an ethical appeal. I quite realize that such appeals are limited in their effect, and yet I am confident that one can appeal to people's consciences and ask them to reflect on the true values of life.

This raises the question whether the unrest and excitability of the general public do not have their roots in the deeper recesses of their consciousness, which can only mean in the still unsolved problems of a free society. I do not believe for one moment that our achievements are being deliberately and maliciously misunderstood. Material living standards have so obviously improved that simple denial is not possible. But that is precisely why it is so surprising that these material improvements should have produced on every side an almost irrational, negative reaction.

On closer reflection we may come to the conclusion that, where a democratic society such as ours has undergone tremendous industrial expansion and has been shaken to its foundations, a special effort is needed to evolve a social policy which will encourage a new approach to life in keeping with the times. Probably all that is needed in many cases is a conscious reappraisal of the bonds that still exist between the individual and his environment, "his" world. Let us not overlook the fact, however, that industrialization, the development of our transport system, the loosening of traditional bonds with the home or the job, and a loss of independence have all had a serious, adverse effect on our society. Our form of society has been described figuratively as a "classless society." This concept, which has undergone a considerable historical change, can be taken to indicate not merely that the rise of the working class led to a process of deproletarization which is still going on, but also that the property-owning and professional layers of society have become fluid and that, throughout the whole range of modern consumer goods right up to the motor-car, the television set and all gadgets designed to lighten the burden of housework, a highly desirable trend, the market for consumer goods is widening, with the result that class privileges are disappearing and will continue to disappear. In this "classless society" the great problem is one not of class but of the individual, the average man, who feels that he is subordinate to the community and therefore has a sense of insecurity. The problem of how and where he finds his rightful place in professional and social life is un-

doubtedly much more difficult to solve than it was in *dirigiste* systems.
There is also the fact that trade cycles, market fluctuations and changes in
production appear to involve him in mechanical processes which are impersonal and leave him dissatisfied because he finds it hard to understand
how these forces work. The more such uncertainty leads to a vague feeling
of anxiety, the less surprising it is that people escape from their sense of
isolation by forming groups and organizations, which in their turn give
public expression, in amplified form, to the individual's inner disquiet.

A process such as this naturally not only produces effects which heighten
the danger both of atomizing and of collectivising life, but also intensifies
the desire of the individual for some kind of bond in which he can find
warmth and security. The more intimate communities of the family and the
church are thus supplemented by social groups of people with common interests in the form of clubs or other associations. I would even go so far as
to say that human nature needs some kind of personal compensation, of
spiritual balance, some way of reconciling the purely practical requirements of one's daily work, which condition one's relationship with society
as a whole, with the desire for peace and security in mental and spiritual
associations. It is asking too much of the Social Market Economy to expect
it to break down the visible social manifestations of our present-day life
and recreate them on an idealistic basis. But it does have an obligation to
live up to the precepts of a Christian social policy and to implement them
in a better society.

Seen in terms of economic policy, the problem is one of working towards a humanization of our environment in all spheres of life but particularly in the economic sphere.

If this is not to remain a mere phrase we must translate our general purpose into specific principles to be actively incorporated in our economic
and social policy. . . . To avoid any misunderstanding, let me say that we
have no intention of renouncing the prevailing principles of the Social Market Economy. Life does not progress by fits and starts, any more than economic and social developments can be reduced to a series of acts; they must
always be seen as a continuing process. The Social Market Economy has
been regarded by its spiritual founders, ever since its inception, as one coherent economic policy. But, in view of the standard of productivity we
have achieved in our industry today, of the steadily improving position of
our national income, and of the hopeful prospects of spreading ownership,
more and more can be done in the future to give concrete expression to that
coherent policy in broad social terms. Although it would be a mistake to
consider this problem solely from the ethical view-point, nevertheless one
should not underestimate the importance and the advisability of ethical values even in the economic sphere. But to imbue our social system with

moral content would be a fruitless task if concrete ways and means could not also be found to create a society of free people. So the Social Market Economy did not prove itself merely by virtue of the idea it represents but essentially because its aim is to combine the practical methods of economic policy with the ideal of social security in economic freedom.

In the spiritually unsettled conditions of the so-called "classless society" it will, therefore, be necessary to build in social stabilizers which are designed to counteract the modern trend towards isolation of the individual and to give him the consciousness, and indeed the objective assurance, that he is living in a unified and coherent society. It is fairly clear that to the average man that is less easy to understand than a *dirigiste* principle, but this does not seem to me a valid criterion. From a political viewpoint, the problem is to overcome the suspicions aroused by a free market economy and to realize that a purely intellectual solution is no longer adequate to meet the problems of our modern society. The flow of its technical expansion and sociological transformation is so rapid and so powerful that it becomes increasingly difficult to take our bearings on the river bank behind us, unless we also study the currents themselves. . . .

It follows from all this that, in the future development of the Social Market Economy, problems of social policy will rank equally with economic problems. The need for our economic system to develop further in this direction has been recognized for years by those intimately concerned with this problem. But it is a problem that must be tackled in its entirety. Efforts to create new forms of property undoubtedly deserve every support, but they are limited in their scope in that they make only a material contribution towards solving the problems of different income and property-owning groups in society. The attempt to interpret our social problems purely and simply in terms of the industrial "middle class" suffers from the same limitation. Important as it is to keep a balance between the various forms of industrial enterprise, we must strive in our social policy not merely to safeguard the existence of independent units at present in being, but perhaps still more to encourage a spread of independence, otherwise we shall find ourselves the prisoners of a backward-looking ideology. From the viewpoint of social policy, the attaining of independence in whatever shape or form must, in fact, take priority over mere survival. This does not mean that our entire attention should not be directed to considering whether present legislation covering, for example, taxation or industrial companies does not unwittingly favour enterprises of a certain kind or size and thereby militate against others.

A social policy which aims to be more than just an ideology and to be realistic and progressive must have as its basis the actual conditions of our economic environment, and this means developing aims which also do justice to the large industrial organizations that have kept pace with modern technology. However clear our purpose might be, we would be frittering away our energy in a purely *pro forma* struggle against concentration of power if we were not prepared to admit that the large industrial units in our economy have achieved a great deal and can rightly claim to have made a major contribution to the general growth of prosperity. It is not the large concern as such but the unbridled lust for power that tends to produce the sort of concentration which is harmful to our national economy and socially undesirable and to which we are therefore opposed. So it is our intention to restrict, and indeed to suppress, all restrictive or monopolistic control of markets by introducing further legislation to protect competition and by pursuing an appropriate taxation policy. But wherever the market is influenced by a lowering of prices and society benefits, then we should acknowledge that such an influence is indispensable. This implies, of course, that even large concerns must recognize that they too have social obligations, especially as they can do much to expand the independent, self-supporting sector of industry. To take only one example, they can leave certain functions and services to independent suppliers. The more liberal our economic system becomes the more importance will accrue to the larger industrial concerns, but this certainly does not mean that intermediate enterprises must go to the wall. Let us also never forget, when we are thinking of our social policy for the future, that we are not alone in the world and that competition will, in fact, increase, from which it follows that our aims must conform to what is actually possible. As no one, either in our personal or our national life, can give more than he has, we would be gambling not only with our future as a nation but also with our social security if we demanded more of the national economy than it is capable of producing to meet its world commitments.

Several attempts have been made, particularly during the last few years, to benefit certain sectors of our society by adjusting taxes. It seems to me, however, that such a social policy, which confines itself to technical measures, is not sufficient to meet the psychological situation we are confronted with. The social blue-print we have to develop must do more than just prescribe certain individual measures to be taken; it must open up a complete vista of social policy, the aims of which can command the moral support of the mass of the people. What this means can best be imagined if we think of the appalling developments in East Germany, where free peasants are enslaved and the independent artisan is deprived of his livelihood. . . .

Although social policy and economic policy must be regarded as not so much coexisting as cohabiting, nevertheless there is bound to be a certain shift of emphasis in that social policy embraces a wider field in which not only the resources of the Federation, the Länder and the Provinces are involved but all private concerns, associations, organizations and enterprises should also participate. This does not mean that we should now make an all-out effort to forget, on principle, the lessons we have learned and break new ground at any price. In many cases it will simply be a question of reinforcing developments which are already under way, of incorporating what we have learned and seen in one coherent scale of values, and of making the individual the conscious purpose and objective of our social policy.

There is no doubt, for example, that modern industrial development requires more specialized production in every department, whether technical or administrative, whether in business, education or in professional training. This almost structural growth in education and training compels us to invest more and more in intellectual capital, in order to make it easier for young people who are trying to find their true place in society to embark on a professional career and gain advancement. . . .

No less important is our responsibility to encourage independence. Here it is not enough simply to think of a "middle-class" policy, however strongly we may defend it. Independence in a free society cannot be confined to specific groups, and it is equally wrong to try to secure existing positions by measures which are likely to debase or even destroy a genuine competitive impulse. The process by which men of the most varied professions become independent is not something that can be institutionalized, nor can we hope to start at every point in exactly the same conditions. In view of the many forms of assistance already being given to the professions, partly by limiting competition, and also in view of the difficulty of entry by means of examination and so on, an effort should be made to offer those who want to be self-supporting certain inducements which will encourage them to accept the risks involved. A policy with this in view would increase the element of competition and would not cut across the basic principles of our market economy. In so far as economic independence rests upon genuine achievement it is a social asset which should be maintained and expanded. In this connection we should consider whether existing legislation does not unwittingly create incentives on the one hand and disincentives on the other.

By and large, of course, the problem of economic independence will be confined to small and medium-sized concerns and to the professions. But it seems to me to be just as important to give the formally dependent employees and workers in heavy industry enough freedom of action to enable them to play their part in a free society. This process must be further developed and expanded from the beginnings that have already been made and every opportunity within the industries themselves must be explored of so organizing the work of both employees and manual labour that groups can be formed and responsibilities allotted which give the individual a sense of relative but nonetheless growing independence. There is a great opportunity here to create a new and genuine middle class in a more modern sense of the word. The state will provide the initial stimulus but will also be in a position to lend practical assistance. What has hitherto been largely dependent on private initiative should, after an experimental period, become an integral part of our social policy. And let us not forget that full employment provides a particularly sound material basis on which to bring such ideas to fruition!

While, therefore, the individual and society can only be reconciled if each person is given the opportunity to find his niche in society by providing him with suitable training and scope, any such policy is incomplete unless an effort is also made to allay people's fears, justified or unjustified, of the machinery of a free economy against which they feel more or less helpless. Most important in this respect is to maintain a stable currency, a factor of increasing sociological importance. When a private citizen earns enough to acquire capital he must be free of anxiety about what he has acquired. If even hard-currency countries could not hold out entirely against the perhaps slight but nevertheless perceptible trend towards devaluation, this imposes on a country's economic policy the responsibility to resist such a softening-up process still more firmly in the future. And it must be taken as a hopeful sign that such an undisputed expert as the President of the International Monetary Fund should have spoken of a new era in which the world must learn to live without price inflation, and added that those who are the first to learn will profit most from the future. . . .

What we are striving for is a social policy inspired by the determination to create a clear and coherent mental image of the sort of environment in which the individual can live in freedom and security. This implies a better over-all view of every sphere of our national life. Whereas in the early period, when we were rebuilding our economy, sheer necessity forced us to concentrate on material problems, as we look to the future we shall give more attention—without neglecting the material side—to improving and, indeed, humanizing our environment. And we are not prepared to hand over the responsibility for developing our economic and social system to a party which has only just begun to grasp what we planned and fought so hard to implement twelve years ago in the teeth of their resistance.

So much importance attaches to working conditions in our factories that we must make an intensive effort to improve them. Until now issues concerning the factory laws have bulked largest. To mention only a few examples, questions of accident prevention, of health, of air pollution, and so on, are increasingly important where severe nervous strain is involved and where demands are made. They point to something like Alexander Rüstow's *Vitalpolitik,* a policy which looks beyond the economic to man as a vital unit. We cannot safeguard this unity of the human environment solely through the family, important as this question is. Modern man is compelled to live in a much wider environment, of which his job forms an integral part. Future legislation must embody the basic assumption that more exacting standards will have to be applied than were in force at a time when the factory was regarded as primarily a mechanical workshop. Yet another indication that the Social Market Economy is on the right lines is the fact that in so many of its principles the production target, even where the internal organization of the factory is concerned, is closely related to the sociological aims.

I am becoming more and more convinced that the problem of social environment must now be tackled in as concrete terms as possible and with the accent on the human element. During the past decade, when our industry and our communications were undergoing enormous development, we released two forces which were answerable, as it were, only to the logic of their own expansion and which did lasting damage to the natural form of life. Despite prolonged scientific and practical experiments, we have not yet succeeded—apart from a few lucky exceptions—in producing even the rudiments of a real solution of our accommodation problem. Romantic visions such as the dispersal of industrial areas have merely served to bring genuine plans for a better utilization of space into disrepute. . . .

In a very interesting analysis which was recently made of the sociological aspects of our urban development it was clearly shown that, while city-dwellers enjoy city life, they avoid the city centres on the grounds that they no longer offer the facilities for orderly public life. Hence the drift into the suburbs and the country by people who are not seeking the beauties of nature but are natural town-dwellers deprived of the kind of life they want to live. The result is a senseless, nerve-wracking human shuttle-service, which makes people restless and excitable, despite the fact that they are enjoying greater prosperity.

This raises problems which should not be dealt with on a casual, hand-to-mouth basis. What we must do is plan urban and rural areas on an ambitious, functional scale. The classification of our towns and cities into commercial and administrative centres, places of education and culture, residential districts and communication-points is something that cannot be left entirely to local authorities but calls for a collective effort which will have to be backed by central funds. . . .

To anyone who appreciates the importance of those facets of our free society which I have outlined must come the conviction that the economic policy of tomorrow will not only have to continue performing its present tasks but will also acquire new ones. Everything points to the fact that the present rate of development of our production will increase still further and that, as a result, the present divergence of views between those who favour the traditional and those who favour a more modern approach to the planning of environment will become even more marked, particularly with the rapid technical advances in industrial production. Social policy, too, will be compelled not merely to continue performing its present functions but also to take account of the change in the over-all situation, for with growing expansion more and more people and even larger categories of people are earning the sort of livelihood that should make them more self-reliant. This means that cases where help is genuinely needed can be treated more generously and more humanely.

But modern social policy in the free world must not be merely inward-looking. Our economic and social life is largely dependent on the world-wide ramifications of our economy, and in consequence our internal national structure can only be properly judged and effectively moulded if we are constantly aware of the implications of our economic dependence on the outside world. Seen in this light, European integration at all levels and in all forms acquires an almost prophetic significance. As you know, we are striving at this very moment to find a solution which will guarantee that the European countries are treated as one and without discrimination, which will foster friendship without having to damage friendship. . . .

I have tried to show how the functions of the Social Market Economy in a free society go far beyond what has in fact been achieved. In view of the fact that personal savings are widespread and on the increase and that our industry can meet at least a considerable proportion of its own production and investment needs, to that extent the state should be relieved of the many subsidies to private industry, which still represent a substantial financial burden. Given this appreciable relief and bearing in mind also that economic expansion provides the state with additional resources, the public services should be reorganized and expanded, both quantitatively and qualitatively, along the lines I have already suggested. For the public services play a major part in shaping the environment in which, quite apart from our domestic and professional routine, we lead much of our lives.

To sum up, we know today that the development of our public services has not kept pace with the growth of industrial production. The means required to plan our environment are treated as residual items in our budget surpluses; they receive no serious consideration because group interests are not prepared to support them.

The fact that, in spite of the growing volume and variety of consumer goods, people are still unsettled can be taken as an indication that material prosperity loses its savour if the life of the individual does not fit organically into an environment which both the individual and society find congenial.

Of course, a mere quantitative increase in the funds set aside for public services is not enough. What is needed is a qualitative reorientation in the direction I have suggested, which will follow a detailed blue-print and will give a new urgency to the search for new standards in planning the structure of our society. . . .

Any liberal system must proceed from the assumption that freedom is one and indivisible and that elementary human freedom in all spheres of life must go hand in hand with political, religious, economic and spiritual freedom. The strategy of collectivist thinking has always been to split up this most essential and most universal of human values as a means of making inroads into the free system itself. So that system can only be made secure if we bring home to the German people that their social and economic life, in all its manifestations and ramifications, is the outward expression of an inner will and a spiritual fulfilment. When our economic and social policy is seen in this light it will be in a position to make a vital contribution to the cause of peace and will thereby satisfy the desire of our people to share in one all-embracing way of life.

39. The Bad Godesberg Program

Meeting in Bad Godesberg in November 1959 the German Social Democratic party (SPD) adopted a new program superseding that approved in Heidelberg in 1925. The program signaled a radical departure for German Socialism from the ways of its ideological past. The program mentioned neither Marx nor Marxism, and explicitly or implicitly slaughtered many of the sacred cows of nineteenth- and early twentieth-century revolutionary socialism. The net effect was to position the SPD as a social reformist, social liberal party which accepted the essential conditions of Erhard's Social Market economy, while striving to widen and deepen the norms of social justice and of social security in German society. As Adolf Sturmthal has noted of a parallel program developed for the German trade unions in 1963, "It may well be said that John Maynard Keynes rather than Karl Marx gave the main inspiration to the program." [1] In the context of the SPD's own history, the Bad Godesberg Program has been seen as a victory of the ethos, if not the form, of Eduard Bernstein's Revisionism over both the centrist orthodoxy of Karl Kautsky and the

1. Adolf Sturmthal, *Left of Center: European Labor since World War II* (Urbana, 1983), p. 63.

revolutionary praxis of Rosa Luxemburg. Rather than a class party, the
SPD now became a "people's party."

The Bad Godesberg Program came after ten years of fruitless opposition by the SPD within the new Federal Republic. Although the SPD
performed respectably in the national elections of 1949, 1953, and 1957,
it remained a minority party, committed (under its first postwar leader
Kurt Schumacher) to a program of anticapitalism, nationalism, and German reunification which proved increasingly anachronistic. The decision
of the key leaders within the SPD to support the new Common Market
signaled that within the party there were powerful forces for change. Following the reforms undertaken at Bad Godesberg, the party accepted
German membership in NATO and acknowledged its support for a bipar-
tisan foreign policy, thereby repudiating another link to Schumacher's
heritage.

Viewed alongside the political moderatism of Adenauer, Erhard, and
the CDU, Bad Godesberg confirmed the fact that the Federal Republic
now had a stable political system based on two mass centrist parties, both
of whom were capable of sustaining and defending the kind of democratic consensus which proved so elusive in the Weimar Republic.

Selections from the Bad Godesberg Program are printed below, in an
official translation produced by the party executive.

Basic Programme of the Social Democratic Party of Germany

Fundamental Values of Socialism

Socialists aim to establish a society in which every individual can develop
his personality and as a responsible member of the community, take part in
the political, economic and cultural life of mankind.

Freedom and justice are interdependent, since the dignity of man rests
on his claim to individual responsibility just as much as on his acknowledgement of the right of others to develop their personality and, as equal
partners, help shape society.

Freedom, justice and solidarity, which are everyone's obligation towards
his neighbours and spring from our common humanity, are the fundamental
values of Socialism.

Democratic Socialism, which in Europe is rooted in Christian ethics,
humanism and classical philosophy, does not proclaim ultimate truths—
not because of any lack of understanding for or indifference to philosophi-

From *Basic Programme of the Social Democratic Party of Germany* (Bonn, Germany:
Social Democratic Party of Germany, 1959), pp. 5–17, 20–22. Reprinted by permission of
the publisher.

cal or religious truths, but out of respect for the individual's choice in these matters of conscience in which neither the state nor any political party should be allowed to interfere.

The Social Democratic Party is the party of freedom of thought. It is a community of men holding different beliefs and ideas. Their agreement is based on the moral principles and political aims they have in common. The Social Democratic Party strives for a way of life in accordance with these principles. Socialism is a constant task—to fight for freedom and justice, to preserve them and to live up to them.

Basic Demands for a Society Worthy of Man

From the acceptance of Democratic Socialism follow certain basic demands which must be fulfilled in a society worthy of man.

All peoples must submit to the rule of international law backed by adequate executive power. War must be ruled out as a means of policy.

All peoples must have equal opportunities to share in the world's wealth. Developing countries have a claim to the help of other peoples.

We are fighting for democracy. Democracy must become the universal form of state organisation and way of life because it is founded on respect for the dignity of man and his individual responsibility.

We resist every dictatorship, every form of totalitarian or authoritarian rule because they violate human dignity, destroy man's freedom and the rule of law. Socialism can be realised only through democracy and democracy can only be fulfilled through Socialism.

Communists have no right to invoke Socialist traditions. In fact, they have falsified Socialist ideas. Socialists are struggling for the realisation of freedom and justice while Communists exploit the conflicts in society to establish the dictatorship of their party.

In the democratic state, every form of power must be subject to public control. The interest of the individual must be subordinated to the interest of the community. Democracy, social security and individual freedom are endangered by an economic and social system in which striving for profit and power are the distinguishing features. Democratic Socialism therefore aspires after a new economic and social order.

All privileged access to educational institutions must be abolished. Talent and achievement should be the sole criteria of advancement.

Freedom and justice cannot be guaranteed by institutions alone. Technology and organisation are exerting a growing influence on all areas of life. This creates new dependencies which threaten freedom. Only diversity in economic, social and cultural life can stimulate the creative powers of the individual without which man's mind is paralysed.

Freedom and democracy are only thinkable in an industrial society if a constantly growing number of people develop a social consciousness and are ready to help shoulder responsibility. A decisive means to this end is political education in its widest sense. It is an essential objective of all educational efforts in our time.

The Order of the State

The Social Democratic Party of Germany lives and works in the whole of Germany. It stands by the Basic Law of the German Federal Republic. In accordance with the Basic Law it strives for German unity in freedom.

The division of Germany is a threat to peace. To end this division is a vital interest of the German people.

Not until Germany is reunited, will the whole people be able freely to determine the content and form of the state and society.

Man's life, his dignity and his conscience take precedence over the state. Every citizen must respect the convictions of his fellow men. It is the duty of the state to protect freedom of faith and freedom of conscience.

The state should create the conditions in which the individual may freely develop his personality, responsible to himself but conscious of his obligations to society. Established fundamental rights do not only protect the freedom of the individual in relation to the state; they should also be regarded as social rights which constitute the basis of the state.

The social function of the state is to provide social security for its citizens to enable everyone to be responsible for shaping his own life freely and to further the development of a free society.

The state becomes a truly civilised state *(Kulturstaat)* through the fusion of the democratic idea with the ideas of social security and the rule of law. It depends for its content on the forces prevalent in society, and its task is to serve the creative spirit of man.

The Social Democratic Party affirms its adherence to democracy. In a democracy the power of the state is derived from the people and the government is always responsible to Parliament whose confidence it must possess. In a democracy the rights of the minority as well as the rights of the majority must be respected; government and opposition have different tasks of equal importance; both share in the responsibility for the state.

The Social Democratic Party aims to win the support of the majority of the people by competing under equal conditions with other democratic parties in order to build a society and a state that accord with the essential demands of democratic Socialism.

Legislature, executive and judiciary should operate separately and it is the duty of each to serve the public interest. The existence of three levels of authority—Federal, State, and Local—ensures the distribution of power, strengthens freedom and through co-determination and co-responsibility gives the citizen manifold access to democratic institutions. Free local communities are vital to a living democracy. The Social Democratic Party therefore supports the principles of local self-government which must be extended and given adequate financial support.

Associations in which people of different groups and sections of the population unite for common ends are necessary institutions of modern society. They must be democratically organised. The more powerful they are, the greater is the responsibility they carry, but the greater also is the danger of their abusing their power. Parliaments, administration and courts must not be allowed to come under the one-sided influence of vested interests.

Press, radio, television and cinema fulfill public tasks. They must be independent and free to gather information wherever they wish, to comment on it and to distribute it, and to form and express their own opinions. Radio and television should remain under the control of public corporations, and be directed by free and democratic boards. They must be safeguarded against pressure from interest groups.

Judges must have outer and inner independence if they are to serve justice in the name of the people. Lay judges should play an equally important part in jurisdiction. Only independent judges can pass judgment on criminal offences. Neither wealth nor poverty should have an influence on people's access to courts or on jurisdiction. Legislation must keep pace with the development of society if justice is to be done and if the people's sense of justice is not to be violated.

National Defence The Social Democratic Party affirms the need to defend the free democratic society. It is in favour of national defence.

National defence must be adapted to the political and geographical position of Germany and therefore stay within the limits imposed by the necessity of creating the conditions for an easing of international tensions, for effectively controlled disarmament and for the reunification of Germany. Protection of the civilian population is an essential part of a country's defence.

The Social Democratic Party demands that the means of mass destruction be banned by international law in the whole world. . . .

The Economy

The goal of Social Democratic economic policy is the constant growth of prosperity and a just share for all in the national product, a life in freedom without undignified dependence and without exploitation.

Constant Economic Expansion The Second Industrial Revolution makes possible a rise in the general standard of living greater than ever before and the elimination of poverty and misery still suffered by large numbers of people.

Economic policy must secure full employment whilst maintaining a stable currency, increase productivity and raise general prosperity.

To enable all people to take part in the country's growing prosperity there must be planning to adjust the economy to the constant structural changes in order to achieve a balanced economic development.

Such a policy demands national accounting and a national budget. The national budget must be approved by Parliament. It is binding on government policy, provides an important basis for the policies of the autonomous central bank, and establishes guiding lines for the economy which keeps its right to make independent decisions.

The modern state exerts a constant influence on the economy through its policies on taxation, finance, currency and credits, customs, trade, social services, prices and public contracts as well as agriculture and housing. More than a third of the national income passes through the hands of the government. The question is therefore not whether measures of economic planning and control serve a purpose, but rather who should apply these measures and for whose benefit. The state cannot shirk its responsibility for the course the economy takes. It is responsible for securing a forward-looking policy with regard to business cycles and should restrict itself to influencing the economy mainly by indirect means.

Free choice of consumer goods and services, free choice of working place, freedom for employers to exercise their initiative as well as free competition are essential conditions of a Social Democratic economic policy. The autonomy of trade unions and employers' associations in collective bargaining is an important feature of a free society. Totalitarian control of the economy destroys freedom. The Social Democratic Party therefore favours a free market wherever free competition really exists. Where a market is dominated by individuals or groups, however, all manner of steps must be taken to protect freedom in the economic sphere. As much competition as possible—as much planning as necessary.

Ownership and Power A significant feature of the modern economy is the constantly increasing tendency toward concentration. Large-scale enterprises exert a decisive influence not only on the development of the economy and the standard of living but also on the structure of the economy and of society.

Those who control large industrial concerns, huge financial resources and tens of thousands of employees do not merely perform an economic function but wield decisive power over men; wage and salary earners are kept in a position of dependence, and not only in purely economic and material matters.

Wherever large-scale enterprises predominate, free competition is eliminated. Those who have less power have fewer opportunities for development, and remain more or less fettered. The consumer occupies the most vulnerable position of all in the economy.

Increased power through cartels and associations gives the leaders of big business an influence on politics and the state which is irreconcilable with democratic principles. They usurp the authority of the state. Economic power becomes political power.

This development is a challenge to all who consider freedom, justice, human dignity and social security the foundations of human society.

The key task of an economic policy concerned with freedom is therefore to contain the power of big business. State and society must not be allowed to become the prey of powerful sectional groups.

Private ownership of the means of production can claim protection by society as long as it does not hinder the establishment of social justice.

Efficient small and medium sized enterprises are to be strengthened to enable them to prevail in competition with large-scale enterprises.

Competition by public enterprise is an important means of preventing private enterprise from dominating the market. Public enterprise should safeguard the interests of the community as a whole. It becomes a necessity where, for natural or technical reasons, economic functions vital to the community cannot be carried out in a rational way except by excluding competition.

Enterprises which are built up on a voluntary collective basis and whose purpose it is to satisfy demand rather than earn private profits help to regulate prices and serve the interests of the consumer. They perform a valuable function in a democratic society and should be supported.

Large-scale publicity should give the people an insight into the power structure of the economy and into business practices in order that public opinion may be mobilised against abuses of power.

Effective public control must prevent the abuse of economic power. The most important means to this end are investment control and control over the forces dominating the market.

Public ownership is a legitimate form of public control which no modern state can do without. It serves to protect freedom against domination by large economic concerns. In these concerns power is held today by managers who are themselves the servants of anonymous forces. Private ownership of the means of production is therefore no longer identical with the control of power. Economic power, rather than ownership, is the central problem today. Where sound economic power relations cannot be guaranteed by other means, public ownership is appropriate and necessary.

Every concentration of economic power, even in the hands of the state, harbours dangers. This is why the principles of self-government and decentralisation must be applied to the public sector. The interests of wage and salary earners as well as the public interest and the interests of the consumer must be represented on the management boards of public enterprises. Not centralised bureaucracy but responsible co-operation between all concerned serves the interests of the community best.

Distribution of Income and Wealth The competition economy does not guarantee by itself just distribution of income and wealth. This can only be achieved through measures of economic policy.

Income and wealth are distributed unjustly. This is not only the result of mass destruction of property through crises, war and inflation but is largely due to an economic and fiscal policy which has favoured large incomes and the accumulation of capital in the hands of a few, and which has made it difficult for those without capital to acquire it.

The Social Democratic Party aims to create conditions in which everybody is able to save part of his rising income and acquire property. This presupposes a constant increase in production and a fair distribution of the national income.

Wage and salary policies are adequate and necessary means of distributing incomes and wealth more justly.

Appropriate measures must ensure that an adequate part of the steadily growing capital of big business is widely distributed or made to serve public purposes. It is a deplorable symptom of our times that privileged groups in society indulge in luxury while important public tasks, especially in the fields of science, research and education, are neglected in a way unworthy of a civilised nation.

Agriculture The principles of Social Democratic economic policy apply also to agriculture. The structure of agriculture, however, and its dependence on uncontrollable forces of nature call for special measures.

The farmer is entitled to own his land. Efficient family holdings should be protected by modern laws on land tenure and leases.

Support of the existing system of co-operatives is the best way of increasing the efficiency of small and medium sized holdings whilst maintaining their independence.

Agriculture must adjust itself to the changing economic structure in order to make its proper contribution to economic development and to assure an adequate standard of living to the people working in it. These changes are determined not only by technical and scientific progress, but also by the changes in the location of the market within the framework of European co-operation and by the fact that the German economy is increasingly linked with that of the rest of the world.

The modernisation of agriculture and its efficiency are a public responsibility.

The interests of the farming population are best served by the integration of agriculture into an economy with high productivity and an ever more widely distributed mass purchasing power. Price and market policies necessary to protect agricultural incomes should take into account the interests of the consumers and of the economy as a whole.

The cultural, economic, and social condition of the entire farming population must be improved. The lag in social legislation must be overcome.

Trade Unions in the Economy All wage and salary earners and civil servants have the right to free association in trade unions. They would be helplessly exposed to those in positions of command in enterprises and concerns unless they were able to confront the latter with the united force of their free and democratically organised trade unions and freely to agree on working conditions.

Trade unions fight to secure wage and salary earners a fair share of the country's wealth and the right to a voice in decisions affecting economic and social life.

They fight for greater freedom and act as representatives of all working people. This makes them an important element in the constant process of democratisation. It is the unions' great task to enable every employee to shoulder responsibility and to see to it that he can make use of his abilities.

Wage and salary earners whose contribution to production is decisive have so far been deprived of an effective say in economic life. Democracy, however, demands that workers should be given a voice and that co-determination be extended to all branches of the economy. From being a servant the worker must become a citizen of the economy.

Co-determination in the iron and steel industry and in coal mining marks the beginning of a new economic structure. The next step should be the establishment of a democratic organisational structure in all large enterprises. Co-determination by employees in the independent administrative bodies set up in the economy must be secured.

Social Responsibility

Social policy must create the essential conditions which allow the individual to unfold himself freely in society and which determine his life according to his own responsibility. Social conditions that lead to individual and social hardship cannot be accepted as inevitable and unchangeable. The system of social security must correspond to the dignity of responsible individuals.

Every citizen has the right to a minimum state pension in case of old age or inability to earn a living, or at the death of the family's provider. This pension is supplemented by other personally acquired pension claims. In this way the individual standard of living will be sustained. Social allowances of all kinds, including pensions for war-disabled and their dependents, must be regularly adjusted to the rise in earned incomes.

Technology and modern civilisation expose people to many dangers to their health. They threaten not only the living generation but future generations as well. The individual is unable to protect himself against these hazards. The Social Democratic Party therefore demands comprehensive health protection. Health policy must be perfected, and the conditions and ways of living must be shaped in a way conducive to making life in sound health possible. Public health protection, especially protection at work and effective methods of preventing damage to health in individuals, must be developed. A sense of personal responsibility in respect of one's health must be aroused and the doctor of one's choice must be given full facilities for the preservation of health and prevention of illness. The professional freedom of decision of doctors must be ensured. The provision of adequately equipped hospitals is a public task.

Since all people should have an equal chance to live, all must have access to the treatment made available through modern technical research when they are in need of it, regardless of their financial position. Such medical treatment must be supplemented by adequate economic assistance in the case of illness.

Working hours should be progressively shortened without prejudice to income levels and in step with the development of the economy. In order to cope with particularly difficult situations in life and in special cases of need, the general social allowances must be supplemented by individual care and social aid. Social aid should be given in co-operation with independent voluntary welfare organisations and institutions for mutual aid and self-help. The independence of free welfare organisations must be protected.

All labour and social legislation should be ordered and compiled in a surveyable code on labour legislation and a code on social legislation.

Everyone has a right to a decent place in which to live. It is the home of the family. It must therefore continue to receive social protection and must not be the mere object of private gain.

The housing shortage must speedily be eliminated through effective building programmes. Public housing must be encouraged and social considerations must be taken into account when determining rents. Speculation in real estate should be prohibited and excessive gains from the sale of real estate taxed away.

Woman—Family—Youth Equality of rights for women should be realised in the legal, economic and social spheres. Women must be given equal opportunities in education and occupational training, in the choice and practice of professions and in earnings. The special psychological and biological characteristics of women should not be disregarded because they have equal rights. The work of the housewife should be recognised as an occupation. The housewife and mother is in need of social assistance. Mothers of children of pre-school age and school-age should not be compelled by economic need to seek gainful employment.

State and society must protect, support and strengthen the family. By supporting the material security of the family, society recognises its moral value. Effective help should be given to the family by generous tax allowances for parents, and by maternity benefits and family allowances.

Young people must be enabled to manage their own lives and grow up ready to assume their responsibilities towards society. It is therefore the task of state and society to strengthen the educational function of the family, to supplement it where it does not suffice, and, if need be, to provide an alternative. A system of grants and scholarships must ensure that special abilities and aptitudes of young people are fully developed in their vocational and professional training.

The protection of the young workers must be adjusted to present-day social conditions and educational experience. If the young people are entrusted at an early stage with a share in the work and responsibilities of adults, they will become well-informed and determined democrats. Progressive youth legislation should guarantee the young people's right to education and development of their personality. In all areas of life which concern education or the encouragement and protection of youth, the welfare of youth must have priority over all other considerations.

Cultural Life

The creative powers of the individual must be given a chance to unfold freely in a full and diverse cultural life. The state should encourage and support all forces willing to make a contribution to cultural progress. The state must protect the citizen against all attempts by power groups or sectional interests at making the people's spiritual and cultural life subservient to their own purposes.

Religion and Church Only mutual tolerance which respects the dignity of all men regardless of differences in belief and conviction, offers a sound basis for political and human co-operation in society.

Socialism is no substitute for religion. The Social Democratic Party respects churches and religious societies. It affirms their public and legal status, their special mission and their autonomy.

It is always ready to co-operate with the churches on the basis of a free partnership. It welcomes the fact that men are moved by their religious faith to acknowledge their social obligation and their responsibilities towards society.

Freedom of thought, of religion and of conscience, and freedom to preach the gospel must be protected. Any abuse of this freedom for partisan or anti-democratic ends cannot be tolerated.

Education Education must give an opportunity to all freely to develop their abilities and capacities. It must strengthen the will to resist the conformist tendencies of our time. Knowledge and the acquisition of traditional cultural values, and a thorough understanding of the formative forces in society, are essential to the development of independent thinking and free judgment.

School and university should bring up youth in a spirit of mutual respect. Youth should be taught to appreciate the values of freedom, independence and social responsibility as well as the ideals of democracy and international understanding. The aim should be to encourage tolerance, mutual understanding and solidarity in our society in which so many philosophical viewpoints and systems of value exist side by side. The curricula of schools should therefore pay proper attention to education for citizenship. . . .

Our Way

The Socialist movement has an historic task. It began as a spontaneous moral protest of wage earners against the capitalist system. The tremendous development of the productive forces with the help of science and technology brought wealth and power to a small group of people, but only destitution and misery to the workers. To abolish the privileges of the ruling classes and to secure freedom, justice and prosperity for all was and remains the essence of the Socialist aim.

The working class had to rely on its own resources in its struggle. It acquired self-confidence by becoming conscious of its own position and by its determination to change this position by united action and the experience of success in its struggle.

Despite heavy setbacks and some errors the Labour movement succeeded in the nineteenth and twentieth centuries in winning recognition for many of its demands. The proletarian who was once without protection and rights, who had to work sixteen hours a day for a starvation wage, achieved the eight-hour day, protection at work, insurance against unemployment, sickness, disability and destitution in old age. He achieved the prohibition of child labour and night work for women, the legal protection of youth and mothers, and holidays with pay. He successfully fought for the right to assemble and to form trade unions, the right to collective bargaining and to strike. He is about to obtain the right to co-determination. Once a mere object of exploitation, the worker now occupies the position of a citizen in the state with equal rights and obligations.

In several countries of Europe the foundations of a new society have been laid under Social Democratic governments. Social security and the democratisation of the economy are being realised to an increasing extent.

These successes represent milestones on the march forward of the Labour movement which has demanded so many sacrifices. The emancipation of the workers helped to enlarge the freedom of all men. From a party of the working class the Social Democratic Party has become a party of the people. It is determined to put the forces unleashed by the industrial revolution and the advance of technology in all spheres of life to the service of freedom and justice for all. The social forces which built the capitalist world cannot tackle this task. Their historical record is one of impressive technical and economic advance, but also of destructive wars, mass unemployment, inflation which robbed people of their savings, and economic insecurity. The old forces are unable to oppose the brutal Communist challenge with a better programme for a new society, in which individual and political freedom is enhanced, and economic security and social justice guaranteed. This is why they cannot satisfy the claims for assistance and solidarity from the young states which are about to throw off the yoke of colonial exploitation, to shape their destinies in freedom and to insist on participation in the world's wealth. These states are resisting the lure of Communism which is trying to draw them into its sphere of influence.

Communists are radical suppressors of freedom and violators of human rights and of the self-determination of individuals and peoples. The people in the countries under Communist domination are increasingly opposing the Communist regime. Even in those countries changes are taking place. Even there, the longing for freedom is growing which no system can wholly suppress in the long run. But the Communist rulers are fighting for their own survival. They are building up military and economic power for which their peoples have to pay the price and which represents an increasing threat to freedom.

Only the prospect of a society based on the fundamental values of democratic Socialism can offer the world new hope, a society resting on respect for human dignity, on freedom from want and fear, from war and oppression, which is built in co-operation with all men of good will.

This message is addressed to all men and women in this country as well as in other parts of the world.

In Germany Socialists are united in the Social Democratic Party which welcomes to its ranks all who accept the fundamental values and demands of Democratic Socialism.

40. The Phenomenon of Gaullism: Selections from de Gaulle

The political history of modern France can be conceptualized as an alter-
nation between parliamentary regimes and "saviors," the former functioning well enough in ordinary times, the latter invoked in times of
crisis. Thus Charles de Gaulle, twice the "savior" of France, comes at
the end of a line which includes Napoleon I, Napoleon III, and Pétain.
All favored a strong executive power which abridged the role of parliament; all had the constitutions of their regimes drawn up by small committees (and then presented to the Assembly for ratification) instead of
being drafted by the Assembly through parliamentary deliberations; and
all but Pétain were practitioners of plebiscitary democracy, bypassing
normal political channels and appealing directly to the people on critical
issues.

Charles de Gaulle was born in 1890 into a family descended from a
long line of impoverished nobles. The family was devoted to Catholicism, regretted the passing of the monarchy, but—a crucial deviation
from the French Rightist stereotype—never nursed a passionate hatred of
the Republic. Charles attended Saint-Cyr, the French equivalent of West
Point, and already at military school began to model his character after
his exceptional height, seeking to tower over others morally as well as
physically. He fought under Pétain in World War I and became the latter's
aide and protégé in the 1920s. With the fall of France in 1940, the two
men became archrivals, Pétain signing an armistice with Germany and
setting up the collaborationist Vichy Regime, de Gaulle announcing by
radio from London that he was leader of the Free French and proclaiming
in a famous poster that "France has lost a battle but France has not lost
the war."

With the liberation of France in 1944, de Gaulle, whose moral authority was now unrivaled in France, emerged as head of the Provisional
Government. But when, as the constitution of the Fourth Republic was
being framed, he sensed its drift away from a strong executive and towards the parliamentarianism and paralyzing party bickering of the Third
Republic, he abruptly resigned in 1946. De Gaulle remained in the political wilderness for the next twelve years. True to his prediction, the
Fourth Republic was a weak and internally divided regime. When it was
toppled in 1958 by a coup in Algeria (then technically part of metropolitan France) in which the French army had played a prominent role,
power passed to de Gaulle. He legitimated himself through popular refer-
endum and installed the Fifth Republic, with its constitution tailored to
powerful executive control. De Gaulle remained President until his resig-

nation in 1969. The Fifth Republic, with its seven-year presidential term, survived him, and in 1981 the French elected its first non-Gaullist president.

De Gaulle's most significant contribution, the political scientist Stanley Hoffmann has written, was "the creation of General de Gaulle, the embodiment of a great style of French leadership, the figure who mobilized old cultural values [and] ancient traits of 'national character' . . . to protect France's integrity and renew France's *grandeur.*"[1] The following selections, from de Gaulle's speeches, display the Gaullist style of leadership at key historical moments, from the first London radio broadcast of 1940 to a 1965 pronouncement on France's refusal to accept a role of dependence on the United States and the NATO alliance. The speeches are prefaced by some general ruminations from de Gaulle's memoirs.

A Way of Thinking about France

All my life I have thought of France in a certain way. This is inspired by sentiment as much as by reason. The emotional side of me tends to imagine France, like the princess in the fairy stories or the Madonna in the frescoes, as dedicated to an exalted and exceptional destiny. Instinctively I have the feeling that Providence has created her either for complete successes or for exemplary misfortunes. If, in spite of this, mediocrity shows in her acts and deeds, it strikes me as an absurd anomaly, to be imputed to the faults of Frenchmen, not to the genius of the land. But the positive side of my mind also assures me that France is not really herself unless in the front rank; that only vast enterprises are capable of counterbalancing the ferments of dispersal which are inherent in her people; that our country, as it is, surrounded by the others, as they are, must aim high and hold itself straight, on pain of mortal danger. In short, to my mind, France cannot be France without greatness.

This faith grew as I grew, in the environment where I was born. My father was a thoughtful, cultivated, traditional man, imbued with a feeling for the dignity of France. He made me aware of her history. My mother had an uncompromising passion for her country, equal to her religious piety. To my three brothers, my sister, and myself a certain anxious pride in our

1. Stanley Hoffmann, *Decline or Renewal? France since the 1930s* (New York, 1974), p. 253.

From *The War Memoirs of General De Gaulle: The Call to Honor (1940–1942)*, translated by Jonathan Griffin (New York: Viking Press, 1955), pp. 3–5; ©1955, 1983 by Simon & Schuster. Reprinted by permission of Simon & Schuster, Inc., and Librarie Plon, Paris.

country came as second nature. As a young native of Lille living in Paris, nothing struck me more than the symbols of our glories: night falling over Notre Dame, the majesty of evening at Versailles, the Arc de Triomphe in the sun, conquered colours shuddering in the vault of the Invalides. Nothing affected me more than the evidence of our national successes: popular enthusiasm when the Tsar of Russia passed through, a review at Longchamp, the marvels of the Exhibition, the first flights of our aviators. Nothing saddened me more profoundly than our weaknesses and our mistakes, as revealed to my childhood gaze by the way people looked and by things they said: the surrender of Fashoda, the Dreyfus case, social conflicts, religious strife. Nothing moved me so much as the story of our past misfortunes: my father recalling the fruitless sortie from Le Bourget and Stains, in which he had been wounded; my mother conjuring up the despair she had felt as a girl at the sight of her parents in tears: "Bazaine has capitulated!"

As an adolescent, the fate of France, whether as the subject of history or as the stake in public life, interested me above everything. I was therefore attracted but also severely critical, towards the play which was performed, day in, day out, in the forum; carried away as I was by the intelligence, fire, and eloquence lavished upon it by countless actors, yet saddened at seeing so many gifts wasted in political confusion and national disunity. All the more so since at the beginning of the century the premonitory symptoms of war became visible. I must say that in my first youth I pictured this unknown adventure with no horror, and magnified it in anticipation. In short, I was convinced that France would have to go through gigantic trials, that the interest of life consisted in one day rendering her some signal service, and that I would have the occasion to do so.

When I joined the Army, it was one of the greatest things in the world. Beneath all the criticisms and insults which were lavished on it, it was looking forward with serenity and even a muffled hopefulness to the approaching days when everything would depend on it. After Saint-Cyr I went through my apprenticeship as officer with the 33rd Infantry Regiment, at Arras. My first colonel, Pétain, showed me the meaning of the gift and art of command. Then, as the hurricane swept me off like a wisp of straw through the shocks of war—my baptism of fire, the calvary of the trenches, attacks, bombardments, wounds and captivity—I was privileged to see France, though deprived of part of her necessary means of defence by an insufficient birth-rate, by hollow ideologies, and by the negligence of the authorities, extract from herself an incredible effort, make up by measureless sacrifices for all she lacked, and bring the trial to an end in victory. I was privileged to see her, in the most critical days, pull herself together morally, at first under the aegis of Joffre, at the end of the drive of the "Tiger." I was privileged to see her, later, though exhausted from losses and devastation, with her social structure and moral balance overthrown, resume with tottering steps her march towards her destiny, while the regime, taking once more its former shape and repudiating Clemenceau, rejected greatness and returned to confusion.

During the years which followed, my career passed through various stages: special duty and a campaign in Poland, a professorship of history at Saint-Cyr, the Ecole de Guerre, attachment to a marshal's personal staff, command of the 19th Battalion of Chasseurs at Trèves, and General Staff service on the Rhine and in the Levant. Everywhere I noted the renewal of prestige which her recent successes had earned for France and, at the same time, the doubts about the future which were being awakened by the erratic behaviour of her rulers. In spite of everything, I found in the soldier's trade the powerful interest it has to offer to the mind and to the heart. In the Army, though a mill without grist, I saw the instrument of the great actions which were approaching.

General de Gaulle's London Broadcast (18 June 1940)

The leaders who for many years have commanded the armies of France have formed a government.

This government, alleging the defeat of our armies, has made contact with the enemy in order to bring the fighting to an end.

Certainly we have been, we are, overwhelmed by the weaponry of the enemy, on the land and in the air.

Infinitely more than their number, it is the tanks, the aircraft, the tactics of the Germans which have driven us back. It is the tanks, the aircraft, the tactics of the Germans which took our leaders by surprise, bringing them where they are today.

But has the last word been said? Must hope disappear? Is the defeat final? No!

Believe me, I speak to you with full knowledge of the facts, from inside information, and I am telling you that nothing is lost for France. The same means that defeated us can bring us one day to victory.

For France is not alone! She is not alone! She is not alone! She has a vast empire behind her. She can join forces with the British Empire, which controls the seas and is continuing the struggle. Like England, she can have unlimited access to the immense industry of the United States.

This war is not limited to the unfortunate territory of our country. This

From General de Gaulle's London broadcast of 18 June 1940. Translated for this volume by Kent Wright.

war will not be decided by the battle for France. This war is a world war. All the mistakes, the delays, the setbacks, the sufferings, cannot alter the fact that the resources necessary to crush our enemies still exist in the universe. Struck down today by the brute force of weaponry, we can in the future conquer with a superior brute force. Therein lies the destiny of the world.

I, General de Gaulle, presently in London, invite French officers or soldiers who are on British territory, or who can make their way to it, with or without their arms; and I invite engineers and skilled workers in the armaments industries who are on British territory or who can make their way to it, to join forces with me.

Whatever happens, the flame of the French resistance must not be extinguished and never will be extinguished.

Tomorrow, as today, I will speak on the radio from London.

Press Conference of General de Gaulle Held in Paris at the Palais d'Orsay on the Conditions of His Return to Power on 19 May 1958

It is almost three years since I have had the pleasure of seeing you. You will remember that, at our last meeting, I told you of my anticipations and anxieties with regard to the probable development of events and also of my determination to remain silent until such time as I could serve the country by speaking.

And indeed, since that time, events have taken a more and more serious turn. What has happened in North Africa during the past four years has been a harsh ordeal. What is now happening in Algeria in relation to Metropolitan France and in Metropolitan France in relation to Algeria may lead to a new and extremely grave national crisis.

But this may also be the beginning of a sort of resurrection. That is why it seems to me that the time may have come when it would be possible for me to be directly useful to France once again.

Useful for what reason? Because some while ago certain things happened, certain things were accomplished, things which the nations associated with ours have not forgotten and which foreign countries have remembered. Perhaps this sort of moral capital, in the face of the difficulties that assail us, the misfortunes that threaten us—perhaps this capital might have a certain weight in political life at a time of serious confusion.

From *Major Addresses, Statements and Press Conferences of General Charles de Gaulle, May 19, 1958–January 31, 1964* (New York: French Embassy, Press & Information Division, n.d.), pp. 1–6.

Useful also because it is a fact of which we must all take note—whoever we may be—it is a fact that the exclusive party system has not solved, is not solving and will not solve the mighty problems which confront us, especially that of the association of France with the peoples of Africa, and also that of the coexistence of the various communities living in Algeria, and even that of internal harmony within each of these communities.

The fact is there. I repeat that everyone must recognize it. The battles that are taking place in Algeria and the fever raging there are but the consequences of this lack.

And if things continue in the way they have started, we all know perfectly well that the system of government, as it now exists, will be unable to find a solution. It may make plans, it may express intentions, it may even take action and make efforts in various directions. I repeat that it will not reach a solution, and consequently we run the risk that one day these solutions will be imposed from without, which undoubtedly would be the most disastrous outcome possible.

Useful, finally, because I stand alone, because I associate myself with no party or organization whatsoever, because for the last six years I have not been politically active and for the last three years I have not issued any statement; in short, because I am a man who belongs to no one and who belongs to everyone.

How can I be useful? Well—if the people wish it—just as I was in the previous great national crisis: at the head of the Government of the French Republic. Having said this, I am now prepared, gentlemen, to answer the questions you wish to ask.

Question: General, you said that you were prepared to assume the powers of the Republic. What exactly do you mean by that?

Answer: When you assume the powers of the Republic, this can only mean those powers that the Republic itself has delegated to you. That seems to me like a perfectly clear statement. Now about the man who made that statement.

The Republic? There was a time when it was denied, betrayed by the parties themselves. And it was I who rebuilt its armies, its laws, its name. I fought the war in order to obtain victory for France, but I did it in such a way that it also was a victory for the Republic. I did this along with all those who, without a single exception, wanted to join me, and as their leader I reestablished the Republic at home. In its name, on its behalf, in accordance with its guiding spirit, my Government accomplished a tremendous task of regeneration. Political regeneration: the vote granted to women, citizenship given to the Moslems of Algeria, the beginning of associating within the French Union peoples who formerly were dependent on us. Economic and social regeneration: the nationalization of the mines, of the gas industry, of the electric industry, of the Bank of France, of the principal credit establishments, of the Renault works; the establishment of labor-management committees, organization of social security on such a scale and in such a manner that the workers would be protected from centuries-old scourges, family allowances granted in such a way that families would be helped and also that the birth rate would rise . . . which it did; the establishment of certain organs for the development, the modernization and the prosperity of the country; for instance, the investment plan which would draw from the resources of the present the means of ensuring the wealth of the future; the Petroleum Bureau, so that exploration could be carried on in Metropolitan France and in the Overseas Territories for this source of energy which we absolutely must have; a start in the development of atomic energy through the establishment of the commission for that purpose.

When all this was done, I gave the people a chance to speak as I had promised to do. And when it had elected its representatives, I passed on to them—without any reservation, without any condition—the powers I was charged with. When I saw that the parties had reacted like the *émigrés* of old, that is to say that they had forgotten nothing and learned nothing, and that consequently, for me as for the others, any genuine Government was impossible, I withdrew. I did not try to force their hand. Subsequently they drew up a poor constitution. They did this in spite of me, against me. I did not attempt to violate it in any way.

Then, in order to try to put an end to the confusion and to create a just and strong state, I instituted the Rally of the French People, inviting everybody to join it, regardless of origin, ideas, or sentiments, or even of party labels; I did this only to obtain, through legal means, the institutions that seemed necessary to me. It so happened that the old system succeeded in leading astray, little by little, the elected representatives of the R.P.F., so that I no longer had any means of action within the law. So I went back home.

Now when there are—and it is not the first time that it has happened in eighteen years—when there are professional saviors of the Republic, who furthermore would not have restored the Republic if they had been alone; when there are professional saviors of the Republic, who impute evil purposes to me, such as violating public liberties, destroying republican institutions, uprooting the rights of the labor unions, I let it go . . . and pass on; which does not prevent me, as well as many others, from asking them what they are doing, these professional saviors, with liberated France and the restored Republic.

Question: How do you judge the current events in Algeria, the revolt of the population, the attitude of the Army?

Answer: In Algeria there is a population of French extraction, as well as Moslem, which for years has been living in the midst of war, murders, and violence. And this population has realized, ever since this situation has been going on, that the present system established in Paris cannot solve its problems. Even more important, it has seen this system recently turn toward [good] offices from abroad. This population has heard a man—a man who, by the way, is my friend and who was at the time the Minister for Algeria—declare publicly, on the spot, "We are headed for a diplomatic Dienbienphu." How could this population, being in such a fever, not revolt in the long run? They see, in Paris, one crisis succeed another indefinitely, and the same representatives of the same parties distribute amongst themselves the same ministerial posts and mingle together, without anything either definite or effective coming out of it. Once more, how could such a population fail to revolt in the long run? Then, this population has sought, it is now seeking, a remedy for its misfortunes outside parliamentary coalitions. It is absolutely normal and natural; and, then, it cries "Vive de Gaulle," as all Frenchmen do, in anguish and in hope.

And besides, this population now offers the magnificent spectacle of an immense fraternization which may afford a psychological and moral foundation for tomorrow's agreements and arrangements—which is infinitely better, of course, than combats and ambushes. Moreover, the best proof that the French of Algeria do not want at any price to break away from Metropolitan France is precisely the fact that they say "Vive de Gaulle." One does not shout "Vive de Gaulle" when one is not on the side of the nation.

The behavior of the Army—in these circumstances, the Army noted this tremendous popular emotion. The Army considered it its duty to prevent this emotion from turning into disorder. This it did and it was right to do so. Furthermore, the Army, as you well know, is also profoundly affected by the tragedy through which the country is passing—that country which it serves very well and often at great sacrifice, sometimes despite a good deal of misunderstanding. The Army, I say, feels in the depth of its being all the disadvantages and the mediocrity which are characteristic of the deficiency [in the system of Government] that I stressed earlier. And then, finally, this Army in Algeria is in close contact with the population and consequently cannot escape or prevent itself from experiencing the same feelings as these people, and the same overwhelming desire as they to see Paris at last solving its problems.

I understand full well the attitude and the action of the military command in Algeria and, in my opinion, it would be absurd and deplorable just because there was no authority left in Algeria except a *de facto* authority— it would be absurd, under this pretext, to cut all forms of communication between Metropolitan France and Algeria. It would be absurd because it would be to the detriment of the Frenchmen who are there, whether they are of French extraction or Moslem, civilians or soldiers, and even to the detriment of many Frenchmen on this side of the sea. It would seriously compromise France's position and it would create a state of affairs, the outcome of which cannot be known. Therefore, I believe that the best thing to do—and even the only thing to do—would be to prevent Algeria from drawing away from France; Algeria must remain with us. As for the Army, it is normally an instrument of the state, providing, of course, that there is a state.

I need not stress the urgency of finding a solution; a decision must be made quickly because events and people's thinking are moving fast.

Question: M. Guy Mollet, after his recent speech in the National Assembly, listed certain questions concerning the procedure for your eventual return to power. Would you like to comment on them?

Answer: I have the highest regard for Guy Mollet. I don't hesitate to say so. During the war he fought for France and for liberty, risking everything. He was one of my companions and I recall that after the Liberation I went to Arras on my way back from visiting our mines which were in a pitiful state. After greeting and expressing our confidence in the miners whom the country so sorely needed, I spoke to the people of Arras from the balcony of the Town Hall on the main square, and I shall always remember that Guy Mollet was there at my side. Those are things that one never forgets. Afterwards, I did not see him again. Why? I do not know. But I have followed his political career from a distance. I will not say that I have always agreed with what he has said and done or tried to do. Moreover, in the regime in its present form, no man of merit can succeed, but what he has done has never altered my esteem for him.

So much for my feelings. And now there are Guy Mollet's questions . . . I have been told and I have read in the newspapers that he raised a certain number of questions: first, second, third, fourth. . . .

My answer is that if de Gaulle were led to assume—or if he should have delegated to him—exceptional powers for an exceptional task, in an exceptional time, it is obvious that this could not be done according to the rites and procedure that are so habitual that everyone is tired of them . . . and a procedure would have to be adopted—also an exceptional one—for investiture from the National Assembly, for example.

You know that events speak very strongly for themselves, and when there is basic agreement procedures can have considerable flexibility. All my public actions are there to prove this.

Should the occasion arise, I would undoubtedly make it known to an authorized person what sort of procedure seemed adequate to me.

In case I should be asked by the French people to arbitrate, that would be all the more reason for me not to specify at the present time what the conclusions of my arbitration would be: indeed, the parties concerned must be heard, a decision must be rendered and we must be in a position to carry it out—all these are factors that do not at present exist. I know of no judge who hands down his decision before hearing the case.

Question: Don't you think that the statement you made on May 15 had the effect of reviving the movement in Algiers which was on the point of dying out?

Answer: I wish to give courage and strength to those French people who want to remake the national unity, whether they are on one side of the Mediterranean or the other. There is no other question. The rest is so much talk—talk from a world that is not mine. Later on we will understand the attitude of those responsible; there is another fact, moreover, and it is that at present generals are being treated as seditious persons, while up to now, as far as I know, no penalty has been inflicted on them by the public authorities, which have even delegated more authority to them. In that case, I who have no public authority—why do you want me to treat them as seditious persons?

You see, in this tragedy, one has to be calm and collected. One has to be serious. It is absolutely necessary. I am endeavoring to be so.

Question: What would be your policy regarding relations with Morocco and Tunisia?

Answer: I have just said that the great problem to be solved is the very question of the association of France with the peoples of Africa, and especially with those whom you have just mentioned. Everybody knows my feelings and purposes in this respect.

Question: What would your attitude be toward basic public liberties?

Answer: Did I ever make any attempt on basic public liberties? On the contrary, I restored them . . . Why should I, at sixty-seven, begin a career as a dictator? . . .

It is not possible to solve the serious national crisis of the present time within the limits of everyday routine. As a matter of fact, one of the politicians recently charged with untangling the famous crisis, which has really been going on for twelve years, this politician himself admitted that it was necessary to form a government but a government which would be different from the others.

I find that our country has been extremely weakened and that it is struggling against great difficulties, and even great threats, in a disturbed world. I find that France holds some good cards for the future: the birth rate; an economy that has gone beyond the stage of routine; French technology, which is constantly developing; the oil which has been discovered in large quantities, and so on.

These cards which we hold may lead, in the near future, to the resurgence of France, to great prosperity in which all Frenchmen must share and in which the people who need and ask for our assistance may also be associated. But it is true that, for the moment, we are in a sad plight, and that is why my last word will be: "I thought it would be useful for the country to say what I have said. Now I shall return to my village and I shall remain there at the disposal of the country."

The Idea of National Independence (General de Gaulle's television and radio broadcast of 27 April 1965)

In the present-day world, riddled with problems and infinite potential dangers, where the needs and ambitions of states clash bitterly, what is the role of France?

Let us recognize that, having once been a colossus among nations in terms of population, wealth, and power, we are now returning, by a narrow squeak, to reclaim our international role. About a century ago our demographic and economic expansion, and at the same time our strength, began to decline. Then followed the two world wars which devastated and ruined us, while two great nations, the United States and Russia, came, in turn, to the summit. In our present diminished situation, the temptation of resignation, which is for an enfeebled people what submission is for a humiliated man, might have carried us irretrievably towards decadence. All the more so, since long accustomed to being in first place—at times not without conceit—we now ran the risk of doubting ourselves excessively. We could have become discouraged by comparing our statistics with those of the total population of the two giant countries, or of the aggregate production of their factories and mines, or of the number of satellites they have launched into orbit around the earth, or the number of megatons their engines of destruction can deliver.

Indeed, after the sudden reawakening of French confidence and pride which pulled us from a fatal abyss in the course of the Second World War, and in spite of the vital forces which reappeared among us with renewed vigor, a tendency towards self-effacement momentarily surfaced, to the point of being established in doctrine and in policy. That is why some partisans advocated giving ourselves over body and soul to the Totalitarian Empire. Or why others claimed that we needed not only to remain the allies of our allies—as is sensible—as long as we were threatened by domination from the East, but also that we should let ourselves be absorbed into the Atlantic system, in whose bosom our defense, our economy, and our com-

From General de Gaulle's television and radio broadcast of 27 April 1965. Translated for this volume by Kent Wright.

mitments would all necessarily depend on American arms, American material ascendancy, and American policy. The same people, with the same intentions, expected that our nation, instead of participating, as is natural, in the organized cooperation of the free nations of the Old Continent, would be literally dissolved into a so-called integrated Europe. And, for want of the jurisdiction that comes with the sovereignty of peoples or the responsibility of states, this integrated Europe would be automatically subordinated to the protector across the ocean. Thus there would doubtless remain French workers, peasants, engineers, teachers, bureaucrats, deputies, and cabinet ministers. But there would be no more France. Well! . . . the main thing about the last seven years is that we have resisted the sirens of surrender and have chosen independence.

It is true that independence comes with conditions attached, none of them easy ones. But, as can be seen, we are successfully meeting those conditions. In the political domain, this means that without disavowing our American friendship, we are conducting ourselves as the Europeans that we are; and that in this capacity, we are attempting to reestablish, from one end of our continent to the other, an equilibrium founded on the mutual understanding and the cooperation of all the peoples that inhabit it. It is good that we are again becoming friends with Germany, that we are proposing a genuine solidarity of the Six to our neighbors on both sides of the Rhine and the Alps, that we are resuming with the Eastern countries, to the extent that they are emerging from their crushing fetters, relations of working understanding that formerly linked us to them. As for the problems of the rest of the universe, our independence leads us to adopt a policy in conformity with our own conceptions, namely that no exercise of hegemony by any power, no foreign intervention in the internal affairs of a state, no attempt to forbid any nation to enter into peaceful relations with any other, can ever be justified. On the contrary, the higher interest of the human race demands that each nation be responsible for itself, free from encroachments, aided in its progress without terms of obedience. From this follows our condemnation of the war in Asia, which intensifies daily. From this follows as well our favorable attitude toward the efforts for human liberation and national organization undertaken by various countries in Latin America, our cooperation in the development of a good number of new African states, the relations we have established with China, and so forth. In short, France now has a policy, and it is made in Paris.

With respect to security in this atomic age, our independence requires that we ourselves possess the necessary means to deter a potential enemy, without dismissing our alliances, but also without leaving our destiny in the hands of our allies. We are providing ourselves with these means. Without doubt, they are thrusting a laudable renewal upon us. Yet they cost us no more than those we would have been obliged to furnish to the Atlantic organization, without necessarily being protected in return, if we continued to belong to it as auxiliary subordinates. Therefore, let us reach the point where no state in the world could deal deathblows to us without receiving them in return; for this is surely the best possible guarantee.

In order to safeguard our independence in the economic, scientific, and technical sphere, while being forced to come to grips with the enormous wealth of some nations, without however refusing relations of exchange with them, we must see to it that our activities remain, by and large, under French administration and management. We must also and at all cost maintain competition in the key sectors—those which determine the value, the autonomy, and the life of the entire industrial apparatus; which call for the most research, experimentation, and improvement of equipment; which require numerous qualified teams of scientists, technicians, and workers. Finally, when the time comes, in a given branch, to combine our inventions, our capacities, and our resources with those of another nation, we ought to choose the one which is closest to us and whom we need not fear will crush us with its own weight.

For this reason, we are imposing upon ourselves a financial, economic, and monetary stability which obviates the necessity of resorting to foreign aid. We are converting into gold the excess dollars that have come our way as a result of the American balance of payments deficit. In the last six years we have increased the funding of research sixfold. We are organizing an industrial and agricultural common market with Germany, Italy, Belgium, Holland, and Luxembourg. We are building a tunnel through Mount Blanc in conjunction with Italy; we are building canals on the Moselle River in association with Germany and Luxembourg. We are joining forces with England to construct the first supersonic passenger airplane in the world; and we are prepared to extend this Franco-British collaboration to other types of civilian and military projects. We have just concluded an accord with the Soviet Union for the development and use of our color-television technology. In short, however large the glass which is offered us from abroad, we prefer to drink out of our own glass, while sharing a toast with the people around us.

Certainly, the independence which we are displaying once again in every area does not fail to astonish, indeed scandalize, many for whom the enfeoffment of France has been a habit and a rule. They speak of Machiavellianism, as if the most clear-sighted conduct did not consist precisely in our following our own path; they are alarmed by our isolation, at a time when we have never been more surrounded by eager activity. On the other hand, the fact that we have reclaimed our faculty of judgment and action with regard to all problems, seems sometimes to offend a State which, by virtue of its power, considers itself invested with a supreme and universal responsibility. But who knows whether, one day, the advantage this friendly nation might find in an independent France, will outweigh the displeasure it is experiencing at present? In the end, our reappearance as a nation with free hands obviously alters the global contest which, since Yalta, seemed henceforth limited to two partners. But since the liberty, equality, and fraternity of peoples decidedly do not profit from this partition of the universe into two hegemonies, and, thus, two camps, a different order and a different equilibrium are necessary for peace. Who can better sustain them than we, provided we remain true to ourselves?

Frenchwomen, Frenchmen, you understand this! For us, for all, more than ever, France must be France!

Long live the Republic!

Long live France!

41. Jean Monnet, *A Red-Letter Day for European Unity*

One of the most inspiring statesmen of the twentieth century, Jean Monnet (1888–1979), more than any other single individual, was responsible for the creation of the European Community in 1956–57. He has been fairly described as a "prophet and a revolutionary in international relations."[1] Monnet was born in Cognac, the son of the owner of a French brandy firm. At eighteen Monnet went to Canada to market the firm's products, beginning a life-long attachment to the New World. During the First World War Monnet served as French representative to the Allied Maritime Transport Committee. From 1919 to 1923 he worked as deputy secretary-general of the League of Nations. In the later 1920s and 1930s he charted a career as an influential international businessman and banker, working on the periphery of high politics.

With the outbreak of the war in 1939 Monnet became the chairman of the Anglo-French Coordinating Committee for economic affairs and after the fall of France worked on the British Supply Council in Washington, where he played a role in the creation of Lend-Lease. As commissioner for supplies and reconstruction on the French National Liberation Committee in Algiers, Monnet mediated between rival French exiled political leaders. Following the war General de Gaulle appointed Monnet the first director of the French Planning Commissariat, where he earned a reputation for brilliant technocratic reforms.

In April 1950 Monnet and several French "Europeanist" colleagues

1. Hans A. Schmitt, *Journal of Modern History* 51 (1979): 793.

drafted a memorandum which was the basis of the Schuman Plan, launching the European Coal and Steel Community (ECSC, which France, West Germany, Italy, the Netherlands, Belgium, and Luxembourg joined) and thus contributed significantly to a profound achievement, impossible between 1870 and 1939: permanent concord between France and Germany. Monnet served as the first President of the ECSC's High Authority between 1952 and 1955. Upon his retirement he organized in October 1955 a semi-public lobbying group of thirty-three high-level European politicians and union leaders, the Action Committee for the United States of Europe, to push the member states of the ECSC toward fuller economic integration. The Action Committee lobbied for a European common market, working in parallel with the official representatives of "The Six," constituted in an intergovernmental committee headed by Paul-Henri Spaak. Monnet's Action Committee has been described as something "like the collective democratic conscience of the European Community." [2]

In the following selection, containing two brief speeches which Monnet presented to the Joint Meeting of the Members of the Consultative Assembly of the Council of Europe and of the Members of the Common Assembly of the ECSC on 22 June 1953, Monnet described the early work of the Coal and Steel Community. But he also reaffirmed his hope that a united Europe would extend beyond the boundaries of The Six, a vision which, in the current membership of the European Community (consisting of twelve member states, including Britain, Spain, and Portugal), ultimately found fruition.

Mr. President, Ladies and Gentlemen, on behalf of my colleagues of the High Authority and myself, I wish to say how very pleased we are to have this meeting to-day with the members of the Common Assembly and the members of the Consultative Assembly. The co-operation between the Council of Europe and the European Coal and Steel Community has now definitely entered a concrete phase. . . .

In respect of coal and steel, the Community has set up a huge European market of more than 150 million consumers, *i.e.* equal in number to the population of the United States of America. Under the terms of the Treaty, customs duties and quota restrictions have been abolished between Germany, Belgium, France, Italy, Luxembourg and the Netherlands; the principal discriminations in respect of transport have been done away with.

2. Quoted (from an anonymous source) in Richard Mayne, "The Role of Jean Monnet," *Government and Opposition* 2 (1967): 369.

From the *Joint Meeting of the Members of the Consultative Assembly of the Council of Europe and of the Members of the Common Assembly of the European Community of Coal and Steel. Official Report of the Debate,* Strasbourg, 22 June 1953, pp. 8–12, 118, 120–23.

Coal and steel, iron-ore and scrap can now circulate freely, without restriction or discrimination, except for such transitional measures as have been taken for the purpose of avoiding too abrupt impacts, and facilitating the necessary readjustments.

At the risk of repeating myself—and I apologise for this to the members of the Common Assembly—I wish to say that the decisions of this first European Executive, which is the High Authority, are being carried out in our six countries as if they were but one country. This is, indeed, one of the essential transformations which our enterprise has brought about, and is the test of its success.

The members of the Assembly of the Community who are sitting here among you are, at this moment, in their own session, exercising their sovereign right of control over the action of the High Authority. The Court of Justice, which has had a number of appeals against the decisions of the High Authority laid before it, will be pronouncing final judgment.

This first Common Market, these first supranational institutions, are the beginnings of a united Europe.

I am happy to welcome here, in this Assembly, the representatives of the countries which have recognized this new reality by accrediting permanent delegations to Luxembourg: Sweden, Norway, Denmark and Austria. I must not forget Switzerland, although she is not a member of the Council of Europe. Great Britain was the first to appoint its delegation in Luxembourg, with instructions to establish an intimate and lasting association with the new Community.

The attitude of the United States is well-known to you; a permanent delegation was appointed to the Community by the President of the United States, and the letters recently exchanged between President Eisenhower and the Foreign Affairs Committees of Congress, which have just been made public, confirm in no uncertain manner the support which the United States is giving to our Community. In this correspondence, President Eisenhower re-affirmed that "the uniting of Europe is a necessity for the prosperity of Europeans and for the peace of the whole world." He says "the Coal and Steel Community appears to me to be the most hopeful and constructive development so far toward the economic and political integration of Europe."

Our Community is an open Community. We want other countries to join on a equal footing with us. I would remind you here that on the very first day when, in the name of the French Government, M. Robert Schuman made his statement of 9th May, 1950, he invited all the nations of Europe to join us, to give up the divisions of the past and, by pooling their coal and steel production, to ensure the establishment of common bases for economic development as the first stage towards the European federation.

This meeting to-day, and the co-operation which we are desirous of developing with the Council of Europe will, I hope, have the effect of persuading certain countries whose delegates are still sitting only in the Consultative Assembly, to take their seats among us in the Common Assembly also, in the very near future. For, as I have said repeatedly before the Common Assembly, and I must say it again before this Assembly, we are not just an association of producers. Ours is the responsibility for setting up the first European Community. It is our ambition to make it as comprehensive as possible. We feel that the association of Great Britain is essential to this undertaking. Now that the Community has become an established fact, I have no doubt that, between us, Great Britain and ourselves will find the right shape and form for this intimate and lasting association for which the British delegation in Luxembourg, so ably led by Sir Cecil Weir, has received instructions to lay the foundations with us. As far as we are concerned, we are resolved to put forward concrete proposals towards the accomplishment of this great task. . . .

All the countries of Europe, even those which are not members of the Community, are interested in the action which we shall now be able to take, with the Common Market set up, and which, as the High Authority has made known to the Common Assembly, will, in addition to the association with Great Britain, be concerned with three main issues:

—to develop production and provide for the financing of this expansion;
—to complete the setting up of the Common Market by putting an end to the cartels which interfere with it;
—to prepare ways and means for enabling the workers to share in the advantages of an improved and increased production.

Our Community embodies the principle underlying all further developments. This principle is very simple: it means the pooling of resources, the acceptance of common rules administered by common institutions vested with effective powers.

The Consultative Assembly has recently been apprised of the proposals which are now being submitted to the six Governments for the setting up of a Political Authority based on a parliament elected by direct universal suffrage, under whose authority both the Coal and Steel Community and the Defence Community will be placed.

Rules and institutions do not change men's natures but they do bring about a change in their behaviour towards one another. That is the lesson which civilisation has taught us. The rules and institutions which we are establishing will contribute essentially towards guiding the action of the peoples of Europe in the paths of peace. (Applause.)

[Jean Monnet spoke again, at the conclusion of the assembly's debates:]

Mr. President, Ladies and Gentlemen, the experiment we have been making to-day will, in my view, make this a red-letter day in the history of the development of European unity.

It is the first time the Representatives to the Common Assembly of the six countries have met together with those of other European countries.

For the first time they have freely, frankly and unreservedly discussed among themselves their common problems. One of the characteristics of the debate which has taken place to-day was the complete freedom of expression not only of members of the Common Assembly and those of the Consultative Assembly, but even—as you have seen—among members of the Common Assembly.

Such freedom of expression, the frankness with which the representatives of countries which are not Members of the Community put their questions, and the frank manner in which Representatives to the Common Assembly stated their objections are, to me, an assurance that in holding this meeting to-day we have succeeded in finding a form of procedure which will, in the not distant future, yield excellent results. . . .

Let me repeat what I have already told the Common Assembly several times, namely that we propose to discuss with the British delegation at Luxembourg without delay concrete forms of association between the High Authority and Great Britain.

I cannot say at this stage precisely what those forms will be; not that I wish to make a mystery out of them. We have fairly clearcut intentions and ideas on this matter, but you will, naturally, understand that we are required to convey them to the British delegation which has been instructed by the United Kingdom Government to co-operate with us in seeking such close and lasting forms of association. You may at least rest assured that in the very near future we shall be taking up this matter with the British delegation in its most concrete form.

Why have I to-day this impression of reality? Why have all the questions seemed to tend towards the reality we embody and the hope we represent?

Because, for men, reality is only satisfactory when it fulfils their hopes at the same time.

The Coal and Steel Community has begun to solve the hitherto insoluble common problems of Europeans, and has done so by overriding national differences and the rigidity of national sovereignties. It has done so by applying, as I said this morning, a very simple principle, which has, indeed, contributed to the spread of civilisation for centuries, namely men's acceptance of common rules.

Our European countries, till now divided, traditionally hostile to one another, transforming questions of prestige into problems such as, in a community governed by common rules, would have settled themselves, found themselves at one period of their history constrained to apply rules of their own. Then, at loggerheads with one another, each operating its own rules, they sought to overstep their narrow frontiers and dominate their neighbours.

The history of Europe, when we stand back to consider it, bears, I suggest, all the signs of one of the world's greatest tragedies.

Let us remember that the territories in which the men who have been meeting together in this Chamber first saw the light of day have for centuries been in the forefront of civilisation, that the greatest thinkers and scientists were born in these lands and that the whole world owes its development to the drive and intelligence of men who were the sons of our countries.

The continent of Europe has not, however, changed. Men were what they were because they were born on European soil and kept abreast of their times. That I believe to be an essential condition of human progress. For men to be themselves, they must be in harmony with the rest of the world.

Europe, however, no longer knows that harmony. Our countries can no longer ensure their nations' prosperity and can no longer, separately, ensure their protection. They are no longer able to give to the world the benefits which their intelligence, earnestness and labour should enable them to supply.

It is my conviction, shared by all the members of the High Authority and by those who, before it came into being, took part in the inception of the first European Community, that the world cannot achieve stability and peace without a strong and prosperous Europe whose sons keep abreast of the times. *(Applause.)*

After all, in this undertaking, which has begun with coal and steel, there is an ultimate objective, namely a human objective. It is the people of Europe who are concerned. Our aim must be to re-establish conditions which eliminate fear and suspicion from human relations—or perhaps I should say suspicion and fear. Just consider what suspicion and fear mean to European activity. For centuries they have been responsible to a vast extent for the anxieties of the inhabitants of Europe, with results with which you are familiar.

The common coal and steel market is a beginning, an experiment. Today's meeting shows us that that experiment is succeeding. Indeed, it is the beginning of a wider, more comprehensive market, leading the way to vast production and the use of technical and material resources within our grasp, whose use depends only upon ourselves, but which the present form of the countries of Europe prevents us from utilising.

However, as I said just now, the purpose of our work is more remote. What we have to do is to create conditions which will enable the inhabitants of Europe to live without fear and suspicion and to keep abreast of world progress. To this end, the new organisation, to which the countries of Europe will surrender a part of their sovereignty, will keep in mind what is best for Europe as a whole and will take decisions under the democratic control of a Political Community and of a European Parliament elected by universal suffrage, solely in the interests of the Community. Only such organisations are likely to show great wisdom.

A long time ago I was struck by a remark made by a Swiss philosopher, who said: "Man's experience is being continually renewed. Only organisations become wiser; they accumulate collective experience and, as a result of that experience and wisdom, man, subjected to the same rules, will undergo no change of nature, but a gradual transformation of behaviour."

It is therein that I would find justification for such common institutions, if any such justification were needed. When I think that Frenchmen, Germans, Belgians, Dutchmen, Italians and Luxemburgers will all follow common rules and, in doing so, will view their common problem in the same light and that, as a result, their behaviour towards one another will have fundamentally changed, I realise that definite progress has been made in relations between the countries and men of Europe.

My colleagues and I were deeply moved by the remarks made by several speakers, particularly by M. Teitgen and M. Wigny. They said how proud they were that for the first time—although there was indeed nothing difficult about it—we were able to go to the United States without having to ask for anything.

I find great comfort and encouragement in this reaction, since it was, above all, a question of the dignity of the people of Europe, rather than of a great market or future security. If by our journey to the United States and in such a simple way we have been able to contribute to their peace of mind, then we are proud and happy to have done so.

Mr. President, Ladies and Gentlemen, before concluding I should again like to say how glad we are that this meeting should have taken place. Everything you have told us, and even the criticisms—in which we have, for reasons I have just explained to you, discerned grounds for feeling encouraged—have convinced us not only that the road along which the six countries of the Community have set out is the right road, but that we must continue to seek even more zealously ways and means of achieving a more complete understanding with the other countries of Europe. When they have seen and understood, as we have done, what this new and living Europe means for them, they will, one of these days, I hope, themselves join in. *(Loud applause.)*

5
Moving Forward

42. Hannah Arendt, *On Humanity in Dark Times: Thoughts about Lessing*

Hannah Arendt (1906–75) was born near Hannover, Germany, and educated at the universities of Marburg and Heidelberg. In 1930 she received her Ph.D. with a thesis on "St. Augustine's Concept of Love," the product of her training under Karl Jaspers and Martin Heidegger. With both men, the former her mentor and patron, the latter (for a time) her close friend, she maintained lifelong intellectual relationships which cut across the disruptions of war and the tribulations of peace. Arendt's grounding in classical literature and German philosophy constituted the principal moorings of her rich, varied intellectual life. She wrote to Gershom Scholem, indignantly denying that she had "come from the German Left" in the 1920s and 1930s: "If I can be said to 'have come from anywhere,' it is from the tradition of German philosophy." [1]

Fleeing the Nazis in 1933 Arendt went first to Paris and in 1941 to the United States, where she worked as a director of the Conference on Jewish Relations and as the executive director of Jewish Cultural Reconstruction, an agency formed to save Jewish cultural materials confiscated by the Nazis. Sympathetic to Zionist ideals, she also offered provocative criticisms of the new Israeli state in the context of her support for federative coexistence between Jews and Arabs in Palestine. A "stateless person" and exemplar of a century whose most typical inhabitants were refugees, she found her second home in America, where, as she commented in 1975, "assimilation is not the price of citizenship." [2]

In 1951 Arendt published her *Origins of Totalitarianism*, which, together with such works as *The Human Condition* (1958) and *Between Past and Future* (1961), established her as a major social and political

---

1. *Encounter* 22 (1964): 53.
2. Quoted in Elisabeth Young-Bruehl, *Hannah Arendt. For the Love of the World* (New Haven, 1982), p. 73.

philosopher of the twentieth century. Arendt's *Eichmann in Jerusalem* (1963), a provocative analysis of the "banality of evil," raised fundamental moral issues involving German culpability and Jewish complicity in the Holocaust which have not been (and perhaps can and should never be) settled. Her work sustained, as Leonard Krieger has noted, "a continuous and explanatory interaction among social criticism, cultural analysis and the philosophical principle in society itself." [3] She aspired to a critical, yet integrated vision of the human community, never losing hold of the threads of intellectual intelligibility, liberal decency, and, in an age she herself recognized as one of an extraordinary destruction of values, a belief in the possibility of joining creative thinking, political action, and moral being.

Between 1963 and 1967 Arendt served as professor on the Committee on Social Thought at the University of Chicago. From 1967 until her death she was associated with the New School for Social Research in New York.

The text below is the lecture which Arendt delivered in 1959, in German, upon receiving the Lessing Prize from the city of Hamburg.

I

The distinction conferred by a free city, and a prize that bears the name of Lessing, are a great honor. I admit that I do not know how I have come to receive it, and also that it has not been altogether easy for me to come to terms with it. In saying this I can ignore entirely the delicate question of merit. In this very respect an honor gives us a forcible lesson in modesty; for it implies that it is not for us to judge our own merits as we judge the merits and accomplishments of others. In awards, the world speaks out, and if we accept the award and express our gratitude for it, we can do so only by ignoring ourselves and acting entirely within the framework of our attitude toward the world, toward a world and public to which we owe the space into which we speak and in which we are heard.

But the honor not only reminds us emphatically of the gratitude we owe the world; it also, to a very high degree, obligates us to it. Since we can always reject the honor, by accepting it we are not only strengthened in our

3. Leonard Krieger, "The Historical Hannah Arendt," *Journal of Modern History* 48 (1976): 674.

From Hannah Arendt, *Men in Dark Times,* translated by Clara and Richard Winston (New York: Harcourt, Brace & World, 1968), pp. 3–31; ©1968 by Hannah Arendt. Reprinted by permission of Harcourt Brace Jovanovich, Inc., and Jonathan Cape Ltd.

position within the world but are accepting a kind of commitment to it. That a person appears in public at all, and that the public receives and confirms him, is by no means a matter to be taken for granted. Only the genius is driven by his very gifts into public life, and is exempted from any decision of this sort. In his case alone, honors only continue the concord with the world, sound an existing harmony in full publicity, which has arisen independently of all considerations and decisions, independently also of all obligations, as if it were a natural phenomenon erupting into human society. To this phenomenon we can in truth apply what Lessing once said about the man of genius in two of his finest lines of verse.

Was ihn bewegt, bewegt. Was ihm gefällt, gefällt.
Sein glücklicher Geschmack ist der Geschmack der Welt.

(What moves him, moves. What pleases him, pleases.
His felicitous taste is the world's taste.)

Nothing in our time is more dubious, it seems to me, than our attitude toward the world, nothing less to be taken for granted than that concord with what appears in public which an honor imposes on us, and the existence of which it affirms. In our century even genius has been able to develop only in conflict with the world and the public realm, although it naturally finds, as it always has done, its own peculiar concord with its audience. But the world and the people who inhabit it are not the same. The world lies between people, and this in-between—much more than (as is often thought) men or even man—is today the object of the greatest concern and the most obvious upheaval in almost all the countries of the globe. Even where the world is still halfway in order, or is kept halfway in order, the public realm has lost the power of illumination which was originally part of its very nature. More and more people in the countries of the Western world, which since the decline of the ancient world has regarded freedom from politics as one of the basic freedoms, make use of this freedom and have retreated from the world and their obligations within it. This withdrawal from the world need not harm an individual; he may even cultivate great talents to the point of genius and so by a detour be useful to the world again. But with each such retreat an almost demonstrable loss to the world takes place; what is lost is the specific and usually irreplaceable in-between which should have formed between this individual and his fellow men.

When we thus consider the real meaning of public honors and prizes under present conditions, it may occur to us that the Hamburg Senate found a solution to the problem rather like that of Columbus' egg when it decided to link the city's prize with the name of Lessing. For Lessing never felt at home in the world as it then existed and probably never wanted to, and still after his own fashion he always remained committed to it. Special and unique circumstances governed this relationship. The German public was not prepared for him and as far as I know never honored him in his lifetime. He himself lacked, according to his own judgment, that happy, natural concord with the world, a combination of merit and good fortune, which both he and Goethe considered the sign of genius. Lessing believed he was indebted to criticism for something that "comes very close to genius," but which never quite achieved that natural harmonization with the world in which Fortuna smiles when Virtù appears. All that may have been important enough, but it was not decisive. It almost seems as if at some time he had decided to pay homage to genius, to the man of "felicitous taste," but himself to follow those whom he once half ironically called "the wise men" who "make the pillars of the best-known truths shake wherever they let their eyes fall." His attitude toward the world was neither positive nor negative, but radically critical and, in respect to the public realm of his time, completely revolutionary. But it was also an attitude that remained indebted to the world, never left the solid ground of the world, and never went to the extreme of sentimental utopianism. In Lessing the revolutionary temper was associated with a curious kind of partiality which clung to concrete details with an exaggerated, almost pedantic carefulness, and gave rise to many misunderstandings. One component of Lessing's greatness was the fact that he never allowed supposed objectivity to cause him to lose sight of the real relationship to the world and the real status in the world of the things or men he attacked or praised. That did not help his credit in Germany, where the true nature of criticism is less well understood than elsewhere. It was hard for the Germans to grasp that justice has little to do with objectivity in the ordinary sense.

Lessing never made his peace with the world in which he lived. He enjoyed "challenging prejudices" and "telling the truth to the court minions." Dearly though he paid for these pleasures, they were literally pleasures. Once when he was attempting to explain to himself the source of "tragic pleasure," he said that "all passions, even the most unpleasant, are as passions pleasant" because "they make us . . . more conscious of our existence, they make us feel more real." This sentence strikingly recalls the Greek doctrine of passions, which counted anger, for example, among the pleasant emotions but reckoned hope along with fear among the evils. This evaluation rests on differences in reality, exactly as in Lessing; not, however, in the sense that reality is measured by the force with which the passion affects the soul but rather by the amount of reality the passion transmits to it. In hope, the soul overleaps reality, as in fear it shrinks back from it. But anger, and above all Lessing's kind of anger, reveals and exposes the world just as Lessing's kind of laughter in *Minna von Barnhelm* seeks to bring about reconciliation with the world. Such laughter helps one to find a place in the world, but ironically, which is to say, without selling one's soul to it. Pleasure, which is fundamentally the intensified awareness of reality, springs from a passionate openness to the world and love of it. Not even the knowledge that man may be destroyed by the world detracts from the "tragic pleasure."

If Lessing's aesthetics, in contrast to Aristotle's, sees even fear as a variety of pity, the pity we feel for ourselves, the reason is perhaps that Lessing is trying to strip fear of its escapist aspect in order to save it as a passion, that is to say, as an affect in which we are affected by ourselves just as in the world we are ordinarily affected by other people. Intimately connected with this is the fact that for Lessing the essence of poetry was action and not, as for Herder, a force—"the magic force that affects my soul"—nor, as for Goethe, nature which has been given form. Lessing was not at all concerned with "the perfection of the work of art in itself," which Goethe considered "the eternal, indispensable requirement." Rather—and here he is in agreement with Aristotle—he was concerned with the effect upon the spectator, who as it were represents the world, or rather, that worldly space which has come into being between the artist or writer and his fellow men as a world common to them.

Lessing experienced the world in anger and in laughter, and anger and laughter are by their nature biased. Therefore, he was unable or unwilling to judge a work of art "in itself," independently of its effect in the world, and therefore he could attack or defend in his polemics according to how the matter in question was being judged by the public and quite independently of the degree to which it was true or false. It was not only a form of gallantry when he said that he would "leave in peace those whom all are striking at"; it was also a concern, which had become instinctive with him, for the relative rightness of opinions which for good reasons get the worst of it. Thus even in the dispute over Christianity he did not take up a fixed position. Rather, as he once said with magnificent self-knowledge, he instinctively became dubious of Christianity "the more cogently some tried to prove it to me," and instinctively tried "to preserve it in [his] heart" the more "wantonly and triumphantly others sought to trample it underfoot." But this means that where everyone else was contending over the "truth" of Christianity, he was chiefly defending its position in the world, now anxious that it might again enforce its claim to dominance, now fearing that it might vanish utterly. Lessing was being remarkably farsighted when he saw that the enlightened theology of his time "under the pretext of making us rational Christians is making us extremely irrational philosophers." That insight sprang not only from partisanship in favor of reason. Lessing's primary concern in this whole debate was freedom, which was far more endangered by those who wanted "to compel faith by proofs" than by those who regarded faith as a gift of divine grace. But there was in addition his concern about the world, in which he felt both religion and philosophy should have their place, but separate places, so that behind the "partition . . . each can go its own way without hindering the other."

Criticism, in Lessing's sense, is always taking sides for the world's sake, understanding and judging everything in terms of its position in the world at any given time. Such a mentality can never give rise to a definite world view which, once adopted, is immune to further experiences in the world because it has hitched itself firmly to one possible perspective. We very much need Lessing to teach us this state of mind, and what makes learning it so hard for us is not our distrust of the Enlightenment or of the eighteenth century's belief in humanity. It is not the eighteenth but the nineteenth century that stands between Lessing and us. The nineteenth century's obsession with history and commitment to ideology still looms so large in the political thinking of our times that we are inclined to regard entirely free thinking, which employs neither history nor coercive logic as crutches, as having no authority over us. To be sure, we are still aware that thinking calls not only for intelligence and profundity but above all for courage. But we are astonished that Lessing's partisanship for the world could go so far that he could even sacrifice to it the axiom of noncontradiction, the claim to self-consistency, which we assume is mandatory to all who write and speak. For he declared in all seriousness: "I am not duty-bound to resolve the difficulties I create. May my ideas always be somewhat disjunct, or even appear to contradict one another, if only they are ideas in which readers will find material that stirs them to think for themselves." He not only wanted no one to coerce him, but he also wanted to coerce no one, either by force or by proofs. He regarded the tyranny of those who attempt to dominate thinking by reasoning and sophistries, by compelling argumentation, as more dangerous to freedom than orthodoxy. Above all he never coerced himself, and instead of fixing his identity in history with a perfectly consistent system, he scattered into the world, as he himself knew, "nothing but *fermenta cognitionis.*"

Thus Lessing's famous *Selbstdenken*—independent thinking for oneself—is by no means an activity pertaining to a closed, integrated, organically grown and cultivated individual who then as it were looks around to see where in the world the most favorable place for his development might be, in order to bring himself into harmony with the world by the detour of thought. For Lessing, thought does not arise out of the individual and is not the manifestation of a self. Rather, the individual—whom Lessing would say was created for action, not ratiocination—elects such thought because he discovers in thinking another mode of moving in the world in freedom. Of all the specific liberties which may come into our minds when we hear the word "freedom," freedom of movement is historically the oldest and also the most elementary. Being able to depart for where we will is the prototypal gesture of being free, as limitation of freedom of movement has from time immemorial been the precondition for enslavement. Freedom of movement is also the indispensable condition for action, and it is in action that men primarily experience freedom in the world. When men are deprived of the public space—which is constituted by acting together and then fills of its own accord with the events and stories that develop into history—they retreat into their freedom of thought. That is a very ancient experience, of course. And some such retreat seems to have been forced upon Lessing. When we hear of such a retreat from enslavement in the world to freedom of thought, we naturally remember the Stoic model, because it was historically the most effective. But to be precise, Stoicism represents not so much a retreat from action to thinking as an escape from the world into the self which, it is hoped, will be able to sustain itself in sovereign independence of the outside world. There was nothing of the sort in Lessing's case. Lessing retreated into thought, but not at all into his own self; and if for him a secret link between action and thought did exist (I believe it did, although I cannot prove it by quotations), the link consisted in the fact that both action and thought occur in the form of movement and that, therefore, freedom underlies both: freedom of movement.

Lessing probably never believed that acting can be replaced by thinking, or that freedom of thought can be a substitute for the freedom inherent in action. He knew very well that he was living in what was then the "most slavish country in Europe," even though he was allowed to "offer the public as many idiocies against religion" as he pleased. For it was impossible to raise "a voice for the rights of subjects . . . against extortion and despotism," in other words, to act. The secret relationship of his "self-thinking" to action lay in his never binding his thinking to results. In fact, he explicitly renounced the desire for results, insofar as these might mean the final solution of problems which his thought posed for itself; his thinking was not a search for truth, since every truth that is the result of a thought process necessarily puts an end to the movement of thinking. The *fermenta cognitionis* which Lessing scattered into the world were not intended to communicate conclusions, but to stimulate others to independent thought, and this for no other purpose than to bring about a discourse between thinkers. Lessing's thought is not the (Platonic) silent dialogue between me and myself, but an anticipated dialogue with others, and this is the reason that it is essentially polemical. But even if he had succeeded in bringing about his discourse with other independent thinkers and so escaping a solitude which, for him in particular, paralyzed all faculties, he could scarcely have been persuaded that this put everything to rights. For what was wrong, and what no dialogue and no independent thinking ever could right, was the world—namely, the thing that arises between people and in which everything that individuals carry with them innately can become visible and audible. In the two hundred years that separate us from Lessing's lifetime, much has changed in this respect, but little has changed for the better. The "pillars of the best-known truths" (to stay with his metaphor), which at that time were shaken, today lie shattered; we need neither criticism nor wise men to shake them any more. We need only look around to see that we are standing in the midst of a veritable rubble heap of such pillars.

Now in a certain sense this could be an advantage, promoting a new kind of thinking that needs no pillars and props, no standards and traditions to move freely without crutches over unfamiliar terrain. But with the world as it is, it is difficult to enjoy this advantage. For long ago it became apparent that the pillars of the truths have also been the pillars of the political order, and that the world (in contrast to the people who inhabit it and move freely about in it) needs such pillars in order to guarantee continuity and permanence, without which it cannot offer mortal men the relatively secure, relatively imperishable home that they need. To be sure, the very humanity of man loses its vitality to the extent that he abstains from thinking and puts his confidence into old verities or even new truths, throwing them down as if they were coins with which to balance all experiences. And yet, if this is true for man, it is not true for the world. The world becomes inhuman, inhospitable to human needs—which are the needs of mortals—when it is violently wrenched into a movement in which there is no longer any sort of permanence. That is why ever since the great failure of the French Revolution people have repeatedly re-erected the old pillars which were then overthrown, only again and again to see them first quivering, then collapsing anew. The most frightful errors have replaced the "best-known truths," and the error of these doctrines constitutes no proof, no new pillar for the old truths. In the political realm restoration is never a substitute for a new foundation but will be at best an emergency measure that becomes inevitable when the act of foundation, which is called revolution, has failed. But it is likewise inevitable that in such a constellation, especially when it extends over such long spans of time, people's mistrust of the world and all aspects of the public realm should grow steadily. For the fragility of these repeatedly restored props of the public order is bound to become more apparent after every collapse, so that ultimately the public order is based on people's holding as self-evident precisely those "best-known truths" which secretly scarcely anyone still believes in.

II

History knows many periods of dark times in which the public realm has been obscured and the world become so dubious that people have ceased to ask any more of politics than that it show due consideration for their vital interests and personal liberty. Those who have lived in such times and been formed by them have probably always been inclined to despise the world and the public realm, to ignore them as far as possible, or even to overleap them and, as it were, reach behind them—as if the world were only a fa-çade behind which people could conceal themselves—in order to arrive at mutual understandings with their fellow men without regard for the world that lies between them. In such times, if things turn out well, a special kind of humanity develops. In order properly to appreciate its possibilities we need only think of *Nathan the Wise,* whose true theme—"It suffices to be a man"—permeates the play. The appeal: "Be my friend," which runs like a leitmotif through the whole play, corresponds to that theme. We might equally well think of *The Magic Flute,* which likewise has as its theme such a humanity, which is more profound than we generally think when we consider only the eighteenth century's usual theories of a basic human na-ture underlying the multiplicity of nations, peoples, races, and religions into which the human race is divided. If such a human nature were to exist, it would be a natural phenomenon, and to call behavior in accordance with it "human" would assume that human and natural behavior are one and the same. In the eighteenth century the greatest and historically the most effec-tive advocate of this kind of humanity was Rousseau, for whom the human nature common to all men was manifested not in reason but in compassion, in an innate repugnance, as he put it, to see a fellow human being suffer-ing. With remarkable accord, Lessing also declared that the best person is the most compassionate. But Lessing was troubled by the egalitarian char-acter of compassion—the fact that, as he stressed, we feel "something akin to compassion" for the evildoer also. This did not trouble Rousseau. In the spirit of the French Revolution, which leaned upon his ideas, he saw *fra-ternité* as the fulfillment of humanity. Lessing, on the other hand, consid-ered friendship—which is as selective as compassion is egalitarian—to be the central phenomenon in which alone true humanity can prove itself.

Before we turn to Lessing's concept of friendship and its political rele-vance, we must dwell for a moment on fraternity as the eighteenth century understood it. Lessing, too, was well acquainted with it; he spoke of "phil-anthropic feelings," of a brotherly attachment to other human beings which springs from hatred of the world in which men are treated "inhumanly." For our purposes, however, it is important that humanity manifests itself in such brotherhood most frequently in "dark times." This kind of humanity actually becomes inevitable when the times become so extremely dark for certain groups of people that it is no longer up to them, their insight or choice, to withdraw from the world. Humanity in the form of fraternity invariably appears historically among persecuted peoples and enslaved groups; and in eighteenth-century Europe it must have been quite natural to detect it among the Jews, who then were newcomers in literary circles. This kind of humanity is the great privilege of pariah peoples; it is the advantage that the pariahs of this world always and in all circumstances can have over others. The privilege is dearly bought; it is often accompanied by so radical a loss of the world, so fearful an atrophy of all the organs with which we respond to it—starting with the common sense with which we orient ourselves in a world common to ourselves and others and going on to the sense of beauty, or taste, with which we love the world—that in extreme cases, in which pariahdom has persisted for centuries, we can speak of real worldlessness. And worldlessness, alas, is always a form of barbarism.

In this as it were organically evolved humanity it is as if under the pressure of persecution the persecuted have moved so closely together that the interspace which we have called world (and which of course existed between them before the persecution, keeping them at a distance from one another) has simply disappeared. This produces a warmth of human relationships which may strike those who have had some experience with such groups as an almost physical phenomenon. Of course I do not mean to imply that this warmth of persecuted peoples is not a great thing. In its full development it can breed a kindliness and sheer goodness of which human beings are otherwise scarcely capable. Frequently it is also the source of a vitality, a joy in the simple fact of being alive, rather suggesting that life comes fully into its own only among those who are, in worldly terms, the insulted and injured. But in saying this we must not forget that the charm and intensity of the atmosphere that develops is also due to the fact that the pariahs of this world enjoy the great privilege of being unburdened by care for the world.

Fraternity, which the French Revolution added to the liberty and equality which have always been categories of man's political sphere—that fraternity has its natural place among the repressed and persecuted, the exploited and humiliated, whom the eighteenth century called the unfortunates, *les malheureux,* and the nineteenth century the wretched, *les misérables.* Compassion, which for both Lessing and Rousseau (though in very different contexts) played so extraordinary a part in the discovery and confirmation of a human nature common to all men, for the first time became the central motive of the revolutionary in Robespierre. Ever since, compassion has remained inseparably and unmistakably part of the history of European revolutions. Now compassion is unquestionably a natural, creature affect which involuntarily touches every normal person at the sight of suffering, however alien the sufferer may be, and would therefore seem an ideal basis for a feeling that reaching out to all mankind would establish a society in which men might really become brothers. Through compassion the revolutionary-minded humanitarian of the eighteenth century sought to achieve solidarity with the unfortunate and the miserable—an effort tantamount to penetrating the very domain of brotherhood. But it soon became evident that this kind of humanitarianism, whose purest form is a privilege of the pariah, is not transmissible and cannot be easily acquired by those who do not belong among the pariahs. Neither compassion nor actual sharing of suffering is enough. We cannot discuss here the mischief that compassion has introduced into modern revolutions by attempts to improve the lot of the unfortunate rather than to establish justice for all. But in order to gain a little perspective on ourselves and the modern way of feeling we might recall briefly how the ancient world, so much more experienced in all political matters than ourselves, viewed compassion and the humanitarianism of brotherhood.

Modern times and antiquity agree on one point: both regard compassion as something totally natural, as inescapable to man as, say, fear. It is therefore all the more striking that antiquity took a position wholly at odds with the great esteem for compassion of modern times. Because they so clearly recognized the affective nature of compassion, which can overcome us like fear without our being able to fend it off, the ancients regarded the most compassionate person as no more entitled to be called the best than the most fearful. Both emotions, because they are purely passive, make action impossible. This is the reason Aristotle treated compassion and fear together. Yet it would be altogether misguided to reduce compassion to fear—as though the sufferings of others aroused in us fear for ourselves—or fear to compassion—as though in fear we felt only compassion for ourselves. We are even more surprised when we hear (from Cicero in the *Tusculanae Disputationes* III 21) that the Stoics saw compassion and envy in the same terms: "For the man who is pained by another's misfortune is also pained by another's prosperity." Cicero himself comes considerably closer to the heart of the matter when he asks (*ibid.* IV 56): "Why pity rather than give assistance if one can? Or, are we unable to be open-handed without pity?" In other words, should human beings be so shabby that they are incapable of acting humanly unless spurred and as it were compelled by their own pain when they see others suffer?

In judging these affects we can scarcely help raising the question of self-lessness, or rather the question of openness to others, which in fact is the precondition for "humanity" in every sense of that word. It seems evident that sharing joy is absolutely superior in this respect to sharing suffering. Gladness, not sadness, is talkative, and truly human dialogue differs from mere talk or even discussion in that it is entirely permeated by pleasure in the other person and what he says. It is tuned to the key of gladness, we might say. What stands in the way of this gladness is envy, which in the sphere of humanity is the worst vice; but the antithesis to compassion is not envy but cruelty, which is an affect no less than compassion, for it is a perversion, a feeling of pleasure where pain would naturally be felt. The decisive factor is that pleasure and pain, like everything instinctual, tend to muteness, and while they may well produce sound, they do not produce speech and certainly not dialogue.

All this is only another way of saying that the humanitarianism of brotherhood scarcely befits those who do not belong among the insulted and the injured and can share in it only through their compassion. The warmth of pariah peoples cannot rightfully extend to those whose different position in the world imposes on them a responsibility for the world and does not allow them to share the cheerful unconcern of the pariah. But it is true that in "dark times" the warmth which is the pariahs' substitute for light exerts a great fascination upon all those who are so ashamed of the world as it is that they would like to take refuge in invisibility. And in invisibility, in that obscurity in which a man who is himself hidden need no longer see the visible world either, only the warmth and fraternity of closely packed human beings can compensate for the weird irreality that human relationships assume wherever they develop in absolute worldlessness, unrelated to a world common to all people. In such a state of worldlessness and irreality it is easy to conclude that the element common to all men is not the world, but "human nature" of such and such a type. What the type is depends on the interpreter; it scarcely matters whether reason, as a property of all men, is emphasized, or a feeling common to all, such as the capacity for compassion. The rationalism and sentimentalism of the eighteenth century are only two aspects of the same thing; both could lead equally to that enthusiastic excess in which individuals feel ties of brotherhood to all men. In any case this rationality and sentimentality were only psychological substitutes, localized in the realm of invisibility, for the loss of the common, visible world.

Now this "human nature" and the feelings of fraternity that accompany it manifest themselves only in darkness, and hence cannot be identified in the world. What is more, in conditions of visibility they dissolve into nothingness like phantoms. The humanity of the insulted and injured has never yet survived the hour of liberation by so much as a minute. This does not mean that it is insignificant, for in fact it makes insult and injury endurable; but it does mean that in political terms it is absolutely irrelevant.

III

These and similar questions of the proper attitude in "dark times" are of course especially familiar to the generation and the group to which I belong. If concord with the world, which is part and parcel of receiving honors, has never been an easy matter in our times and in the circumstances of our world, it is even less so for us. Certainly honors were no part of our birthright, and it would not be surprising if we were no longer capable of the openness and trustfulness that are needed simply to accept gratefully what the world offers in good faith. Even those among us who by speaking and writing have ventured into public life have not done so out of any original pleasure in the public scene, and have hardly expected or aspired to receive the stamp of public approval. Even in public they tended to address only their friends or to speak to those unknown, scattered readers and listeners with whom everyone who speaks and writes at all cannot help feeling joined in some rather obscure brotherhood. I am afraid that in their efforts they felt very little responsibility toward the world; these efforts were, rather, guided by their hope of preserving some minimum of humanity in a world grown inhuman while at the same time as far as possible resisting the weird irreality of this worldlessness—each after his own fashion and some few by seeking to the limits of their ability to understand even inhumanity and the intellectual and political monstrosities of a time out of joint.

I so explicitly stress my membership in the group of Jews expelled from Germany at a relatively early age because I wish to anticipate certain misunderstandings which can arise only too easily when one speaks of humanity. In this connection I cannot gloss over the fact that for many years I considered the only adequate reply to the question, Who are you? to be: A Jew. That answer alone took into account the reality of persecution. As for the statement with which Nathan the Wise (in effect, though not in actual wording) countered the command: "Step closer, Jew"—the statement: I am a man—I would have considered as nothing but a grotesque and dangerous evasion of reality.

Let me also quickly clear away another likely misunderstanding. When I use the word "Jew" I do not mean to suggest any special kind of human being, as though the Jewish fate were either representative of or a model for the fate of mankind. (Any such thesis could at best have been advanced with cogency only during the last stage of Nazi domination, when in fact the Jews and anti-Semitism were being exploited solely to unleash and keep in motion the racist program of extermination. For this was an essential part of totalitarian rule. The Nazi movement, to be sure, had from the first tended toward totalitarianism, but the Third Reich was not by any means totalitarian during its early years. By "early years" I mean the first period, which lasted from 1933 to 1938.) In saying, "A Jew," I did not even refer to a reality burdened or marked out for distinction by history. Rather, I was only acknowledging a political fact through which my being a member of this group outweighed all other questions of personal identity or rather had decided them in favor of anonymity, of namelessness. Nowadays such an attitude would seem like a pose. Nowadays, therefore, it is easy to remark that those who reacted in this way had never got very far in the school of "humanity," had fallen into the trap set by Hitler, and thus had succumbed to the spirit of Hitlerism in their own way. Unfortunately, the basically simple principle in question here is one that is particularly hard to understand in times of defamation and persecution: the principle that one can resist only in terms of the identity that is under attack. Those who reject such identifications on the part of a hostile world may feel wonderfully superior to the world, but their superiority is then truly no longer of this world; it is the superiority of a more or less well-equipped cloud-cuckoo-land.

When I thus bluntly reveal the personal background of my reflections, it may easily sound to those who know the fate of the Jews only from hearsay as if I am talking out of school, a school they have not attended and whose lessons do not concern them. But as it happens, during that selfsame period in Germany there existed the phenomenon known as the "inner emigration," and those who know anything about that experience may well recognize certain questions and conflicts akin to the problems I have mentioned in more than a mere formal and structural sense. As its very name suggests, the "inner emigration" was a curiously ambiguous phenomenon. It signified on the one hand that there were persons inside Germany who behaved as if they no longer belonged to the country, who felt like emigrants; and on the other hand it indicated that they had not in reality emigrated, but had withdrawn to an interior realm, into the invisibility of thinking and feeling. It would be a mistake to imagine that this form of exile, a withdrawal from the world into an interior realm, existed only in Germany, just as it would be a mistake to imagine that such emigration came to an end with the end of the Third Reich. But in that darkest of times, inside and outside Germany the temptation was particularly strong, in the face of a seemingly unendurable reality, to shift from the world and its public space to an interior life, or else simply to ignore that world in favor of an imaginary world "as it ought to be" or as it once upon a time had been.

There has been much discussion of the widespread tendency in Germany to act as though the years from 1933 to 1945 never existed; as though this part of German and European and thus world history could be expunged from the textbooks; as though everything depended on forgetting the "negative" aspect of the past and reducing horror to sentimentality. (The world-wide success of *The Diary of Anne Frank* was clear proof that such tendencies were not confined to Germany.) It was a grotesque state of affairs when German young people were not allowed to learn the facts that every schoolchild a few miles away could not help knowing. Behind all this there was, of course, genuine perplexity. And this very incapacity to face the reality of the past might possibly have been a direct heritage of the inner emigration, as it was undoubtedly to a considerable extent, and even more directly, a consequence of the Hitler regime—that is to say, a consequence of the organized guilt in which the Nazis had involved all inhabitants of the German lands, the inner exiles no less than the stalwart Party members and the vacillating fellow travelers. It was the fact of this guilt which the Allies simply incorporated into the fateful hypothesis of collective guilt. Herein lies the reason for the Germans' profound awkwardness, which strikes every outsider, in any discussion of questions of the past. How difficult it must be to find a reasonable attitude is perhaps more clearly expressed by the cliché that the past is still "unmastered" and in the conviction held particularly by men of good will that the first thing to be done is to set about "mastering" it. Perhaps that cannot be done with any past, but certainly not with the past of Hitler Germany. The best that can be achieved is to know precisely what it was, and to endure this knowledge, and then to wait and see what comes of knowing and enduring.

Perhaps I can best explain this by a less painful example. After the First World War we experienced the "mastering of the past" in a spate of descriptions of the war that varied enormously in kind and quality; naturally, this happened not only in Germany, but in all the affected countries. Nevertheless, nearly thirty years were to pass before a work of art appeared which so transparently displayed the inner truth of the event that it became possible to say: Yes, this is how it was. And in this novel, William Faulkner's *A Fable,* very little is described, still less explained, and nothing at all "mastered"; its end is tears, which the reader also weeps, and what remains beyond that is the "tragic effect" or the "tragic pleasure," the shattering emotion which makes one able to accept the fact that something like this war could have happened at all. I deliberately mention tragedy because it more than the other literary forms represents a process of recognition. The tragic hero becomes knowledgeable by reexperiencing what has been done in the way of suffering, and in this *pathos,* in resuffering the past, the network of individual acts is transformed into an event, a significant whole. The dramatic climax of tragedy occurs when the actor turns into a sufferer; therein lies its peripeteia, the disclosure of the dénouement. But even non-tragic plots become genuine events only when they are experienced a second time in the form of suffering by memory operating retrospectively and perceptively. Such memory can speak only when indignation and just anger, which impel us to action, have been silenced—and that needs time. We can no more master the past than we can undo it. But we can reconcile ourselves to it. The form for this is the lament, which arises out of all recollection. It is, as Goethe has said (in the Dedication to *Faust*):

Der Schmerz wird neu, es wiederholt die Klage
Des Lebens labyrinthisch irren Lauf.

(Pain arises anew, lament repeats
Life's labyrinthine, erring course.)

The tragic impact of this repetition in lamentation affects one of the key elements of all action; it establishes its meaning and that permanent significance which then enters into history. In contradistinction to other elements peculiar to action—above all to the preconceived goals, the impelling motives, and the guiding principles, all of which become visible in the course of action—the meaning of a committed act is revealed only when the action itself has come to an end and become a story susceptible to narration. Insofar as any "mastering" of the past is possible, it consists in relating what has happened; but such narration, too, which shapes history, solves no problems and assuages no suffering; it does not master anything once and for all. Rather, as long as the meaning of the events remains alive— and this meaning can persist for very long periods of time—"mastering of the past" can take the form of ever-recurrent narration. The poet in a very general sense and the historian in a very special sense have the task of setting this process of narration in motion and of involving us in it. And we who for the most part are neither poets nor historians are familiar with the nature of this process from our own experience with life, for we too have the need to recall the significant events in our own lives by relating them to ourselves and others. Thus we are constantly preparing the way for "poetry," in the broadest sense, as a human potentiality; we are, so to speak, constantly expecting it to erupt in some human being. When this happens, the telling-over of what took place comes to a halt for the time being and a formed narrative, one more item, is added to the world's stock. In reification by the poet or the historian, the narration of history has achieved permanence and persistence. Thus the narrative has been given its place in the world, where it will survive us. There it can live on—one story among many. There is no meaning to these stories that is entirely separable from them—and this, too, we know from our own, non-poetic experience. No philosophy, no analysis, no aphorism, be it ever so profound, can compare in intensity and richness of meaning with a properly narrated story.

I seem to have digressed from my subject. The question is how much reality must be retained even in a world become inhuman if humanity is not to be reduced to an empty phrase or a phantom. Or to put it another way, to what extent do we remain obligated to the world even when we have been expelled from it or have withdrawn from it? For I certainly do not wish to assert that the "inner emigration," the flight from the world to conceal-ment, from public life to anonymity (when that is what it really was and not just a pretext for doing what everyone did with enough inner reserva-tions to salve one's conscience), was not a justified attitude, and in many cases the only possible one. Flight from the world in dark times of impo-tence can always be justified as long as reality is not ignored, but is con-stantly acknowledged as the thing that must be escaped. When people choose this alternative, private life too can retain a by no means insignifi-cant reality, even though it remains impotent. Only it is essential for them to realize that the realness of this reality consists not in its deeply personal note, any more than it springs from privacy as such, but inheres in the world from which they have escaped. They must remember that they are constantly on the run, and that the world's reality is actually expressed by their escape. Thus, too, the true force of escapism springs from persecu-tion, and the personal strength of the fugitives increases as the persecution and danger increase.

At the same time we cannot fail to see the limited political relevance of such an existence, even if it is sustained in purity. Its limits are inherent in the fact that strength and power are not the same; that power arises only where people act together, but not where people grow stronger as individu-als. No strength is ever great enough to replace power; wherever strength is confronted by power, strength will always succumb. But even the sheer strength to escape and to resist while fleeing cannot materialize where real-ity is bypassed or forgotten—as when an individual thinks himself too good and noble to pit himself against such a world, or when he fails to face up to the absolute "negativeness" of prevailing world conditions at a given time. How tempting it was, for example, simply to ignore the intolerably stupid blabber of the Nazis. But seductive though it may be to yield to such temptations and to hole up in the refuge of one's own psyche, the result will always be a loss of humanness along with the forsaking of reality.

Thus, in the case of a friendship between a German and a Jew under the conditions of the Third Reich it would scarcely have been a sign of human-ness for the friends to have said: Are we not both human beings? It would have been mere evasion of reality and of the world common to both at that time; they would not have been resisting the world as it was. A law that prohibited the intercourse of Jews and Germans could be evaded but could not be defied by people who denied the reality of the distinction. In keep-

ing with a humanness that had not lost the solid ground of reality, a humanness in the midst of the reality of persecution, they would have had to say to
each other: A German and a Jew, and friends. But wherever such a friendship succeeded at that time (of course the situation is completely changed,
nowadays) and was maintained in purity, that is to say without false guilt
complexes on the one side and false complexes of superiority or inferiority
on the other, a bit of humanness in a world become inhuman had been
achieved.

IV

The example of friendship, which I have adduced because it seems to me
for a variety of reasons to be specially pertinent to the question of humanness, brings us back to Lessing again. As is well known, the ancients
thought friends indispensable to human life, indeed that a life without
friends was not really worth living. In holding this view they gave little
consideration to the idea that we need the help of friends in misfortune; on
the contrary, they rather thought that there can be no happiness or good
fortune for anyone unless a friend shares in the joy of it. Of course there is
something to the maxim that only in misfortune do we find out who our
true friends are; but those whom we regard as our true friends without such
proof are usually those to whom we unhesitatingly reveal happiness and
whom we count on to share our rejoicing.

We are wont to see friendship solely as a phenomenon of intimacy, in
which the friends open their hearts to each other unmolested by the world
and its demands. Rousseau, not Lessing, is the best advocate of this view,
which conforms so well to the basic attitude of the modern individual, who
in his alienation from the world can truly reveal himself only in privacy and
in the intimacy of face-to-face encounters. Thus it is hard for us to understand the political relevance of friendship. When, for example, we read in
Aristotle that *philia,* friendship among citizens, is one of the fundamental
requirements for the well-being of the City, we tend to think that he was
speaking of no more than the absence of factions and civil war within it.
But for the Greeks the essence of friendship consisted in discourse. They
held that only the constant interchange of talk united citizens in a *polis.* In
discourse the political importance of friendship, and the humanness peculiar to it, were made manifest. This converse (in contrast to the intimate
talk in which individuals speak about themselves), permeated though it
may be by pleasure in the friend's presence, is concerned with the common
world, which remains "inhuman" in a very literal sense unless it is constantly talked about by human beings. For the world is not humane just
because it is made by human beings, and it does not become humane

just because the human voice sounds in it, but only when it has become the object of discourse. However much we are affected by the things of the world, however deeply they may stir and stimulate us, they become human for us only when we can discuss them with our fellows. Whatever cannot become the object of discourse—the truly sublime, the truly horrible or the uncanny—may find a human voice through which to sound into the world, but it is not exactly human. We humanize what is going on in the world and in ourselves only by speaking of it, and in the course of speaking of it we learn to be human.

The Greeks called this humanness which is achieved in the discourse of friendship *philanthropia*, "love of man," since it manifests itself in a readiness to share the world with other men. Its opposite, misanthropy, means simply that the misanthrope finds no one with whom he cares to share the world, that he regards nobody as worthy of rejoicing with him in the world and nature and the cosmos. Greek philanthropy underwent many a change in becoming Roman *humanitas*. The most important of these changes corresponded to the political fact that in Rome people of widely different ethnic origins and descent could acquire Roman citizenship and thus enter into the discourse among cultivated Romans, could discuss the world and life with them. And this political background distinguishes Roman *humanitas* from what moderns call humanity, by which they commonly mean a mere effect of education.

That humaneness should be sober and cool rather than sentimental; that humanity is exemplified not in fraternity but in friendship; that friendship is not intimately personal but makes political demands and preserves reference to the world—all this seems to us so exclusively characteristic of classical antiquity that it rather perplexes us when we find quite kindred features in *Nathan the Wise*—which, modern as it is, might with some justice be called the classical drama of friendship. What strikes us as so strange in the play is the "We must, must be friends," with which Nathan turns to the Templar, and in fact to everyone he meets; for this friendship is obviously so much more important to Lessing than the passion of love that he can brusquely cut the love story off short (the lovers, the Templar and Nathan's adopted daughter Recha, turn out to be brother and sister) and transform it into a relationship in which friendship is required and love ruled out. The dramatic tension of the play lies solely in the conflict that arises between friendship and humanity with truth. That fact perhaps strikes modern men as even stranger, but once again it is curiously close to the principles and conflicts which concerned classical antiquity. In the end, after all, Nathan's wisdom consists solely in his readiness to sacrifice truth to friendship.

Lessing had highly unorthodox opinions about truth. He refused to accept any truths whatever, even those presumably handed down by Providence, and he never felt compelled by truth, be it imposed by others' or by his own reasoning processes. If he had been confronted with the Platonic alternative of *doxa* or *aletheia,* of opinion or truth, there is no question how he would have decided. He was glad that—to use his parable—the genuine ring, if it had ever existed, had been lost; he was glad for the sake of the infinite number of opinions that arise when men discuss the affairs of this world. If the genuine ring did exist, that would mean an end to discourse and thus to friendship and thus to humanness. On these same grounds he was content to belong to the race of "limited gods," as he occasionally called men; and he thought that human society was in no way harmed by those "who take more trouble to make clouds than to scatter them," while it incurred "much harm from those who wish to subject all men's ways of thinking to the yoke of their own." This has very little to do with tolerance in the ordinary sense (in fact Lessing himself was by no means an especially tolerant person), but it has a great deal to do with the gift of friendship, with openness to the world, and finally with genuine love of mankind.

The theme of "limited gods," of the limitations of the human understanding, limitations which speculative reason can point out and thereby transcend, subsequently became the great object of Kant's critiques. But whatever Kant's attitudes may have in common with Lessing's—and in fact they do have much in common—the two thinkers differed on one decisive point. Kant realized that there can be no absolute truth for man, at least not in the theoretical sense. He would certainly have been prepared to sacrifice truth to the possibility of human freedom; for if we possessed truth we could not be free. But he would scarcely have agreed with Lessing that the truth, if it did exist, could be unhesitatingly sacrificed to humanity, to the possibility of friendship and of discourse among men. Kant argued that an absolute exists, the duty of the categorical imperative which stands above men, is decisive in all human affairs, and cannot be infringed even for the sake of humanity in every sense of that word. Critics of the Kantian ethic have frequently denounced this thesis as altogether inhuman and unmerciful. Whatever the merits of their arguments, the inhumanity of Kant's moral philosophy is undeniable. And this is so because the categorical imperative is postulated as absolute and in its absoluteness introduces into the interhuman realm—which by its nature consists of relationships—something that runs counter to its fundamental relativity. The inhumanity which is bound up with the concept of one single truth emerges with particular clarity in Kant's work precisely because he attempted to found truth on practical reason; it is as though he who had so inexorably pointed out man's cognitive limits could not bear to think that in action, too, man cannot behave like a god.

Lessing, however, rejoiced in the very thing that has ever—or at least since Parmenides and Plato—distressed philosophers: that the truth, as soon as it is uttered, is immediately transformed into one opinion among many, is contested, reformulated, reduced to one subject of discourse among others. Lessing's greatness does not merely consist in a theoretical insight that there cannot be one single truth within the human world but in his gladness that it does not exist and that, therefore, the unending discourse among men will never cease so long as there are men at all. A single absolute truth, could there have been one, would have been the death of all those disputes in which this ancestor and master of all polemicism in the German language was so much at home and always took sides with the utmost clarity and definiteness. And this would have spelled the end of humanity.

It is difficult for us today to identify with the dramatic but untragic conflict of *Nathan the Wise* as Lessing intended it. That is partly because in regard to truth it has become a matter of course for us to behave tolerantly, although for reasons that have scarcely any connection with Lessing's reasons. Nowadays someone may still occasionally put the question at least in the style of Lessing's parable of the three rings—as, for example, in Kafka's magnificent pronouncement: "It is difficult to speak the truth, for although there is only one truth, it is alive and therefore has a live and changing face." But here, too, nothing is said of the political point of Lessing's antinomy—that is, the possible antagonism between truth and humanity. Nowadays, moreover, it is rare to meet people who believe they possess the truth; instead, we are constantly confronted by those who are sure that they are right. The distinction is plain; the question of truth was in Lessing's time still a question of philosophy and of religion, whereas our problem of being right arises within the framework of science and is always decided by a mode of thought oriented toward science. In saying this I shall ignore the question of whether this change in ways of thinking has proved to be for our good or ill. The simple fact is that even men who are utterly incapable of judging the specifically scientific aspects of an argument are as fascinated by scientific rightness as men of the eighteenth century were by the question of truth. And strangely enough, modern men are not deflected from their fascination by the attitude of scientists, who as long as they are really proceeding scientifically know quite well that their "truths" are never final but are continually undergoing radical revision by living research.

In spite of the difference between the notions of possessing the truth and being right, these two points of view have one thing in common: those who take one or the other are generally not prepared to sacrifice their view to humanity or friendship in case a conflict should arise. They actually believe that to do so would be to violate a higher duty, the duty of "objectivity"; so that even if they occasionally make such a sacrifice they do not feel they are acting out of conscience but are even ashamed of their humanity and often feel distinctly guilty about it. In terms of the age in which we live, and in terms of the many dogmatic opinions that dominate our thinking, we can translate Lessing's conflict into one closer to our experience, by showing its application to the twelve years and to the dominant ideology of the Third Reich. Let us for the moment set aside the fact that Nazi racial doctrine is in principle unprovable because it contradicts man's "nature." (By the way, it is worth remarking that these "scientific" theories were neither an invention of the Nazis nor even a specifically German invention.) But let us assume for the moment that the racial theories could have been convincingly proved. For it cannot be gainsaid that the practical political conclusions the Nazis drew from these theories were perfectly logical. Suppose that a race could indeed be shown, by indubitable scientific evidence, to be inferior; would that fact justify its extermination? But the answer to this question is still too easy, because we can invoke the "Thou shalt not kill" which in fact has become the fundamental commandment governing legal and moral thinking of the Occident ever since the victory of Christianity over antiquity. But in terms of a way of thinking governed by neither legal nor moral nor religious strictures—and Lessing's thought was as untrammeled, as "live and changing" as that—the question would have to be posed thus: *Would any such doctrine, however convincingly proved, be worth the sacrifice of so much as a single friendship between two men?*

Thus we have come back to my starting point, to the astonishing lack of "objectivity" in Lessing's polemicism, to his forever vigilant partiality, which has nothing whatsoever to do with subjectivity because it is always framed not in terms of the self but in terms of the relationship of men to their world, in terms of their positions and opinions. Lessing would not have found any difficulty in answering the question I have just posed. No insight into the nature of Islam or of Judaism or of Christianity could have kept him from entering into a friendship and the discourse of friendship with a convinced Mohammedan or a pious Jew or a believing Christian. Any doctrine that in principle barred the possibility of friendship between two human beings would have been rejected by his untrammeled and unerring conscience. He would instantly have taken the human side and given short shrift to the learned or unlearned discussion in either camp. That was Lessing's humanity.

This humanity emerged in a politically enslaved world whose foundations, moreover, were already shaken. Lessing, too, was already living in "dark times," and after his own fashion he was destroyed by their darkness. We have seen what a powerful need men have, in such times, to move closer to one another, to seek in the warmth of intimacy the substitute for that light and illumination which only the public realm can cast. But this means that they avoid disputes and try as far as possible to deal only with people with whom they cannot come into conflict. For a man of Lessing's disposition there was little room in such an age and in such a confined world; where people moved together in order to warm one another, they moved away from him. And yet he, who was polemical to the point of contentiousness, could no more endure loneliness than the excessive closeness of a brotherliness that obliterated all distinctions. He was never eager really to fall out with someone with whom he had entered into a dispute; he was concerned solely with humanizing the world by incessant and continual discourse about its affairs and the things in it. He wanted to be the friend of many men, but no man's brother.

He failed to achieve this friendship in the world with people in dispute and discourse, and indeed under the conditions then prevailing in German-speaking lands he could scarcely have succeeded. Sympathy for a man who "was worth more than all his talents" and whose greatness "lay in his individuality" (Friedrich Schlegel) could never really develop in Germany because such sympathy would have to arise out of politics in the deepest sense of the word. Because Lessing was a completely political person, he insisted that truth can exist only where it is humanized by discourse, only where each man says not what just happens to occur to him at the moment, but what he "deems truth." But such speech is virtually impossible in solitude; it belongs to an area in which there are many voices and where the announcement of what each "deems truth" both links and separates men, establishing in fact those distances between men which together comprise the world. Every truth outside this area, no matter whether it brings men good or ill, is inhuman in the literal sense of the word; but not because it might rouse men against one another and separate them. Quite the contrary, it is because it might have the result that all men would suddenly unite in a single opinion, so that out of many opinions one would emerge, as though not men in their infinite plurality but man in the singular, one species and its exemplars, were to inhabit the earth. Should that happen, the world, which can form only in the interspaces between men in all their variety, would vanish altogether. For that reason the most profound thing that has been said about the relationship between truth and humanity is to be found in a sentence of Lessing's which seems to draw from all his works wisdom's last word. The sentence is:

JEDER SAGE, WAS IHM WAHRHEIT DÜNKT,
UND DIE WAHRHEIT SELBST SEI GOTT EMPFOHLEN!

(Let each man say what he deems truth,
and let truth itself be commended unto God!)

43. Michel Foucault, *The Subject and Power*

For at least a decade and a half before his untimely death in 1984, Michel
Foucault (born 1926) was one of those figures more often found in Paris
than anywhere else—an intellectual with a large public following. He
held a chair at the Collège de France, the most prestigious institution in
the French academic system, and an idiosyncratic one which offers no
formal courses or degree programs but opens all its lectures to the general public. Foucault's lectures were a weekly "event," consistently drawing overflow crowds. Once his books began to appear in English translation, his popularity spread to the United States, and in the 1980s he was
visiting American universities with increasing frequency.

Foucault was a combination philosopher and historian, fitting neither
of those categories entirely easily. Much of his work was devoted to
studying areas long regarded as peripheral to the historical processes
which shaped the modern Western world but which, Foucault argued with
great persuasiveness, were in fact absolutely central. In a series of books
which appeared from 1961 until just weeks before his death, he addressed the history of psychiatry, of medical epistemology and the hospital, of prisons, and of human sexuality. As he articulated perhaps most
clearly in *Discipline and Punish: The Birth of the Prison* (1975), he was
concerned to show that the "sciences of man" (e.g., medicine, psychiatry, penology, pedagogy), supposed to be a part of the liberal, humanitarian flowering of the Enlightenment, were actually agencies of power,
less conspicuous than the "macro-power" of the state but all the more
insidious for touching the individual more immediately and intimately.
These "human sciences" and their correlative institutions—hospitals,
asylums, prisons, schools—defined the individuality of the people they
enclosed, indeed *created,* through detailed record-keeping, the very idea
that ordinary, lowly people were individuals and had individual biogra-
phies. Thus these forms of "micro-power" not only acted on individuals
(as does the state) but also mediated the relationship of individuals to
themselves, constituting their very sense of self, or subjectivity. Foucault
called these micro-powers "disciplines" and stressed that they had become necessary from the nineteenth century on in order to undergird the

modern liberal state, to make it effective despite its own reliance on "gentle" constitutional practices.

Thus Foucault's philosophical history functions as cultural criticism, revealing patterns in our social environment that we had not noticed before and sources of modern malaise in places we had not thought to look. Whether Foucault offers a way out of the entrapments he so brilliantly describes is, however, less clear.

The essay reprinted below was written by Foucault in English in 1982 for oral presentation in this country. It is a kind of interim progress report, Foucault's own attempt to discuss the main thrust of his work to date. He situates his intellectual project as a response to the fascist and Stalinist episodes of the earlier twentieth century and suggests how deeply rooted in the history of Western civilization the mode of disciplinary power is.

Why Study Power: The Question of the Subject

The ideas which I would like to discuss here represent neither a theory nor a methodology.

I would like to say, first of all, what has been the goal of my work during the last twenty years. It has not been to analyze the phenomena of power, nor to elaborate the foundations of such an analysis.

My objective, instead, has been to create a history of the different modes by which, in our culture, human beings are made subjects. My work has dealt with three modes of objectification which transform human beings into subjects.

The first is the modes of inquiry which try to give themselves the status of sciences; for example, the objectivizing of the speaking subject in *grammaire générale,* philology, and linguistics. Or again, in this first mode, the objectivizing of the productive subject, the subject who labors, in the analysis of wealth and of economics. Or, a third example, the objectivizing of the sheer fact of being alive in natural history or biology.

In the second part of my work, I have studied the objectivizing of the subject in what I shall call "dividing practices." The subject is either divided inside himself or divided from others. This process objectivizes him. Examples are the mad and the sane, the sick and the healthy, the criminals and the "good boys."

From Hubert L. Dreyfus and Paul Rabinow, *Michel Foucault: Beyond Structuralism and Hermeneutics* (Chicago: University of Chicago Press, 1982), pp. 208–216; ©1982 by The University of Chicago.

Finally, I have sought to study—it is my current work—the way a human being turns him- or herself into a subject. For example, I have chosen the domain of sexuality—how men have learned to recognize themselves as subjects of "sexuality."

Thus it is not power, but the subject, which is the general theme of my research.

It is true that I became quite involved with the question of power. It soon appeared to me that, while the human subject is placed in relations of production and of signification, he is equally placed in power relations which are very complex. Now, it seemed to me that economic history and theory provided a good instrument for relations of production; that linguistics and semiotics offered instruments for studying relations of signification; but for power relations we had no tools of study. We had recourse only to ways of thinking about power based on legal models, that is: What legitimates power? Or we had recourse to ways of thinking about power based on institutional models, that is: What is the state?

It was therefore necessary to expand the dimensions of a definition of power if one wanted to use this definition in studying the objectivizing of the subject.

Do we need a theory of power? Since a theory assumes a prior objectification, it cannot be asserted as a basis for analytical work. But this analytical work cannot proceed without an ongoing conceptualization. And this conceptualization implies critical thought—a constant checking.

The first thing to check is what I should call the "conceptual needs." I mean that the conceptualization should not be founded on a theory of the object—the conceptualized object is not the single criterion of a good conceptualization. We have to know the historical conditions which motivate our conceptualization. We need a historical awareness of our present circumstance.

The second thing to check is the type of reality with which we are dealing.

A writer in a well-known French newspaper once expressed his surprise: "Why is the notion of power raised by so many people today? Is it such an important subject? Is it so independent that it can be discussed without taking into account other problems?"

This writer's surprise amazes me. I feel skeptical about the assumption that this question has been raised for the first time in the twentieth century. Anyway, for us it is not only a theoretical question, but a part of our experience. I'd like to mention only two "pathological forms"—those two "diseases of power"—fascism and Stalinism. One of the numerous reasons why they are, for us, so puzzling, is that in spite of their historical uniqueness they are not quite original. They used and extended mechanisms already present in most other societies. More than that: in spite of their own internal madness, they used to a large extent the ideas and the devices of our political rationality.

What we need is a new economy of power relations—the word *economy* being used in its theoretical and practical sense. To put it in other words: since Kant, the role of philosophy is to prevent reason from going beyond the limits of what is given in experience; but from the same moment—that is, since the development of the modern state and the political management of society—the role of philosophy is also to keep watch over the excessive powers of political rationality. Which is a rather high expectation.

Everybody is aware of such banal facts. But the fact that they're banal does not mean they don't exist. What we have to do with banal facts is to discover—or try to discover—which specific and perhaps original problem is connected with them.

The relationship between rationalization and excesses of political power is evident. And we should not need to wait for bureaucracy or concentration camps to recognize the existence of such relations. But the problem is: What to do with such an evident fact?

Shall we try reason? To my mind, nothing would be more sterile. First, because the field has nothing to do with guilt or innocence. Second, because it is senseless to refer to reason as the contrary entity to nonreason. Lastly, because such a trial would trap us into playing the arbitrary and boring part of either the rationalist or the irrationalist.

Shall we investigate this kind of rationalism which seems to be specific to our modern culture and which originates in *Aufklärung?* I think that was the approach of some members of the Frankfurt School. My purpose, however, is not to start a discussion of their works, although they are most important and valuable. Rather, I would suggest another way of investigating the links between rationalization and power.

It may be wise not to take as a whole the rationalization of society or of culture, but to analyze such a process in several fields, each with reference to a fundamental experience: madness, illness, death, crime, sexuality, and so forth.

I think that the word *rationalization* is dangerous. What we have to do is analyze specific rationalities rather than always invoking the progress of rationalization in general.

Even if the *Aufklärung* has been a very important phase in our history and in the development of political technology, I think we have to refer to much more remote processes if we want to understand how we have been trapped in our own history.

I would like to suggest another way to go further towards a new economy of power relations, a way which is more empirical, more directly related to our present situation, and which implies more relations between theory and practice. It consists of taking the forms of resistance against different forms of power as a starting point. To use another metaphor, it consists of using this resistance as a chemical catalyst so as to bring to light power relations, locate their position, find out their point of application and the methods used. Rather than analyzing power from the point of view of its internal rationality, it consists of analyzing power relations through the antagonism of strategies.

For example, to find out what our society means by sanity, perhaps we should investigate what is happening in the field of insanity.

And what we mean by legality in the field of illegality.

And, in order to understand what power relations are about, perhaps we should investigate the forms of resistance and attempts made to dissociate these relations.

As a starting point, let us take a series of oppositions which have developed over the last few years: opposition to the power of men over women, of parents over children, of psychiatry over the mentally ill, of medicine over the population, of administration over the ways people live.

It is not enough to say that these are antiauthority struggles; we must try to define more precisely what they have in common.

1) They are "transversal" struggles; that is, they are not limited to one country. Of course, they develop more easily and to a greater extent in certain countries, but they are not confined to a particular political or economic form of government.

2) The aim of these struggles is the power effects as such. For example, the medical profession is not criticized primarily because it is a profit-making concern, but because it exercises an uncontrolled power over people's bodies, their health and their life and death.

3) These are "immediate" struggles for two reasons. In such struggles people criticize instances of power which are the closest to them, those which exercise their action on individuals. They do not look for the "chief enemy," but for the immediate enemy. Nor do they expect to find a solution to their problem at a future date (that is, liberations, revolutions, end of class struggle). In comparison with a theoretical scale of explanations or a revolutionary order which polarizes the historian, they are anarchistic struggles.

But these are not their most original points. The following seem to me to be more specific.

4) They are struggles which question the status of the individual: on the one hand, they assert the right to be different and they underline everything which makes individuals truly individual. On the other hand, they attack everything which separates the individual, breaks his links with others,

splits up community life, forces the individual back on himself and ties him to his own identity in a constraining way.

These struggles are not exactly for or against the "individual," but rather they are struggles against the "government of individualization."

5) They are an opposition to the effects of power which are linked with knowledge, competence, and qualification: struggles against the privileges of knowledge. But they are also an opposition against secrecy, deformation, and mystifying representations imposed on people.

There is nothing "scientistic" in this (that is, a dogmatic belief in the value of scientific knowledge), but neither is it a skeptical or relativistic refusal of all verified truth. What is questioned is the way in which knowledge circulates and functions, its relations to power. In short, the *régime du savoir.*

6) Finally, all these present struggles revolve around the question: Who are we? They are a refusal of these abstractions, of economic and ideological state violence which ignore who we are individually, and also a refusal of a scientific or administrative inquisition which determines who one is.

To sum up, the main objective of these struggles is to attack not so much "such and such" an institution of power, or group, or elite, or class, but rather a technique, a form of power.

This form of power applies itself to immediate everyday life which categorizes the individual, marks him by his own individuality, attaches him to his own identity, imposes a law of truth on him which he must recognize and which others have to recognize in him. It is a form of power which makes individuals subjects. There are two meanings of the word *subject:* subject to someone else by control and dependence, and tied to his own identity by a conscience or self-knowledge. Both meanings suggest a form of power which subjugates and makes subject to.

Generally, it can be said that there are three types of struggles: either against forms of domination (ethnic, social, and religious); against forms of exploitation which separate individuals from what they produce; or against that which ties the individual to himself and submits him to others in this way (struggles against subjection, against forms of subjectivity and submission).

I think that in history, you can find a lot of examples of these three kinds of social struggles, either isolated from each other, or mixed together. But even when they are mixed, one of them, most of the time, prevails. For instance, in the feudal societies, the struggles against the forms of ethnic or social domination were prevalent, even though economic exploitation could have been very important among the revolt's causes.

In the nineteenth century, the struggle against exploitation came into the foreground.

And nowadays, the struggle against the forms of subjection—against the submission of subjectivity—is becoming more and more important, even though the struggles against forms of domination and exploitation have not disappeared. Quite the contrary.

I suspect that it is not the first time that our society has been confronted with this kind of struggle. All those movements which took place in the fifteenth and sixteenth centuries and which had the Reformation as their main expression and result should be analyzed as a great crisis of the Western experience of subjectivity and a revolt against the kind of religious and moral power which gave form, during the Middle Ages, to this subjectivity. The need to take a direct part in spiritual life, in the work of salvation, in the truth which lies in the Book—all that was a struggle for a new subjectivity.

I know what objections can be made. We can say that all types of subjection are derived phenomena, that they are merely the consequences of other economic and social processes: forces of production, class struggle, and ideological structures which determine the form of subjectivity.

It is certain that the mechanisms of subjection cannot be studied outside their relation to the mechanisms of exploitation and domination. But they do not merely constitute the "terminal" of more fundamental mechanisms. They entertain complex and circular relations with other forms.

The reason this kind of struggle tends to prevail in our society is due to the fact that since the sixteenth century, a new political form of power has been continuously developing. This new political structure, as everybody knows, is the state. But most of the time, the state is envisioned as a kind of political power which ignores individuals, looking only at the interests of the totality or, I should say, of a class or a group among the citizens.

That's quite true. But I'd like to underline the fact that the state's power (and that's one of the reasons for its strength) is both an individualizing and a totalizing form of power. Never, I think, in the history of human societies—even in the old Chinese society—has there been such a tricky combination in the same political structures of individualization techniques, and of totalization procedures.

This is due to the fact that the modern Western state has integrated in a new political shape, an old power technique which originated in Christian institutions. We can call this power technique the pastoral power.

First of all, a few words about this pastoral power.

It has often been said that Christianity brought into being a code of ethics fundamentally different from that of the ancient world. Less emphasis is usually placed on the fact that it proposed and spread new power relations throughout the ancient world.

Christianity is the only religion which has organized itself as a Church.

And as such, it postulates in principle that certain individuals can, by their religious quality, serve others not as princes, magistrates, prophets, fortune-tellers, benefactors, educationalists, and so on, but as pastors. However, this word designates a very special form of power.

1) It is a form of power whose ultimate aim is to assure individual salvation in the next world.

2) Pastoral power is not merely a form of power which commands; it must also be prepared to sacrifice itself for the life and salvation of the flock. Therefore, it is different from royal power, which demands a sacrifice from its subjects to save the throne.

3) It is a form of power which does not look after just the whole community, but each individual in particular, during his entire life.

4) Finally, this form of power cannot be exercised without knowing the inside of people's minds, without exploring their souls, without making them reveal their innermost secrets. It implies a knowledge of the conscience and an ability to direct it.

This form of power is salvation oriented (as opposed to political power). It is oblative (as opposed to the principle of sovereignty); it is individualizing (as opposed to legal power); it is coextensive and continuous with life; it is linked with a production of truth—the truth of the individual himself.

But all this is part of history, you will say; the pastorate has, if not disappeared, at least lost the main part of its efficiency.

This is true, but I think we should distinguish between two aspects of pastoral power—between the ecclesiastical institutionalization which has ceased or at least lost its vitality since the eighteenth century, and its function, which has spread and multiplied outside the ecclesiastical institution.

An important phenomenon took place around the eighteenth century— it was a new distribution, a new organization of this kind of individualizing power.

I don't think that we should consider the "modern state" as an entity which was developed above individuals, ignoring what they are and even their very existence, but on the contrary as a very sophisticated structure, in which individuals can be integrated, under one condition: that this individuality would be shaped in a new form, and submitted to a set of very specific patterns.

In a way, we can see the state as a modern matrix of individualization, or a new form of pastoral power.

A few more words about this new pastoral power.

1) We may observe a change in its objective. It was no longer a question of leading people to their salvation in the next world, but rather ensuring it in this world. And in this context, the word *salvation* takes on different meanings: health, well-being (that is, sufficient wealth, standard of living),

security, protection against accidents. A series of "worldly" aims took the place of the religious aims of the traditional pastorate, all the more easily because the latter, for various reasons, had followed in an accessory way a certain number of these aims; we only have to think of the role of medicine and its welfare function assured for a long time by the Catholic and Protestant churches.

2) Concurrently the officials of pastoral power increased. Sometimes this form of power was exerted by state apparatus or, in any case, by a public institution such as the police. (We should not forget that in the eighteenth century the police force was not invented only for maintaining law and order, nor for assisting governments in their struggle against their enemies, but for assuring urban supplies, hygiene, health and standards considered necessary for handicrafts and commerce.) Sometimes the power was exercised by private ventures, welfare societies, benefactors and generally by philanthropists. But ancient institutions, for example the family, were also mobilized at this time to take on pastoral functions. It was also exercised by complex structures such as medicine, which included private initiatives with the sale of services on market economy principles, but which also included public institutions such as hospitals.

3) Finally, the multiplication of the aims and agents of pastoral power focused the development of knowledge of man around two roles: one, globalizing and quantitative, concerning the population; the other, analytical, concerning the individual.

And this implies that power of a pastoral type, which over centuries—for more than a millennium—had been linked to a defined religious institution, suddenly spread out into the whole social body; it found support in a multitude of institutions. And, instead of a pastoral power and a political power, more or less linked to each other, more or less rival, there was an individualizing "tactic" which characterized a series of powers: those of the family, medicine, psychiatry, education, and employers.

At the end of the eighteenth century Kant wrote, in a German newspaper—the *Berliner Monatschrift*—a short text. The title was *Was heisst Aufklärung?* It was for a long time, and it is still, considered a work of relatively small importance.

But I can't help finding it very interesting and puzzling because it was the first time a philosopher proposed as a philosophical task to investigate not only the metaphysical system or the foundations of scientific knowledge, but a historical event—a recent, even a contemporary event.

When in 1784 Kant asked, Was heisst Aufklärung?, he meant, What's going on just now? What's happening to us? What is the world, this period, this precise moment in which we are living?

Or in other words: What are we? as *Aufklärer,* as part of the Enlightenment? Compare this with the Cartesian question: Who am I? I, as a unique but universal and unhistorical subject? I, for Descartes is everyone, anywhere at any moment?

But Kant asks something else: What are we? in a very precise moment of history. Kant's question appears as an analysis of both us and our present.

I think that this aspect of philosophy took on more and more importance. Hegel, Nietzsche. . . .

The other aspect of "universal philosophy" didn't disappear. But the task of philosophy as a critical analysis of our world is something which is more and more important. Maybe the most certain of all philosophical problems is the problem of the present time, and of what we are, in this very moment.

Maybe the target nowadays is not to discover what we are, but to refuse what we are. We have to imagine and to build up what we could be to get rid of this kind of political "double bind," which is the simultaneous individualization and totalization of modern power structures.

The conclusion would be that the political, ethical, social, philosophical problem of our days is not to try to liberate the individual from the state, and from the state's institutions, but to liberate us both from the state and from the type of individualization which is linked to the state. We have to promote new forms of subjectivity through the refusal of this kind of individuality which has been imposed on us for several centuries.

44. Raymond Williams, *The Long Revolution*

Raymond Williams (born 1921) is an English man of letters who is also one of the most distinguished socialist literary and political critics of the mid-twentieth century. Born in Wales, the son of a railway signalman, he was educated at Trinity College, Cambridge, in English literature. After service in Europe with the British Army during World War II Williams worked for the Workers' Education Association, wrote novels and literary criticism (*Reading and Criticism* [1950]; *Culture and Society* [1958]; *Communications* [1962]), and contributed to various journals, including *Highway* and the *New Left Review*. In 1961 he assumed a lectureship in English literature at Cambridge; in 1974 he was appointed Professor of Drama.

Long active in Labour party affairs, Williams resigned from the party in 1966 in protest of what he felt were the reactionary foreign and domestic policies of the government of Harold Wilson. The *May-Day Manifesto* of 1967 expressed his sense that the Labour party was "no longer just an inadequate agency for socialism, it was now an active collaborator in the process of reproducing capitalist society." [1]

In 1961 Williams published *The Long Revolution,* in which he argued that modern society was characterized by three concurrent, interactive, and transformational movements—a democratic revolution, an industrial revolution, and a cultural revolution—which together constituted a historical process which Williams called the "long revolution." The essay below is part of the final chapter of this book. Williams himself has described the project of this work:

> I drew on various kinds of alternative evidence in my own response to the very fiercely fought and agitated debates between right and left within the labour movement through the fifties. But what I essentially felt about them was that, although I was very much nearer the one than the other, neither really answered to the social experience to which they were attempting to speak. That is what explains the no doubt exaggerated judgement that socialism had almost lost any contemporary meaning. What I was trying to say was that it was above all necessary not to pretend that there was a strong, well-rooted socialist movement which was in a position to change society and that the first duty was affiliation to it. It was a time, on the contrary, when the real need was to contrast very rapidly changing social relations with the prevailing formulations which were helpless before them. I think out of that came certain directions for a relevant cultural practice. . . . [2]

Britain in the 1960s

1

As we enter the 1960s, the effective historical patterns of British society seem reasonably clear. The industrial revolution, in an important technical phase, is continuing. The cultural expansion, again with new technical developments, also continues. In the democratic revolution, Britain has recently been mainly in a defensive position, as the colonial peoples move to emancipation. At home it is generally assumed that the democratic process has been essentially completed, with parliamentary and local government

1. Raymond Williams, *Politics and Letters: Interviews with the New Left Review* (London, 1981), p. 373.

2. Ibid., pp. 172–73.

From Raymond Williams, *The Long Revolution* (New York: Columbia University Press, 1961), pp. 293–304, 305–16, 317–26, 347–55. Reprinted by permission of Columbia University Press and Chatto & Windus.

solidly established on universal suffrage, and with the class system apparently breaking up. Britain seems, from these patterns, a country with a fairly obvious future: industrially advanced, securely democratic, and with a steadily rising general level of education and culture.

There is substantial truth in this reading. It is not only the general consensus, but most attempts to challenge it seem unreasonable; even powerful local criticisms do not fundamentally disturb the sense of steady and general advance. Yet in deeper ways, that have perhaps not yet been articulated, this idea of a good society naturally unfolding itself may be exceptionally misleading. It is perhaps an intuitive sense of this that has given such emotional force to the total denunciations, the sweeping rejections, so characteristic of recent years, for even when these can be shown to be based on selective evidence and particular minority tensions, the experience they attest is still not easily set aside.

It seems to me that the first difficulty lies in the common habit of supposing our society to be governed by single patterns, arrived at by averaging the overall trends in familiar categories of economic activity, political behaviour and cultural development. As I see the situation, we need quite different forms of analysis, which would enable us to recognize the important contradictions within each of the patterns described, and, even more crucially, the contradictions between different parts of the general process of change. It is not only that the analysis should be more flexible, but that new categories and descriptions are needed, if all the facts are to be recognized. In particular fields we have made some progress with these, but in our most general descriptions we are all still visibly fumbling, leaving an uncertainty easily exploited by the blandest versions of a natural and healthy evolution, and certainly not redeemed by such general nostrums as the fight for socialism, which remains, after all, in terms of this country, almost wholly undefined.

We have to observe, for example, that the ordinary optimism about Britain's economic future can be reasonably seen as simple complacency. It is very far from certain that on present evidence and given likely developments the directions and rate of growth of the economy guarantee us, over say fifty years, a steadily rising standard of living in this economically exposed and crowded island. Both the rapid rate of economic growth elsewhere, and the certainty of steady industrialization of many areas now undeveloped, seem ominous signs for a country so dependent on trade and in fact given its prosperity by its early industrial start (now being rapidly overtaken) and by its Empire (now either disappearing or changing its character). Long-term thinking of this kind is in fact beginning, but the gap between thinking and vigorous action to implement it seems no ordinary inertia, but the consequence of habits which, in other parts of our life, seem satisfactory and even admirable. The deep revulsion against general planning, which makes sense again and again in many details of our economic activity, may be really disabling in this long run. And this revulsion is itself in part a consequence of one aspect of the democratic revolution—the determination not to be regimented. Here is a substantial contradiction that I think now runs very deep. The very strong case for general planning, not simply to avoid waste but to promote essential development, research and reorganization, is practically nullified by a wholly creditable emotion: that we reject the idea of this kind of economic system controlling our lives. True, we are controlled now and will continue to be controlled by a quite different system, with its own denials and rigidities, but in the first place this is very much harder to identify, and secondly, by its very structure and ideology, it appears to offer, and in just enough places does offer, the feeling of freedom. It seems unlikely that the case for general planning will ever be widely accepted until not only do its forms seem sensible, but also its methods seem compatible with just this feeling of freedom. Democratic planning is an easy phrase, but nobody really knows how it would work, and the spectacular successes of economic planning elsewhere have after all not co-existed with any general democracy. This is the severe damage of the contradiction, because it is then easy to suppose that we have found good reasons for not planning, when in fact the need remains urgent and the problems will not disappear because on balance we find them too difficult to solve.

It remains very difficult, in fact, to think about our general economic activity at all. Both its successes and its failures remain obstinately local, and to this kind of description (particular successes announced by their makers, particular failures not announced until they erupt in crisis) the only ordinary alternative is an almost useless measurement of total production, as if some single thing were being produced. Economists have done a good deal to make these questions significant, but in ordinary thinking it is either this success and that failure, or this misleadingly simple general graph. We can only think in real terms if we know what real things are being produced, and ask relevant questions about need and quality. Some part of the production may be truly unnecessary, but the more likely situation is that the balance between various kinds of production will be wrong or even absurd. The usual answer to this kind of question is a particular description, the market, which supposedly regulates questions of need and quality. "It is needed because it is bought; if it were not bought, it would not be made." Of course this leaves out one major consideration: whether need and ability to buy are matched. But in any case the description is crude, because it leaves out too much. To match the block figure of production, we are offered another block figure, the consumer. The popularity of "consumer" as a contemporary term deserves some attention. It is significant because, first, it unconsciously expresses a really very odd and partial version of the purpose of economic activity (the image is drawn from the furnace or the stomach, yet how many things there are we neither eat nor burn), and, second, it materializes as an individual figure (perhaps monstrous in size but individual in behaviour)—the person with needs which he goes to the market to supply.

Why "consumer," to take the first point? We have to go back to the idea of a market, to get this clear. A market is an obviously sensible place where certain necessary goods are made available, but the image of the place lingers when the process of supply and demand has in fact been transformed. We used to go to markets and shops as customers; why are we regarded now as consumers? The radical change is that increasingly, in the development of large-scale industrial production, it is necessary to plan ahead and to know the market demand. What we now call market research was intended as a reasonable provision for this: demand is discovered so that production can be organized. But in fact, since production is not generally planned, but the result of the decisions of many competing firms, market research has inevitably become involved with advertising, which has itself changed from the process of notifying a given supply to a system of stimulating and directing demand. Sometimes this stimulation is towards this version of a product rather than that *(Mountain Brand is Best),* but frequently it is stimulation of a new demand *(You Need Pocket Radio)* or revival of a flagging demand *(Drinka Pinta Milka Day).* In these changing circumstances, the simple idea of a market has gone: the huckster stands level with the supplier. It is then clear why "consumer," as a description, is so popular, for while a large part of our economic activity is obviously devoted to supplying known needs, a considerable and increasing part of it goes to ensuring that we consume what industry finds it convenient to produce. As this tendency strengthens, it becomes increasingly obvious that society is not controlling its economic life, but is in part being controlled by it. The weakening of purposive social thinking is a direct consequence of this powerful experience, which seeks to reduce human activity to predictable patterns of demand. If we were not consumers, but users, we might look at society very differently, for the concept of use involves general human judgements—we need to know how to use things and what we are using them for, and also the effects of particular uses on our general life—whereas consumption, with its crude hand-to-mouth patterns, tends to cancel these questions, replacing them by the stimulated and controlled absorption of the products of an external and autonomous system. We have not gone all the way with this new tendency, and are still in a position to reverse it, but its persuasive patterns have much of the power of our society behind them.

An equally important effect of the "consumer" description is that, in materializing an individual figure, it prevents us thinking adequately about the true range of uses of our economic activity. There are many things, of major importance, which we do not use or consume individually, in the ordinary sense, but socially. It is a poor way of life in which we cannot think of social use as one criterion of our economic activity, yet it is towards this that we are being pushed by the "consumer" emphasis, by the supposed laws of the market, and by the system of production and distribution from which these derive. It is beginning to be widely recognized, in Britain in 1960, that a serious state of unbalance between provision for social and individual needs now exists and seems likely to increase. It is easy to get a sense of plenty from the shop windows of contemporary Britain, but if we look at the schools, the hospitals, the roads, the libraries, we find chronic shortages far too often. Even when things are factually connected, in direct daily experience, as in the spectacular example of the flood of new cars and the ludicrous inadequacy of our road system, the spell of this divided thinking seems too powerful to break. Crises of this kind seem certain to dominate our economy in the years ahead, for even when late, very late, we begin thinking about the social consequences of our individual patterns of use, to say nothing about social purposes in their own right, we seem to find it very difficult to think about social provision in a genuinely social way. Thus we think of our individual patterns of use in the favourable terms of spending and satisfaction, but of our social patterns of use in the unfavourable terms of deprivation and taxation. It seems a fundamental defect of our society that social purposes are largely financed out of individual incomes, by a method of rates and taxes which makes it very easy for us to feel that society is a thing that continually deprives and limits us—without this system we could all be profitably spending. Who has not heard that impassioned cry of the modern barricade: *but it's my money you're spending on all this; leave my money alone*? And it doesn't help much to point out that hardly any of us could get any money, or even live for more than a few days, except in terms of a highly organized social system which we too easily take for granted. I remember a miner saying to me, of someone we were discussing: "He's the sort of man who gets up in the morning and presses a switch and expects the light to come on." We are all, to some extent, in this position, in that our modes of thinking habitually suppress large areas of our real relationships, including our real dependences on others. We think of my money, my light, in these naïve terms, because parts of our very idea of society are withered at root. We can hardly have any conception, in our present system, of the financing of social purposes from the social product, a method which would continually show us, in real terms, what our society is and does. In a society whose products depend almost entirely on intricate and continuous co-operation and social organization, we expect to consume as if we were isolated individuals, making our own way. We are then forced into the stupid comparison of individual consumption and social taxation—one desirable and to be extended, the other regrettably necessary and to be limited. From this kind of thinking the physical unbalance follows inevitably.

Unless we achieve some realistic sense of community, our true standard of living will continue to be distorted. As it is, to think about economic activity in the limited terms of the consumer and the market actually disguises what many of us are doing, and how the pattern of economic life is in any case changing. Even now, one person in four of the working population is engaged neither in production nor in distribution, but in public administration and various forms of general service. For a long time this proportion has been steadily rising, and it seems certain that it will continue to rise. Yet it is a kind of economic activity which cannot be explained, though it may be distorted, by such descriptions as the consumer and the market. A further one in thirteen work in transport, and it is significant that the ordinary argument about our transport systems, especially the railways, is unusually difficult and confused, as the problem of finding any criterion more adequate than consumption, any method of accounting more realistic than direct profit and loss in the market, inevitably shows through. As for administration and general services, from medicine and education to art, sport, and entertainment, the argument is almost hopelessly confused. The product of this kind of work, which one in four of us give our time to, is almost wholly in terms of life and experience, as opposed to things. What kind of accounting is adequate here, for who can measure the value of a life and an experience? Some parts of the process can be reduced to more familiar terms: medicine saves working days, education produces working skills, sport creates fitness, entertainment keeps up morale. But we all know that every one of these services is directed, in the end, to larger purposes: doctors work just as hard to save the life of a man past working age; every school teaches more than direct working skills, and so on. To impose an accounting in market terms is not only silly but in the end impossible: many of the results of such effort are not only long-term and indirect, but in any case have no discoverable exchange value. The most enlightened ordinary reaction is to put these activities into a margin called "life" or "leisure," which will be determined as to size by the shape of "ordinary" economic activity. On the other hand, if we started not from the market but from the needs of persons, not only could we understand this part of our working activity more clearly, but also we should have a means of judging the "ordinary" economic activity itself. Questions not only of balance in the distribution of effort and resources, but also of the effects of certain kinds of work both on users and producers, might then be adequately negotiated. The danger now, as has been widely if obscurely recognized, is of fitting human beings to a system, rather than a system to human beings. The obscurity shows itself in wrong identification of the causes of this error: criticism of industrial production, for example, when in fact we should starve without it; criticism of large-scale organization, when in fact this extension of communication is the substance of much of our growth; criticism, finally, of the pressures of society, when in fact it is precisely the lack of an adequate sense of society that is crippling us.

For my own part I am certain, as I review the evidence, that it is capitalism—a particular and temporary system of organizing the industrial process—which is in fact confusing us. Capitalism's version of society can only be the market, for its purpose is profit in particular activities rather than any general conception of social use, and its concentration of ownership in sections of the community makes most common decisions, beyond those of the market, limited or impossible. Many industrial jobs, as now organized, are boring or frustrating, but the system of wage-labour, inherent in capitalism, necessarily tends to the reduction of the meaning of work to its wages alone. It is interesting that the main unrest of our society— the running battle which compromises any picture of a mainly contented and united country—is in this field of wages. Whenever there is an important strike, or threat of a strike, we tend to react by defining a different conception of work—service to the community, responsibility to others, pulling together. The reaction is quite right: work ought to mean these things. But it is hypocritical to pretend that it now does, all the way through. While the light comes on when we press the switch, we take for granted just these qualities, but ordinarily fail to acknowledge, with any depth, the needs of the man who made the light possible. If we want to stop strikes, we have to carry the reaction right through, for this system of bargaining for labour necessarily includes, as a last resort, as in all other bargaining, the seller's refusal of his labour at the price offered. Strikes are an integral part of the market society, and if you want the advantages you must take the disadvantages, even to the point of dislocation and chaos. While we still talk of a labour market, as despite long protest many of us continue to do, we must expect the behaviour appropriate to it, and not try to smuggle in, when it becomes inconvenient, the quite different conception of common interest and responsibility. The moral disapproval of strikers is shallow and stupid while the system of work is based on the very grounds of particular profit which we there condemn.

What is happening to capitalism in contemporary Britain? We are told that it is changing, but while this is obviously true it can be argued that the patterns of thinking and behaviour it promotes have never been more strong. To the reduction of use to consumption, already discussed, we must add the widespread extension of the "selling" ethic—what sells goes, and to sell a thing is to validate it—and also, I think, the visible moral decline of the labour movement. Both politically and industrially, some sections of the labour movement have gone over, almost completely, to ways of thinking which they still formally oppose. The main challenge to capitalism was socialism, but this has almost wholly lost any contemporary meaning, and it is not surprising that many people now see in the Labour Party merely an alternative power-group, and in the trade-union movement merely a set of men playing the market in very much the terms of the employers they oppose. Any such development is generally damaging, for the society is unlikely to be able to grow significantly if it has no real alternative patterns as the ground of choice. I remember that I surprised many people, in *Culture and Society,* by claiming that the institutions of the labour movement—the trade unions, the co-operatives, the Labour Party—were a great creative achievement of the working people and also the right basis for the whole organization of any good society of the future. Am I now withdrawing this claim, in speaking of moral decline? The point is, as I see it, that my claim rested on the new social patterns these institutions offered. I recognize that the motives for their foundation, and consequently their practice, must be seen as mixed. Sectional defence and sectional self-interest undoubtedly played their part. But also there was this steady offering and discovery of ways of living that could be extended to the whole society, which could quite reasonably be organized on a basis of collective democratic institutions and the substitution of co-operative equality for competition as the principle of social and economic policy. In the actual history, there has been a steady pressure, from the existing organization of society, to convert these institutions to aims and patterns which would not offer this kind of challenge. The co-operatives should be simply trading organizations, the trade unions simply industrial organizations with no other interests, each union keeping to its own sphere, and the Labour Party simply an alternative government in the present system—the country needs an effective opposition. This pressure could not have been as successful as it has if just these aims had not been part of the original impetus of the institutions: certain elements in their patterns have been encouraged, certain elements steadily opposed and weakened. And in every case, of course, to accept the proposed limitation of aims may lead to important short-run gains in practical efficiency; the men within these institutions who accept the limitation often make more immediate sense. But it is quite clear, as we enter the 1960s, that the point has been reached when each of these institutions is discovering that the place in existing society proposed for it, if it agrees to limit its aims, is essentially subordinate: the wide challenge has been drained out, and what is left can be absorbed within existing terms. For many reasons this has sapped the morale of the institutions, but also, fortunately, led to crisis and argument within them. The choice as it presents itself is between qualified acceptance in a subordinate capacity or the renewal of an apparently hopeless challenge. The practical benefits of the former have to be balanced against the profound loss of inspiration in the absence of the latter. If I seem eccentric in continuing to look to these institutions for effective alternative patterns, while seeing all too clearly their present limitations, I can only repeat that they can go either way, and that their crisis is not yet permanently resolved.

The situation is complicated by the fact that real changes have occurred in the society, through the pressure of these institutions aided by reforming elements within the existing patterns. The extension of social services, including education, is an undoubted gain of this kind, which must not be underestimated by those who have simply inherited it. But it remains true not only that the social services are limited to operation in the interstices of a private-ownership society, but also that in their actual operation they remain limited by assumptions and regulations belonging not to the new society but the old (a situation brilliantly described by Brian Abel-Smith in *Conviction*). The other substantial change, the nationalization of certain industries and services, has been even more deeply compromised. The old and valuable principle, of production for use and not for profit, has been fought to a standstill in just this field. The systems taken into public ownership were in fact those old systems no longer attractive in profit terms (coal, railways), new systems requiring heavy initial investment (airways) and systems formerly municipally or publicly developed (gas, electricity). Some of these systems have been much more successful than is generally allowed, but it remains true, first, that they have not only failed to alter the "profit before use" emphasis in the general economy but have also been steadily themselves reduced to this old criterion; and, second, that they have reproduced, sometimes with appalling accuracy, the human patterns, in management and working relationships, of industries based on quite different social principles. The multiplication of such effects is indeed uninviting, and the easy identification of these institutions, as types of the supposed new society, has added to the general confusion. In being dragged back to the processes of the old system, yet at the same time offered as witnesses of the new, they have so deeply damaged any alternative principle in the economy as to have emptied British socialism of any effective meaning. The proposal to admit this formal vacuity, by detaching the Labour Party from any full commitment to socialism, then makes sense of a kind, the practical acknowledgement of an existing situation, until perhaps one remembers that the containment and eventual cancellation of any real challenge to capitalist society has been, for more than a century, the work of capitalist society itself. . . .

The central point, in this contentious field, is that the concepts of the organized market and the consumer now determine our economic life, and with it much of the rest of our society, and that challenges to them have been so effectively confused that hardly any principled opposition remains, only the perpetual haggling and bitterness of the wage claim and the strike. It is difficult to believe that we shall remain satisfied by this situation, which is continually setting us against each other and very rapidly promoting patterns of crude economic cynicism, yet to which no clear and practical alternative exists. The challenge to create new meanings, and to substantiate them, will have to be met if that apparently obvious future is in fact to be realized.

2

The progress of democracy in Britain is deeply affected by what is happening in the economy, but also by other factors. The aspiration to control the general directions of our economic life is an essential element of democratic growth, but is still very far from being realized. Beyond this general control lies a further aspiration, now equally distant and confused. It is difficult to feel that we are really governing ourselves if in so central a part of our living as our work most of us have no share in decisions that immediately affect us. The difficulties of a procedural kind in ensuring this share are indeed severe, and because of the variety of institutions in which we work there is no single answer. Yet if the impulse is there, some ways can be found, and steadily improved from experience. I know from my own experience, in helping to work out such ways in my own job, some of the difficulties yet also some of the real gains. From practical experience alone, I agree with Burke that

> I have never yet seen any plan which has not been mended by the observations of those who were much inferior in understanding to the person who took the lead in the business.

Even the smallest human group produces leaders, though not always the same leaders for all projects. The difficulty lies in interpreting just what this leadership means. The majority patterns of our society, especially in work, offer an interpretation which not only fixes leaders, for all sorts of circumstances, but encourages them to believe that it is not only their right but their duty to make independent decisions and to be resolute in carrying them out. After all, a dog doesn't keep a man and then take the lead himself.

There are still many natural autocrats in our society, and the trouble they cause is beyond reckoning. More dangerous, perhaps, because less easily identified, are those skilled in what was called in the army "man management." The point here, as I remember, is that of course you have to command, but since a leader has to be followed he must be diligently attentive to the state of mind of those he is leading: must try to understand them, talk to them about their problems (not about his own, by the way), get a picture of their state of mind. Then, having taken these soundings, having really got the feel of his people, he will point the way forward.

I know few greater social pleasures, in contemporary Britain, than that of watching man-management, for indeed its practitioners are almost everywhere. It is true that they are usually very bad at it, although they invariably think themselves very good. The calmly appraising eyes (narrowed about an eighth of an inch; more would look suspicious), the gentle silences, the engaging process of drawing the man out: although I have watched these so often, I find them better than most plays. And these are the heroes of our public life, with a solid weight of mutual admiration behind them. An exceptionally large part of what passes for political commentary is now a public discussion of a party leader's command of this skill: how will the Prime Minister or the Leader of the Opposition "handle" this or that "awkward element"; how will he time his own intervention; if he says this, how can he avoid saying that? The really funny thing about this kind of commentary is that it is public; printed and distributed in millions of sheets; read by almost everybody, including the "awkward elements." The delicate art has become public myth, and it is rare to see it challenged. This, evidently, is what democratic leadership is supposed to be.

In fact, of course, it is the tactic of a defensive autocracy (and people do not have to be born into an autocracy to acquire its habits). The true process of democratic decision is that, with all the facts made available, the question is openly discussed and its resolution openly arrived at, either by simple majority vote or by a series of voluntary changes to arrive at a consensus. The skills of the good listener and the clarifier are indeed exceptionally necessary in such a process, but these are crucially different from the stance of the leader who is merely listening to the discussion to discover the terms in which he can get his own way. The intricate devices worked out by democratic organizations, to ensure the full record of facts, the freedom of general contribution, the true openness of decision, and the opportunity to review the ways in which decisions are executed, are indeed invaluable (some people thought I was joking when I mentioned committee procedure as part of our cultural heritage, but the joke is on them, if they are serious about democracy, for these are the means of its working). Yet just because they are intricate, they are easily abused by the man-managers:

one even hears boasts about the ways in which this or that committee has been "handled." I would only say that I have never seen such handling, reputedly practised as a way of "avoiding trouble," lead to anything but trouble. For once men are reasonably free, they will in the end assert their interests, and if these have not been truly involved in the decision (as opposed to collected and "borne in mind") the real situation will eventually assert itself, often with a bitterness that shows how bad the man-managers really are. Our main trouble now is that we have many of the forms of democracy, but find these continually confused by the tactics of those who do not really believe in it, who are genuinely afraid of common decisions openly arrived at, and who have unfortunately partly succeeded in weakening the patterns of feeling of democracy which alone could substantiate the institutions.

We must add a note on the tones of contemporary discussion, if this situation is to be fully understood. Most people who pass through universities learn certain conventions of discussion which pass into the public process. The most important of these is a habit of tentative statement, characteristically introduced by such phrases as "I should have thought that" or "I don't know but it seems to me." This manner is sometimes merely superficial, like the gambit of the Oxford lecturer who begins by saying that he knows practically nothing about the subject of the lecture, and in any case has forgotten his notes (I once saw this practised, by three lecturers running, on an audience of foreign graduates; they were not charmed, and indeed concluded that the lecturers were not quite as good as they supposed themselves to be—a "not wholly inaccurate" diagnosis of a stance of modesty which in fact came through as insulting). These defects are evident, but elsewhere, for certain kinds of discussion, the conventions have their advantages. These can most easily be seen by contrast with the conventions of argument of many wage-earners (particularly manual workers, but not always trade union officers, who have sometimes learned tortuousness to a really amazing proficiency). At first, the bluntness of statement and assertion is refreshing after too long a course of "I should have thought." But one notices how easily, in such discussions, points of view become involved with the personal prestige of the speaker; the opinion cannot be attacked without attacking him as a man, and he cannot modify it without what looks like climbing down. I have listened in despair to many arguments of this kind, where in the end it would really be easier to adjourn and fight it out in the yard, all the signs of physical aggression and challenge being already more evident than the issues—except, of course, that tomorrow the discussion would only have to begin again. The value of the convention of tentative statement is that opinion can be reasonably detached from the personal prestige of the speaker, in a way that is ultimately necessary if a common opinion is to be arrived at. The frank speaking of the Labour movement has been, on balance, a great gain: the issues are forced into the open, away from the man-managers and the cupboarded autocrats. But at the same time the workings of democracy have been severely damaged by habits of aggressive assertion (personified in many a roaring old man at the rostrum) which must be seen quite clearly as pre-democratic: the language of unequals, shouting for their place in the world, and sometimes ensuring, by turning a common process into a series of personal demonstrations, that common improvement will not be got.

It is clear, on balance, that we do not get enough practice in the working of democracy, even where its forms exist. Most of us are not expected to be leaders, and are principally instructed, at school and elsewhere, in the values of discipline and loyalty, which are real values only if we share in the decisions to which they refer. Those who are expected to be leaders are mainly trained to the patterns of leadership I have been discussing, centred on the general development of confidence—but in fact that a leader should be self-confident enough to be capable of radical doubt is rarely mentioned and rarely taught. The necessary practice of the difficult processes of common decision and execution is left, on the whole, to hit or miss, and the result, not unexpectedly, is often both. A weakening of belief in the possibility of democracy is then inevitable, and we prefer to lament the "general indiscipline" (trade-union leaders cannot control their members, party leaders are not firm enough; it is all sloppy discussion, endless talk, and then people behaving unreasonably) rather than nourishing and deepening the process to which in any case, in any probable future, we are committed.

The counterpart of this feeling, reinforced by the actual history of democratic institutions in this country, is an approach to government which in itself severely limits active democracy. A tightly organized party system and parliament seem to have converted the national franchise into the election of a court. As individuals we cast one national vote at intervals of several years, on a range of policies and particular decisions towards which it is virtually impossible to have one single attitude. From this necessarily crude process, a court of ministers emerges (in part drawn from people who have not been elected at all), and it is then very difficult for any of us to feel even the smallest direct share in the government of our affairs. Approaches through the party organizations, taking advantage of the fact that at least there are alternative courts, are more practicable, but not only is it generally true that inner-party democracy is exceptionally difficult in both large parties, it is also the case that the right not to be tied, not to be precisely committed, is increasingly claimed by both sets of leaders. The general influence of public opinion counts for something, since in the long run the court has to be re-elected. But the period is exceptionally long, given the rate and range of development in contemporary politics. In the four and a half years between the elections of 1955 and 1959 several wholly unforeseen major crises developed, and public opinion in fact violently fluctuated, to be met in general only by the bland confidence of the court in its own premises: that the duty of the government is to govern, for the Queen's government must be carried on. It is fair to say that this does not even sound like democracy, and we must be fair to our leaders, conceding them at least consistency, in their obvious assumption that direct popular government is not what democracy is about. It is true that any administration should have reasonable time to develop its policies, but this is not the same thing as the current uncritical belief in the importance of "strong government": certainly one hopes that a good government will be strong, but a government that is both strong and bad (most people are agreed that we had such governments in the 1930s; I think we have had one or two since) is almost the worst possible public evil. I see no reason why two-year intervals of re-election of at least a substantial part of the House of Commons should not be our immediate objective, since it seems vital for the health of our democracy that more of us should feel directly involved in it. Such a change, coupled with working reforms now being canvassed in Parliament, and with an improvement of the democratic process within the parties, would be a substantial yet reasonable gain. The alternative is not only the rapid extension of man-management, monstrously magnified by the use of modern communications as its general device, but also the unpleasant development of organized pressure-groups, pushing into the anterooms of the court. One further necessary amendment seems to be a fixed date for the periodic elections, for to concede choice of this date to the court itself is psychologically quite wrong: we should not have to wait, within broad limits, for the court to ask our approval; the right of election is not theirs but ours.

These changes in themselves would make only a limited difference, but they would at least go some way towards altering the present atmosphere of British democracy, which seems increasingly formal and impersonal, and powered by little more than the belief that a choice of leaders should be periodically available. The next field of reform is obviously the electoral system, which seems designed to perpetuate the existing interpretations. Its most obvious characteristic is that it exaggerates, sometimes grossly, comparatively slight tendencies in opinion. Post-war electoral history suggests a violent fluctuation of opinion, from a very strong Labour to a very strong Conservative government. But actual opinion, reckoned in terms of people, has changed much less. What I notice more about current political commentary is that it is preoccupied by results at the level of the court, rather than by the registered opinion of actual persons; and this, however natural it may be to people who like living in anterooms, is quite un-democratic in spirit. It is ridiculous to talk of an overwhelming endorse-ment of Conservatism in the election of 1959, when less than half the people voting in fact voted Conservative, and when of adults entitled to vote only just over a third in fact approved the nevertheless very strong gov-ernment to which all of us are committed for as long as five years. The same is true, of course, of previous "overwhelming" Labour victories, and the mode of description suggests that we are not, in these terms, thinking about real people at all. I believe that the process of common decision, even as crudely registered by single occasional votes, must be carried through without such distortion into the formal process of government, if we are to have any honest democracy. The weight of conventional thinking by politicians is against this tendency, but such conventional thinking, when it is traced to its sources, is again the tactical wisdom of a defensive autocracy, carried on, through inertia and lack of challenge, into what is claimed to be a very different society. It is difficult, as we look over this whole field, to assent even in passing to the ordinary proposition that the democratic revolution is virtually complete.

At this critical point, the relative absence of democracy in other large areas of our lives is especially relevant. The situation can be held as it is, not only because democracy has been limited at the national level to the process of electing a court, but also because our social organization else-where is continually offering non-democratic patterns of decision. This is the real power of institutions, that they actively teach particular ways of feeling, and it is at once evident that we have not nearly enough institutions which practically teach democracy. The crucial area is in work, where in spite of limited experiments in "joint consultation," the ordinary decision process is rooted in an exceptionally rigid and finely-scaled hierarchy, to which the only possible ordinary responses, of the great majority of us who are in no position to share in decisions, are apathy, the making of re-spectful petitions, or revolt. If we see a considerable number of strikes, as the evidence suggests, as revolts in this sense, we can see more clearly the stage of development we have reached. The defensive tactic, once again, is man-management, now more grandly renamed personnel management. This is an advance on simple autocracy, but as an answer to the problems of human relations at work only shows again how weakly the democratic im-pulse still runs. It seems obvious that industrial democracy is deeply re-lated to questions of ownership; the argument against the political vote was always that the new people voting, "the masses," had no stake in the coun-try. The development of new forms of ownership then seemed an essential part of any democratic advance, although in fact the political suffrage eventually broke ahead of this. The idea of public ownership seemed to be a solution, but there is some truth in the argument that little is gained by substituting a series of still largely authoritarian state monopolies for a series of private monopolies (something is gained, however, to the extent that the state is itself democratically directed). It is obvious that in a complex large-scale economy, many central decisions will have to be taken, and that their machinery easily becomes bureaucratic and protected from general control. At this level there can be no doubt that the separate democratic management of industry is unworkable. The true line of advance is making this machinery directly responsible to the elected government, probably through intermediate boards which combine representation of the industry or service with elected political representatives. With this framework set, as for example it is to some extent set in educational administration, the development of direct participation in the local decisions of particular enterprises could be attempted. The difficulties are severe, and there is no single solution. It seems to me that a government which was serious about this would initiate a series of varied experiments, in different kinds of concern, ranging from conventional methods such as the reform of company law, promoting actual and contractual membership, with definite investments and rights in the concern, to methods that would be possible in concerns already publicly owned, in which elected councils, either from a common roll or at first representing interests in an agreed proportion, would have powers of decision within the accepted national framework. It is commonly objected that modern work is too technical to be subjected to the democratic process, but it is significant that in certain fields, notably education and medicine, the necessarily complicated processes of involving members in self-government are already much further advanced than in work where the "service" criterion is not accepted, though in fact it is claimed. Education and medicine are not less technical or specialized, but they have a less obvious class structure, which is undoubtedly important. The necessary principle is that workers of all kinds, including managers, should be guaranteed the necessary conditions, including both security and freedom, of their actual work, in precise ways that are perfectly compatible with general decisions about the overall direction of the enterprise. Boards of directors elected by shareholders now give such directions, ordinarily with less security and freedom for all kinds of workers, since these are not represented. In publicly owned industries and services, and in reformed companies, the principle of boards elected by the members of the industry or service, to operate within the agreed national framework, is surely not difficult. There would be a long and continuous process of setting-up and improving such machinery, and many serious and largely unforeseen problems would undoubtedly arise. But the basis of the whole argument for democracy is that the substance of these problems would in any case exist, and that participation in the processes of decision leads to more rational and responsible solutions than the old swing between apathy, concession, and revolt.

One other field in which the growth of democracy seems urgently necessary is the ordinary process of decision about the development of our communities. This has been approached, but is still very muddled, and it is unfortunately true that there is even more dissatisfaction, and consequent apathy, about local government than about the national court. Authoritarian patterns at the centre seem to be widely reproduced in our local councils, where much more of the process is in the open and within our ordinary experience, unfortunately in its ordinary course giving far too much evidence of how easily democracy is distorted. Still, the problems here are quite widely understood, and the active struggle against distortion is encouraging. More seriously, behind this struggle is a familiar inertia of old social forms. Housing is an excellent example, because the common provision of homes and estates is so obviously sensible, in principle, and is already extending beyond the mere relief of exceptional need. Why then does such an extension, or further extension, leave many of us quite cold? One answer, certainly, is the way such houses and estates are commonly managed, by supposedly democratic authorities. I have seen letters to tenants from council housing officials that almost made my hair stand on end, and the arbitrary and illiberal regulation of many such estates is justly notorious. While this can still be fairly said even of Labour authorities, it is difficult to feel that the spirit of democracy has been very deeply or widely learned. Why should a public official, often a perfectly pleasant man to meet, transform himself so often into the jack-in-office who has done extraordinary harm to the whole development of social provision? Partly, I suppose, because he sees so many jacks-in-office above him. More generally, I think, because the patterns and tones of leadership and administration are still pre-democratic. The businessman, dealing with customers, has learned to be pleasant; so, usually, has the public official, at that level. But there are public officials who regard such people as council-house tenants as natural inferiors, and they speak and write accordingly. The remedy, of course, is not to teach them man-management, but to try to develop democratic forms within these areas of public provision. Why should the management of a housing estate not be vested in a joint committee of representatives of the elected authority and elected representatives of the people who live on it? While general financial policy obviously rests with the whole community, there is a wide area of decision, on the way the houses are used and maintained, on estate facilities, and on any necessary regulations, which could be negotiated through such channels more amicably and I think more efficiently. If this experiment has been tried, we should know more about it and consider extending it. If it has not been tried, here is an immediate field in which the working of democratic participation could be tested. Labour councils, in particular, ought continually to be thinking in these ways, for there is great danger to the popular movement if its organizations are persistently defensive and negative (as in the ordinary Tenants' Association), and it is Labour which has most to lose if it allows democracy to dwindle to a series of defensive associations and the minimal machinery of a single elected administration. The pressure has been to define democracy as "the right to vote," "the right to free speech," and so on, in a pattern of feeling which is really that of the "liberty of the subject" within an established authority. The pressure now, in a wide area of our social life, should be towards a participating democracy, in which the ways and means of involving people much more closely in the process of self-government can be learned and extended.

3

Behind any description of the patterns of our economy and of our political and social life lie ways of thinking about "class," which in Britain in the 1960s seem exceptionally uncertain and confused. Here, as a matter of urgency, we must go back from our ordinary meanings to our experience. . . .

Most people in Britain now think of themselves as "middle class" or "working class." But the first point to make is that these are not true alternatives. The alternatives to "middle" are "lower" and "upper"; the alternative to "working" is "independent" or "propertied." The wonderful muddle we are now in springs mainly from this confusion, that one term has a primarily social, the other a primarily economic reference. When people are asked if they belong to the working class many of them agree; when they are asked if they belong to the lower class many less agree. Yet the persistent suggestion of "middle" is that the working class is "lower," and it is hardly surprising that many wage-earners want to think of themselves as "middle class" if "lower" is explicitly or implicitly the alternative description. Again, many "middle class" people are indignant at the suggestion or implication that they do not work because they do not belong to the "working classes." They are quite right to be indignant, but they have only themselves to blame if they have contributed in any way to the confusion between the economic description—the wage-earning "working classes," and the social implication that these people are the "lower" class. It seems that we have to ask not only what purposes are served by the classification, but also what purposes are served by so persistent a confusion.

The fact is that we are still in a stage of transition from a social stratification based on birth to one based on money and actual position. The drive towards the latter kind of society is very strong; it is both built into our economic system and continually stimulated by it. But we do not have to look far, in Britain, to find older ways of thinking. The principal function of the otherwise insignificant "upper" class is to keep distinction by birth and family alive. A simple description of power in Britain might show the irrelevance of this, but there are still, after all, the monarchy, the House of Lords, and a system of honours involving change of family name and status. So far from these systems being regarded as merely the vestiges of an older society, they are now so intensively propagated that their practical effect is still considerable. By their very removal from the harsh and controversial open exercise of power, their social prestige is even enhanced. But why is this so, in a changing society? The intense propaganda of monarchy (by a shrewd mixture of magnificence and ordinariness which in its central incompatibility bears all the signs of functional magic) seems a conscious procedure against radical change. The emphasis on the unity, loyalty and family atmosphere of the Queen's subjects is not easy to reconcile with the facts of British life, but as an ideal, though silly, it catches just enough real desires, and just sufficiently confuses consciousness of real obstacles, to be a powerful reserve of feeling in favour of things as they are. This mellow dusk then spreads over the ancillary power system, still important in many areas of actual decision, in which people chosen by family status and not by the democratic process carry on in a special position, whether in the House of Lords or as chairmen of many official and unofficial but influential committees (a process still curiously known as voluntary public work, in which if the practitioners are discovered to have the common touch the magic is even more potent).

This could hardly have happened if the rising middle class had remained independent, or retained any real confidence in itself. Somewhere in the nineteenth century (though there are earlier signs) the English middle class lost its nerve, socially, and thoroughly compromised with the class it had virtually defeated. Directed personally towards the old system of family status, it adopted as its social ideal a definite class system, blurred at the top but clear below itself. The distinction of public schools from grammar schools led to a series of compromises: in the curriculum, where just enough new subjects were introduced to serve middle-class training, but just enough old subjects kept to preserve the older cultivation of gentlemen; and in social character, where just enough emphasis on the superiority of the whole class was shrewdly mixed with a rigorous training in concepts of authority and service, so that a formal system could be manned and yet not disturbed. The principal difficulty, in preserving this system, was that new middle-class groups kept rising behind those who had made their peace. However closely the grammar schools imitated those few of their number that had been renamed public schools, it was necessary for distances to be kept, and "grammar school," in some ears, soon sounded like "soup kitchen." The principal tension, in recent English social life, has been between the fixed character of the arrived middle class, with its carefully conditioned ways of speaking and behaving, and the later arrivals or those still struggling to arrive. The worst snobberies still come, with an extraordinary self-revealing brashness, from people who, if family were really the social criterion, would be negligible. The compromise takes care of that, for it had included (what the aristocracy was not unwilling to learn) the accolade of respectability on work and especially the making of money by work. This enabled the pattern to be kept mobile, without altering its character. It is true now, as Mr. Ralph Samuel has argued, that the captain of industry has become the social hero, but distinctively, in Britain, the captain of industry provides himself with a family title and status express-ing prestige in older terms. And since honours are easy, in the sense that they can be continually created and extended, it has been possible to work out a system whereby the results of individual effort and merit can be con-firmed in terms of hereditary values. There is even a very nice grading, quite formalized in the public service, in which the particular point reached in climbing the bourgeois-democratic ladder is magically transformed into a particular feudal grade: a Prime Minister equals an Earl, a permanent Secretary a Knight and so on. This fundamental class system, with the force of the rising middle class right behind it, requires a "lower" class if it is to retain any social meaning. The people cast for this lower rôle keep turning round, it is true, and pointing the same finger at those below them. This is the basic unreality of the "middle class" in Britain, and also the explanation of its vagueness. I remember sitting with a group of small shopkeepers who were trying to explain to me how you could never trust "that class of people" (shop assistants): it seemed, in the most colourful phrase, that they always had their fingers in the toffees. The particular cli-max of this discussion, for me, was a description of the group, by one of its members, as "tip-top business men"; this went down very well. Here, in fact, was a solid assumption of middle-class membership and distinction by a group of people who if they moved only a little way up this same middle class would at once be placed and despised, much as the shop as-sistants were placed and despised (they would probably call the waitress "Miss," which as the normal mode of address to a young unmarried woman by the eighteenth century gentry is of course now obviously "low"). But so long as a group can find another group to turn round and point at, the contradictions seem hardly to be noticed. All class distinction in Brit-ain is downward, under the mellow dusk from the very top. And it seems very doubtful if it will simply wither away, for the confusion noted earlier, between social and economic description, has, as explained, been built into the system. The drive for money, power and position, which might have created the separate ideal of self-made prestige, has been neatly directed into the older system, at a cost in confusion which we are all still paying.

In this respect, I belong to the awkward squad who have been discussed a good deal since the war. Many people have told us that the reason for our interest in class is that we are frustrated to find that educational mobility is not quite social mobility; that however far we have gone we still find an older system above us. This is a very revealing account of the class-feeling of someone born just too far down in the middle class but still accepting its ethos. That sense of differential mobility is just the confusion that many middle-class groups encounter, if they are thinking in their own class terms. I can only say for myself that I have never felt my own mobility in terms of a "rise in the social scale," and certainly I have never felt that I wanted to go on climbing, resentful of old barriers in my way: where else is there to go, but into my own life? At the same time, the particular history of going from a wage-earning family to one of the old universities takes one on a very rapid traverse of this same social scale, which seems largely to survive with the confusions it now has because really, when it comes to it, movement along it is normally quite limited, and the divisions are quite carefully kept. It is then less the injustice of the British class system than its stupidity that really strikes one. People like to be respected, but this natural desire is now principally achieved by a system which defines respect in terms of despising someone else, and then in turn being inevitably despised. In my own traverse, I have seen so much of this, aware of the standards of one group while watching another, in a truly endless series, that I should have to be very odd indeed to be bitter: the predominant feeling is of pathos. The more widely this is experienced the better; we might even get back our nerve. But then we cannot stop at this stage of the analysis; we have still to look at what the system is for, in the actual running of our kind of society.

In part, as noted, it is for respect, though in making this respect differential it is often self-defeating. Still, as we move around in our own country, the operation of differential respect is evident enough to tempt some people into accepting the scale so long as they can improve their own position on it. Anyone who wants to experience the reality of the differential has only to put himself, physically, at a point on the scale other than that he is used to, changing some of the signals by which the ordinary exchange is operated, and he will feel the difference quickly enough. Let any middle-class man who thinks class distinction has died out put aside, if only for a day, his usual clothes, his car, his accent, and go to places where he is not known but where he knows how he would be normally received: he will learn the reality quickly enough. Let him go in the working clothes of a manual worker, but with his "standard" accent, to a shop, an office, a pub, and watch the confusion as the contradictory signals are sorted out. In daily experience this complicated differential goes on, but we have to cross the borders to appreciate it fully, for we normally get used to the rate of respect our evident market value commands. Is this differential anything to worry about, though, in its patent hypocrisy? Not personally, of course, but it would be a change to have a community in which men and women were valued either as real individuals or, where that closeness is impossible, by a common general respect.

There are many signs that money, in the form of conspicuous possession of a range of objects of prestige, is rapidly driving out other forms of class distinction, and it is this change which is behind the argument that class distinction is diminishing. This is a simple confusion of meanings, for it is the reality of differential treatment, rather than the particular forms through which it operates, that makes a class system. The point is particularly important in that the money we earn, to set the differential system going, is itself subject to built-in differentials of an especially complicated kind. The differential for extra skill and extra responsibility is part of this system, but only part, and all arguments about pay become hopelessly confused if this basis of differential is assumed to be the only one generally operative. There is the first obvious fact that a radical differential is imposed by the general financial position of the industry or service in which a man is working. The teacher and the engine-driver start on different total scales, in services where money is short, from the copywriter or the car-assembly worker, where money is easier. And if standing in the community is increasingly assessed in straight money terms, this situation is a very serious distortion from the outset. The next radical differential is more closely tied to class. Most of us live by selling our labour, but in some cases the pay is called salary, in other cases a wage. In practice this is much more than a verbal difference: we hear of wage demands from one kind of man, but of requests for a review of remuneration from another. Public indignation, or what passes as such in the newspapers, is quite regularly reserved for the "wage demands," while much larger "adjustments" in the pay of salaried men pass with little comment. When workers in one industry agitate for more pay, there is too little comparison with the whole range of pay, and too much with other workers no better off. Or one reads the public discussions, in some minority newspapers, of the level of percentage increase which wages can be confined to in a given year. In the same year quite different and much larger percentage increases are discussed in relation to salaries, but hardly ever within the same terms of reference. It is difficult to know what else to call this but a practical class system.

Many of the lower-salaried workers are in practice treated as wage-earners: there is great confusion at that point in the scale. But at a certain level a whole world of difference begins, not only in straight money, but in such critical factors as an automatic incremental scale, a contract of service conferring important rights in such things as payment in sickness and protection against dismissal, and differential facilities in many things from cups to carpets. The system is almost infinitely graded within itself, but the class-line, below which these benefits are not available, is ordinarily quite clear.

Once again, however, it is misleading to confine such analysis to comparison between salaried and wage-earning employment. Many salaried people consider themselves unjustly treated, in such matters as tax-relief for expenses, by comparison with salary-earners or employers in different parts of the economy. Between all these groups there is enough resentment to ensure a cynical community for generations. I support those economists who believe that in spite of the immense difficulties the attempt to establish some general principle of equity, to which particular arguments about pay can be referred, must be made. The present resentments, and the crude ways in which they are fought out, are more than a healthy community can afford.

Meanwhile, to finance the system of conspicuous expenditure, an extraordinary credit network has been set up, which, when considered, reveals much of our real class situation, and the ways in which it is changing. The earners of wages and salaries are alike in this, that most of them become quickly involved in a system of usury which spreads until it is virtually inescapable. How many supposedly middle-class people really own their houses, or their furniture, or their cars? Most of them are as radically unpropertied as the traditional working class, who are now increasingly involved in the same process of usury. In part it is the old exaction, by the propertied, from the needs of the unpropertied, and the ordinary middle-class talk of the property and independence which make them substantial citizens is an increasingly pathetic illusion. One factor in maintaining the illusion is that much of the capital needed to finance the ordinary buyer comes from his own pocket, through insurance and the like, and this can be made to look like the sensible process of accumulating social capital. What is not usually noticed is that established along the line of this process are a group of people using its complications to make substantial profit out of their neighbours' social needs. The ordinary salary-earner, thinking of himself as middle class because of the differences between himself and the wage-earners already noted, fails to notice this real class beyond him, by whom he is factually and continually exploited. Seeing class-distinction only in the limited terms of the open differential, he is acquiescing in the loss of his own freedom and even, by the usual upward identification with which the struggling middle class has always been trapped, underwriting his real exposure, as one of the unpropertied, as if it were his system and his pride.

As we move into this characteristic contemporary world, we can see the supposed new phenomenon of classlessness as simply a failure of consciousness. The public discussion is all at the level of the open differential and its complicated games, but if this were eventually resolved, into a more apparent equity, there would still be no real classlessness; indeed there can be none until social capital is socially owned.

It is in this context that the distinction between middle class and working class must always be considered. The line between them, always difficult to draw, is now blurred at many more points by a common involvement which the remaining distinctions not only disguise but in part are meant to disguise. Is the working class becoming middle class, as its conditions improve? It could as reasonably be said that most of the middle class have become working class, in the sense that they depend on selling their labour and are characteristically unpropertied in any important sense. The true description is one that recognises that the traditional definitions have broken down, and that the resulting confusion is a serious diminution of consciousness. New kinds of work, new forms of capital, new systems of ownership require new descriptions of men in their relations to them. Our true condition is that in relation to a complicated economic and social organization which we have not learned to control, most of us are factually servants, allowed the ordinary grades of upper, middle, and lower, insistent on the marks of these grades or resentful of them, but, like most servants, taking the general establishment for granted and keeping our bickering within its terms.

This situation is clearly reflected in contemporary politics. The Conservative Party is still basically the party of the propertied and the controllers, with an old and natural genuflection to the mellow dusk in which these processes are blurred. But it is felt to be the party of most of those who still anxiously call themselves "middle class," preoccupied as always with the upward identification and the downward keeping-in-place, the latter now fortunately expressible in precise wage percentages. The Labour Party, with vestigial ideas of a different system, offers little alternative to this structure of feeling, and upward identification, it is now learning, can spread a long way down. This is no sudden and dramatic change, though particular voting results may appear dramatically to reveal it. It is part of the logic of a particular system of society, which will operate so long as there is no adequate rise and extension of consciousness of what the system is and does. . . .

5

The human energy of the long revolution springs from the conviction that men can direct their own lives, by breaking through the pressures and restrictions of older forms of society, and by discovering new common institutions. This process necessarily includes both success and failure. If we look back over recent centuries, the successes are truly spectacular, and we ought to keep reminding ourselves of them, and of the incomprehension, the confusion, and the distaste with which the proposals for things now the most ordinary parts of reality were received. At the same time the failures are evident: not only the challenging failures, as new and unrealized complexities are revealed, but also the straight failures, as particular changes are dragged back into old systems, and as ways of thinking deeply learned in previous experience persist and limit the possibility of change. We tend to absorb the successes and then to be preoccupied by the hard knots of failure. Or as we approach the failures, to see if anything can be done, we are distracted by the chorus of success.

I am told by friends in the United States that in effect the revolution is halted: that my sense of possibility in its continued creative energy is a generous but misleading aspiration, for they in America are in touch with the future, and it does not work—the extension of industry, democracy and communications leads only to what is called the massification of society. A different stance is then required: not that of the revolutionary but of the dissenter who though he cannot reverse the trends keeps an alternative vision alive. I hear this also in Britain, where the same patterns are evident, and it is true that in a large part of recent Western literature this is the significant response: the society is doomed, or in any event damned, but by passion or irony the individual or the group may preserve a human enclave. Meanwhile I am told by friends in the Soviet Union that the decisive battle of the revolution has been won in nearly half the world, and that the communist future is evident. I listen to this with respect, but I think they have quite as much still to do as we have, and that a feeling that the revolution is over can be quite as disabling as the feeling that in any case it is pointless. To suppose that the ways have all been discovered, and that therefore one can give a simple affiliation to a system, is as difficult, as I see it, as to perform the comparable act of ingratiation in Western societies: either the majority formula of complacency, or the minority announcement (tough, hard, realistic) that we are heroically damned.

In the long revolution we are making our own scale, and the problem of expectations seems crucial in every society that has entered it. "That's enough now" is the repeated whisper, and as we turn to identify the voice we see that it is not only that of the rich, the dominant and the powerful, who want change to stop or slow down, but also that of many others, who have no further bearings and are unwilling to risk their real gains. "That's enough now; we've got rid of poverty, we've got the vote, every child can be educated." And there it all is, for once these were all seemingly impossible expectations. Even to shape them took many men's lives, and to realize them took the work of many generations. "But that's enough now; let's tidy up and consolidate."

We have to distinguish three kinds of thinking by which the long revolution is continually limited and opposed. The first and most important, though it is often left unnoticed, is the steady resistance of privileged groups of many kinds to any extension of wealth, democracy, education or culture which would affect their exceptional status. In the early stages this is usually quite open, but later it becomes a very delicate strategy, using the advances that have been gained as reasons for doing no more, and above all creating the maximum of delay. It is because of the existence of this conscious and highly skilled opposition that the process is still as much a revolution, though in different forms, as when earlier expectations were met with open violence. Recent arguments and measures against African democracy are very similar to the history of early nineteenth-century Britain, but a further relation is even more important, that the arguments and measures against, say, the extension of education in Britain on any adequate scale are part of the same historical process. This strategy must obviously be defined and opposed at every stage.

Yet the privileged groups, again at all stages, find strange allies. The ordinary tactic of attaching the leaders of one phase to its achievements, and encouraging them to identify with the existing order, is extremely successful. The history of the labour movement is full of such cases, in which former leaders become determined opponents of further change, and give much of their energy to fighting new elements coming up through their own movement. This is still going on, in very much its old forms, though the reality of what such men are doing is usually not generally recognized until they are dead. In our own generation we have a new class of the same kind: the young men and women who have benefited by the extension of public education and who, in surprising numbers, identify with the world into which they have been admitted, and spend much of their time, to the applause of their new peers, expounding and documenting the hopeless vulgarity of the people they have left: the one thing that is necessary, now, to weaken belief in the practicability of further educational extension. They could find plenty of vulgarity and narrowness where they are, if they had the nerve to look, just as the knighted trade-union leader, indignant about shop-stewards and communists and all kinds of disruptive elements, could find plenty of arbitrary and ignorant power and conscious intrigue in the world in which he now moves. In our own period it is impossible to over-look this body of people who are effectively limiting and opposing the revolution by which they themselves have benefited.

The third kind of thinking which limits and opposes is much the most difficult to understand. What the Americans call the "massification" of so-ciety can only happen, however hard the new élites may work, if a majority of the people whom they regard as "the masses" accept this version of themselves. But then it is a fact that for long periods, given sufficient skill in the élites in confusing and flattering, such a majority can for practical purposes be got. I remember watching in a backstreet fish-and-chip shop, the man and his wife, obviously not well off, with obvious local accents, looking in, with what seemed pleasure, at a television play in which people like themselves and their customers, with the same local accent, were made nonsense of, as a class of obviously ignorant clowns. This is not an iso-lated example of a human version of ordinary people which is regularly and widely presented for the enjoyment of the very people whom the ver-sion misrepresents and insults. It is from evidence like this that some people resign themselves to "massification": the masses will create them-selves, take any inferior position that is offered them, and that is the end of any hope of change. I am conscious of the weight of the evidence, but I think it is ordinarily misinterpreted. There is a very skilful obliquity in all such versions: it is always other people who are inferior, the practical iden-tification is never with oneself. While no significant version of other people is there as an alternative, the degrading version makes easy headway. But this version of other people is, precisely, a social expectation. The version of ordinary people as masses is not only the conscious creation of the élites (who work very hard at it, by the way). It is also a conclusion from actual experience within the forms of a society which requires the existence of masses. The framing of different expectations of others has to be carried out, always, against the pressures of an existing culture which is teaching, often very deeply, incompatible patterns. A good example of this is the popularity of "I'm all right, Jack" as an interpretation of our majority so-cial feelings. Whatever moral notes may be added on the selfishness of this attitude, the fact is that this is a version of ordinary people which the terms of our society need people to accept: if everyone is only out for himself, why bother about social change? Very few people, however, would accept this attitude as an adequate description of their *own* feelings. It is how the others are, and the irony is that some real behaviour in the society, against which there might otherwise be principled protest, feeds in to this cynical version to promote and confirm the safe attitudes it embodies.

The central problem is that of expectations. I do not think the "I'm all right, Jack" attitude correctly describes our majority social feelings; it is, rather, a skilful stabilization of achieved expectations. Facing real contradictions, which cannot be argued away but need long and difficult effort for any solution, it makes sense to very many of us to concentrate on an area of immediate living where the relation between desire and achievement is straight and practical. If you accept your place and work hard at your job, you *can* make a big improvement in your life, as things now are. Any alternative effort will not only make less visible progress, but it is by no means clear what in fact the effort would be for. The main pressure of the last three generations of social criticism has been towards the abolition of individual poverty, and the point has now been reached where the social conditions for this have been largely achieved, and can then be taken for granted, the immediate climb from poverty seeming now an individual effort. And the point is not so much to remind ourselves that unless the social effort had been made the individual effort, as in the past, would have been normally fruitless. Most people, understandably, will not take much notice of the past. The point is always to frame new expectations, in terms of a continuing version of what life could be. Thus the crucial definition, in the coming generation, is that of social poverty, which in overcrowded hospitals and classrooms, inadequate and dangerous roads, ugly and dirty towns, is as evident in a supposedly prosperous Britain as were the rags and hunger we have abolished. But it is characteristic of all cultural growth that the intensity with which the old patterns have been learned is itself a barrier to the communication of new patterns. Everything will in any case be done, by those opposed to social change, to keep the old patterns alive, even if originally these were bitterly opposed in their turn. And since these patterns are not abstractions, but deeply learned ways of thinking and feeling and forms of behaviour, it is not surprising that for some time a majority in their favour can usually be got. The long effort to communicate new patterns must continue, but it can be cut short and weakened if, falling into old types of despair, those who wish to communicate them dismiss other people, who are under real pressures, as the ignorant and selfish masses who are deliberately prolonging their own condition.

The definition of social poverty, and the revolt against it, have in fact already begun. Parallel definitions of cultural poverty and of inadequate democracy are also being actively shaped. These ways of thinking require not only new kinds of analysis of the society, but also new versions of relationship and new feelings in human expectation. Characteristically, much of the first phase of this growth of consciousness has been negative. The new feelings of the middle 1950s were not in themselves creative; they were a stage of dissent from old formulations, and contempt, sickness and anger were the predominant impressions. These feelings, rooted in a brittle boredom, were indeed strange counterparts of the more general reasoned catalogues of an achieved Utopia. It was comparatively easy to isolate this kind of protest, and to discount it as the expression of an eccentric minority out of touch with the mood of a society which had gathered its energies to a pattern of known expectations. Yet the patterns of real communication in a society are always changing, and people thinking in the old ways suddenly found that a generation had grown up behind them which was similarly isolated, and which found little meaning in the achieved patterns that had seemed so satisfactory. The new feelings, if still only at the stage of disbelief, boredom and contempt, were getting through with surprising speed. New areas of feeling and expectation were being actively reached, if only in the sense of the touching of an exposed nerve. As this was realized, the old kind of attempt to dilute, contain and direct the new feelings was hurriedly made. "Youth" became a problem, and the more this was said the more contemptuous and insulted most young people felt: "Can't they see that they're a problem too?" A process very familiar to any historian of cultural change emerged with unusual clarity. People tied to the old definitions and expectations assumed, as always, that the new feelings were either irresponsible or a misunderstanding. "Perhaps we ought to explain to them that people are earning good wages, that every child gets his chance in education, that we all have the right to vote. Men struggled for these things, so can't these young people show a bit of respect?" "Or if we trained them more carefully, some wiser investment in qualified leadership perhaps, until they share our values." But this kind of reaction, characteristically passed through many committees, is in fact useless. Consciousness really does change, and new experience finds new interpretations: this is the permanent creative process. If the existing meanings and values could serve the new energies, there would be no problem. The widespread dissent, and growing revolt, of the new young generation are in fact the growth of the society, and no reaction is relevant unless conceived in these terms. The most useful service already performed by the new generation is its challenge to the society to compare its ideals and its practice. This comparison, as we saw earlier, is the first stage of new learning. People get a sense of reality, and of their own attitudes to it, from what they learn of a whole environment. It is one thing to offer certain meanings and values and ask people to consider and if possible accept them. Yet we all naturally look, not only at the meanings and values, but at their real context. If, for example, we are to be co-operative, responsible, non-violent, where exactly, in our actual world, are we expected to live? Is the economy co-operative, is the culture responsible, are the politics non-violent? If these questions are not honestly answered, propagation of the values as such will have little effect. The degree of evasion will be matched by a degree of contempt, and this can as easily degenerate into cynical apathy as grow into protest and new construction. The only useful social argument is that which follows the meanings and values through to the point where real contradictions are disturbing or denying them. Then, with the real situation admitted, the stage of contemptuous comparison and dissent may pass into constructive energy. For my own part, I see the present situation as a very critical phase in the long revolution, because it is by no means certain, in the short run, whether the new and constructive stage will be reached in time. There are many warning signs of dissent and boredom being capitalized, as a new kind of distraction. The cult of the criminal, the racketeer, the outsider, as relevant heroes of our society, is exceptionally dangerous, because it catches up just enough real feelings to make the heroism seem substantial, yet channels them towards those parodies of revolution often achieved in modern history in the delinquent gang or even in fascism. These destructive expressions can only occur when, in the widest sense, the society is in a revolutionary phase. It is not time then for the reasoned catalogues of sober achievement, but for new creative definitions. The contradiction between an apparently contented society and a deep current of discontent emerging mainly in irrational and ugly ways is our immediate and inescapable challenge.

A growing number of people, in recent years, have been trying to describe new approaches and to make them practical. They have, of course, been widely dismissed as utopians or extremists. But how did they seem at the time, those men we look back to who "in opposition to the public opinion of the day," "outraging their contemporaries," "challenging the general complacency," somehow live with us and even seem tame and "limited by their period"? Working for something new, a writer or thinker easily identifies with these men, and of course may be wholly wrong: not everything new is in fact communicated and lived. But the reasonable man, tolerantly docketing the extremists of his day: who is he exactly? For he too identifies with these figures from the past; it is usually where he learned to be reasonable. And then who is left for that broad empty margin, the "public opinion of the day"?

I think we are all in this margin: it is what we have learned and where we live. But unevenly, tentatively, we get a sense of movement, and the meanings and values extend. I have tried to describe some possible ways forward, and ask only for these to be considered and improved. But what I mainly offer is this sense of the process: what I have called the long revolution. Here, if the meaning communicates, is the ratifying sense of movement, and the necessary sense of direction. The nature of the process indicates a perhaps unusual revolutionary activity: open discussion, extending relationships, the practical shaping of institutions. But it indicates also a necessary strength: against arbitrary power whether of arms or of money, against all conscious confusion and weakening of this long and difficult human effort, and for and with the people who in many different ways are keeping the revolution going.

Index